A HISTORY OF WOMEN'S EDUCATION IN THE UNITED STATES

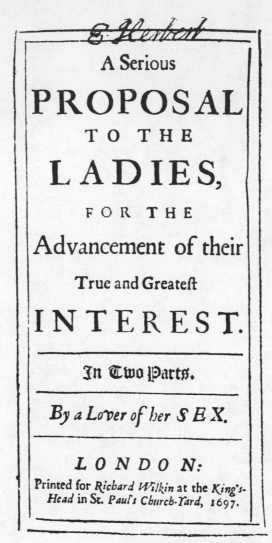

E. Herbert

A Serious

PROPOSAL

TO THE

LADIES,

FOR THE

Advancement of their

True and Greateſt

INTEREST.

In Two Parts.

By a Lover of her SEX.

LONDON:

Printed for *Richard Wilkin* at the *King's-
Head* in St. *Paul's Church-Yard,* 1697.

A HISTORY OF WOMEN'S EDUCATION IN THE UNITED STATES

By

THOMAS WOODY

VOLUME II

1966

OCTAGON BOOKS, INC.

New York

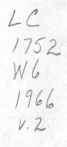

TO

FRANK PIERREPONT GRAVES

INSPIRING TEACHER, COLLEAGUE AND FRIEND

*"Then as far as the guardianship of a state is con-
cerned, there is no difference between the natures of
the man and of the woman, but only various degrees
of weakness and strength.*

"Apparently there is none.

*"Then we shall have to select duly qualified women
also, to share in the life and official labours of the
duly qualified men; since we find that they are competent to the work, and of kindred nature with the
men."*—PLATO.

TABLE OF CONTENTS

VOLUME II

ILLUSTRATIONS

CHAPTER I

CHANGING ECONOMIC STATUS OF WOMEN

I. "Superfluous" Women

In Colonial America, women were at a premium. Many Virginian gentlemen were still unmarried when, in 1619, Sir Edwin Sandys caused ninety "young maidens to make wives of" to be sent into the colony.[1] In 1624, one authority states, there were 432 free males and 176 females; 441 male servants and 46 female.[2] Similar conditions prevailed elsewhere. Women generally married, and the home was, consequently, regarded as the true sphere of women, even though they engaged in a large number of occupations outside of it, as has been shown.[3]

Glancing at the statistics of male and female whites in the United States, with the excess of males reported after 1790, one might assume that women would have continued to marry, and be given in marriage, rather than turn to anything but housekeeping for a living. But, while men were in excess in the country at large, by 1860 there were eight Eastern states—Connecticut, Maryland, Massachusetts, New Hampshire, New Jersey, New York, North Carolina and Rhode Island—in which the excess of women was marked, totalling 74,360 more than men.[4] At once there arose the cry, "What shall we do with the superfluous women?" In New York State, by the same census, women of marriageable age exceeded men by 38,783, and, in Massachusetts, by 27,001. These figures brought home to many a realization of the fact that home life, in the normal sense, was no longer even a possibility for a large number of women. Especially in the large cities, the excess of women compelled attention.[5] One writer de-

---

[1] *Virginia Company Records,* I, 66.

[2] Compare Brown: *First Republic,* 611–27; and the *Virginia Magazine of History,* VII, 364.

[3] See Vol. I, 162 *ff.,* 192 *ff.,* and 259 *ff.*; and Dexter: *Colonial Women of Affairs.*

[4] *Census of the United States* (1860), XXXIII, 36, 210, etc.

[5] The following table shows the excess of female population in certain cities of the East:

1

clared: "Marriage—the only aim in life to which hundreds of
thousands of women of the New England and middle states are
taught to look forward—is already a failure before their education is begun . . . it becomes a most serious question to society
as well as to the sex to determine what they shall do."[6]

The cry of "give us labor" was raised especially in behalf of
these "superfluous" women. Society must find something for
them to do and train them to do it. Up to 1850, the only real
profession into which they had entered was teaching in the common schools and seminaries. Now there was a more general assertion of their "right to labor" in many new fields. These activities represented an extension of the sphere generally attributed
to woman. "Give woman some pursuit which men esteem important, and see if their work is not well done, provided they are
suitably trained," represents a view held in many quarters.
But any desire to undertake man's work was decried by the cau-
tious. "We only want our sex to become fitted for their sphere,"
but we believe this includes preparation for physicians, nurses,
teachers, social workers and managers of savings banks.[7]

Caroline H. Dall emphatically championed woman's claims to
labor. To prove their willingness and capacity for all work, she
cited cases of girls working on Ohio farms at 62½ cents a day,
and others at Media, Pennsylvania; the menial tasks of women in
New York, the heroic efforts of some at a fire in the Lawrence
mills, the exploits of Mary Patton at Cape Horn, the intrepidity
of Mrs. Clark who stayed a mutinous crew on board the *Maria*;
and the ingenuity of the Quaker manufacturess, Ann Scofield, as

TABLE I

	Males	Females	Excess
New Bedford	9,039	10,895	1,856
Lowell	14,635	22,151	7,516
Boston	84,185	91,394	7,209
New York	392,309	413,359	21,050
Brooklyn	125,399	136,049	10,650
Jersey City	13,998	14,893	895
Hoboken	4,626	4,998	372
Pittsburg	23,962	24,101	239
Philadelphia	260,156	286,188	26,032

—*Harper's New Mo. Magazine* (1868), XXXVII, 548.

6 *Ibid.*

7 *Godey's Lady's Book*, March, 1852, 228.

evidence of woman's versatile capacity.[8] She declared the necessity of opening all fields of labor:

"I ask for woman, then, free, untrammelled access to all fields of labor; and I ask it, first, on the ground that she needs to be fed, and that the question which is at this moment before the great body of working women is 'death or dishonor:' for lust is a better paymaster than the mill-owner or the tailor, and economy never yet shook hands with crime.

"Do you object, that America is free from this alternative? I will prove you the contrary within a rod of your own doorstep.

"Do you assert that, if all avenues were thrown open, it would not increase the quantity of work; and that there would be more laborers in consequence, and lower wages for all?

"Lower wages for *some*, I reply; but certainly higher wages for women; and they, too, would be raised to the rank of partners, and personal ill treatment would not follow those who had positions and property before the law.

"You offer them a high education in vain till you add to it the stimulus of a free career.'"[9]

The slow change of attitude towards women as workers, and the reluctance to believe they could be anything but housewives, was described by Lucy Larcom in *A New England Girlhood*:

"In the olden times it was seldom said to little girls, as it always has been said to boys, that they ought to have some definite plan, while they were children, what to be and do when they were grown up. There was usually but one path open before them, to become good wives and housekeepers. And the ambition of most girls was to follow their mothers' footsteps in this direction; a natural and laudable ambition. But girls, as well as boys, must often have been conscious of their own peculiar capabilities,—must have desired to cultivate and make use of their individual powers. When I was growing up, they had already begun to be encouraged to do so. We were often told that it was our duty to develop any talent we might possess, or at least to learn how to do some one thing which the world needed, or which would make it a pleasanter world.

"When I thought what I should best like to do, my first dream —almost a baby's dream—about it was that it would be a fine

[8] *College, Market and the Court*, 172–5.
[9] *Ibid.*, 135–6.

thing to be a school-teacher, like Aunt Hannah. Afterward, when I heard that there were artists, I wished I could some time be one.''[10]

But if some were told it was their duty to develop any talent they might possess and learn to do something the world needed, there were many rebuffs waiting for those who attempted to break into occupations hitherto closed to women. Public sentiment was against it. Dall declared: ''No woman of rank can find work, if she does not happen to be philanthropic, literary, or artistic in her taste, without braving the influence of home, or, what is next dearest, the social circle, and earning for herself a position so conspicuous as to be painful to the most energetic.''[11] The truth of her contention cannot be questioned when one recalls the painful experiences of Elizabeth Blackwell who, just before the middle of the century, had begun to knock at the doors of the medical profession.[12]

Equally illuminating was the experience of Jennie C. Croly, who, shortly before the Civil War, sought to enter in a modest way upon a journalistic career. Only two papers offered an opportunity, and in both of them her work was limited to realms wherein it was judged women would be at home. One paper paid three dollars a week for a department called ''Gossip with and for the Ladies,'' while the other offered five for ''Parlor and Sidewalk Gossip.'' It is significant that art, music, science, drama, and politics were tabooed for her, simply because her department was for women.[13]

In business, too, prospects were not bright. *Harper's New Monthly Magazine* described the difficulty with which a young woman had contended in her effort to gain a position as bookkeeper:

''To this end she entered a Commercial College. She had studied bookkeeping before; but she was determined to be thorough, and if patience, perseverance, and the closest application ever accomplish any thing her purpose was attained. And the Principal must have thought so; for when she received her di-

[10] *Op. cit.*, 157.

[11] *Op. cit.*, 178.

[12] For further reference to her work, see pp. 346 *ff.*

[13] Referred to by McNaught in The Enfranchised Woman Teacher [*N. E. A. Proceedings* (1917), LV, 245].

ploma he stated that she was among the best book-keepers who had ever left his College.

"Now, then, she thought her trials and difficulties were nearly over. But how was she amazed to find it not only difficult—it might have been that even to a man—but utterly impossible, to obtain a situation. She traversed the whole city; she bore coldness, rudeness, misconstruction, absolute insult, all to no purpose. The very idea of a woman wanting to keep books was ridiculed as something beyond belief; and the woman who could think of it was looked on with suspicion; and the friends whose influence had obtained for her the situation she held were particularly wrathful."[14]

There were, of course, numerous enthusiastic advocates of women's freedom to labor, who believed that their service would constitute a most important reform. Louis A. Godey (1853) was employing eighty-eight female operatives, and more in the capacity of contributors in various departments, to publish the *Lady's Book*. The magazine often urged the need of high school education for girls so that they might be better fitted for "general employment." In 1853, the *Lady's Book* published, with great approval, a quotation from the *American and Gazette* relative to the social benefit to be derived from the education and labor of women.

"This is a grievous wrong, which is daily crushing hope out of the hearts of the young women of the land, burying faculties which might be converted by cultivation and exercise to the great benefit of the public, and causing an amount of physical and moral suffering which, could it be computed, would amaze and sadden the community. There is a plain and easy remedy for this evil, and the obligation to correct it rests upon society. Wherever the labor of females can be substituted for that of males, it should invariably be preferred; and we believe that, were the policy once fairly put in practice, and carried out to the farthest limits of which the capacity of the sex would admit, it would be the most benevolent and perhaps important reform that it is possible to introduce into the industrial economy of every civilized State."[15]

[14] *Op. cit.* (1869), XXXVIII, 666.
[15] *Godey's Lady's Book* (1853), 84–5.

II. Factors Producing a Change in Women's Economic Status

Among the primary factors which influenced the withdrawal of women from the home was the rise of factory production.[16] This system grew rapidly, for it meant quantity production and great profits for those whose money was invested. When Hamilton made his Report on Manufactures, in 1791, he enumerated 17 industries which had grown up and, as he said, afforded "assurance of success in future attempts." Besides these industries, he described "a vast scene of household manufacturing" which contributed largely to supplying community wants. "Great quantities of coarse cloths, coatings, serges and flannels, linsey woolseys; hosiery of wool, cotton, and thread; coarse fustians, jeans, and muslins; checked and striped cotton and linen goods; bed ticks, coverlets and counterpanes; tow linens, coarse shirtings, sheetings, toweling and table linen, and various mixtures of wool and cotton, and of cotton and flax, are made in the household way, and, in many instances, to an extent not only sufficient for the supply of the families in which they are made, but for sale, and even, in some cases, for exportation. It is computed in a number of districts that two thirds, three fourths, or even four fifths of all the clothing of the inhabitants are made by themselves."[17] Though we have no statistics of that date on the subject, it is clear that much of this household manufacturing was the work of women. They had done it since the day of the earliest colonists, but it had been given a new impetus by the Revolutionary War. When the manufacture of textiles, and clothing in general, passed from the home, women followed it into the factories.

At the opening of the nineteenth century the factory system, in contrast to the domestic, had practically no vogue in the United States; but considerable impetus was given to it by the events leading up to the War of 1812. From then on, the manu-

16 Important sidelights on economic, social, political background of the early nineteenth century are to be found in Fish: *The Rise of the Common Man,* Chaps. on "Manners and Morals" and "Education for the People"; Adams: *New England in the Republic,* Chaps. XIV and XV; Schlesinger: *Political and Social History of the United States,* Chaps. I and V; and, for the broadest view of the field, 1815 to 1848, Channing: *History of the U. S.,* V, Chaps. I–IX.

17 Hamilton's Report on the Subject of Manufactures, *Works of Hamilton,* I, 210–11.

facture of cotton and woolen goods passed speedily from homes to mills; but not until the decade of 1840 to 1850, was the factory system dominant. The census of 1810 gave the value of cotton, flax, and woolen manufactures, "in families and otherwise," as $26,076,997 and $25,608,788, respectively.[18] The next census (1820) did not include the manufacture of cotton and wool in families, with the result that the figures decreased to $4,834,157 for the former and $4,413,068 for the latter. The difference between the figures for the two decades suggests the important rôle still played by the domestic and small shop manufacturers. In 1830, when domestic and factory production were apparently lumped together again, the value of cotton manufactures was given as $22,534,815 and that of woolen as $14,528,166. No separate figures were obtained in 1810, 1820, or 1830 as to the value of household manufactures, but in 1840 they were valued at $29,023,380. At the same date, the factory output of cotton and woolen materials, exclusive of the value of domestic productions, was valued at $46,350,453 and $20,696,-999, respectively. These make a total of $67,047,452. The total value of cotton, flax and wool, in 1810, $51,685,785, represented chiefly the domestic output; but by 1840, as noted, domestic output of all sorts amounted only to twenty-nine million dollars. From these figures, it is evident that the home as a place of production was becoming unimportant, and that its functions were slowly but surely being absorbed by the new institution of the industrial state.[19]

Advocates were not wanting to spread the gospel of the great service to be rendered to old and young by the factory. One thought the new cotton mill ". . . a never failing asylum for the friendless orphans and the bereft widows, the distribution of labor and the improvements in machinery happily combining to call into profitable employment the tender services of those who have just sprung from the cradle, as well as those who are tottering to the grave. . ."[20]

18 These and following figures appear in the *Twelfth Census of the United States* (1900), VII, pp. LI–LIII.

19 Calhoun: *Soc. Hist. of the Am. Family*, II, 171, properly calls attention to the fact, however, that household production continued well into the nineteenth century and was particularly persistent in rural districts.

20 A speech of Mr. Lloyd, of South Carolina, relative to proposed cotton mills. Reprinted by permission of the publishers, The Arthur H. Clark Company, from Calhoun's *Social History of the American Family*, II, 173.

In general, the Civil War resulted in an unsettling of the usual relation of the sexes in the fields of labor. Calhoun[21] quotes one source, to the effect that, in Iowa, the writer had seen more women than men driving teams and working in the fields. In Kansas, because of shortage of men, they drove the reapers at harvest, took care of the stock, and performed the routine duties of the farm. Elsewhere it has been noted that even the most conservative localities, due to the circumstances of war, began to see the value of women as teachers.

Women of the South were similarly affected. A traveller stated that Southern women had taken to work, and thousands might be seen in Richmond, and elsewhere, going to and from the factories. In North and South there was an evident shift of emphasis from the delicate and lady-like occupations and pastimes to serious labours formerly thought proper only for men. In no place was the contrast more marked than in the South.[22] Besides all this, it should be remarked that during the war, both in the North and South, women were given opportunity for public employment in hospitals, camps, and in centers for the preparation and distribution of food and clothing.[23]

III. Progress of Women in Industrialism

The last half of the past century saw great advancement by women, so far as entrance into new fields was concerned. Harriett Martineau declared (1836) that American women were free to engage in only seven occupations,—teaching, needlework, keeping boarders, working in cotton mills, book-binding, type-setting, and housework.[24] While this statement was certainly not true in detail—Calhoun mentions that women were, at that time, employed in more than one hundred industrial occupations—[25] there were decidedly few opportunities for educated women and they were generally denied the necessary training,

[21] *Ibid.*, II, 357.

[22] See Brockett and Vaughan: *Woman's Work in the Civil War*, Introductory chapter; Underwood: *Women of the Confederacy*, 117; and Calhoun: *Soc. Hist. of the Am. Fam.*, *II*, Ch. XIV.

[23] Moore: *Women of the War* and Brockett and Vaughan: *Woman's Work in the Civil War*.

[24] Martineau: *Society in America*, II, 257.

[25] *Op. cit.*, II, 182.

except in the case of teaching.[26]   By 1845, there were 75,710 women, and but 55,828 men, employed in the textile industries of the United States. A like proportion was to be found in other factories. Up to 1850, "women formed, roughly speaking, two-thirds to three-fourths, and in some places as much as nine-tenths, of the total number of factory operatives. . .".[27] About sixty per cent of the cotton operatives from Virginia northward, in 1831, were women.[28] But is is significant that women were more numerous only as employees, not as employers. The secret of the large number of women employed in the factories lay in the lower wage for which they labored. One case may be given to illustrate. Lynn, Massachusetts, in 1850, employed 3,729 men and 6,412 women in shoe factories. Although women were nearly twice as numerous they received but $37,000 a month, while the men were paid $75,000.[29]

Let us note some of the figures indicating woman's entrance into the factory world. As suggested, women followed their work thither as it was removed from their households. The city of Lowell, a mill town from the beginning, was made famous by its factory girls.[30]   In fact, wherever mills opened, women found a place. One "intelligent friend of manufactories" asserted there were about 200,000 females employed in various factories as early as 1830.[31] In 1850 there were 1,074 cotton factories in twenty-five states, employing 32,295 males and 62,661 females.[32]   In 1860, there were 1,091 factories in twenty-nine states, wherein 46,859 males and 75,169 females were employed.[33] In 1870, males above sixteen numbered 42,790 and females over fifteen, 69,637. Nearly twenty-three thousand "youth" were also employed.[34]

[26] For the development of higher professional training, see pp. 321 ff.

[27] Reprinted by permission of the publishers, The Arthur H. Clark Company, from Calhoun's Social History of the American Family, II, 175.

[28] Schlesinger: Polit. and Soc. Hist. of the United States, 7.

[29] Dall: op. cit., 202–7.

[30] The Lowell Offering, a product of the mill girls, was very favorably commented on by Dickens, Martineau, and others.

[31] Am. Annals of Education, VI, 219–23.

[32] In the Census of 1870 the figures were slightly different, due presumably to corrections that had been made—See volume on Industry and Wealth, p. 597, table X.

[33] Eighth Census of the U. S. (1860), volume on Manufactures, p. IX.

[34] Ninth Census (1870), volume on Industry and Wealth, 596–7.

In 1850, 16,574 women and 22,678 men were employed in manufacturing woolen goods; in 1860, there were 16,519 women and 24,841 men. In 1870, women above fifteen years of age numbered 27,682; men above sixteen, 42,728; and "youth," 9,643.[35]

GIRLS MAKING FRINGES

In all manufactures, in 1850, there were 732,157 men and 225,-922 women; in 1860, there were 1,040,349 men and 270,897 women; and, in 1870, the total of males above sixteen was 1,615,-598, while women over fifteen numbered 323,770, and "youth" 114,628.[36]

While women thus entered the factory to do their productive work of clothing the family, they also became contributors of in-

[35] *Ibid.*, 631.
[36] *Ibid.*, 392–3.

ventions.   The first American patent right issued to a woman bore the date of 1808; another was issued in 1815; but progress was slow, and from 1808 to 1833 only fifteen patents were granted women.   Among these were a baby jumper, fountain pen, deep sea telescope, a cook stove, and a globe for teaching geography. From 1834 to 1859, women took out only thirty-five patents; but in the next twenty-five years they were granted 1,503.   By the eighties, they were being issued at the rate of more than a hundred per annum, and, in the next decade, about one a day.   By 1910, 8,596 patents had been issued to women.[37]   These figures would have delighted the heart of Catherine Beecher as she planned her scientific cook stove.   They would, no doubt, have proved to Mrs. Willard that she was right in thinking higher mathematics enabled women to use their reason.

A concise view of women's progress as inventors, since the patent law of 1790, may be obtained from table II.[38]

Notwithstanding low wages and a public mind generally hostile to the idea of women working for wages, they continued increasingly to enter various kinds of employment.   They have been mentioned as teachers and typesetters.   They are seen coming forward to take up the work of authors,[39] doctors,[40] librarians,[41]

[37] See Women as Inventors [*Educational News*, Oct. 7, 1899, 246 *ff*.]; also the *North American Review*, Vol. 136, 478–89; Sykes: *Soc. Basis of New Education for Women* (1917), 3–5.

[38] An interesting pamphlet on *Women's Contributions in the Field of Invention*, No. 28, published by the Women's Bureau in 1923.   By permission of the Women's Bureau, Department of Labor.

[39] As early as 1851 women's authorship was becoming noticeable, and the following comment upon it was made: ''It is apparent to any one who will take the trouble to look over the books which make up the burden of a bookseller's counter, that it has become a wonderfully common piece of temerity for a lady to make a book.   Apart from the consideration, that a female author puts much of her personal individuality into her book, being more prone to express emotions than ideas, it may be said that in taking any public stand for praise or blame, a woman risks more than a man.   From the time when the boy finds himself struggling among fifty or a hundred other boys, to find the level accorded to his measure of strength, tact, and talent, till the day when the man must cope with men in the crowded avenues to fame and wealth,—he is sheltered by no prescriptive immunities.''—*North American Review* (1851), CL, 151–2.

[40] Women physicians, surgeons, and osteopaths in 1910 numbered 9,015. Elizabeth Blackwell found that women doctors had to fight opposition and discrimination in many forms.   Discrimination against women is still

TABLE II

NUMBER OF PATENTS ISSUED TO WOMEN AND TO MEN AND THE PER CENT.
INCREASE IN SUCH ISSUANCE IN EACH DECADE
OR PERIOD SINCE 1790

| Periods following enactment of patent law, 1790 | Patents issued to— | | | |
| | Women | | Men | |
	Average number annually	Per cent. increase over previous period	Average number annually	Per cent. increase over previous period
Forty-five years prior to commencement of present series of numbers of letters patent (1836)	0.4	....	220.9	....
Nine and one-half years ending 1845	.7	85.0	456.9	106.8
Decade ending 1855	1.3	75.7	964.8	111.2
Decade ending 1865	10.1	676.9	3,767.4	290.5
Decade ending 1875	67.3	566.3	11,918.4	216.4
Decade ending 1885	106.0	75.5	16,079.3	34.9
Nine years ending 1894[42]	229.8	116.8	21,784.0	35.5
Ten selected years from 1905 to 1921	501.6	118.3	34,836.9	59.9

actresses in increasing numbers, railway officials, professional cake-makers for Presidents, deans, presidents of colleges, police-women,[43] bootleggers, civil service clerks[44] and consular agents,[45]

charged. Thus recently, Texas women charged the Texas University Board of Regents with refusing internships to two women at the John Sealy Hospital. Discrimination, it was said, was due to the idea that women should not attend male patients.—An article in [Phila.] *Evening Public Ledger*, Jan. 20, 1926.

[41] By 1892, women had become prominent in this field as catalogers, assistants, and as chief librarians. Of 508 members of the American Library Association, 237 were women, and, of these, 93 were at the head of libraries. But 125 libraries represented by the American Library Association had men as head librarians.—*R. C. E.*, 1892–93, I, 748.

[42] The last published report on women inventors to whom patents had been granted did not give complete figures for 1895; consequently this year was omitted from the figures.

[43] Mary E. Hamilton, first New York City police woman, has published a book: *The Police Woman: Her Service and Ideals*—F. A. Stokes Company; see also Owings: *Women Police*—N. Y.: Hitchcock, 1925.

linemen for telephone companies, bankers, barbers, and magistrates.[46]   This general invasion of fields, once thought man's
exclusive domain, has appeared throughout the Western world.
Even the muffin man of London is said to be passing and is being
replaced by "woman, trim, neat, quick." So common has it
become for the wife to contribute to, and sometimes supply the
main body of, the budget, that a woman's magazine has said, with
a measure of truth and humor, that 'any man who expects to go
ahead must save a part of his wife's wages and that he should
not allow her to give up one position until she has secured
another.' There is, of course, a vague theory in the common
mind that women are the home "makers" and men the "providers." But when one considers that one out of every four
persons gainfully employed is a woman, the truth is impressed
that they are, in reality, "providers." A recent publication of
the Women's Bureau, *The Share of Wage-Earning Women in
Family Support,* states that few people realize that the single
woman worker "is often the chief bread winner for her family,"
that "almost every married woman wage earner" supplements
her husband's income by turning over her entire wage to meet
the family expenses, and that "many families get as much financial help from daughters as from sons."[47] The Manchester study
showed that of the "women . . . who were living at home, 67.9
per cent. contributed all their earnings" to the family.[48] This
means they do not have that "economic independence" which is

---

[44] When General Spinner, Treasurer of the United States, proposed to
employ some women as clerks in his department he was, doubtless, considered
a little unbalanced. But there was no law against it, and so it was done.
In 1870 an act was passed, providing that "women may, at the discretion of
the head of any department, be appointed to any of the clerkships . . . upon
the same requisites . . . conditions and . . . compensation, as . . . prescribed for men." [Sec. 165, Act of July 12, 1870, quoted by Helen H.
Gardiner, first woman member of the U. S. Civil Service Commission, 1920–
1925—in *Journal of the Assoc. of Univ. Women* (Oct. 1925), XIX, 17 *ff.*]

[45] Pattie Field, first woman "Foreign Service Officer" of the U. S., made
Vice-Consul at Amsterdam.

[46] A young lady, Justice of the Peace in Vancouver for but one year, has
proved so charming in her official capacity that, it is alleged, motorists are
pleased to be fined; and many couples have come within the year for her
official sanction.

[47] Bulletin No. 30, 1923, 1.

[48] *Ibid.,* 12.

so often boastfully proclaimed. They have only changed the place of servitude; they have not left the state of it behind them. Of the married women, in the same study (they constituted 15.4 per cent. of all interviewed), nearly every one contributed all earnings to the family. At Passaic (N. J.) about half the women wage earners studied were married. One study of a group of "working mothers" revealed that, where "both mother and father" worked, "nearly a third of the family income came from the mothers"; where "mother, father, and children" worked, "slightly less than one sixth" was contributed by the mothers.[49] It should not be overlooked, certainly, that these women who contributed their earnings, won outside the home, generally did their household tasks also.

Evidence of the growing professionalism of women may be found in numerous books published as guides to future occupations, such as Church's *Money Making for Ladies* (1882), Manson's *Work for Women* (1883), Rayne's *What Can a Woman Do* (1884), *Occupations for Women* (1897),—edited by Willard, Winslow and White,—and Alden's *Ways of Earning Money* (1904). In this century the literature has become voluminous. Lack of space forbids description of these recommendations concerning ways of earning a living,—or a wage,—but a glance below will indicate the range of occupations covered.[50] Willard's book discussed the following occupations very definitely, and alluded to many others: preserve making and pickling, professional menders, dressmaking, women as farmers, bee culture, poultry culture and silk culture, caring for pets, lunch and tea rooms, telegraph and telephone girls, stenographer and typewriter, the faithful saleswoman, women in advertising, real estate, banking, insurance, temperance work, women in medicine, politics, in the

[49] *Ibid.*, 13.

[50] Rayne's book included the following headings: business education, women as hotel clerks, the professions of literature, journalism, law, medicine, music, government clerkship, a lady government official, women of enterprise (miscellaneous occupations), women as photographers, women as wood engravers, profession of telegraphy, lady book canvassers, art and industrial exchanges, profession of elocution, profession of nursing, women in gardening, raising poultry, bee keeping for women, dressmakers and dressmaking, the housekeeper, how a working girl lives, science of cookery, the new cook, keeping boarders, value of personal appearance, the influence of wife and mother, women as poets, the mother begins, the good wife, female beauty, and toilet medicines.

THE FAITHFUL SALESWOMAN

pulpit, piano and organ tuning, public singers, in choir and concert, pianists and composers, in orchestra work, women as photographers, women in interior decoration, women as teachers, college presidents, professors, and principals, in the lecture field, newspaper women, editors, magazine writers and paragraphers, in the dramatic profession, women in science, women in unusual paths, cooking-school teachers, kindergarten teachers, women as inventors, business managers, and in government service.[51]

The foregoing suggestions regarding occupations and professions must have been decidedly heartening to their readers at the time of their publication. Many of the so-called "higher" professions listed, however, were but slowly made accessible to women. Massachusetts passed a law permitting women to prac-

[51] Willard: *Occupations for Women.*

tice as attorneys-at-law in 1882.[52] Two years later, she enacted
that "in each of the State lunatic hospitals . . . an educated
female physician shall be appointed assistant physician,"[53] thus
providing an official and remunerative encouragement to those
daring women who had braved the terrors of medicine.

For the past fifty years, there have been many 'scare' headlines and perturbed fathers, mothers, preachers, teachers and
reformers, ready to tell of dire consequences to follow the entrance of women into new occupations. Today when one woman
enters a new work it is the occasion for a full page in Sunday
supplements. This tendency to make a great noise, when a slight
infringement of man's domain is noticed, has, without doubt, led
the public mind to believe changes were being made more rapidly
than they really were. The figures since 1880 are not so startling
as newspaper headlines; they do show, on the contrary, that the
entrance of women into industry, commerce, and so on, was not
caused suddenly by the War but was a gradual growth. In fact,

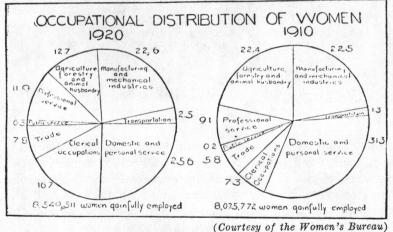

(Courtesy of the Women's Bureau)
OCCUPATIONAL DISTRIBUTION OF WOMEN

progress in this direction has been constant since 1830. In 1880,
the total number of women gainfully employed, ten years of age
and over, was 2,647,157, or 14.7 per cent. of that age group of
our female population; in 1890, there were 4,005,532, or 17.4 per
cent.; in 1900, 5,319,397, or 18.8 per cent.; in 1910, 8,075,772,

52 *Laws of Massachusetts,* 1882, 100.
53 *Ibid.,* 1884, 101.

or 23.4 per cent.; and in 1920, 8,549,511, or 21.1 per cent.[54] The number of women gainfully employed has increased since 1910; but, considering the increase in population, the proportion of women thus employed has actually decreased more than two per cent.

Though the numerical increase of women is not startling, there has been a great shifting of women from one occupational group to another, and this is what has attracted public attention. Women in domestic and personal service decreased 13.6 per cent.; but those in clerical positions, transportation, mechanical and manufacturing industries, and professional service, increased 140.4, 99.8, 6, and 38.5 per cent., respectively.[55] Conspicuous increases were made by women as bankers (152.8 per cent.), real estate agents (214.6 per cent.), teachers in higher institutions (240.6 per cent.), and many others might be added.[56] It is worth noting that, in a number of professions requiring special training, marked increases occurred. As designers, draftsmen and inventors they rose from 3,012 to 7,664; as healers, from 4,672 to 7,902; as authors, editors, reporters, from 6,239 to 8,736; as college heads and professors, from 2,958 to 10,075; as librarians, from 5,829 to 13,502; as religious, charity, and welfare workers, from 8,889 to 26,927; and as trained nurses, they increased from 76,508 to 143,664.[57] The figures for welfare workers and nurses were, doubtless, greatly increased by the War. The number of women musicians, artists, sculptors, and physicians and surgeons decreased slightly during the decade. The limit of the expanded woman's sphere is suggested by the fact that the Census Bureau lists 678 possible occupations, only 33 of which are not represented by women. From 1880 to 1910, women workers increased 205.1 per cent. and men, 104.1 per cent.[58]

IV. Conditions of Labor

It is quite possible that the conditions of women laborers, in factories of the early period in the United States, never were as bad as that of English laborers in mines depicted by Lord Ash-

[54] *Abstract of the Fourteenth Census of the United States*, 1920, 481.

[55] *The Occupational Progress of Women*, Bulletin of the Women's Bureau, 1922, No. 27, 1–5.

[56] Black: Jobs for Women [*The Nation* (Dec. 9, 1925), Vol. 121, 648–9].

[57] *Occupational Progress of Women*, 16 f.

[58] Anderson: Women in Industry [*N. E. A. Proceedings* (1922), 707–8].

ley's Commission (1842) and most vividly portrayed by Disraeli in *The Sibyl*.[59]

Much has been said, however, about the bad conditions faced by American laboring women. In what has been written one naturally finds extremes. It is impossible to get a complete picture—each article is but a flash that lights up a particular location—but such as can be obtained is, for the most part, harrowing. A few cases may be noted. Child labor became common. The census of 1870 noted 114,628 "youth" employed. In 1830, about 7 per cent. of cotton operatives were children under 12 years. A little girl stated, in 1845,[60] that: "I go to work before daylight in the morning and never leave it until it is dark, and don't make enough to support mother and baby."

Hours were extremely long, generally from morning light till dark. Lighting, heating and ventilation of factories were bad and the housing of operatives entirely inadequate. One of the delegates to the National Trades Union Convention, in 1834, described cotton manufacturing plants as inimical to health and extremely miserable places to work.[61] Housing of the Lowell operatives was described by an Associationist (1846) as follows: "The young women sleep upon an average six in a room; three beds to a room. There is no privacy, no retirement here; it is almost impossible to read or write alone, as the parlor is full and so many sleep in the same chamber. [One said] that if she had a letter to write, she did it on the head of a band box, sitting on a trunk, as there was not space for a table. So live and toil the

[59] The latter described them as follows: "They come forth. The plain is covered with the swarming multitude: bands of stalwart men, broad-chested and muscular, wet with toil, and black as the children of the tropics; troops of youth, alas! of *both sexes*, though neither their raiment nor their language indicates the difference. All are clad in male attire, and oaths that men might shudder to hear issue from lips born to breathe words of sweetness. Yet these are to be, some *are*, the mothers of England! Can we wonder at the hideous coarseness of their language, when we remember the savage rudeness of their lives? Naked to the waist, an iron chain fastened to a belt of leather runs between their legs, clad in canvas; while, on hands and feet, an English girl, for twelve, sometimes for sixteen hours a day, hauls and hurries tubs of coal along subterranean roads, dark, precipitous, and plashy."

[60] From the *Voice of Industry* (Fitchburg, Mass., 1845). Reprinted by permission of the publishers, The Arthur H. Clark Company, from Calhoun's *Social History of the American Family*, II, 180.

[61] *Ibid.*, 183–4.

young women of our country in the boarding houses and manufactories which the rich and influential of our land have built for
them.''[62]

Many began to fear the effect this would have on the succeeding generations. Catherine Beecher, referring to the plea of
Mathew Carey for factories (because they would remedy evils),
declared:

''I have made the situation of our sex in shops and mills a
distinct subject of inquiry and of personal investigation; and
it is my solemn conviction that if there is no other way to relieve
our sex but to remove them from their appropriate vocations
to labor in manufactories and shops, it would be far better for
woman, and for the coming generation, that she should follow
the example of the Germans at the West, and toil in the open
air in horticulture and farming. It would be better for her
health, better for her morals, and better for her children.

''If I should state all I can prove on this subject, and that,
too, in reference to our best-conducted manufacturing establishments, it, probably, would make a great hue-and-cry among
capitalists; yet nothing is needed but to go to these places and
converse with the most intelligent and candid female operatives,
to learn what would abundantly establish my position—that, as
the general rule, it would be far better for women to be employed
on farms and gardens than in shops and manufactories.''[63]

Speaking of children employed in factories, it was asserted
(1834) that ''to look at the pale and dirty, and spiritless beings,
as they pour out of the factory to their hurried meals at the
sound of a bell . . . to see the lazy motion of their jaded limbs
and the motionless expression of their woebegone countenances,
must give a pang to the feeling heart . . .''

A visitor at the Lowell factories (an Associationist), who had
talked with operatives, and eaten with them, so as to learn facts
at first hand, stated there were from seven to eight thousand
young women, mostly the daughters of farmers, working there.
They labored thirteen hours in summer and from daylight until
dark in winter. ''At half past four in the morning the factory

[62] Reprinted by permission of the publishers, The Arthur H. Clark Company, from the *Documentary History of the American Industrial Society*,
VII, 134–5.

[63] *True Remedy*, 37–9.

bell rings, and at five the girls must be in the mills. A clerk
. . . observes those . . . a few minutes behind time, and effectual means are taken to stimulate to punctuality." At seven
there are thirty minutes for breakfast, and at mid-day from
thirty to forty-five minutes, varying with the time of year.
Work stops at seven in the evening. Numerous girls are "so
fatigued . . . that they go to bed soon after their evening meal
and endeavor by a comparatively long sleep to resuscitate their
weakened frames for the toils of the coming day. . . . It would
be a poor speculation in an industrial point of view to own the
operative; for the trouble and expense of providing for times
of sickness and old age would more than counterbalance the
difference between the price of wages and the expense of board
and clothing. The far greater number of fortunes, accumulated
by the North in comparison with the South, shows that hireling
labor is more profitable for capital than slave labor."[64]

As to the character of the work done by these women, and the
conditions of labor, the same observer stated the largest room
they visited was in Manchester. ". . . It is four hundred feet
long, and about seventy broad; there are five hundred looms,
and twenty-one thousand spindles in it. The din and clatter of
these five hundred looms under full operation, struck us on
first entering as something frightful and infernal, for it seemed
such an atrocious violation of one of the faculties of the human
soul, the sense of hearing. After a while we became somewhat
inured to it, and by speaking quite close to the ear of an operative
and quite loud, we could hold a conversation, and make the
inquiries we wished.

"The girls attend upon an average three looms; many attend
four, but this requires a very active person, and the most unremitting care. However, a great many do it. Attention to two
is as much as should be demanded of an operative. This gives
us some idea of the application required during the thirteen
hours of daily labor. The atmosphere of such a room cannot of
course be pure; on the contrary it is charged with cotton fila-
ments and dust, which, we were told, are very injurious to the
lungs. On entering the room, although the day was warm, we

[64] Reprinted by permission of the publishers, The Arthur H. Clark Company, from the *Documentary History of the American Industrial Society*,
VII, 132 *ff*.

remarked that the windows were down; we asked the reason, and a young woman answered very naively, and without seeming to be in the least aware that this privation of fresh air was anything else than perfectly natural, that 'when the wind blew, the threads did not work so well.' After we had been in the room for fifteen or twenty minutes, we found ourselves, as did the persons who accompanied us, in quite a perspiration, produced by a certain moisture which we observed in the air, as well as by the heat. . . .''[65]

The Hamilton Manufacturing Company's rules (1848) forbade an overseer to give leave of absence to an operative unless there were "spare hands" to take her place, or if it were an "absolute necessity." All operatives were to board in the Company's boarding houses. None who did not attend church, or who were immoral, would be employed. The contract with the Company was for twelve months. Free vaccination was offered by the Company to those who "need" it. The boarding-house keepers, judging from their complaints, were as closely bargained with, by the mill owners, as were the factory girls themselves.[66]

One method of getting girls for factory labor was described in the *Voice of Industry*, Jan. 2, 1846, as follows:

''. . . We were not aware until within a few days, of the *modus operandi* of the Factory powers in this village, of forcing poor girls from their quiet homes, to become their tools, and like the southern slaves, to give up her life and liberty to the heartless tyrants and task-masters. Observing a singular looking 'long, low black' wagon passing along the street, we made inquiries respecting it, and were informed that it was what we term 'a slaver.' She makes regular trips to the north of the state, cruising around in Vermont and New Hampshire, with a 'commander' whose heart must be as black as his craft, who is paid a dollar a head, for all he brings to the market, and more in proportion to the distance—If they bring them from such a distance that they cannot easily get back. This is done by 'hoisting false colors,' and representing to the girls, that they can tend more machinery than is possible, and that the work is

[65] Reprinted by permission of the publishers, The Arthur H. Clark Company, from the *Documentary History of the American Industrial Society*, VII, 134.

[66] *Ibid.*, 138–40.

so very neat, and the wages such, that they can dress in silks and spend half their time in reading. . . .

"Let us say a word in regard to the manner in which they are stowed, in the wagon, which may find a similarity only in the manner in which slaves are fastened in the hold of a vessel. It is long, and the seats so close that it must be very inconvenient. Is there any humanity in this? Philanthropists may talk of negro slavery, but it would be well first to endeavor to emancipate the slaves at home. Let us not stretch our ears to catch the sound of the lash on the flesh of the oppressed black while the oppressed in our very midst are crying out in thunder tones, and calling upon us for assistance."[67]

To meet the extortionate demands of employers was hard for individuals. Soon, we find a measure of cooperation, on the part of women, seeking to resist oppression and secure better conditions, better pay. In 1846 the Massachusetts Corporation proposed that weavers should tend four looms and that wages be reduced one cent a piece. A meeting of the operatives was arranged at which they declared: "We will not tend a fourth loom (except to oblige each other) unless we receive the same pay per piece as on three, and . . . we will use our influence to prevent others from pursuing a course which has always had a tendency to reduce our wages."

In 1845, *The Workingman's Advocate* described a meeting of women industrial workers, called to remedy the evil conditions and oppression under which they labored. About seven hundred attended. The following statement was agreed upon as representing the true status of female laborers:

"Whereas, the young women attached to the different trades in the city of New York, having toiled a long time for a remuneration totally inadequate for the maintenance of life, and feeling the truth of the Gospel assertion, that 'the laborer is worthy of his hire,' have determined to take upon themselves the task of asserting their rights against unjust and mercenary employers. It must be remembered by those to whom we address ourselves, that our object is not extortion; our desire, not to reap advantages which will be denied to our employers. The boon

[67] Reprinted by permission of the publishers, The Arthur H. Clark Company, from the *Documentary History of the American Industrial Society*, VII, 141.

we ask is founded upon right, alone! The high prices demanded by tradesmen for their goods renders them amply able to advance wages to a standard, which, while it obviates the present cause of complaint, will render laborers only the more cheerful at their work, and still more earnest and willing to serve their employers. The scarcity of employment, and the low rates of pay which have so long prevailed, have, undoubtedly driven many virtuous females to courses which might, otherwise, have been avoided. Many of the female operatives of this city have families dependent upon their exertions; aged fathers and mothers—young brothers—helpless sisters, who, but for their exertions, must inevitably starve, or betake themselves to that scarcely less horrible alternative—the poor house! Such a picture is enough to bestir the most inert to active exertion; the love of life is a passion inherent in us all, and we feel persuaded that we need no better excuse for the movement to which the glaring injustice of our employers has driven us! . . .'' It was further resolved to hold a benefit for the aid of workers and to prepare an address to the public presenting the wrongs of female workers in "the true and proper light."[68]

A much lighter touch was given the picture of factory girls' existence by Lucy Larcom. Still, even from her cheerful interpretation, one can see that life was not easy.

". . . I know that sometimes the confinement of the mill became very wearisome to me. In the sweet June weather I would lean far out of the window, and try not to hear the unceasing clash of sound inside. Looking away to the hills, my whole stifled being would cry out, 'Oh, that I had wings!' "[69]

As one of the "younger girls" of her family, she was compelled to leave school when nearly prepared for high school, beginning to work in the mills at twelve years of age. She described the "home-life" of the employed girls, as follows:

"Work began at five o'clock on summer mornings, and at daylight in the winter. Breakfast was eaten by lamplight, during the cold weather; in summer, an interval of half an hour was allowed for it, between seven and eight o'clock. The time given for the noon meal was from a half to three quarters of an hour. The only hours of leisure were from half past seven or

[68] *The Workingman's Advocate*, March 8, 1845.
[69] Larcom: *A New England Girlhood*, 182.

eight to ten in the evening, the mills closing a little earlier on Saturdays. It was an imperative regulation that lights should be out at ten. During those two evening hours, when it was too cold for the girls to sit in their own rooms, the dining-room was used as a sitting-room, where they gathered around the tables, and sewed, and read, and wrote, and studied. It seems a wonder, to look back upon it, how they accomplished so much as they did, in their limited allowance of time. They made and mended their own clothing, often doing a good deal of unnecessary fancy-work besides. They subscribed for periodicals; took books from the libraries; went to singing-schools, conference meetings, concerts, and lectures; watched at night by a sick girl's bedside, and did double work for her in the mill, if necessary; and on Sundays they were at church, not differing in appearance from other well-dressed and decorous young women. Strangers who had been sitting beside them in a house of worship were often heard to ask, on coming out, 'But where were the factory girls?' "[70]

She points out that these mill girls supported churches and charities, paid home debts, and kept sisters at school and brothers at college—all so quietly as to be unnoticed by outsiders. They had no thought of amusements for they were able to entertain themselves, she adds, naively, "in their brief hours of leisure." But evening classes were formed, and paid for by them, wherein they continued studies begun elsewhere. Many became teachers in the primary and grammar schools of the city. A minister was of the opinion that "about five hundred" of the mill girls there would have been acceptable as teachers. Lucy, herself, found relaxation in "a lead pencil and a bit of paper." Her activity was contagious, and as the habit of writing became more common, contributions were made to a little sheet, *The Diving Bell*. As an outgrowth of this early effort, a maturer production, *The Lowell Offering*, made its appearance in April, 1841. This literary contribution achieved a considerable reputation, attracting the attention of English writers like Martineau, and Dickens in his *American Notes*; and parts of the *Offering* were republished in England as *Mind Among the Spindles* and *American Factories and their Female Operatives*. The *North American Review*, through its editor, John G. Palfrey, passed

[70] *Atlantic Monthly* (1881), XLVIII, 599 *f*.

a most favorable judgment, looking upon it as something that would "bear criticism" and "reward perusal."[71] The *Offering* and Lucy Larcom, without doubt, give a rosier view of mill life than generally prevailed. They make even sordid conditions appear less so. Martineau summed it up when she wrote of the girls at Waltham: "Twice the wages and half the toil would not have made the girls I saw happy and healthy, without the cultivation of mind which afforded them perpetual support, entertainment, and motive for activity. Their minds were so open to fresh ideas as to be drawn off from thoughts of themselves and their own concerns. . . ."[72]

To see that Martineau's judgment is largely true we have only to turn to the *Offering* itself. Some of the descriptions of the mill girl's life, given there, are perhaps as accurate and fair as can be found; and certainly they reveal young women who faced life with wide open eyes and minds. We cannot pass these by without giving an example, which describes "A Week in the Mill":

"Much has been said of the factory girl and her employment. By some she has been represented as dwelling in a sort of brick-and-mortar paradise, having little to occupy thought save the weaving of gay and romantic fancies, while the spindle or the wheel flies obediently beneath her glance. Others have deemed her a mere servile drudge, chained to her labor by almost as strong a power as that which holds a bondman in his fetters; and, indeed, some have already given her the title of 'the white slave of the North.' Her real situation approaches neither one nor the other of these extremes. Her occupation is as laborious as that of almost any female who earns her own living, while it has also its sunny spots and its cheerful intervals, which make her hard labor seem comparatively pleasant and easy.

"Look at her as she commences her weekly task. The rest of the Sabbath has made her heart and her step light, and she is early at her accustomed place, awaiting the starting of the machinery. Everything having been cleaned and neatly arranged on the Saturday night, she has less to occupy her on Monday than on other days; and you may see her leaning from the window to watch the glitter of the sunrise on the water, or

[71] Robinson: *Loom and Spindle*, 150–1.
[72] *Atlantic Monthly* (1881), XLVIII, 599–608.

looking away at the distant forests and fields, while memory wanders to her beloved country home; or it may be that she is conversing with a sister-laborer near, returning at regular intervals to see that her work is in order.

"Soon the breakfast bell rings. In a moment the whirling wheels are stopped, and she hastens to join the throng which is pouring through the open gate. At the table she mingles with a various group. Each dispatches the meal hurriedly, though not often in silence; and, if, as is sometimes the case, the rules of politeness are not punctiliously observed by all, the excuse of some lively country girl would be, 'They don't give us time for manners.'

"The short half-hour is soon over. The bell rings again, and now our factory girl feels that she has commenced her day's work in earnest. The time is often apt to drag heavily till the dinner hour arrives. Perhaps some part of the work becomes deranged and stops. The constant friction causes a belt of leather to burst into a flame; a stranger visits the room, and scans the features and dress of its inmates inquiringly; and there is little else to break the monotony. The afternoon passes in much the same manner. Now and then she mingles with a knot of busy talkers who have collected to discuss some new occurrence, or holds pleasant converse with some intelligent and agreeable friend, whose acquaintance she has formed since her factory life commenced; but much of the time she is left to her own thoughts. While at her work the clattering and rumbling around her prevent any other noise from attracting her attention, and she must think, or her life would be dull indeed.

"Thus the day passes on, and evening comes, the time which she feels to be exclusively her own. How much is done in the three short hours from seven to ten o'clock. She has a new dress to finish, a call to make on some distant corporation, a meeting to attend. There is a lecture or a concert at some one of the public halls, and the attendance will be thin if she and her associates are not present; or, if nothing more imperative demands her time, she takes a stroll through the street or to the river with some of her mates or sits down at home to peruse a new book. At ten o'clock all is still for the night.

"The clang of the early bell awakes her to another day, very nearly the counterpart of the one which preceded it. And so the week rolls on, in the same routine, till Saturday comes. Saturday! the welcome sound! She busies herself to remove every particle of cotton and dust from her frame or looms, cheering herself meanwhile with sweet thoughts of the coming of Sabbath; and when, at an earlier hour than usual, the mill is stopped, it looks almost beautiful in its neatness.

"Then approaches the Sabbath—the day of rest! If the factory girl keeps it well, it must be at church; for there are some in every boarding-house who find an excuse for staying at home half the day at least. One of her room-mates is indisposed, another says she must write a letter to one of her friends, another has to work so hard during the week that she thinks she ought to make this literally a 'day of rest,' so that retirement and meditation are out of the question. But in the Sabbath school and sanctuary her time is well spent. No one is more constant at church or earlier in her seat than the operative who has been trained to know the value of the institution of the gospel. The instructions which she receives sink deep into her heart, giving her a fund of thought for the coming week. Her pastor and her Sabbath-school teacher are felt to be her best friends and their kindness is a strong allurement to her spirit, often keeping her long from her less-favored home. If it is said that many a one has here found a grave, shall it not also be said that many a one has here found the path to heaven?

"The writer is aware that this sketch is an imperfect one. Yet there is very little variety in an operative's life, and little difference between it and any other life of labor. It lies 'half in sunlight—half in shade.' Few would wish to spend a whole life in a factory, and few are discontented who do thus seek a subsistence for a term of months or years."[73]

Since the inauguration of the factory system and the entrance of women into the commercial world, there has been a well-sustained effort to improve conditions. But they are still bad, in many places, for women as well as men. That women in modern business concerns were subjected to bad working conditions was shown, for example, by Elizabeth B. Butler,[74] who pointed out, in her survey of Baltimore stores, that (1) base-

[73] *The Lowell Offering* [*Old South Leaflets*, No. 157, Vol. VII, 129–31 and 150–1].

[74] *Saleswomen in Mercantile Stores* (1912).

ments had very poor ventilation, (2) stores requiring artificial illumination were very badly lighted, (3) most stores did not comply with the laws requiring that seats be furnished for women clerks, and (4) that 54 per cent. of the women in the different wage groups earned $5 or less per week. A recent bulletin of the Women's Bureau, on the *Health Problems of Women in Industry*,[75] reproduced photographs of women (a) working at benches, sitting all day on high stools with no back rests; (b) standing on very narrow platforms, leaning over benches, cutting for the shoe industry. It is impossible here to survey the evil conditions in shops of the present day, and it is unnecessary. All who observe at all, as they visit our great cities, see the woe-begone, starved, haggard expression on the faces of wage-slaves. Sometimes it is thinly disguised by flapper devices, but it is there nevertheless.

Many laws have been passed by the states to secure better laboring conditions, but there has been great variation of opinion as to what ought to be recognized as legal conditions in the several states. The Women's Bureau has undertaken to set up "definite standards" to "serve as a guide to the many groups . . . working for the better protection of wage-earning women." Briefly these are:

"The eight-hour day.

"Saturday half holiday.

"No nightwork.

"A living wage based on occupation and not on sex, with the minimum rate sufficient to cover the cost of living for dependents and not merely for the individual.

"Good working conditions, including adequate washing facilities; adequate and sanitary toilet accommodations; dressing rooms, rest rooms, and lunch rooms; clean workrooms with carefully adjusted lighting, ventilation, and heating; plentiful and sanitary drinking facilities; chairs, machines, and work tables adjusted so that the workers can either stand or sit at their work; carefully guarded machinery; elimination of the necessity of constant standing or other posture causing physical strain, repeated lifting of heavy weights or other abnormally fatiguing motions, and the operation of mechanical devices requiring undue strength; exposure to excessive cold, or to dust, fumes or

[75] No. 18, 1921, 10–11. Washington: Govt. Printing Office.

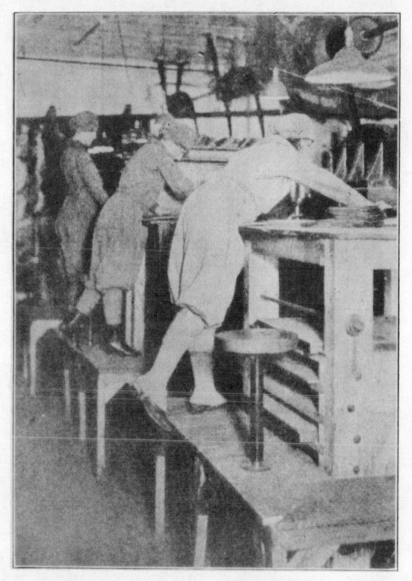

(*Courtesy of the Women's Bureau*)

WOMEN CUTTERS IN THE SHOE INDUSTRY

other occupational poisons without adequate safeguards against disease.

"Prohibition of employment of women in occupations involving the use of poisons which are proved to be more injurious to women than to men.

"Prohibition of home work.

"Establishment of systems of employment management.

"Cooperation of workers in establishing standards."[76]

It is seen from several sources that employers offered great encouragement to young prospective workers by giving false promises of great rewards and picturing them dressed in silk and having sufficient leisure to read and study. One of the Lowell mill girls wrote bitterly of the proprietors and agents who allured "us from our homes—from the peaceful abodes of our childhood. . . ."[77] This feeling of dissatisfaction was to be found in many quarters but work in the mill, in spite of disappointments, did offer a way to earn a little money; and this was a stepping-stone to something better for many of them. To earn and have real money did, no doubt, greatly impress the little girls just arrived from village and local countryside. They hoarded their meager savings—many of them—and went back to school, helped assist other members of the family to do so, or paid family expenses for destitute parents. But when the glamor of the new occupation wore away, it was quite evident even to the girls themselves that they were miserably paid—underpaid, judging by the pay given to men.[78] The low wages and inequality were dwelt upon by *The Man* in many issues. Inequality of pay for the mill girls was asserted to be a wrong of the first magnitude and liable to result in many grave consequences for society. It is not to be wondered at, therefore, that when it was proposed to reduce wages because of the *"unusual pressure of the times"* about six or seven hundred girls held a great meeting and drew up resolutions of protest:

"1st Resolved, that we will never consent to work for the Cocheco Manufacturing Company at their reduced *'Tariff of Wages.'*

[76] *Ibid.*, 4–5.
[77] *The Man*, March 20, 1834.
[78] See the protest of women workers referred to, p. 21.

"2d Resolved, that we believe the '*unusual pressure of the times*' . . . to have been caused by artful and designing men to subserve party purposes, or . . . to promote their own private ends.

"3d Resolved, that we view with feelings of indignation the attempt made to throw upon us, who are least able to bear it, the effect of this *pressure,* by reducing our wages, while those of our overseers and agent are continued . . . at their former high rate."

Fourth, it was declared this reduction was but a part of a scheme to reduce the female employees to a genuine state of slavery; fifth, vigorous dissent was asserted to the accusation, made by the employers, that the girls had formed "riotous combinations"; sixth, it was declared that no matter how often they might be called "factory slaves" they would never justify the application of the term by any "base and cringing submission to proud wealth or *haughty insolence.*"[79]

Another article in *The Man* dealt with the same question: "The price of female labor is already too low, and the amount of labor that females have to perform too great. Many of these young women have poor and aged parents depending on the earnings of their children for support. Others who are not obliged to assist their parents, can receive no assistance from them, and must, out of their small earning, which rarely exceeds two dollars and fifty cents a week, provide board and clothing, and lay by something to support themselves when they are sick or unemployed."[80]

Some thought that if women were better educated they would then be better paid. Horace Mann called attention to the fact that the forty thousand female operatives, estimated as engaged in cotton and straw platting and so on, received on the average $100 a year; and that the best educated girls average 50 per cent. more than the least educated. Superficially, he argued that if all girls were given "mental cultivation" the total wages paid "would rise to the sum of six millions of dollars, annually."[81]

Further recognition was given the wage question, by the workers themselves, about 1863, when "thirty thousand girls"

[79] *The Man,* March 8, 1834.
[80] *Ibid.,* March 4, 1834.
[81] *Com. Sch. Jour.,* IV, 376.

in New York were reported to be working for "from one dollar to three dollars a week each," with board alone costing within twenty-five cents of their total wages; and a similar development took place at Boston. *Littell's Living Age*[82] used this occasion to publish, among other things, the following lines, under the name of Woodbury Fernard:

"She asks for bread, for clothes, for more!
"For comfort, culture, virtue, peace.
"She asks—and by the heavens so pure,
"By God's great arm, by man's increase,
"By all the powers above, below,
"Her righteous prayer, so long deferred,
"Shall soon be answered: earth shall know
"The judgments which its crimes have stirred.

"Yes, patient ones, 'tis not alone
"One form of bondage now that falls;
"Jehovah makes thy cause his own,
"And man shall tremble when he calls.
"Oh, long account of labor crushed!
"Of honest, anguished, starving toil!
"And who art thou, O man, so flushed
"At such a price, with such a spoil!

"See! rising thousands, hear their tramp,
"From seats of weariness and pain,
"From gloomy garrets, cellars damp,
"And crowded streets—a numerous train—
"Who do not threaten, cannot take
"The bolder measures man employs,
"But simply ask of him to make
"Life's burden lighter, more its joys."

Others had much less sympathy with the laboring woman's plea for better conditions and wages. W. B. F., writing in the *Common School Journal*,[83] apropos of the excitement created by an exposure of the oppression of seamstresses in New York, declared there were two sides to the question; and, while she was astonished at the avarice of employers who would pay so little for service rendered, she nevertheless felt that the women were partly to blame for not relieving themselves at once, as they very easily could do. Her suggestions, often made by others—

[82] (1863), LXXIX, 482.
[83] X, 297–9.

and they are sometimes repeated today with minor changes—
may best be given directly:

"When I am told that a worthy and virtuous girl is obliged
to toil from sunrise to sunset for twelve and a half, or twenty
cents, and board herself, I sometimes ask, why she does not go
into some respectable family, where, without half the labor, she
can obtain more money, and be fed and lodged in a far more
comfortable manner. The difference between a good American
girl and such girls as now constitute almost the whole of our
domestics, is so great that they always have the preference, and
when they are faithful, they are hardly treated as inferiors by
their employers. When, therefore, they can obtain constant
employment, good pay, and good treatment—and the deserving
may always do this—it may admit of doubt whether they are
entitled to all the sympathy that is bestowed upon them, if they
choose to suffer.

"A great change has come over this community within a quarter of a century. When the writer of this became a housekeeper,
few or no foreigners were employed as domestics. With the
exception of a few colored persons, who were often preferred to
white American girls, and were far superior to the foreigners
that have now usurped all Kitchendom, the domestics of New
England were not always the children of poor persons, for the
daughters of respectable farmers often went out to service for a
few years, to obtain enough to form a marriage portion, or to
clothe them comfortably for years after their return to the
paternal mansion.

"But all this is changed. The foreigners came, and the
American girls retired before them. It soon was considered dis-
reputable to live out as domestics, and though a large number
found employment in our factories, from which the foreigners
were excluded by their ignorance; still, a very large number,
not liking a factory life, have endeavored to obtain a living by
needle-work; and as the number of laborers has always been
more than sufficient for the work to be done, and as this class
of laborers has constantly increased, competition has as constantly reduced the price of labor, and the employers have not
shrunk from taking every advantage of the necessity which they
did not create, and which, I fear, they cannot remove.

"Far be it from me to complain of the reception which has been given to the wretched immigrants who have swarmed hither; yet, I cannot but think it was a sad day for this community when the intelligent and virtuous females of New England were driven from our families to make room for them. . . . The question arises, how far is the present condition of our female work-women to be attributed to their education, and how far may a better education remedy the existing evil. There can be no doubt, I think, that all our improvements in education have not led our children to place a right estimate on the dignity of labor. They have not learned that every honest employment is respectable, and that he who is greatest of all may be the servant of all without losing his own self-respect or the respect of the wise and good. I see no reason why a large portion of the distressed females, whom it is fashionable to commiserate, may not at once find employment and high wages, and kind treatment in respectable families; and who does not see, that by this movement our families would be improved, our children benefitted, the demand for a wretched class of foreigners reduced, and then, such females as cannot leave their homes to reside in families, would be able to find full employment, and obtain sufficient compensation for their needle-work. If our teachers would take more pains to teach the young the true basis of respectability, and if our charitable societies, instead of railing at the employers of the poor seamstress, would teach her better, and induce her to seek other employment where it may be had, a great benefit would be conferred upon society, and one of the true ends of a right education would be secured."[84]

Many were quick to point to inadequate pay as a contributing factor in the growth of prostitution. Well may prostitution take its toll when wages are so miserable that a whole day's work brings only a few pennies, while a smile will buy a dinner. Dall was a stanch champion of the right of women to equal pay— a living wage. She declared that "of two thousand cases [of prostitution] in the City of New York, five hundred and twenty-five pleaded destitution as the cause." At that time, of two thousand women who worked for their daily bread, in that city, "five hundred and thirty-four receive[d] a dollar a week."[85]

[84] *Ibid.*
[85] Dall: *College, Market and the Court*, 142–3.

"How many men would keep off death and conquer the Devil on such wages?"

But, if many realized in low wages a crime against womanhood, progress towards a better situation was slow. Yet some advancement was made, the details of which cannot be chronicled here. Brief reference has already been made to the demand for equal pay for men and women teachers.[86] This was regarded by many as certain to influence the equalization of wages for other workers.[87] California, progressive in many things, as early as 1860, had accepted the idea of equal compensation for equal work, regardless of the sex of the laborer.[88] Gradually public interest was aroused and became an influential factor in bringing about better wage conditions. A writer on the topic stated that the "reiterated declaration" in favor of "equal pay" had achieved results; that the injustice of "the present inequality" was more generally felt.[89]

The dawn of the next century, however, found the struggle still going on. In New York (1907), a mass meeting was held at Carnegie Lyceum to demand congressional investigation of the status of women workers. Appeals made by two organizations, for equal pay for men and women teachers, the forming of women's trade unions, and demands for the vote by laboring women, showed the ferment that was going on in the ranks of workers.[90] Alice Salmon, in a study of unequal wages, advanced the idea that the lower wage was due to the fact that young women did not like the long apprenticeship necessary for skilled trades; and she was convinced that proper training for skilled work would raise wages more effectively than agitation and the work of unions.

In the table below are wage figures for a few industries, showing the situation in 1890 and 1900. These facts, collected in a special inquiry by the Bureau of the Census,[91] show that in some industries where women had long been employed—such

86 See Vol. I, 460, 490–6, 505, 512.

87 See N. A. R. (1895), CLX, 416–17.

88 Littell's Living Age (1860), LXIV, 528.

89 N. A. R. (1895), CLX, 416–17.

90 Comment in The Nation (1907), LXXXIV, 72–3.

91 Twelfth Census of the United States: Special Report on Employees and Wages. See page 36.

as woolen, cotton, and knitting—their wages compared more favorably with those of men. Facts like these partially formed the basis of Salmon's contention. In bakeries, breweries, candy, cigars, clothing, paper and shoe industries, there appear great discrepancies between wages of men and women. If the complete analysis of the figures collected by the Census Bureau could be displayed here, it would also be seen, at a glance, that low wage medians for women were closely allied to the fact that women were performing many of the least skilled tasks.

Still the agitation for equality of men and women in the industrial world goes on. Recently a delegation of women wage earners brought a petition to the White House, and a mass meeting was held at a nearby theater for a discussion of the subject.[92]

That the agitation for better conditions, hours and wages has indeed had an influence can be seen in the growth of state legislation relative thereto, especially since the Civil War. A few laws may be named to illustrate the sort of things they attempted to secure. New York, in 1867, enacted that ''no property now exempt by law shall be exempt from levy or sale, under an execution, issued upon a judgment obtained in any court in the city of New York, for work, labor or services . . . performed by any female employee when such amount does not exceed the sum of fifteen dollars exclusive of costs.''[93] The next year (1868) a law was passed incorporating the Working Women's Protective Union, the purpose of which was ''to promote the interests of women who obtain a livelihood by employments other than household service, and especially to provide them with legal protection from the frauds and impositions of unscrupulous employers . . .''[94] An act of 1886 provided that no minor under eighteen and no woman under twenty-one be employed in manufacturing concerns more than sixty hours per week, unless for making necessary repairs. Not less than fifty, nor more than one hundred dollars, was named as a fine; and in default thereof, imprisonment from thirty to ninety days was to be the sentence.[95]

---

92 Article in [Phila.] *Evening Public Ledger*, Jan. 4, 1926.
93 Passed Apr. 22, *Laws of N. Y.*, 1867, 1399.
94 Passed May 5, *Laws of N. Y.*, 1868, 1205.
95 *Ibid.*, 1886, 629.

TABLE III

Industry	Median Earnings per Week (Dollars) Over 16 years of age only	
COTTON MILLS	*1890*	*1900*
Men	7.00	7.50
Women	5.00	6.00
DYEING AND FINISHING TEXTILES		
Men	7.50	7.50
Women (few employed)	6.00	5.50
KNITTING MILLS		
Men	8.00	8.00
Women	5.50	6.00
WOOLEN MILLS		
Men weavers	7.50	8.50
Men sorters	11.00	12.50
Women weavers	7.00	8.00
Tenders and beamers	5.50	6.00
BAKERS		
Men	11.00	12.00
Women (few employed)	5.00	4.50
BREWERIES		
Men	13.00	14.00
Women (few employed)	3.50	3.50
CANDY		
Men	8.00	8.00
Women	3.50	3.50
CIGARS		
Men	10.00	12.50
Women	5.00	5.50
CLOTHING		
Men	11.50	10.00
Women	4.50	4.00
PAPER MILLS		
Men	9.00	9.00
Women	4.50	4.50
SHOES		
Men	11.00	11.50
Women	2.50	3.00

A Pennsylvania statute, of 1885, provided that no woman should be employed in the coal mines and the manufactories thereof in the state, save for clerical work in offices connected with the industry. Fines of from one hundred to five hundred dollars and six months in prison, either or both, were to be meted out to offenders.[96]   Two years later an act was passed to compel manufacturing, mercantile, and mechanical establishments to provide suitable seats for the use of female employees, and to permit them to use them.   A fine of twenty-five to fifty dollars was provided.[97]

A law relative to the provision of seats for female employees had been passed by Massachusetts five years before that of Pennsylvania.   In this law the fine was from ten to thirty dollars.[98] In 1887, the Bay State required that uniform and proper meal times should be set aside for children, young people and women, employed in factories.[99]   In 1890, a law prohibited women's and minors' employment in factories at night, between ten o'clock and six.[100]

Connecticut, in 1887, prohibited the employment of minors, under sixteen, and women, in manufacturing and commercial concerns, more than ten hours a day, except when necessary repairs must be made to prevent interruption of business, and certain cases in which hours might be apportioned so as to make one day of the week shorter than the rest.[101]   Virginia, in 1890, passed a similar ten-hour day law.   Fines of five to twenty dollars were to be levied on the offenders.[102]

It would be useless to catalog more individual cases.   By 1908, nineteen states had passed similar ten-hour laws.   Oregon provided a test case as to the constitutionality of such enactment.   In 1903, she passed a ten-hour law.   Curt Muller, of Portland, contested the law's constitutionality, maintaining it violated the Fourteenth Amendment.   The Oregon Supreme Court's decision upheld the law, and the Federal Supreme Court did likewise.   The ground for the favorable judgments was found in social welfare.   The Industrial Commission, in 1900, had declared that "industrial progress cannot be built upon physical exhaustion of women and children."   Now the courts decided the question on the basis of moral and social justice rather than

[96] *Laws of Pa.*, 1885, 202.
[97] *Ibid.*, 1887, 7.
[98] *Laws of Mass.*, 1882, 109.
[99] *Ibid.*, 1887, 832–4.
[100] *Ibid.* (1890), 152.
[101] *Laws of Conn.*, 1887, 692–3.
[102] *Laws of Va.*, 1890, Ch. 193, 150–1.

economic expediency or inexpediency. Brewer, rendering the decision, declared legislation designed for the protection of women laborers could be sustained "even when like legislation is not necessary for men, and could not be sustained."[103]

In less than a decade after this decision, five states and the District of Columbia had established the eight-hour day for women in industry. California passed her laws securing the eight-hour day and forty-eight-hour week for women in 1911 and 1913.[104] The Supreme Court of the United States sustained the laws of California, and thus gave validity to the acts of Arizona, Colorado, Washington and Wyoming, who soon followed the lead of their Western neighbor. Five other states—Massachusetts, New York, Pennsylvania, Indiana and Nebraska—had, by 1916, provided for rest periods at night.[105]

By 1924, there were but four states—Alabama, Florida, Iowa and West Virginia—which did not have some law regulating the hours of women's work. Indiana, Georgia, North Carolina, and South Carolina had made limited prohibitions,—the first relative to night work in manufacturing, and the last three by limiting definitely the hours per week, or by providing for increased rates for overtime employment.[106] Nine states—Arizona, California, Colorado, Kansas, Montana, Nevada, New Mexico, Utah, and Washington—have the eight-hour day; as also the District of Columbia and the Territory of Porto Rico. Most of the other states have nine-hour and ten-hour laws, while a few permit from ten to twelve hours a day.[107] Approximately a fourth of the states prohibit or regulate home work. Thirteen[108] have minimum wage laws, operating in a variety of ways.

[103] Quoted in *The Nation* (1908), LXXXVI, 184.

[104] *Laws of California*, 1911, Ch. 258; and 1913, Ch. 352.

[105] The Eight Hour Day and Rest at Night, by Florence Kelly [*Educational Foundations*, XXVIII, 414–16].

[106] Women's Bureau, Bulletin No. 40, 1924, on *State Laws Affecting Working Women*, 1.

[107] New Hampshire, 10¼-hour day, 54-hour week; Vermont, 10½-hour day, 56-hour week; Tennessee, 10½-hour day, 57-hour week; North Carolina, 11-hour day and 60-hour week for men and women in textiles; South Carolina allows a twelve-hour day to women in mercantile concerns but limits labor to ten hours in the cotton factories.—From the bulletin of the Women's Bureau, cited above.

[108] Arizona, Arkansas, California, Colorado, Kansas, Massachusetts, Minnesota, North Dakota, Oregon, South Dakota, Utah, Washington, and Wisconsin—Bulletin No. 40, 1924, 6.

V. Effects of Women's Entrance into Industry

Thus, step by step with the progress of the factory system, and to a large degree, doubtless, as a result of it, women have entered widely different occupations.   Once it was urged, when women first entered the work-a-day factory world, that certain tasks were too onerous for them.   This is sometimes true today, but, for the most part, one may say that now labor knows no sex lines. There is still marked discrimination in some fields of work. Agitation against it is, however, gradually gaining ground. Modern women are resolved that ability alone be the determiner. In a measure it is true, as Gilbert Murray wrote, that women are as a rule "worse paid and harder driven."[109] So completely has the position of woman been changed by the rise of industrial society, that those tasks which once were believed to constitute her greatest glory are no longer expected of her.   Higginson depicted the transformation in Women and Men.[110]

"Even the home made shirts . . . have come within the domain of the shop-keeper.   The sister would not weave or spin for her brother if he wished it; and he . . . would rather gratify her in any other way than by wearing garments of her spinning or weaving.   The reign of Alcinous and his white armed daughter has passed."   Hannah no longer binds shoes at the window, nor does Delia braid straw hats there; but they go to the factories and elsewhere and perform functions comparable to those done heretofore.   There is another essential difference.   They no longer work for their board, but receive a wage.   So common has wage earning of women become that it is no longer disgraceful, meretricious.   There arise, naturally, many questions concerning the advantages and disadvantages of this change.   Are men and women living more completely since machines have increased production?   Are women happier because they slave in the factory, or elsewhere, rather than in their fathers' or husbands' houses?   The machine-filled factory has drawn women from those to whom they were bound by the strongest natural tie, and has, by their labor, increased output.[111] Is life essentially

109 Interesting views of women in industrial society are presented in Sykes: Soc. Basis of the New Education for Women, 3–5; Murray: The Weaker Sex [Ed. Rev. (1910), XL, 514–16].

110 Pp. 9–10.

111 Hamilton: A New Atmosphere, 78–9.

richer because we have three suits rather than one; cover three hundred miles a day rather than forty; eat the white bread of idleness and worry rather than the corn bread of industry and content? It is said that "he most lives who thinks the noblest, acts the best." To what extent has the entrance of women into new spheres of action, from lowest factory "hand" to highest clerkship, improved the character of thought and action? No one knows the truth of this matter,—but there are many opinions as to the good and ill derived from this new venture.

It being an innovation of no small proportion, and our social and individual minds being unusually conservative, there naturally arose all sorts of predictions; and many final judgments were given, setting forth the consequences of a "reform against nature," economic, physical, social, and moral. The approximate unanimity of certain judgments has, with reason, given pause; others, representing a strong individual bias, have passed with slight attention.

Having been blamed for almost all the evils that beset modern society, it is quite within the range of plausibility that the entrance of women into almost all occupations may have been the cause of some of them, or at least contributory thereto. Female wage earners have from time to time been blamed for the increase of crime—due to the decrease of mother's influence; race suicide—women become so wealthy and independent they will not have children; lowered marriage rate—having an income, they do not need a husband and prefer to slave for one rather than two; increase of divorce and wife desertion—men cannot live with such independent and disrespectful creatures; denuding home life of its pleasures—having an independent income, they can go to the movies and grand opera; the disappearance of a reliable domestic servant class—women are too proud to do housework;[112] the ruin of men's wages—by insinuating themselves in the good graces of his employers; and the decline of women's morals—not being protected, as in the homes of yore, from the force of bad examples. Up to about 1906 little effort was made to look into these serious charges. Then the General Federation of Women's Clubs, Women's Trade Union League, and others interested in social problems, urged the study of in-

[112] The inevitable servant problem, referred to by Starrett: *Letters to Elder Daughters*, 96–7.

dustrial women by the Department of Labor, securing the endorsement of Roosevelt for their demand.[113]

One of the very early fears expressed was that woman's health would suffer in the factories, due to long hours and the nature of the work. The following view was expressed at a national Trade Union Convention in 1834: "For a few years past, the sons of our farmers, as soon as they are of sufficient age, have been induced to hasten off to the factory where for a few pence more than they could get at home, they are taught to become the willing servants, the servile instruments of their employer's oppression and extortion! The daughter, too, must quit the farm house, the scene of ruddy health and former content, for a confined and baneful workshop, where to be sure, she earns a little more money, for a short time; but as surely loses health, if not her good character, her happiness."[114] That the fear of such effects was well grounded there is no question. From that day to this, efforts have been made to curb greedy employers by setting reasonable, standard, conditions and wages. The early, and some later, efforts to regulate these by law have, however, been far from successful.

The factory operators wanted cheap labor and learned to find it in women. Soon the effect upon men as laborers appeared. In *The Working Class Movement in America,* the Avelings showed that because of female and child labor men's compensation was so reduced as to make it impossible for the family to live upon it.[115] John Swinton wrote, in *Striking for Life,* "A father . . . finds . . . he cannot earn enough . . . for the maintenance of his household; he asks his daughter, or, in many a case, his wife, to help him to eke out a living; and she does her best for their mutual benefit. . . . I know that the pay in the cheap clothing trades, at which between thirty and forty thousand people are employed in New York City alone, has become so pitiful that the work of both the husband and wife, both the boy and the girl of the family, for the livelong day, is needed for the payment of rent and the purchase of food that is often unfit for consumption."[116]

[113] *The Nation* (1906), LXXXII, 152–3.

[114] Reprinted by permission of the publishers, The Arthur H. Clark Company, from Calhoun's *Social History of the American Family,* II, 196.

[115] Chapters V and VI.

[116] *Op. cit.,* 63–4.

Such were the conditions about a generation ago, when the Avelings and Swinton wrote; and that the situation in New York was similar to that in other large industrial centers is suggested by studies of Massachusetts, to which reference will shortly be made. In the present century, married women have continued to increase in many occupations outside the home—not always from choice, it appears, but because their families must have their slender earnings. In the chart, below, which has been carefully prepared by the Women's Bureau, it is shown that of all women, in all occupations, almost one-fourth are married (23%). The proportion of married women is lowest in clerical occupations (9.1%) and highest in agricultural pursuits (39.7%).

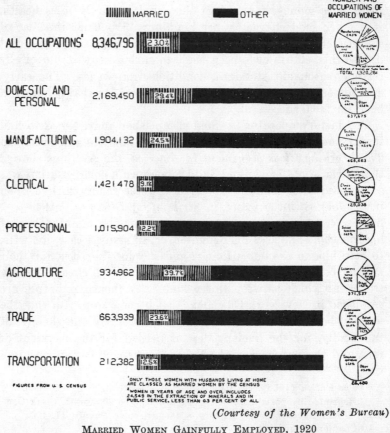

(*Courtesy of the Women's Bureau*)

MARRIED WOMEN GAINFULLY EMPLOYED, 1920
PER CENT OF ALL EMPLOYED WOMEN

At the beginning of the last quarter of the nineteenth century, in Massachusetts, a study of 397 families showed that but approximately 36 per cent. could live on the earnings of the father. Still the general situation is the same. Married women, and single, are generally observed to contribute all or a large part of their earnings to pay family expenses, and this is explicitly pointed out by recent studies.[117] The conclusions of the Massachusetts study were:

"*First*. That in the majority of cases workingmen in this Commonwealth do not support their families by their individual earnings alone.

"*Second*. That the amount of earnings contributed by wives, generally speaking, is so small, that they would save more by staying at home, than they gain by outside labor.

"*Third*. That fathers rely, or are forced to depend, upon their children for from one-quarter to one third of the entire family earnings.

"*Fourth*. That children under fifteen years of age supply, by their labor from one-eighth to one-sixth of the total family earnings.

"*Fifth*. That more than one-half of the families save money, less than one-tenth are in debt, and the remainder make both ends meet.

"*Sixth*. That without children's assistance, other things remaining equal, the majority of families would be in poverty or debt." Elsewhere it was stated: "That savings, by families and fathers alone, are made in every branch of occupation investigated; but that in only a few cases is there evidence of the possibility of acquiring a competence, and in those cases it would be the result of assisted or family labor."[118]

The use of children has been common from the beginning of factories. The continuance of their labor has most stubbornly been held to by employers in spite of attempted legal control. Even today a child labor amendment to the constitution of the United States has failed. In the thirties, educators of America were already becoming alarmed at the tendency to employ children—and women. The *American Annals of Education* described

[117] See Bulletin No. 30, 1923, of the Women's Bureau.

[118] Mass. Bur. of Statistics of Labor, *Sixth Annual Report*, Part IV, 441 *ff*.

the facts in a long article, quoting a committee report on education, whence the following is taken:

"In four large manufacturing towns, not, however, including the largest, from which we have no information upon that topic, containing, by the last census, a population of a little less than twenty thousand, there appears to be *eighteen hundred and ninety-five children* between the ages of *four and sixteen,* who do not attend the common schools any portion of the year. And from this number there is but a very slight deduction to be made for those who attend private schools. If full and accurate answers were given by all the towns in the Commonwealth, to the question designed to obtain this information, it is believed there would be developed a state of facts, which would at once arrest the attention of the Legislature, and not only justify, but loudly demand legislative action upon the subject. And this state of facts as appears by the returns, is peculiar in degree and almost in kind to the manufacturing towns. . . .

"Human labor, which no perfection of machinery can wholly dispense with, of every variety of form, must inevitably be dearer in a country like our own, abounding in cheap, productive and uncultivated lands, than in those countries where the land has been for centuries appropriated, and which are now full to overflowing of people, who are already crowded hard upon the bare means of subsistence. Labor being dearer in this country than it is in any other, with which we are brought in competition in manufacturing, operates as a constant inducement to manufacturers to employ female labor, and the labor of children, to the exclusion of men's labor because they can be had cheaper.

"The families usually collected in our large manufacturing establishments, are either those that have been unfortunate, or from some cause, unsuccessful in agriculture or other employments, and are there collected in despair of obtaining more than a comfortable support, or a bare subsistence; or they are families formed around the establishments, on the strength of the then present prospect of gaining a certain support, by those young people, who depend solely upon their daily wages, and have nothing to expect but what they can obtain from day to day, or week to week. Of course, when such families, numerous and indigent as they generally are, begin to increase, and when their wants begin to press upon their scanty means of comfort, or perhaps even of necessary subsistence, there is a strong interest and an urgent motive to seek constant employment for their children; at a very early age, if the wages obtained can aid them even but little in bearing the burden of their support.

"These two causes or principles of interest, in the employer on the one hand, and in the employed, on the other, are operating, silently perhaps, but steadily and powerfully, to deprive young females particularly, and young children of both sexes, in a large and increasing class in the community, of those means and opportunities of mental and moral development and cultivation, which are essential to their becoming the intelligent mothers and educators of the next generation, and good citizens of the republic."[119]

The committee, quoted above, reported a bill imposing fifty dollars fine on any who employed a child under fifteen years of age in manufacturing "who has not attended some public or private day school for at least three months of the twelve months preceding."[120] The bill was passed, but with slight, if any, results.

In spite of early efforts to protect them, the use of children's labor continued in Massachusetts. About 1870, recognizing, merely from general observation, that laws were laxly enforced, if at all, the legislature appointed a commission, with General H. K. Oliver at its head, to investigate the situation carefully. One factory woman stated:

"There are many children under ten years of age employed in my mill and in others, and some not over seven. They work eleven hours, and sometimes till half-past nine at night. Boys have to walk not less than twenty miles a day. I know of no case where the legal schooling has been had. The influence of factory life on children is very bad; they are always of a sickly look, and it disqualifies girls for household duties and for mothers."

Again, it was stated by an "overlooker": "To the best of my knowledge there are one hundred and fifty children under fifteen years of age in the room in which I am employed; none of them have attended school during the past year. Six years ago I ran

[119] *Op. cit.*, VI, 219 *ff.*
[120] *Ibid.*

night work from 6:45 P. M. to 6 A. M., with forty-five minutes for meals in the room. The children were drowsy and sleepy; I have known them to fall asleep while standing up at their work. Some of these children are now working in the mill, and appear under fifteen years of age. I have had to sprinkle water in their faces to arouse them, after having spoken to them till hoarse." Another observer declared that, in a Rhode Island mill, drowsy children were aroused to their work with a "leather strap, with tacks driven through the striking end."[121]

The view that laws were not, and could not be, enforced was further corroborated by the report of the Massachusetts Bureau of Statistics of Labor, in 1874, though the burden for failure was not laid entirely on the factories. It appears from this statement that ". . . the law in relation to the employment of children neither is, nor can be, enforced. Should the managers of mills cooperate heartily with the officers of the cities and towns, or of the state, the law could not well be enforced. The testimony of the school boards in some of the manufacturing places is, that often as much difficulty arises from parents as from mill-owners and managers.

"The interest of parents, and, alas, too frequently the necessity of the case, compels the father or mother, or both, to register a falsehood, in order to keep the wolf from the door; but so long as children of tender age, more fit for the hospital than the mill, are allowed to have a place in our factories, their employment will be tolerated, and the cheapness of their labor materially affects the wages of older persons. . . .

". . . At least twenty-five thousand children between the ages of five and fifteen do not receive the slightest education either in our public or private schools."[122]

It is not the purpose of this work to study the child labor problem; but it has been alluded to because of its intimate connection with another of the effects of the upheaval in economic life; the change of the American home. With women and children in the factory all day—and sometimes at night—the home, for thousands upon thousands, literally ceased to be. Respect, love, reverence for domestic life came to an end, when that life itself became non-existent. The dissolution of that life dissolved

[121] Quoted in *Godey's Lady's Book*, Sept. 1870, 374.
[122] *Op. cit.*

the bonds that made it.   It was this transformation of the relationships formerly existing between wife, husband, and children
that appears to have stimulated the most universal alarm.   Men
were generally most alarmed, for the old family ideal and practice had placed them as heads over the wives and children.   But
when each and all began to earn a wage, real economic equality
of husband and wife became a not remote possibility; and the
headship of the former as well as the obedience of the latter,
reverently referred to in marriage forms, began to be questioned,
winked at, ridiculed and, at last, deleted.[123]

Very early in women's independent labor career the baleful
effect on the home was decried.   The *American Annals of Education* quoted approvingly a lengthy article from the *British
Education Magazine,* a part of which follows:

"The moral influence of woman upon man's character, and
domestic happiness, is mainly attributable to her natural and
instinctive habits.   Her love, her tenderness, her affectionate
solicitude for his comfort and enjoyment, her devotedness, her
unwearied care, her conjugal attractions, exercise a most enno-
bling impression upon his nature, and do more towards making
him a good husband, a good father, and an useful citizen, than
all the dogmas of political economy.   But the factory woman
cannot have this beneficial agency upon man's character.   Her
instincts, from their earliest birth, have been thwarted and
pushed aside from their proper channels; they have had no

---

[123] It is interesting to compare the gradual transformation of the American family with the more rapid change of the Russian.   Industrial equality
and equality of man and woman in the family have presented there, as elsewhere, the most difficult problems.   In *Problems of Life,* 49-9, Trotsky
wrote: " . . . To institute the political equality of men and women in the
Soviet State was one problem and the simplest.   A much more difficult one
was the next—that of instituting the industrial equality of men and women
workers in the factories, the mills and the trade unions, and to do it in such
a way that the men should not put the women to any disadvantage.   But to
achieve the actual equality of man and woman within the family is an in-
finitely more arduous problem.   All our domestic habits must be revolution-
ized before that can happen.   And yet it is quite obvious that unless there
is actual equality of husband and wife in the family, in a normal sense as
well as in the conditions of life, we cannot speak seriously of their equality
in social work or even in politics.   As long as woman is chained to her housework, the care of the family, the cooking and sewing, all her chances of
participation in social and political life are cut down to the extreme."

field in which they could be lavished. On the reverse, her passions have been prematurely developed, her physical organization stimulated into precocious activity, her social affections
utterly blighted, her person rendered unworthy by its want of
feminine gracefulness; her occupation has destroyed the delightful sympathies of home, as also her maternal affections; and,
finally, in place of seeking her pleasures, enjoyments, and happiness, in ministering to the wants, and promoting the welfare
of her household, she seeks gratification in other less pure and
less womanly stimuli, fatal alike to her health and her comfort.

"Nothing would tend more to elevate the moral condition of
the manufacturing population, than the restoration of woman
to her proper social rank; nothing would exercise greater influence upon the form and growth of her offspring, than her
devotion to those womanly occupations, which would render her
a denizen of home. No great step can be made, till she is
snatched from unremitting toil, and made what nature meant
she should be, the center of a system of social delights. Domestic
avocations are those which are peculiarly her lot. The poor
man who suffers his wife to work separate from him, and from
home, is a bad calculator. It destroys domestic economy, without which, no earnings are sufficient to render him comfortable;
it produces separate interests, and separate sets of feelings;
they lose their mutual dependence upon each other; their offspring is suffered to starve or perish; to become, even as a child,
the imitator of their bad example; to have its frame prematurely
injured, to acquire bodily conditions, which it must in its turn,
transmit to its own children; till in the end a point of physical
declension is reached, from which the return of a condition
approximating to that of the more perfect and more valuable
part of the species, must be by slow and painful gradations.
When women are thus reduced below the grade of savage life,
we can no longer wonder that all household virtues are utterly
extinct; and thus we have to lament the want of regard for
conjugal obligations of bashful reserve, of a cultivation of those
few sensibilities which can and do shed a bright gleam of pure
radiance over married life, when composed of its proper
elements."

As for "love of helpless infancy" and attention to its wants,
"the system of factory labor has . . . gone far towards annihil-

ating this great and beautiful principle in woman's moral organization; it has torn asunder those links of instinctive affection, which, under almost every other circumstance, have bound a mother to her offspring, and, in doing this, it has deprived woman of that moral characteristic, the most influential in rendering her a loveable and loving being.

"Compelled to rise early; no opportunity for visiting home during the day, but at scanty and hurried meal-times; her mind and body alike enthralled by her occupation; her social affections destroyed; her frame, little calculated to furnish her child with support, she becomes inaccessible to its appeals to her tenderness, leaves it to the care of an hireling or young person—a mere infant—and as its faculties develope, takes no interest in keeping it from the contagión of vice and grossness.

"If a mother's love is thus injured, a love springing as it does from the very groundwork of her moral nature, no wonder can be excited that the relations of husband and wife are perverted; and, in place of presenting a perfect picture of what love and domestic felicity should be, developing a scene of disorder, wanting everything which should render home a place of pure and chaste delights.

"The delicacy of comportment, which is the palladium of married love, has no existence; separated the whole of the day, exposed to vicious example, surrounded by a stimulant yet enervating atmosphere, the intercourse of man and wife loses its protecting influence upon the animal appetites, and ceases to become a bar to licentiousness and even profligacy.

"If the domestic manners of the parents are thus depraved, their example cannot tend to remove the influence of the evil lessons taught their children. . . .[124]

When the above was first read in America, the family had lost few of its Colonial characteristics. The changes were only foreseen, somewhat hazily in the future. As, more and more, women went into industry, some of the anticipated characteristics of the changing family life appeared. Economic changes are so fundamental that they cannot occur without influencing other phases of life as well. The family of Colonial and post-Revolution days was an economic unit, whatever else it was; when its economic function was impaired, and in many instances destroyed, it

[124] *Op. cit.*, VI, 174–7.

began to disintegrate. Many other factors helped promote this tendency. The influence of industrialism upon the family has been a destructive one. Calhoun, after extensive study, drew the following conclusions concerning its effect on marriage:

"1. Woman's access to industry lowers the wage scale and makes it harder for men to assume the burdens of matrimony. 2. Industrial opportunity makes women independent of the necessity of marriage. 3. Employment in specialized industry tends to create distaste for housekeeping and so may be a factor in checking marriage. 4. The experience of wage-earning may raise a girl's standard of living so that she will hesitate to marry an ordinary man. 5. Experience in the world brings her in touch with the vice and disease prevalent among men and may cause fear of marriage. 6. Delay of marriage may lead to an irregular sex life, which is very likely to prevent marriage altogether. 7. Women are crowding particularly into professional and other high positions where ambition makes the current against matrimony strongest."[125]

Judge MacNeille, of the Municipal Court, Philadelphia, whose daily duties bring him in contact with domestic infelicities and juvenile delinquency, has expressed his conviction that economic independence of women is "one of the large factors which is contributing to the gradual breakdown of the American home. . . . Eventually, under the present trend of economic conditions, the marriage relation and the family unit will be eliminated. . . . It will probably not better our present civilization, because now we have that fundamental altruism which has been the outgrowth of family love and Christianity. The new civilization will be selfish. Of course, some people believe that selfishness is better than altruism, but I believe that any idealism which can be built up to combat the trend toward that selfish civilization is justified.

"It is only through ideals that we can hope to save altruism, and yet all history proves that the economic conditions will outrule the ideals, and the standard of civilization will change. Even now people are urging the state control of children."[126] Edith Clarke, one among the few women who have entered

125 Reprinted by permission of the publishers, The Arthur H. Clark Company, from Calhoun's *Social History of the American Family*, III, 205–6.
126 Quoted from the [Phila.] *Evening Public Ledger*, Feb. 3, 1926.

engineering, has declared it to be well-nigh impossible "to have a successful home and a successful profession at one and the same time. If you choose one, it is necessary to sacrifice the other."[127] This view seems perfectly sound; but others are just as certain that professions and families may be had by women who want them. Whichever view one is inclined to hold, since it is perfectly certain that women of the industrial state are, and will be increasingly, professional, it is necessary to recognize that the ancient home is passing. Murray wrote, just a short while ago: "The plain fact is that our present social system is no longer one based on the patriarchal family, in which all women are the belongings or the dependents of some man and have to be fed by him. It is a system in which the independent wage-earning women form a cardinal factor, a factor which neither reaction nor revolution can eliminate."[128]

[127] Quoted in the [Phila.] *Sunday Ledger*, Feb. 10, 1924.
[128] *Ed. Rev.* (1910), XL, 514–16.

CHAPTER II

VOCATIONAL EDUCATION FOR WOMEN

I. Domestic Economy

Following upon numerous changes in economic and social life, there occurred many innovations in the educational world; several of them were concerned with vocational preparation. There appeared courses in cooking, sewing, budget making, care of children, nursing, commercial training, house planning, home decoration, and so on. This movement towards special courses was in response to newly felt needs of society; it was also in accord with the changing conception of education. Formerly, faith was put in general disciplines which were thought to train for life; but new psychological insights, from Herbart to Thorndike, caused faith in formal discipline to decline, and substituted therefor a reliance upon specific disciplines. Educators revived the time-honored doctrine of Comenius that we learn to do by doing.[1] The reaction against the general discipline of the seminary, academy and early woman's college is suggested by the imaginary conversation of a father with a daughter, just returned from school: "I have made 100 in algebra, 96 in Latin, 90 in Greek, 88½ in mental philosophy and 95 in history; are you not satisfied with my record?" To which the father replied: "Yes, indeed, and if your huband happens to know anything about housekeeping, sewing and cooking, I am sure your married life will be very happy." It was generally agreed that one must marry.

The rise of domestic training in the schools may be traced to the exit of mothers from the home, the decline of the family's importance as an economic unit. When the home was the center of almost all life-activities, it was naturally the place for apprenticeship of the girl to her future occupation. But in the past century women gradually left housekeeping and began to earn money for the support of the family. As a result, girls of the the present day are without homes and domestic training in the

[1] Compare the *Great Didactic* (Keatinge's translation, 1910), 194 *ff.*

old-time sense. To take the place of it there are so-called "matrimony courses" of high schools and colleges, designed, as were mothers' courses, to enable the daughter to hold a husband after catching him. Under the former system older daughters practiced on baby brothers and sisters; today large painted babies, or borrowed babies, are used for demonstration.[2] There may also be noted here and there a tendency to emphasize college courses to fit young men for matrimony. Dr. McCracken of Vassar, Mrs. Roman, Martha Van Rensselaer, and others, have been credited with enthusiastic support of such domestic training.[3]

Recognition of the need of domestic training, and the possibility of putting it on a scientific basis, appeared in the work of Emma Willard, who declared: "It is believed that housewifery might be greatly improved by being taught, not only in practice but in theory."[4] Catherine Beecher, too, began a crusade for domestic education[5] and called attention to its importance by the publication (1840) of her *Treatise on Domestic Economy for the Use of Young Ladies at Home and at School.* The book proved popular, and went through many editions. That it was considered important by educational leaders is suggested by the fact that the revised edition of 1843 was given a thorough six-page review in the *Common School Journal.*[6]

Still, there were few or no schools teaching the subject. Julia Ward Howe wrote of the time: "I especially remember one summer which I resolved to devote to the study of cookery, for which there was then no school, and no teacher to be had at will. Having purchased Miss Catherine Beecher's Cook-book, I devoted some weeks to an experimental following of its recipes, with no satisfactory result."[7] Even at the time Beecher and Stowe published their *Principles of Domestic Science* (1870) they felt justi-

[2] Courses in matrimony at the Carl Schurz High School (Chicago)— *Evening Bulletin* [Philadelphia], Apr. 9, 1924; very valuable vocational program has been carried on by the American Association for the Study and Prevention of Infant Mortality since about 1910. See *Annual Reports.*

[3] An article in Philadelphia [Sunday] *Public Ledger.*

[4] Barnard: *Memoirs of Teachers and Educators,* 140.

[5] Compare also the views of Mrs. A. Mott, in *Observations on Female Education* (1825).

[6] V, 340.

[7] *Reminiscences,* 215–16.

fied in offering the following criticism of woman's vocational preparation:

"The Authors, while they sympathize with every honest effort to relieve the disabilities and sufferings of their sex, are confident that the chief cause of these evils is the fact that the honor and duties of the family state are not duly appreciated, that women are not trained for these duties as men are trained for their trades and professions, and that, as the consequence, family labor is poorly done, poorly paid, and regarded as menial and disgraceful.

"To be the nurse of young children, a cook, or a housemaid, is regarded as the lowest and last resort of poverty, and one which no woman of culture and position can assume without loss of caste and respectability.

"It is the aim of this volume to elevate both the honor and the remuneration of all the employments that sustain the many difficult and sacred duties of the family state, and thus to render each department of woman's true profession as much desired and respected as are the most honored professions of men.

"When the other sex are to be instructed in law, medicine, or divinity, they are favored with numerous institutions richly endowed, with teachers of the highest talents and acquirements, with expensive libraries, and abundant and costly apparatus. With such advantages, they devote nearly ten of the best years of life to preparing themselves for their profession; and to secure the public from unqualified members of these professions, none can enter them until examined by a competent body, who certify to their due preparation for their duties.

"Woman's profession embraces the care and nursing of the body in the critical periods of infancy and sickness, the training of the human mind in the most impressible period of childhood, the instruction and control of servants, and most of the government and economies of the family state. These duties of women are as sacred and important as any ordained to man; and yet no such advantages for preparation have been accorded to her, nor is there any qualified body to certify the public that a woman is duly prepared to give proper instruction in her profession."[8]

8 Beecher and Stowe: *op. cit.*, 13–14; the interesting character of this preeminent book for the household is suggested by the following chapter head-

Livermore frequently expressed belief in the desirability of training for motherhood: "She needs to know all that science can teach of the prenatal laws of being, and of the laws of heredity. Her acquaintance with physiology should not be the superficial knowledge given in the ordinary school or college. . . . It should be a thorough exposition of the mysteries of her own physical being, with a clear statement of the hygienic laws she must obey, if she would grow into healthy, enduring, glorious womanhood. She should be taught the laws of ventilation and nutrition; what constitutes healthful food; the care of infancy; the nursing of the sick; and in what that vigilant and scrupulous cleanliness consists, which almost prohibits certain forms of disease from passing under one's roof."[9] Claghorn[10] and numerous others might be quoted, who took the position that the various tasks of the housewife and mother were sufficiently complex and exacting to require the most "varied talent and the most thorough training."

In the discussion of needed specific vocational training there also appeared sharp criticisms of the existing system. Some have been referred to. Starrett pointed out (1888) that girls were not always to blame for not being better prepared for the responsibilities of wifehood. "Too many things are, in these days, pressed upon the attention of young girls . . . too many studies, too many diversions, too much going about, too much seeing people. . . . Nearly all households are suffering today from over-pressure of some kind or other that prevents mothers from giving that care to the training of their daughters in habits of industry or in knowledge of household arts which all young girls

ings:—"The Christian Family; A Christian House; A Healthful Home; Scientific Domestic Ventilation; Stoves, Furnaces, and Chimneys; Home Decoration; The Care of Health; Domestic Exercise; Healthful Food; Healthful Drinks; Cleanliness; Clothing; Good Cooking; Early Rising; Domestic Manners; Good Temper In The Housekeeper; Habits of System and Order; Giving In Charity; Economy of Time and Expenses; Health of Mind; The Care of Infants; The Management of Young Children; Domestic Amusements and Social Duties; Care of the Aged; The Care of Servants; Care of the Sick; Accidents and Antidotes; Sewing, Cutting, and Mending; Warming and Ventilation; Care of the Ignorant, The Homeless, The Helpless, and the Vicious; The Christian Neighborhood, Appeal to Teachers and Pupils; Questions and Suggestive Hints."

[9] *What Shall We Do With Our Daughters* (1883), 74–5.

[10] *College Training for Women* (1897), 201.

should receive.''[11]   Beecher had long advocated that schools make a place for such domestic instruction, no longer given in the home. She pointed out that education should be regulated on the vocational principle: ''It should secure to every young girl first and chiefly the kind of training which will best prepare her to become a housekeeper, wife, mother, and school teacher; and also ensure to her a self-supporting profession *suited to her capacities and tastes.*''[12]   Then she asked how the public schools might be modified so as to meet this requirement, and declared: ''Our public schools are now so graded that the *primary* branches might be taught in a much shorter time were the enormous accumulations of useless *details* in our school books greatly reduced. There is no use filling the memory with what excites no interest as *practically* useful and therefore soon forgotten. Let this reduction be made to give room for a *practical* training that would be interesting to all who should be trained for women's distinctive profession.''[13]

Not only should formal studies and ''useless details'' be reduced to make a place for practical training, but a new institution (Practice House) should be created to make domestic training real. ''. . . Let a model house be built for the scientific and practical training of young girls as future housekeepers, mothers, and teachers, and an endowment of $50,000 invested to support a lady Principal of Domestic Science, who shall choose her own Associate Principal. Then let a family be instituted, consisting of these two principals and ten of the most deserving pupils of the public schools, who shall receive *gratuitous* instruction in all the duties of the family state, both practical and scientific, and at the close receive diplomas certifying that they have been instructed in all that a woman needs to know should she become housekeeper, wife, mother, or school teacher. Then ten others might follow in rotation, and none be allowed to graduate till this course is completed, either at home or at school.

''This might be done so that this course of domestic education could be combined with intervals for reading the standard works

11 *Letters to Elder Daughters,* 17.

12 *Educational Reminiscences,* 203–5.

13 The question of reducing the time allotment of other subjects for the sake of domestic science was raised by many schools. This was true, for example, at Bridgeport about 1898.—See *Educational News,* Oct. 15, 1898, 278–9.

of English literature, and thus cultivating a taste for a higher course of reading than is now prevalent. Such an establishment might become a popular feature not only of the public school system, but be widely imitated in woman's colleges and private schools, so that as the result every young girl will, either at home or in such an establishment, be properly trained for her future duties."[14]

Briefly stated, the demands for vocational training of women in the schools depend upon the following: (1) Expansion of the sphere of women's activities in an industrial society now includes many things beyond the home, leaving less opportunity for giving instruction to the young. (2) The application of science to the tasks of the household requires systematic instruction, which cannot be given at home because many mothers are not trained for the purpose, even though they are not employed outside the home in any other occupation. (3) Its teaching constitutes a reform measure. Healthy people are apt to be happy. Healthy, happy people are valuable social assets. Scientifically planned meals, child hygiene, harmonious decoration, scientific regulation of ventilation, heating and plumbing systems, and skillful expenditure of the family funds, it is maintained, conduce to this end. (4) If women are to enter occupations outside the home, there must be preparation for them, and guidance in making the choice.

It is an old, old saying that "God sends meat and the devil sends cooks"; and there was, doubtless, back of the movement to open cooking schools, the idea that waste might be prevented and digestion spared. But it requires some boldness, as we have often noted, to set up to teach a thing scientifically that has been thought to reside in an individual naturally, or not at all. To wrest the supply of cooks from demonic control, no school committee dared; so it remained for individual experiment to prove it could be done. It was in 1874 that Joanna Sweeney began her work in Boston, and three years later Maria Parloa opened a cooking school. The Boston Woman's Educational Association undertook, in 1879, to support a cooking school, which, some years later (1903), was merged with Simmons College. Two cooking schools were started in 1885, supported by Mrs. Hemmenway, Mrs. Shaw, and Sarah Fay. In 1888 one school was

14 *Ibid.*

n over by the city and the other in 1892. All grammar
ols were provided for by 1893.[15]

About 1873 Juliet Corson, who was secretary of a philanthropic institution concerned with preparing women for useful
occupations, became convinced of the desirability of directing
female labor back into domestic affairs. In 1876, she opened a
cooking school in New York City, giving lessons to cooks and
housewives, as well as very young girls. In 1877, she did a great
deal to popularize the idea of economy through scientific buying

LADIES' CLASS IN COOKING

and preparing of foods, by the publication and circulation of
fifty thousand copies of her little pamphlet on *Fifteen Cent
Dinners for Working Men's Families*. After two years of
marked success the cooking school was incorporated.[16] In 1880
the Kitchen Garden Association of New York was incorporated
which, four years later, was to become the Industrial Education
Association. From this, in 1888, there was organized the College

[15] See the *Commissioner's Report*, 1893–4, I, 908.
[16] See an interesting illustrated account in *Harper's New Mo. Mag.*
(1879–80), LX, 22–9.

An Early Cooking Class

for the Training of Teachers. The School of Practical Arts, of Teachers College, was separated from the other departments in 1911. The influence of the early experiments of Miss Corson is to be seen in the fact that cooking became a part of public school instruction in 1888. While dealing with New York, reference should be made to the founding of Pratt Institute in Brooklyn in 1887, where attention was given home economy from the start.

Developments similar to those of Boston and New York appeared elsewhere. Philadelphia had classes in cookery at the New Century Club in 1878. From these developed the Cooking School of Mrs. Rorer, which lasted almost a generation; and the city, encouraged by private example, adopted cooking as an elementary school study a few years later.

Of the experimental introduction of cooking into Chicago schools the *Educational News* wrote in 1898: "It is pleasant to note that an experiment has been made in teaching cooking in three Chicago public schools. The results have been so satisfactory that domestic science is to be introduced into sixteen other schools scattered throughout the city. It is assumed therefore that cooking and sewing will become in the future a regular part of the educational work of the Chicago public school system. The object of public school education is to prepare children to become useful members of society. There are many things necessary besides knowledge to be obtained from books and it is with much interest that the study of domestic science in the Chicago schools will be watched by those interested in such subjects.

"The majority of girls grow up without a proper knowledge of housework, and, as the larger number have to do such work, it is a pity to enter on what becomes the chief occupation of life without any preparation whatever. There is no reason why the ability to cook and sew should not be considered an accomplishment which may properly become a part of the education taxpayers pay for in public schools. Instructions in such branches will do much to improve the conditions in many homes and to raise the standard of health and comfort without increasing the cost of living. At present much food is wasted because the average woman does not know how to cook it properly."[17]

By 1900, 4,372 pupils were receiving instruction in cooking

[17] *Op. cit.*, 278–9.

in Chicago schools, in eleven of which kitchens had been equipped. In closing an enthusiastic paper on Domestic Science, Henry Tibbits characterized its position at Chicago and prophesied its future:[18]

"Domestic science has been styled a fad by a certain portion of the public, along with drawing, music, physical culture, manual training, and German, and has endured with them the storm and stress period in Chicago. One week ago the board of education raised the salaries of teachers of Chicago, as one expressed it, 'scraping together' all the money they could for the teachers. At the same time they scraped off two months of the term of domestic science, providing this year for only eight months' instruction. This will be restored; but shows the necessary nursing which the subject requires. The most helpful sign of the progress of domestic science in Chicago is the increasing interest in the subject among teachers and principals, and especially among the pupils. It is easy to predict that another generation will take a more generous interest and largely increase the teaching of this subject."

At the end of the next ten years, sewing and cooking were to be found in ninety-five elementary school systems and in two hundred and seven high schools. By 1916–17, about 20 per cent. of the public high schools offered courses in home economics; about 10 per cent. of the girls in these institutions were in domestic science courses, and 6 per cent. of boys and girls combined.[19]

An interesting indication of the spread of domestic science is seen in the attention given it in colleges and technical schools. Pioneer work was done by the Young Woman's Christian Association, the American School of Home Economics of Chicago, Lake Placid Conference of Home Economics, Boston Trade School, the Manhattan Trade School, Simmons College, Pratt Institute, the School of Practical Arts of Teachers College, and Drexel Institute of Philadelphia. In 1869, Iowa required women students to work in dining room and kitchen, a practice of Mt. Holyoke College since its foundation, though for a different purpose; and lectures on food were given at Kansas Agricultural College in 1875–1876. At the University of Illinois, a course

[18] *N. E. A. Addresses and Proceedings,* 1901, 261.
[19] *Biennial Survey,* 1916–18, IV, 169.

was offered in 1875. Courses soon appeared at other state universities as well as in private institutions, but the growth, while general, was not rapid. In 1905, there were but 213 students of domestic economy at universities and colleges for men and for both sexes. At the same date, there were 636 attending such courses at schools of technology.[20] In the next five years the gain was more rapid, there being 1,934 students; by 1916 there were, in 195 institutions, 17,778 students; and, in the year following, 773 degrees in home economics were conferred.[21]

Home economics, the modern designation for the earlier domestic economy, has come to include many things. At the outset, when introduced into elementary and secondary schools, cooking and sewing were frequently bracketed together. In Colonial days, teachers taught "all sorts of needle work," "plain work," "marking" and "pattern drawing"; but not until the latter part of the nineteenth century was an effort made to incorporate this form of training in the work of the schools. About 1854, Boston experimented with the teaching of sewing. After 1866 the success of the effort was recognized and the way opened for general introduction of the subject. Of this "industrial training" the Commissioner's *Report* said, in 1873:

"The Winthrop School, in Boston, began last October an experiment of a most important character in the industrial education of girls. A sewing teacher was employed, who was paid the maximum salary given to other teachers and whose whole time was devoted to giving instruction in family-sewing. The results have been in the highest degree satisfactory and successful. Two hours each week are devoted to this study. Each class receives separate instruction suited to its advancement and all grades of work are carried on from simple hemming to cutting and fitting a dress. In teaching cutting, the pattern is drawn upon the blackboard and the several measurements are given. The diagrams are drawn and properly marked by the pupils, who submit them to the teacher for approval before cutting the cloth. All the work is supervised by the sewing-teacher and

---

[20] *R. C. E.* (1905), I, 552 and 568.

[21] Woody: "Vocational Education" [in *Twenty-Five Years of American Education* (edited by Kandel), 287].

class-teacher, and the pupils obtain marks for progress as in other studies."[22]

Two years later, Elizabeth Emmons, writing in the *New England Journal of Education,* explained that the Boston Committee was considering introducing sewing as a regular branch of instruction, and made an ardent plea for such action: "Is not a needle a woman's weapon emphatically, and have not our girls a right to be educated to its use? As I believe every woman who marries, is joined by that act to a necessity for the use of the needle, I ask that every man who values the home he makes should give his influence to this cause."[23]

The following extract from the *Annual Report* of the Boston School Committee indicates the enthusiasm of that body for the innovation because of its anticipated effect on future domestic economy and happiness and its influence on the character of the usual academic work of the school:

"The remarkable success which has attended the experiment of extending instruction in sewing to all the classes of the Winthrop School, in place of limiting it, as the rules prescribe, to the fourth, fifth, and sixth classes, is a subject for sincere congratulation among the friends of a comprehensive education. It furnishes an illustration of the principle long known among enlightened educators, that a change from mental to manual exercises within limits, is favorable to the best intellectual attainments; for the children of the Winthrop School have surpassed their former standing in scholarship, while they have gained in addition a most useful accomplishment. We believe that the thorough education of our girls in sewing and the cutting and making of garments, as now carried on by the Winthrop School, will have a marked effect upon the domestic economy and happiness of the rising generation, and we trust the movement thus skillfully and successfully begun, will not stop until all our grammar schools containing girls are in complete accord with it. The committee appointed by the board to investigate this subject, having consulted both the masters and sewing teachers, have reported in favor of introducing instruction in sewing into all the classes of the grammar schools where girls are taught. We heartily commend this report, and hope their recommenda-

22 *R. C. E.* (1873), CXXXIX–CXL.
23 *Op. cit.,* I, 158.

tion will be adopted."[24] The Commissioner's *Report* for 1880 stated that in the past year 70,948 pieces had been finished in the 39 Boston grammar schools.[25]

The article of Miss Emmons, referred to above, made clear that she looked upon sewing as an important subject because of the economies it would effect for poor families. Thus cooking and sewing were on the same ground. Sewing was experimented with by several New York churches after 1870 and, in 1888, both cooking and sewing became part of the regular school work. Sewing was first introduced into the Philadelphia schools in 1885. The Commissioner's *Report* for 1889–90, doubtless incomplete, showed that sewing was taught in the public schools of seventeen cities, usually from the third to the sixth year, and cooking in the schools of thirteen cities, generally in the seventh and eighth grades and sometimes in the high school.[26]

Considerable influence may have derived from foreign example. For many years the reports of the Commissioner of Education contained full references to the development of special instruction[27] in foreign schools. In 1893, the Chicago World's Fair showed what was going on elsewhere and stimulated the formation of the New York Association of Sewing Schools (1893), which as a national body was influential in causing the general acceptance of sewing as a school study throughout the United States.

In the present century, evidence appears on all sides to show the importance now attached to domestic education. Domestic science organizations have been numerous. In 1904, the Domestic Science Association of Illinois stated as its purpose the awakening of women to "a greater interest in their work," that they might be better informed about it and be able to use such current aids as government bulletins more intelligently.[28] In general, the purposes of others have been the same.

As some voluntary clubs have sought to improve domestic knowledge on the part of adult women, so others have endeavored to improve the teaching of domestic arts in the schools. The

[24] *Ibid.*, 170.
[25] P. CXXXVIII.
[26] Vol. II, 1351–6, Table 3.
[27] See, for example, *R. C. E.*, 1889–90, I, 91, 129, 244, and 532.
[28] *The Intelligence*, Jan. 1, 1904, 830.

Home School Plan, as worked out at Providence, in the Willard Avenue Home School, was an effort in this direction. Condon declared in his report before the School Committee that "Comparatively little has been done in public schools as yet to prepare girls for the most important and most difficult of all feminine vocations, that of the housewife and mother. I want the teachers in the Home School to feel that they have a big family of girls to be brought up in the old-fashioned way. Since the home is of more importance than the shop or factory, it is even more necessary to educate girls for motherhood and the home pursuits than to educate them for the industries or the professions."[29]

It has been stated that the purpose of the Home School was not merely to increase earning capacity of the girl, but "rather to develop from the stratum where economic pressure is greatest a new type of woman—clean, intelligent, industrious and competent."[30] As to character, "The home school represents all the possibilities of the neighborhood, or rather it is a means of giving expression to all the talents of the people through the resources of the locality. It is typical, showing what may be accomplished in any home of the neighborhood, through well directed effort; and in every phase of activity it preaches a new economy and thrift that must become a habit of mind before any lasting prosperity can be enjoyed."[31]

Another indication of the established position of home economics in American schools is to be seen in the provisions made by the Smith-Hughes Act. From 1918 to 1923, the number of schools benefitting by the funds appropriated by the Act had increased from 323 to 914 (no reports received from Wisconsin), and the number of students therein, from 30,799 to 63,806. Schools training teachers of home economics increased from 60 to 79 in the same years, and students attending increased from 3,319 to 4,954.[32]

II. Commercial Education

John Wingfield appealed to the women of New York (1759) to recognize the commercial value of a knowledge of writing,

[29] Trowbridge: *Home School*, 58–9.

[30] *Ibid.*, 42 *ff.*

[31] *Ibid.*, 26 *ff.*

[32] Woody: "Vocational Education" [in *Twenty-Five Years of American Education*, 299].

and lamented the fate of many "in the melancholy state of widowhood" who could not, because of ignorance of the pen, look after their own affairs.[33] Commercial studies, such as shorthand and bookkeeping, flourished under the influence of private masters in the large Eastern cities throughout the eighteenth century,[34] contrary to the oft-quoted assertions that private commercial education began with Bartlett in Philadelphia, about 1843, and James Bennett or James Gordon Bennett, between 1818 and 1836, in New York. But not much importance attaches to these early offerings, so far as woman's commercial education in the modern sense is concerned. Wingfield clearly had in mind the mastery of the pen so that women might manage their own affairs rather than be fitted as secretaries for some-one else.

Towards the latter part of the century the demand for women to enter freely all manner of occupations was vigorously voiced. Mrs. Dall's work has been referred to.[35] Livermore declared that "indolence is always demoralizing." Another cried, "A poet may say that men must work and women must weep; but the stern realities of life teach us that women must work and also weep." Since there was a growing feeling that women must work, there arose dissatisfaction with the general education of the public schools. The new cry was, as Carnegie put it, for "handication" versus "headication."[36] Livermore pleaded for distinctly vocational preparation for women, comparable with that offered to men:

"As the theory that 'all men support all women' does not fit the facts, it is time for us to reform our theory as well as our practice. I would give to all girls equal intellectual and industrial training with boys. I would not give them the same training unless they were fitting for the same work, business, or profession; but I would, in all cases, give to them equal advantages. If I were able, I would change the public sentiment so radically, that no girl should be considered well-educated, no

[33] See Vol. I, 223.

[34] Some of the early advertisements have been published by Seybolt: *Notes on the Curriculum in Colonial America,* reprinted from the December, 1925, *Journal of Educational Research.*

[35] See p. 2.

[36] See Livermore: *What Shall We Do With Our Daughters* (1883), 82–4.

matter what her accomplishments, until she had learned a trade, a business, a vocation, or a profession. Self-support would then be possible to her, and she would not float on the current of life, a part of its useless driftwood, borne hither and thither by its troubled waters. There would then be fewer heavily taxed fathers and brothers, toiling like galley-slaves to support healthy and vigorous human beings in stagnating idleness—idle for no earthly reason than that God has made them women.''[37]

Ezra S. Carr, in 1876, had stated similar views: ''There is not an argument for the industrial education of boys which does not apply with equal force to the education of their sisters. Whatever else is omitted from woman's training, just ideas of the dignity of labor, and a practical acquaintance with some of its many branches should be gained. She should be taught to recognize the necessity of it for the moral development of man, that labor is his mission, his destiny, his consummation, that the right to labor corresponds with the right to live. Viewed from a moral stand-point it is an obligation, from a social one it is a necessity—in both these aspects she should be taught to look upon herself as an equal partner.''[38]

Julia S. Tutweiler, of Alabama, discussed the same problem.[39] Under normal conditions, she recognized that ''the true profession of every woman is that of 'queen,' '' but pointed out that the ''forty thousand anxious and aimless women'' of Massachusetts would never enter into their domain. Everyone is consumer, producer, or both. The unmarried, untrained women consume only, and for this state of things society must find the remedy. . . . ''Technical education of our surplus women'' is the answer; they must be ''not only self-supporting, but contributors to the general wealth of the community. Let our girls, who have no means, be able to begin life as cheerfully and hopefully as their brothers, feeling that avenues of honorable labor are open to them in many directions. . . .''

In the latter half of the nineteenth century the employment of women in commercial establishments became more common. Manson (1883) said that the employment of women ''as amanuenses has grown very largely of late years; . . . fifteen

---

[37] *Ibid.*, 62–5.
[38] *N. E. A. Proc.*, 1876, 242–6.
[39] *Education* (1882), III, 201–7.

years ago there were but five females in the city of New York who made their living by writing shorthand; at the present time there are, as nearly as can be estimated, between one hundred and fifty and two hundred.''[40] Pay ranged generally from eight, for beginners, to fifteen or eighteen dollars a week for the more experienced, but twenty to twenty-five dollars was reported in certain exceptional cases.

That the employment of women was increasing cannot be doubted; it may be that Manson was too conservative in his estimate of the number employed. At any rate, private commercial colleges and other business schools were training many women. It should be noted, however, that commercial concerns favored young men rather than women; and, for that reason, many who did prepare themselves had difficulty in securing employment. In 1871, 84 business colleges, having 6,460 pupils, were reported by the Commissioner of Education.[41] The figures were incomplete, but some are suggestive for the present inquiry.

TABLE I

| Institutions | Students | | |
	Men	Women	Total
Bryant & Stratton, Chicago	400	25	425
Burlington Business College, Iowa	184	18	202
Bryant & Stratton, Boston	400	20	420
" " " Detroit	321	11	332
Gaskell, Bryant, Stratton, Manchester, New Hampshire	239	45	284
Trenton Business College	290	7	297
Packard's Business College, N. Y. C.	400	25	425
Scientific and Business Institute	16	21	37
Clark, Bryant & Stratton, Brooklyn	100	10	110
Nelson's Business College, Cincinnati	335	6	341
Union Business College, Cleveland	425	23	448
Bryant, Stratton & Smith, Meadville, Pa.	60	15	75
Warner, Bryant & Stratton, Providence	225	55	280
	3395	281	3676

Thus in the thirteen schools which mentioned women at all, there were 281 female and 3,395 male students, the latter being

40 *Work for Women*, 10–18.
41 *R. C. E.* (1871), 53.

about twelve times as numerous. Probably the proportion would not be changed greatly if figures were available for all schools engaged in this work. Twenty-seven of the eighty-four institutions reporting gave dates of foundation, all between 1852 and 1871, except Crittenden's, opened in 1844. Eight female teachers were named, though here, as for students, but very incomplete returns were made. Six schools mentioned courses from five months to two years. Most schools allowed pupils to enter "any time."[42]

The number of business colleges reporting increased steadily between 1871 and 1882, there being, at the latter date, 217, with 44,834 students.[43] Of these, approximately fifteen per cent. were female.[44] Ten years later (1893) there were 518 "commercial and business colleges," with 115,748 students, of whom 37,295 were female.[45] The female students were distributed as follows: 399 studied telegraphy; 6,932, the "English Course"; 14,201, the "Amanuensis Course"; and 11,893 the "Commercial Course."[46]

After 1893 there occurred a decrease in the number attending private business schools and an increase elsewhere. The Commissioner's report, of 1872, had said: "School officers have too often yielded to these demands [for commercial training] with reluctance if at all. The business colleges . . . have come forward and measurably furnished a supply."[47] This was true and continued to be so for some time. In the nineties the public high schools began to play a more important rôle. Edmund J. James, in 1892, made an appeal for public commercial high schools. The newly created university schools of commerce, such as the Wharton School at the University of Pennsylvania, needed commercial secondary schools as feeders.[48] Many separate com-

[42] *Ibid.*, 610–13.

[43] *Ibid.*, 1882, CII.

[44] *Ibid.*, totals from Table IV, 399–407.

[45] *Ibid.*, 1893–4, 2170 *ff.*

[46] The discrepancy between the total of these figures and the entire number of women attending is explained by the fact that many schools did not quote distribution according to studies.

[47] P. XXXIII.

[48] Courses in commerce at New York University, Louisiana State University, Dartmouth College, University of Vermont, University of Wisconsin, Ohio State and Michigan Universities were mentioned by the *R. C. E.*, 1899–1900, II, 1861.

mercial high schools exist today in larger cities, such as San Francisco, Washington, Louisville, Boston, Brooklyn, New York City, Cleveland, Springfield, Worcester, Columbus, Portland, (Oregon) and Syracuse. Elsewhere, commercial courses are maintained in high schools.

In 1893-4, there were but 15,220 students in commercial courses of public high schools.[49] How many were girls we do not know, but it seems probable that, even at this early date, a greater proportion of girls attended than in the private commercial schools. In 1898-99, there were 38,134 in public high school commercial courses, and of these 18,737 were girls. Since this date it appears the public high school has opened the way for large numbers of girls to enter commercial occupations. The following table indicates what was done by other agencies than public high schools.[50]

Besides instruction in the usual courses of bookkeeping and stenography, there developed, at an early date, a great interest in telegraphy to meet the demand for women operators. By 1883, it was estimated that in New York City alone there were "about two hundred ladies engaged in this occupation." They were mainly employed by the Western Union Telegraph Company, but some were in the service of private individuals, such as brokers. Pay ranged, as a rule, from $25 to $65 a month. In New York, Cooper Union formed special free classes in telegraphy, and with such success that it was besieged by a host of applicants. In 1878-9 they admitted thirty-five,[51] and one hundred and sixty applied for entrance in 1882 and were accepted. Its graduates were in demand. Kansas Agricultural College was among the earliest state schools to introduce telegraphy. The chief agency preparing for such a skilled occupation, however, was the business college. By the early eighties, telegraphy was being offered in at least two score of these, throughout the United States.[52] In 1900, the private schools reported 1,319 students in telegraphy; in 1905, 3,923; in 1910, 2,094; in 1915, 3,059; and in 1920, 5,188.[53]

[49] R. C. E. (1893-4), II, 2171 ff.

[50] Ibid. (1898), II, 2174; 1905, II, 1219; 1909-10, II, 1251 and 1258; 1916, II, 529.

[51] R. C. E. (1879), CXXIX.

[52] Manson: Work for Women, 21 ff.

[53] Biennial Survey, 1918-1920, Bul. 1923, No. 29, 553.

TABLE II

	1898–99		1904–05		1909–10		1915		1919–20	
	Men	Women	Men	Women	Men	Women	Men	Women	Men	Women
Universities and Colleges	5,127	1,336	7,909	2,468	5,073	727	Not reporting	Not reporting		
Public and Private Normal Schools	4,023	2,103	1,561	1,071	797	825				
Private High Schools and Academies	7,136	3,473	8,178	5,216	5,753	4,438	9,360	8,346	21,710	38,815[54]
Public High Schools	19,397	18,737	42,636	47,673	35,155	46,094	92,226	116,379	299,187	605,286[55]
Commercial and Business Schools	46,421	23,765	84,621	61,465	72,887	61,891	94,870	88,416	139,551	196,481[56]

[54] *Biennial Survey*, 1920–22, II, 623–4.
[55] *Ibid.*, 593–5.
[56] *Ibid.*, 1918–20, Bul. 1923, No. 29, 553.

Numerous criticisms have been levelled at commercial training since its introduction into the schools. Eliot, in 1899, characterized it as "hopelessly inferior to the other courses [in the American high school] being made up by substituting bookkeeping, stenography, typewriting and commercial arithmetic for some of the languages, history, mathematics, or science of the Classical or English scientific course. This course exists in our public schools because it has for committee men and parents a practical sound. The so-called commercial schools supplement for many young people a defective elementary education, but they seldom train anybody for service above that of a clerk."[57] Such views are found on all sides, and still hold true to a considerable extent. Girls need to have more than a narrow skill with pencil and typewriter or ledger if they are to do a high grade of work intelligently.

Thompson,[58] though writing from a different viewpoint in 1915, declared there was need for a clearer statement of the aims of commercial schools and courses; but recognized the difficulty of doing so inasmuch as commercial education has always suffered from the cross fire of school people and men of business. The former want general culture to predominate, allowing 25 per cent. of time and energy to distinctly commercial studies, 25 more to "related" subjects and 50 to "general information" and "conventional culture"; the latter demand well developed skills. The school people have, no doubt, generally won out. The commercial teachers of Boston described the situation as follows:[59]

"Every secondary school in the city wherein commercial education is offered gives a general culture course in science, history, mathematics, English, and other languages, and in addition offers courses in commercial subjects. These latter may be divided into two groups: First, courses designed to liberalize the pupils' attitude toward business; and, secondly, those courses that issue in skill in clerical pursuits. Hence the education now given in commercial courses in this city's general schools is threefold: First, to enable a graduate to enter into the inheritance of all educated people and to understand the meaning of democracy, of citizenship, and of opportunity; second, to give him

---

[57] R. C. E. (1898–9), I, 677–8.
[58] Ibid. (1916), I, 219 ff.
[59] Ibid., 221.

a professional point of view that will enable him to see his work in the light of the whole and lift it out of drudgery in an awakened spirit of service; third, to enable him to succeed in his first humble position.''

May Allinson, in 1914, summed up, most concisely, our experience with commercial education for women. After a thorough study of the situation in Boston, covering the school and its problems, character of office service, wages, home life and responsibilities, she concluded:

''Training for this occupation has been a long series of experiments, with little systematic or scientific study of the requisites of the occupation for which preparation was offered. The private business schools which sprang up about the middle of the nineteenth century attempted to meet, in as short a time as possible, the demands of increasing business for skilled office workers on the one hand, and on the other, the needs of prospective workers for training to meet the requirements of the business office. These schools, however, provided training for specific processes or machines rather than for the vocation in a large sense. Nor was vocational fitness, adequacy of preliminary education, or the desirability of establishing a uniformly high standard, a matter of serious consideration.

''The public high schools almost half a century later began on a large scale to cater to public demand for 'practical courses,' and at first tacked on the regular high school curriculum an occasional course in bookkeeping, stenography and typewriting. Two year courses followed by three year courses which were, in turn, supplanted by four and occasionally five year courses of training in commercial subjects all have had their place in the history of public school commercial education. Recently, 'intensive' two year and three year courses are again being offered, attempting to compete with the short courses offered by the private commercial schools. These various educational schemes have been attempted with little or no intimate knowledge of the needs and demands of the business office, nor of the suitability or adaptability of the students electing these courses. All who desired might elect the 'curriculum of commercial subjects,' ranging from two to five years in length, or under a very elastic system, might elect any number of particular commercial subjects. As a result, pupils with a preparation ranging from two to five years in high school and a vocational equipment based on from four to thirty-six points in commercial subjects have been going out from the public high schools as prospective office workers. And the pupil has been left to choose her course or her particular subjects largely at will with little or no knowledge of the requirements of office work and of the varying demands of the business offices themselves. At the opposite extreme are the women's technical colleges which are turning out the 'college trained secretary' with a four year technical college course or four year academic college education with one year's intensive preparation for office service.

''So-called commercial education has been handicapped by its introduction before the real significance and the fundamental principles of *vocational training* were understood or appreciated. Efficiency has been endangered by the lack of a standard or definitely formulated program for 'commercial education.' The sponsorship for commercial education assumed by private business schools of all grades of efficiency has produced the problem of many workers with inadequate general education and limited technical skill. The introduction of 'commercial' subjects in the general high school course or even a 'commercial curriculum' in the control of academic schoolmen has produced the worker with inadequate technical and vocational preparation.''[60]

III. Nurses' Training

One of the most lucrative professions opened to women, and one to which not much objection was raised, was that of nursing. Women had been, in their own homes, the nurses of mankind throughout all time. Now that there were many women without homes of their own, and the custom of a maiden aunt taking care of a brother's children falling into disuse, it was quite natural for them to become professional nurses. The American Women's Education Association called attention (1852) to ''care of the human body in infancy and sickness'' as one of the true professions of women, and announced a determination to see women prepared for that and other appropriate professions.[61] In 1883, however, Manson wrote, ''It may not be known to many that, of

60 Women's Educational and Industrial Union, Boston: *The Public Schools and Women in Office Service* (1914), 172–4.

61 See Vol. I, 113.

late years, nursing has come to be a regular profession. Women are trained to become nurses by going through a regular course of study in what are called training schools, and they receive on their graduation a diploma. . . . For some women this is an excellent occupation. The work is hard, but the pay is exceptionally good.''[62]

The development of training schools for nurses in the United States received the greatest encouragement from (1) the example of Pastor Fliedner's School for Deaconesses at Kaiserwerth on the Rhine, (2) the notable success of Florence Nightingale, and (3) the opportunity given American women, in the Civil War, to demonstrate the significance of the nurses' work. Early attempts at nurses' schools were made by Friends at Philadelphia in 1839, and the Woman's Hospital in 1861. A school was also opened at Roxbury, Massachusetts, at the Women's and Children's Hospital, in 1862. But the most conspicuous step forward was taken by New York and Boston, in 1873, when schools were established in connection with Bellevue Hospital and the Massachusetts General Hospital. The same year the Connecticut Training School was opened at New Haven.[63] In the institution at Boston, the provisions for training were as follows:[64]

''Among other followings of Pastor Fliedner's practical training-schools at Kaiserwerth is a school opened in Boston November 1, 1873, for giving a systematic training to women who wish to become nurses. With a small and manageable number for a beginning, an influential body of ladies and gentlemen has made arrangements with the trustees of the Massachusetts General Hospital for exercise of the pupils in their wards. Lodging and boarding at a house near the hospital, these pupils are to receive instruction there in the theoretic part of their profession and in the preparation of diet for the sick, and for a year will practice in the wards under the direction of the hospital-physicians. During that year they will receive $10 a month for clothing and personal expenses. At the expiration of the year they will become full nurses and receive as such a salary sufficient for their sup-

---

[62] *Work for Women*, 47–8.

[63] Incorporated with privilege of holding property to the amount of $50,000—see *Laws of Conn.*, 1873, 58–9.

[64] The plan at Bellevue Hospital and at the Connecticut school was much the same—see *R. C. E.*, 1873, 45–6 and 293.

port, but must remain another year for further practice and instruction. This full term of two years completed, they will, if approved, receive diplomas certifying their knowledge of nursing, their physical ability, and good character.''[65]

The merits of these schools were at once recognized, in spite of the fact that some doctors opposed women as nurses, almost as strenuously as they did women doctors. By 1880, there were fifteen training schools, 323 pupil nurses, and 157 graduates. The total number of students reported by the fifteen schools, since their respective dates of foundation, was 1,303; the total number of graduates, to 1880, was 663.[66] In the next decade schools increased to 35, with 1,552 pupils (only 93 male). There were 471 graduates in 1889–90.[67] Eleven schools had a 100 weeks' course; ten, a 104 weeks' course; five, 80 weeks; two, 72 weeks; two, 52 weeks; two, 48 weeks; and three had 70, 78, and 108 weeks, respectively. The following table presents some of the figures for nurses' training since 1900:

TABLE III

	Schools	Students	Graduated
1899–1900	432	11,164	3,546[68]
1909–1910	1,129	32,636	8,140
1919–1920	1,755	54,953	14,980[69]

Gradually the length of training school courses has been increased, especially in the past fifteen years, and the requirements for admission have been raised. Whereas, at first, a year of theoretical training, plus a year of practice, was considered ample—and many schools had less—in 1920, 86 per cent. of the general hospital schools had 3 years or more; and three institutions reported four year courses.[70]

IV. Art and Industrial Art Schools

In the early female seminaries considerable attention was paid to art, in one form or another, chiefly because a smattering of

[65] Ibid., 1873, 186.
[66] Ibid. (1880), CLXVII.
[67] Ibid. (1889–90), II, 1024 and 1042.
[68] Ibid. (1899–1900), II, 1965.
[69] Biennial Survey, 1918–1920, Bul. 1923, No. 29, 566.
[70] Ibid.

it was considered an accomplishment. But the art instruction
of some was not unimportant nor lacking in influence. Julia Du
Pré, educated at the Troy Seminary, travelled abroad and completed her art education under foreign masters. On returning
to the United States she and her mother opened a school for
young ladies at Charleston, South Carolina, but she devoted much
of her time to painting. Such pieces as *The Love Letter, The
Liaison* and *L'Espagnole* were highly praised.[71]   Others, such as
Miss Withers, who painted in oil and water color and cut cameos,
Charlotte Cheves, and Ellen Cooper of Columbia, South Carolina,
might be mentioned as partial proof of the effect of the elementary study of the arts in seminaries of the South. But the
work of the seminary was limited, and few had sufficient wealth
to continue studies abroad; almost no opportunities for thorough
study existed in the United States. *Godey's Lady's Book* mentioned the Art School of Mr. Van der Wielen, in Philadelphia,
heading the article "An Employment for Young Ladies." It
was judged a thorough school:

"Beginning with first principles, it aims to conduct the pupil
through all the legitimate and essential steps of study and practice to the higher branches of finished culture. It is no 'Painting
in Twelve Easy Lessons' affair, but an honest working school,
where all who are willing to apply themselves and go through a
certain amount of patient work, may attain the highest degree of
excellence that their native abilities fit them for. The rooms are
large, well-ventilated, and admirably lighted; the supply of objects and models full and carefully chosen, and the supervision
of the master constant and severely critical. The majority of his
pupils are young ladies, many of whom, of course, have simply
entered upon the study as amateurs, while quite a number intend
making art their profession and means of livelihood."[72]

In Philadelphia, about the middle of the century (1844), Mrs.
Peter, wife of the British consul, began an experiment that may
be regarded as the forerunner of the industrial art schools of the
United States. She selected young girls of limited education,
who, as a class, usually depended on the needle for a living. To
these she gave a room in her own house for instruction, until the
increased number made necessary the use of a special apartment.

[71] *Littell's Living Age* (1859), LXIII, 616.
[72] *Op. cit.*, March, 1870, 287.

With no knowledge of art, a beginning was made in the "simplest principles of drawing"; then others took up wood engraving, a business hitherto monopolized by men.[73] After a year, reports were current that the School of Design had been closed for wants of funds, but this was emphatically denied:

". . . This school is flourishing, has an endowment of fifty thousand dollars in expectation—about half the sum already contributed—and has every prospect of continued success. It offers great advantages to intelligent young women, who desire to educate themselves for the profession of teachers in drawing or as artists."[74]

The work of the School of Design was greatly stimulated by the exposition of 1876. In the early eighties it offered instruction in "architecture, engraving, lithography, and practical design," and had about three hundred students per year. These went out as teachers of art or were employed by industrial concerns.[75]

The Woman's Art School of New York, opened as a private, independent association in 1852, and merged with Cooper Institute in 1859, may be regarded as a pioneer in the field of industrial art in that city. It also suggested the chief direction which art was to follow for some time in America. Designing and wood engraving played an important part in the studies. Of the art work at the school, Townley wrote (1871) that it had been successful "only when the efforts made were unmistakably with a view to add grace of form or charm of color to the products of our industries . . . where the knowledge needed is scientific rather than artistic. . . . It is true that the schools have accomplished a good deal toward refining the taste of the workmen and workwomen, and in educating their hands, but that they could have accomplished very much more had they been intelligently managed, is also true."[76] In New York, pioneer work was also done by the Art Students' League (1875), the Ladies Art Association—both of which charged tuition—and the National Academy of Design, which offered free instruction. At

73 *Ibid.*, September, 1852, 275 *ff.*

74 *Ibid.*, Aug., 1854, 176.

75 Livermore: *What Shall We Do With Our Daughters*, 100 *ff.*; also see *R. C. E.*, 1879, 208.

76 *R. C. E.*, 1871, 514 and 522.

Vassar College, conspicuous opportunities were offered to women in this field.[77]

The success of early experiments led to others. The New England School of Design for Women was (1853) granted an appropriation of $1500 annually for three years.[78] The art school of Cooper Institute, New York, had 231 women pupils and the wood engraving department, 25.[79] The Boston Normal Art School (1879) reported 1,543 pupils since its creation in 1873, one hundred and thirteen of whom had become teachers.[80] The San Francisco School of Design, organized in 1873 under the auspices of the Art Association of that city, reported 69 pupils attending throughout 1879. It was open to pupils 14 years of age, and required payment of a tuition fee. Instruction was given in drawing and painting.[81] The Lowell Free School of Industrial Design, in connection with the Boston Institute of Technology, also afforded opportunities for women's education. Other cities, ten at least, such as Cincinnati, Chicago, St. Louis, Milwaukee, Providence, Washington and Minneapolis, had similar schools. Smith and Wellesley College caught the growing interest in art and followed the lead already taken by Vassar. Of the thirty-eight schools for art instruction, reported in 1880, there were seven that had been founded by women, and nine were especially for women. Most of them were open to women as well as men.[82]

Finally, legislatures began to take notice of the industrial art movement. Massachusetts provided (1870) that every city of 10,000, or over, should offer industrial drawing, and recommended that it be taught in all.[83] New York required (1875) that industrial and free-hand drawing be included in normal school courses and "in some department of each city school." Vermont (1876) added free-hand drawing to the list of required studies in public schools. Similar provisions appeared elsewhere. The tendency was to emphasize mechanical drawing in connection with manual training courses. In fact the art seems to have

[77] *Ibid.*, 1879, 177.
[78] *Laws of Mass.*, 1853, 681.
[79] *R. C. E.*, 1870, 60.
[80] *Ibid.*, 1879, 109.
[81] *Ibid.*, 1879, 19.
[82] *Ibid.*, 1880, 824–9.
[83] *Ibid.*, 1880, CCXXXV *ff*.

suffered because of the training. H. C. Ives, director of the art exhibits at Chicago (1893) and at St. Louis (1904), declared that "although much has been said and written about industrial art . . . little [has been] done."[84]

In 1905 there were, at various schools of technology in the United States, 336 students in art and 704 in music. In universities and colleges for men and for both sexes there were 5,462 students in art and 20,912 in music.[85]

That the schools which opened up industrial art as a field for employment, or prepared teachers of art subjects in the schools, were a great boon to women cannot be denied. They were expected to do much. Mary Livermore declared that the woman "who has a thorough art education can to-day [1883] easily find employment. The demand for art teachers is in excess of supply. . . . Occupation in the useful and ornamental arts will give to the rising ambition and talent of American girls a large and noble scope."[86] Others recognized that it would be an up-hill fight for women, for men already dominated the field. Manson wrote:

"I do not think she can hope to get a permanent salaried position, at least just at present. For this profession, albeit a good one, is a new one for women. . . . Men still hold the best positions, and they receive large salaries, from $1,000 to $4,000 a year. In the present condition of affairs, hedged in as the female industrial designer is by the masculine doubt of the employer as to her ability, and the masculine jealousy of the employee whose work she seeks to do, it would be the best plan for her to do piece-work at her own home, or office. Her earnings, under this plan, cannot even be stated approximately. The pay for a good carpet design would be $20 to $30, and the design can be made in two and a half days. Wall-paper designs bring $10 to $15; an oil-cloth sketch, $8 or $10—the technicalities to be mastered in this latter branch are not so great as in the others."[87]

But, if it was up-hill work, women achieved a good measure of success. Mrs. Wheeler and Revere Johnson became well

84 *Ibid.* (1905), I, XXVIII, and also pp. 155–83.
85 *Ibid.*, 552 and 568.
86 *Op. cit.*, 100 *ff.*
87 *Work for Women*, 8–9.

known. Maria Longworth Nicholas founded the Rockwood pot-
teries of Cincinnati and maintained a school, while Louise
McLoughlin was credited with "re-discovering" the Haviland
underglaze.[88] In later years their accomplishments in the field
of industrial, as in other forms of art, are quite too numerous
to catalog.

At the World's Fair at St. Louis (1904) the exhibit of Pratt
Institute showed how women were prepared for industrial life
by training in "costume design, sewing, millinery, dressmaking,
embroidery, and domestic science for dietitians, matrons, housekeepers, and probationary nurses."[89] The exhibits of the evening school made it clear that those employed during the day
could fit themselves for advancement in their occupations by
special study at night.

V. Trade, Evening and Other Schools

Art has entered into many employments. In 1850 women
sought chiefly to be fitted as industrial designers. No one
thought of beauty culture courses. Yet to-day such courses are
included in the wide range of offerings of the modern girls' trade
school, which has become an important agency for girls' vocational education. The Manhattan Trade School for Girls was
founded under philanthropic auspices in 1901, and taken over
by the Board of Education in 1910, being now "a free public
vocational school entirely supported by the municipality."[90]
The Philadelphia Girls' Trade School, till recently, occupied two
buildings not designed for the purpose. The school began about
1914, due to the efforts of Helen Fleischer, Mary M. Friedley,
and G. C. Crawford, and came under control of the Board of
Education in 1918. A new building has been erected, costing
over a million dollars and accommodating 1,200 pupils, who have
either completed the elementary school or have reached the age
of fourteen and wish to prepare for a trade. Ruth Sill, Principal of the Trade School, is reported in favor of introducing a
"beauty culture course": "There is a definite need for reputable
training in the field of hair culture and manicuring. . . . There
have been repeated requests for such a course. . . . [In the new

88 *North Am. Rev.* (1892), CLV, 382 *ff*.
89 *R. C. E.* (1904), I, 981.
90 Letter of Florence M. Marshall, Principal, October 30, 1924.

building we] will be thoroughly equipped for hairdressing and kindred arts. . . ."[91] A head of a modern chain of beauty schools says, ". . . Modern faces are resembling masks and comic valentines."[92] No one who values the truth will gainsay her. And, if the making of a beautiful face has become as technical a performance as the manufacture of a fine silk dress, or approaches it in difficulty, there must be schools to train for the vocation. Private beauty schools to-day train embryo beauty shop owners much as private "female" schools of design, and business colleges, prepared women to take up certain vocations seventy-five years ago. Public institutions eventually took over much of that training and are planning now to prepare the beauty doctor.

The State of New Jersey has had under consideration the establishment of such vocational training. The ends to be attained by it are suggested in the following extract from a report of the Assistant Commissioner in charge of Vocational Education :[93]

"Manicuring and care of the skin and hair is a rapidly developing field with many opportunities for employment open to girls and women. The Newark telephone directory lists 170 shops, exclusive of the department stores, where this work is done.

"A need for reputable training exists in this work such as has been found in no other occupation in which women are employed. This is due to the fact that girls commonly pay from $40.00 to $150.00 to be taught the different phases of the business with no guarantee that they will receive adequate instruction in return for their money. Girls who go into low grade shops giving time and money with the expectation of learning the trade, generally lose whatever they invest. The instruction given them is so meager that they are not qualified for desirable employment. One very intelligent woman stated that the tuition fee which she paid merely gave her an opportunity to get into the shop. She then had to 'steal the trade' by devising opportunities to watch or help more experienced workers.

[91] *Phila. Inquirer*, Dec. 9, 1925.
[92] *Ibid.*, Jan. 7, 1925.
[93] Kindly furnished by John H. Logan, Commissioner of Education, State of New Jersey.

"A number of so-called 'schools' exist in connection with different systems of beauty culture. Just what they teach depends on the proprietor, as they are under no supervision or regulation.

"The better shops do not take learners, as their trade will not endure unskilled service. It is these shops which offer desirable conditions of employment and a good wage.

"The existence of high grade instruction in a good public school would eventually become a protection to all learners in this occupation. It would cure the private establishment which takes the girl's money and teaches her as little as possible and would set a standard of training which some of the so-called 'schools' would have to meet. In addition to this, by teaching certain things which are ignored by the trade, the school would establish protection to the public."

The Camden County Council of the Parent Teachers' Association recently approved the move for beauty culture, by appointing a committee to prepare a plan for introducing "beauty culture in the vocational schools."[94]

Other institutions that have become of great significance in the vocational preparation of girls are evening, full-time day vocational and trade schools, and part-time vocational, trade and continuation schools. Manual training schools might be mentioned also. In eighteen schools reported in 1887–8, there were 293 girls and 3,246 boys, distributed in the several courses designated as "literary," "drawing," and "manual training."[95] Evening schools were of course known in our early history. To-day they educate thousands who work during the day. While varied forms of evening schools appear, the following examples will illustrate very well their founding and their nature.

Night schools were opened by the Common School Board of Cincinnati, 1840–1, the first year's expenses amounting to $299. Few attended the schools; and few cities at this early date established them. The philanthropic influence on the opening of some evening schools is shown in the following:

"During the past winter [1885–6] a night-school for working girls was held in the S. S. room of St. Mary's Church, West Philadelphia. The Rev. T. Yarnall, Rector of the Parish, gave

94 [Phila.] *Evening Bulletin*, Feb. 26, 1926.
95 *R. C. E.*, 1887–8, 904.

his personal attention to the work, and is much encouraged by the result.

"The school, which was intended for the girls employed in mills and factories, was opened December 4th, and there have been in all 112 pupils connected with it, of whom more than half were regular attendants. The average has varied with the weather, from 15 to 35. The instruction was confined to the elementary English branches, while one evening of each week was devoted to plain sewing. On Saturday evening a class of 16 met to take writing lessons from a paid instructor. There have been 30 ladies connected with the school, as volunteer teachers. Some of these belong to the Church of the Saviour, and two or three to the Presbyterian church, but the majority of them to St. Mary's.

"Such is a brief synopsis of this truly Christian charity. This is the first attempt, we believe, to give fitting culture to Working Girls. The Institute now needs funds to establish it permanently, and *books for a library*. Shall it fail, for want of patronage, in the rich and liberal city of Philadelphia?"[96]

In Providence, an evening school especially for ladies was established and maintained by a philanthropic women's association widely known as the "Irrepressibles." It was taught by Harriet Metcalf, and attended by thirty students. The public school authorities furnished books. In 1870, at the close of the school, the valedictory was delivered by Eliza A. Boyle, who for four years had attended school in the evening, after working at the mill from early morning till a quarter of seven in the evening. She completed this work at the age of 19, in spite of handicaps; and it was said "her education will compare favorably with not a few who graduate at the high school."[97]

Statistics on evening schools for women are not available for this early period, though it is quite clear that they were established in a somewhat desultory fashion. New York (1849) had eleven evening (elementary) schools for men and four for women. The latter were manned by eighteen teachers and served 1,757 students. Besides regular classes, special lectures "on various useful subjects" were given, designed to awaken the desire for knowledge. The rules for evening schools pro-

[96] *Godey's Lady's Book*, July, 1886, 82.
[97] *R. C. E.*, 1870, 283.

vided that women's schools open and close a half hour earlier than those of the men, "to prevent any improper meetings outside the schoolhouse."[98]

The evening schools, found mostly in commercial and industrial centers, had become numerous by 1880. They were of both elementary and secondary grade. As a rule, wherever established, the success of evening schools was marked. Albany seems to have been an exception. Complete statistics are not available, but San Francisco had five and St. Louis, forty-one, with an enrollment of over 6,000. High schools were maintained by New York, Boston, Providence, Patterson, and Chicago, in addition to lower evening classes.[99] The number of girls attending was not reported separately. By 1889–90, 165 cities of the United States, each with a population over 4,000, reported 808 schools, 150,770 pupils, and were employing 3,678 teachers.[100] Of the pupils, approximately one-sixth were girls.[101] In 1921–22, evening schools (in towns of over 10,000) were classified as elementary, high and vocational. The total of female students in all combined was 390,561; the number of males, 439,953.[102]

The full-time day vocational and trade schools enrolled, in 1921–22, 24,963 boys and 17,249 girls.[103] Part-time vocational, trade, and continuation schools, at the same time, had 92,230 male and 85,388 female students.[104]

VI. Horticultural Schools

The farmerette is not so ultra-modern as she sometimes appears. A horticultural school for women was opened near Newton Center, Massachusetts, in 1870. A year later it was incorporated and so continued until 1885, when the corporation was dissolved by law, though its continuance was permitted until 1888.[105] The purpose of the school was to afford women "a thorough education in the theory and practice of horticulture including the culture of fruit, vegetables, and flowers, both in

98 Siljeström: *Education in the United States,* 130–2.
99 *R. C. E.* (1879), CCX–CCXI.
100 *Ibid.* (1889–90), II, 616.
101 *Ibid.* From Table 2, 1346 *ff.*
102 *Biennial Survey of Education,* 1920–1922, II, 170–81.
103 *Ibid.,* 160–2.
104 *Ibid.,* 166–9.
105 *Laws of Mass.,* 1885, 552.

the open air and under glass.''[106]   A secondary purpose, or hope
at least, was that outdoor work would greatly improve health,
benefitting directly those who were at the school, and indirectly,
by example, benefitting the health of women generally.   A two-
year course of lectures and practice was offered, on the day or
boarding plan, to those having a good elementary education and
who were sixteen years of age.   Tuition was $100 a year.   Of
the first efforts, Mrs. F. B. Fay, visitor, wrote:

''The land was not ploughed until after the 20th of May, when
the young ladies, five in number, put in the seeds for the vegetable garden, and, with the exception of the first hoeing of the
potatoes, they have taken the entire charge of the garden.   The
success of their labors can be judged by the fact that they have
not only supplied their own table with eight or ten varieties of
excellent vegetables, but have also made sales to parties outside
the school.   From cuttings, the pupils have raised, and now have
for sale, fifteen hundred plants of various kinds, and they have
been wonderfully successful even with those varieties which are
the most difficult of propagation.   One fact will be interesting,
especially to those persons who have been somewhat doubtful
upon the point, viz., that young women, in out door work, are
able to endure the severe heat of summer.   With the exception
of four or five days, our pupils have worked out of doors, and
there is but one opinion among them in regard to the health-
fulness of the employment.''[107]

That the experiment was not entirely out of harmony with the
times, in spite of its early dissolution, is suggested by the fact
that women have shown an interest in agricultural courses at
various universities and professional schools whenever these
opportunities have been opened to them.   At Groton, Massachusetts, a woman's agricultural and horticultural school was
established and some women's colleges (Wellesley, for example)
have come to include instruction in this and allied subjects.   In
1921–1922, 67 first degrees in agriculture[108] were granted to
women by universities, colleges, and professional schools.[109]

[106] *R. C. E.*, 1870, 169.
[107] *Ibid.*
[108] Horticulture is usually a part of the agricultural course.
[109] *Biennial Survey*, 1920–1922, II, 316.

VII. Refuges, Reformatories and State Industrial Schools

A movement to take care of girls, delinquent in one way or another, has also contributed somewhat to their vocational education. Reformers and humanitarians have desired to substitute the school for prison and punishment treatment of youth of both sexes. In most of the state industrial schools—and most schools of this class are under public control or receive some public money for their support—there is an effort to give the rudiments of education and teach a trade. The purposes have long been recognized. In New York, a House of Refuge was established and opened January 1, 1825. Manual labor was stressed. Following a careful inspection of this institution, a charter was applied for in Pennsylvania (1826), which represents the beginning of the Glen Mills and Sleighton Farm schools of the present day. Massachusetts incorporated the State Industrial School for Girls in 1855. It was for "training to good conduct and instructing in household labor destitute or neglected girls . . . who shall be surrendered to them. . . ."[110] Waterbury Industrial School (Connecticut) had for its object the "instruction of indigent girls in useful occupations, and in morals and religion."[111] The Connecticut Industrial School for Girls was to act as guardian to any girl committed according to law, between the ages of eight and sixteen years, "for the physical, mental and moral training of such girl."[112] In 1871, instruction in elementary branches was being given three hours a day and Bible lessons on Sunday. There were 48 inmates, but the school had capacity for seventy.[113]

The Indiana Reformatory for women and girls reported (1879) that "in the educational department the advancement was encouraging. . . . A general knowledge of housework, laundry work, knitting, sewing, and cane seating of chairs is also given to the girls."[114]

In 1881, 71 reform schools were reported to the Bureau of Education. There were 11,961 male and 3,665 female inmates. Teachers and officers employed numbered 539 men and 581

110 *The Glen Mills Schools*, 1826–1926, 1 *ff.*; and *Laws of Mass.*, 1855, 504.
111 *Laws of Conn.*, 1872, 234.
112 *Ibid.*, 1868, 228–9.
113 *R. C. E.*, 1871, 98.
114 *Report* for 1878–1879.

women. The libraries contained 69,178 volumes, and the annual earnings of the institutions amounted to $353,441.[115] The situation from 1900 to 1918, as reported to the Commissioner's office, is shown in the following table:[116]

TABLE IV

	1900	1910	1918
Institutions	80	115	135
Female Inmates	4,933	12,961	14,102
Male Inmates	18,968	43,702	49,660
Female Teachers	(538	624	655
Male Teachers	Total)	493	482
In School Classes	21,626	39,877	51,937[117]
Learning a Trade	15,946	36,262	43,410[117]

VIII. Special Courses for Workers

During the recent war, women had an opportunity to enter positions previously held almost exclusively by men. The War Industries Board declared there was a real need for women to replace men as employment managers. College courses were designed and offered free, under the direction of the government, to prepare women for these new responsibilities.[118] The candidates for such instruction were to be twenty-five years of age at least, and must have had a high school or, preferably, a college education, and at least three years' experience as a worker or executive in shop work.

Some of the work of colleges and universities, since the war, has been developed more for cultural purposes than vocational. Thus the *Extension Leaflet*[119] of the University of North Carolina, for 1918, described this branch of work as follows. The purposes were: to correspond with women of the state, old and young, relative to plans for higher education; to be a clearing house of information for women of the state; to help make and

[115] *R. C. E.*, 1881, CCXXII–III.

[116] *Biennial Survey*, 1916–1918, IV, 744–5.

[117] Men and women not separated in the report given.

[118] *School and Society*, VII, 765, mentioned courses beginning, or to begin, at Rochester, Harvard, Boston University, and the Massachusetts Institute of Technology.

[119] Division for Women Series, No. 1, 1918.

carry out programs for civic leagues, clubs, parent teachers' associations, study circles and literary clubs; and to prepare special study outlines for women's clubs.[120]

A most significant experiment with the higher education of women workers has been in process at Bryn Mawr College since 1920. The plans for the experiment were drawn and approved by representatives of the college board, faculty, alumnae, and women in industry,—that is, women who "work with the tools of the trade and not in a supervisory capacity,"—the last being named by Mary Anderson of the Women's Bureau. The college and the women of industry were equally represented. Scholarships worth $200 were provided by the combined philanthropy of collegiate alumnae and women in industry, individually and coöperatively, through trade unions and women's clubs. Eighty students were selected from 212 applicants, all being required to be able to read and write the English tongue, have the equivalent of a common school training, good health and a medical certificate. Women between 21 and 35 were admitted. They were drawn from all levels of industrial life, representing various labor groups. Ten leaders in industry were accepted at the college for advanced work.[121]

The purpose of the experiment is to give workers a chance "to study liberal subjects and to train themselves in clear thinking; to stimulate an active and continued interest in the problems of industry. It is expected that thus the students will gain a truer insight into the problems of industry and feel a more vital responsibility for their solution." The work, which lasts eight weeks, is in the fields of economics, English composition, public speaking, literature, science, history, hygiene, and appreciation of music.[122]

At the annual convention, held at Boston, 1925, the National Federation of Federal Employees, recognizing the importance of the labor college movement, acknowledged the leadership of Dr. Martha Carey Thomas in this movement to educate workers, and adopted a resolution to ". . . coöperate especially with those developing the opportunity afforded women workers by the Bryn

[120] Thus, in 1917–18, Latin America was studied, 25 clubs participating.

[121] Reported by H. W. Smith, Dean of Bryn Mawr College, in *N. E. A. Proceedings*, 1922, 713.

[122] *Sch. and Soc.*, May 9, 1925, 555.

Mawr Summer School.''[123] While it is manifestly of great personal benefit to those women workers elected to receive the scholarships; and the association, in study, of women of diverse religions, nationalities, and occupations ought to be an effective means of disseminating a truer understanding of industrial problems, too little has transpired to permit a judgment as to the ultimate influence of the movement. Conversation with a few students discovers some who are enthusiastic about the work and others who are not.

A significant educational opportunity was offered women in industry at the opening of Brookwood Labor College (1921) at Katonah, New York, which was incorporated in 1925. About a third of the graduates have been women. The purpose of this coeducational, resident labor college is ''to train active members of labor organizations for more intelligent and efficient service to their organizations.'' Its conception of its function is further described as follows:

''As an educational institution, Brookwood has not considered it to be its job to promulgate without analysis the views or policies of any particular organization or faction in the labor movement. It tries, rather, to assist its students to an understanding, by means of study, analysis and discussion of the philosophy and policies of the American Federation of Labor and other organizations and groups in the labor movement of America and of the world, endeavoring primarily to teach students how to think, not to tell them what to think.''

The full course requires two years for completion. Courses cover trade union administration, labor legislation, labor history, organization methods, economics, public speaking, parliamentary law, history of civilization, psychology, labor journalism, English, and so on. Summer conferences and special institutes are held.[124]

Other less advanced experiments with education for women in industry are being tried here and there. Last year, a school under the direction of Louise Leonard was held at Sweet Briar, Virginia, for six weeks and this year (1928) it was at Burnsville, North Carolina. After study, which was chiefly economics, writing, and speaking—with recreational activities and health edu-

[123] *Ibid.*, Sept. 19, 1925.
[124] Leaflets and announcements of the Brookwood Labor College.

cation—the students returned to their various employments to work for 'organization, better wages, and shorter hours.' Union and non-union workers were represented.[125]

IX. Vocational Guidance

One of the most complicated and perplexing problems precipitated upon us by the complexity of modern industrial life is that of vocational guidance. In truth, the problem is not new, but it has become more unavoidable. We have heard of fitting individuals for their proper functions ever since Plato told of the men of iron, silver, and gold. *A General Description of All Trades . . . by which Parents, Guardians and Trustees, may, with greater Ease and Certainty, make choice of Trades agreeable to the Capacity, Education, Inclination, Strength and Fortune of the Youth under their Care* appeared in London, in 1747. Lysander Richards published a little volume called *Vocophy* in 1881, and Parsons began his work at Boston in 1908. The demand of industrial society cannot be silenced or ignored. Women have fled from the household to the market place. They wish to find the best place possible, and the employer wants the best service. Guidance and placement of workers must satisfy the two parties to the agreement.

Vocational, or educational, guidance for women is faced by three great problems: the analysis of individual capacities; analysis of the occupational world; and the development of such educational means whereby the individual may satisfactorily fit into it. Brewer has said that guidance involves six things: "(1) laying a broad foundation of useful experiences, (2) studying occupational opportunities, (3) choosing an occupation, (4) preparing for the occupation, (5) entering upon work, (6) securing promotions and making readjustments."[126]

The first is a problem for the psychologist. It is now generally accepted that women can do almost all things that men do; some they do better, others less well. They are found in all but thirty-three of the six hundred and seventy-eight "gainful" occupations listed by the Census Bureau.[127] Psychologists have

[125] Some account is given in *The Federated Press Labor Letter*, Aug. 30, 1928; many other articles in the *Labor Letter*, Vols. I–XVI.

[126] Woody: "Vocational Education" [in Kandel's *Twenty-Five Years of American Education*, 296].

[127] See p. 17.

thus far found (recognizing of course that there are divergent opinions among them) little justification for the ancient belief in widely different capacities of men and women. The greater variability of men has been questioned.[128] If it is true, then, that woman possesses much the same variable capacities as man, we may say that what is known or unknown of the mental capacities of the one for a particular occupation, or group of occupations, may be fairly accurately deduced in the case of the other, barring differences which would disqualify women, though possessed of intelligence. This, at any rate, is the basis on which the vocational guide must work at present, whenever the mental traits of men and women are involved in a question of guidance.

But to be assured by the psychologist that men and women do not differ widely, certainly not more widely than one man or woman does from another of the same sex, does not help the vocational counsellor as much as might be surmised. For, as to fitness of men for one employment rather than another, there may be great disagreement among psychologists. The wide divergence of their views may excuse ordinary mortals for not completely trusting in them. Caution in too readily attaching great weight to the results of various tests must be reckoned the virtue of some psychologists; others, Bagley and Lippman aver, have not exhibited this virtue.

Colvin cautiously summarized the prognostic value of tests, recently:[129] "We must, therefore, conclude that on the whole, psychological tests have justified their use as prognostic of academic achievement. . . . The army tests have indicated the probability at least, that there are certain intelligence levels for various occupations, ranging from below average intelligence for day laborers to decidedly above average for the professions. It is not altogether certain that these results can be taken unreservedly at their face value, but they are at least suggestive and may be employed together with other data in assigning men to occupational groups and in advising pupils in regard to various life callings."

[128] Thorndike: *Educ. Psychology*, III, 205 and 193–6; and Parsons: Sex and Genius [*Yale Review*, July, 1925, 745–6].

[129] *Ed. Rev.*, Nov., 1922, 331, 334–5.

Arps put a conservative estimate upon the accomplishments of the testing movement when he said:[130]

"I very much doubt whether we can at present take the existing crop of children and with easy conscience classify them even roughly into large groups on the basis of native fitness. Theoretically, it would seem that the variety of such human groups should correlate perfectly with the variety of occupational groups found in the environment. The first safe step in guidance has *not* been taken if we cannot say to John, 'Thou art by endowment, by native inclination and interest foreordained to labor in the general field of mechanic arts'; to William, 'Analysis points unerringly that your native inclination is in the direction of the learned professions.' If we stand helpless before the problem of rough group classification who is there so bold as to venture advice for specific vocations, as carpentry, law, medicine, electrical engineering, banking, or any one of hundreds of particular vocations?"

Many have been quite unable to accept Cutten's enthusiastic interpretation that analysis of capacities by use of intelligence tests will result in the establishment of a true intellectual aristocracy and the destruction of American democracy.[131] The quoted *Credo* of Whipple, however, is subscribed to by most psychologists and workers in the field of education, and is the faith which guides those who are attempting to work out more reliable measures of intelligence and vocational fitness at the present day:

"1. I believe that the existence of fundamental and relatively permanent individual differences in intellectual capacity has been incontrovertibly demonstrated.

"2. I believe that these differences are in the main inherited differences.

"3. I believe that intelligence tests, properly devised, properly administered and properly interpreted offer a feasible and valuable device for measuring these differences in capacity.

"4. I believe that an enormous amount of time, money and energy is now being wasted in the attempt to teach the same material by the same methods and at the same rate to pupils of distinctly different inherent capacity.

[130] *National Vocational Guidance Association Bulletin* No. 4, June, 1922, 12.

[131] *School and Society*, Oct. 28, 1922, 481; and Nov. 4, 1922, 519.

"5. I believe that in our present educational system, the gifted child in particular is given far less opportunity to develop his potential promise than is the average child, and that segregation or at least special educational measures must be used to give him this fair opportunity.

"6. I believe that the real meaning of democracy *is* properly safeguarded in the notion of 'equity of opportunity' and if any nation is destined to perish it is that one which fails to provide the best possible educational training for those of its rising generation that show promise of intellectual leadership."

Proctor, after studying the value of mental tests in guidance, concluded that they were worth consideration, along with teachers' judgments of the individual's ability and vocational desires.[132] That each of the three must be used with caution is well known. The erratic judgment of teachers has been studied. Crathorne, studying those who entered high school, found that of 57% who had a vocational objective in mind, about one-half changed their minds by the time they were freshmen at college.[133] Other studies have been made of the use of mental tests in advising students in the selection of high school courses, but they are by no means conclusive.[134] Significant beginnings have been made by endeavoring to give intelligence standards for nearly a hundred employments, on the basis of army studies, and checked by others at the Central Y. M. C. A., Brooklyn, New York.[135] These various studies convince even the most skeptical that there is something that may be done by scientific study of guidance, but that extreme care must be used in employing the instruments thus far devised for the discovery of vocational aptitudes.

An insight into the progress of vocational guidance in the schools may be secured from McDougall's study.[136] Of 130 high

[132] Proctor: *Psychological Tests and Guidance of High School Pupils,* Journal of Educational Research Monographs, No. 1.

[133] Change of Mind Between High School and College as to Life Work [*Sch. and Soc.,* XI, 28–30].

[134] For example, see Weisman: Use of Stanford Revision of Binet-Simon Test in Selection of High School Courses [*Jour. Ed. Research* VII, 137–44]; Powers: Intelligence as a factor in election of high school subjects [*Sch. Rev.,* XXX, 452–5]; Dickson: Use of group mental tests in guidance of eighth grade and high school pupils [*Jour. of Ed. Research,* II, 601–10].

[135] See Allen: *Guide to the Study of Occupations;* Freyer: Occupational Intelligence Standards [*Sch. & Soc.* (1922), XVI, 273–6].

[136] McDougall: Vocational Guidance in High School [*Industrial Arts Magazine* (April, 1922), XI, 133–5].

schools, in 32 different states, 92 had some special vocational
courses; 54 made available, to the student, surveys of local vocational openings; 46 had pre-vocational work in grades 7 and 8;
54 reported that teachers were urged to act as vocational coun-
sellors; and a considerable number reported using English
courses to locate vocational abilities, "vocational civics," written
reports on local industries, observation of local businesses, and so
forth, as means of assisting in choosing fields of work.   Only
thirty-six schools reported use of mental tests.   The work of
guidance was handled by the principal in 62 schools, by deans in
26, by employment bureaus in 86, and by central bureaus in
charge of educational boards in 43.

Activity in vocational guidance is on the increase; the need
for it is unquestioned.   It requires more exact knowledge, however, before it can measure out justice to the employee and the
employer.   It is the realization of this that accounts in large
measure for the frantic researches after facts at the present day.
How scientific guidance can become is yet undetermined.   Kitson
recently declared, "Particular attention is being paid to vocational guidance of college women.   This is due to our changing
attitude towards college education in general.   Once it was believed it must fit one for anything; now, that it must fit one for
something."[137]

Analysis of the occupational world has been going on ever
since women began to seek new fields to conquer.   We have seen
that concerted efforts were made to analyze their tasks as teachers and to give that training which enabled them to achieve success therein.   Beecher's books on domestic economy attempted
to describe the occupation and show the need of genuine training for it.   In the eighties, numerous books were written to
serve as vocational guides for women.   Some titles, such as
Money Making for Ladies (1882), *Work for Women* (1883),
and *What Can A Woman Do?* (1884), make clear that they
hoped to introduce the new woman to sufficiently rewarded congenial employment.[138]   They covered practically all occupations
open to women at the time.   Books of the present, which aim

137 Kitson: Progress and Coördination in Vocational Guidance [*Nat. Voc.
Guidance Assoc. Bulletin I*, No. 8, March, 1923, 123 *ff.*]; for a special bibliography on vocational guidance see the *Biennial Survey*, 1920–1922, I, 564.
138 See also p. 14.

at the same objective, are numerous. They have changed to some extent, due to the fact that they are for women of a different generation, and describe occupations, and means of getting into them, which did not exist for women a generation ago.[139]

Today, the complexity of the field requires that many specific studies be made as to vocational opportunities, as these vary greatly in different places. Vocational surveys are now common occurrences. More than ten years have passed since Dr. E. K. Adams, of the Committee on Vocational Opportunities of the Association of Collegiate Alumnae, issued the pamphlet on *Vocational Training*. In this was given a list of institutions offering training for occupations other than teaching. This truly pioneer piece of work was destined soon to be out-of-date, due to the fact that the decade of the War saw such rapid expansion of women's vocational opportunities; but the utility of such a publication was demonstrated, as also the necessity of continued revision from time to time. Since then, such practical studies as that of Dorothy Weir, on the *Training Opportunities for Connecticut Women*,[140] are of vital importance. She dealt in a brief, pointed manner with agriculture, applied art, business, clerical workers, economics, household economics, industry and trade, languages, fine arts, engineering, law, journalism, library work, medicine, dentistry, nursing, religious work, teaching, physical training, scientific work, and social workers. Following a brief statement on each of the above, schools, with their purposes, subjects taught, admission require-

---

[139] *Vocations Open to College Women,* pamphlet of the University of Minnesota; *Talks to Women on Essentials to Success in the Business World,* by Cora B. Frazier; *Social Service as a Vocation for Women,* issued by Women's Educational and Industrial Union, Boston; E. W. Weaver: *Vocations for Girls; Opportunities for Vocational Training,* by the Woman's Municipal League, Boston; *Vocations for the Trained Woman,* by A. F. Perkins, issued by the Woman's Educational and Industrial Union, Boston; *Finding Employment for Girls Who Have to Work,* by the Chicago School of Civics and Philanthropy; *Psychology and Industrial Efficiency,* by Hugo Münsterberg; Ruth M. Weeks: *The People's School,* Ch. 5; Elizabeth B. Butler: *Woman and the Trades,* Chaps. 21 and 22; C. W. Alden: *Woman's Ways of Earning Money;* McKeever, W. A.: *The Industrial Training of the Girl* and *Training the Girl;* E. K. Adams: *Women Professional Workers;* and a host of others.

[140] Published by Woman's Division, Connecticut State Council of Defense, n.d.

ments, degrees, fees, and length of term or course, were listed as the best available avenue to the desired occupation. Such a knowledge of training facilities is indispensable to the seeker, as also to the one who wishes to help her. In 1924, a valuable work on a national scale, rather than state, was published by the Bureau of Vocational Information, New York City. It offered facts regarding "facilities available to women in the United States" for *Training for the Professions and Allied Occupations*.

Another important study, in 1921, undertook to investigate the "agencies, other than academic appointment bureaus, concerned with the vocational guidance and placement of professional women."[141] Questions were sent to "twenty-one noncommercial bureaus, including fifteen Bureaus of Occupations for Trained Women" with a view to taking "a practical first step towards . . . improvements in the training of women for professional service . . . and investigating their status in professional and professionalized occupations." Eighteen bureaus replied to the questions.[142] Another task contemplated by the Committee was the study of "what educational institutions themselves are doing . . ." for the placement of women. The present study asked the various agencies to indicate whether they did the following types of work: "placement; information; research; training; publicity; recruiting." Fifteen, of the eighteen replying, reported "placement"; fifteen, "information"; eight reported "research" but this term is variously interpreted. Five reported "training courses"; and two, "incidental recruiting." Clearly placement, giving information, and research regarding vocations are the activities that are judged most necessary by the agencies actually engaged.

The "development of such educational means whereby the individual may satisfactorily fit into" vocations has been conspicuous in woman's education of the nineteenth and twentieth centuries. Normal schools and seminaries fitted her to be a teacher; schools of design, trade schools, commercial schools, and others, have given specialized training for vocations more recently opened. The Federal Board for Vocational Education, under the Smith-Hughes Act, administers $4,140,000 each year, after 1926, in trade, household economics, industrial education and teacher training, in which fields many women are occupied;

141 *Educational Record,* III, 66–109.
142 Those replying are listed on pp. 67–9 of the Committee's report.

and, of course, the federal expenditure is only a fraction of that expended from combined state and local sources.[143] There is a marked tendency towards industrial education for girls and women. According to most recent figures, "more than one worker out of every six engaged in mechanical and manufacturing pursuits is a woman, the number of such . . . being approximately 2,000,000.[144]

In the field of general higher education offered by colleges, there have been many changes, and others proposed.[145] Gradually the tendency to practicability and professionalism in college studies has made its appearance, so that Miss Thomas has declared the old college course very much worm-eaten.[146] A straw here and there shows the wind's direction. Wellesley girls were recently reported as playing the stock market—but "with theoretical money."[147] Lange, in 1916, wished for a reorganization of women's collegiate education around the "fountain head of all progress, the home." Most young women would be required to take such foundation courses, but they would not be vocational. After completing such, "every young college woman is . . . to . . . put on her working-program pursuits with a vocational turn. For women . . . a higher education that prepares only for leisure and perhaps a purely decorative or parasitic life should be a thing of the past. . . . Every college woman, whatever her . . . economic status, . . . should, during the latter part of her course, concentrate effort about a vocational aim, and subject herself to specific training for specific doing." How far has college education for women students followed the direction indicated by Lange and others? There has been some shifting of views, some introduction of new courses, and so forth, in response to vocational demands. But general training, especially in the woman's college, is strongly entrenched. A thoroughly renovated woman's college education, capable of being defended by reason rather than tradition, has recently been proposed.[148]

[143] See *Biennial Survey*, 1920–1922, I, 348 *ff*.

[144] *Ibid.*, 351.

[145] Opportunities developing for higher professional education are discussed pp. 321 *ff*.

[146] See p. 220.

[147] *N. Y. Times*, Sunday, Mar. 7, 1926.

[148] See pp. 214–16.

CHAPTER III

PHYSICAL EDUCATION

I. General Lack of Physical Education

Our Colonial ancestors knew nothing of organized physical education. As it had not yet developed in their old homes, there was no system to be transplanted to the new. Life itself, in a primitive environment, offered abundant useful activity; and the Puritan conscience was apt to be troubled by frivolous sports, exercises, and "merrymakings" which were regarded as snares of the devil. Where Puritan sentiment did not prevail, however, as in South Carolina, Virginia and New York, for example, considerable attention was given to sports and games of their mother country. Bowling, skating, coasting, running races, riding, boxing, wrestling, cock fighting, and similar entertainments, contemporary records assure us, were not without recognition, and increased greatly in the eighteenth century, in spite of the warnings issued against them by ministers and churches. Most significant, from the standpoint of physical education of girls, was the invasion of American cities by the dancing masters whose offerings were advertised in considerable numbers after 1725 and, by 1776, were to be found in all cities irrespective of previous religious opposition.

Not many years ago, women were criticized, and not without reason, for their dress: gowns were too heavy, tight, and long. Now they are taken to task by moralists who insist that dresses are too loose, too light, and too short. The changes that have come about are not traceable to fickle fashion alone. The movement to introduce hygiene and physical education into the schools, and the entrance of women into more active life, have been effective in suggesting the necessity of more sensible clothing.

When seminaries, normal and high schools first opened to girls, they emphasized book-learning to the almost total exclusion of provisions for health. Critics of these institutions were numerous. They did not fail to point out the significance of

98

the lack of attention to health. The result was an energetic movement on the part of the leading seminaries and their promotors to institute regular systems of physical exercise. Calisthenics, physiology, and hygiene began to appear here and there.

The *American Annals of Education*[1] quoted a long article from the Boston *Medical and Surgical Journal* of December, 1837, to the effect that "there is something radically wrong in the present system of education among young ladies. Their physical condition does not receive from parents or teachers that consideration which it deserves." Briefly, the faults are these: girls go to school early and are confined there long hours; they have not enough exercise in the open air; they have too many studies; they finish their education too young and are hastily prepared by anxious mothers for society. For this debut "their bodies are encased in whalebone, [and] their faces are veiled if they venture into the open air. . . ."[2] Pelopio, writing on female education, declared they have been "taught more concerning the structure of the earth, the laws of heavenly bodies, the habits and formation of plants, the philosophy of language and the art of cutting awkard capers to music, than concerning the structure of the human frame and the laws of health and reason."[3]

A similar criticism was made by Nathan Allen in *Education of Girls*, which fairly represents the views of many:

"From six to sixteen years of age, girls are confined closely to school, except about twelve weeks' vacation each year. No systematic provision for physical culture is made at the school, neither is there sufficient exercise taken outside for a proper and healthy development of the body. These ten years constitute also the principal time in life for the growth and development of all parts of the system. The period from twelve to sixteen is especially a critical time in the growth and health of girls. These years in the high school or seminary are crowded with most difficult studies, combined with examinations, reviews, and exhibitions, which make a ruinous strain upon the brain and the nervous system. . . In no part of female education is there so

[1] VI, 100–5.
[2] *Ibid.*
[3] *Conn. Com. Sch. Jour.*, IX, 284.

much need of reform as in *physical culture*. If the standard of scholarship is to be raised higher and higher in all our schools for girls, and no greater attention is to be paid to the laws of health and life, grave consequences may well be apprehended. . . . With rare exceptions, there is no system of gymnastics, or calisthenics, provided in schools for girls, and, generally speaking, no regular and systematic exercise that is adapted to promote their highest physical development.''

Coxe, too, argued that girls should be ''educated in such habits of physical exertion as shall fit them for their station in life . . . and not in the inaction, which will incapacitate them for the allotted duties, and abridge essentially the comfort, happiness and usefulness of those with whom their future destinies may be connected.''[4]

With the encouragement of Dr. Bellows, Elizabeth Blackwell published her lectures on *The Laws of Life in Reference to the Physical Education of Girls*, 1852.[5] These were republished, ''at the request of friends,'' in 1871. In them she called special attention to the restrictions on girls' activity and the almost exclusive attention to school duties. ''The school-hour closes, the child returns home, but not racing merrily along, with shout and frolic; for the little girls must not run, or slide on the ice like a boy. . . . Can there be a more melancholy spectacle than that of the girls in a boarding school taking their afternoon walk? There is no vigor in their step, no pleasure in their eye; the fresh air is certainly good for their lungs, but the unattractive exercise is of most questionable benefit. . . . No opportunity is given for the healthy action of those bodily powers which are, as we have seen, of the first importance to the young, and whose neglect is the source of prolonged suffering and incapacity. . . .

''Until a girl is sixteen, it is much more important that she should possess a healthy body, an honest, loving heart, good sense, and a clear intellect, than that she should be able to answer questions on every science, play tolerably on the piano, speak

---

4 *Claims of the Country on American Females*, II, 100–2; for other criticisms of negligence relative to physical education and recommendations for improvement, see *Am. Annals Ed.*, VI, 84–6; V, 262–6; VII, 449–51; *Am. Jour. Ed.*, I, 349–52, and II, 339–43; also *Com. Sch. Jour.*, I, 282–3, and X, 266.

5 Blackwell: *Pioneer Work*, 158.

DIO LEWIS

French and embroider, if these acquisitions are to necessitate physical and mental weakness in after life."[6]

On every hand the evils of too little attention to physical training were seen and commented upon. The editor of the Boston *Courier*, having attended a school festival (1858), noted that "not one girl in ten had the air and look of good health. . . . If we neglect the body, the body will have its revenge. And are we not doing this? Are we not throwing our whole educational force upon the brain? Is not a healthy city-born and bred woman getting to be as rare as a black swan? And is it not time to reform this altogether? Is it not time to think something of the casket as well as the jewel—something of the lantern as well as the light?"[7]

Of the prevailing mode of education, Dio Lewis wrote: "In most seminaries, physical exercise is optional with the pupil. . . . The average American girl has a delicate body. . . . The school which does not provide in its curriculum for this average and fundamental condition, seems to me strongly deficient in its educational provisions."[8] Upon attending a commencement and being told that a certain group of girls had "finished" their education, he retorted: "If you had said the girls themselves were *finished*, I should have understood you; but if you mean that their *education* is *finished*, I can only say that it seems to me they have not laid the first stone in the foundation of a true education."

"Pale, thin, bent—they had been outrageously humbugged. What amount of languages and music could compensate for this outrage upon the very foundations of their being?"[9]

Dress was conceded by many to be an important factor, and a dress reform movement arose, which progressed hand in hand with the reform of girls' schools in regard to exercise. The *American Annals of Education*[10] noted: "Two societies of this kind have been formed, and are successfully going on, putting down the wicked slavery to fashion, which destroys so many females." All the ladies, save three, in Peterborough, New

[6] Blackwell: *Lectures on the Laws of Life*, 124, 125, 127, and 172.
[7] *New York Teacher*, Jan., 1858, 148; also 394.
[8] Lewis: *Our Girls*, 357–8.
[9] *Ibid.*, 359–60.
[10] 1835, V, 331–2.

York, "signed the pledge." At Atkinson, Maine, a similar movement started with the students of a boarding school. Dr. Mary Safford wrote, later, "It does not require the foresight of a seer, to diagnose a chronic case of tight lacing and of heavy skirts." They produce what are called "women's diseases," but should be "termed 'women's follies.' "[11]

While it was generally recognized that prevailing fashion was in the main responsible for the unsuitable dressing of young ladies, it was well known that the seminaries were seats of juvenile fashion as well as learning. Holmes deftly portrayed them in "My Aunt":[12]

> "They braced my aunt against a board,
> "To make her straight and tall;
> "They laced her up, they starved her down,
> "To make her light and small;
> "They pinched her feet, they singed her hair,
> "They screwed it up with pins;—
> "Oh, never mortal suffered more
> "In penance for her sins."

Some critics gave teachers the chief credit for the prevailing tight-lacing habit and declared that "lady-teachers' waists" were smaller than those of any other class of "women who earn their daily bread." Teachers and principals of seminaries, it was thought, could not break up the fashion, for "mothers enforce it, young ladies advise it, gentlemen frequently encourage it . . . [and] society favors it," but they could, at least, not encourage it by their own example.[13]

Dio Lewis was an ardent champion of the women's movement; and he denounced their dress as a chief cause of illness and weakness, which in turn hindered women from playing an independent rôle. He decried the "wasp-waist"—but was, at the same time, intolerant of low necks and short sleeves.[14] He set out, in his school at Lexington, to encourage physical exercise and did much to promote the idea of the "Home Gymnasium."[15] At his Family School for Young Ladies, 140 pupils were in attendance the third year. They were a selected group—those

---

[11] Livermore: *What Shall We Do With Our Daughters?* 28–9.

[12] Page: *The Chief American Poets,* 357.

[13] *N. E. Jour. of Education,* I, 207.

[14] *Our Girls,* 64 *ff.* and 191 *ff.*

[15] *Ibid.,* 284 *ff.,* wherein he described the Pangymnastikon of Schreber.

JUST THE STYLE IN 1860

who could not, because of "delicate constitutions," stand the strain of exclusive application to studies. The girls wore no corsets, ate but twice a day of very simple food, exercised twice a day, and danced a good deal. Of the latter, he wrote: ". . . We danced from two to four evenings a week . . . beginning about half past seven o'clock . . . till half past eight, which was always our bed time." Only the square dances were used, the "round" or the "German" being not admitted because "the rotary motion is injurious to the brain and spinal marrow" and "the peculiar contact between the man and the woman *may* suggest impure thoughts."[16] The results were immediately noticeable. Chests, arms, and waist were measured at the begin-

THE FAMILY SCHOOL OF DIO LEWIS (Lexington, Mass.)

ning; after eight months there was a gain of two and a half inches in chest, five inches in waist, and one and one-half inches in arm measurements. Lewis attributed the success, however, in large measure, to the long hours of sleep required at the school.

Lewis' *New Gymnastics* laid considerable emphasis on proper dress and, being widely introduced into girls' schools, was unquestionably an influential factor in improving health, if not in reforming ideas of dress. "The most essential feature of the dress is perfect liberty about the waist and shoulders. . . . It is worn without hoops. . . ."[17] Woolson, twenty years later, though favoring more emphasis on free exercises and athletic sports, such as their brothers indulged in, commented favorably

16 *Ibid.*, 226 *ff.*
17 *New Gymnastics*, 16 *ff.*

GYMNASIUM COSTUMES APPROVED BY DIO LEWIS

on the "gymnastic evolutions of late" which have required girls "to don a loose blouse for their performance" and which, if it does nothing else, makes them "conscious twice a week of some comparative freedom and comfort in dress."[18] Some college girls happened to appear in class in bloomers at Northwestern, in 1895. Gradually, it has been accepted that women should dress comfortably, even outside the gymnasium.[19] Nevertheless, in recent years school officials have been known to protest against school girls attending classes in "knickers."

II. Prevailing Ill Health

The criticisms of schools suggest that the ill health of women was due, partly at least, to the lack of school facilities for pro-

[18] Woolson: *Woman in American Society* (1873), 197–8, 205–6.
[19] *Educ. News*, Dec. 14, 1895, 715.

moting physical health. Frances P. Cobbe, however, attributed the great prevalence of ill health largely to the fashion of the day. "Another source of *petite santé*, I fear may be found resulting from a lingering survival among us of the idiotic notion that there is something particularly 'lady like' in invalidism, pallor, small appetite and a languid mode of speech and manners. The very word 'delicacy', properly a term of praise, being applied vulgarly to a valetudinary condition, is evidence that the impression of the dandies of sixty years ago, that refinement and sickness were convertible terms, is not yet wholly exploded."[20] Other causes of ill health, she thought, were (1) blind devotion to their families, which caused sacrifices of sleep, food and rest, (2) dress, and (3) occupations.

In the middle of the past century, this matter of ill health was taken very seriously. Today, when the health of American girls is almost a by-word and their athletic prowess thrills the world, it is indeed strange to read that, in 1858, some held, though unable to give the cause, that "the fact is certain that the American girl is a very delicate plant . . . not generally strong in nerve and muscle, and too ready to fade before her true mid-summer has come."[21]

Catherine E. Beecher declared the "Standard of health among American women is so low that few have a correct idea of what a healthy woman is. . . . A woman who has tolerable health finds herself so much above the great mass of her friends . . . that she feels herself a prodigy of good health."[22] By some, Miss Beecher was considered an alarmist; but they admitted, in the same breath, that her "facts" could "not be questioned" and the "dark side" they represented "must still be recognized." She tabulated these facts from reports made by women in 45 towns in New England and central Eastern states. Each woman named for her town ten women who she knew best and then described their health as "strong and perfectly healthy," "delicate or diseased" and as "habitual invalids." Thus 450 women were described in the 45 towns. Miss Beecher checked up the descriptions personally and discarded judgments which were clearly misinformed. She found 23 5/9 per cent. were strong and per-

20 Quoted by Starrett: *Letters to Elder Daughters*, 131 *ff.*
21 *Harper's New Mo. Mag.* (1858), XVI, 73.
22 *Letters to the People on Health and Happiness*, 122.

fectly healthy; 41 7/9 per cent. were "delicate" or "diseased";
while 34 3/9 per cent. were "habitual invalids." Her conclusion was that—

"The present generation of parents, then, have given their
children, so far as the mother has hereditary influence, feebler
constitutions than the former generation received, so that most
of our young girls have started in life with a more delicate organization than their mothers. Add to this the sad picture given
in a former letter of all the abuses of health suffered by the young
during their early education, and what are the present prospects
of the young women who are now entering married life?

"This view of the case, in connection with some dreadful developments which will soon be indicated, proved so oppressive
and exciting that it has been too painful and exhausting to attempt any investigation as to the state of health among young
girls. But everywhere I go, mothers are constantly saying,
'What shall I do? As soon as my little girl begins school she has
the headache.' Or this—'I sent my daughter to such a boarding-
school, but had to take her away on account of her health.'

"The public schools of our towns and cities, where the great
mass of the people are to be educated, are the special subject
of remark and complaint in this respect.

"Consider also that 'man that is born of woman' depends on
her not only for the constitutional stamina with which he starts
in life, but for all he receives during the developments of infancy
and the training of childhood, and what are we to infer of the
condition and prospects of the other sex now in the period of
education?"[23]

III. Remedial Measures

Various proposals were made for remedying the ill health of
women. Starrett made a homely proposition, which doubtless
would have proved beneficial to the families whose "females"
were "delicate" because it was the fashion. "No such healthful
exercise has ever been invented as ordinary housework . . .
nothing is so conducive to health." The "movement cures" of
the physicians and the gymnasium are similar to the movements
of climbing stairs, wielding the broom, and moving furniture.
"If ordinary housework greatly fatigues any ordinary young

[23] *Ibid.*, 132–3.

THE "DAILY DOZEN" IN 1856

woman, it is a sign that she has flabby, undeveloped muscles;
. . . if she will practice such work a reasonable amount of time
every day with spirit and cheerfulness, she will inevitably reap
the reward of an invigorated body. . . . The truth is that one
good speeping of an ordinary parlor is worth a dozen carriage
rides . . . it will bring the color to her cheeks and send the blood
coursing through her veins as scarcely any other exercise will.
If it tires her she should practice it (like any gymnastic exercise)
till it does not tire her."[24]

Less prosaic, and probably more fruitful, remedies were recommended by several ladies' magazines which presented cuts and

[24] Starrett: *Letters to Elder Daughters*, 20–2.

lengthy dissertations setting forth, with all the precision of a present day promoter of the daily dozen, exactly the way in which "the general health of persons of sedentary habits and employments" could be improved. The renowned *Godey's* closed a series of illustrated articles with an injunction to "implicit obedience to His will, which, as we may readily ascertain by contemplating the course of nature, is opposed to slothfulness and inactivity."[25]

Another agency developed for promoting the health of women, outside of the schools, was the public gymnasium and playground. In 1889, Boston opened a public gymnasium for men; and on June 1, 1891, one was opened for women, under the direction of Elizabeth C. McMartin, a student in Sargent's Normal School. By September, 97,000 women and girls had availed themselves of its facilities.[26] The great success of the public gymnasium for the female sex, it was felt, must enforce "the demand for making compulsory physical training a part of public school education, beginning with the primary schools and continuing through all the grades." The *Baltimore Sun* complimented the progressive spirit of Boston, which had been first in establishing libraries and schools as well as gymnasiums, and hoped that Baltimore would also further physical education. Since 1890, there has been a marked development of public gymnasiums for women; but private agencies have contributed much. A valuable service for the physical education of women has been performed by such organizations as the Young Women's Christian Association and the Young Women's Hebrew Association.

The beginning of physical education ought to be with the very young. Until recently, however, the public state school systems took little cognizance of physical training. Ohio passed a physical education law in 1904, influenced by the Women's Christian Temperance Union. Up to 1922, twenty-seven other states passed physical education laws, with varying success so far as practical outcomes are concerned. Twelve states were reported in 1922 as having state supervisors of physical education. Recent interest in physical education in public schools has been increased by the War. Seventeen of the twenty-eight state laws

25 *Lady's Book,* November and December, 1852, 448 and 529.
26 *Educational News,* Sept. 12, 1891, 500; Leonard and McKenzie: *History of Physical Education,* 341.

(to 1922) have been passed since 1917.[27]   In 1926, thirty-three states had laws requiring the teaching of physical education; and fifteen states had appointed state directors of this work.[28]

IV. Introduction of Physical Exercise into Seminaries

More significant than any of the foregoing suggestions and practical efforts was the leadership of women and men prominent in the movement for the education of women.   These in their own schools, and others through them, began to introduce regular physical exercise and did much to make health popular.

William Bentley Fowle (1795–1865) was a prominent promotor of monitorial education, and was for a time connected with girls' education.   He was among the earliest of those who experimented with calisthenics in girls' schools.   In the following article from the *Medical Intelligencer,* quoted (1826) in the *American Journal of Education,*[29] he told the story of his crude beginnings and set forth the obstacles he had to overcome:

". . . I will endeavor to furnish you with a brief account of my humble attempts to introduce gymnastic exercises into the Monitorial School; and perhaps not the least gratifying circumstance in my relation will be the fact, that my attempt takes date from the delivery of one of your lectures on Physical Education, early in the spring of 1825.   I had long before noticed the feeble health of many of my pupils, and encouraged them to take more exercise, but they wanted means and example, and little or nothing was effected.   The very day after the delivery of your first lecture, I procured two or three bars, and as many pulleys, and after I had explained the manner of using them to the best advantage, my pupils needed no further encouragement to action.   The recess was no longer a stupid, inactive season; all were busy and animated.   My chief difficulty was in the selection of proper exercises for females.   You know the prevailing notions of female delicacy and propriety are at variance with every attempt to render females less feeble and helpless,—and the bugbears of rudeness, romping, &c. are sure

[27] *Biennial Survey,* 1920–1922, I, 56 and 169–70; also *Recent State Legislation for Physical Education,* Bul. Bur. Ed., 1922, No. 1.

[28] Mimeographed circular of the Bureau of Education on *Requirements of State Departments for Directors and Supervisors of Physical Education,* No. 8247.

[29] I, 698–9.

to stare every such attempt in the face. I read all the books I could find, but met with very little applicable to the instruction of females. It seemed as if the sex had been thought unworthy of an effort to improve their physical powers. But the beneficial effects of what I had already introduced led me to persevere, and I have finally succeeded in contriving apparatus and exercises enough to keep all employed in play hours. Besides the ordinary exercises of raising the arms and feet, and extending them in various directions, we have various methods of hanging and swinging by the arms, tilting, raising weights, jumping forward, marching, running, enduring, &c. &c. I have no longer any anxiety about procuring suitable exercises, or in sufficient variety, for my pupils; and I believe the few parents whose more prim education led them to shudder at my innovation, have surrendered their prejudices.

"As to the effect of the exercises on the character and conduct of the pupils, it may be recorded for the encouragement of others, that many weak and feeble children have at least doubled their strength, and now disdain the little indulgences which were then thought necessary to them. Some very dull children have become more animated, and some over sprightly ones have found an innocent way of letting off their exuberant spirits; the discipline of the school has not been impaired, nor has my participation in the exercises of the children lessened their respect for me or my orders. I do not pretend that every dull child has been completely excited, or that every wild one has been tamed, nor every vicious one reformed, but I do believe that no child has been made worse than she would have become without the exercises, while many, very many, have been essentially benefitted. I would not conceal the fact that many hands have been blistered, and perhaps a little hardened by the exercises, but I have yet to learn that the perfection of female beauty consists in a soft, small, and almost useless hand, any more than in the cramped, diminutive, deformed, and useless feet of the Chinese ladies. But some of the old school say, why not let the children walk much, and exercise themselves in useful household labors. I should recommend both these methods of exercise, but do not think they would be a complete substitute for gymnastics, though a very useful aid to them. But the fact is the children of the present day are not thus employed at home, but on the contrary are engaged in the health destroying business of committing books to memory, and filling the mind with indigestible food, that it may be a suitable companion for its dyspeptic envelope. *I hope the day is not far distant when gymnasiums for women will be as common as churches in Boston,* and when our young men, in selecting the mothers of their future offspring, will make it one condition of the covenant that they be healthy, strong, capable of enduring fatigue, encountering danger, and helping themselves, and those who will naturally and of right, look to them for assistance." (*Italics mine.*)

The editor of the *Intelligencer* considered this the first account of gymnastics "successfully practiced in any school for girls, in any part of the United States"; it was also the first proof that his "feeble, though persevering efforts" to encourage physical education for girls had "produced any good effect."

Emma Willard, founder of Troy Female Seminary, was an enthusiastic believer in health education; and advocated fresh air, exercise, bathing, suitable diet, and regular hours of sleep. Proper posture and graceful movement could, by attention, be acquired. Dress should be elegant in simplicity.[30]

Contemporary with the labors of Fowle and Willard was that of Catherine Beecher, who after 1823 had been engaged in creating a girls' school at Hartford, Connecticut. In her account she told of the origin of her interest in calisthenics, which was stimulated by the visit of an English woman to her school. The latter gave demonstrations of exercises, many of which were later incorporated in Beecher's *Physiology and Calisthenics* (1856), and assured the school that she had corrected curvature of the spine by the use of them. "The whole school took lessons of her . . . and though the results were not conspicuous, they convinced me that far more might be done in this direction. . . . From this came the system of Calisthenics which I invented, which spread all over the country, and which Dio Lewis, courteously giving me due credit, modified and made additions to, some of which I deem not improvements but objectionable. . . . "[31]

---

[30] Barnard: *Am. Teachers and Educators*, 151.

[31] *Educational Reminiscences*, 42–3; Miss Beecher does not mention in this account a book, *Calisthenie ou Gymnastique des jeunes Filles* (Paris, 1828), which was enthusiastically reviewed in *American Annals of Education* (May, 1831), I, 229, and which doubtless influenced many leaders, certainly Emma

When she left this school and began a seminary at Cincinnati, Miss Beecher "invented a course of Calisthenic exercises . . . an improvement on the . . . [system] adopted at Hartford. . . . These were extensively adopted in schools, both East and West. . . ." The chief objections to her early systems were that they required a large floor without furniture, and the use of a piano. To meet these criticisms, she later adopted exercises to be used "in a school room without removing desks . . . to be performed with or without music. . . ." These were incorporated in her *Physiology and Calisthenics,* referred to above. The advantages of the system, she believed to be as follows:

"1. This system can be practiced in schools of every description, in the family, in nurseries, in hospitals, and in health establishments, *without apparatus,* and *without a room set apart for the purpose.*

"2. It excludes all those severe exercises that involve danger, either from *excess* or from *accidents.* It is maintained that many athletic exercises suited to the stronger sex are not suited to the female constitution. This is a system that contains all that either sex needs for the *perfect development* of the body. Any more severe exercises are useful only for men whose professions require some unusual physical strength or endurance. This method is adapted to mixed schools, so that both sexes can perform them together.

"3. This system is arranged on *scientific principles,* with the design of exercising *all* the muscles, and of exercising them *equally* and *harmoniously.* It embraces most of what is to be found in the French and English works that exhibit the system of *Ling,* the celebrated Swedish Professor, whose method has been widely adopted in European schools and universities.

"It also contains, in addition, many valuable exercises that have been employed in Health Establishments for the cure of disease and deformities.

"4. This system is so illustrated by drawings, and so exactly arranged as to mode and time, that *any* person, young or old, can practice it without aid from a teacher, and in any place."[32]

Willard and Mrs. Phelps, if not Miss Beecher herself; elsewhere she mentions "French and English works that exhibit the system of Ling."

[32] *Physiology and Calisthenics,* IV–V.

That one must regard Miss Beecher's appraisal of her system as that of an enthusiastic reformer, is doubtless true. There is some exaggeration. It is nevertheless certain that her book was for a time the textbook for courses in physiology, hygiene, and calisthenics in the leading seminaries and some of the women's colleges. She, like Mrs. Phelps and others, was chagrined to note the prevailing apathy on the part of the public, parents, and even the girls themselves. At the close of her life she was still looking forward to the time "when physical education . . . [would take] . . . the proper place in our schools . . ."; when "these exercises, set to music . . . [would be] sought as the most agreeable of school duties."[33]

Mrs. Phelps, who assisted Mrs. Willard for a time at Troy, and was later head of the Patapsco Female Institute, devoted sixteen pages of her *Lectures to Young Ladies* (1833) to a discussion of physical education. "Calisthenics, or female gymnastics," she said, "is very properly becoming a branch of education." Like Mrs. Willard, she considered the purpose of physical education to be the promotion of health and beauty. "Beauty is essentially connected with health: exercise, neatness and temperance are essential to both." Walking, cultivation of flowers, horseback riding, dancing, proper posture when writing or at the piano were recommended; in addition there should be attention to proper, comfortable clothing. Women should have some knowledge of botany and chemistry; also an acquaintance with "medical knowledge, both with reference to their individual maladies and the diseases of those around them."[34]

Few phases of the early higher education of women in the United States can be examined without finding the trace of Mary Lyon's influence. After her education under Joseph Emerson, she assisted Zilpah Grant at the Ipswich Seminary, where a systematic course of calisthenics was followed. When she succeeded in founding the new seminary at South Hadley, proper physical exercise occupied a prominent place in her plans, the system employed at Ipswich being introduced. Not only were formal ex-

[33] *Educational Reminiscences,* 84–6; also Barnard's *Journal,* XXVIII, 83–4.

[34] *Lectures to Young Ladies,* 49–65; also *Hours With My Pupils* (1859), 110–11; see also Abbot Academy *Catalog,* 1844, 13, regarding physical education provided.

ercises provided, but the purposes back of the system of labor were healthful exercise and a democratic atmosphere, as well as financial economy. Speaking of the value of domestic work as exercise, she wrote, after some experience in the school, it is "worth very much more than I anticipated, especially in winter. The daily work brings one hour of regular exercise, coming every day, and the same hour of the day. The exercise is peculiarly fitted to the constitution of females. . . . I did fear that the washing would be a loss of time, but we take it on our recreation day, and it only seems to make the day more effectual in meeting its object. The studies of the best scholars are broken in upon more effectually, and after washing they are willing to sew or read or write instead of continuing to pore over their books."[35]

Formal physical exercises, called calisthenics but essentially quadrilles, were proposed in a circular published by Miss Lyon in 1835, and practiced regularly from the opening of the seminary till 1862, when the New Gymnastics of Dio Lewis were adopted to take their place. The early calisthenic drills were directed by teachers who had learned them from their predecessors; little special training was required. In 1853 they were assembled and published by Miss Titcomb, under the title of Calisthenic Exercises.[36]

Informal recreation out of doors was at first secured chiefly through walking, both in rainy and sunny weather. The Book of Duties stated: "The young ladies are to be required to walk one mile per day till the snow renders it desirable to specify time instead of distance, then three quarters of an hour is the time required."[37] Tennis and boating were introduced about 1875.

In 1862, at the suggestion of Abner Kingman, Miss Evans, teacher of calisthenics at Mt. Holyoke, went to Boston to learn the New Gymnastics of Lewis. Some had raised objections to the calisthenic exercises because they resembled dances. In 1863, at graduation exercises, Ellen C. Parsons read, as her essay, a plea for a gymnasium. Governor Andrews, who was present, started a subscription; fifteen hundred dollars was raised at the church, and before night, nineteen hundred. The new gym-

---

[35] McCurdy: Physical Training at Mt. Holyoke [Am. Phys. Ed. Rev. (March, 1909), XIV, 139–40].

[36] Ibid., 141–3.

[37] Ibid., 145.

nasium was opened in 1865. In it the Lewis system of exercises, adopted in 1863, was used and the Lewis dress, with "Zouave" trousers, was worn. After 1863, domestic work was somewhat lightened. After 1891, it was still further reduced and more attention given to corrective gymnastics, apparatus work, and dancing.

After Miss Evans, gymnastics were under the direction of Alice Gordon Gulick and then of Cornelia Clapp, later professor of biology. In 1888, Dr. Hitchcock of Amherst was influential in causing the introduction of physical measurements. Three years later a department of physical training was established in charge of Eliza Clarke, a pupil of the Sargent School in Boston. Miss Spore, graduate in physical education at Oberlin College, came (1894) to take charge of the department, and served until 1908. As in most seminaries, hygiene was not at first taught as a formal subject; but it is said that Miss Lyon gave advice as to bathing, eating, and proper dress. Since 1862, there has been a resident physician and lecturer on physiology, anatomy, and personal hygiene.[38]

One of the most remarkable seminaries for girls was established by Dio Lewis at Lexington about 1866. This Home School, as he called it, offered all the usual studies of the female seminary in a four-year course. There was a distinguished faculty of thirty-two. Catherine E. Beecher was selected to teach the "ethics of home life." But its chief novelty was the emphasis on health, which was the first objective. The *Catalog* of 1866 explained:[39]

"It is the special and earnest aim of this school to give physical culture an honorable place in its course of instruction. American girls, especially of the higher classes, are too often pale, nervous, and fragile, with stooping shoulders, weak spines and narrow chests. In studying under the ordinary systems of education, such girls imperil their chances of health, compromise their enjoyment of life, and often break down in the midst of their labors. . . . We are resolved . . . to insist upon such a style of life in our school as shall give to the body stregth, endurance and grace and shall help each one of our graduates to go forth

[38] *Ibid.*, 149–50.
[39] P. 7.

with 'a sound mind in a sound body.' " To carry out this purpose, Lewis proposed to rely upon the following means:

(1) Regular and thorough instruction in anatomy and physiology and frequent lectures on practical hygiene; and attention to personal habits of pupils.

(2) Two to four half-hours each day of the New Gymnastics;
also exercise in the Swedish movement cure—for pupils
needing special treatment.

(3) Plain and nutritious food.

(4) Fixed hours for rising and retiring.

(5) Baths, warm and cold.

(6) Regular morning and evening walks in favorable weather;
also indoor sports and amusements.

(7) A "physiological dress such as shall properly protect the
body without hindering its growth. . . ."

In high schools, as well as seminaries, efforts were soon made
to provide for the physical education of girls. While the first
experiments gave little or no attention to it, the plan of Bache
(1840) suggested that "the ground should be provided with a
circular swing, with parallel bars and perhaps other simple and
safe modes of exercise." For, he thought, "A play-ground is
hardly less essential in a school for girls than in one for boys,
though the modes of exercise are different."[140] It is hardly necessary to add, however, that the provision of playgrounds in
secondary schools, for boys as well as for girls, made little advancement till the present century.

V. Physical Education in Early Women's Colleges

When a seminary education was proposed for girls, many objected that the mental strain would be too severe. We have seen
the initial efforts of some seminary leaders to guard against loss
of physical and mental health by a liberal provision of physical
exercises and out-of-door recreation. When the more arduous
discipline of college mathematics and classic languages was advocated, those who frequently called themselves "friends of the
female sex" stood aghast at the prospect of a host of broken
down women whose "gossamer intellects" and frail bodies
surely could not stand the strain. It was undoubtedly due

---

[40] *Report on the Organization of a High School for Girls, and Seminary
for Female Teachers,* Oct. 5, 1840, 10.

largely to this form of antagonism to the women's college movement that these women's institutions, almost without exception, provided for some sort of health oversight, and for more or less formal calisthenics, walks, boating, and various forms of gymnastics. A gymnasium, if not the first thing provided, was soon added, as a precaution against ill health; and an infirmary, to care for the girls when ill, was considered an essential part of the equipment of the college.

At Elmira (1855) an effort was made to utilize domestic tasks for the benefit of health:

"Careful attention will be paid to health and physical culture. Exercise in the open air, for which the extensive grounds of the Institution afford ample opportunity, will be encouraged. There is also an arrangement by which a moderate amount of domestic occupation will be apportioned to each pupil, in the care of rooms, and in connection with the boarding department, the more severe portions of the labor being performed by domestics. A lady peculiarly fitted for this important department has under her charge the direction of the young ladies in their domestic duties, and also in respect to health, deportment and all that may promote their comfort and happiness, as members of a well regulated family. The experience of the past year has more than satisfied the expectations of the Institution and its friends, as to the expediency and value of the present arrangements of the domestic department. It has exerted a most happy influence upon the health and cheerfulness of the young ladies, giving them a daily practical lesson of useful industry; so that instead of proving a hindrance, or disagreeable interference with the studies and general improvement of the young ladies, as some have feared, it has contributed to both moral and mental development."[41] Later it appears that more emphasis was put on formal gymnasium work:

"Careful attention is paid to health and physical culture. In addition to the exercise gained in domestic duties, all students are expected to engage in regular gymnastic exercises at least twice each week, in divisions. The system of gymnastics is that of Dr. Dio Lewis. For this class a suitable dress will be needed."[42]

[41] Elmira College *Catalog,* 1855–6.
[42] *Ibid.,* 1864.

At the founding of Vassar College, every effort was made to safeguard health. The first *Report on Organization,* drawn up in accord with the desire of the trustees at their second annual meeting, June 30, 1863, declared, ''A sound mind in a sound body is received as a first truth among educators. All right education looks to this result. . . . In our plan of education, then, we must include Anatomy . . . Physiology . . . Hygiene, by which we are taught the laws of health and the art of preserving it.'' These must be taught, not medically or professionally, but ''with a practical reference to the laws of life and health as affecting every individual pupil.''[43] Thus physical training was ''placed first, not as first in intrinsic importance, but as fundamental to all the rest.''[44]

The first catalog stated:

''The Gymnasium will be furnished with every variety of apparatus required to make it attractive and useful, and placed under the direction of an experienced and successful lady instructor. The system of Light Gymnastics, as perfected by Dr. Dio Lewis, will be taught to all the College without extra charge, and all possible encouragement given to healthful feminine sports in the open air. Each student is required to provide herself with a light and easy-fitting dress adapted to these exercises.

''The Riding-School will be supplied with properly trained saddle-horses and the necessary caparison, and regular instruction in horsemanship given to such as desire it, by a competent master, at reasonable rates.''[45]

Even before the gymnasium was completed ''classes for physical training had been organized and instructed in the corridors of the college building, by Elizabeth M. Powell. . . .''[46] By the second year the gymnasium was ready and the riding school was in operation under an ex-cavalry officer of the Prussian army, Leopold von Seldeneck.

The elaborate gymnasium was adequate to house the riding school, stables, calisthenic hall, bowling alley, and music hall. The riding school room alone was sixty by one hundred and twenty feet, forty-six feet high, well lighted and ventilated. It

---

[43] *Op. cit.,* 7–8.

[44] Robinson: *Curriculum of the Woman's College,* 11.

[45] *Catalog,* 1865–6, 28.

[46] Lossing: *Vassar College and Her Founder,* 111.

VASSAR'S CALISTHENIC HALL (1866)

was, indeed, as Lossing declared, "a new thing under the sun, to have a riding school a part of the instrumentalities of a seminary for the education of young women."[47] The calisthenic hall was thirty by eighty feet and completely supplied with the equip-

[47] *Ibid.*, 153–4.

ment necessary for the practice of the Lewis system of gymnastics.

Outside there was ample space for gardening; horse-back riding on the open road was encouraged, likewise boating and skating; while walking over the countryside, and playing croquet, were the recreations of those who desired less vigorous exercise.

The prospectus of Smith College[48] called attention to the fact that "in addition to lectures on Physiology and Hygiene, regular exercises in the gymnasium and the open air will be prescribed under the direction of an educated lady physician. These exercises will be designed not merely to secure health, but also a graceful carriage and well-formed bodies. "The number and arrangement of studies, and the mode of life will be carefully adapted to the demands of an enlightened physiology."[49]

In his inaugural address Dr. Seelye took cognizance of, and issue with, the objections to women's colleges on the ground of health, which were attracting particular attention just then, due to the statements published by Dr. Clarke.

"We admit it would be an insuperable objection to the higher education of woman, if it seriously endangered her health. We admit also that many requirements of our schools have been directly opposed to known physical laws. All this we grant and still maintain there is no more danger in an intelligently arranged system of higher education for women than there is for men. Imprudence in study is subject to the same penalty as imprudence in other things, but study properly pursued is healthy. Intelligence is a benefit to the body. Educated men are the longest lived. Students, as a class, are less exposed to disease. . . ."[50] In accord with the ideas of her president and in keeping with what was soon to be universal practice, Smith College opened (1875) with physical education occupying a place of importance, on a level with other departments, and a teacher of gymnastics, Lucy D. Hunt, in charge of it.[51]

Wellesley College, opened the same year as Smith, aimed to receive students "who have vigorous health, more than ordinary ability, and the purpose to give themselves faithfully to the pur-

[48] October, 1874.
[49] Seelye: *History of Smith College*, 22.
[50] *Ibid.*, 29–30.
[51] *Ibid.*, 37.

suit of knowledge. . . ."[52]   The following statement shows clearly the emphasis put on health, how to attain and keep it:

"Good health is essential to good scholarship.   The prevailing ill-health of American school-girls is not due to hard study, but is in most cases due to the violation of the plain laws of nature as to fresh air, simple and nourishing food, daily exercise, sufficient sleep, and suitable dress.   Diligent study benefits the health of young women who regulate their lives by these laws. The vigorous health of the great majority of the students at Wellesley College . . . is satisfactory proof that healthy young women are usually capable of constant hard study, without injury.   During the first year, many students were received in poor health, and the improvement, even in many of these, was remarkable. . . . If it is to be considered as an experiment whether girls can bear the strain of a collegiate education, then it would be wrong to make the experiment with students broken down in advance by violation of the fundamental laws of nature. . . . The charge is frequently made against colleges and seminaries that the health of the girls is destroyed by hard study. We will not submit to this odious injustice.   If students enter in good health, and obey the simple regulations, they will usually become stronger in body as well as in mind."[53]

The calendar, 1877–8, made no reference to courses in physiology or hygiene, but in 1883–4 the curriculum was changed considerably, more electives being allowed, and lectures on hygiene and physiology "were given for the first time to freshmen." Outdoor recreation was encouraged from the first.   Converse, in her entertaining *Story of Wellesley,* quotes the diary of Florence M. Kingsley, who was much concerned over having to explain to Mr. Durant how she broke an oar while rowing.   Again she relates their experience while walking.   Mr. Durant's spirit dominated the college in the early days.   Girls should exercise vigorously, if he had anything to say about it: "That isn't the way to walk, girls. . . . You need to make the blood bound through your veins; that will stimulate the mind and help to make you good students.   Come now, I'll . . . show you what I mean."[54]

[52] Robinson: *op. cit.,* 19.
[53] *Catalog,* 1876–7, 19–20.
[54] Converse: *Story of Wellesley,* 40.

Left to their own devices, however, with no formal physical education required, it seems that many avoided following the vigorous example set by Mr. Durant and fell into the habit of taking little exercise. Of a class of one hundred and four, who graduated in 1891, "only two had been in the habit of taking outdoor exercise for two hours every day, while eight did not average an hour, or one and a half, daily. Forty-five averaged about one hour a day, and the remaining forty-nine, less than one hour."[55]

In 1908–9, the Boston Normal School of Gymnastics was consolidated with the physical education department of Wellesley, making it possible, by five years of work, to obtain the A.B. degree and a Certificate in Physical Education.[56] Beginning with the fall of 1891, physical training became a regular department of college work and three hours of work per week were required of all members of the Freshman class. No gymnasium was as yet erected, but there was a large hall equipped with the apparatus necessary for the Sargent system of gymnastics.

By the last decade of the nineteenth century, most girls' colleges had adopted physical education and equipped themselves with gymnasiums. We have briefly noted Vassar's equipment in 1865. President Seelye visited Europe in order to be better able to select the best equipment for the Smith College gymnasium. Other later colleges, among them Bryn Mawr and the Woman's College of Baltimore, were provided with the most up-to-date buildings and equipment. The Zander machines of the latter were installed at a cost of $8,000. The women of the Harvard "Annex" utilized Dr. Sargent's gymnasium for a time but were provided with a new building in 1898.

Two systems of gymnastics were favored. The Woman's College of Baltimore followed the Swedish system of Ling under the direction of Dr. Alice H. Chapman, who was assisted by two women trained in the schools of Stockholm. In the wake of Dio Lewis' New Gymnastics, at Mt. Holyoke and Vassar, had come the Sargent system, which, with some variations, was adopted also by Smith, Wellesley, Bryn Mawr, and others.

While it is true that physical training came into the women's colleges, in the latter part of the nineteenth century, on a great

55 McCabe: *American Girl at College*, 20–1.
56 Robinson: *op. cit.*, 27.

tidal wave of popularity, some there were who pointed out that women were still not on an equality with men. Women's colleges, said Annie Payson Call, "would efface all intellectual distinctions of sex. In one particular only is there an obvious discrimination. The part which athletics plays in college life for men has no answering equivalent in college life for women. . . ."[57] Others decried formal gymnastics as a fad and thought it was carried to extremes. Such criticism, however, has not until recently resulted in a noticeable decline of its popularity. There has been, however, a conspicuous development of competitive sports among college women. Dr. Clarke believed, apparently, that if women did not suffer from their intellectual efforts while there, the vigorous methods of the gymnasts would surely be harmful to them. Another critic was of the opinion that more attention ought to be given to feeding girls properly and less to drilling them in gymnastics. The "genteel starvation" of the old-fashioned boarding school, she felt, had not entirely passed into oblivion. Kristine Mann declared confidently (1921), however, that "students in women's colleges were never so hygienically housed and fed . . . as at present."[58]

In 1897, Claghorn noted that "not many years ago systematic athletics under regular supervision was unknown in colleges for women; no definite courses in physical education were given, little gymnastic drill of any kind was practiced; . . . [but] today nearly every college has its well-equipped gymnasium; . . . attendance and exercise . . . [are] obligatory . . . [and] courses in physical training and . . . [organized] athletic sports [are] under competent direction. . . ." She concluded there was "little danger" that "the importance of this element in college life" would not be adequately recognized.[59] In fact, she believed too much faith was put in formal exercises: "Of late years liberal sacrifice has been paid to the gymnasium fetich. Exercise in the gymnasium has been made compulsory . . . in the belief that it will be of benefit to every student engaging in it. . . . In many instances, however, gymnasium work of any kind is felt as an additional task, heaped upon the task of study, not the refreshment and restorative after study that it is meant

[57] The Greatest Need of College Girls [*At. Mo.* (1892), LXIX, 102].

[58] *Ed. Rev.* (1921), LXII, 46–7.

[59] Claghorn: *College Training for Women*, 77–8.

to be. To do good, exercise must be attended by two circumstances, one mental and one physical; namely, enjoyment and fresh air. To many students no enjoyment whatever is afforded by gymnasium work—it seems a stupid, aimless performance in all its diversities; and as for air, that which floats casually through opened upper windows is but a poor substitute for the wide and sunlit expanse of the great ocean of atmosphere that bathes all out-of-doors in its invigorating currents.

"Gymnasium work is considered necessary from the mistaken but widespread notion that muscular development is in itself a good thing. The process of developing the muscle is attended by heightened respiration, and a consequent enrichment of the blood, whereby is offered increased nourishment to the organs and tissues in general, including that greedy bloodsucker, the brain. But the muscles themselves are greedy also; and if the process of their development is carried on so vigorously that they absorb for their own needs the greater part of the nourishment afforded by the freshened blood, the worker is left with a sense of fatigue in the mind instead of the renewed strength and power she ought to feel.

"Many students have this sense of fatigue after work in the gymnasium, but feel a decided refreshment after out-of-door exercise, which quickens and purifies the blood at least as well as, if not better than, gymnasium practice. That student is wise, then, who after suitable trial, finding this to be the case with her, frankly and deliberately gets rid of the gymnasium all she can, and walks, rides, drives, wheels, and plays tennis or basket-ball, changing the current of her thought as well as of her blood, so that she will return to her books with fresh delight and zest."[60]

Considering the lackadaisical manner in which some go through exercises today, it is not hard to agree with Claghorn that little or no benefit results from such physical training. Still more dubious is the benefit when the lazy individual is even able to avoid a bath after exercise.

Although colleges and universities have come to adopt the practice of requiring physicians' certificates and proofs of vaccination of entering students, and though courses in personal hygiene, as well as regular physical exercises, are generally required, it is felt in some quarters that still greater improvement

[60] *Ibid.*, 112–15.

is desired. One writer on hygiene in the woman's college is of the opinion that the "increase of liberty" given students at college has resulted in a lower standard of health than should be expected, considering the great care that is expended upon formal health education. "Lights out at ten" has fallen into the discard; there is too much spending of money without any restriction by elders; collegiate candy and ice cream parlors are "rushed" too much. In a large woman's college, in a thirty-day period, 42 per cent had missed work on account of illness, mostly of inconsequential nature. Of the total hours missed (516), 83 per cent "were probably avoidable." The causes were: colds, 34 per cent; menstrual disturbances, 20; headache, 16; fatigue, 4; and indigestion, 5 per cent.[61]

The several "complaints" just named could easily be remedied or avoided. The more serious physical defects among college women, which require the special knowledge of qualified physicians and physical directors, rather than greater care on the part of chaperones and house mothers, were listed under nine heads by Baer:

"1. Psychic nervous conditions, sensitiveness, neuralgic headaches, fainting, insomnia, and continuous worry.

"2. Defects of posture—scoliosis, kyphosis, and lordosis, drooping head, flat chest, and ptosis.

"3. Defects of the respiratory organs—usually an inability to breathe normally and an utter lack of the fundamental principles of breathing; rigid chest with lack of muscular development of chest; also cases with inherited tendency to tuberculosis.

"4. Derangements of the digestive organs—chief of which is constipation with its attendant ills, where frequently the student has no real understanding of how to remedy conditions. Here we often find a lack of practical knowledge as to diet and water and their bearing upon health and efficiency, although lectures on dietetic hygiene have been given them during their college course.

"5. Disturbances of the pelvic organs with functional irregularities.

"6. Skin troubles, especially those that can be traced to constipation, diet, pelvic disturbances, and general lack of care of the body, due in many instances to a want of understanding of

[61] *Ed. Rev.* (1921), LXII, 46-7.

the efficient use of water as a therapeutic agent, and of the fundamental principles of personal hygiene.

"7. Defects of the feet—especially flat foot.

"8. Sprains, old and new.

"9. Obesity, rarely serious, but affecting the student's general efficiency."[62]

VI. *Effect of Physical Education on College Women*

The foregoing array of ailments of college girls may suggest that physical education has not proved its efficacy. But each college generation brings its health problems; and no health education, no matter how satisfactory in its effect upon the present students, will eliminate the problems of the next generation, though it may modify them considerably. Here we are concerned only with getting an estimate of the results of physical training upon those who shared in the first experiments.

It may be that to physical education is due the credit for the fact that those for whom early disaster was prophesied, if they underwent the discipline of colleges, have lived to relate their experiences! Though we cannot be sure how far this may be true, it is clear that much credit has been given to physical exercise for the good health which college women kept on stubbornly exhibiting, even at the end of the four years when, according to all the prophecies, they should have been in their graves! Mary Carpenter, after she had witnessed the amazing intellectual attainments of Vassar College girls, emphatically asserted: ". . . We must admit that they have superior health—it is most extraordinary."[63] Caroline H. Dall, writing on the same subject, believed "the world may be challenged to produce, in any one neighborhood, four hundred young women of so great physical promise"; furthermore, it seemed to her a fact well known to parents and teachers that "the health of the girls continued to improve up to the hour of graduation."[64]

Summarizing the experience of the first four years at Smith College, Seelye concluded: "The health of the students had not been impaired. All of them were as well and most of them stronger physically than when they entered college. There had

---

[62] Baer: Health of College Women [*N. E. A. Proc.*, 1916, 692].

[63] Howe: *Sex and Education*, 100–1.

[64] *Ibid.*

been neither death nor serious illness among them, nor had they grown apparently less womanly or less winsome as a result of higher education."[65] In 1884, the Commissioner of Education reviewed the facts assembled by the collegiate alumnae, and tabulated by the Massachusetts Bureau of Statistics of Labor, and concluded: "It is sufficient to say that the female graduates of our colleges and universities do not seem to show, as a result of their college studies and duties, any marked difference in general health from the average health likely to be reported by an equal number of women engaged in other kinds of work, or, in fact, of women generally, without regard to occupation followed." It is clear that the Commissioner believed these favorable results due, in part at least, to the safeguards of physical education, as he said, "Only 12 institutions were included in the above examination . . ." but ". . . while they are colleges or universities that maintain high standards [of work], they are so managed as to offer peculiar facilities for physical culture and for healthful living."[66] It was pointed out that "undoubtedly the mode of life affects the health of students much more than their studies" and that "a large proportion of the institutions for the superior instruction of women are deficient in respect to the means for promoting physical vigor."

After 1891, gymnasium work was required of students at Wellesley. "The results of a year and a half of the experiment" were said to be "most satisfactory, not only in the development of physique, improvement in carriage and vigor of the young women, but also in the increased capacity for mental application."[67] The establishment of systematic study of cases, use of measurements and charts, and comparison of abnormal with normal developments, was an important step forward. Special exercises came to be recommended for specific defects; measurements and tests, at set periods, showed what results had been effected. McCabe stated that a study of the effect of Swedish exercises, on one hundred cases at the Woman's College at Baltimore, showed chest development varying from one to five inches.[68] Most physical directors could produce similar or more

[65] *Hist. of Smith College*, 51.
[66] *R. C. E.*, 1884–5, CLXVIII–CLXIX.
[67] McCabe: *American Girl at College*, 20 *f.*
[68] *Ibid.*

startling figures. Britan quoted figures (1908) showing the effects of rowing at Wellesley. After training and a month of actual rowing, chest measurements increased on the average from 31.5 to 33.4 inches; shoulder measurements increased .9 inches; and strength of back, 17 pounds.[69] Voluminous figures, showing different sorts of physical improvement, might be cited.

When "friends of the sex" had been forced to admit the ocular demonstration that women could and did live through the course of the separate women's colleges, there was still another objection that they should not be subjected to the *identical* studies and conditions in the same colleges and universities with men. Objections on moral grounds, as well as intellectual and physical, have been reviewed elsewhere.[70] Dr. Clarke, and other medical men, were frequently called upon to witness what would surely happen if the practice were persistently followed. Howe pointed out to these gentlemen that possibly it was not the "identity of the intellectual education given to girls and boys in America" that caused the ill health of girls, but the "dissimilarity of their physical training."[71] While boys were out of doors, girls spent more time shut up in houses. The movements of boys were free; those of girls impeded by ridiculous dress.

T. W. Higginson and other prominent men, as well as women who were interested in the movement for higher and equal education for women, joined in an effort to show the unscientific nature of the conclusions which had been so hastily drawn by Clarke and other self-styled "friends of the sex." Mrs. Dall, Mrs. Horace Mann, John Bascom, and Elizabeth S. Phelps were among those who contributed to a little volume, *Sex and Education,* which was sent out under the editorship of Mrs. Howe to counteract the influence of Clarke's book, which bore the same name. Their arguments and criticisms were generally scintillating but not always illuminating; sometimes they were both. They had the advantage of poking at a man of science who had clearly overstated his case; the opportunity for jibes was not overlooked. One of the contributors noted that:

[69] What Physical Education Is Doing for Women [*Education* (1908), XXIX, 35 *ff.*].

[70] See pp. 266–80.

[71] Howe: *Sex and Education,* 27–8.

"Before this pet theory of the incompatibility of health with intellectual activity, for women only, was discovered, men of science speculated concerning the deficient busts of American women. The dry, stimulating climate was supposed, in a great measure, to account for it. The fact itself reaches back to the grandmothers of the grandmothers of today. It was and is chiefly observable in the northern and eastern States. As you go south, you find fuller forms, but not always combined with emptier heads. . . ."[72]

More potent than their arguments were the statements issued by those who had attended or presided over the coeducational colleges. Olympia Brown asserted that at Antioch she had "never heard of a young lady in the college requiring a physician's advice. Among the seven girls in my class, . . . [not] an instance of illness. . . . The ill-health of the women of our time is not due to study or regularity in study; it is due to the want of regularity, and want of aim and purpose, and want of discipline. If you should take the whole number of women in this country who have graduated from a regular college with men, and place them side by side with the same number of women who have not had that course of study, select them where you will, the college graduates will be stronger in mind and body, able to endure more and work harder than the others. This I am sure of, as I am acquainted with many of the somewhat small number of women graduates; and I know something of other women, having belonged to various female seminaries at different times."[73]

In 1882, President Thwing gathered facts and impressions relating to women students' health from a number of coeducational institutions. The President of Oberlin replied: "Our impression has been . . . that our young women endure the strain . . . as well as the young men." Angell, of Michigan, stated: "Women have been here since 1870, . . . have done every kind of work successfully and without injury to character or health." Lee, of St. Lawrence University, found "their health has generally improved during their college course. There have been exceptions but . . . few." Bascom, of Wisconsin, reported, by actual count, that girls had lost only a third as much time proportionally as the boys; also that most of the girls who missed

[72] *Ibid.*, 23–5.
[73] *Ibid.*, 197–9.

classes were from the lower classes. "The young women do not, then, seem to deteriorate with us in health but *quite the opposite*; . . . it has long seemed to me plain that a young woman who withdraws herself from society and gives herself judiciously to a college course is far *better* circumstanced in reference to health than the great majority of her sex."[74] At a more recent date (1908) when the reaction against coeducation at Wisconsin was strong, Olin declared that "the fact that more than 95 per cent of the 1500 women, . . . graduated from the Wisconsin University during the last forty years, are alive, indicates that the strain of competition . . . has not been dangerously severe."

VII. Emphasis on Athletics

In the twentieth century there has been a marked tendency to increase attention to sports; this is reflected in the physical education of girls as well as that of boys. The same thing has been true in England. In 1921, an English committee studied the situation by sending a questionnaire to physicians, school principals, and women students. In the replies, "there was general approval of games . . . as beneficial not only to the health of girls, but to disposition and character as reflections of health. Tennis, net ball, and lacrosse received general approval." Hockey, some thought, was suitable only for older girls. Cricket was held not injurious. "Football was generally disapproved. . . ."

A similar movement has been set on foot in the United States. In 1923, 200 leaders in physical activities for girls convened in Washington and, as a result, the Women's Division of the National Amateur Athletic Federation was formed. Resolutions were drawn up, expressing what the leaders believed most necessary to strive for in athletics and as a suggestion to those "who must make decisions as to the participation of girls in school sports." These resolutions were published by the Bureau of Education as follows:

"1. *Resolved,* That it be noted that the term 'athletics' as used in this conference has often included the problems connected with all types of noncompetitive as well as competitive physical activities for girls and women.

[74] Thwing: Women's Education [*Education* (1883), IV, 55-7].

"2. Whereas the period of childhood and youth is the period of growth in all bodily structures, and

"Whereas a satisfactory growth during this period depends upon a large amount of vigorous physical exercise, and

"Whereas the strength, endurance, efficiency, and vitality of maturity will depend in very large degree upon the amount of vigorous physical exercise in childhood and youth, and

"Whereas normal, wholesome, happy, mental, and emotional maturity depends in large part upon joyous natural, safe-guarded, big muscle activity in childhood and youth; Therefore be it

"*Resolved,* That vigorous, active, happy, big muscle activity be liberally provided and maintained and carefully guided for every girl and boy, and that all governments—village, county, State, and National—establish and support adequate opportunities for a universal physical education that will assist in the preparation of our boys and girls for the duties, opportunities, and joys of citizenship and life as a whole.

"3. *Resolved,* That there be greater concentration and study on the problems and program of physical activities for the pre-pubescent as well as for the adolescent girl.

"4. *Resolved,* In order to develop those qualities which shall fit girls and women to perform their functions as citizens,

"(a) That their athletics be conducted with that end definitely in view and be protected from exploitation for the enjoyment of the spectator or for the athletic reputation or commercial advantage of any school or other organization.

"(b) That schools and other organizations shall stress enjoyment of the sport and development of sportsmanship and minimize the emphasis which is at present laid upon individual accomplishment and the winning of championships.

"5. *Resolved,* That for any given group we approve and recommend such selection and administration of athletic activities as makes participation possible for all and strongly condemn the sacrifice of this object for intensive training (even though physiologically sound) of the few.

"6. *Resolved,* (a) That competent women be put in immediate charge of women and girls in their athletic activities even where the administrative supervision may be under the direction of men.

"(b) That we look toward the establishment of a future policy that shall place the administration, as well as teaching and coaching of girls and women, in the hands of carefully trained and properly qualified women.

"7. *Whereas* a rugged, national vitality and a high level of public health are the most important resources of a people: Therefore be it

"*Resolved,* That the teacher training school, the colleges, the professional schools, and the universities of the United States make curricular and administrative provisions that will emphasize—

"(a) Knowledge of the basic facts of cause and effect in hygiene that will lead to the formation of discriminating judgments in matters of health:

"(b) Habits of periodical examination and a demand for scientific health service; and

"(c) Habits of vigorous developmental recreation.

"To this end we recommend that—

"(1) Adequate instruction in physical and health education be included in the professional preparation of all elementary and secondary school-teachers;

"(2) Suitable instruction in physical and health education be included in the training of volunteer leaders in organized recreation programs;

"(3) Definite formulation of the highest modern standards of professional education for teachers and supervisors of physical education and recreation and the provision of adequate opportunity for the securing of such education.

"8. *Resolved,* That in order to maintain and build health, thorough and repeated medical examinations are necessary.

"9. *Resolved,* Since we recognize that certain anatomical and physiological conditions may occasion temporary unfitness for vigorous athletics, therefore effective safeguards should be maintained.

"10. Whereas we believe that the motivation of competitors in athletic activities should be that of play for play's sake, and

"Whereas we believe that the awarding of valuable prizes is detrimental to this objective: Be it

Resolved, That all awards granted for athletic achievement be restricted to those things which are symbolical and which have the least possible intrinsic value.

11. *Resolved,* That suitable costumes for universal use be adopted for the various athletic activities.

12. Whereas we believe the type of publicity which may be given to athletics for women and girls may have a vital influence both upon the individual competitors and upon the future development of the activity: Be it

"*Resolved,* That all publicity be of such a character as to stress the sport and not the individual or group competitors.

"13. Whereas certain international competitions for women and girls have already been held, and

"Whereas we believe that the participation of American women and girls in these competitions was inopportune: Be it

"*Resolved,* That it is the sense of this conference that in the future such competitions, if any, should be organized and controlled by the national organization set up as a result of this conference.

"14. *Resolved,* That committees be appointed for study and report on the following problems:

"(a) Tests for motor and organic efficiency.

"(b) The formulation of a program of physical activities adapted to various groups of the population.

"(c) The relation of athletics to the health of prepubescent and postpubescent girls.

"(d) Scientific investigation as to anatomical, physiological, and emotional limitations and possibilities of girls and women in athletics, and a careful keeping of records in order that results may be determined."[75]

The action taken by the convention, it appears, will not be without influence. Already some effect is to be noted. In 1925, a conference on girls' athletics was held at the University of Cincinnati. A representative group of about 200 were present. After free discussion, "The group unanimously voted to go on record as supporting the policies of the National Amateur Athletic Federation."[76]

VIII. *Training Teachers of Physical Education*

When calisthenics was first introduced into girls' seminaries, there were no properly prepared teachers of physical training.

[75] *Athletics for Women*—Bur. of Ed., Phys. Ed. Series No. 4, April, 1924.
[76] Reported in *Sch. and Soc.* (December 26, 1925), XXII, 820–1.

From the time of Fowle's experiment (1825) to 1860, there was no completely developed system of exercise, though that of Miss Beecher had been adopted in many schools.   Teachers of academic studies merely "caught on" to the exercises and then took charge of groups.   The formal exercises, quadrilles, used at Mt. Holyoke were not printed until 1853.   Miss Beecher's *Physiology and Calisthenics for Schools and Families* was published in 1856.

Though the North American *Turnerbund* was proposed as early as 1856, its operation did not begin till 1866.   In 1860, Dio Lewis established classes in gymnastics in Boston.   The same year, he says, "I was so fortunate as to be invited to appear before that most august of educational bodies [American Institute of Instruction] to explain my new system of gymnastics." With such a favorable introduction the new system was destined to spread rapidly.   The next year (1861) his Normal Institute for Physical Education was incorporated, which enlisted the sympathetic coöperation of numerous prominent men of the state. Here, in seven years, over four hundred men and women were given training, and went out into schools as apostles of the Lewis system.   As the *Announcement* of the second year's program stated, all received into the institution were to be at once "critically examined, with reference to strength, form and health; and any deficiency thus disclosed will be at once placed under the most thorough treatment."   All were to "be drilled by Dr. Lewis in person, with such care that he or she cannot fail to become a competent teacher of gymnastics. . . . All will be made familiar with at least two hundred different exercises. . . ."[77]   The course was ten weeks long; provision was made for practice in conducting small classes, as a part of the training.

Shortly after opening the Institute, Dr. Lewis published his *New Gymnastics* (1862), which contained, in addition, free renditions of Kloss' *Dumb-Bell Instructor* and Schreber's *Gymnastikon*. He introduced it as "a new system. . . . Novel in philosophy, and practical details, its distinguishing peculiarity is a complete adaptation, alike, to the strongest man, the feeblest woman, and the frailest child.   The athlete finds abundant opportunities for the greatest exertions, while the delicate child is never injured. Dispensing with the cumbrous apparatus of the ordinary gymnasium, its implements are all calculated not only to impart

[77] *Announcement,* 1861.

strength of muscle, but to give flexibleness, agility and grace of movement. None of the apparatus (with one or two slight exceptions) is fixed. Each and every piece is held in the hand, so that any hall or other room may be used for the exercises.'"[78]

In 1882, Mary E. W. Jones completed the one-year course for physical training teachers, under Dr. Sargent, at Cambridge; four women were graduated from a two-year course in 1884, and by 1905 nearly 300 women had finished the one-year course. A three-year course was offered in 1902. In 1887, Harvard University offered a summer course of five weeks in physical education, open to men and women. In 1886, William Gilbert Anderson organized the Brooklyn Normal School for Physical Education, in connection with Adelphi Academy. The Boston Normal School of Gymnastics was opened in 1889, and in 1909 was merged with Wellesley College. The Savage School for Physical Education, first incorporated by New York (1890) as the Savage Physical Development Institute, became the New York Normal School of Physical Education in 1898, and was chartered by the State Board of Regents upon application made in 1914. It was the first school of physical education to become a member of the University of the State of New York.[79] Candidates for admission are required to hold the diploma of an approved four-year high school and are graduated upon completion of 108 semester hours of work.[80]

Beginning with California (1898), Nebraska (1899), and Oberlin (1900), there has been a considerable growth of facilities for training physical instructors in colleges and universities in the United States. Teachers' College, Columbia University, offered similar opportunities in 1903, and the University of Wisconsin, in 1911.[81]

Britan, commenting upon the development of facilities for training teachers of physical education, said, in 1908:

". . . To-day a normal course in physical culture takes two years, eight months each, on a basis of at least a high school, far preferably, a college education, and at least three summers of six weeks each of as hard and careful study as most will care

[78] Lewis: *New Gymnastics*, 9.
[79] *Catalog*, 1927–8.
[80] *Ibid.*, 31–4.
[81] *Catalog*, Univ. of Wisconsin, 1911.

to enter.   A course is required in physiology, anatomy, hygiene, kinesiology, anthropometry and physical examination; theory of gymnastics, orthopedics, medical gymnastics, first aid to the injured, etc., to say nothing of the actual practice of all the various forms of gymnastics and athletics."[82]

The quarter century just elapsed has witnessed an almost complete acceptance of the task of training physical education teachers on the part of colleges and universities, as well as by teachers' colleges, normal schools, and junior colleges.   Information available at the Bureau of Education (1926) showed that practically all state universities, and a large number of private colleges and universities, provided such courses.   Thirty-five public and twenty-nine private colleges and universities, and twenty-nine teachers' colleges offered four-year courses with a major in physical education, leading to the A.B. or B.S. degree. Fifteen institutions offered four-year courses leading to these degrees, with physical education as a minor subject.   Nine teachers' colleges and normal schools offered three-year professional training courses for teachers of physical education. Twenty-eight institutions—colleges, teachers' colleges, and junior colleges—offered two-year courses; and thirteen special private normal schools of physical education gave courses, usually three years in length.   In addition, fourteen institutions offered (1926) special summer courses (one offered a year course) for the preparation of teachers and gave certificates for this work.

[82] What Physical Education Is Doing for Women [*Education* (1908), XXIX, 36–7].

CHAPTER IV

COLLEGES FOR WOMEN

". . . I would build
"Far off from men a college like a man's,
"And I would teach them all that men are taught."

I. Rise of the "Female College" Idea

In 1636, Lucy Downing suggested, in a letter to Governor Winthrop, the desirability of creating a college in New England. As she said: "I believe a college would put no small life into the plantation."[1] What this woman proposed was for the good of the plantation in general, and of men in particular. At that time, such an educational scheme for women, as suggested in Mary Astell's *Proposal*, would have staggered the imagination. Two centuries later a movement arose to establish colleges especially for women, but in general for the welfare of society. In this interval there were no institutions for women's "collegiate" education. Some few girls, by irregular means, private teachers, academies, and seminaries, prepared themselves sufficiently to enter collegiate institutions. But "convention beat them down"; they were not allowed to enter. When, on December 22, 1783, Lucinda Foote, twelve years old, was examined "in the learned languages, the Latin and Greek" it was found she had made "commendable progress," being able to give the "true meaning of passages in the Aeneid of Virgil, the Select Orations of Cicero and in the Greek Testament." She was accordingly declared "fully qualified, *except in regard to sex* [italics mine], to be received as a pupil of the Freshman class of Yale University."[2]

Other cases might be mentioned, if it were necessary to prove the existence of antagonism to woman's college education; but it is a well known fact, and calls for no lengthy proof at this point. Indeed, even in the nineteenth century, this same oppo-

[1] Quoted in Earle: *Margaret Winthrop*, 227-8.

[2] Given in the College Library, Dec. 22, 1783—quoted by Stephens in Advanced Education for Women [*The Forum* (1889), VII, 41-51].

sition still prevailed.   It was feared that, as one asserted, women might forsake their infants for quadratic equations.

The last quarter of the eighteenth, and the first quarter of the nineteenth, century witnessed a rapid growth of the female seminary idea.[3] This institution offered girls a more liberal education than they had received before. When girls all over the country were just beginning to take advantage of the new opportunity, there was comparatively little dissatisfaction with it. After a longer acquaintance, however, many evils and short-comings appeared in the seminary system.[4] Many critics arose. Among them two groups may be distinguished: (1) those who would reform the seminary thoroughly; (2) those who would create a new institution for women. The first group, of which Emma Willard was a prominent member, did not favor a college education for women; but they did demand that the seminary emphasize substantial subjects rather than accomplishments. The second group, led by Beecher, urged an institution which would imitate the men's college. We may judge, then, that the "female college" idea arose, in part, as a criticism of the female seminary. For the accomplishments of the latter, it would substitute the discipline of hard studies; for professionalism, a liberal education; for impermanence, permanence; for poor in-stitutions, those with endowments; and for the principal-proprie-tor with his subordinate teachers, a college system of "co-equal" teachers. It will be well to examine the ideal institution pro-posed by these critics.

Two things were necessary before genuine women's colleges could be realized; first, seminaries and the new high schools had to give a more substantial preparation so that women could actually enter upon more advanced studies, and to this end the first group of critics rendered valuable service; second, the propagandists of college education for women had to win the approval of influential people to such an extent as to support it financially. The attainment of these prerequisites required time. A complete realization of an ideal is generally not achieved at a single stroke; and this case is no exception. The fact is that we find a period of experimentation, roughly fifty years (1825–1875), during which the college idea was advocated by several

[3] See Chapters VIII and IX, Vol. I.
[4] Pp. 441–56, Vol. I, for criticisms of the seminary.

able leaders and experimental attempts at its realization were made, with varying vigor and success. After considering several conspicuous efforts to advance the idea, certain individual experiments aimed at its realization may be noted.

A zealous advocate of "equal educational opportunity" for women appeared early in the person of Duncan G. Campbell, of Georgia. He came to Wilkes in 1807 and opened a girls' school. Later he became a member of the state legislature.[5] At the session of 1825, he proposed a bill "to establish a public seat of learning in this state for the education of females."[6] He did not employ the term "College." It is significant, however, that he pointed out: (1) "in no part of this vast confederation has the education of females been the object of public munificence"; and (2) that Georgia cannot rely on existing seminaries in other states. Fifteen men and fifteen women were named in the bill as trustees. Though passed by a large majority in the House, the Senate opposed it strongly and defeated its passage. The importance of this movement, for our consideration, lies in the fact that it proposed an institution where women could have the same educational advantages as men, and that it would put such an institution on a permanent basis. The failure to become law indicates that as yet public sentiment was not quite ready to support equal education for women.

In 1834, Daniel Chandler, son-in-law of Duncan Campbell, made an address at the University of Georgia, wherein he advocated, in enthusiastic terms, that the same educational facilities should be accorded to women as to men. The address was printed and distributed and must have been influential if one may form an opinion from the numerous references made to it and the fact that it was widely and favorably quoted.

Speaking of "female education," he said, "legislation neglects it and learning itself . . . casts upon its humble pretensions, the withering smile of cold recognition. It is now an outlaw in our State, and persecution with all its ancient rigor still impedes its struggling march. . . . How many . . . [women] have enjoyed the inestimable benefits of an enlightened education? Are they familiar with general or natural History—with natural and moral Philosophy—with Chemistry, Geometry, and practical

[5] White: *Hist. Collections of Georgia,* 685.
[6] Butler: *Hist. Rec. of Macon,* 118–19.

Mathematics—with Chronology, Belles-Lettres, and Rhetoric? How many of them have never heard Newton's Principia or Bacon's Organum. . . . These questions come home to our feelings and interests, and could satisfactory answers be obtained, they might awaken the public mind to the consideration of the most important subject, that has ever engaged its attention. . . . In our country, there are 61 *colleges,* containing expensive philosophical and chemical apparatus, valuable cabinets of minerals, and libraries that embrace more than 300,000 volumes— and to the disgrace of the nation be it spoken, *not one is dedicated to the cause of female education."* (Italics mine.)[7]

Two years later the legislature was ready to endorse the college experiment by chartering the Georgia Female College which was launched at Macon.[8] That it was the idea of the founders to establish an institution superior to the well-known academy or seminary is clear. George F. Pierce, the first president, wrote in 1840: "Two years ago the notion of a female college was laughed at as a Platonic idea—a mere dream—an impracticable fancy born in the reverie of some speculative mind, well meaning perhaps, but utterly ahead of sober sense and prudent wisdom. A Female College!—Anomalous, absurd. A Town Academy with its thirty or forty pupils, was the 'Ultima Thule'; all beyond was fairyland."[9] "Schools have been multiplied but they are all located upon the same level. Increase and not elevation has been the aim. Although much has been done, it has been rather in the way of extension than exaltation. The demand, in both respects, has been great, urgent and augmenting; and in the one case the action of society has corresponded with the want and the obligation—in the other the only essay (among us) has been the Institution, the history of which is here appended. The project is novel; it stands out on the map of the world's history alone—isolated—a magnificent example of public spirit and Catholic feeling—of devotion to literature, and of zeal for Female Education."[10] Elsewhere he declared: "Universities are endowed for the education of sons, while daughters are overlooked or forgotten."[11]

[7] Chandler: *Address on Female Education,* 4.

[8] See pp. 160 *ff.* for further critical examination of this experiment.

[9] *Southern Ladies' Book,* I, 4.

[10] *Ibid.,* 65 *ff.*

[11] Also, on the origin of the College, see *Macon Telegraph,* June 2, 1840, 2, col. 4.

George F. Pierce

Occasionally, the newly proposed institution was referred to as the "Female University." The *Macon Telegraph* announced: "We are requested to state that the Reverend Charles Hardy has been appointed agent of the Macon Female University."[12]

A second proponent of the woman's college idea in the South appeared at Winchester, Tennessee, a little more than ten years after the opening of Georgia Female College. Z. C. Graves was born in Vermont (1816); at the age of twenty-one he went to Ashtabula, Ohio, where he opened an academy; and shortly thereafter, became principal of Kingsville Academy, where he taught till his removal to Winchester, Tennessee. There he became president of Mary Sharp College for Women, first called Tennessee and Alabama Female Institute, which was organized in 1850 and opened in 1851, largely through the influence of his brother, J. R. Graves.[13]

As early as 1848, a charter had been granted to certain fifteen trustees, among them J. R. Graves, B. Kimbrough, J. H. Eaton, J. Sykes, I. Burleson, T. Mosely (?), incorporating Tennessee Female Institute, and providing "that in case of a donation of $10,000 . . . made to the Institute by any person or persons then the Institute may, by an act of the Board of Trustees, receive a name in honor of such benefactor . . . and by that name shall and may have continual succession hereafter. . . ." The trustees were empowered to "select and appoint a President" and "grant all such literary honors and degrees . . . as are usually granted by any similar institution or seminary of learning in this state or in the United States and in testimony . . . to give suitable diplomas under their seal and the signature of the president and board of trustees, which diplomas shall entitle their possessors, respectively, to all the immunities and privileges which either by usage or by statute are allowed to possess[ors?] of similar diplomas from any other similar institute or seminary of learning."[14] In 1851 the Tennessee and Alabama Female Institute opened, J. R. Graves and others named above being among its promoters. By act of 1852, the Tennessee Baptist Female Institute was incorporated, Eaton, Sykes, Kimbrough, Burleson, and Mosby(?) being among those

---

[12] Feb. 11, 1836, 3, col. 1.
[13] *Z. C. Graves and the Mary Sharp College*, 1850–1896, 17 *ff*.
[14] *Laws of Tenn.*, 1848, 290–2.

named as trustees, with all the powers and privileges previously granted to the trustees of Tennessee Female Institute in 1848.[15] The financial way was rough and precipitous. Finally, Mary Sharp, deeply interested in the freedom of women's minds as well as freedom of the Negroes, gave more freely than any other contributor,[16] and it was accordingly named in her honor. Catalogs bearing the new name appeared, and the first diplomas of 1855 were issued in the name of "Maria Sharpius Collegium." It appears that no further legal authorization, beyond the Acts of 1848 and 1852, was given the trustees until 1857, when the name was changed to Mary Sharp College and the same powers were continued. Six of the eight trustees who signed the diplomas in 1855 were named among the twenty-one to be in charge of Mary Sharp in 1857. W. P. Marks, Professor of Mathematics, was also one of the new trustees.[17]

The first catalog of the new institution that has come down to us (1853) indicates clearly enough that Graves' conception of women's education was that it should be "as thorough as their brothers have been acquiring at their colleges and universities." He distinguished between the private academy and the permanent college. His was to be "a school for young ladies of a higher grade than any previously known to exist . . . a college where ladies may have the privilege of a classical education." Women were to have "the same knowledge, literary, scientific and classical, that has been for so many generations the peculiar and cherished heritage of the other sex." The sister was to be "on an equality with the brother, for the developing and unfolding of all the qualities of her mind, thus making her what she was designed to be by her Creator, a thinking, reflecting, reasoning being, capable of comparing and judging for herself and dependent upon none other for her free unbiased opinions."[18] The success which attended his efforts to realize this ideal may be noted later.[19]

15 *Ibid.*, 1852, 486.
16 $5,000, which was later increased.—Letter from Pearl W. Kelly, Tenn. State Library, Dec. 7, 1928.
17 *Ibid.*, Dec. 21, 1857, 30.
18 *Mary Sharp Catalog*, 1853–1854.
19 See p. 171.

Z. C. GRAVES

It is not our purpose at present to deal with the influence of such prominent institutions as the Elizabeth Female Academy of Washington, Mississippi; the Salem Female Academy of Winston-Salem, North Carolina; Elias Marks Female Academy near Columbia, South Carolina; or the Judson Female Institute at Marion, Alabama, under the leadership of Milo P. Jewett. That these and others helped to make women's college education a possibility is not to be denied. They were not, however, primarily efforts at college education.[20] The same may be said of the most prominent seminaries of the West and North.

There was one leader, however, in the Northern seminary movement who, though she started several famous seminaries, distinguished herself by her writing as an advocate of colleges for women. From the day she began her little school for girls at Hartford, Connecticut (1823), Catherine E. Beecher showed a tendency to be very critical of the existing views and practices of "female education." Near the end of her experience there, she published her critical observations—*Suggestions Respecting Improvements in Education* (1829). Between the time of her going to Cincinnati (1832) and the beginning of the effort to establish the Institute at Milwaukee (1848) her ideas about a new institution for women's education were crystallized. In 1851, the *True Remedy for the Wrongs of Women* appeared, in which she set forth the chief *desiderata*: permanence, the college system, endowment, equipment, and co-equal teachers. At some length, she criticized existing high schools and demanded the college:

"I now wish to point out some of the measures which might be aimed at, in attempting to secure a liberal education and remunerative employ to our own sex, by an organization for this direct end. And in this, we shall be very properly guided by the experience of the other sex, in securing similar advantages for themselves.

"The first and most important measure would be the establishment of permanent female institutions on the college system.

"The main features of the college system are these: In the first place, permanent endowments, buildings, library, and apparatus, with a corporation whose duty it is to perpetuate the institution on a given plan. The effect of this is, to secure

[20] See pp. 341, 380 f., 384, 386, 390, 422, 435, Vol. I.

the highest class of teachers, by insuring them a liberal and permanent support, posts of high honor, the means of self-improvement, and only such an amount of labor as is consistent with such improvement. It also secures protection from those vacillations of public favor which are constantly destroying all institutions not thus sustained.

"The next feature of this system is, a regular course of study, and such a division of labor and modes of classing the pupils, that only two or three branches are ever given to one teacher, and ordinarily not more than two hours of service are required in the recitation-room. This method tends to promote a much higher style of instruction for the pupils, and greatly increases the opportunities of self-improvement to the instructors.

"The third feature is a division of responsibilities, so that no individual ever is obliged to assume those which rest upon the principals of institutions which are not on the college plan. In colleges, each professor is the head of his own department; and neither the president nor any of his colleagues have a right to interfere—not so much even as to give advice—much less to control. The corporation is the only body that can exercise the power of advice and control over the faculty. The president has no more power than any of his colleagues. He is only primus inter pares . . . and acts as the presiding officer of the faculty. In some of our universities, and in most of our professional institutions, the office of president is omitted entirely, as needless. In these cases the presiding officer is appointed by his colleagues, and often is the youngest member of the faculty.

"Institutions for women, embracing these main features of the college plan, are as indispensable for the liberal education of our sex as they are for the other. Some modifications, which I will hereafter suggest, would increase the advantages thus secured.

"Those female institutions in our land, which are assuming the ambitious name of colleges, have, not one of them, as yet, secured the real features which constitute the chief advantage of such institutions. They are merely high-schools, with one or two principals, employing subordinates, who are entirely subject to the control of the head of the institution."[21]

The practical effect of Miss Beecher's utterances and her restless activity is to be seen in the formation of the American

21 *True Remedy*, 52–5.

Women's Education Association (1852), one of its objects being the encouragement of such collegiate projects as she had suggested. Speaking of the Association's work, in 1854, *Godey's Lady's Book* pointed to the efforts to found institutions at Dubuque and Milwaukee. The Association tried to collect an endowment of $20,000. They declared: "Woman has waited until the middle of the nineteenth century for the endowment of the first institution for her education. Millions upon millions have, from time immemorial, been invested to enrich and render most valuable the colleges for the other sex. This ought to have been done and the other not left undone."[22]

In 1851, the idea of "a real college for women" was discussed by a group of prominent clergymen and laymen at Albany, New York. The result was the chartering of Auburn Female University, 1852.[23] The ideas stressed in this movement, which was largely due to the leadership of Mr. and Mrs. Harvey A. Sackett, as in others mentioned, were (1) a higher grade of education than yet provided, (2) permanent organization, (3) endowments, and (4) the college faculty. Among the trustees named were Dr. Wyckoff, Amos Dean, Luther Tucker, Dr. Beman, Dr. Mandeville, Dr. Hickok, Dr. Hogarth, Professor Boyd, and Dr. Kendrick. Like every other effort, it encountered financial difficulty. Because of pecuniary encouragement from Elmira, the location was changed from Auburn; and a new charter, secured in 1855, designated it as Elmira Female College.[24] That education equal in value and leading to a degree equal to that given men, was the objective, was made clear by the provision that "no degree shall be conferred without a course of study equivalent to a full ordinary course of study as pursued in the colleges of this state shall have been completed; . . . said college shall be subject to the visitation of the Regents of the University of the State of New York in the same manner and to the same extent as the other colleges of the state."[25] The first degrees were conferred in 1859.[26]

[22] *Godey's Lady's Book*, Aug., 1854, 175–6.
[23] *Laws of New York*, 1852, 8–9.
[24] *Laws of New York*, 1855, 775.
[25] *Ibid.*
[26] Diploma of Helen Ayres.

Another step was taken by the New York Legislature of 1857, when it changed the name of Ingham Collegiate Institute, established at Leroy, New York, in 1841, to Ingham University. Only women were admitted. There was a four-year course and, by charter, it was authorized to grant degrees.[27] Its catalog of 1857 shows Latin grammar as the only classical requirement for admission. In the four-year course, the Latin reader, the *Aeneid*, Cicero, and Horace were studied; Greek was mentioned only in the last year. The University continued until 1892, when her charter was revoked by the Regents of the State of New York.[28]

At the time the college idea was gaining in New York, a similar movement was on foot in Pennsylvania. In 1848, J. W. Sunderland, a graduate of Wesleyan College, Middletown, Connecticut, accepted a position as teacher of mathematics and classics at Freeland Seminary,[29] Collegeville, Pennsylvania. Montgomery Female Seminary—the branch for young women—issued its first catalog in 1851. Two hundred girls attended during its first two years. In the meantime, Sunderland planned a more advanced institution for which the Female Seminary was to prepare students. This was chartered as Pennsylvania Female College, April 6, 1853.[30] Like other institutions which aspired to raise the level of women's education, it offered its degree—"A *Laureate* as significant and valuable as that conferred on young men at institutions of a corresponding grade."[31] Two other colleges were chartered by Pennsylvania—one later in 1853, at Harrisburg, the other, in 1854, at Pittsburgh.[32]

In Ohio, three early institutions must be mentioned for their efforts to establish college education for women—Wesleyan Female College at Cincinnati (1843), Oxford Female College (1852), and Ohio Wesleyan Female College at Delaware (1853).[33] The Cincinnati institution was largely a result of the forward views of Catherine Beecher and the liberal ideas of women's education disseminated by the College of Teachers, plus the influence of the Methodist denomination. Ohio Wes-

---

27 *Laws of New York*, 1857, I, 504–5.
28 Sherwood: *Higher Ed. in New York*, 445; *Catalog*, 1857, 16 *ff.*
29 Now Ursinus College.
30 *Laws of Pa.*, 1853, 327–8.
31 *Catalog* of 1853.
32 *Laws of Pa.*, 1853, 562–4; and 1854, 58–60.
33 *Catalogs*, 1852–3; and 1853–4, respectively.

leyan opened, in 1853, with 36 listed as members of the collegiate, and 123 in the preparatory department. It continued as an independent woman's college till 1877, when it became a part of Ohio Wesleyan University.[34] Oxford Female College grew out of a female academy of the same name, established (1830) by Bethania Crocker, who was encouraged by the president and Professors Scott and McGuffey, of Miami University, to undertake the task of improving girls' education. It was first incorporated in 1839,[35] and ten years later reincorporated as Oxford Female Institute,[36] to be, as later said, "literally and truly a female college, coördinate in rank with our regular colleges and universities for males."[37] Its first catalog, however, under the name of Institute, declared it was "designed to embrace the whole field of a complete and thorough female education."[38] Generally, "a complete and thorough female education" bore slight resemblance to the course of the men's colleges. In 1852, the institution received its charter as Oxford Female College.

In Illinois, two early institutions promoted the idea of women's collegiate education: the first, Illinois Conference Female Academy (1847),[39] which was changed to "College" in 1851;[40] the second, Rockford Female Seminary (1847),[41] which, though not officially known as a college till 1892, offered a strong "collegiate course" in 1854-5, and improved it consistently thereafter.[42]

Without further enumeration of instances, it is clear from the foregoing that by 1855 the idea of college education for young women, in an institution like those established for men, had been promoted in Southern, Western and Northern sections of the United States; and that efforts had been made in all to create institutions able to give such an education. Certainly, by this date, the "absurdity of sending ladies to college," which Emma Willard said must "strike everyone," had been dispelled in many and wide circles. That these earliest efforts were not

[34] Knight and Commons: *Higher Education in Ohio*, 79 *ff*.
[35] *Laws of Ohio*, Feb. 27, 1839, 80.
[36] *Ibid.*, March 23, 1849, 238.
[37] *Catalog*, Oxford College, 1925-26, 9.
[38] *Catalog*, Oxford Female Institute, 1849-50.
[39] *Laws of Illinois*, 1847, 52-4.
[40] *Ibid.*, 1851, 35.
[41] *Ibid.*, Feb. 24, 1847.
[42] See pp. 372 and 374-5, Vol. I.

as successful as later ones would be expected. That their fame was chiefly local accounts partially for the fact that institutions arising much later regarded themselves as pathfinders of the new movement. Every institution founded during the decade of the sixties, and shortly after, continued, like its forerunners, to aim at being a "college like a man's."

The action finally taken by Matthew Vassar, after full consideration of the advice of Lydia Booth and Milo P. Jewett,[43] was, in his judgment, warranted by the fact that "the project . . . [had] received the warmest commendations of many prominent literary men and practical educators as well as the universal approval of the public press. . . ."[44] While a perusal of newspapers and magazines of the time does not warrant our acceptance of his statement of "universal approval"—certainly there were some who scoffed—it is undeniably true that such stern opposition of unbelievers as met the earliest attempts did not manifest itself in 1860. Mr. Vassar recognized that there was "not in the world, so far as is known, a single fully endowed institution for the education of women"; and that there was a "great felt, pressing want . . . [for] ample endowments to secure to female seminaries the elevated character, the stability and permanency, of our best colleges."[45] As a result, he declared: ". . . I have come to the conclusion that the establishment and endowment of a college for the education of young women is a work which will satisfy my highest aspirations, and will be, under God, a rich blessing to this city and state, to our country and the world. . . . It is my hope to be the instrument, in the hands of Providence, of founding and perpetuating an institution which shall accomplish for young women what our colleges are accomplishing for young men."[46]

About ten years after the chartering of Vassar, the idea of a woman's college like a man's was set forth in the will of Sophia Smith. As early as 1861, Greene says, the idea of a woman's college was approved; and in her will of 1868, most of her prop-

[43] Haight: *Autobiography and Letters of Matthew Vassar*, 3.

[44] Matthew Vassar on the Founding of Vassar College, quoted in *Harper's New Mo. Mag.* (1875–6), LII, 549–50; also Lossing: *Vassar College and Its Founder*, 81 *ff*.

[45] *Ibid.*

[46] Lossing: *op. cit.*, 92.

erty was set aside for its endowment.[47]   According to the will, as finally probated, she provided "for the establishment and maintenance of an Institution for the higher education of young women, with the design to furnish for my own sex means and facilities for education equal to those which are afforded now in our Colleges to young men."[48]

That the novelty of the idea had worn off somewhat is suggested by the fact that this proposal occasioned slight comment, compared with earlier ventures.   Dr. Greene, in his address on *Smith College*,[49] attributed its origin not to a crusader for woman's education, but to the *Zeitgeist* which had developed, favorable to the higher education of women.   Seelye, too, noted that "the advent of a new college for women excited little attention or comment."[50]   There was, however, this much of novelty: It was the first time a woman had devoted a fortune towards the endowment of a college for her sex.   Smith College was chartered in 1871[51] and opened in 1875.

Wellesley College, originated in the mind of Henry F. Durant as early as 1867, was incorporated in 1870[52] as Wellesley Female Seminary; but, in 1873, it was changed to Wellesley College by an act of the legislature, and under this name opened in 1875.[53] In founding the college, Durant was unquestionably influenced by the death of his son, his conversion, and the firm belief that women could be educated as well as men.   He was, moreover, convinced that social questions of the future could not be answered save by the assistance of enlightened women, whose influence in the public schools, even then, was a great factor.   To prepare them for this larger sphere into which he foresaw they would go in ever greater numbers, he believed they must be educated as thoroughly as men.   "There can't be too many Mt. Holyokes," he is reported to have said; and, in planning the

[47] Greene: Origin of Smith College [in *Quarter Centennial Anniversary* (1900), 8].

[48] Seelye: *Early Hist. of Smith College*, Appendix I, 224.

[49] *Op. cit.*, 79.

[50] *Ibid.*, 7.

[51] *Laws of Mass.*, March 3, 1871.

[52] *Ibid.*, 1870, 64.

[53] *Ibid.*, 1873, 519.

new institution, he was guided largely by the experience of Mt. Holyoke and Vassar.[54]

In the case of Mills College (California), established as a seminary in 1871 and incorporated as a college in 1885, an effort was made "to build up a school in no respect inferior to the highest of the eastern colleges for women." Mount Holyoke was the model upon which the youthful college of the West was patterned. Thus indirectly, while not so specifically stated, we find that the purpose of the institution was to imitate the college courses already devised for men.[55]

From the foregoing it is evident that the ideal of a woman's college, "like a man's," had been consistently pursued for at least fifty years (1825–1875). Bryn Mawr, founded after that period (1880), had the same objective;[56] and so have a multitude of colleges founded more recently. When, in 1891, the Randolph-Macon Board of Trustees sought to establish an institution for the higher education of girls, they declared their purpose in the well known words of the preceding generation:

"We wish to establish in Virginia a college where our young women may obtain an education equal to that given in our best colleges for young men, and under environments in harmony with the highest ideals of womanhood; where the dignity and strength of fully-developed faculties and the charm of the highest literary culture may be acquired by our daughters without loss to woman's crowning glory—her gentleness and grace."[57]

It should be mentioned, however, now that women have so conclusively demonstrated their ability to pursue the same curriculum as men, that a movement has arisen to provide a women's collegiate education based on utility rather than tradition.[58]

[54] Converse: *The Story of Wellesley*, Ch. I; Palmer: *Life of Alice F. Palmer*, 90 *ff.*; and Kingsley: *Life of Henry F. Durant*, Chaps. XII, XIII and XIV; also Kincaid: Wellesley College [*Education* (1887), VII, 305–16].

[55] Mills College *Catalog*, 1885–6, 32.

[56] Joseph W. Taylor, in his will, said: "I have been impressed with the need of such a place for the advanced education of our young female Friends, and to have all the advantages of a college education, which are so freely offered to young men."—Quoted in the *Bryn Mawr Bulletin*, May, 1925, No. 5.

[57] Reprinted in the *Catalog*, 1925–6.

[58] Kelly: *A Curriculum to Build a Mental World* (1927).

II. *Opposition to College Education of Women*

Noah Webster, of spelling-book fame, defined a good education for ladies, about 1790, as that which renders them "correct in their manners, respectable in their families, and agreeable in society. That education is always wrong which raises a woman above the duties of her station. . . . Some . . . arithmetic is necessary for every lady and geography should never be neglected." As for books, novels were roundly condemned, but "the Spectator should fill the first place in every Lady's library"; other periodicals, "though inferior to the Spectator, should be read." At that date, a "seminary" education was a luxury; girls studied little beyond the rudiments, English grammar, geography, and a considerable array of "accomplishments." There was decided opposition to higher studies because it was thought they led beyond woman's sphere. At length, however, a fair array of "solid" studies came to be encouraged in female seminaries and parents were gradually accustomed to such institutuitions, so that they viewed with equanimity a girl's leaving home to obtain a seminary education.

Besides the opposition to seminaries, which had its root in prejudice, there was another sort of objection, founded upon their numerous defects and shortcomings. Because of these, in part, there arose a demand, voiced at first by a few only, for women's colleges, that would be all to women that colleges were to men.

The new name, "female college," caused consternation in the hearts of some and ridicule in others. Ridicule was the chief weapon used against it. In general it is true that the objections to the college idea were less vigorously urged than those against the earliest seminaries, and were decidedly ineffective. The latter had prepared the way, to some extent, for a more advanced institution; but the shafts of ridicule could not be completely turned aside from those who would go so far as to open genuine colleges for women. Old arguments were thrown into the breach, worn epithets hurled at the reformers' heads, by those who opposed the innovation.

It has been a popular idea that "man loves a learned scholar, but not a learned wife." Pierce encountered essentially the same argument when he began raising funds for the Georgia

Female College in 1836: "No, I will not give you a dollar; all that a woman needs to know is how to read the new Testament, and to spin and weave clothing for her family. . . . I would not have one of your graduates for a wife, and I will not give you a cent for any such object."[59]   Then, too, the objection found expression throughout the century, and appears even today, that "if, and after, a woman marries," her higher education is wasted. Lyman Abbott restated the question raised in the discussion of higher education of women: "After your college girl has graduated, she may, possibly, spend three years in teaching. By that time she is tolerably certain to marry. And *then* what becomes of her higher education?"[60]   A "foreign gentleman," having visited Wellesley College, is reported to have said, "This is all very fine, but . . . how does it affect their chances?"[61]

Ouida, writing of *The New Woman* (1894), objected to the belief held by so many at that date, that "there is no good education without a college curriculum"; this idea, the writer thought "as injurious as . . . erroneous."   Though college education "may have excellencies for men, . . . for women it can only be hardening and deforming.   If study be delightful to a woman, she will find her way to it as the hart to water brooks. The author of Aurora Leigh was not only always at home, but she was an invalid; yet she became a fine classic, and found her path to fame.   A college curriculum would have done nothing to improve her rich and beautiful mind; it might have done much to debase it.

"The perpetual contact of men with other men may be good for them, but the perpetual contact of women with other women is very far from good.   The publicity of a college must be odious to a young girl of refined and delicate feeling."[62]

President Thomas, of Bryn Mawr, bore witness to the existence of a belief that college education would destroy womanly nature. "Before I myself went to college I had never seen but one college woman.   I had heard that such a woman was staying at the house of an acquaintance.   I went to see her with fear.   Even if she had appeared in hoofs and horns I was determined to go to col-

59 Quoted from Meyer: *Woman's Work in America*, 89.
60 Quoted from Kingsley: *Life of Henry F. Durant*, 161.
61 Brackett: *Woman and the Higher Education*, 191.
62 *No. Am. Rev.* (1894), CLVIII, 614–15.

lege all the same." Later, she wrote of those who believed in women's education, we were convinced that "women, like men, are quickened and inspired by the same study of the great traditions of their race, by the same love of learning, the same love of science, the same love of abstract truth; that women, like men, are made vastly better mothers, as men are made vastly better fathers, by subordinating the distracting instincts of sex to the simple human fellowship of similar education and similar intellectual and social ideals."[63]

Miss Thomas declared that after she went to study in Germany, her name was never mentioned to her mother by women of her acquaintance. It appears she had, in some way, disgraced herself. Marion Talbot asserted that when she entered Boston University, she was "completely ostracized" by her friends and was welcome nowhere, except at Washington, where "women were kind to me, for they did not know that I was a college graduate."[64]

It was, no doubt, the alleged "hardening and deforming" influence of college studies which Alice Miller celebrated with gentle irony in "The Maiden's Vow":

> "I will avoid equations,
> "And shun the naughty surd,
> "I must beware the perfect square,
> "Through it young girls have erred:
> "And when men mention Rule of Three
> "Pretend I have not heard.
>
> "Though Sturm's delightful theorems
> "Illicit joys assure,
> "Though permutations and combinations
> "My woman's heart allure,
> "I'll never study algebra,
> "But keep my spirit pure."[65]

Although Ouida, and many others, feared the "hardening" and "deforming" influence of college education on women's character,

[63] Present Tendencies in Woman's Education [*Ed. Rev.* (1908), **XXXV**, 65–6].

[64] Selden: Sex and Higher Education [*Ladies' Home Journal*, Oct., 1924, 69].

[65] *Are Women People?* 27. Copyright, 1915, by George H. Doran Company. Reprinted by permission of the publishers.

others were more affrighted at the probability—nay, the certainty
—of physical and mental weaknesses that would appear.   Alexander Black, in *Miss America,* portrayed the general view of the
college versus health question, in the words of the conservative
who questioned the woman professor: "Ah . . . !   When we
forget sex are we not in danger of a costly transgression?   Are
we not combatting Nature?"[66]   Martha Carey Thomas related,
in 1908, that as a young woman she had been "terror-struck,"
after reading the seventh and seventeenth chapters of Hall's
Adolescence, lest she "and every other woman . . . were doomed
to live as pathological invalids . . . " because of her pursuit of
higher studies.[67]   It was not until after these women had made
the experiment that they felt reassured; that they convinced
others that their health was not impaired, mentally or physically,
by four years of mental culture.[68]

III. Ability to Do College Work

Besides the foregoing objections another was stressed which,
had it proved valid, would have brought the college movement
to an early end.   Women, it was confidently asserted, simply
could not do college work; they did not have minds like those of
men.   These sex differences in mind were said to be an insuperable barrier, against which no propaganda for the equality of
women could be effective.

Todd asserted, "As for training young ladies through a long
intellectual course, as we do young men, it can never be done.
They will die in the process. . . . "   He appears to have admitted that women have enough intelligence for a college course,
but saw danger "in forcing the intellect of women beyond what
her physical organization will possibly bear. . . . In these years
the poor thing has her brain crowded with history, grammar,
arithmetic, geography, natural history, chemistry, physiology,
botany, astronomy, rhetoric, natural and moral philosophy, metaphysics, French, often German, Latin, perhaps Greek, reading,
spelling, committing poetry, writing compositions, drawing,
painting, &c., &c., *ad infinitum.*   Then, out of school hours, from

[66] (1898) Pp. 44–6; see also pp. 273–80.

[67] Present Tendencies in Women's Education [*Ed. Rev.* (1908), XXXV,
65–6].

[68] See pp. 126–30, chapter on "Physical Education."

three to six hours of severe toil at the piano. She must be on the strain all the school hours, study in the evening till her eyes ache, her brain whirls, her spine yields and gives way, and she comes through the process of education, enervated, feeble, without courage or vigor, elasticity or strength. Alas! must we crowd education upon our daughters, and, for the sake of having them 'intellectual,' make them puny, nervous, and their whole earthly existence a struggle between life and death?''[69]

It is strange, considering the immediate and very evident success of women in doing college work, that this belief in their mental inferiority and physical weakness continued as long as it did. Its persistence in the face of facts was one of the best proofs of the social prejudice that opposed women's collegiate education. Thwing noted this (1894), and asserted that ''the question should have been laid on the shelf more than fifty years ago''when Mary Lyon successfully subjected her young protégées to Paley's *Natural Theology*, Whateley's *Logic* and *Rhetoric*, Wayland's *Moral Philosophy* and *Political Economy*, as well as Butler's *Analogy of Natural and Revealed Religion*.[70] He might as well, however, have expected it to have disappeared seventy-five years earlier, when Emma Willard led her young ladies to love higher mathematics and showed they could master it.

Notwithstanding what might or might not have been expected, it is true that the notion of incapacity lingered long. *Littell's Living Age* (1860) quoted an article from *The Saturday Review* which derided the idea that, just because there have been a few cases like Mary Somerville, Rosa Bonheur, and Lady Jane Grey, women have equal powers of mind and should have a changed education which would bring out the best capacities in them. After magnanimously granting that ''any plausible view on the subject is . . . worth examining . . . ,'' the writer concluded: ''The great argument against the existence of this equality of intellect in women is, that it does not exist.''[71] President Eliot, too, asserted more than a decade later: ''Now, women differ more from men that men differ from each other; . . . there is a fundamental pervading difference . . . which extends to their minds

[69] Hamilton: *Woman's Wrongs*, 51–4; see also ''Lob-Sided,'' an essay by Rev. John Todd, in Orton: *Liberal Education of Women*, 178 *ff*.

[70] *The College Woman*, 11–12.

[71] LXIV, 184.

quite as much as to their bodies. . . . ''[72]   Thomas wrote: ''We
were told that their brains were too light, their foreheads too
small, their reasoning powers too defective, their emotions too
easily worked upon, to make good students.''[73]   Like Mr. Stell-
ing, it seems many men continued to believe that women ''can
pick up a little of everything. . . . They have a good deal of
superficial cleverness; but they couldn't go far into anything.
They're quick and shallow.''[74]   The persistence of such views
justified fully the assertion of Nesta H. Webster, a few years ago,
that ''the strangest feature of masculine intelligence is man's
abysmal ignorance on the subject of woman. . . . ''   He knows
bees, wasps, ants, and other insignificant creatures, but ''the
mentality of woman . . . and the purpose she should serve, are
subjects on which he seems unable to arrive at any satisfactory
conclusion.''[75]

Although most of the world was skeptical, a few were apparently as much convinced of the equal mental ability of men and
women to do college work as are teachers and psychologists of
today, who have endeavored to look into the question with scientific impartiality.[76]   Branagan deplored the fact that the ''female
claim to mental equality is questioned, and their reasoning faculties depreciated . . . even by Christian philosophers. . . . How
astonishing it is that a man of Lavater's ingenuity and celebrity
could believe . . . 'that women know not how to think; they perceive, and can associate ideas, but can go no further.' ''[77]   With
the views of Rush, Willard, Clinton, Beecher, Lyon and others,
we are already familiar.

George F. Pierce, advocate of the Georgia Female College experiment, would not argue the question of equality of mind but
stood ready to give women every opportunity to demonstrate the
ability he believed they possessed: ''Girls can learn, and they
deserve to be taught.   Adopt enlightened plans of instruction—
grant sufficient time—afford the necessary facilities, and though

[72] Orton: *Liberal Education of Women*, 321.

[73] *Ed. Rev.* (1908), XXXV, 70–1.

[74] Eliot: *Mill on the Floss*.

[75] Woman and Civilization [*Nineteenth Century Mag.*, Nov., 1920].

[76] E.g., Thorndike: *Educational Psychology*, III, Ch. IX; also Hollingworth: Variability as related to sex differences in achievement [*Am. Jour.
of Soc.*, XIX, 510–30].

[77] Branagan: *Excellency of the Female Character*, 81–3, 101, 118–19.

there will be no struggle for supremacy, there will be advancement, corresponding in grade, and equivalent in effect, to anything ever realized from the most generous arrangement for the Lords of Creation."[78]

Sunderland, too, to quote one of the less known promoters of female college education, stated unequivocally his belief in woman's mental capacity: "We are among those who believe that the female mind is endowed with powers and capabilities quite equal to those of the other sex. . . . It will, therefore, be a primary object with us, to arouse public attention to the importance of a more practical and liberal education for woman. . . ."[79] Mr. Sunderland touched upon the most important point: "to arouse public attention." T. W. Higginson, in a paper read before the Social Science Convention, May 14, 1873, reviewed the "ghostly sentinels, all individually powerless as you approach, but collectively formidable to the imagination."[80] These "ghostly sentinels"—fallacies in the minds of men—continued, until examined and tested, to effectually keep woman out of her heritage. The second fallacy discussed was "the assumption of the hopeless intellectual inferiority in the case of women."[81]

Higginson properly called the inferiority of women an assumption, asserting, " . . . there is no class of facts directly sustaining it, and the class of facts which have most to do with it . . . [public school records] look just the other way." He quoted a school superintendent who, on the basis of his observations, asserted it "a pretty safe inference that they will not drop far behind in university studies. . . . " He felt he could adopt as a general formula the certificate of a school committee of a New Hampshire town: "This is to certify that Fanny Noyes stands on a medium with other girls of her age . . . and for what I know is as good as folks in general."[82]

The "inference" was soon recognized to be more than "pretty safe" by those who had the opportunity to know what girls

[78] Georgia Female College—Origin, Plan and Prospects. *So. Ladies' Book* (1840), 65 *ff*.

[79] Pa. Female College *Catalog*, 1853.

[80] Orton: *Liberal Ed. of Women*, Appendix, 309.

[81] *Ibid.*, 310.

[82] *Ibid.*

could do at college.   Maria Mitchell corroborated to her own satisfaction the findings of Emma Willard and Mary Lyon, in the work of her Vassar girls in mathematics.   Thwing stated (1894), "the old and tiresome question . . . of intellectual ability is closed."[83]   The Commissioner's *Report* on education (1897), recognizing that, but twenty-five years before, there had been a great dispute as to the possibility of women mastering the subjects of a man's education, stated: "Since that time, where girls and boys have been educated together, it has become an historical fact that women have made rapid strides, and captured a greater number of honors in proportion to their number than men. . . . "[84]   Thwing says that Ballard, in 1903, stated that "of sixteen elections [to Phi Beta Kappa] this commencement . . . at Boston University, fifteen were women.   At the University of Chicago, in the ten years which closed June, 1902, women secured a greater representation in Phi Beta Kappa than men.   The record was: Bachelor's degree, men, 53.9 per cent.; Bachelor's degree, women, 46.1 per cent.; Phi Beta Kappa admissions, men, 43.7 per cent.; Phi Beta Kappa admissions, women, 56.3 per cent.

"Though the women graduates were 6.9 per cent. less than half of the total number of graduates, they contributed 6.3 per cent. more than half of the Phi Beta Kappa members.   In the ten years at the University of Chicago, women also secured a greater share of the honors and prizes."[85]

Martha Carey Thomas doubtless had the same and additional facts in mind when she wrote (1908): "We should have been satisfied if they had been proved to be only a little less good than men college students, but tested by every known test of examination or classroom recitation, women have proved themselves equal to men, even slightly superior."[86]   Besides the testimony of men connected with coeducational colleges, quoted elsewhere,[87] mention should be made of recent statements of James R. Angell and W. A. Neilson, both to the effect that women are better college

[83] *College Woman*, 9–10.
[84] *R. C. E.* (1897–98), I, 631–2.
[85] *Jour. of Educ.* (1903), LVIII, 115.
[86] *Ed. Rev.*, XXXV, 70–1.
[87] See pp. 298–300.

students than men.[88]   Dr. Neilson stated his observation, however, which I have found corroborated by the experience of several others, though not by my own, that "in post-graduate courses men students are able to make a better showing than women." For this fact he assigned economic and social reasons: men have specialized for economic reasons, while marriage draws many of the women from post-graduate work.   The number of graduate women students, both in general and technical courses, is, however, increasing markedly.

W. D. Hyde went much further than Dr. Neilson, asserting that women lacked the qualities essential for productive scholarship.[89]   That women do succeed well, when they attempt higher specialized courses, few, who have had experience with both men and women, will be inclined to deny.   In 1910, Marion Talbot published figures concerning the rank of men and women candidates for the Doctorate at the University of Chicago, before July, 1909.   Women made up 15.6 per cent. of those receiving the degree (80 women and 434 men); they made up "8.9 per cent. of the *rite* grade; 10.8 per cent. of *cum laude;* 15.5 per cent. of *magna cum laude,* and 20.7 per cent. of *summa cum laude.*"[90] Of the women, 11.2 per cent. received the *rite*, compared with 21.2 per cent. of the men; 41.3 per cent. of the women, and 33.4 per cent. of the men, received the *cum laude;* practically the same per cent. of women and men receivd the *magna cum laude* (40% and 40.1%); while 7.5 per cent. of the women and 5.3 per cent. of the men received the *summa cum laude.*[91]

Thus evidence seems to show that women are not only successful in undergraduate studies, but also highly successful in graduate study, though as to the latter there is greater variation in opinions.   It should be pointed out that while the greater part of the evidence and opinions generally submitted points to such a conclusion, there are some studies reported, in recent days, purporting to show that while girls can do algebra well, because they learn "type forms" by rote and "in many instances the only ingenuity required is the recognition of the type in the indi-

[88] As reported in *Collier's Weekly*, Oct. 3, 1925, 25; and *Phila. Inquirer*, Oct. 19, 1925.

[89] *College Man and the College Woman*, 207.

[90] *Education of Women*, 20–1.

[91] *Ibid.*

vidual example or problem,'' they cannot succeed in geometry, wherein they are "called upon to reason absolutely . . . [and] to offer original demonstrations. . . . ''[92]

IV. Success of Early "Female College" Experiments

It has been shown that the idea of a woman's college "like a man's'' was developing in several sections of the United States between 1825 and 1875; and that contributions influencing the growth of the idea were made by practical efforts as well as by

GEORGIA FEMALE COLLEGE

the theoretical defense of it. It is necessary to evaluate the earliest efforts to see how nearly they were able to measure up to generally accepted standards of college education for men. By this standard they must be judged, as imitation of the men's college was the universally expressed objective. For this reason studies offered in men's colleges have been placed parallel with those offered in female institutions. In order to compare the relation of the professed female college to the female seminary,

[92] See, for instance, Felter: Education of Women [*Ed. Rev.* (1906), XXXI, 355–7].

as well as the male college, some of the best seminary courses also have been placed parallel. The catalogs of the institutions and an extensive table based thereon are before me.

As the earliest experiment in woman's collegiate education in the United States, Georgia Female College is the first to draw our attention. The high grade seminaries, such as Elizabeth, Mount Holyoke, Troy, and Marks', need not be discussed here, as in their incorporation there was nothing to suggest they were to make an effort at collegiate education. The Georgia institution was, without doubt, chartered as a college and authorized to "confer all such honors, degrees, and licenses as are usually conferred in colleges or universities. . . . "[93] The president, Pierce, was elected in 1838 and the college opened on January 7, 1839. To the college came Mr. Slade, with some of his students from the Clinton Female Institute. Several contemporary accounts give flattering estimates of the new institution, its teachers, students and standards of work.[94] It will be necessary, however, to examine carefully other evidence in order to judge how effectually the new institution strove to be a college.

The first class, of which Catherine Brewer was a member, graduated in July, 1840, a year and a half after the college opened. The "Testimonial of the Georgia Female College," issued to her, was in English and recited that "after having passed through a Regular Course of Study . . . embracing all the Sciences which are usually taught in the Colleges of the United States, with such as appropriately belong to Female Education in its most ample range," Miss Brewer "was deemed worthy of the First Degree conferred by this Institution, and accordingly it was conferred upon her on the 16th of July, 1840." This testimonial was signed by Pierce, President; Ellison, professor of mathematics; Slade, professor of natural science; and Maussanett, professor of languages. Evidently, this female college diploma did not imitate those of the male as to the language employed, for the latter were in Latin. Latin diplomas of the period generally mentioned *Gradum Primum in Artibus Liberalibus,* or some similar phrasing, and went on to specify the holder's right to the title *Artium Baccalaureus.* On the other

---

[93] *Charter,* approved December 23, 1836.
[94] Buckingham: *Slave States,* I, 195 *f.;* and Burke: *Reminiscences of Georgia,* 203–4; not to mention various newspaper accounts.

DIPLOMA ISSUED BY GEORGIA FEMALE COLLEGE (1840)

hand, though not in Latin, and though it does not go on to specify the *Artium Baccalaureata,* as might be expected, the diploma differs from those granted generally by seminaries of the day in that it specifies the "First Degree."[95]   It is worthy of notice that, in common usage, "first degree" has been used to refer to the baccalaureate; and "second degree" to the master's.

No record shows exactly what studies were completed by the recipient of this "First Degree"; but it is stated that "all the Sciences which are usually taught in the colleges of the United

[95] Compare with other seminary diplomas, pp. 455–6, Vol. I.

States, with such as appropriately belong to Female Education"
were included in her course.[96] This would suggest that attention had been given to the usual college studies and other studies
usually emphasized in female seminaries, such as "accomplishments," perhaps. Additional evidence, to 1840, on which to base
a further deduction, is lacking. However, we may compare the
studies outlined in the *Catalog* of 1842, which, in all probability,
were the same as those required of the students who graduated
in 1840.[97] How do these studies compare with those of men's
colleges of that day, and with those of nearby female seminaries?

The fairest comparison that can be made is with neighboring
male colleges and female seminaries, rather than with those at a
great distance. Let us note entrance requirements. In 1828,
Augusta College, Kentucky, required English grammar, arithmetic, including vulgar and decimal fractions and the extrac-
tion of roots, Latin grammar, parts of Caesar's *Commentaries,*
Virgil's *Aeneid,* Greek grammar, and the Greek Testament for
admission.[98] The University of Georgia named English grammar, arithmetic, Virgil, *Select Orations* of Cicero, Livy, *Graeca
Minora* and *Majora,* Greek reader, Greek Testament, and geography as its specific requirements for admission in 1834. The
catalogs of William and Mary (1841–2) did not state entrance
requirements specifically. Generally, however, admission requirements of male colleges covered parts of Caesar, Virgil,
Cicero, the *Anabasis,* the *Iliad,* algebra and geometry. History,
geography, English grammar and composition, ancient history
and United States history, and physical geography were gradually recognized as admission studies also, between 1820 and 1870.
The requirements for admission to Judson Female Institute in
1841 were reading, spelling, writing, English grammar, arithmetic, United States history, geography, and natural history.
The Mooresville, Alabama, Young Ladies' Seminary, in 1838,
added to these, defining, geometry, botany, elementary astron-

---

[96] Notice that the copy of the diploma given in Taylor's *Before Vassar
Opened,* 21, is inaccurate and misleading; moreover, the author states that
no professor of literature signed the diploma. The professor of languages
did, however.

[97] An advertisement published in the *Florida Sentinel,* issues of August 4
and September 10, 1841, shows that much the same studies were offered.

[98] *Catalog,* 1828, 32–3.

omy, natural theology, and philosophy.[99]   Georgia Female College named reading, writing, English grammar, and arithmetic as her entrance studies in 1842.

From this it appears that so far as entrance studies were concerned, the Georgia Female College was far below the male colleges around her; and at least two female seminaries of the South demanded higher entrance attainments than did she.   Pierce stated the facts: "The standard of admission especially is reduced so low as to present an incongruity between the high character of a college (at least so far as the name may be considered a distinction) and the requisitions laid down in our plan, as published in the catalog. . . . To one uninformed of the facts in the case [the admission requirements seem] . . . quite too academic to accord with the preconceived views of a college." But "the alternative submitted to us was, by elevating the standard of admission to diminish the number of scholars, and consequently, the receipts from tuition, and thus burden the Institution (dependent on its patronage for its very existence,) with the responsibility of paying the salaries of its officers without any corresponding means, or by reducing the grade of scholarship necessary for admission to increase the number of pupils and the amount of receipts, and thus enable the Board of Trustees to meet their unavoidable engagements."[100]

The age for entrance at the University of Georgia, in 1834, was fourteen; at Oberlin, in 1838, and at Maryville College, Tennessee, in 1854, it was the same.   From fourteen to sixteen was the usual age for admission to college, the age being gradually advanced as the century progressed.[101]   Female seminaries varied greatly as to the age of admission, ranging from twelve to sixteen.   After 1835, the age of admission, if specified, was usually given as from fourteen to sixteen, though at some pupils were admitted at ten, twelve, or thirteen.   The Georgia Female College, in 1839, permitted entrance at twelve and thus seems to be more in keeping with the practice of the seminaries for girls than with the colleges for men.   This early age of admission had a distinct bearing on the entrance studies, for, as President

[99] *Catalog*, 1838.
[100] *So. Ladies' Book*, I, 65–74.
[101] Kirkland: *Higher Education in the United States*, 9–10.

Pierce pointed out, the studies prescribed had to "correspond with the common acquisitions at that period of life."[102]

The accepted length of the college course was then, as now, four years. In this, the institution at Macon followed the men's colleges. Reference to the table of female seminaries shows that, after the organization of courses with specific requirements, the prevailing standard of length was three years; only a few attempted a four-year course. Georgia seminaries were no exception to this general rule. Hence, in planning the four-year course, Pierce clearly endeavored to go beyond the usual academies. He pointed out that "a College can confer no higher literary distinction, as to real acquisition, than an academy, *if forced upon the usual hasty method of instruction:* [Italics mine] . . . the academy, on paper, proposes oftentimes to teach a greater variety of branches than the college."[103] One cannot read the various utterances of Pierce without being convinced that he was striving for a higher institution different from the seminary. To accomplish this he made the course longer, and, in the interest of greater thoroughness, reduced the number of studies far below what most academies thought respectable. "The specific difference, and that which should deservedly give the College preeminence is, that its diploma should be the voucher of a superior education." Pierce saw also, apparently, one of the greatest difficulties that stood in the way of perfectly satisfactory college performance: the need of better, systematic, early instruction. As he said, "Primary learning should become more accurate and extensive, and the standard of admission into a college should be elevated—a regular uniform system adopted so that the course of learning might be graduated. . . . "[104]

This prevailing lack of standardization was very embarrassing to the youthful aspiring college. Because of "the endless diversity of the modes of teaching that are prevalent in the country" it proved impossible to adopt a rigid standard. "A rigid adherence to our best judgment, as to the proper collegiate gradation, would have excluded well nigh all the applicants, or ranged them in classes so low as to have dissatisfied our patrons. . . . We were compelled, moreover, to have respect not only to the age

102 *So. Ladies' Book*, I, 65–74.
103 *Ibid.*, I, 11–13.
104 *Ibid.*

of the candidate, but in many cases, to the probable duration of her stay.   Resolved to do the very best that time and circumstance allowed in the exercise of unusual labor and painstaking, without any very specific grade of acquisition being defined, we made up our opinion, in every individual case, taking into consideration all the facts legitimately entitled to affect our decision.''[105]   Pierce was forced to recognize the necessity of compromise, for a time; and that the ''mere existence of the Institution, however lofty its design or beneficial its ultimate results, could not revolutionize the popular system of teaching, and the mode of elementary education must be changed before the College can be brought to the high ground in all respects we trust it is destined to occupy.   The impulse must be general before the work of reform can be consummated.''[106]

An examination of the catalogs shows that, so far as Greek and Latin were concerned, Georgia Female College did not reach the standard of Augusta College or the University of Georgia, several years earlier.[107]   These were almost universal requirements. William and Mary College was a notable exception in that, according to the *Catalog* of 1841–2, it did not specify Latin and Greek for the A.B., but did require Latin for the Master's.   At Georgia Female College, ancient and modern languages could be studied if elected.   The fact that Maussanett, Professor of Languages, signed Miss Brewer's diploma, may indicate that she had studied ''languages,'' but not necessarily Latin or Greek.   As for mathematical, English, historical, religious and scientific studies, this ''female college'' compared favorably with the male.   It should be noted, however, that, with the exception of Latin and Greek, many seminary courses compared favorably with the number and kind of subjects offered by male colleges, though instruction in the latter was in some cases doubtless much more advanced.[108]

From the foregoing one cannot escape the conclusion that, because of (1) the early age of admission, (2) low entrance re-

---

[105] *Ibid.*

[106] *Ibid.*

[107] Augusta *Catalog*, 1828, 32; Univ. of Ga. *Catalog*, 1834; and Ga. Female College *Catalog*, 1842, 3–13; also *So. Ladies' Book*, I, 65–74.

[108] Comparing Judson Female Institute (1841) in the college table and the courses of female seminaries.

quirements, (3) the sacrifice of standards of work and classification, in order to get students whose fees would help pay expenses (115 were in the college department by the end of the first half year, though Pierce says, if requirements had been rigidly adhered to, almost all students would have been kept out), (4) failure to *require* Latin and Greek, and (5) granting of a diploma more like contemporary seminary certificates than those of male colleges, this first great experiment failed to attain its objective—an education equivalent to that offered men in colleges of the day. The Reverend George F. Pierce confessed the inability of the pioneer to attain that goal, in the midst of so many unfavorable circumstances. He was honest in his endeavor. Facing the shortcomings of the institution, he declared: ''Gradually, yet certainly, we hope (and we think with good reason) to effect our purpose, thus giving to the Institution a character worthy its cognomen, and to Female Education a loftier aim and a wider range.''[109] Considering his integrity, his high ideal, his early recognition of the impossibility of its immediate fulfillment, as also the prevailing antagonism to college education for women, and the jealous outcry that would doubtless have greeted the granting of a diploma exactly like a man's, based on the completion of what were admitted to be inferior studies, is it not conceivable that he felt better satisfied in awarding a diploma not in all respects like those issued by male colleges of the day, and which the charter given by the Georgia legislature authorized him to award? This conjecture may be entirely erroneous; but it seems a reasonable interpretation.

Wesleyan Female College at Cincinnati, Ohio, the next notable effort at providing education for women equal to that of men's colleges, had a three-year course in 1842–3. Miami, Oberlin and Antioch College had standard four-year courses. There were seven teachers, but four probably taught only elementary studies. In 1843, the library had 615 volumes which, by 1860, were increased to 1000.[110] Admission requirements (age was not mentioned) included English grammar and composition, arithmetic, Latin grammar, Latin reader, the *Commentaries* of Caesar, Greek grammar and reader, mythology, general history and history of the United States, geography, and some natural history.

109 *So. Ladies' Book*, I, 65–74.
110 *Alumna*, II, 123.

Though not equal to, they compare favorably with the requirements of Miami University and Antioch College a full ten years later; they are far beyond those demanded at Macon at the same time; they are not, however, equal to the classical requirements of Augusta College in 1828, nor those of the University of Georgia in 1834. In history and geography, however, the Cincinnati college went beyond the men's colleges of the South.

The degrees, at first, were Mistress of English Literature and Mistress of Liberal Arts. At just what date the first A.B. was awarded is not known. The studies of the three-year course, on completion of which graduation depended, included Greek grammar, some of Virgil, Cicero, and Sallust, which is quite meagre if compared with Oberlin requirements of 1838, or with those of Miami and Antioch at a slightly later date. Mathematical studies were decidedly weak, compared with those required in men's colleges. English studies, religion, and the sciences were more nearly on a par with men's colleges, but history was neglected. It is readily apparent that though some advancement had been made, the Cincinnati Wesleyan Female College was far from a plane of equality with contemporary local men's institutions.

The Oxford Female College, which had developed from the Academy (1830), and was chartered as a college in 1852, had a four-year course in 1855. Admission requirements, as to studies, were decidedly lower than at Wesleyan Female College of Cincinnati. No Latin or Greek was required. Both the entrance studies and those of the four-year course were decidedly inferior to the courses of men's colleges. The classical requirements of the four-year course, however, were better than those of (Cincinnati) Wesleyan, as they included Greek grammar, reader, Testament, Latin grammar, reader, Caesar and Virgil. Other studies were about on a par with those of Wesleyan and seminaries throughout the United States.

On the completion of the course a diploma was awarded which certified that "having completed the Higher Course of Study prescribed in this institution" and attained "an acquaintance with the several branches of *Literature* and *Science*" the recipient was entitled to the "rank of a Graduated Pupil of the College of the Second Degree."[111] This certificate, issued on the

[111] See diploma of Julia Rogers, June 26, 1856.

DIPLOMA ISSUED BY OXFORD FEMALE COLLEGE

basis of the studies prescribed, clearly does not indicate college work, in the generally accepted sense.

At Delaware, the Ohio Wesleyan Female College was established according to the "Articles of Association," April 1, 1853.[112] It grew out of the desire of patrons of Wesleyan University to "educate their daughters in the same vicinity with

[112] Ohio Wesleyan Female College, *Circular*, 1853, 4–5.

their sons.'' Apparently, too, denominational prestige was at stake, as the *Circular* recited: ''. . . The only point left for us to decide, was, not whether there should be such a College in Delaware, but whether the Methodist church, which is entitled to the ground by first colonization, should proceed to occupy it.''[113] This institution offered a four-year course, either scientific or classical. To enter the classical course, Latin and Greek, ''first and second books,'' were required, besides the usual reading, arithmetic, geography, grammar, physiology, penmanship, and so on. In the four-year classical course, Nepos, the *Anabasis*, Cicero's *Orations*, Greek Testament, Virgil, Livy and Strong's *Harmony* (Greek) were covered. Science, mathematics, geography, history and philosophy had approximately the same representation as in other colleges discussed.[114] It is seen at once that the classical course, in which the catalog of 1854 showed thirty-six students, went beyond the usual range of female education. The strength of the course was weakened, however, by the admission that modern languages ''may be substituted for Greek.''[115] It must have been difficult to keep up the Greek requirement of the classical course, for the catalog of 1863 shows that no Greek was required. The early catalogs, 1854 and 1863, do not mention the granting of degrees, but those completing scientific or classical courses were to receive ''appropriate diplomas''; that of 1876 stated that those who had completed the course, ''including ancient and modern languages, receive the degree of Baccalaureate of Arts.''[116] That the course was not equal to that of the male college, required for the A.B., is indicated by the fact that when merged with Ohio Wesleyan University, in 1877, the course was modified and the degree of B.L. given on completion of it.[117]

The Illinois Conference Female Academy (1847) was changed to ''College '' in 1851. In 1854, it provided a four-year course. Its admission requirements were high, but did not include Virgil, Cicero's *Select Orations* and Sallust, as did Illinois College for men at the same date. More emphasis was placed on elementary

113 *Ibid.*, 1.

114 *Catalog*, 1854, 13 *ff.*

115 *Ibid.*, 15.

116 *Catalog*, 1876, 16 *ff.* and 24.

117 Knight and Commons: *Hist. of Higher Ed. in Ohio*, 82 [Bur. Ed., Circ. Inf., No. 5, 1891]; Burns: *Ed. Hist. of Ohio*, 342 *f.*

English studies, however, than by the men's college; and newer subjects, such as natural philosophy, mental philosophy, and bookkeeping, were required, whereas the male college ignored them.

As for the Greek studies of the four-year course, the requirements of the female college were decidedly lower than the male; in Latin, the same was true. In mathematics, also, the offering of the female college was weaker; and only in higher English studies and the sciences was it practically on a par with the male. Compared with the four-year collegiate course offered at Rockford Female Seminary (1854), the three-year course of Jacksonville Female Academy (1856) and the St. Louis Female Institute (1854), it is seen to be somewhat stronger than the best of these, Rockford, as to Latin and Greek; but as far as the other studies are concerned, they are all substantially equal, allowance being made, of course, for minor variations. Thus while Illinois Female College and the collegiate course of Rockford were distinctly better than most seminaries, they were still far below the college level as to classical studies.

Mary Sharp College, at first known as the Tennessee and Alabama Female Institute, opened (1851) at Winchester, Tennessee, was (1853) decidedly below the admission requirements of the University of Tennessee, as stated in 1851–52; or those of Maryville College, 1854. She stood distinctly above the best secondary schools, but somewhat below the men's colleges of the day in that locality. As to classical studies of the four years, they were decidedly in advance of female seminaries, generally; yet they compare unfavorably with the men's institutions, Maryville and the University of Tennessee. The latter had Livy, Tacitus, Horace, the *de Oratore, de Officiis, de Amicitia, Oedipus Tyrannus, Iliad, Odyssey, Memorabilia* and the *Anabasis*, whereas Mary Sharp required only Greek grammar, Testament, Latin grammar, Virgil, Cicero and Horace. These were but little better than the admission studies of some men's colleges, but they constituted a step towards the college level.

On the completion of the four-year course, the first diplomas were given (1855) to three ladies,—Nannie Meredith, Mary A. Farmer, and Matilda Winford.[118] The diploma, in Latin, issued

[118] *Z. C. Graves and the Mary Sharp College*, 137; Merriam's *Hist. of Higher Education in Tenn.* quotes a letter from John Eaton, Commissioner

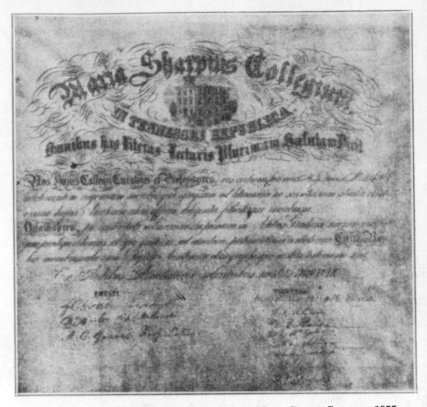

DIPLOMA ISSUED TO NANNIE MEREDITH BY MARY SHARP COLLEGE, 1855

to Miss Nannie Meredith, lies before me. It is signed by eight trustees, the President, Graves, and the professors of Mathematics and Latin. It recites that having satisfactorily completed her studies, literary and scientific, she is, by the authority of their charter, admitted to the *"Primum in Artibus Gradum"* and is entitled to all the "rights, privileges and honors everywhere pertaining to that degree." This diploma is the earliest found to date, *issued by a woman's college*,[119] which, in form,

---

of Education (p. 247), in which two graduates are mentioned as early as 1853. The "3" may have been an error in typesetting or some may have come to Mary Sharp with advanced standing and have graduated in less than four years after the opening. However, no diploma of 1853 has yet been found. Neither does the memorial volume of Z. C. Graves show any graduates in 1853. Probably there were none.

119 Oberlin, a coeducational institution, issued the first diploma to a woman in Latin, and based on completion of a good four-years' standard college

content, and the work for which it stood, can compare at all favorably with the Bachelor's degree of male colleges.[120] But it must be remembered that in this college, and in many others which gave Bachelor's degrees in the succeeding two decades, the studies for which the degree stood were decidedly narrower in range than those of most men's colleges.

Notwithstanding the unquestioned merit of the Mary Sharp experiment, there is no doubt but that much was left to be attained before women could stand on equal academic footing with men. Material facilities, in general, were inadequate; there was no endowment, sufficient to sustain her through the crisis through which she must pass. Still, she struggled on, after the Civil War, against financial difficulties, until the last decade of the century, when the doors were closed. Her experience, recalling the financial obstacles that beset the earlier experiment in Georgia, reinforces strongly the judgment that Catherine Beecher was entirely correct in declaring that, without endowments comparable with those given to men's colleges, collegiate institutions for women could not be established and successfully carried on from generation to generation. The vision, clearly caught, and energies, liberally expended, were doomed to fade and decline, without an organization, backed by financial resources, sufficient to meet the storm and stress of adverse years.

At the same time that Graves was founding Mary Sharp College, Sunderland at Perkiomen Bridge, Pennsylvania, was similarly engaged in promoting the idea of a college for women.[121] Admission to the college department was generally from the seminary, which had been in operation for a few years before the college charter was obtained.[122] This Montgomery Female Seminary had a strong three-year course of modern studies, but required no classical languages.[123] Hence those entering the college, in all probability, as a general rule, presented no Latin or Greek. They entered at thirteen or fourteen. The "college course" outlined (1853) was to cover only three years; but the catalog of 1857 showed a four-year course. The classical studies of 1857, while fairly numerous and representative of college grade work, were, however, not all *required* for the A.B. degree.

[120] See facsimile on opposite page.
[121] See p. 146.
[122] *Laws of Pa.*, 1853, 327–8.
[123] See *Catalog*, 1851, 9–11.

It was specified that candidates who had reached the age of seventeen, and had completed all studies save Greek, mathematics, and other languages of the senior year, could be admitted to the A.B. Those eighteen years old and who had completed all studies could receive the Master's degree: *Magistra in Bonis Artibus*.[124] The Bachelor's degree was therefore inferior, based on but three years of college work and probably no prerequisite of classical preparation. The work for the Master's was comparable to what would be expected for the Bachelor's degree; indeed, it makes a poor showing alongside of the requirements of Dickinson College or the Arts College of the University of Pennsylvania. Except for Greek, it was not better than Patapsco Female Institute; in some respects it was inferior to the Institute.

While Mary Sharp was getting under way and Pennsylvania was experimenting, Auburn Female University was chartered by New York, 1852.[125] In 1855, a new charter was granted and the institution, now as Elmira Female College,[126] was actually opened in that year. The first class graduated in 1859, the young ladies being granted a diploma, which mentioned admission to the *Gradum Primum* and designated the recipient as *Artium Baccalaureata*. Seventeen were granted in 1859, and fifteen in 1860. To 1865, 96 had received Elmira's A.B. What were the conditions under which this degree was obtained? How did the requirements compare with contemporary and neighboring male colleges?

Elmira specified sixteen as the age of entrance—a maturity beyond that required at most female seminaries, beyond many men's colleges, and equal to the best of the day. There were eight teachers, three holding the Bachelor's and three the Master's degree. The library had about 1,000 volumes. For science work there was a set of "philosophical and chemical apparatus." The Legislature voted $10,000 for its support; and Simeon Benjamin made a total donation of about $80,000. The charter of the college was given on condition that "no degree shall be conferred without a course of study equivalent to a full ordinary course of study as pursued in the colleges of this state

124 *Catalog*, 1857, 27.
125 *Laws of N. Y.*, 1852, 8–9.
126 *Ibid.*, 1855, 775.

Elmira Female College

DIPLOMA ISSUED BY ELMIRA COLLEGE (1859)

shall have been completed.'' It was to be subject to the Regents' visitation. For admission to the college course leading to the A.B., a candidate had to complete the studies of the preparatory course. This included analysis, English grammar, rhetoric, criticism, arithmetic, algebra, Latin grammar, the *Aeneid*, Roman and Grecian antiquities, as well as geography, natural philosophy, zoölogy, physiology, anatomy, bookkeeping, hygiene, and the Bible.[127] These compare favorably with admission studies of Amherst (1856) but are not equal to them, the latter specifying either Sallust or Caesar's *Commentaries*, and *Select Orations* of Cicero, as well as Greek grammar, the *Anabasis*, and two books of the *Iliad*. About the same relation existed between Elmira's and Columbia's admission requirements (1859) as between the former's and Amherst's. Comparing her admission requirements of 1855 with those of two other female institutions, Wesleyan Female College, Macon, Georgia, 1855, and Oxford Female College, Ohio, 1864, they are seen to be more like those of the men's colleges than those of female institutions—the latter not specifying Latin. If we compare Elmira's prerequisites of 1855 with those of Vassar in 1865, they are about the same, except that the latter named Latin prose, two books of Caesar and two orations of Cicero, whereas the former specified only Virgil's *Aeneid* and Roman antiquities in addition to the Latin grammar. Vassar named French; Elmira did not. In history, geography, and the several sciences, Elmira's requirements were superior to those of Vassar, ten years later. From 1855 on, Elmira's preparatory work increased. In 1857–8, it included Latin reader and Caesar's *Commentaries*, in addition to those already named.

As for the work of the four collegiate years, from sixteen to twenty, the number of classics specified by Elmira were decidedly fewer than those named by Amherst, Columbia or Oberlin, being particularly weak in Greek. Nevertheless, Greek grammar, exercises and composition and Greek Testament were required. In Latin, Cicero's *Orations*, or Sallust, and the *Germania* and *Agricola* of Tacitus were read. These, though not exactly equal to, approximated the Oberlin requirements ten years later. And though they were less numerous and advanced than the courses specified by Amherst and Columbia, they formed a justifiable basis for issuing the Bachelor's degree.

[127] *Catalog*, 1855–6.

Diploma Issued by Maine Wesleyan Seminary and Female College

Two years after Elmira had graduated the first class, the college course of Maine Wesleyan Seminary was opened for young women.[128] After completing a four-year course, the first class graduated in 1865, the year of Vassar's opening. The diploma, of the eighth of June, 1865, specified the recipient was admitted to the *Gradum Primum* and was a properly qualified *Baccalaureata Artium*.[129] What were the course requirements leading to this distinction? Students were admitted from the seminary course. The age was not definitely stated. In Latin, the requirements were exercises, composition, and prosody; and *de Officiis, de Amicitia, de Senectute,* some of Horace, Plautus, and Livy, and the *Germania* and *Histories* of Tacitus were read. Greek was not required, but students were advised they could substitute it for modern language; if so, they would read the *Anabasis, Iliad, Gorgias,* and *de Corona* of Demosthenes.[130] How many, or whether any, chose to substitute Greek is not known. So far as Latin studies, modern languages, higher English studies and sciences are concerned, however, the course compared favorably with those of men's colleges. The Latin requirements were greater than those of Elmira; but no Greek was demanded.

Lindenwood College, at St. Charles, Missouri, was the outgrowth of a girls' school, established by George C. and Mary Easton Sibley, in 1827. By 1863, the collegiate department offered a full four-years' course. Students were prepared for it in a special department, which was supposed to afford a thorough course "in all the branches of an ordinary English education." This was by no means equal to the entrance requirements of men's colleges of that day. The studies of the collegiate years included (1863) Caesar, Virgil, Tacitus, Ovid, Cicero, Greek grammar, reader, and some of Homer.[131] In science, mathematics, history, modern language, and Bible study, the course was similar to others of the day. This compares favorably with the courses of Mary Sharp and Elmira, but the catalog states that "students may omit some of the studies in the regular [course] when studying the Languages, or *several* ornamental branches." The classics stated, then, were not indispensable to

128 French: *Hist. Maine Wesleyan Seminary*, 35 *ff.*
129 Issued to Louisa Frances Allen and signed by Henricus P. Torsey.
130 *Catalog*, 1863.
131 *Catalog*, 1863, 8–10.

Matthew Vassar

the attainment of the degree; and the degrees given were (M.E.L.) Mistress of English Literature and (M.A) Mistress of Arts, the latter for those who completed the scientific, literary, and classical studies.[132] This last, though all studies had been finished, was not the kind of diploma issued to graduates of men's colleges.

Vassar College, incorporated January 18, 1861, and opened in 1865, had an endowment such as no other women's college up to that day. Considering purely material equipment, she had all that could be desired.[133] The first president was Milo P. Jewett, formerly of the Judson Female Institute, Marion, Alabama, and, from 1855 to 1860, the Principal of Cottage Hill Seminary, at Poughkeepsie.[134] There was a faculty of thirty: president, lady principal, eight professors, and twenty assistant instructors. The college was authorized to grant "honors, degrees and diplomas" such as are "granted by any university, college or seminary of learning in the United States."[135] In the first half year after opening, there was 353 students. As with other female colleges, a preparatory department was found to be absolutely necessary, due to inadequate facilities for secondary education elsewhere. On the whole, the wealth that had been so generously poured out by Mr. Vassar, the excellent library, buildings and grounds, broad course of studies planned, and the large faculty—note, too, there were twenty-two women to eight men—left the enthusiastic advocates of women's equality with only one reason for complaint: it was, in spite of all these good gifts, "Vassar Female College." "Let this misnomer be corrected," said one prophetess of the women's movement, "then VASSAR COLLEGE FOR YOUNG WOMEN would be an example of moral fitness of perfect words to express the honor due to the NAME of the illustrious Founder."[136]

Students were admitted at fifteen years of age. An earnest effort had been made to reach the standards prevailing in New England men's colleges; and Milo P. Jewett had been in correspondence with President Cowles of Elmira, then a struggling

[132] *The Sibleys*, 22.—Published by Lindenwood College.
[133] *Education*, VIII, 73 *ff.*; Raymond: *op. cit.*, 6–7; and Lossing: *op. cit.*, 86 *ff.*
[134] *Poughkeepsie Eagle*, Aug. 23, 1856.
[135] *Laws of N. Y.*, Jan. 18, 1861, 8–10.
[136] *Godey's Lady's Book*, Aug. 1866, 170.

VASSAR FEMALE COLLEGE

infant of six years, about to graduate her third class. On May 18, 1861, Jewett wrote: "Charged with the duty of organizing this institution, I desire to avail myself of the experience of our most eminent practical Educator." To this letter he appended twenty-one questions, dealing with the constitution of the faculty, responsibilities of superior and inferior officers, discipline, requirements for a diploma; with the extent to which languages and literature, ancient and modern, mathematics, and natural science should be pursued; how moral and religious culture, physical culture, aesthetic culture, theory and practice of domestic economy, conversation, and agreeable manners should be taught; and whether dancing should be encouraged and premiums or prizes offered. Advice was also sought on the admission of day, irregular, and preparatory students.[137]

One cannot examine Jewett's first plan of studies at Vassar without raising the significant question as to the origin of his scheme, which recognized "departments" or "schools," similarly organized as at the University of Virginia and later (1885) at Mary Sharp College. The presumption is not without some foundation that he got the idea and cherished it throughout the long years of his service at Judson Female Institute, in Alabama, and welcomed the opportunity to share it with Mr. Vassar, who was ready to endow magnificently an institution for the collegiate education of women.[138]

The prerequisites for entrance to the collegiate course at Vassar (1865) included Latin grammar, syntax, Latin prose, two books of the *Commentaries* of Caesar, two orations of Cicero, French, and a few other modern studies. From this it is seen that Vassar in 1865, like Elmira in 1855, did not exactly reach the men's college standard which required Greek for admission.[139] Two courses were offered in the college: classical and

[137] Letter dated May 18, 1861, in Elmira Archives.

[138] It is conceivable that future researches may bring definite evidence to light, showing a connection between the first female college movement in Georgia and those in other parts of the South. Vassar, Elmira and Judson archives may still contain some fragments that, through Jewett, link Vassar more conclusively to a movement in favor of collegiate education for women, which spread in the South between 1825 and 1855 but was unable to attain practical success for lack of funds.

[139] Columbia *Catalog*, 1859; Vassar *Catalog*, 1865–1866; and Amherst *Catalog*, 1856–7.

scientific. The latter, which led to the A.B., as well as the former, required no Greek.[140] The Latin requirements of the scientific course, though not equal to those of local men's colleges, were fair, about on the same level as those of her sister college. The latter, however, with her Greek requirement, as indispensable to the A.B., stood a fair first. Vassar's classical course, leading to the A.B., as outlined in 1867–8, included Felton's Historians, Kuhner's Grammar, syntax, Arnold's Prose Composition, six books of the Iliad, Agamemnon, Ajax and Plato's Phaedon in Greek; in Latin, Livy, Cicero, Horace, and Tacitus were read. This was in its day the strongest classical course offered by a woman's college, leading to the A.B.

Students who completed either one of the "regular courses," the classical with Greek or the scientific without it, were to receive "a Diploma of the First or Baccalaureate Degree"; if they completed a "Post Graduate Course," they were to be rewarded with "a Diploma of the Second Degree."[141]

Wells College,[142] according to the catalog of 1868, had a four-year course with requirements for admission only slightly below those of Vassar and Elmira. The Latin requirements for the completion of the four-year course, however, were inferior to those of Vassar; and the Greek requirements were not as extensive at at Elmira. Graduates of the classical course received the A.B.; the B.S. was given to graduates of the scientific course.

It was not until Smith College opened (1875) that we have opportunity to see a women's college beginning at the very outset of her career to provide a course of study almost identical with that of the best men's colleges. It should be mentioned, too, that Wellesley, opening the same year, was a close second to Smith. The former did not, however, demand Greek for admission till 1881;[143] Smith College admission studies, with but few exceptions, matched those of Amherst (1874–5) and Harvard (1873–4). A similar parallelism is to be noted in the work of the four years. This is true of both Smith and Wellesley.[144]

[140] Catalog, 1867–8, 12–21.

[141] Ibid., 21.

[142] Chartered in 1868 as a seminary but changed, in 1870, to college—Wells College, General Catalog 1868–94, 5.

[143] Wellesley Catalogs, 1880 and 1881.

[144] Amherst Catalog, 1874–5; Harvard Catalog, 1873–4; and Smith College Circular, 1873 and Catalog of 1879.

Smith College

WELLESLEY COLLEGE

Of the success with which later colleges such as Bryn Mawr, Mount Holyoke,[145] and Goucher measured up to the college standard, it is unnecessary to speak. The period of experimentation, during which female colleges had earnestly striven, but with varying degrees of success, to reach male college standards, may be said to have come to an end in 1875, when Smith was so conspicuously successful. Thereafter, it is impossible to read the literature of a single year without finding some one criticizing the women's colleges for so successfully imitating the men's. In the opening of Wells, Smith, and Wellesley, too, we recognized the passing of the era of the "Female College," which had been the prevailing ideal for fifty years. But the hated "female" recurred but seldom after 1875. Smith was simply a

145 College charters received in 1888 and 1893.

"College," "the leading object of which shall be the higher education of young women. . . ."[146]

V. Increase of Women's Colleges

Though the Georgia Female College was the first chartered in the United States to confer on girls "all such honors degrees and licenses as are usually conferred in colleges and universities, . . . " Mary Sharp (1851) was the earliest college for women only, in the United States, which required both Latin and Greek, though in meager amount, in a four-year course, and gave an A.B. degree comparable, both in form and significance, to those issued by men's colleges. After a great brave struggle, following the Civil War, Mary Sharp came to an end in 1896. Elmira College (1855) is the oldest existing women's college in the United States which succeeded in attaining standards in a fair degree comparable with men's colleges at the very beginning of her career. Vassar, ten years thereafter, likewise attained fairly comparable standards and was the first women's college that was adequately endowed. Ten years later, Smith College formed the culmination of the effort to found "a college, like a man's . . . to teach them all that men are taught." The praiseworthy pioneer efforts, of the twenty-five years preceding 1851, must, so far as data at present available are concerned, be regarded as falling short of their goal in one way or another. Since 1855, the opportunities for genuine college work for women have been steadily increasing in number; and the standard of the work, in the earlier as well as in later established colleges, has, so far as it may be judged by requirements on paper, been improved. This increase in variety of courses afforded, improvement of faculties, and the material aids, such as buildings, libraries, laboratories, and so on, has come about as a result of (1) the increase of wealth, (2) the universally accepted notion that women should be educated in colleges as well as men, and (3) the development of adequate secondary schools, preparing young women for college. Interwoven with these are basic economic, political, social and professional factors, which have developed to such an extent that women of to-day recognize the advantage of higher education just as certainly as do men.

[146] Act of incorporation, *Laws of Mass.*, 1871, 475–7.

About twenty years after the opening of Elmira, 209 institutions for the "superior" education of women were reported to the Bureau of Education. Many reporting were not more than secondary schools; and the vast majority were not equipped to do standard college work. Taking into account a few well known colleges for women which did not file a report, and those on the list which were fairly able to meet accepted college standards, there were probably not more than a half dozen in the entire country.[147] In the *Report* for 1886–7, the Commissioner called attention to the need for distinguishing between seminaries and collegiate institutes, and those colleges which "as is well known are organized and conducted in strict accordance with the plan of the arts college. . . ." The latter, forming "Division A," included seven institutions—Bryn Mawr, Vassar, Ingham University, Wells College, Wellesley, Smith, and the Society for Collegiate Education of Women, at Cambridge.[148] One hundred and fifty-two were included in "Division B." Both lists were obviously incomplete. In 1888, there were eight in "Division A," Mount Holyoke having been granted a college charter; and one hundred and ninety were reported in "Division B."[149] The *Report* for 1890 included fifteen in the first group— Mills College, Woman's College of Baltimore, Evelyn College (at Princeton, New Jersey), Elmira, Barnard, Rutgers, and Cleveland having been added.[150]

In 1907, "Division A" included Mills, Trinity, Rockford, Woman's College of Baltimore, Simmons, Smith, Mount Holyoke, Wellesley, Wells, Elmira, Vassar, Bryn Mawr and Randolph-Macon Woman's College, as well as the coördinate colleges, Sophie Newcomb and Radcliffe. One hundred and ten institutions were included in Division B. Combining the figures of these two groups, we have a fair picture of the women's colleges, fifty-five years after the opening of Mary Sharp. Too much weight should not be attached to the classification of the institutions; it is not for the sake of the classification that the figures are reproduced here. Indeed, it was admitted in 1911, "the

[147] *R. C. E.*, 1874, 660 *ff.*
[148] *Ibid.*, 1886–7, 643 and 645.
[149] *Ibid.*, II, 1888–9, 1073 and 1078 *ff.*
[150] *Ibid.*, 1890–1, II, 1414.

basis of classification" had "become uncertain, and therefore unsatisfactory"; and its discontinuance was announced.[151]

A large proportion—75, or 68 per cent.—of the 110 institutions designated in "Division B," in 1907, were located in

TABLE I[152]

	A	B
NUMBER OF INSTITUTIONS	16	110
NON-SECTARIAN	13	33
SECTARIAN	3	77
Professors and Instructors		
PREPARATORY DEPARTMENT		
Men	2	23
Women	30	223
COLLEGIATE DEPARTMENT		
Men	340	193
Women	489	593
TOTAL NUMBER (EXCLUDING DUPLICATES)		
Men	352	375
Women	528	1,520
Total	880	1,895
Students		
TOTAL NUMBER	8,164	21,284
PREPARATORY	327	7,010
COLLEGIATE	7,436	12,561
GRADUATE	176	102
EDUCATION	....	865
MUSIC	....	10,808
ART	....	2,533
Income		
FROM STUDENT FEES		
For tuition and other educational services	$1,010,372	$1,531,752
For board and other non-educational services	$1,234,635	$1,129,640
Total student fees	$2,245,007	$2,661,392
FROM PRODUCTIVE FUNDS	$513,150	$37,704
FROM PRIVATE BENEFACTIONS		
For increase of plant	$294,531	$326,570
For endowment	$185,042	$75,529
For current expenses	$25,735	$7,434
FROM ALL OTHER SOURCES	$204,503	$28,808
TOTAL RECEIPTS EXCLUSIVE OF PRIVATE BENEFACTIONS FOR ENDOWMENT	$3,282,826	$3,081,340

[151] *R. C. E.* (1911), II, 884.
[152] Adapted from *R. C. E.* (1907), II, Tables 69–72, pp. 840–52.

TABLE I—(*Continued*)

	A	B
Property, Scholarships, and Fees		
LIBRARIES		
Volumes	341,992	246,314
Value	$615,162	$302,242
VALUE OF SCIENTIFIC APPARATUS, MACHINERY, AND FURNITURE	$1,031,264	$733,929
VALUE OF GROUNDS AND BUILDINGS	$12,768,451	$11,651,521
AMOUNT OF ENDOWMENT FUNDS	$11,697,624	$1,206,078
NUMBER OF FELLOWSHIPS	33	5
AMOUNT GIVEN IN FELLOWSHIPS	$17,725	$1,000
NUMBER OF SCHOLARSHIPS	614	257
AMOUNT GIVEN IN SCHOLARSHIPS	$99,969	$16,186
AVERAGE ANNUAL CHARGE FOR TUITION	$129.06	$61.15

Southern states. Mrs. Ellis stated, in 1915, speaking for the Southern Association of College Women, that there were 140 institutions[153] in the South calling themselves "colleges for women"; but "only six have been recognized as standard colleges. . . .'"[154] They were Agnes Scott, Converse, Goucher, Randolph-Macon, Sophie Newcomb and Westhampton. A report by the Association was promised for the succeeding year, wherein the different types of higher institutions, with their requirements, were to be clearly differentiated. This report, by Elizabeth Avery Colton, appeared in 1916.[155] Seven institutions[156] were listed as standard colleges, being accepted as such by the Association of Colleges and Secondary Schools of the Southern States.[157] Baylor, Hollins, Hood, Meridith, Sweet Briar, Salem, Tennessee and Wesleyan were designated as "approximate colleges" because "not sufficiently well organized and not sufficiently equipped in 1915–16 to conform to all the regulations of the Association of Colleges and Secondary Schools of the

[153] Note that a year later Miss Colton gave the total of "colleges" as 124.

[154] *N. E. A. Proc.* (1915), 1110–11.

[155] *Bulletin* No. 2, 1916, published by the Southern Association of College Women.

[156] Florida State College for Women had been added to the above-named six.

[157] For the college standards of the Association, see pp. 255–7 of the *Proceedings of the Thirty-First Annual Meeting*, 1926.

Southern States . . ."; but, it was admitted, they offered "four years of work which might justly entitle especially good students to graduate standing in first class institutions." The distinctions drawn between the "standard" and the "approximate" colleges were based on the fact that the latter had (1) preparatory departments, (2) more "special-study pupils," (3) "poorer library and laboratory equipment," and (4) did "not pay as good salaries" nor "secure as many professors distinguished for creative and research work." Entrance requirements were equal to, in two cases stronger than, those of the first class. Other classes into which the remaining higher institutions of the South were placed, such as normal and industrial colleges, junior colleges, "unclassifiable colleges," and imitation and nominal colleges, need not concern us here. Since the publication of this report, nearly a dozen institutions, some of them almost of the first rank then, have been admitted to the Southern Association.[158] The report was vigorously assailed by many colleges which felt themselves unjustly treated by Miss Colton. A recent investigation, and requests for information to show wherein her classification was erroneous, have, however, failed to uncover any substantial reason for questioning the validity of her work.[159]

The cause of the poorer library, laboratory and salaries, mentioned above, was poverty. Compared with those which were rated as "standard," the "approximate" colleges were poor; compared with colleges for women in the North, all Southern colleges for women were poor; and compared with the best men's colleges, the women's colleges of the North were poor. Sykes found the ratio of gifts for men and women, in four great men's and four great women's colleges to be: in 1910–11, 21 to 1; 1911–12, 13 to 1; 1912–13, 13 to 1; and in 1913–14, 5–1.[160] Small wonder, then, that it should cost so much more to send a daughter to college than a son.[161] When the War came, even the

[158] See *Proc., Thirty-First Annual Mtg. of Southern Association*, 1926, 8–11.

[159] Grinstead: Materials collected relative to the work of E. A. Colton; also a biographical sketch in the *Dictionary of American Biography*.

[160] Sykes: *Social Basis of New Education for Women*, 15–16.

[161] Eliot stated in 1904 that it cost nearly twice as much to send a girl to Radcliffe as to send a boy to Harvard.—*Harvard Graduate Magazine*, XII, 424; see also Can a Poor Girl Go to College? [*No. Am. Rev.* (1891), CLII, 624 *ff.*].

wealthiest women's colleges faced the mounting costs with productive funds of less than three million dollars. Smith, which began in 1875 with $393,000, had $2,225,000; Vassar, $2,330,000; Wellesley, $2,700,000; and Bryn Mawr, $2,373,000. As a result, salaries were low, compared with the best men's colleges; and improvement of physical plant was, in some cases, long delayed.

Significant efforts have been made recently, however, to relieve the financial stress. Mount Holyoke launched a campaign for $3,000,000, Smith for $4,000,000, Wellesley for $2,750,000, Vassar and Radcliffe for $3,000,000 each, and Bryn Mawr for $2,000,000.[162] Recently Wesleyan has secured a one hundred and thirty-two acre site, at Rivoli, six miles from Macon. The "Greater Wesleyan" will care for 700 students; the present buildings will house the conservatory, with places for 500 students. A campaign for a million dollars, nearly a half of which had been raised, was in progress in 1925.[163] It was expected that the new site would be occupied by the beginning of the 1927–8 session. Though they have increased in wealth, they are still poorly supported, compared with men's colleges, and urgent appeals have been made that something be done to adequately support the women's colleges.[164]

Closely connected with women's colleges is the Association of Collegiate Alumnae, which was founded in January, 1882, largely due to the efforts of Dr. Talbot and her daughter. At the outset there were seventeen members, graduates of Vassar, Wellesley and Smith, and the coeducational institutions, Oberlin, Universities of Michigan, Cornell, Boston and Wisconsin. The original purpose was to "better . . . utilize their privileges in personal education, and to perform their duty in respect to popular education," and to do "practical educational work." The Association has increased in size consistently, though at a modest pace, strict standards having always been required for admission. Only twenty-four institutions were represented in 1908.[165] There were over three thousand alumnae members,

[162] As reported in *Sch. and Soc.*, XIV, 72.

[163] *The Wesleyan Alumnae*, Oct. 1925, 3 ff.

[164] Article, *At. Mo.*, Nov. 1927, 577 ff.

[165] Barnard, Bryn Mawr, Chicago, Leland Stanford Junior, Massachusetts Institute, Northwestern, Radcliffe, Syracuse, Wesleyan, Western Reserve, and, of the state universities, California, Illinois, Kansas, Minnesota, Missouri and Nebraska, had been added to the eight charter members.

located in about thirty-five branches. Today there are 414 branches and 28,237 individual members.[166]

Since its founding, the Association has rendered valuable services to the cause of women's higher education in general, as well as to its individual members. Among the problems in which they have been interested, and on some of which they have made valuable reports, already referred to, are health of college women, women on coeducational faculties, endowment of colleges, college administration, withdrawals from college, development of home economics, admission to colleges, guidance of college women, and the founding of scholarships for women both at home and abroad.

In the question of scholarships and fellowships the Association took an early interest. Though women's colleges have been steadily increasing since 1875, and coeducational facilities, too, have been vastly increased, the provision of endowments and stipends of one form and another for women has by no means been liberal. The Commissioner's *Report* for 1891–2[167] pointed out that there was a marked discrimination against women in this respect. In 1889, of the colleges for women, Bryn Mawr was the only one provided with fellowships. This institution had six foundations, one with an annual income of $500, available for a year's residence and study at a foreign university. The other five gave free tuition, free room, and a stipend of $350 yearly.[168]

In 1907, the total number of scholarships in women's colleges, "Division A," was 614; in those of "Division B," 257. There were thirty-three fellowships reported for the sixteen institutions of "Division A" and five for the 110 institutions in "Division B."[169] The women of the South, where nearly seventy per cent. of the "B Colleges" were located, were very poorly provided for, and efforts were made to encourage such foundations.[170]

In 1889, the Association of Collegiate Alumnae proposed to devote "$500 every year towards paying the expenses of some young woman who wishes to carry on her studies in a foreign

166 Letter, Executive Secretary, Nov. 4, 1927.

167 P. 796.

168 *R. C. E.*, 1888–9, I, 654.

169 See Table I, p. 187.

170 Tuttle: A Plea for Scholarships for the Young Women of the South [*Jour. A. C. A.*, Feb. 1906, 24–5].

country.'' The candidate was to be a graduate of an associated institution, give promise of genuine distinction, and be approved by a committee of seven members named to make the award.[171] Other fellowships were added, and a report of the work of the thirty-one women who had held them was presented in the *Twenty-Fifth Annual Report*.[172] In 1914, the Association listed five fellowships, two available for foreign study and three for study in Europe or the United States.[173] In 1921, when the Association of Collegiate Alumnae was consolidated with the Southern Association of College Women, the name was changed to the American Association of University Women.[174] At that date there were 96 institutions whose graduates were eligible to membership. This organization announced eleven fellowships to be awarded to women for 1927–28, and three for the year following.[175] The whole number of fellowships awarded by the American Association of University Women is fifteen.

The scope of the Association's work today was summarily described by Mina Kerr, in 1924, as follows:

''(1) Provides, through local branches, scholarships for undergraduate women in colleges and universities; (2) administers and awards eleven scholarships for graduate work in the United States and in foreign countries; (3) improves, by the stimulus of recognition on an accredited list of institutions the conditions for women students in physical education, medical supervision, housing and social life; (4) upholds, by the pressure of the accredited list of colleges, women members of faculties in getting proper salary, promotion and tenure; (5) encourages international relationships among university women, by exchange of

[171] *R. C. E.* (1888–9), I, 654.

[172] *Jour. Assoc. Coll. Alumnae,* Feb. 1907, 74 *ff.*

[173] *Ibid.,* Jan. 1914, 9 *ff.*

[174] Letter, Executive Secretary, Nov. 4, 1927.

[175] *Sch. and Soc.* (Nov. 13, 1926), XXIV, 606. They were: Alice Freeman Palmer Memorial Fellowship, $1500; Sarah Berliner Research and Lecture Fellowship, $1000 to $1200; Anna C. Brackett Memorial Fellowship, $1000; Mary Pemberton Nourse Memorial Fellowship, $1500; Gamma Phi Beta Social Service Fellowship, $500; Phi Mu Fellowship, $1000; Boston Alumnae Fellowship, $800; A. A. U. W. European Fellowship, $1500; Margaret E. Maltby Fellowship, $1500; A. A. U. W. Fellowship, $1500; A. A. U. W. International Fellowship, $1500; Alpha Xi Delta, $1000; Rose Sidgwick Memorial Fellowship, $2000; and the Julia C. G. Platt Memorial Fellowship, $1000.

professors and fellows, by a biennial international convention, and by the exchange of information and courtesy; (6) supports a national and international club house in Washington, D. C., as a center for work and fellowship among university women of the United States and foreign countries; (7) publishes a magazine devoted to information and discussion concerning subjects of interest and importance to university women; (8) suggests educational policies for national work, prepares an educational program for over 250 local branches of the association, and carries on educational research, through the office of an educational secretary; (9) stimulates university women to continue intellectual growth after graduation, and to contribute to the welfare of their communities; [and] (10) maintains a national headquarters in Washington, D. C., for the business of the association, for cooperation with other national organizations, and for a center of information and of service to university women.''[176]

The Association has, at certain periods, given its attention to the problems of special current interest. This ready yielding to demands of the day is reflected in the program of the Portland Convention, according to which the Association was to devote five to ten years to study of public elementary education and the revision of its curriculum, the education of women in liberal arts colleges, promotion and tenure of college and university faculties, problems of pre-school education, and international educational problems.

VI. Objectives of the Women's Colleges

The purposes of women's education in the United States may be systematically arranged under the following heads, according to their historical development: (1) preparation for home duties; (2) cultivation of formal gentility and grace for their social value, through a variety of accomplishments; (3) discipline of the "mental powers," so that women might be ready for any emergency in life; and (4) more specific preparation for a variety of professional opportunities.[177] Concurrent with all, except the last, there has been (5) a constant emphasis on religious and Christian purpose.

[176] *Sch. and Soc.*, XIX, 314.
[177] Vol. I, 311, 326, 377, 452, 460 *ff*.

These periodic purposes arose and had their day approximately as follows: the first prevailed in most early Colonial groups, and was accomplished, chiefly without the aid of schools. A home and husband were the divinely appointed ends for women, so they served an apprenticeship in cooking, sewing, sweeping, dusting, and bed-making.[178]

The first purpose was gradually superseded, after the middle of the eighteenth century, by the second, which prevailed, with but slight opposition, for three quarters of a century and dominated the practice of a vast majority of academies and seminaries till the middle of the nineteenth century. The sphere of women continued to be the home; the path to it, matrimony. But, in more prosperous families, it was felt that special encouragements to matrimony and preparation for the social world into which the husband would take the wife should be provided. The accomplishments that were added to the home training prepared the way for a formal or informal debut into the matrimonial market. With a hint at the story of the virgins who lighted their lamps and went out to meet the bridegroom, Abbot suggested that the maiden "went to school that she might light her lantern and better look for a husband."[179]

Largely because of dissatisfaction with the shallowness of showy accomplishments, partly, too, because of the general spread of disciplinary theory, Pestalozzianism, and the ideas of other educational reformers, with which we were becoming increasingly familiar, the third purpose, discipline gained from the pursuit of "solid" studies, was gradually accepted. Women must be prepared for "life"—not simply for "society." The disciplinary purpose appeared in the best seminaries, such as the Elias Marks' Female Academy (1820), Elizabeth Female Academy (1819), and those of Willard, Beecher, and Mary Lyon. It was vigorously advocated in the earliest educational periodicals, after 1826;[180] but found its universal acceptance in the earlier

---

[178] Abbott: Education of Women [in the *Woman's Book*, I, 344, 346–7]; see also Vol. I, Chapters IV, V, and VI on Colonial education.

[179] *Ibid.*, 339–40; Female Education, II, *Am. Annals of Educ.*, V, 314–16; see also Vol. I, Chapters VIII and IX.

[180] *Am. Journal Ed.*, I, 349–52, contained an argument for discipline in the education of females.

as well as in the later women's colleges.   The gradual infiltration
of disciplinary ideas into the seminaries has been noted.[181]   In
them, the new purpose caused no early and complete denial of
the education of social accomplishments; rather, the two developed side by side, the former rising into ascendancy, the latter
declining.

In the women's colleges, since they were endeavoring to offer
women the same facilities for higher education as were offered
to men, the accomplishments were renounced more promptly and
completely; in fact, in some they scarcely had a place, except
as electives; in others they did not appear at all.   Where music,
painting, and so on, were pursued in colleges, they stressed the
idea that the result was to be higher ethical culture (or even
professional development) rather than an accomplishment to be
paraded in the drawing room.[182]   As a rule, the general discipline of the faculties of the mind was heartily embraced as the
end of women's collegiate education.

Z. C. Graves, of the Mary Sharp College, declared the "aim
is not only to impart knowledge, but to direct for a time the
powers of the mind which this knowledge has nourished and
stimulated.   He [the teacher] marshals these powers, not for a
single field but for life's campaign.   Pupils should be taught
how to study, and that it is not the number of hours spent with
books in hand, but close thinking that secures thorough discipline, good lessons, and sound learning.''[183]   More explicitly,
the ends of learning are the ''power of fixing the mind,'' mastery
of elementary principles, precision of thought, power of language, acquisition of facts—the ''materials of thought''—to
cultivate the judgment and the memory, ''teaching the mind
how to take up a subject, investigate it and draw conclusions,''
and an understanding of where to go for information.[184]

Besides the proofs of the accepted disciplinary purpose, found
in the case of each individual institution, and which need not be
catalogued here, there is also the store of assertions made by

[181] Vol. I, 398 and 405 *ff*.

[182] For example, the cultivation of interest in drama, painting, and music
in American women's colleges, McCabe believed, might prove of large significance in American life—*American Girl at College*, notes on Chapter III.

[183] *Z. C. Graves and the Mary Sharp College*, 37.

[184] *Ibid.*, 58–9.

those writing for and against the college education of the past seventy-five years. *Godey's Lady's Book* voiced a severe criticism of the Vassar College course of study, which it reprinted, pointing out that "the system of education appears to be in many respects eminently a false one. It is based, not on a consideration of the real needs of the students, but on the semi-obsolete systems . . . [of] Oxford, Cambridge, Harvard and Yale. . . . The scientific course is much better . . . yet . . . leaves the impression that it was framed not so much with a view to the actual needs of the students . . . as with the idea of furnishing a well rounded scheme of study in the sciences and modern languages."[185] E. L. S., writing in *The Nation* (1879),[186] lamented the existing "want of reasoning capability, impetuosity in forming judgments," and other "unlovely" traits of the female sex; and expressed the belief that the most hopeful and practical way to remedy the weaknesses is by giving "our daughters the mental discipline and the breadth of outlook which young men get in a good college. . . ." Thwing set forth the supreme end of college education as "teaching the girl to think";[187] and Mrs. Agassiz appears to have had general discipline in mind when she spoke to Radcliffe students of the necessity of education to "enrich a woman's life, and help her in her appointed or her chosen work, whatever that may prove to be. . . ."[188] McCabe, too, declared the college was not tinctured with professional motives, but aimed "to impart to women through liberal studies, the discipline, the culture of the powers of observation, perception, reflection. . . ."[189]

Mere mental discipline, or ability to think, was not a sufficiently definite or practical objective for Catherine Beecher. In her proposals for an institution on the "college plan," she stressed the professional purpose of higher education; and the justice of this emphasis was recognized by the American Women's Education Association. In the formation of the Association (1852) and the influence of Miss Beecher may be seen the rise of the fourth purpose, professional preparation, which was destined,

185 April, 1870, 347–9, 382.
186 XXIX, 365.
187 The *School Journal*, LXVIII, 699.
188 *Journal of Ed.* (1897), XLV, 304–5.
189 *Am. Girl at College*, 4–5, 14.

after little more than a generation, to result in the honeycomb-ing of the curriculum of the liberal arts college, referred to by Dr. Thomas. The above reference to McCabe bears witness to the fact that the pressure of professionalization of courses was beginning to be felt. In 1852, the American Women's Associa-tion had approved of the college idea and professional prepara-tion.[190] The college came, but for the most part paid little heed, at the outset, to professions. Gradually, however, the college responded to the social need.

All colleges have been nurseries of teachers. Early women's college graduates often entered this field, but the colleges did not aim primarily at such professional preparation. Wellesley Col-lege is rather unique in that her first *Calendar* evinced a definite interest in the then profession of women (teaching) and instead of merely tolerating the professional spirit, encouraged it: "One prominent purpose in organizing the college has been to give peculiar advantages to students of limited means, who intend to prepare themselves to be teachers. . . . To assist . . . they are allowed to suspend their studies for a year for the pur-pose of teaching, and then to return and resume them and take their degrees."[191]

The professional purpose became more clearly discernible in the college education of women in the final decade of the nine-teenth century. This tendency to practical professional courses was most marked in coeducational institutions and coördinate women's colleges; in the separate women's colleges, the changes came more slowly. In the twentieth century, specialization and professionalization called forth sharp criticism from those who defended the disciplinary value of a general education. Anne C. E. Allinson, in 1907, expressed, in summary fashion, the view of these critics:

". . . The principle is the same whether the college recognizes self-support as the particular end of some students, or the details of domestic life as the particular end of others. That technical education in separate institutions or in added years may be a desirable supplement to college training, we are not interested in denying. But that the four precious years of 'liberal pur-

[190] Account of 3rd annual meeting—*Godey's Lady's Book,* Sept. 1855, 276–7.

[191] *Calendar,* 1876–77, 5.

suits' should be intruded upon is an educational blunder of the first magnitude. Yet the intrusion is stealthily made. Sweetness and light are unmarketable commodities. Pedagogy, household economics, and other lo heres and lo theres, if we but heed them, will make us 'practical.' Poetry, they tell us, does not remove the microbes of the pantry, neither does philosophy ventilate a school room. Therefore let literature and metaphysics be abandoned, while good housekeepers and good teachers are evolved.

"It is a significant fact that the separate colleges for women raise this cry less persistently than the women's colleges connected with men's universities, or than the coeducational universities. Among men the tendency toward an ultilitarian conception of education is obvious. Perhaps they exercise a late revenge in offering the apple of 'practical knowledge' to the Eves in their garden.

"A more idealistic plea does not disregard the fact that many girls in this vast country will need later to apply their powers to self-support. Neither does it disregard the fact that society must be efficiently served or homes well managed by the women who are to have no technical occupations, but are to be engaged in a work that is without money and without price. It rather seeks to cleave through the pedagogical fallacies that ideas should be applied coincidently with their acquisition, or that second-rate ideas can result in first-rate activities; and to urge the sacred truth that life in whatever form it is handled is greater than an easy matter of methods and of facts. The world itself, for all its clamor, unconsciously demands something better than mechanical equipment, for it gives its largest prizes, whether of position or of favor, to those who possess a personal power that is not the outcome of 'practical courses.' How much more clearly, then, should colleges see from the mountain peak what is only dimly surmised in the valley!"[192]

As stated above, the religious purpose is to be found throughout, but the earlier women's colleges stressed it more than the later. Georgia Female College was deeply affected by "a gracious revival in Macon";[193] the Wesleyan Female College at Cincin-

[192] Quoted from *The Nation*, LXXXIV, 151 *f.*

[193] Smith: *Life and Times of George Pierce*, 97; Pierce: Origin, Plan and Prospects of Georgia Female College [*So. Ladies Book*, I, 17].

nati, Ohio Wesleyan at Delaware, and the Female College of
Maine Wesleyan Seminary, at Kents Hill, Maine, were deeply
imbued with religious and sectarian interests. Mount Holyoke
College, the outgrowth of the seminary, was fed by the religious
fervor of Mary Lyon. Wellesley, in early years, was dominated
by Durant, whose change of heart and religious zeal had led
him to found it.[194] Candler, in 1889, called attention to the very
widespread influence of the churches in Southern female colleges.[195] In 1881, it was asserted that "with few exceptions they
[women's colleges] are conducted under the auspices of religious
denominations. . . ."[196] Twenty-five years later, thirteen of the
sixteen institutions listed in Division A were non-sectarian; but
of the one hundred and ten listed in Division B, only thirty-three
were non-sectarian, while seventy-seven were under sectarian
auspices.[197]

VII. Government of College Students

An interesting change has taken place in the government of
students since the earliest experiments with women's colleges.
The management of the student body in the earliest colleges was
patterned after that of the female seminary,[198] which was then at
its height. The seminary had many rules; so did most of the
early colleges; but in later institutions the idea of greater freedom, and even student government, began to appear.

Georgia Female College was an early exception to the general
rule. Discipline appears to have been mild and rules few, government being "founded on mutual confidence and affection between teacher and pupil."[199] Many rules, it was thought, would
"multiply offences." Young ladies were, however, compelled to
rise at sunrise and attend prayers in the chapel. It was stated
that "no difficulties" had arisen "of serious magnitude" and
that "acts of disorder" were of "the mischievous kind rather
than the rebellious—ebullitions of playful feeling—the giddy

194 Porter: *The Christian College*, an address at Wellesley, 1880.

195 Educational Progress in the South [*N. E. A. Proceedings*, 1889, 343];
see also Thwing: *Am. Colleges*, 64 *ff.*, for treatment of religious life at
women's colleges.

196 *R. C. E.*, 1881, CL–CLI.

197 See Table I, 186.

198 See Vol. I, 434–41.

199 *So. Ladies Book*, I, 1840, 65–74.

thoughtlessness of a spirit full of life, rather than the wicked disrespect of authority and rule.''[200]   Typical of the more general habit of fixing everything by a rule was the Wesleyan Female College, of Cincinnati. The rules published in 1857–8 follow :[201]

"Young Ladies are required to rise at the ringing of the bell—have their rooms in order by the time appointed—be prompt and regular at all their meals—retire, and have their lights extinguished by ten o'clock, P. M.

"No loud talking or laughing permitted in the rooms or halls, but that gentle deportment required which ever marks the refined lady.

"All 'nicknames,' by-words, and cant expressions are deemed highly unbecoming, and therefore will not be allowed.

"During study hours no unnecessary conversation allowed—no visiting in public or private rooms, and no reading or writing not directly required in school duty, without permission.

"Boarding pupils are not allowed to attend parties or picnics—to walk, ride, or correspond with any gentleman, other than father, brother, uncle, or guardian ; nor to be absent on the Sabbath, except with parents or near relatives.

"They must not, without permission from the Governess, leave the College premises, or make any purchases.

"They are not allowed to visit in the city or country, except in those families where the parents or guardians have, by note or otherwise, given their consent.

"They will receive all calls from those not resident in the family in the public parlor; and under no circumstances invite friends to their private rooms without permission from the Governess.

"Students are not permitted to receive calls from citizens except on Friday evening, and during Saturday. Friends residing out of the city they can see when most convenient. But they can not receive calls at any time from young gentlemen, other than very near relatives, except by the especial permission of parents or guardians, given to the President or Governess.

[200] *Ibid.*

[201] For similar lists, compare *The Sibleys* (Lindenwood College, St. Charles, Mo.), 26 *ff.;* Ohio Wesleyan Female College, *Catalog*, 1863, 19 *f.;* and Mary Sharp College, *Catalog*, 1861, 22–3.

"All are required to take daily exercise in the open air under the supervision of a teacher, and cultivate active and industrious habits in social as well as scholastic duties.

"Each one must be provided with an umbrella and pair of over-shoes, have every article of apparel fully and distinctly marked with her name, and discard all jewelry as a mere ornament from daily use. Indeed, they are most earnestly advised to leave at home all jewelry and expensive clothing, not only as troublesome, but injurious, and altogether unnecessary in a schoolgirl's outfit.

"No borrowing, lending, or exchanging any articles, except in peculiar cases, and then by permission only of the Governess.

"The occupants of rooms will be held responsible for all injury done to them or the furniture, as well as for any rudeness or impropriety in them.

"Under no circumstances can the duties of the week or letter or composition writing be permitted on the Sabbath.

"Calls upon the Sabbath are not allowed, except upon very urgent occasions.

"Each one must be furnished with a Bible, and, in usual health, attend church with the family at least once upon the Sabbath.

"Neatness in person, clothing, and room must be strictly observed at all times.

"Politeness and due respect must ever be manifested to teachers, companions, and all others with whom they are associated."[202]

The government of the students at Mary Sharp College in its earliest years was one of manifold prohibitions. Each day was begun with "a short moral lecture . . . to the pupils . . . by the president, upon some text of Scripture. . . . Right and wrong . . . [were] to be made the foundation of school discipline, and the pupils [were] carefully taught to govern themselves, thus early acquiring habits of self-reliance and independence of character." Pupils were forbidden to make purchases at stores without special permission of parents or guardians, and likewise forbidden to go out at night except "in special circumstances." All funds of the students had to be deposited

[202] Catalog, 1857–8, 31–2.

with the institution. For the rest of their conduct, it was to be according to the following specific rules:

"1st. No pupil will be permitted to sit up at night later than 10 o'clock, and in every instance, except in sickness, will be required to rise at 5 o'clock in the morning.

"2d. The pupils will be required to pay due regard to the counsel and advice of the heads of the family in which they reside.

"3d. No pupil will be permitted to leave her boarding house to spend nights or leisure days, without permission from one of the male members of the Faculty.

"4th. They will be disallowed to make or receive visits, to go to parties, or to entertain the company of young gentlemen, either in going to or from Church, or School, or at their boarding places.

"5th. They will not be permitted to go to the stores, or to make purchases, without being accompanied by one of the family in which they board.

"6th. They will be required to spend at least four hours in study out of school: two and a half at night, and one and a half in the morning."[203]

Nineteen regulations encircled the life of Elmira students in 1858. These covered attendance at college exercises, presence in their rooms, visiting kitchen and store rooms, making and receiving calls, study hours, walking, damage to furniture, use of gas and heat, inspection of rooms, order of rooms, borrowing ornaments or articles of dress, and the use of lamps, candles, pails, and pitchers. It was specially improper to visit "stores, shops, or other places of refreshment" without parent, guardian, or near relative; to "indulge in light and trifling conversation" or "visit each other's rooms" on the Sabbath; to "hold correspondence by writing with persons in the village"; and "to meet in companies in each other's rooms for purposes of festivity."[204]

It would appear that as more thought was given to physical health and as recreational facilities were more liberally afforded, there came a decrease in the number of stringent rules. It is, at least, true that at Vassar, where recreation and health were

[203] Mary Sharp College *Catalog*, 1858, 18–9.
[204] *Catalog*, 1858–9, 33 *f*.

given a conspicuous place, there were fewer hard and fast rules. The same was true, in general, of such later colleges as Wells, Wellesley, Smith, and Goucher.

Though student government gained a few friends in women's colleges in the latter part of the nineteenth century, it was most completely developed at Bryn Mawr, where the system was begun about 1891. All students were *ipso facto* members of the association for self government. They elected an executive committee, which had large responsibilities; it could recommend that members be not allowed to live in the college halls, or even that they be expelled. Such recommendation, Saunders stated, was equivalent to a sentence, though as a matter of form the decree was signed by the president of the college on behalf of the board of trustees.[205] Student government at Bryn Mawr grew out of the students' own desire and petition for it; consequently, it has had a genuine hold upon them. The control of conduct at the college has always been regarded by the authorities as subject to the same principles as the government of any democratic society. It was a great innovation, however; and the president of Harvard, upon first seeing it in operation, declared to Miss Thomas, "If this continues, I will give you two years, and no more, in which to close Bryn Mawr College."[206] The dire prophecy has not been fulfilled; and student government has been in continuous operation.

Just recently the genuineness of the democratic government at Bryn Mawr was tested and not found wanting. In many, probably most, women's colleges, as well as in coeducational institutions, girls' smoking had become a problem, frequently dealt with by the authorities in a wholly arbitrary manner.[207] Bryn Mawr shocked the women's collegiate world in the United States, particularly the West, by approving the student government's recommendation that smoking rooms be set aside, that those who wished might smoke without sneaking.[208] The move-

[205] Govt. of Women Students in College and University [*Ed. Rev.* (1900), XX, 478–80].

[206] Present Tendencies in Women's Education [*Ed. Rev.* (1908), **XXXV**, 68].

[207] See for example: *Ev. Public Ledger*, Nov. 27, 1925; Nov. 24, 1925; May 16, 1924; Apr. 26, 1926; Mar. 2, 1925.

[208] *Phila. Inquirer*, Dec. 9, 1925; Nov. 24, 1925; *Ev. Public Ledger*, Nov. 26, 1925; the question was reviewed by *The New Student*, Dec. 9, 1925.

ment to change the old regulation was led by a non-smoker, and supported by many of them; otherwise it could not have been adopted, for probably less than half the students smoke. The change was made as a concession to individual liberty, rather than to satisfy a universal desire for smoking. President Park defended her action, in approving the change, as necessary if student government is to mean anything:

"A change in the attitude toward smoking by women has come in twenty-five years and is naturally reflected among college students. A regulation prohibiting smoking can no longer depend on the authority of conscience and convention, which make up public opinion, and it is no longer effective in a self-governing commonwealth. Attempts to enforce it begin to affect their relations to other regulations otherwise unquestioned. I agree with the overwhelming majority of the Self-Government Association, a majority made up of many students who do not smoke themselves or wish to smoke, that no democracy can keep on its books a regulation which stands apart from its other regulations in that it is no longer resting solidly on intelligent public opinion."[209]

The idea of student government spread to many women's and coeducational institutions. In 1908, Miss Thomas asserted it was "working well in thirteen eastern colleges where women study" and she believed it was "destined to spread."[210] Some form of student participation in government exists in most women's colleges to-day, though frequently to a rather limited extent. Baldwin, Greene, and Messner found, for example, in 1915, that some of the best colleges did not favor the honor system in examinations.[211] In some places, it was felt that too much individual freedom had been granted and that greater, rather than less, restraints should be imposed.[212]

VIII. Effect of College Education on Women

In many ways it is clear that early college education of women had results. Women were prepared to be teachers of seminaries

209 [Phila.] *Sunday Ledger*, Jan. 3, 1926.
210 *Ed. Rev.* (1908), XXXV, 68.
211 *Status of the Honor System*, 20–1.
212 Jordan: Home and Student Government [*Phila. Inquirer*, Dec. 8, 1926].

and high schools in large numbers; they were, undoubtedly, personally benefitted by more extended culture; socially and politically, they were better able to stand independently and with new self-assurance;[213] and, financially, a college education came to have a more definite value, though at first college girls had some difficulty in turning it to use.[214]   That a college education had little to do with great personal achievements to 1886, was pointed out by Thwing, who found but nineteen college women in a total of 633 who had been listed in Appleton's *Cyclopedia of American Biography.*[215]

While these results were useful to the individuals concerned, enabling them to secure a much greater degree of freedom from the usual limited sphere of woman, other evil results were anticipated by those who opposed women's entrance to college.   Dr. Eliot recalled, in 1908, the fears that women could not master the traditional studies; that their health would fail, and their womanly nature be destroyed.   All these expected results failed to make an appearance after college education had been given a fairly long trial.[216]

When the predicted results of women's collegiate education did not appear, a new and more terrible outcome was discerned, which many had not even anticipated: the decline in the marriage rate of college women, and the decline of the birth rate in alumna's family.   This fact, real or apparent, has been much discussed since 1895, interest in it being so great that editors have accepted all kinds of essays on the subject.   The bulk of the literature is purely opinion and scarcely worth review. Some significant papers have been published, however, scientific in character, which have pointed out other more reasonable causes of decline in marriage and birth rates.   The leading views on both sides of the subject are presented below.

213 Miss Wooley discussed influence on character [*Jour. A. C. A.* (1905), 10].

214 Compare the figures of Abbott: Generation of College Women [*Forum* (1895), XX, 377–84]; most women entered teaching, writing, and advanced study.

215 What Becomes of College Women [*N. A. R.*, Nov. 1895, 546–53].

216 Catt: The Home and the Higher Education [*N. E. A. Proc.*, 1902, 100]; *Jour. A. C. A.*, Jan. 1908, 101–5; the question of physical health of women has been dealt with in Chapter III of this volume.

First, let us begin with the prevailing opinions, some of which seem to have taken very seriously an old Oxford rhyme:

"'Who will marry you, my pretty maid?'
"'Advanced women don't marry, sir,' she said."

Others seem to have been sure that should a college woman marry, her education would immediately be lost.[217] As a rule, however, there was a general agreement that women would be lost to the race rather than education lost to her. Münsterberg declared, not long ago, that "from whatever side we look at it, the self assertion of woman exalts her at the expense of the family—perfects the individual but injures society, makes the American woman perhaps the finest flower of civilization, but awakens at the same time serious fears for the propagation of the American race."[218]

Johnson and Stutzmann, writing of "Wellesley's Birth-rate," were of the opinion that "there are at least three causes for this abnormally low birth-rate: lack of coeducation; the failure of their education to make them desirous of having homes of their own and efficient in these homes; [and] excessive limitation of the student's opportunities for social life."[219] A. L. Smith wrote in 1904:

"First of all, is education being carried on at present to such a degree as to at all affect the bodily or physical health of women? This is an important question, because the duties of wifehood, and still more of motherhood, do not require an extraordinary development of brain, but they must absolutely have a strong development of body. Not only does wifehood and motherhood not require an extraordinary development of brain, but the latter is a decided barrier against the performance of these duties. Any family physician could give innumerable cases, out of his experience, of failures of marriage directly due to too great a cultivation of the female intellect, which results in the scorning to perform those duties which are cheerfully performed and even desired by the uneducated wife."[220]

Dr. Smith claimed most ill health was due to "over education" because it takes blood to the brain which is needed for muscular

[217] Higginson: *Women and Men*, 232–3.
[218] Münsterberg: *The Americans*, 583.
[219] *Jour. of Heredity*, June, 1915, 250–3.
[220] *Pop. Sci. Mo.*, LXVI, 467.

and generative organs; it overdevelops the nervous system, causes women to lead abnormal lives, and not to marry till twenty-six or twenty-seven, if at all, whereas they ought to marry at eighteen; finally, education raises women's standards so high that no man can afford to marry them. He is so much impressed with this tendency that he apparently approves of the advice of Punch, to those about to marry: "Don't."

D. C. Wells, writing on some questions relating to higher education of women, in 1909, concluded that "to speak plainly, children have become, to many women, a nuisance, or at least unwelcome beings of an alien domestic world, which years of intellectual training have unfitted the college woman to like or understand. Their environment has awakened their interests and then these imperious interests dominate their lives. Various as are the causes of this low birth rate, the effect is a comparative sterilization of presumably superior stocks. This . . . is sure to become alarming with the growth of the college habit among girls.' "[221]

This terrifying influence of education on the family has been commented on for more than a century.[222] "Why don't people marry? Why are there so many antiquated damsels and superannuated bachelors?" The answer is that it results from "errors of education" and "extravagance of fashion." This was in 1819.[223] By the end of the century, scientists were counting noses to see if the college influence on the family was really as bad as depicted. Gordon showed (1895) that out of an entire group of seven hundred and twenty, only 120 married; and, at Girton, only forty-six out of three hundred and thirty-five married. The conclusions were (1) that those who went to college were more likely to become teachers than wives; (2) that those who took pass courses were more likely to marry than those who took honors courses; (3) women became more "particular" in choosing a husband; and (4), being independent, they avoided uncongenial marriages.[224]

[221] *Am. Jour. Sociology*, XIV, 731–9; and a similar article by Linton: The Higher Education of Women [*Pop. Sci. Mo.*, Dec. 1886, XXX, 168–80].

[222] Westermarck: *Short History of Marriage*, 51–2.

[223] An article quoted in the *Ladies' Magazine* (Savannah, Ga.) 1819, from the *National Advocate*.

[224] Gordon: After Careers of College Women [*Nineteenth Century* (June, 1895), XXXVII, 955–60].

Millicent W. Shinn, in 1895, studied the records of 1805 members of the Association of Collegiate Alumnae and came to about the same conclusions as Gordon as to the causes of the lower marriage rate.[225] She found that only 28.2 per cent. married, —compared with about 80 per cent. for women, over twenty, in the country at large. This comparison, she pointed out, did not, however, represent the whole truth; for, if we take those over twenty-five years of age, 32.7 per cent. are married; of those past thirty, 43.7 per cent. are married; of those past thirty-five, 49.7 per cent.; while of those beyond forty years, 54.5 per cent. are married. Truly, then, one must compare a marriage rate of 55 per cent. for college women with that of 80 to 90 per cent for the non-collegians. Among other facts, the study showed that only 25.7 per cent. of those from the separate woman's college married, compared with 32.6 per cent. of coeducational graduates. Percentages in each group, from twenty-five to forty, were higher in the case of graduates of coeducational than in separate colleges. Studied by location, the figures showed that only 26.6 per cent. of those graduated from colleges of the North Atlantic section married, as compared with 37.1 per cent. of those graduated in the middle Western colleges. Finally, Miss Shinn concluded that the low marriage rate was not due to a desire for an exciting career, for most of the members became school teachers! She felt, however, that subsequent occupation,—becoming a resident teacher in a girls' boarding school,—was a very effective bar to marriage. In the West, where graduates taught chiefly in public high schools, marriages were more frequent. As to college women, Miss Shinn believed them a "more conspicuous success as mothers than in any other calling they have tried; . . . it is doubtless here, and not in the learned professions, in letters or in public life, that the main effect of the higher education of women is to be looked for."[226] A few years later she would possibly have modified her belief about their success in professions, letters, and public life.[227]

Frances M. Abbott studied a generation of Vassar College women,[228] including 1,082, of whom 409, or nearly 38 per cent.,

[225] Marriage Rate of College Women [*Century* (Oct. 1895), L, 546–8].
[226] *Ibid.*
[227] Compare Felter: Educ. of Women [*Ed. Rev.* (1906), XXXI, 360 *ff.*]; and an article in *Education* (1902), XXII, 351–62.
[228] *Forum* (Nov. 1895), XX, 377–84.

had married. She, too, pointed out, as did Miss Shinn, that college girls marry late; "but", as Maria Mitchell added, "they marry well." Of the first graduating class of Vassar, (4) 75 per cent. married; of the second class, (25) 60 per cent. married; of the third class, (34) 62 per cent. married; and of the fourth class, about the same per cent. Taken all together, 63 per cent. of the graduates of the first four classes had married at the end of twenty-five years.[229]

Hall and Smith, after studying marriage and fecundity of college men and women, came to the conclusion that "although the marriage rates are higher for men than for women graduates, the disparity is far less than was supposed. Indeed, considering the facts that in our social system man makes the advances and that woman is by nature more prone than man to domesticity and parenthood, it is not impossible that men's colleges do more to unfit for these than do those for women."[230]

In the more recent studies of the facts, which have continued to show about the same per cent. of marriages as were set forth in the earlier investigations, there has been a decided denial of a causal relation between attendance at college and tendency to remain unmarried or have small families. Mary Roberts Smith compared 343 college-bred and married women with 313 of their married relatives and friends, but found mostly negative results: ". . . that there is by no means the degree of difference between the two classes in the matters of health, marriage and child-bearing capacity that has been looked for both by the friends and by the enemies of the college education of women."[231] Emerick pointed out that the causal relation had not been proved and that it probably did not exist. The significant fact is that alumnae of women's colleges are chiefly native stock and come from parents who are wealthier than the average. It is well known that this native stock and the upper classes do not marry as often or have as large families as the foreign poorer families. Emerick declared that "due allowance should be made for the fact that in entering college women give expression to their circumstances, ideals and character as well as subject them-

229 *Ibid.*
230 *Ped. Sem.* (1903), X, 273–314.
231 *Publication American Statistical Association* (1900–1), VII, 1–26.

selves to certain formative influences."[232] Statistics do not reveal a causal connection between the two sets of facts, and "the results at which some writers arrive can be reached only by reading into statistical data the conclusions they wish to show."[233] Later he published the conclusion that "the diminishing birth rate is primarily volitional, and that the various factors which make for involuntary sterility are of minor importance."[234]

Thorndike, in 1903, published figures for Middlebury, Wesleyan, New York University, and Harvard showing a gradual decline in the size of families of college graduates from 1803 to 1879. Middlebury's figures were the most complete, showing a decline from an average of 5.9 children per family (1803–1809) to 1.8 children (1875–1879). The averages were based on sufficiently large numbers of families to be reliable; and while figures for all other institutions were not as complete as Middlebury's, the tendency revealed was substantially the same. Thorndike recounted the reasons generally assigned to explain the decrease, including voluntary restriction, but concluded "that the changes in distribution actually found decade by decade have far more likeness to those that would result from a decrease in fertility than to those that would result from restriction."[235]

Engelmann, using Thorndike's figures and others, showing a decline in the size of families since 1700, concluded: "Family shrinkage seems clearly referable to the strenuous nerve wracking life of the day, to the struggle, not for existence, but for a luxurious existence, to the ever-increasing desire for the luxuries of life and morbid craving for social dissipation and advancement. . . . Let us no longer beat about the bush and attribute the low fecundity now prevailing to later marriages and higher education."[236]

The general conclusion of the whole matter seems to be: "If only half of the college women marry it is because they come

[232] College Women and Race Suicide [*Polit. Sci. Quart.* (1909), XXIV, 269–83].

[233] *Ibid.*

[234] *Pop. Sci. Mo.* (1911), LXXVIII, 71–80.

[235] *Pop. Sci. Mo.*, LXIII, 64–70; see also Alumna's Children [*Pop. Sci.* (1904), LXV, 45–51].

[236] Education Not the Cause of Race Decline [*Pop. Sci. Mo.* (1903), LXIII, 172–84]; compare Russell: *Why Men Fight*, 195–6; Caullery: *Universities in the U. S.*, 84 *ff.*; Thwing: *Higher Ed. in America*, 352–3.

from a social class in which only half of the women marry.''[237]
As Jordan said: "There is not the slightest evidence that highly
educated women are necessarily rendered sterile or celibate by
their education. . . .''[238] Another author has said that "educated women are not shunning marriage or maternity; but they
are declining to view matrimony as a profession, as their sole
vocation, or to become merely childbearing animals. Let us not
worry about the destiny of college women. It is simply wrong
wedlock which they are avoiding.''[239] Companionate marriage,
many think, may remove some of the difficulties that stand in the
way of old-fashioned marriage.[240]

IX. Reaction Against a "College Like a Man's"

In a certain sense it might be said that women's colleges were
founded as places where women might prove their minds. It
was generally believed they were not capable of such discipline
as were men's.[241] Therefore, an effort was made to establish a
rigid curriculum, as much like the men's colleges as possible.
Women came and demonstrated they were not inferior. But
scarcely had the women's colleges succeeded fully in imitating
the men's, when numerous criticisms were made of this policy.
Some of these have been referred to specifically.[242] These critics
wanted to know why such a straight-laced curriculum was so
strictly followed; why education especially designed to meet the
needs of women was not provided. Surely, it was said, they did
not need to swallow so many lexicons and grammars or master
the intricacies of differential and integral calculus in order to
learn how to operate a household, bring up children, or even to
prepare themselves for newly opening professions.

The first release from slavery to the rigidly fixed curriculum
was provided in the questioning and gradual overthrow of the
theory of formal discipline. With it, in the last twenty-five
years of the past century, came a progressive—but sometimes
grudging—acceptance of the elective system. More recently the

---

237 *The Nation,* Apr. 24, 1890, 330–1.
238 *Munsey's Mag.,* XXXIV, 683 *ff.*
239 Hollister: *The Woman Citizen,* 90.
240 Lindsey: *Companionate Marriage.*
241 See pp. 154 *ff.*
242 See p. 216.

demands of professional life, into which women have increasingly entered, have given impetus to a belief on the part of many, that the woman's colleges should map out work, a part of which at least should serve as pre-vocational preparation. The colleges themselves, however, conservative like other institutions, have moved but slowly in this direction. Dr. Zook, in 1923, pointed out the failure of the liberal arts colleges in regard to meeting vocational needs:[243]

"No real change in the curriculum has been made as a result of the new social and economic demands for women workers or the young women's own eagerness to meet their responsibilities either by Mount Holyoke or Wellesley. A possible change is pending at Wellesley since there is a faculty committee considering vocational training. Wellesley College has shown an interest in vocational education in the publication of a bulletin in 1918 on *Occupations toward which Wellesley College Courses may Lead.*"

Dr. Zook continued:

"A large percentage of the graduates of women's colleges in Massachusetts enter some gainful occupation, or become homemakers or both." But "there is a very low correlation between the major subjects taken in college and the occupation pursued by the women graduates of Massachusetts colleges, except in the case of teaching and among the graduates of Simmons College." Technical and vocational courses, such as fit the needs of women, are "limited in kind and restricted to a few of the colleges, Simmons College and the Massachusetts Institute of Technology offering the most varied choice." A change is to be seen, however, in the post-graduate training for social work at Smith and in Wellesley's suggestion "that students select their courses with a view to promoting their professional or vocational interests subsequent to graduation." Nevertheless it is obvious that "facilities for the higher education of young women along vocational lines are at present inadequate. . . ."[244]

There are at least three ways in which this need may be met: (1) by transforming the women's colleges' offerings; (2) by development of intelligent guidance programs in them; and (3)

---

[243] *Report of the Commission for an Investigation Relative to Opportunities . . . for Technical and Higher Education* [in *Massachusetts House Document*, No. 1700, Dec. 26, 1923].

[244] *Ibid.*

by the creation of new institutions designed not to imitate some existing college, but to prepare women to do what they want to do, assuming at least a fair degree of natural fitness therefor.

Some changes in existing colleges have been brought about; others seem certain to follow. The need for guidance and placement has been felt; but it is increasingly necessary that the women's colleges give attention to intelligent choice of work, correlation of studies with it, and the placement of graduates. Free election of subjects does not solve questions as readily as the early protagonists of election thought. It may be very bad for the student. Flexner has pointed out, truly enough, that once a right course has been chosen, there is no longer any choice for the student; for it is not to be expected that a student can construct a better course of study, toward some vocational end, than those who are older and more experienced.[245] Already there is here and there a tendency to swing towards fundamental courses, having definite objectives rather than the general objective of culture, but which do not exclude the latter. Some say, "Let us make use of the powerful vocational motive and we shall find better work in every study that is taken up." But to choose between courses with vocational objectives, students need guidance; there is no longer one road, but many. The students themselves feel the need keenly enough. About ten years ago an inter-collegiate conference was called and attended by representatives of twenty-eight colleges, both coeducational and for women only, east of the Mississippi. In 1919, a constitution was adopted, which declared the purpose of the association to be "to facilitate the interchange of vocational information; to hold an annual conference on vocational subjects of interest to college women; to study vocational opportunities for college women; and to further the cooperation of appointment bureaus and students." Numerous institutions became affiliated with this organization, though it was without faculty assistance or supervision.[246]

What is vocational guidance for college women supposed to do? Miss Leigh's statement is fairly representative. After setting aside the faulty notion of guidance as a ready-made system for

[245] Flexner: *The American College*, 125.
[246] Leigh: Voc. Guidance for College Women [*Ed. Rev.* (1921), LXII, 43–4].

telling one at once what she will be able to do in life, she stated the nature of guidance and its purposes to be as follows:

"It is assisting a girl to make the necessary adjustment between education and work after graduation; it is supplying her with the broad knowledge of openings and their demands that will serve as background for an intelligent choice; it is bridging over the gap between life in college and life outside; it is helping a girl to make the best possible correlation between the subjects studied in college and the vocation chosen; it is saving from one to ten years of wasteful experiment, while a girl tries herself out in one thing after another; it is a continuous process designed 'to help the girl to choose, to plan her preparation for, to enter upon and to make progress in an occupation'; it is enhancing the cultural aim of the college by introducing a high type of vocational appeal; it is a conscious attempt to guide a girl into the best position she can fill in view of her training and background; and, in the last analysis, it is a means of helping a girl to be her own guide under the best conditions for efficiency that human experience can provide.'"[247]

How is guidance generally carried on? Generally, through deans of women, but specially prepared vocational advisors have increased greatly in the past ten years; in many places little is done save by an employment bureau. Although the methods employed still range from the "common sense, applied in patch work fashion, to the very latest word in forward-looking, scientific method," the latter is undoubtedly on the increase.[248] It is evident from the complicated nature of the problem that it needs the service of a staff as much as the teaching of any subject in the college course. The head of vocational service must eventually be recognized as one of the faculty, must handle such course or courses as are needed to open up vocational opportunities, and bring the professor into as intimate a knowledge of the whole group of students as possible. There must be a liberal allotment of time for personal interviews. Otherwise guidance cannot be brought above the level of the land-office-like operations of appointment bureaus, which reckon their success chiefly, if not wholly, by the number of positions filled.

[247] Ibid., 36–7.
[248] Ibid., 39–40.

The third means, a new college, is also to be given one trial at least. New England, already the mother of many of the best women's institutions, will have a new college at Old Bennington, Vermont. Being sponsored by several leading progressive educators of the day, such as Professor William Heard Kilpatrick, Dr. Frank P. Graves,[249] President Neilson of Smith, and Dr. Willystine Goodsell of Teachers College, all of whom have been deeply concerned directly or indirectly with women's education for the past generation, and a committee of nineteen others, it is to be expected that the new institution will not seek to imitate the old, except where reason so directs. A few, at least, would turn the light of science on the colleges, even as it is being turned on the elementary and secondary schools; others see the newly proposed college as one which shall be free to offer higher education to girls who do not, necessarily, possess capacities and desires for higher mathematics or ancient languages.

With the support of friends of Bennington College, a survey of curriculum problems has been prepared by Amy Kelly, after personal visitation of "every College and University in America where promising educational experiments" have been recently tried out, as well as the women's colleges of Oxford and Cambridge. Her conclusions are embodied in *A Curriculum to Build a Mental World: A Proposal for a College of Liberal Arts for Women.*[250] In brief, the central theme of the pamphlet is *integration*, which, it is felt, must be reintroduced into college education to counteract recent disintegrating tendencies and specialization. An effort is made to sketch the features and estimate the values of such experiments as at Reed College and the University of Wisconsin; the tutorial system at Radcliffe, Harvard, and Princeton; the survey courses in contemporary civilization at Columbia, Chicago, and elsewhere; Antioch College; the experiment of Dr. Meiklejohn at Amherst; and the Oxford system in various places. All these indicate a revolt

249 In an editorial [*Ed. Rev.*, Feb. 1924, 98] which tersely characterized the development of women's colleges since the earliest foundations were laid, the *Educational Review* raised the significant question: "May we not venture the hope that some serious attention will be given to the curriculum of the new college and that it will be based upon recognized principles of education?" and proceeded to urge that a scientific study of the problem be made before answering the question.

250 Baltimore, 1927.

against the piecemeal "course," "subject," "department," "major," "elective," "prerequisite," and other well known causes of chronic indigestion of college students of today. The remedy, in the new college, as far as this pamphlet outlines it tentatively, would be an orientation course in each of the following great schools or divisions: physical sciences, life sciences, institutions (social sciences), languages, aesthetics, and philosophy.[251] "The six orientation courses and the study of 'personal fitness and human relationships' would be the only definite provisions for background or distribution, and the only requirements fixed alike for all. . . . For concentration a student would in general elect specialization in a school," or division.[252] Within the school, for the student specializing therein, there would be an orientation course, prerequisites, and adequate definition and mastery of the tools of the field. The purpose, however, is not to "lead, like the program of the University, to the practice of a vocation or profession," for it is to be in fact a liberal arts college. It is recognized, nevertheless, that the "liberal arts college . . . should and commonly does perform the important incidental service of indicating where some of these [vocational] values may be found, and of helping students to assemble from the whole program courses relevant to their vocational aims."[253]

Robert Devore Leigh, who has been identified with progressive movements in collegiate education, has been named President of the new institution. A brief announcement has just stated that, so far as educational policy is concerned, emphasis will be placed "on the individual student and her expanding interests, learning through activity and living, a curriculum planned for women in the modern world, organization of community life

[251] Apropos of Miss Kelly's formulation of the curriculum of the new Woman's College, designating certain "schools" of subject matter, it is interesting to note the marked similarity between her suggestion and the practice of the University of Virginia; and of Mary Sharp College, which, several decades ago, recognized the same divisions: School of Philosophy, School of Ancient Languages, School of Mathematics, School of Natural Science, the School of English—*Catalog*, 1885–86—the School of Music, the School of Art, and the School of Modern Languages,—the last three, listed as independent of the college course; and the original plan of studies, organized according to "schools," presented by Milo P. Jewett at Vassar.

[252] *Op. cit.*, 37.

[253] *Ibid.*, 44–5.

designed to break down the artificial barriers between teacher
and student and between curriculum and extra-curriculum [and]
a conscious elasticity in educational plans."[254]

X. Criticism of the Women's College

Criticism of the woman's college has dealt chiefly with the
following questions: the undermining of mental and physical
health, the imitation of the man's college, and the failure to
imitate the man's college. The first has been touched upon in
discussing physical education as related to the health of college
women.[255]

Imitating, and failing to imitate, the man's college has called
forth two sets of critics, each taking sides, according as they
wished to see women educated exactly like men, or given studies
considered especially suitable to women. These criticisms are,
in fact, but two sides of the one question: What shall the
woman's college teach? In the formative period of the women's
colleges, the imitation of the men's curriculum was derided or
praised, according to taste; in later years, the question appeared
in a clearer light as the struggle between the proponents of a
liberal education and those who desired professional specialization.

The need for a professional education was stressed by some of
the earliest critics. Beecher felt that the higher seminaries
"too closely copied" the course of study of men's colleges.[256]
Mrs. Child declared, "Our girls have no *home* education."
They are educated in schools where "no feminine employments,
no domestic habits, can be learned."[257] Such attacks were made
upon the colleges directly when it was seen that the most wealthy
of all of them had adopted a course of study as nearly like the
best men's colleges as possible. Beecher, in her *Reminiscences,*
declared: ". . . The 'curriculum' . . . is very nearly the same
as that of Yale and Cambridge and nothing withdrawn or added
with reference to the preparation of woman for her distinctive
profession as housekeeper, mother, nurse, and chief educator of
infancy and childhood. Nor is there any recognition of the addi-

254 *Official Circular,* 1928.
255 See p. 116.
256 *True Remedy,* 56–8.
257 *Godey's Lady's Book* (July, 1853), 86.

tional demands on a young woman from which the young man is free.''[258] This same criticism of a lack of attention to professional needs was made by Horace Greeley.[259] Beecher carried her criticisms of the imitative tendency further, remarking upon the evil effect of having only men on the board of trustees, a man for president, and only two women teachers (six men), only one of whom had ''any experience in teaching or governing young girls. . . .''[260] She quoted with approval, and very rightly too, Agassiz's criticism of our colleges in general, which she thought even more of a fault in the new colleges for women:

''The fact that there is no university in the United States *the intellectual* interests of which are managed by the professors, but *always by a corporation outside,* shows that we do not understand what a university is. The men who are *in it* must know better what are the wants of an institution than outsiders. Every college is got up by outsiders and has *their* curriculum and the professors have to teach that.''[261]

Godey's Lady's Book (1866) sums up: ''To that *half* education which our countrywomen now receive—the education in science and ornamental arts—add the education in useful arts and domestic knowledge necessary to fit them for the duties of their proper sphere, and they will not merely be, as at present, the 'queens of society,' but will be far better, the adored rulers of well-ordered and happy households.''[262] The editors noted with pleasure a promise of improvement, in the fact that Vassar's prospectus proposed a ''department of Domestic Education,'' which would receive special attention. But four years later, though they found ''much to admire,'' they feared ''the munificent provision made by the lamented founder, may not produce the beneficial results . . . expected from it . . .'' for the system is eminently ''a false one,'' *not* based on the real needs of the students.[263]

Until fairly recent years the women's college took small cognizance of these criticisms, though the effect of the elective

258 P. 184.
259 P. 115, Vol. I.
260 *Reminiscences,* 184.
261 *Ibid.,* 182.
262 March, 1866, 278–9.
263 *Godey's Lady's Book,* April, 1870, 347–9; also 382.

system was such that women were able to select more practical
studies than they could have done otherwise. The failure to
respond readily to demands of the professionally-minded accounts for the fact that this type of criticism runs throughout
the period of early colleges and down to the present. Elizabeth
Bisland lamented (1894) that women entered "life's calling
absolutely unprepared by any special training."[264] Starrett
related the experience of four Vassar graduates returning home.
with nothing to do and unable to enter any profession—a $3,000
education to do work in a house which a moderately paid servant
could do as well.[265]   Girls should have occupations when they
graduate and should, of course, be prepared for them. The
same demand for professional education, the same dissatisfaction
with the imitation of the classical course of men's colleges, was
voiced by Felter, Sachs, and McMurry in the first decade of the
twentieth century.[266]   Sachs declared: "I am sure that the need
of great modifications in the present college courses of women
is fully realized in more than one instance, but each individual
head of a college seems reluctant to incur the odium that at first
attaches to a radical change of front."

But a few years ago Agnes L. Rogers found that four classes,
studied at Goucher College, showed ". . . a marked tendency
to select the humanistic studies. It is especially noteworthy that
relatively few women are concentrating in the natural sciences
and that almost half are majoring in the social sciences."[267]
Substantially the same facts were reported by Dr. Thomas in
the case of Bryn Mawr College.[268]

Dealey, too, pointed out the neglect of sciences and professional courses at Smith, Wellesley, and Vassar:

"There is a clear lack of interest in the study of Education.
At neither Wellesley nor Smith is Education elected by at least
one-half the students of a given class, while the majority of those
electing in the department limit themselves to a year's work.
Vassar has merely a semester course hidden away in the depart-

264 *No. Am. Rev.*, CLIX, 628.

265 Starrett: *After College What?* (1896).

266 Felter: Education of Women [*Ed. Rev.* (1906), XXXI, 351–2]; Sachs:
Intellectual Reactions of Coeducation [*Ed. Rev.* (1908), XXXV, 467–9];
McMurry's criticism in *Am. Educ. Rev.*, XXXIV, 447.

267 What Women in Colleges Specialize in [*Sch. & Soc.*, XX, 700–2].

268 *Ed. Rev.* (1908), XXXV, 72–3.

ment of Philosophy. The important practical branch of Educational Hygiene, for instance, seems entirely neglected at these colleges.

"Vassar leads in the emphasis on Psychology, with more than six times the number of courses elected at Wellesley and Smith, exclusive of their requirement. On the other hand, the total number of courses, exclusive of requirements, elected in Philosophy at Wellesley approximates those of Smith and Vassar combined.

"With the exception of a few courses at Smith, the science of Sociology is sadly neglected. The perusal of any good text of Sociology should eliminate the fallacy that other subjects of less value should have precedence in the quantity and quality of courses.

"Little importance is yet attached to the Science departments. This contention is supported by the lack of concentration in the sciences, by the slight attention devoted by students of Phi Beta Kappa grade and by the relatively small percentage of students electing science work beyond the requirement."[269]

In 1885, Jane Bancroft called attention to law, journalism, industrial branches of the fine arts, architecture, medicine, pedagogy, and several fields of science—biology, chemistry and physics—as professions into which college-bred women should be able to go.[270] M. M. Whitney also urged the great need for more attention to scientific studies in 1882;[271] and, though McCabe labeled as "erroneous" the impression that "the literary and classical course leads in popularity," there can be no question about the slight attention to scientific preparation for future occupations.[272] Facilities preparing therefor were but slowly found. Zook, in his study of opportunities for the higher education of women in Massachusetts (1923), pointed out the "extensive facilities for the higher education of young women in the cultural realm," whereas "in the vocational and professional realm . . . there is by no means such a wealth of institutions." Nevertheless, he found that "a large percentage of the graduates

[269] Dealey: Comparative Study of the Curricula of Wellesley, Smith and Vassar Colleges [*Ped. Sem.*, XXII, 372–4].

[270] *Education* (1885), V, 486–95.

[271] *Ibid.*, III, 58–69.

[272] McCabe: *Am. Girl at College*, notes on Ch. VII.

of women's colleges in Massachusetts . . ." enter "some gainful occupation, or become homemakers or both."[273]

The above conclusion, based on a full examination of available facts, is but a culminating criticism of the women's college's tendency to imitate the institution already long established for men. Robinson, too, after particular study of curricula of the women's colleges, stated that "the growth of the curriculum of the women's college has been marked by no particular originality; that is the woman's college cannot be pointed out as the source of any single tendency in the American college today. . . . Able from the beginning to take advantage of the hard won experience of the older colleges, they have incorporated into the American colleges as yet little which could be designated as their original contribution."[274]

As stated before, the elective system enabled some women to pursue courses most closely related to what they hoped to do, and broke down the practice of following a single path to the coveted A.B. Though the elective system had been introduced in the University of Virginia in 1825 and Harvard, after 1869, took the lead in promoting its acceptance, some prominent leaders in women's education deplored its influence in their colleges, pointing out the havoc that had been wrought at Harvard, Cornell, Columbia, or Pennsylvania. Back of this opposition, there was, in some quarters, a feeling that women must prove their ability to do college work equal to men's, and the only way to do this was by pursuing a single, set, and, generally believed, difficult, course of study. Martha C. Thomas, of Bryn Mawr, expressed vigorously her disapproval of this system which was ruining the traditional college curriculum.

". . . In many colleges everything that is desirable for a human being to learn to do counts towards the bachelor's degree—ladder work in the gymnasium (why not going upstairs?), swimming in the tank (why not one's morning bath?), cataloging in the library (why not one's letter home?).

"People who used to believe in the free elective system used to believe also that all studies one could elect were equally good for purposes of mental training and discipline. Indeed, the free

273 See p. 211.
274 Robinson: *Curriculum of the Woman's College*, 108.

elective system could not have existed for a moment on any other hypothesis. There never was any real reason given for this belief. The presidents of Harvard and of other free elective colleges just said so, and said so over and over again, until every one came to think that it must be so.

"Now, however, we have been trying the experiment of acting as if it were so in our men's colleges for over a generation, and we know that it is *not* so. No one can read the educational articles and addresses based on practical experience with college students which have appeared, say since 1900, and not become convinced of this.

"Indeed, I personally have come to regard this vitally important question in education as now settled by this very costly method of practical experience for most truly intelligent and open-minded people. I am in consequence astounded to see the efforts which have been made within the past few years, and perhaps never more persistently than during the past year, to persuade, I might almost say to compel, those in charge of women's education to riddle the college curriculum of women with hygiene and sanitary drainage and domestic science and child-study, and all the rest of the so-called practical studies."[275]

Dealey pointed out some weaknesses of the elective system: "Preferences of certain faculty members" may be a determining factor; the influence of friends and the fact that certain courses are rated as "easy" may determine a choice in other cases. To bring order out of the chaos of the elective system, she suggested that:

"Certain constructive suggestions looking towards a definite basis for the elective system are, first, a required course in College Life, descriptive of the curriculum but emphasizing scientific and vocational motives; second, an adequate system of faculty advisers to bring the student into personal relationship; finally, organized vocational guidance."[276]

In the above points of view may be recognized the preconception of various individuals as to what college studies ought to be. What do the conditions of women's life seem to demand? We have noted before the increasing number of women entering

[275] Present Tendencies in Women's Education [*Ed. Rev.* (1908), XXXV, 76–7].

[276] Dealey: *op. cit.*, 372–4.

all kinds of occupations.[277] Surely, the college must make clear
to the individual the range of opportunities afforded by life, and
not merely leave her to stumble upon them, or not, as the case may
be. Realization of an opportunity to do a particular thing may
transform the whole mental life by furnishing an adequate motive.
Olive Schreiner caught the spirit of women's demand: they ask
the right to labor. To complete the satisfaction of this desire
women must have adequate professional training thereto. This
may be accomplished without throwing out of the college all the
old studies. Rather, present studies may come to have a new
meaning, may be raised to a new standard of excellence by a life
motive. Substitution of a definite direction, and purpose, for
aimlessness and the general conception of liberal culture, may
prove more acceptable in a society which sends, among the
brightest flowers, a considerable number of very ordinary mortals
to college.

Recognizing the facts of the present situation, Robinson noted,
with apparent approval, a tendency to "specialization of courses,
which the interests of the students appear to be forcing . . ."[278]
and again the "practical tendencies of the content of the
courses" in chemistry.[279] But change in the nature of courses
is not enough. There should be ". . . in the regular sophomore
year a course of regular academic standing . . . the content of
which is concerned with vocations open to women." Herein
should be presented "an accurate conception of the special occupation and the group of coordinated occupations . . . the qualities demanded by the work . . . the preparation required in
special outside courses and that acquired by intelligent grouping of college electives . . . [and] the advantages and disadvantages of the occupation . . ."[280]

Of the women's colleges in the South, the most common criticism has been that many of them failed to measure up to the
standard—the men's college. In 1916, Elizabeth Avery Colton
found but "seven standard colleges for women" out of a total
of one hundred and twenty-four "bearing the name College for
Women." These were Agnes Scott, Decatur, Georgia; Converse,

[277] Pages 8–17.
[278] *Op. cit.*, 66.
[279] *Ibid.*, 103.
[280] *Ibid.*, 129–30.

Spartanburg, South Carolina; Florida State College for Women, Tallahassee; Goucher, Baltimore, Maryland; Sophie Newcomb, New Orleans; Randolph-Macon, Lynchburg, Virginia; and West-hampton College, Richmond, Virginia. Since the publication of the above study, and probably largely due to its influence, the approximate colleges, with the exception of Tennessee,[281] have met the requirements of the Southern Association of Colleges and Secondary Schools. A few others, from Colton's lower groups, such as Coker, Hartsville, South Carolina; Judson, Marion, Alabama; Shorter, Rome, Georgia; North Carolina College, Greensboro, North Carolina; Winthrop College, South Carolina; and Georgia State College for Women, have also become members of the Southern Association.

[281] Baylor College for Women was admitted, 1926.

CHAPTER V

COEDUCATION

"Rise or sink
"Together, dwarfed or godlike, bond or free."

I. Origin and Progress of Coeducation

Coeducation has meant many things to different people: education of the sexes together in the same college (but not necessarily the same education for both); identical education of the sexes together; and education in coördinate colleges. Among coeducationists, of one type or another, there has been general sympathy with the age-old view of Plato that women have like capacities with men, but differ quantitatively.[1] They have consistently denied the Aristotelian assertions as to qualitative differences;[2] they have put no faith in the dictum of Thomas Elyot that man is by nature "fiers, hardy, stronge in opinion, Couaitous of glorie, desirous of knowledge"; while woman is "milde, timerouse, tractable, benigne, of sure remembrance."[3] Denial of qualitative differences and acceptance of quantitative left them quite free, however, to assert the social interdependence of man and woman. In fact, the stress upon this social relationship has been great. The argument, that since men and women must live together, they should therefore be educated together, has been convincing to many. Education must approximate the conditions of life; and this obtains only under a system of coeducation which simulates life as portrayed by the poet:

"As unto the bow the cord is,
"So unto the man is woman,
"Though she bends him, she obeys him,
"Though she draws him, yet she follows:
"Useless each without the other."

Though the question of similar, or the same, education for men and women is an old one, the term "coeducation" has been gen-

[1] *Republic*, Book V.
[2] *Politics*, Book I, Ch. XIII.
[3] *The Boke named the Governour* (1531).

erally employed in America only in the past seventy-five years. Murray's *New English Dictionary* describes the term as of United States origin, as does also the *Standard Dictionary*. Foreign critics of education have generally regarded coeducation as a peculiar characteristic of American schools. Scott, of the University of Michigan, contributed a note to the *Nation,* wherein he stated the earliest use of it he had found was in a circular issued by Mayhew to the Union Schools of Michigan in 1857. An investigation of educational periodicals would have discovered it earlier. The subject was discussed, pro and con, in the *Pennsylvania School Journal*[4] in 1854, and many other citations might be made.

Practice was much older than the name, certainly. In New England, girls were generally excluded from the town schools because, as Hopkins' rule said, their attendance was "improper and inconsistent with . . . the design" thereof. But, in 1790, Boston admitted girls to equal privileges with boys, and the change was general in this direction after the Revolution. The dame school was from its earliest appearance attended by girls and little boys. In New Netherlands, Dutch boys and girls attended the same elementary schools.[5] In Quaker communities it was not universal, but very common, for boys and girls to attend the same elementary schools in the Colonial period. When the free-school movement arose, championed by such men as Mann, Barnard, Seward, Potter, Stevens, Stowe, and others, there was no thought of excluding girls from the benefits of the public system. The new common schools followed the example of the dame school and district school. By the end of the nineteenth century the practice of coeducation in public elementary schools was almost universal. To answer inquiries made on the subject the Commissioner of Education made a study (1882–1883), and stated that in rural districts "their schools are everywhere for both sexes."[6] As to the "graded schools of the villages, towns, and smaller cities," they are "like those of the rural districts."[7]

4 III, 87 *ff.* and 211 *ff.*

5 See Vol. I, 196.

6 *Circular of Information,* No. 2, 1883, U. S. Bur. of Ed., 9.

7 Statistics were given for 144 such towns and smaller cities having less than 7,500 inhabitants.

In larger cities, coeducation was the rule; but 19 of 196 cities reported separation of sexes for at least a part of their course.[8] In 1891, only 41 out of 628 cities (6%) from which information was obtained practiced separation in some grades. Ten years later the situation of the elementary schools was practically the same.[9] In 1910, separation in elementary schools was not practiced in more than four per cent, and that chiefly in the East where public education had developed first for boys, and where later demands for girls' education had been met by building new and separate accommodations.[10]

It may be worth while to consider, briefly, the reasons assigned for adopting coeducation in elementary schools. In 1883, twenty-five cities practiced coeducation because it was the most "natural" way. "It is the natural arrangement that boys and girls should be together in school as they are in the family," wrote H. E. Sawyer, of New Britain, Connecticut. Forty-five replies indicated that it was the most "customary or legal method." "Our schools have always been mixed," wrote Clarke, of Chicopee, Massachusetts; and Booher, of Virginia City, Nevada, said, "It is the law of the State." Du Shane, of South Bend, Indiana, wrote: "We never knew any other way; it grew up naturally as the city schools developed from the township schools." Five authorities suggested "justice to both sexes" as the reason. Hutchins, of Fond du Lac, averred that "there is no appreciable difference in the mental capacity of boys and girls during public school life." Seven cities regarded coeducation the most "economical way." Slauson, of Houghton, Michigan, said: "Economy is the chief reason. To obtain the same excellence in grading and instruction would require a much larger teaching force were the sexes separated." Seven others thought coeducation a "convenient method," Rahway, New Jersey, especially naming "convenience in grading and facility in discipline" as a reason for adoption. Fifty cities named "beneficial results" for both sexes as the reason for their preference. To quote but two, Clar-

[8] The cities were Mobile, Ala.; Wilmington, Del.; Macon, Ga.; Belleville, Ill.; New Orleans; Baltimore; Marblehead and Newburyport, Mass.; Vicksburg, Miss.; New Brunswick, N. J.; Brooklyn; Allentown, Easton, Harrisburg, and York, Pa.; Charleston, S. C.; Knoxville, Austin, and Alexandria, Va.—*Op. cit.*, 24.

[9] *R. C. E.* (1900–1), II, 1220–1.

[10] *Ibid.* (1910), I, 126.

endon, of Freemont, Nebraska, asserted that "the result is a more harmonious development of both sexes"; and Barnes, of Little Falls, New York, felt that "better results can be obtained; the influence of each sex upon the other is helpful." Twenty-two places favored it because of "economy and benefit"; nineteen because of "convenience and benefit"; eighteen because of "economy and convenience"; twelve mentioned "natural character and beneficial effect"; seven specified "economy and custom"; seven, "customary and beneficial"; fifteen, "economy, convenience and benefit"; seven grouped "natural, cheap and beneficial" as the causes; five practiced it because it was "customary, cheap, convenient and beneficial"; five others thought it "customary, economical, and beneficial"; and five others, including Chicago, mentioned that it was "natural, convenient and beneficial."[11]

Summarizing its findings, the report said: "Combining these opinions with those of 139 towns and of 285 cities and towns practicing coeducation, 158 favor it as "beneficial," 101 as "economical," 81 as "customary," 78 as "convenient," 59 as "natural," and 14 as "impartial."[12]

A number of cities indicated some definite opposition to coeducation, though practicing it to some extent. Dickson, of Mobile, had been convinced by experience that "separation is the safer plan of education, especially in cities." At Wilmington, Delaware, the opinion was held "by a very large majority of our people that it is better that the sexes should be separate after the age of twelve." Wise, of Baltimore, felt "popular sentiment" was decidedly in favor of "separate schools for the sexes." Allentown, Pennsylvania, was reported "strongly opposed to it," probably because "we never had it in the public schools of this city." Seven other cities gave somewhat similar replies. Of Alexandria, Virginia, it was asserted: "There is not, and there never has been, coeducation of the sexes in the public schools here."[13]

Colonial secondary educational institutions were chiefly for boys; and it was not until female seminaries and academies arose that girls participated in higher learning, except as it was im-

---

[11] *Circular of Information*, No. 2, 1883, 16 *ff*.

[12] *Ibid.*, 23.

[13] *Ibid.*, 26.

parted by a private tutor in the families of liberally minded gentlemen, or purchased of an adventure master at "reasonable"
prices. Among the new academies there were many, both for
male and female pupils, in the late eighteenth and early nineteenth centuries: Leicester Academy (1784) was one of the
oldest, while Westford (1793) was also coeducational. Bradford
(1803) was for girls and boys, as also the Friends' Academy at
New Bedford (1812). Another famous coeducational institution
was the Greenfield Hill Academy, under the leadership of
Dwight, who never doubted but that men and women were
equally capable of being educated. The lack of statistics for the
early part of the century renders impossible a statement as to the
exact proportion of coeducational seminaries and academies; but
they were certainly less numerous than the separate institutions
and, at first, were regarded as interesting experiments, not only
in the East but in the West.

The early high schools followed the lead of the first academies,
being separate institutions, as we have already noted.[14] Any
wide acceptance of coeducation in practice had obviously to wait
upon more general approval of the idea that girls should have
more than rudimentary education. Hence the first academies
and high schools, insofar as they promoted the educational interests of women, had to do it on the separate plan. The high
schools, once under way, soon changed, however, and became
chiefly coeducational. They benefitted by the great faith in
girls' education that was gradually built up by the seminaries
from the middle of the eighteenth to the middle of the nineteenth
centuries. Believing in equal education for their sons and daughters, communities began to seek an institution to offer it. The
high school was preëminently the choice; and most localities, for
reasons of "economy," "convenience," "benefit," "natural-
ness," "refinement," and so forth, began to favor coeducation in
it. The cities that held to separate high schools regarded their
age-old "traditions," "buildings," "impropriety," "vicious influence of boys," "unequal capacities," "corporal punishment
necessary for boys," "size of schools" and the variant character
of those attending them, as sufficiently weighty reasons for continuing their practice.[15] In some cities, changes came quickly.

14 See Vol. I, 519, 521, 524.
15 R. C. E. (1901), II, 1258 ff.

The High School at Cleveland, Ohio, was opened (1846) for boys only; a year later girls were admitted, though "against the protest of the principal."[16]

According to Commissioner Harris, there were eleven public high schools in 1850, organized distinctly as such, having two to four-year courses. The next decade saw thirty-three more and, by 1870, there were 160. In these, the tendency was overwhelmingly in favor of coeducation, after the Civil War; by 1891-2, information from 628 cities showed but fifteen with separate high schools for girls and boys; ten years later, three of these had shifted their practice to coeducation.[17] In 1900, reports received from 6,005 public high schools showed 5,933 (98%) mixed. In these schools, 93.6 per cent of the pupils attending high schools were enrolled. In 1910, 34 separate public high schools for boys were reported, and 26 for girls, in a total of 10,213; in 1920, there were 78, equally divided for the sexes, in a total of 14,326 public high schools reported.[18] Of the private secondary schools, at that date, 1,121 out of 1,978 (56.7%) were mixed.[19] By 1910, coeducational private high schools and academies declined to 51 per cent, or 922 in a total of 1781.[20] In 1919-20, the proportion was further changed, there being 980 private secondary schools coeducational (46.8%) out of a total of 2,093.[21]

In view of the rapid development of coeducation in public high schools, it is interesting that slight efforts have been made to test its various claims. The reason for failure to subject it to experiment, doubtless, has been largely in the fact that the common judgments of schoolmen were overwhelmingly in its favor. There were, indeed, a few doubting Thomases; but their unfavorable criticisms were no more clear-cut and logical than those which favored it. On both sides there was almost nothing but personal views and experiences, to support the favored contention. A few slight exceptions may be made.

Englewood (Chicago) High School (1906) attempted segregated instruction with an entering class of 150 pupils, but con-

16 *Ibid.* (1903), I, 1054.
17 *Ibid.* (1900-1), II, 1221.
18 *Biennial Survey*, 1918-20, Bul. 1923, No. 29, 497.
19 *R. C. E.* (1900-1), II, 1227.
20 *Ibid.* (1910), II, 1168.
21 *Biennial Survey*, 1918-20, Bul. 1923, No. 29, 547.

tinued the mixed school, save in recitations. Each teacher had a boys' class and a girls' class, to permit them to compare effects on the two sexes. After six months, parents were asked whether their children had benefitted by the segregation, and whether they wished the plan used in the next incoming class. Ninety per cent answered the two questions in the affirmative. Their wishes were respected; and a referendum, a year later, showed that 85% of the parents favored segregation. With this favorable reaction, the system was extended to the second-year class and, in 1909, "about 1,000" boys and girls were taught in separate classes, during the first two years. In general, it was judged that (1) the new plan improved boys' scholarship and increased the number of them in school in the second and third years; (2) boys did better under men teachers during early adolescence; (3) pupils and parents liked the plan; (4) leading traits of the sexes became more marked and hence the work better adapted to each; (5) such grouping made grading more perfect; (6) more reserve was shown by the sexes and less tendency for the "smart boy" to "show off"; (7) boys' discipline could be more severe without the danger of becoming too much so for girls; and (8) in physiology, history, mathematics, languages, and so on, the work was better suited to the sexes when separated. "In mixed classes neither one helps the other, as each is impatient to go on in his or her own course. . . . My conviction is that we should keep the boy and the girl in the same high school so as to preserve the same social environment, but teach them in different classes so as to adapt the work to the highest needs of each."[22] The above judgments were all favorable to segregation; they were, however, just another set of judgments, though perhaps more reliable for having been the result of especial observation over a four-year period, and because they represented a consensus of opinion. No thoroughgoing effort has yet been made to study the question experimentally.

As coeducation may be said to have grown up into the high school from the general practice in the elementary schools (this was asserted to be the case by numerous superintendents in Western towns and cities), so in colleges the influence of the earlier seminary or academy may sometimes be seen, and is probably greater than can be proved by direct evidence. Sug-

[22] Reported in the *R. C. E.* (1909), I, 178 *ff.*

gestion is powerful. There were numerous coeducational seminaries which, in the minds of common people, stood for "higher" education. The college and the seminary were often linked together in speaking and writing. Catherine Beecher established "seminaries" and always aimed to get them founded on the "college" plan—but did not succeed. Seminaries were often privileged by charter to grant some proper reward to the student, such as a degree or diploma. Also, it should be said that it was often difficult to know what to call a new institution— seminary, academy, or college—and that, undoubtedly, as the vogue of "college" became established, many which were typical seminaries, so far as the curriculum was concerned, called themselves by the new, fashionable name. The line of demarcation between seminary and college being thus indistinctly drawn,[23] it was most natural that coeducation, a practice of the secondary school, should appear, here and there, in institutions of higher grade which, we recognize today, deserved the name of college.

Though Blount College was coeducational for a time, Oberlin is the oldest college in the United States that has consistently and continuously practiced coeducation. It was opened in 1833, but was, at first, coeducational only in the secondary or preparatory department. Not until 1837 were ladies ready to be enrolled in the college course. "The first year," President James H. Fairchild said, "it was a high school, with something over a hundred pupils, more than one-third of whom were ladies; . . . one-half of the students at least were from New England and New York." The second year there were nearly 300, and college classes were in complete operation. About a fourth of the 300 were women. Soon the annual level of 500 was reached and maintained until about 1852, when the number approached 1,000. From 1852 to 1867 the annual average was something over that figure. The number of women was generally not less than a third nor more than a half of the total, except during the Civil War.[24]

[23] As an example of hazy notions about college and seminary, even in circles constantly in touch with the changing ideas of the time, we may mention an article in *Godey's Lady's Book*, Dec. 1853, 554, in which the *four colleges*, Patapsco, Milwaukee, Cincinnati and Oberlin, were highly praised for their service to 1200 young ladies who were pursuing courses.

[24] Merriam: *Higher Educ. in Tenn.*, 63; Fairchild: Coeducation of the Sexes, an address before a meeting of college presidents, Springfield, Illi-

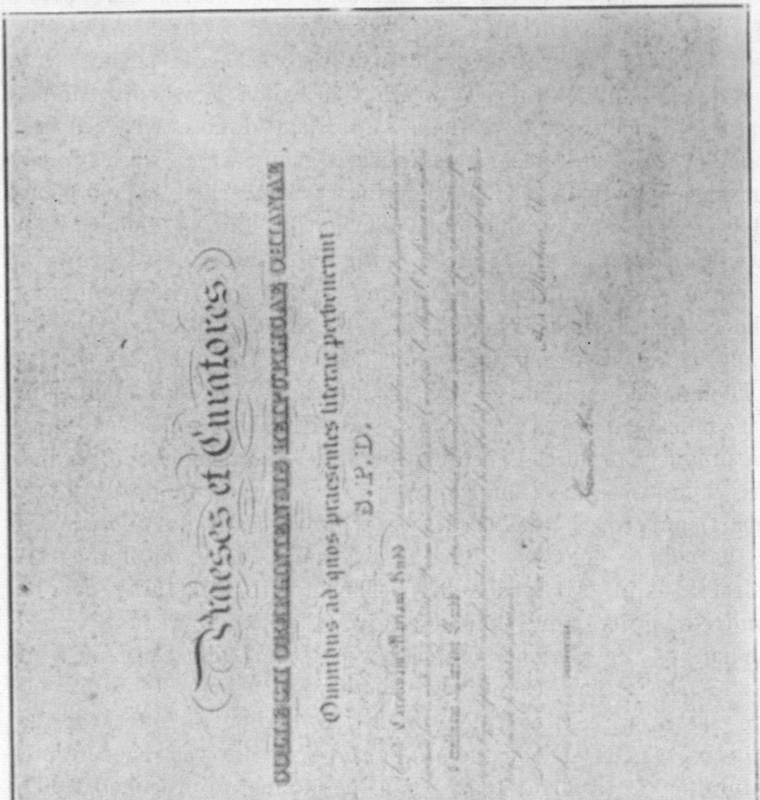

Diploma Issued by Oberlin College (1841)

College education, it was originally thought, would not be demanded for girls; but in 1837, four had been sufficiently prepared, asked for admission, and were accepted as Freshmen in the College Course. Their presence thereafter was taken as a matter of course, though the proportion was small: one in ten to one in four, at times, were women. Women received, on completing the course, the regular arts degree, eighty-four having been granted up to 1866. In the theological department, which was not opened to women as a rule, there were two women students "who attended all the exercises . . . through a three years course," early in its history, but "not as regular members."[25]

Where the studies of men and women were the same they were taught together; but, as Fairchild said, "the larger number of both sexes are found in our preparatory department" rather than in college or ladies' courses. In the first thirty-four years the diploma of the Ladies' Course was given to three hundred and ninety-five, and the Bachelor's degree to but eighty-four. To enter the Ladies' Course, a year of Latin and an "elementary English education" were required. Four years were necessary to complete it, the subjects being the same as those of the College Course, save that all Greek, calculus, and nearly all Latin were omitted, and French, drawing, and some natural science were added. Where studies of the college and ladies' courses were the same, co-instruction was the rule.

The sexes were allowed to mingle socially, though some restrictions may now cause a smile. Separate dormitories were erected; but male students ate at the tables with women at the women's hall. Some students were permitted to live in private homes, some taking women or men alone, while others were approved to receive both sexes for board and lodging. Supervision and discipline of the women was in the hands of the "lady Principal," though the advice of the college faculty might be sought where desired. Fairchild described the limitations on social activities as follows:[26]

". . . Young gentlemen call on ladies in a social way at the parlors of the Ladies' Hall and of private families, between the

nois, reprinted in the *R. C. E.*, 1867–8, 385 *ff.*; see Orton: *The Liberal Education of Women*, Ch. XXV.

[25] *R. C. E.*, 1867–8, as cited above.

[26] *Ibid.*, 1867–8, 388.

hour for tea and half-past seven in the winter, and eight o'clock in the summer. They walk in groups from one class-room to another, as convenience and their sense of propriety may dictate, with the help of a suggestion, if needed, from thoughtful and observing friends. Now and then the young ladies have permission to attend an evening lecture given under the auspices of the College, and in such case to accept the attendance of young men. No such association is permitted in the case of religious meetings. They do not ride or walk together beyond the limits of the village, except on a holyday, under special arrangements. There is no association of the sexes in literary societies, or other voluntary and independent organization.''

This interesting experiment, both in coeducation and manual labor, drew considerable attention and, of course, was regarded as eccentric by many. The following description appeared in a circular of 1834:

''The system embraces instruction in every department, from the Infant School to a Collegiate and Theological course. Physical and moral education are to receive particular attention. The institution was opened in December last, and has sixty students; about forty in the academic, and twenty in the primary department. All of them, whether male or female, rich or poor, are required to labor four hours daily. Male students are to be employed in agriculture, gardening, and some of the mechanic arts; females in housekeeping, useful needle-work, the manufacture of wool, the culture of silk, certain appropriate parts of gardening, &c. The Institution has five hundred acres of good land, of which, though a complete forest a year ago, about thirty acres are cleared, and sown with wheat. They have also a steam mill, and a saw mill, in operation. During the present year it is contemplated to add fifty acres to the cleared land, to erect a flouring mill, shingle machine, turning lathe, a work shop with an extensive boarding house (which together with the present buildings will accommodate about one hundred and sixty students), furniture, farming, mechanic, and scientific apparatus; and begin a library.

''During the winter months, the young men are at liberty to engage as agents, school teachers, or in any other occupation they may select. The expenses of students in the seminary for board at the table spread only with vegetable food, are eighty cents a

JAMES H. FAIRCHILD, PRESIDENT OF OBERLIN COLLEGE (1866–1889)

week; and ninety-two cents a week for the same with animal food twice a day. Tuition is from fifteen to thirty-five cents a week. The avails of the students' labors have thus far varied from one to eight cents an hour. The average has been five cents. A majority of the male students have, by their four hours' daily labor, paid their board, fuel, lights, washing and mending, and some even more; and this without any interference with their progress in their studies.

"The time to be spent at this institution, in preparation for the various professions and employments, of life is not yet defined, nor a single course of study marked out as the only one through which an individual can attain a desired station. Diplomas are not to be given according to the time spent in study, but to the student's real acquirements."[27]

In summing up the early experience of Oberlin, Fairchild gave what he believed was the unanimous opinion of all responsibly connected with the school, rather than his personal view alone. As advantages he listed, "economy of means and forces" and "convenience to the patrons of the school" who are able to send sons and daughters to the same place. (He has noted the fact that where men's colleges have been established, frequently prominent girls' schools have arisen nearby, requiring "a good degree of vigilance" to prevent the meeting of students of both places.) "Wholesome incitements to study which the system affords" operated on all members of the community the same as in life and, he believed, were more effective than the rewards and honors often distributed to a few in other schools; "Social culture which is incidental to the system is a matter of no small importance" and "the tendency to good order which we find in the system" was also praised. Exclusion for misconduct in classes of the college and ladies' courses did not average over one in five years, and, in one period of over ten years, none were dismissed. "Good order and morality in the town outside the school"; a "manifest advantage . . . in the relation of the school to the community— a cordial . . . good will, . . . [an] absence of that antagonism between town and college"; and, finally, "the fact that young people educated under such conditions are kept in harmony with society at large, and are prepared to appreciate the responsibilities of life" were added guarantees of the value of coeducation.[28]

[27] *Am. Annals of Education*, IV, 242–3.
[28] *R. C. E.*, 1867–8, 388–92.

Such were the advantages, considered unanimously agreed upon after an experiment of thirty-four years' duration, and which, as Fairchild said, had "forced themselves upon our attention." To several questions which had been raised relative to women's higher education, he gave answers, dictated by Oberlin's experience. First, are women not a check to the progress of men? After eight years as teacher of Latin, Greek and Hebrew, eleven as teacher of Mathematics, and eight years in Philosophy and Ethics, it was his judgment that "the strong and the weak scholars are equally distributed between the sexes." Second, do not women break down? "A breaking down in health does not appear to be more frequent than with young men." Third, do not ladies "need a course of study adapted to their nature and their prospective work?" To this he replied, "The education furnished is general, not professional, designed to fit men and women for any position or work to which they may properly be called." The general discipline theory avoided manifold, complex, perturbing questions. Some variation, on the basis of choice, was allowed by choosing the Ladies' instead of the College course. Do not young girls become coarse and young men effeminate? It makes "men of boys and gentlemen of rowdies." As for women, they are neither coarsened nor caused to disdain the usual lot of woman. Most of the graduates of the college married.[29] Three, it was admitted, were "somewhat distinguished lady lecturers," sometimes classed as "strong-minded women"; but, while he could not agree with their radical views, he counted these ladies among his friends, and pointed out that they never gave Oberlin any credit for their advanced views on "woman's rights." Does not association in college at this age tend to "foolish love affairs?" There is as little of this "as is found in any general society" and it is generally believed that the association from day to day, in ordinary work of the school, offers "favorable conditions for sensible views and actions," whereas monastic institutions heighten the imagination of youths, filling their minds with fanciful creations, unlike the realities which must be faced when they return to normal social life. Will not acquaintances formed at school result in matrimony, either in school or after leaving it? "Undoubtedly . . . and if this is a fatal objection, the system must be pronounced a

[29] All except 23 living and four deceased at an early age.

failure." But the question is raised whether unions after college association do not promise at least as happy, probably more happy, results than those made under other circumstances, often less favorable. May not "positive immoralities" occur? Yes, but "is the moral atmosphere of the best and most approved Eastern colleges perfectly free from every taint of impurity?" and the "most carefully guarded female seminary . . .?" Can the system of Oberlin succeed elsewhere; or does it depend on local conditions and "peculiar features of the School and of the place," not to be reproduced elsewhere? There was an original advantage in that the town and school grew together, coeducation was practiced at the outset, and the community was bound together by homogeneity of people and purpose. None of the founders, however, had had experience with such a coeducational institution; and homogeneity did not long prevail, for people, cultivated and uncultivated, came from all parts of the country and there were five to seven per cent of Negroes. Continued success under these changing circumstances pointed to the adaptability of the scheme to other localities. On this point, too, there were, by 1867, many other institutions of higher grade to prove that success was not due to "peculiar features" of the Oberlin community.

Another experiment with coeducation was undertaken by Antioch College, at Yellow Springs, Ohio, in 1852. Here, from the first, it was Mann's idea "to secure for the female sex equal opportunities of education with the male, and to extend those opportunities in the same studies, and classes, and by the same instructors, after the manner of many academic institutions in different parts of the country "[30] The continuance of this coeducational college through its early troublous years was due to the heroic courage, unflagging energy and wisdom of Horace Mann. In keeping with his purpose, which never wavered, young men and women had the same courses and recited together in class. His antagonism to emulation as a motive power was a safeguard to the health of women as well as men, and helped to avoid the censure of those who said women would ruin their health at college. Mrs. Mann wrote that the health of girls was much better than that of the men:[31]

[30] Barnard: *American Teachers and Educators*, 396.
[31] In *Sex and Education* (1874) (Ed. by J. W. Howe), 66-9.

"Young women who came with their systems out of order, through ignorance and unhealthy living, were greatly benefitted, and sent home to spread the knowledge they had gained. But one death of each sex occurred in six years . . . and they were both cases of poisoning by food in metallic vessels; yet the hardships were great during the first years, and the exposures rather exceptional, owing to the poverty of the food and the inadequacy of the buildings as to ventilation and water supply."[32]

Dr. Hubbell wrote of the student body: "It was a motley group. Ministers had given up their parishes; husbands and wives were there to enter side by side that they might be fitted to rear and teach their children. Sons and daughters of eminent men, east and west, gathered there for the teaching of this man of renown in education."[33] Women were employed as teachers as well as men, two being mentioned by Mann in 1859. Had not Mann expressed his firm faith in the efficacy of an equal education and opportunity for women? In the first *Announcement*[34] it had been stated that:

"In some particulars of its aim and scope, this college differs from most of the higher literary institutions of the country. It recognizes the claims of the female sex to equal opportunities of education with the male, and these opportunities it designs to confer. Its founders believe that the labors and expenditures for the higher education of men will tend indirectly to elevate the character of women; but they are certain that all wise efforts for the improved education of women will speed the elevation of the whole human race."

Other beginnings with coeducation were made by the state universities. Iowa was coeducational from its opening in 1856.[35] Elsewhere, as at Washington (1862), much the same policy was followed, though frequently with some delay and opposition.

32 *Ibid.*

33 *Horace Mann,* 182.

34 P. 14.

35 Iowa, established 1847, but not opened till 1856, was coeducational in the normal department from the first but an effort was made by the trustees to exclude women in 1858. This was unsuccessful. Three women received diplomas from the normal department in 1857–8; and eleven, in 1859. The first bachelor's degree issued to a woman was granted in 1863. Phoebe Sudlow taught English and literature at the University about 1879—see *Catalogues,* University of Iowa, 1856, 1857, and 1858; also Aurner: *Hist. of Ed. in Iowa,* IV, 20, 21, and 58.

Antioch College

In general, however, the Western state universities were influential leaders in the movement, though not much importance attaches to it until after 1870. In Wisconsin and Michigan, considerably more significance lay in their experience because of the struggle for coeducation in the former, and the effect that the example of both had in establishing it firmly in other institutions.

In Wisconsin, as early as 1850,[36] the regents proposed a normal department for the University wherein men and women were to share all benefits equally; but this was not at once realized on account of lack of an appropriation. In 1856 the first lectures in this department were held, eighteen students attending, of whom *none* were women. In 1857, there were 28 students, all men.

In 1857, three years after the first class had been graduated, the Regents of the University declared in their report that: "The completion of the central edifice will open the way to the admission of female pupils to the normal and other departments of the university. It is a question now much agitated whether the liberal culture of the female mind is an end most appropriately attained under the existing agency of separate educational establishments, doubling the array and quadrupling the expense of the instruction. The entire success which has attended the common education of the sexes in the normal schools and higher academies of the eastern states goes far toward settling the question for the university. There is not wanting collegiate experience of some authority in the same direction, and the whole question is now being conclusively tested at Antioch College under the presidency of Horace Mann. It may be alleged that public sentiment in Wisconsin is not yet ripe for dispensing with separate female schools; still the board deem it right to prepare to meet the wishes of those parents who desire university culture for their daughters by extending to all such the privileges of the institution."

No women were admitted, however, until 1860, when in a class of fifty-nine there were thirty women who attended normal classes.[37] The beginning of the Civil War increased the attendance of women, their number at times actually exceeding that

---

[36] See *Regent's Report* for Jan. 16, 1850.
[37] Olin: *Women of a State University*, 22.

of men at the University. In the autumn of 1863, there were 117 women and 110 men in all departments. They were not, of course, regular college students; but it was stated in the catalog (1863) that "all members of the normal school[38] in addition to the proper exercises of that department will, without additional charge, have access to the lectures and other exercises of such other university classes, as with the approbation of their Principal, they may elect to attend." This privilege, Olin found by interview with former students, was readily made use of by the young women.[39] In 1864–5, all students of the normal department were women. The war period then, with the urgent demand for women to prepare themselves as teachers, and the scarcity of men students at the University, represents the real origin of coeducation at Wisconsin.

In the reorganization act of 1866[40] "the University in all its departments and colleges" was declared open to men and women equally. But upon attempting to secure Paul A. Chadbourne as president, it was found that he objected to the coeducational feature of the law, under which he would be forced to work. Therefore the regents appealed to the legislature for modification, thus forsaking their previous consistent advocacy of coeducation. The amended reorganization act stated that the University was "open to female as well as male students under such regulations and restrictions as the board of regents may deem proper."[41]

Under this law, Chadbourne planned a female college with a different course and separate instruction, save that "university lectures" were to be attended by both men and women. Until this scheme could be actually begun, however, the women students of the normal department (numbering over a hundred) continued to utilize the privilege previously announced by University publications that "students in this [normal] department may attend all university lectures and . . . elect any study in the college of arts and letters." Under "this freedom" six

[38] The Normal School was created in 1863, under Professor Charles H. Allen, and seventy-six women at once made use of it. See Allen and Spencer: *Higher Education in Wisconsin, Circular of Information*, No. 1, 1889, Bur. of Ed., 28.

[39] *Women of A State University*, by Mrs. H. M. Olin, used by courtesy of the publishers, G. P. Putnam's Sons, New York. P. 25.

[40] *Laws of Wisconsin*, 1866, Ch. 114, 153 *ff.*

[41] *Ibid.*, 1867, Ch. 117.

women completed the work for the degree in arts, graduating in 1869. In fact, the new president found great difficulty in forcing the young women into the course prescribed for the "female college" and announced in the catalog (1869) that upon completing the same work as men the same degree would be granted; also, that "in addition to the prescribed course in this college young ladies are instructed in any study taught in the college of letters and arts . . ." if prepared for it. Olin declared, a few years ago, that no woman ever "availed herself of any of the opportunities" of Chadbourne's "female college," and none graduated from it.[42] After the inauguration of Twombly (1871), the catalog fiction of a separate college continued for a time; but no effort was made to provide such separate instruction, and there was no demand for it by students. Public sentiment had generally been in favor of coeducation, judging by the legislative step of 1866. The same sentiment, and some dissatisfaction with Chadbourne's policy, was reflected in the *Visitors' Report* of 1871:

". . . Your committee would also suggest the propriety of allowing the ladies and gentlemen pursuing the same studies to unite in classes together. Accepting the fact that they are to be educated together, we fail to see the necessity of having a distinct department known as the 'female college.' Such an arrangement would save the time and strength of the professors, and would accord with general public sentiment."[43]

In 1870, $50,000 was appropriated to build a dormitory for young women;[44] and from this date the attendance of women ranged between 30 and 39 per cent up to 1877, when it fell to 28. Between 1878 and 1892, it fluctuated between 27 per cent and 40; and, after 1892, rose through the forties until 1906–1907, when university officials were alarmed to note that women constituted 50.8% of the whole student body.[45] This was the signal for a reaction against coeducation.[46]

[42] *Women of A State University*, by Mrs. H. M. Olin, used by courtesy of the publishers, G. P. Putnam's Sons, New York. P. 47.

[43] *Visitors' Report*, 1871.

[44] *Laws of Wisconsin*, 1870, Ch. 54; *Regents' Report*, 1870, 49.

[45] Complete figures for the period, 1871–1907, are given in Olin: *op. cit.*, 152.

[46] See pp. 280 *ff.*

In 1870, it was still the expressed purpose of the regents that "recitations and studies of the two sexes" be kept "entirely separate"; but, as before, the policy of allowing women to attend "any study taught in the college of letters" and "all university lectures" was continued. The latter was what the ladies wanted to do; consequently the former purpose to carry on separate college classes was never realized. The view of the State Superintendent was that "more thorough instruction would be given the ladies, and expense of carrying on the institution [would] be greatly lessened, if both sexes were generally to recite together. The coeducation of the sexes in the collegiate department is no longer a matter of experiment."[47]   In 1872, it was stated:[48]

"In the management of this branch of the university the regents have endeavored not only to carry out that provision of the organic law which requires that female students shall have all the advantages of the university, but they have also conceded to them the privilege of a distinct ladies' education. The sexes are not required to recite together, but a preference in this respect, required by parents and students, is granted to the ladies, and competition for all the honors of the university is open alike to both male and female students." The *Visitors' Report*, for the same year, expressed approval of the liberal provisions of the regents, which shows clearly that in their judgment, at least, coeducation was both a fact and a success at Wisconsin:

". . . It is too late, amid the noontide splendours of the nineteenth century, to ignore the claims of woman to higher education. We hold that every human being has a natural and inalienable right to cultivate and use, as circumstances permit, the powers and faculties which the Creator has bestowed. Woman possesses a rational soul, and in this very fact she has a divine warrant for the exercise and improvement of her powers. Her development should be limited only by her capacities and powers. Whatever will make her wiser and better, that she may learn; whatever knowledge she may be able to use, either in adding to her own happiness, or in promoting the happiness of others— that knowledge she may rightfully acquire. . . . These questions . . . [of different courses, etc.] you have bravely and wisely met. You have thrown the doors of the university wide open and

47 *R. C. E.*, 1871, 374–5.
48 *Regents' Report*, 1872, 4; also *R. C. E.*, 1873, 418.

ladies are permitted to pursue any course of instruction or elective study in which they may show themselves prepared to enter. If one should wish to take the law course, no interdict of yours will forbid. But you have prescribed a curriculum of study for the ladies' college which will meet the wishes of the great majority of young women. It offers a broad and generous culture in letters, science, and art. At the same time it recognizes the feminine character. . . . You have made the ladies' college independent of the other departments of the university so that, when desired, instruction shall be imparted by the professors within the college walls. . . . This may be well, but . . . we believe it will be found that young women who are pursuing the same studies with young men will prefer to share in the same recitations. And we are not surprised to learn that after a trial of one year, this course has been attended with the most satisfactory results. On careful inquiry, we are convinced that any apprehensions of danger or difficulty from the coeducation of the sexes are groundless. The evils feared are imaginary; the benefits substantial.''[49]

It was in the spring of 1874 that John Bascom,[50] of Williams College, and an enthusiastic advocate of coeducation, became president. In that year, the ladies graduated, receiving the degree of Bachelor of Arts, numbered fourteen.[51] The coming of Bascom was marked by the beginning of unrestricted coeducation. At the commencement, he announced to the young women receiving degrees that in another year ''the graduates of the university would appear as a unit'' and the ladies would not be ''a separate element.'' His first report stated: ''The young women have been put, in all respects, on precisely the same footing in the University with the young men. No difficulties have arisen from it. . . . Their average scholarship was certainly as high as that of the young men and they were apparently in good health.''[52]

[49] *Visitors' Report*, 1872, 16.

[50] Dr. Bascom had, in 1872, made a minority report at Williams in favor of coeducation. This report was an eloquent plea based upon considerable study, as well as in accord with his view of elemental justice. David Field collaborated with him in this report.

[51] *R. C. E.*, 1874, 454.

[52] *Report* of President Bascom, as quoted in *Women of A State University*, by Mrs. H. M. Olin, used by courtesy of the publishers, G. P. Putnam's Sons, New York. P. 75; see also *Visitors' Report* to Regents, 1874, 11.

Bascom's faith in their scholarship was rewarded. At the first "new-style" commencement, a lady took the honors for the best oration. The visitors stated (1876) that in the present class, 17 men and 19 women, "the percentage of young women to be graduated with honor in respect of higher scholarship is, relatively to their whole number, decidedly larger than that of the young men," and therefore the ability of women to do the college work of men cannot be doubted.[53] The catalog and *Report* of the board of regents for 1878–79 stated: "The scholarship of the young ladies, as a whole, appears to be fully equal to that of the other sex."[54]

Of the effect on moral conditions, the visitors reported in 1876: "The moral effects of this combination are no less happy. If absence of rudeness and ready subordination in the young men may be in any degree justly ascribed to the restraining presence of the more refined sex, it is as fairly inferable that the latter must derive from the association, thoughtful disposition, serious purpose, and desire for respect; and, if to the observant presence of either sex is traceable the decorous demeanour or competitive ambition of the other, this alone might well lead to their early association in common pursuits."[55] Again it was said that "the work of discipline seems to have been made easier by the presence of both sexes"; and, "so far as discovered, no disadvantages have arisen from this union in the classroom, while many advantages have accrued."[56]

About the mid-century an earnest effort was made to open the facilities of higher education at the University of Michigan to women. Memorials were addressed to the legislature on several occasions. In 1853, one of these lamented that "no provision is made by the state for the education of young women beyond the Primary School unless they wish to become teachers." The state superintendent in his *Report* for 1855–6[57] pointed out that if "persons" means female as well as male, as Dr. Webster asserts, there is no way to keep the former out of the state university.

[53] Olin: *op. cit.*, 76–7.
[54] *R. C. E.*, 1879, 260.
[55] *Women of A State University,* by Mrs. H. M. Olin, used by courtesy of the publishers, G. P. Putnam's Sons, New York. P. 77.
[56] *R. C. E.*, 1879, 260.
[57] Pp. 30–1.

In 1857–8, petitions were presented, desiring that the University of Michigan offer its advantages equally to men and women; but no such favor was granted until 1870, when the regents announced (somewhat cryptically to be sure, but they were readily understood) "that no rule exists in any of the University statutes for the exclusion of any person from the University who possesses the requisite literary and moral qualifications."[58] The first year there were 17 in the medical, 10 in the literary, and 1 in the legal department. These twenty-eight came from six states besides Michigan: three each from Massachusetts and New York, two from Indiana, one each from Connecticut, Illinois, and Wisconsin, and seventeen from Michigan.[59] Acting President Frieze, in spite of his early conservatism, declared: "We have already ceased to fear the dangers which were apprehended from this action . . . the loss of reputation and caste among universities, the decline of scholarship, and the corruption of morals."[60]

The system at once vindicated itself against all charges, according to the judgment of Michigan's distinguished president. He was convinced that the "effect of the admission of these young women" upon the general spirit and life of the University was much the same as would have come from the "addition of the same number of earnest, intelligent young men." Women at this early date, of course, formed but a small part of the student body, there being but about thirty in the arts college, which had nearly four hundred students.[61] "So far the women show themselves entirely competent to master any of the studies of the course, and without injury to their health. . . . There is no department of study in which some of our female students do not excel; and in none have they, as a class, failed to do fine work." Two years later, he wrote: "The history of our work during the past year has only deepened the impression made during the two preceding years. . . ."[62] After nine years of experiment, Angell's analysis of the origin and success of coeducation was published in the *Pennsylvania School Journal*. It was a significant statement, often referred to by the "pros" and the "antis":

[58] Hinsdale: *Hist. of the Univ. of Michigan*, 132.

[59] Article by Moses Coit Tyler, in *The Independent*, Dec. 1870.

[60] *Ibid.;* also Stone: Hist. of Coeducation at the Univ. of Mich. [*Mich. Pioneer and Hist. Collections*, XVIII, 411–18].

[61] Orton: *Liberal Education of Women*, 268.

[62] *R. C. E.*, 1873, 196–7.

"It is nine years since the first woman was formally admitted to this university. It is proper to say that usages in the West had fairly prepared the way for the admission of women to this institution. The idea of coeducation was familiar to the public. Public opinion expressed itself, both in the legislature and otherwise, so strongly in favor of the admission of women to the university, that it was deemed wise to defer to it.

"I think the opposition to receiving women was due to the fear (1) that some young men might be turned away from here; (2) that the health of the women would suffer from the attempt to pursue a thorough course of study here; (3) that the women would not be able to master the severer studies; and (4) that embarrassments might arise from the lack of thoughtfulness and discretion on the part of some of the young men and the young women, left largely to themselves and away from home.

"We have now had nine years' experience in coeducation. We have had women studying in every department—the Literary or Collegiate, the Medical Schools (the Old School and the Homeopathic), the Law School, the Pharmacy School, and the Dental College. The number has risen from 34 in 1871, to 132 in 1879. We now have 129. We have never made a single new law or regulation in consequence of their coming.

"What, now, can we say of the fears which were entertained at the outset? First, I think it possible that some young men who had thought of coming here were at first turned from us to some other college; but I cannot say that I know of any such case. Second, I think the solicitude concerning the health of the women has not proved well-founded. On the contrary, I am convinced that a young woman, coming here in fair health, devoting herself to her appointed work, not going too much into society, but living with reasonable prudence and care of herself, is quite as likely to be in good health at the time of her graduation as she would have been if she had remained at home. The regularity of the life and the deep interest which it awakens and maintains, are manifestly conducive to mental and bodily health.

"Third, there is no branch of study pursued in any of our schools in which some women have not done superior work. It was soon found that in those studies which are thought to make the most strenuous demand on the intellect, some of the women took equal rank with the best men. They have desired and have received no favors. After graduation, a fair proportion have secured positions of eminent usefulness, especially as teachers and as physicians. Some of them have been engaged in teaching the Greek and the Latin in our preparatory schools. Five of our graduates have been called to the Faculty of Wellesley College.

"Fourth, the relations of the sexes to each other here are those of well-bred men and well-bred women, and are not, in fact, in the least degree embarrassing to us."[63]

Two other early experiments in coeducation, less significant than that at the University of Michigan, were carried on in the state—one at Olivet College and the other at Hillsdale College, both beginning about 1844. The first was under the leadership of Shipherd, previously associated with the experiment at Oberlin. In 1858, Rev. Fairfield came to take charge of Olivet College and, in 1859, the institution was opened under a new college charter. Three ladies were granted diplomas from the "ladies' course" in 1863, and received the degree L.C.; but the first class graduated from the classical department, according to one authority, was in 1867.[64] Official records of the College do not show that any woman received the A.B. from Olivet before 1882. One received a B.S. in 1874.[65]

The institution which became Hillsdale College, was first opened at Spring Arbor (1844) but was closed (1853) and transferred to Hillsdale. The institution was coeducational from the beginning, following the influence of Oberlin. Moreover it was open to all, "irrespective of nationality, creed or color." In 1851, Elizabeth D. Camp graduated from the scientific course and received a degree; but Livonia E. Benedict was the first graduate in the classical course, 1852, receiving the Bachelor of Arts degree.

Cornell University, modelled to some extent after Michigan, and depending much upon the labors of A. D. White and Charles Kendall Adams, both Michigan men, was destined to become a new center of the struggle for coeducation. The practice of coeducation was implied in Ezra Cornell's wish to "found an institution where any person can find instruction in any study";

[63] Op. cit. (1881), XXIX, 281.
[64] Early History of Olivet College [Michigan Pioneer and Historical Collections (1881), III, 410–11].
[65] By letter from the President, Dec. 9, 1927.

and more explicitly, "I hope we have made the beginning of an institution which will prove highly beneficial to the poor young men and the poor young women of our country." *Godey's Lady's Book* commented with approval on Cornell's wish "to see at least five thousand boys and girls studying within its walls" and remarked that the time had passed for "the Oriental system of separating the sexes," which was "based on a mistaken view of human nature."[66]

The early entrance of women to Cornell was made possible by the gift of a building and an endowment of $250,000 by Henry W. Sage. On the day of President White's inauguration, he said to him: "When you are ready to carry out the idea of educating young women as thoroughly as young men, I will provide the endowment to enable you to do so."[67] The wisdom of such a step was carefully questioned, and opinions were sought from far and near by the committee of which Andrew White was chairman. In the *Report of the Committee on Mr. Sage's Proposal to Endow a College for Women* (1872), the idea was approved. Curiously enough, as it doubtless appeared to some, one of the purposes which it was felt would be served by the education of women was the reformation of taste in dress. It was planned to open Sage College in 1874. Somewhat later the University published an *Answer to Inquiries about Facilities for the Education of Ladies at Cornell University*, in which the view (very commonly quoted at the time) was expressed, that "the difference between a college where ladies are not admitted and one to which they are admitted is the difference simply between the smoking car and the one back of it."

But if the University was officially strongly in favor of coeducation, the student body—at least that small part of it that makes itself conspicuous by much talking—was and has continued to be opposed, proposing, at one time or another, to exclude "coeds" from ordinary college activities, such as elections, class publications, and places on committees. A professor, sympathizing with the complete separation idea, was reported to have said at a banquet of the students of Arts and Sciences: "It is to be effected in a gentlemanly way, but effected it must be. The situation is due, perhaps, to the fact that the girls have a civilization and in-

66 *Op. cit.*, Dec. 1870, 556.
67 *R. C. E.* (1903), II, 1058.

terests of their own and do not share in those of the boys. Their sports, views, and habits differ so that they have little in common. Enforced association under the circumstances is irksome. It is promised in regard to coeducation that it will 'refine' the boys, but college boys want their fling and don't wish to be refined. They prefer congenial savagery.''[68]

But women have increased in importance at Cornell. Ten years ago, the Cornell Women's Club of New York City sent a petition to the Trustees requesting (1) that opportunities for vocational training for women at Cornell be increased and (2) that "a distinguished woman scholar" be put on the faculty of Arts and Sciences. A committee, appointed to handle the petition, recommended (1) that such vocational courses be organized, (2) that a woman scholar be appointed, and (3) that "as vacancies occur" women be considered as well as men. The first was taken under consultation, and the third adopted. As to the second, the faculty of arts and sciences, on Jan. 8, 1915, resolved as follows:

"1. The faculty would regard as unfortunate the appointment of any woman or her exclusion from consideration as a candidate for appointment on the ground of sex.

"2. The faculty recognizes the difficulties and dangers which have been pointed out in discussions of the subject, such as the temptation to appoint women from motives of economy. It is in full accord with that portion of the report of the committee of the trustees read to the faculty by the president which insists upon preëminence in productive scholarship and creative ability as the necessary qualification of any woman who may be considered.''[69]

Another effort to enhance the position of women was made by Mrs. Moody, who requested that the title, Adviser of Women, be changed to Dean of Women and that the salary be not less than five thousand dollars. After full consideration, the faculty concluded:

"1. The coeducational system, to which Cornell University is committed, assumes that women do not constitute a separate class educationally; and accordingly that it is not desirable or necessary to entrust their education to a separate faculty or to appoint a dean or director of women's education.

[68] Quoted in *The School Journal*, LXXIV, 550.
[69] Reported in *Sch. & Soc.*, I, 237.

"2. It is undesirable to change the title of Adviser of Women to that of Dean of Women.

"3. It is undesirable to attempt to solve the problems which the presence of women in the university involves, by ignoring existing conditions, and copying the system in vogue at some other institution.

"4. The determination of educational policies and the educational direction of all students, both men and women, should remain in the hands of the faculties.

"5. It is highly desirable that the Adviser of the Women should be an active teacher of experience and reputation in her profession, or that (as at present) the position should be filled by a woman who is also the medical officer in charge of the health of women students.

"6. The Adviser of Women should ex-officio be a member of the instructing staff of one of the colleges of the university, she should also be a member of the faculty of that college.

"7. The relation of the adviser of women to educational matters should be the same as that of any other member of the university faculty; but she should not ex-officio have any jurisdiction over educational policies, and should not in virtue of that office have any responsibility for the education of women students.

"8. It would not be in accordance with the present scale of salaries at Cornell to appropriate so large an amount as $5,000 for this position.'"[70]

The period from 1833 to 1870 was one of experimentation with coeducation, usually beginning on a small scale as at Oberlin and Antioch. The adoption of the principle by such influential institutions as Michigan and Wisconsin in the West, and Cornell in the East, exerted a powerful influence on its general acceptance elsewhere. Then, too, there were advances in conservative centers. In 1869, action was taken which resulted in Boston University. President William F. Warren stated, regarding it, that "a university should exist not for one sex merely, but equally for the two. . . . Boston University, therefore, welcomes to all its advantages young women and young men on precisely the same conditions. It welcomes women not merely to the bench of the pupil, but also to the chair of the professor. It is the first insti-

[70] *Ibid.*, VI, 136.

tution in the Commonwealth of Massachusetts to admit the two sexes to common advantages in classical collegiate studies; the first in the world to open the entire circle of post-graduate professional schools to men and women alike. Nor is any fear whatever felt lest the newly enfranchised class prove in the end incapacitated, either intellectually or by physiological constitution, for making a wise and beneficent use of these new-found facilities.''[71]

Limited coeducation appeared officially at the University of Pennsylvania; and the Philadelphia *Telegraph* announced hopefully that ''if females avail themselves of this exceptional opportunity'' there can be no doubt, ''if the plan succeeds, . . . that the entire university course will eventually be as open to women as to men.''[72] It had already been tried on a small scale. The *Ledger* said: ''Some women students who worked in Professor Genth's laboratory last winter acquitted themselves well, their work comparing favorably with that of the boys and their presence proving to be by no means a disturbing element—rather a regulating one in fact. The University Classes in Harmony and the Science of Music, in the afternoons, for two years, have been attended by both men and women students. Thus the 'making haste slowly' of the old institution has proven the wisdom of the step.''[73] The prophecy of the *Telegraph* has not been completely fulfilled, but the prophet saved his face, perhaps, by ''eventually.'' The *Ledger* was convinced that ''what this old, conservative, Philadelphia University can do may be safely followed by every other university and college in the state.''

The force of example on the part of the conservative cannot be denied. But coeducation had the fortune to be encouraged both by old, conservative and radical, new institutions. At its very foundation, the aspiring University of Chicago elected to go upon the full coeducational plan, albeit in later years a reaction against coeducation occurred.

In 1873, forty years after the beginning of the first experiment at Oberlin, the returns to the Commissioner's office showed a total of 8,141 women students in ''mixed colleges,'' of whom 5,622 were in ''preparatory'' and 2,519 in regular college courses. Of

71 *R. C. E.* (1903), I, 1059.
72 Quoted by the *Pennsylvania School Jour.* (1877), XXVI, 177-8.
73 *Ibid.*

97 institutions, which reported 7,357 of the 8,141 women students, 5 were in the New England, 8 in the middle, 67 in the Western and 17 in the Southern states.[74]   Making allowance for inaccuracy and incompleteness of returns, and the false claims to collegiate rank, which would tend to correct each other, it is obvious that widespread sanction had been accorded coeducation. The figures are also sufficiently accurate to show the location of conservative opinion in the Eastern, Southern and Central states, and the presence of a freer, progressive attitude in the West. By 1870, women had been admitted to 30.7% of the whole number of colleges (excluding the technical schools and the colleges established expressly for women).   Ten years saw the proportion of coeducational institutions reach 51.3%; and, in 1890 and 1900, they constituted 65.5% and 71.6% of the whole number, respectively.[75]   Significant as is this increase of coeducational institutions from thirty to seventy per cent between 1870 and 1900, the number of students is of even greater importance. Women in coeducational schools increased from 3,044, in 1875, to 19,959 in 1900 (a sixfold increase), whereas students at women's colleges increased only from 9,572 to 15,977.   Another fact which was rather terrifying to anti-coeducationalists was that the number of men at coeducational institutions increased but threefold (26,352 to 81,084), while the number of women increased six.[76]

In the nineties, the action of a number of Eastern institutions showed to what an extent the demand for women's education in men's institutions had been felt.   The trustees of Tufts College voted to open all departments to women in 1892–3.   Yale opened the Graduate School in 1891–2.[77]   Brown admitted women to examinations of the university in 1890, after discussing proposals for fully five years.   To prepare them to pass examinations, "women's classes in all Freshman studies were formed outside of college and received instruction substantially the same as that received by Freshmen in College."[78]

[74] R. C. E., 1873, LVIII.
[75] Ibid., 1889–90, II, 764; 1899–1900, II, 1880; and 1902, II, 2388–9.
[76] Ibid., for the dates mentioned.
[77] See p. 335.
[78] R. C. E. (1890–91), II, 814–15.

So convincing is the argument of popularity and numerical majority, that by the beginning of the new century the question of coeducation was often referred to as "a dead issue." Butler, in 1902, declared: "The American people have settled the matter," and he gave the above figures to prove his statement.[79] An editorial in the *New England Journal* regarded it "an innocent diversion to discuss the question," but hazarded the opinion that "public schools will never be less coeducational than they are today." Van Hise pointed out, in 1907, that it was the "immediate success of coeducation in the older of the state universities of the middle west" that caused "its establishment as a matter of course in the newer." It was this dominant sentiment that was responsible for the coeducational basis upon which such great private institutions as Stanford and Chicago were founded.

Only in the South has coeducation been slow of adoption. In 1869, the chief obstacles said to stand in the way of "an efficient system of free schools" in South Carolina were "want of funds," "indifference resulting from the ignorance of the people," and "deeply rooted prejudice against mixed schools."[80] Other expressions of contempt for coeducation in public schools have already been referred to.[81] Scarcity of funds was not such an insuperable obstacle to communities which either did not harbor the "prejudice" or, if they did, sacrificed it. Higher education in the South was also inclined to follow the principle of separate education. In 1910, of the 108 class A and class B women's colleges, 66 per cent were in the South Atlantic and South Central states.[82] Of the state universities in the South, and east of the Mississippi, only Alabama, Kentucky, Mississippi, North Carolina, Tennessee and West Virginia were coeducational. To the west of the Mississippi, Louisiana alone was non-coeducational.[83] In 1921–22, Florida reported none as attending the university, but mentioned over four thousand women taking "summer school, short winter courses, extension and correspondence courses." Florida State College for Women had 658

---

[79] *Journal of Education* (1902), LVI, 314.

[80] *R. C. E.*, 1870, 285.

[81] See p. 227.

[82] *R. C. E.* (1910), II, Tables 46 and 51, pp. 870 and 876.

[83] Van Hise on Educational Tendencies in State Universities [*Ed. Rev.* (1907), XXXIV, 511].

students.[84]   The University of Georgia had 132 women, whereas the Georgia State College for Women had 1,081.   Louisiana had 276 women; the University of Maryland, 222; the University of South Carolina, 109; and the University of Virginia, 36.[85]

Though Barbara Blount and a few others attended Blount College—the University of Tennessee—in its early days, the fact is not in any way an index to sentiment prevailing in the South on the subject of coeducation.   Probably no struggle for the admission of women to a state university was longer drawn out, or developed more bitterness, than that at the University of Virginia.   About 1879, a resolution was offered in the Senate by C. T. Smith, asking that something be done by Virginia to provide higher education for women, since she "has never, at any period of her history, made any provision whatever" for them, though she "has liberally provided for the higher education of her sons."[86]   Even at this early date, as his speech indicated, there were two distinct parties interested in the question: "The oppostion has said that this was a proposition 'to drag the women of Virginia into politics.'   I cannot see the matter in that far-fetched vain light, and there is no power on earth that can drive our noble women in that direction."[87]   Smith's resolution, which was adopted, required the Superintendent of Public Instruction to make an investigation and report.   Ruffner's reply dismissed the coeducational idea as "repugnant to the prejudices of the people" and proposed a female college similar to Girton, Smith or Vassar.[88]

About ten years later, A. D. Mayo made an eloquent appeal for the women of Virginia to "demand the establishment of a genuine woman's university. . . ."[89]   This was the beginning of an active, continuous, and concerted movement to secure the admission of women to the University of Virginia.   The immediate cause which precipitated the whole question was Caroline P. Davis' request (1892) for permission to take the regular examinations required of candidates for the A.B. in the School of

84 *Biennial Survey*, 1920–1922, II, 335–6.
85 *Ibid.*, 336, 340, 351, 354.
86 *Jour. Ed. of Va.* (1879), X, 212–3.
87 *Ibid.*
88 As quoted in the *R. C. E.* (1903), I, 437–8.
89 *Ibid.* (1890–1), II, 920–1.

Mathematics. The request was granted and the whole question of women's freedom to take such examinations was submitted to a special committee. The result was faculty approval of the exercise of this examining function on the part of the University. But because it was later voted "ineffective," the plan was never put into general practice. From 1892 to 1920–1, the struggle resolved itself into a question of a state college for women, full coeducation, or a coördinate college. During this period all the old arguments were brought forth which had done duty in many another controversy over coeducation. Women would encroach on the rights of men; there would be new problems of government, perhaps scandals; the old honor system would have to be changed; standards would be lowered to those of other coeducational schools; and the glorious reputation of the university, as a school for men, would be trailed in the dust.

Both sides were earnest. Bills were introduced regularly, favoring the establishment of a coördinate institution.[90] The organized opposition of alumni met each bill as introduced and defeated it. Such was the legislative record each biennium from 1910 to 1920. The president thoroughly favored a coördinate college, as the only safe and sure way to forestall complete coeducation. Finally, after many failures, one of the leaders of the woman's movement, Mrs. Munford, came to accept the view that the best step was to follow R. W. Moore's suggestion that the question of women's admission be restricted to their entrance into professional and graduate instruction. Acting accordingly, a measure of success was achieved in 1920–1, when women were admitted on a coeducational basis to study in graduate and professional departments.[91]

II. Arguments for and against Coeducation

Facing the figures of today, 115 institutions for the higher education of women only, with 31,769 students, and 354 coeducational universities and colleges, with 162,558 male and 96,908 female students,[92] and, recalling that, at present, scarcely an article appears either for or against coeducation, it is rather curi-

90 Text of one resolution in favor of the coördinate college published in *Sch. & Soc.*, III, 274.

91 Bruce: *Hist. of Univ. of Va.*, IV, 63–9; and V, 86–103.

92 *Biennial Survey*, 1918–1920, Bul. 1923, No. 29, 281.

ous to find what a thin partition separates the present complacent indifference from the agitation and widely divergent views of the recent past. "The American people," Butler said, "have decided in favor of coeducation." But that they "have decided" implies that there was a time of indecision. What were the arguments or proofs that carried the day for coeducation; what adverse views had to be met before it was "decided"? It is impossible to measure precisely the weight and influence of each argument pro and con, but all that appear to have carried weight may be mentioned; and, insofar as it is possible to judge the importance of ideas by the attention devoted to them, in the order of their significance.

The reason most often assigned for coeducation's success was its economy. Hosmer, in 1874, wrote that "for economical reasons, the highest education makes necessary coeducation."[93] As an influential factor, it has been very generally accepted, though not universally. Olin came to the conclusion that "economy in providing for . . . women . . . was not, in the origin of the present system, influential in Wisconsin."[94] Bryce clearly was led to believe that money was a factor, for he said of coeducation: "The need for it is at any rate not urgent [in the East] because the liberality of founders and benefactors has provided in at least five women's colleges . . . an excellent education," which he believed surpassed that of the state universities.[95] This "liberality" in the case of Vassar had been exhibited long before Wisconsin, Michigan, and many other state universities established coeducation. Van Hise, too, contrary to Olin, accepted the economic explanation: "The reasons which led to coeducation were then purely economic. The western states in these early days were too poor to support two high grade educational institutions. Yet the justice was recognized of the women's demand that they have equal opportunity with men. There was no way to afford such opportunity but to adopt coeducation, and this was the solution which was gradually forced upon the older state universities of the middle west."[96] Bascom, the enthusiastic sup-

[93] *N. E. A. Proc.*, 133.

[94] *Women of A State University*, by Mrs. H. M. Olin, used by courtesy of the publishers, G. P. Putnam's Sons, New York. Pp. 54–5.

[95] *American Commonwealth*, II, 734.

[96] Educational Tendencies in State Universities, by Van Hise [in *Ed. Rev.* (1907), XXXIV, 509–11].

porter of coeducation, and President of Wisconsin, judged the
economic reason sound: "Coeducation is the most simple and
economical method and has an advantage both in attainment and
extension over separate colleges. These reasons of equality and
economy greatly helped coeducation in the Western States in
their early history. . . . That a University should be provided
for young men, while young women were left to shift for themselves, was not to be thought of."[97] Thwing wrote, also, in 1883:

"A reason for coeducation that might be urged in advance of
any trial of the system, and yet one which practice has found to
be valid, is its economy of means and forces. A professor can
lecture to a hundred as well as to fifty students. Libraries and
laboratories once established can be used by a larger number
without a correspondingly larger expense. It is this fact of
economy to which President Eliot refers when, in expressing his
opinion that young men and women from fifteen to twenty years
of age are not 'best educated in intimate association,' he yet
acknowledges that this 'method may nevertheless be justifiable
in a community which cannot afford anything better.' "[98]
Again, in 1894, he declared: "Coeducation has the advantage of
economy. Numbers increase pecuniary cheapness. Many of the
colleges of the West were established for both men and women
because the churches or the people could not afford two colleges
in a single commonwealth."[99] Garber, in 1902, said: "The
necessities of frontier conditions and the influences of education
by the state paved the way for educating them together."[100]
Sachs, too, was of the opinion that "the fundamental considerations that underlie are of a purely economic character. Coeducation is the first, the most obvious, the cheapest way of satis-
fying the just demands of women that they be given every
intellectual opportunity they crave for."[101] While his statement
did not reach beyond the usual limits of the argument of economy, the manner of it did challenge the thought of some. "Suppose," he asked, "it were definitely shown that coeducation were
a more expensive scheme than separate school organizations,

[97] Bascom: Coeducation [*Ed. Rev.* (1908), XXXVI, 444 *ff.*].
[98] Women's Education [*Education* (1883), IV, 54–5].
[99] *The College Woman*, 111 *ff.*
[100] Garber: Coeducation [*Education* (1902), XXIII, 236 *ff.*].
[101] *Ed. Rev.* (1908), XXXV, 467.

would its advantages still be as forcibly urged, because of the ethical and social presumptions which commend it, because of the influence on quality and content of instruction, because of its efficacy as a preferable means of discipline?"[102]   It is possible that Bascom emphasized equality more and economy less than he should.   In the case of Wisconsin, from 1850 to 1860, no women were admitted on any basis; and during the War they were in normal courses, but attended college classes when approved.   The legislature did express its belief in offering equal advantages in 1866, but not till 1874 was coeducation fully recognized in practice.   Alabama (1831) was not coeducational until 1893; Illinois (1868) admitted women in 1870; Indiana (1820) did not admit women till 1868; Maine (1868) admitted women in 1872; and Mississippi (1848) was not coeducational till 1882.   Others might be named.   These suffice, however, to point out that equality of provision was not universal at first, even in state schools.   Those established early usually waited a long time for the admission of women; those established later were coeducational from the start or changed in the course of a few years.

Usually the economic factor was involved in one way or another.   Michigan had been in operation since 1841.   In 1867, the legislature expressed its opinion that the high purposes of the institution could never be fully realized till women were admitted.   In the next report, President Haven made a quick change of view, expressing himself in favor of the admission of women on the same footing as men.   This change, it is believed, was due partially to the fact that he did not wish to make another plea for appropriations until the legislature's expressed preference for coeducation had been given a favorable reply.[103]   There can be no question as to the rôle played by this economic factor.   Van de Warker asserts that after the legislature had approved the "two sex college" the faculty objected to the extra expense and the "women of Michigan raised $100,000. . . ."[104]   Cornell did not open its doors to women until Sage had made a special endowment for them.[105]   A considerable amount was

[102] *Ibid.*
[103] Hinsdale: *Hist. of the Univ. of Michigan*, 131–2.
[104] *Woman's Unfitness for Higher Coeducation*, 8.
[105] See p. 248.

given by women to gain a place in Johns Hopkins.[106] Susan B. Anthony is said to have nearly lost her life raising money to subsidize the University of Rochester, that women might be admitted.[107] The economic factor cannot be denied by any candid judge. It is true, of course, that saving money was not stressed by those who actually established coeducation. Oberlin, Knox, Antioch, and their successors found many more ideal reasons for coeducation than mere economy. But it is evident to all that the people of the West, in 1833, 1846, or 1852, could not have erected separate colleges for women. To extricate even a single coeducational college from its financial troubles, and keep it alive, cost the life of one man. Thwing was justified in saying "the churches" and "the people" were too poor to "afford two colleges."

Grant and Hodgson, in *The Case for Coeducation,*[108] pointed to the accepted economic factor, but rightly asserted it was not entirely responsible. With it they coupled our fundamental democracy. As a single factor, however, democracy has been overrated. It is customary for visitors to see the natives worse or better, rather than as they are. De Tocqueville said, in his *Democracy in America,* "The Americans have done all they could to raise woman morally and intellectually to the level of man, and in this respect they appear to me to have excellently understood the true principle of democratic improvement." He did not know, or possibly had forgotten, our New England forebears, who very generally excluded the "maids" from the town schools, and only after many years began to allow them to attend in the early morning or after the school hours of the boys; and that girls generally, throughout the land, had no opportunities for a college education. Still the "Americans" may have done "all they could"; and it is certainly true that there were many champions of such justice and equality as De Tocqueville mentioned, who recognized this "true principle of democratic improvement." These champions, however, appeared only at intervals, and among those who possessed some leisure. They became more numerous with the expansion of the industrial

[106] See p. 358.

[107] Harper: *Life and Work of Susan B. Anthony,* III, 1224–6; see also Van de Warker: *op. cit.,* 8–9.

[108] 160 *ff.*

changes which helped to increase and concentrate wealth, freed some women from household activities, and gave to others freedom to engage in new occupations, as well as the incentive thereto. It is not chance that the nineteenth century had its Blackwells, Beechers, Willards, Dalls, Lockwoods, Lyons, Grants, Stantons, Motts, and Anthonys, while the eighteenth could point to but few outstanding women. But it is also improbable that their appearance was due, in any great measure, to an enlargement of that democracy in which we had declared our faith, for it actually began to shrink rather than grow larger. The democratic principle, though frequently invoked, could not free women and educate them, contrary to the devout wishes of our New England ancestors; nor could it free and educate them in the midst of poverty and hard work. The Southern gentleman of Colonial days was less Puritanic and more wealthy than his Northern neighbor; along with these differences he retained a chivalric conception of woman, and consequently educated her more liberally. The Quakers held a doctrine of equality of the sexes, which, rather than "democracy," accounts for their attitude towards the education of girls.

Given certain environing conditions such as (1) the change in the economic situation[109] and (2) the decline of a religious doctrine that made man the head and woman the body, it was then possible for a cry in the name of democracy to be of some avail. Such a cry had been unavailing when Mrs. Adams spoke to John on the subject. "All men are created free and equal," it was agreed. But as for women, that was a different question.

The two conditions mentioned above were satisfied gradually. The opening of new avenues to women has been pointed out. Wealth increased phenomenally in the nineteenth century. Theological taboos against women declined. Oberlin admitted women to its theological school. This was but a symptom; and while the church, here and there, became more liberal towards women, its complete sway over both men and women began to decline.

This new economic independence made woman an equal of man, and sturdier virtues began to be demanded of her. She became "companion and co-laborer," in a new and more complete sense than before. As an equal she demanded an equal

[109] See Ch. I.

education. This claim to equal opportunity, this demand that America give heed to the "true principle of democratic improvement," was proclaimed with marked vigor by Caroline Dall, in 1861. The plea appears in many places, and is especially characteristic of the suffragist's position. Its importance warrants quotation here:

"We have already said, that the coeducational rights of women are simply those of all human beings,—namely, 'the right to be taught all common branches of learning, a sufficient use of the needle, and any higher branches, for which they shall evince either taste or inclination; the right to have colleges, schools of law, theology, and medicine open to them; the right of access to all scientific and literary collections, to anatomical preparations, historical records, and rare manuscripts.'

"And we do not make this claim with any particular theory as to woman's powers or possibilities. She may be equal to man, or inferior to him. She may fail in rhetoric, and succeed in mathematics. She may be able to bear fewer hours of study. She may insist on more protracted labor. What we claim is, that no one knows, as yet, what women are, or what they can do,—least of all, those who have been wedded for years to that low standard of womanly achievement, which classical study tends to sustain. Because we do not know, because experiment is necessary, we claim that all educational institutions should be kept open for her; that she should be encouraged to avail herself of these, according to her own inclination; and that, so far as possible, she should pursue her studies, and test her powers, in company with man. We do not wish her to follow any dictation; nor ours, nor another's. We ask for her a freedom she has never yet had. There is, between the sexes, a law of incessant, reciprocal action, of which God avails himself in the constitution of the family, when he permits brothers and sisters to nestle about one hearth-stone. Its ministration is essential to the best educational results. Our own educational institutions should rest upon this divine basis. In educating the sexes together under fatherly and motherly supervision, we avail ourselves of the highest example; and the result will be a simplicity, modesty, and purity of character, not so easy to attain when general abstinence from each other's society makes the occasion of re-union a period of harmful excitement. Out of it would come a quick perception of mutual proprieties, delicate attention to manly and womanly habits, refinement of feeling, grace of manner, and a thoroughly symmetrical development. If the objections which are urged against this—the divine fashion of training men and women to the duties of life—were well founded, they would have been felt long ago in those district schools, attended by both sexes, which are the pride of New England. The classes recently opened by the Lowell Institute, under the control of the Institute of Technology, are an effort in the right direction, for which we cannot be too grateful. Heretofore, every attempt to give advanced instruction to women has failed. Did a woman select the most accomplished instructor of men, and pay him the highest fee, she could not secure thorough tuition. He taught her without conscience in the higher branches; for he took it upon himself to assume that she would never put them to practical use. He treated her desire for such instruction as a caprice, though she might have shown her appreciation by the distinct bias of her life. We claim for women a share of the opportunities offered to men, because we believe that they will never be thoroughly taught until they are taught at the same time and in the same classes."[110]

The argument touched on in the last lines was developed by John Bascom, one of the few men who were absolute friends of coeducation in colleges. "As the need of woman for more generous training was recognized, there arose slowly and painfully colleges fitted to meet it. These institutions, owing their origin to a sentiment which only partially and reluctantly recognized the underlying claim, though excellent in themselves, have always, as educational centers, been inferior to those provided for young men. The East . . . can never regard its colleges for women as standing on any terms of equality with its universities. The only ground on which an unalloyed satisfaction can be taken in them is that the claims of young women are not only different from those of young men, but inferior to them.

"The inferiority of women's colleges will not be limited to the curriculum, or to its possible lines of development, but will extend to the purpose and temper of instruction. There are few colleges in which any rare excellence of instruction is reached. To speak of genius in a teacher may be thought to approach an

[110] *College, Market and the Court*, 6–8.

absurdity; the dullness of routine nowhere prevails more than in the recitation room.   Teachers of unusual guiding and stimulating power are great wealth.   An institution that is possest of even a few of them begins at once to take preeminent rank. These persons will be found almost exclusively in men's colleges. The demand, opportunity, and reward are greater there than elsewhere.   Here the superiority is most likely to be achieved and recognized.   But if we cut off half the human household from the best inspiration which comes to it, we do it an irreparable wrong."[111]   Continuing, he said:

"A recent article averse to co-education gathers up its conclusions in the following words: 'The time has come, I believe, to base a rational educational scheme upon an analysis of girls' nature; it should recognize their potentialities, their methods of thought, their defects, and their merits; should strengthen, control, direct their energies.'   This summation not only carries no weight with the advocate of co-education, it is simply a concise statement of what he fears.   It rejects what the lovers of liberty desire, that the powers of election and use should have free play in working out personal life.   The opportunities of one-half the race are about to be measured out to them under some existing notion of their proper extent."[112]

In the minority report on coeducation at Williams College, Bascom had definitely declared that "the graduates [of Vassar] . . . are not prepared to take charge even of our high schools. They cannot fit young men for college."[113]   This inequality in institutions was generally recognized.   Tarbell, in 1884, declared: "Coeducation is at present a necessity for those young ladies who desire to be accredited with thorough scholarship.   A diploma from Michigan University is of much more value to a lady than one from any of the colleges for women."[114]   Women needed the university stamp as well as men.   For that reason, the univer-

---

[111] Bascom: Coeducation [Ed. Rev. (1908), XXXVI, 444 ff.].

[112] Ibid.; also Olin: Women of a State University, 66–70, for the minority report on coeducation at Williams College.

[113] To this it was replied that Vassar was not a normal school and did not aim at "manufacturing teachers"; its entire and only aim was a liberal education.   As to what this was, no two colleges agreed, which surely left Vassar free to have her own opinion.   Other critics asserted that Vassar taught too much Greek.   Greek was elective.

[114] Coeducation, by Tarbell [Education (1884), IV, 428–9].

sities of England, and Harvard and Brown in the United States, conservatively admitted them to examinations, before admitting them to instruction.

Apropos of equal education for women, and of exceptional interest, coming from one long a leader in women's college circles, is the recent statement of Martha Carey Thomas. "The very first next step seems to me to be the demand for unqualified, true, out and out coeducation. Only by having the schools and universities coeducational can we ensure the girls of the world receiving a thoroughly good education. There is not enough money in the world to duplicate schools and universities for women, and if we could duplicate them they would soon become less good. It requires endless vigilance to keep women's universities as good as coeducational universities. It would be tragic if now, after coeducation has been tried on a tremendous scale, we university women should accept separate universities for women. We must uncompromisingly refuse an offer so vicious and reactionary as that made by your great university of Cambridge for the establishment of a separate women's university."[115]   Ada L. Comstock, of Smith College, after discussing the question, hoped the International Federation of University Women would "express its belief in the coeducation of men and women in higher institutions of learning." Her proposed resolution was endorsed by Dr. Thomas.

A third argument which appeared repeatedly was that coeducation was in accord with nature. Though minor variations on the theme occurred, the statement of Blanchard, of Knox College (1846), may be taken as representing the gist of this plea:[116]

"If I were giving, as the lawyers would say, an argument 'upon the case,' I should say this: That God has united the sexes in the family, and that man and Satan have separated them in the convent and the camp; that love between the sexes cannot be shut in or out by seminary walls, and least of all when it has

---

[115] International Federation of University Women, Bul. No. 1. *Report of First Conference*, July, 1920, 56–7.

[116] *Independent*, Jan. 1870; other statements of the "natural" argument may be found in an article by Thwing in *Education* (1883), IV, 54–5; an article by Higginson in *Educational News*, June 14, 1890, 373; touched upon also by authorities of Bennett College, *R. C. E.* (1892–3), II, 1559; also see part of the minority report on coeducation at Williams College, in Olin: *op. cit.*, 66 *ff.*

festered and soured into lust; that shutting the sexes apart to keep them pure is a mistake; that monks, as a class, are more passionate and corrupt than merchants; that imagination of the absent sex in the separate schools is worse than its presence in the mixed; and that the history and habits of the lower animals prove that as horses are known to work quietly in teams which rage and neigh when kept solitary in stalls; and that, therefore, by the laws of Nature and the workings of the mind, we ought to expect a college of young men or of young ladies kept separate and apart, would be more disorderly, harder to manage, more unreasonable, and every way worse than where the two are united in an institution sanctified by Christ's presence, and governed by conscience and God's fear. And the institution where the latter conditions are not, however constructed or conducted, is a curse.''

A fourth claim of coeducationists was the refining influence exerted upon both boys and girls. They were fond of quoting Richter's *Levana*, wherein he asserted: ''To insure modesty I would advise the educating of the sexes together; for two boys will preserve twelve girls, or two girls twelve boys, innocent amid winks, jokes, and improprieties, merely by that instinctive sense which is the forerunner of matured modesty. But I will guarantee nothing in a school where girls are alone together, and still less where boys are.'' The *Pennsylvania School Journal* reported the conclusions of a committee appointed to investigate the question, in 1854. Of this advantage, the committee remarked that ''it is a fact, lamented by teachers, but existing despite their efforts, that in schools for boys, the college and academy, the state of morals is more loose than in society in general; that young men confined with others of their own sex, will habitually engage in improprieties if not vices of which they would not dare to be guilty in other circumstances. . . . The same is true of schools for females, if not to the same extent. . . . In society at large, much good is owing to female influence . . . and if the admission of both sexes into our schools will have a tendency to produce this effect, it seems to us a strong argument in its favor.''[117] Extremely few articles in favor of coeducation failed to mention the purifying influence as an argument.

A fifth advantage, represented almost universally by protagonists of coeducation, was ''that it renders school government

[117] *Pa. Sch. Jour.* (Aug. 1854), III, 90.

more easy''; a sixth, that "it acts as a stimulus to study''; seventh, that "it enables the sexes to form a just estimate of each other.''[118]   Another claim put forth by Bascom, and occasionally referred to approvingly, sounds strange today, when most institutions are overburdened with students: ". . . Many colleges . . . would be improved financially and educationally, would experience . . . a bracing tonic in the acquisition of twenty, forty, sixty, students, though not a single dollar were added to their endowments.''[119]   Thus we have returned to the argument of economy, but this time from a slightly different angle.

Most of the advantages claimed for coeducation became disadvantages—even rank improprieties—in the minds of its opponents. In the list of metamorphosed boons, it was, however, possible for the opponents to capitalize many fears, which the coeducationalists hoped to avoid. And when the "coeducators" could quote Richter, their adversaries could summon a whole cloud of German witnesses. In fact, from almost any country of Europe arguments could be mustered against this "unnatural" system of education. Let us note their views: they are important, for it was at least partially due to such opinions, which were widely circulated, that the reaction to coeducation appeared. It was in consonance with the views of the opponents of coeducation that an institution, the coördinate college, was set up as a half-way house between coeducation and the woman's college.

The opponents, almost without exception, admitted that coeducation was "thoroughly in place in the elementary schools," but insisted that in the secondary schools and colleges "its value is at least doubtful.''[120]   The objections to coeducation in the secondary schools, voiced prominently by Sachs and Hall, and the limited movement to try out at least partial segregation at Englewood, have already been referred to.[121]

It is true that the early experiments did not cause so much public discussion as the later. Van Hise and Angell agreed that at first "the only real difficulty" was that "the women were not welcome to the students and professors." In this there was

---

[118] *Ibid.*

[119] Orton: *Liberal Education of Women*, 215 *f.*

[120] *Ed. Rev.* (1907), XXXIII, 304–5.

[121] See pp. 229 and 270 *ff.;* Cleveland might also have been included, where vocational specialization was emphasized by Harris.

some truth. How skeptical the professors were, at Geneva Medical College, about Elizabeth Blackwell! Chadbourne was reluctant to admit women to his botany class. Even today, a professor refused women admittance to his seminar,—because he would not feel free to smoke for two hours!

Closely allied to the fear that coeducation would "coarsen," "demoralize," or in some way destroy feminine sensibility was a second apprehension, perhaps springing out of the failure of the first to materialize, that women would "feminize" the institutions of learning; that even the course of study would become influenced. Some colleges found certain courses overrun by women. Men avoided them. President Van Hise, in 1907, gave figures for 13 state institutions showing that in the liberal arts departments of seven of them the women outnumbered the men. In three institutions they were "nearly twice as numerous as the men." In the thirteen universities, 52.7% of the students of the liberal arts were women. Michigan had 41.3% women, while Washington had 69.9%. Cornell, a semi-state university, had 40.8% women in the liberal arts.[122] The feminization of the public school system has already been referred to.[123] The Amherst students, anticipating from afar the advent of women as a possibility, declared they would treat them "with respect and courtesy . . . if the trustees shall deem it best to make the experiment." But they saw the end of free college life: "No such intimacy or friendship, as now exists among classmates, could or would be encouraged or permitted between students of different sex. We would inevitably be placed under stricter surveillance, our actions would be more sharply scrutinized and our privileges materially abridged. . . ."[124] Livermore wrote, in 1883, "A scholarship has been founded at Amherst, the income of which will be given to a woman when women are admitted to the institution. But that day waits."[125] Cornell men, a small and snobbish set of them at least, have been, and still are, credited with a great deal of contempt for women students.[126] Olin quotes a Wis-

[122] Tendencies in State Universities [*Ed. Rev.* (1907), XXXIV, 512–13]; consult also *Education* (1902), XXIII, 239–40.

[123] See Vol. I, 505; and Grant and Hodgson: *The Case for Coeducation* (1913), 170.

[124] *Amherst Student*, Oct. 1871, quoted by Orton: *op. cit.*, 204.

[125] *What Shall We Do With Our Daughters?* 43 *ff.*

[126] Compare Slosson: *Great American Universities*, 332 *f.*

consin alumnus, of 1864, as saying: "The feeling of hostility was exceedingly intense and bitter. As I now recollect the entire body of students were without exception opposed to the admission of the young ladies, and the anathemas heaped upon the regents were loud and deep. Some of the students left for other colleges, and more of us were restrained only by impecuniosity from following their example. During the remaining year of my own college life the feeling of intense and bitter indignation caused by the change continued almost unabated."[127]   As recently as 1907, F. W. Hamilton, President of Tufts College, wrote: "The average young man will not go to a coeducational institution if other things are anywhere near equal. . . . He is not comfortable with the women in the classroom."[128]

In the reactions of the student body and professors may be detected a large element of devotion to old tradition. The preserves of Amherst, Williams, Michigan, and Cornell must not be encroached upon by these female "thirsty knowledge seekers." Do they not have their Vassar, Smith, Mount Holyoke, Bryn Mawr, and other colleges which are "likely to meet the wants . . . for some time to come?"[129]   But some leaders of the educational world were equally opposed to change; indeed, some thought they were incapable of seeing changes already come to pass.[130]   Higginson, with great scorn, pointed out this blindness on the part of his Boston neighbors:

"I suppose that those born and bred in New England can never quite abandon the feeling that this region should still lead the nation, as it once led, in all educational matters. For one, I cannot help a slight sense of mortification, when, in an assemblage of Boston professors, undertaking to discuss a simple practical matter, everybody begins in the clouds, ignoring the facts before everybody's eyes, and discussing as a question of theory only, what has long since become a matter of common practice. The mortification is not diminished when the common-sense has to be at last imported from beyond the borders of New

127 The *Madison Democrat*, June 20, 1877—quoted from *Women of a State University*, by Mrs. H. M. Olin, G. P. Putnam's Sons, New York. Used by courtesy of the publishers. Pp. 101–2.

128 *New England Journal of Education* (1907), LXVI, 485–6.

129 *Amherst Student*, Oct. 1871, quoted by Orton: *op. cit.*, 203.

130 See, for example, the review of C. W. Eliot's address at Smith College in the *New England Jour. of Educ.* (1879), X, 149.

England, in the shape of a college president from Central New York. To him alone it seems to have occurred to remind these dwellers in the clouds that what they persisted in treating as theory had been a matter of daily experience in half the large towns in New England for the last quarter of a century."[131] Colonel Higginson made it clear that it was only a question of tradition. The only question to be answered is—since normal schools, high schools and endowed academies have proved its workability for many years—whether we may "widen the course of instruction a little and call the institution a college."

The conservatism of the South relative to coeducation has been mentioned. In 1888, Smith, writing of coeducation, pointed out the lingering opposition and the importance of the whole question for the State:

"In North Carolina the opposition to the co-education of the sexes in the higher institutions of learning is so manifest that no one would dare propose, with any hope of success, that women be admitted to the University and leading denominational colleges of the State. But coeducation is making headway in the institutions for secondary instruction, and its friends claim that good results have been manifest. The rank that women are taking in some of the best of the English and American universities precludes the argument that they can not maintain themselves in intellectual competition with the sterner sex, and so the objection that their admission would necessitate the lowering of the educational standard is not valid. The expediency of their admission is an open question which the writer is not prepared to advocate; but at this time when a number of the female teachers of the State are seeking admission to the normal department of the University, endowed by the State for the express purpose of giving the teachers of the State, a large proportion of whom are women, a better opportunity for special preparation in their profession, the question is practical to all North Carolinians and is worthy of careful study."[132]

While the enthusiastic coeducationist was declaiming on the improved morality of the two-sex colleges, his opponent was throwing up his hands at the prospect of dire results. At the women's colleges it was felt the scholarly standard was to be

---

[131] *Common Sense About Women* (1882), 227–8.
[132] Smith: *Ed. in North Carolina*, 130–1.

attained "with less heartburning and disquietude than in the coeducational university, while the students preserve a sweet womanly innocence that is difficult of preservation where the girl student is thrown into close daily association with men . . . and the delicate bloom of womanhood is lost in the enforced familiarity."[133] Van Hise says it "must unquestionably be added that in the minds of many there was doubt in reference to the maintenance of the proprieties if coeducation were adopted."[134] Many seemed to have no doubt. Bennett College authorities regretted that some families were "reluctant to send their daughters to schools for both sexes," chiefly because they were ignorant of the facts.[135] The authorities were thoroughly convinced that coeducation was right and conducive to normal life, as at home. Sachs insisted that whether this refining influence "is in truth a profound or merely a superficial one, is a matter of doubt in many quarters,"[136] and if there is impairment of either sex in any way, "we should feel ourselves compelled to care for the separate education of the two sexes on parallel lines, however great the cost."

It may be well to point out that many who opposed coeducation had had no experience with it. In the Boston investigation, of 421 masters, 254 were opposed to coeducation; and of these, 122 were teachers of girls only, and 109 taught boys only. The committee thought these views were *ex parte* and should be thrown out.[137] A similar situation appeared in college circles. Michigan, before becoming coeducational, sought opinions from many college men, some of whom, of course, had had no experience with it. Almost without exception they were hostile to the idea and believed it "demoralizing"; that it would lead to "corruption of manners and morals" and destroy "the delicacy of female character."[138]

The evils just referred to are capable of many interpretations. Some believed that the combined demoralizing influences on manners, morals, and delicacy of female character had a direct bearing on woman's relation to the matrimonial state. Hall and

133 *Educational News*, July 16, 1892, 438.
134 *Ed. Rev.* (1907), XXXIV, 509–11.
135 *R. C. E.* (1892–93), II, 1559.
136 *Ed. Rev.* (1907), XXXIII, 300.
137 *R. C. E.* (1901), II, 1255.
138 See *Education* (1883), IV, 54–5; also Orton: *op. cit.*, 233.

Smith exclaimed: "It surely can hardly be called an ideal education for women that permits eighteen out of one hundred college girls to state boldly that they would rather be men than women."[139] The new education was frequently charged with destroying romance and leading to disillusionment, and hence to "less probability of marriage."[140] "Coeducation has done more than anything else to rob marriage of its attractions, by divesting the man of most of his old-time glamour and romance. This early contact with the other sex on a footing of equality, which the majority of girl students more than maintain intellectually, has tended to produce that contempt of the much vaunted superiority of man that is as a rule reserved for those post nuptial discoveries which make marriage such an interesting venture."[141] One must not forget, of course, that other opponents of coeducation were overwhelmed with a fear of early and too many marriages. Thus Livermore, in *What Shall We Do With Our Daughters*, gave as the second objection: "Were girls and boys to study together, flirtations and early marriages would be the inevitable result; the girls would become masculine and unwomanly, and the boys effeminate and unmanly. Co-education would, therefore, lower the standard of morals."[142] Still other arguments suffered this chiastic transposition.

The dictum that coeducation was an advantage because more natural, and just like the home, was somehow twisted; and coeducation became a positive evil because it was so unlike nature. Sachs maintained that "the family and the home recognize the differences of the two sexes; they are differentiated in their occupations, their games, their tastes; why do our schools exert themselves to wipe out this distinction?"[143]

It was also assumed, finally, that since woman was the "weaker vessel," the intellectual standards of coeducational colleges would be lowered. And, as universities prized their scholastic reputation highly, many doubted the wisdom of admitting

[139] Marriage and Fecundity in College Men and Women [*Ped. Sem.*, X, 308 *ff.*].

[140] Grant and Hodgson: *op. cit.*, 193 *ff.*

[141] Laurvik: Articles on The American Girl, quoted in *Am. Ed. Rev.*, XXXIII, 428–9.

[142] *Op. cit.*, 43 *f.*

[143] *Ed. Rev.* (1907), XXXIII, 302.

women. A faculty report at Wisconsin, in 1865,[144] stated: "There has been an apprehension that the standard of culture would be lowered in consequence," but so far the institution was saved by the fact that there had been no such "mingling of classes in the higher and more recondite subjects. . . ." Van Hise said, in 1907, that he had been asked the question, "by prominent educational men," whether this had not been so; and "notwithstanding my denial, which has since been sustained by a score of letters from state university presidents, it was still held that a deterioration of intellectual standards in coeducational institutions could hardly be avoided."[145] Livermore also noted as one of the first objections to coeducation that it would, because of woman's weakness of mind and body, "lower the grade of scholarship."[146] Hall declared, "It is utterly impossible without injury to hold girls to the same standards of conduct, regularity, severe moral accountability and strenuous mental work, that boys need." Again, we find it asserted dogmatically that "romance is inevitably bred wherever young men and women come into close association [a moment ago it was destroyed by the same circumstance] and when the little winged god comes in the window, study flies out."[147]

In view of the great skepticism about women's ability to do college work, it is proper to note here that those who had experience with coeducation reported almost without exception to the contrary. In fact, in due time, the superior scholarship of women and girls, in some subjects, became a new objection to coeducation. For the boys did not do so well competing with girls. This argument, though obviously an embarrassing one, was very frequently used. It became the target of ridicule in Alice D. Miller's lines on "The Protected Sex":

> "There, little girl, don't read,
> "You're fond of your books, I know,
> "But Brother might mope
> "If he had no hope
> "Of getting ahead of you.

[144] From *Women of a State University*, by Mrs. H. M. Olin, G. P. Putnam's Sons, New York. Used by courtesy of the publishers. P. 32.

[145] *Ed. Rev.* (1907), XXXIV, 509–11.

[146] *Op. cit.*, 43–5.

[147] *Educational News*, July 16, 1892, 438–9, quoting the *San Francisco Examiner*.

"It's dull for a boy who cannot lead.
"There, little girl, don't read."[148]

At Englewood, the "school officials . . . noted that a large portion of the boys fail to attain the same degree of scholarship that a majority of the girls reach." The officials tried segregation to save the boys' scholarship, and found it "greatly improved thereby."[149]

Many of the fears about coeducation were probably imaginary. Of these, one of the most conspicuous was that women would not be able to carry the studies of men, because unable to bear the physical strain of college work.[150] But, imaginary or not, this argument of physical weakness, coupled with the other objections named, formed the basis of the agitation for segregation, and was partly responsible for the "reaction against coeducation" which appeared in several institutions. The idea of segregation was founded everywhere on a belief in such great fundamental differences—physical, mental, and vocational—that education must be greatly modified for the two sexes, in both high school and college.[151] E. E. White, in 1872, gave a premonition of the movement for limited segregation in high schools, saying: "While we would give a daughter an education every whit as thorough and complete as a son, we are not sure that we would have this education in every respect precisely the same. The diversity would not, however, be sufficiently great to necessitate their attending separate schools." In 1885, Philbrick, of Boston, put out a circular strenuously advocating segregation because the "greatest evil in the high school [coeducational] was the risk of injury to the health of girls"; further, he argued that to attempt any readjustment in the two-sex school, that would be effective

[148] From *Are Women People?* by Alice Duer Miller, copyright 1915 by George H. Doran Company. Pp. 34–5.

[149] Grant and Hodgson: *op. cit.*, 179–81.

[150] *Ed. Rev.* (1907), XXXIV, 509–11; see also Thwing: Women's Education [*Education* (1883), IV, 54–5].

[151] The character of this argument may be seen fairly well by reference to a few of the following: Clarke: *Sex in Education* (1874); Livermore: *What Shall We Do With Our Daughters?* 43–5; Sachs: Coeducation in the U. S. [*Ed. Rev.* (1907), XXXIII, 303–4]; *Ed. Review* (1906), XXXII, 410–11; and XXXI, 353–6; *Education* (1886), VI, 647 *ff.*; Hall: Coeducation in the High School [*N. E. A. Proc.*, 1903, 446–60]; Van de Warker: *Woman's Unfitness for Higher Education*, 29, etc., etc.

in saving the girls, would be "endangering that hardihood of the boys." This led to an investigation by the Boston school committee in 1890, the result of which was that, contrary to the views of Dr. Philbrick, the separate system was held to be "an error which may take years to fully eradicate."[152] Hall and Smith were of the opinion that woman, "so long as she strives to be manlike . . . will be inferior and a pinchbeck imitation; . . . it is high time to ask ourselves whether the theory and practice of identical coeducation, especially in the high school, . . . has not brought certain grave dangers . . . and whether it does not interfere with the natural differentiations everywhere seen in home and society."[153] Elsewhere Hall said: "Coeducation in the middle teens tends to sexual precocity. This is very bad; in fact, it is one of the subtlest dangers that can befall civilization. There are momentous changes in boys at the age of fourteen. Adolescence is a crisis in their lives. The first danger to a woman is over-brainwork. It affects that part of her organism which is sacred to heredity. This danger is seen in the diminishing number of marriages. The postponement of marriage is very unfortunate in its influence upon civilization."[154]

When the fear of grave danger to health became acute, many people thought it wise' to go to the doctors. Sachs said their opinion was the only one to be considered. From many doctors the protagonists of segregation were able to get good arguments. Several books were written, one of the earliest vigorous denunciations of coeducation, for health reasons, being written by Dr. E. H. Clarke, former professor at Harvard. This appeared in 1874; *Building a Brain*, by the same author, appeared in 1880; and Maudsley's *Sex in Mind and Education*, in 1884. Clarke's first work became widely known and reached eleven editions in six years. It was vigorously attacked by physicians and educators, the latter feeling that their experience belied his statements. It was widely quoted. As late as 1903, Van de Warker, in a tirade against coeducation,[155] used Clarke's work as a conclusive argment. But it was also effective in stirring the camp of coeducation to action, provoking an early inquiry

152 Report on Coeducation, *R. C. E.* (1901), II, 1217–1315.
153 *Ped. Sem.*, X, 308 *ff.*
154 *N. E. A. Proc.* (1903), 460.
155 *Op. cit.*

on the part of the Association of Collegiate Alumnae into the health of college women.[156] It also brought forth a direct denial of its alleged facts in a book called *Woman's Education and Health*.[157] In this book the authors demolished the arguments set up previously by Dr. Clarke, and showed that most of his reasoning was *a priori*. A few statements of physicians are given at the end of the book, in which they say they cannot agree with Clarke. Most of them disagreed with him as categorically as the following:

"You cannot state too strongly my disapproval of the reasoning and conclusions of Dr. Clarke, in his book entitled 'Sex in Education.' An extended observation of thirty years has led me long since to the decided opinion that young women who study in our schools while in their teens are as a class more healthy in after life than those who do not. The causes of poor health among American women are to be found elsewhere than in uninterrupted or excessive study while in their teens. Of this I could write very largely, but will content myself with simply stating my utter disapproval of Dr. Clarke's conclusions."[158]

Lack of space will not permit a full examination of the material of *Sex in Education,* but a fair view of its contentions may be seen in the following:

"Co-education, then, signifies in common acceptation identical co-education. This identity of training is what many at the present day seem to be praying for and working for. Appropriate education of the two sexes, carried as far as possible, is a consummation most devoutly to be desired; identical education of the two sexes is a crime before God and humanity, that physiology protests against, and that experience weeps over. Because the education of boys has met with tolerable success, hitherto—but only tolerable it must be confessed—in developing them into men, there are those who would make girls grow into women by the same process. Because a gardener has nursed an acorn till it grew into an oak, they would have him cradle a grape in the same soil and way, and make it a vine. Identical education, or identical co-education, of the sexes defrauds one sex or the other, or perhaps both. It defies the Roman maxim, which physiology

---

[156] See p. 127.

[157] By G. F. and A. M. Comfort (1874).

[158] P. 146.

has fully justified, *mens sana in corpore sano.* The sustained regimen, regular recitation, erect posture, daily walk, persistent exercise, and unintermitted labor that toughens a boy, and makes a man of him, can only be partially applied to a girl. The regimen of intermittance, periodicity of exercise and rest, work three-fourths of each month, and remission, if not abstinence, the other fourth, physiological interchange of the erect and reclining posture, care of the reproductive system that is the cradle of the race, all this, that toughens a girl and makes a woman of her, will emasculate a lad. A combination of the two methods of education, a compromise between them, would probably yield an average result, excluding the best of both. It would give a fair chance neither to a boy nor a girl. Of all compromises, such a physiological one is the worst. It cultivates mediocrity, and cheats the future of its rightful legacy of lofty manhood and womanhood. It emasculates boys, stunts girls; makes semi-eunuchs of one sex, and agenes of the other.''[159]

In *Building A Brain,* to support his views of possible, nay certain disaster, Doctor Clarke quoted the results of a study of school hygiene by the Massachusetts State Board of Health.[160] These questions among others were submitted to ''teachers, physicians and others,'' with the results given below:

''1. Is one sex more liable than the other to suffer in health from attendance on school?

''2. Does the advent of puberty increase this liability?''

*   *   *

''Replies were received from one hundred and sixty persons, of whom one hundred and fifteen are stated to be physicians; nineteen, physicians and members of school committees; fourteen, teachers of experience; and six, superintendents of schools. The Circular of the Board requested that all the replies should be 'based on personal observation.' The result of this inquiry, so far as it concerns the relation of sex to education, may be gathered by looking over the following extract from the *Report,* which also presents the conclusion that Dr. Winsor reached upon the subject we are considering:

[159] Pp. 127–9.
[160] See *Fifth Annual Report,* 1873.

"*Question* 1 [was] answered substantially as follows:

Females more liable than males... 109
Males more liable than females................................... 1
Both alike liable.. 31
Neither is in danger... 4
Not in district schools.. 1
Not if both sexes exercise alike in the open air...... 1
Unable to answer... 5

* * *

"*Question* 2 [was] answered substantially as follows:

Yes 120
No 12
Uncertain 9

"Of those who answer, 'Yes,' many add, 'for girls'; and it is evident that nearly all have the same limitation in mind."[161]

On the basis of the "facts," Clarke prophesied that "if these causes should continue for the next half-century, and increase in the same ratio as they have for the last fifty years, it requires no prophet to foretell that the wives who are to be the mothers in our republic must be drawn from transatlantic homes. The sons of the New World will have to react, on a magnificent scale, the old story of unwived Rome and the Sabines." Similar gloomy vistas were beheld by many prominent doctors, whom Maudsley quoted. Dr. N. Allen said:

"Formerly such an organization was generally possessed by American women, and they found but little difficulty in nursing their infants. It was only occasionally in case of some defect in the organization, or where sickness of some kind had overtaken the mother, that it became necessary to resort to the wet-nurse, or to feeding by hand. And the English, the Scotch, the German, the Canadian, the French, and the Irish women who are living in this country, generally nurse their children; the exceptions are rare. But how is it with our American women who become mothers? It has been supposed by some that all, or nearly all of them, could nurse their offspring just as well as not; that the disposition only was wanting, and that they did not care about having the trouble or confinement necessarily attending it. But this is a great mistake. This very indifference or aversion shows something wrong in the organization, as well as in the disposi-

---

161 Clarke: *op. cit.*, 71–3; and 75.

tion; if the physical system were all right, the mind and natural instincts would generally be right also. While there may be here and there cases of this kind, such an indisposition is not always found. It is a fact that large numbers of our women are anxious to nurse their offspring, and make the attempt; they persevere for a while—perhaps for weeks or months—and then fail. . . . There is still another class that cannot nurse at all, having neither the organs nor nourishment necessary to make a beginning.''

The reasons for the difference between American and other women, Allen found as follows:

''In consequence of the great neglect of physical exercise, and the continuous application to study, together with various other influences, large numbers of our American women have altogether an undue predominance of the nervous temperament. If only here and there an individual were found with such an organization, not much harm comparatively would result; but when a majority, or nearly a majority have it, the evil becomes one of no small magnitude.''

Dr. Weir Mitchell was also quoted:

''Worst of all, to my mind, most destructive in every way, is the American view of female education. The time taken for the more serious instruction of girls extends to the age of eighteen, and rarely over this. During these years they are undergoing such organic development as renders them remarkably sensitive. . . . To-day the American woman is, to speak plainly, physically unfit for her duties as woman, and is, perhaps, of all civilized females, the least qualified to undertake those weightier tasks which tax so heavily the nervous system of man. She is not fairly up to what Nature asks from her as a wife and mother. How will she sustain herself under the pressure of those yet more exacting duties which nowadays she is eager to share with man?''[162]

Maudsley stated his own belief in the following terms:

''. . . There is sex in mind as distinctly as there is sex in body; and, if the mind is to receive the best culture of which its nature is capable, regard must be had to the mental qualities which correlate differences of sex. To aim, by means of education and pursuits in life, to assimilate the female to the male

[162] Maudsley: *Sex in Mind and Education*, 19, 22–4.

mind, might well be pronounced as unwise and fruitless a labor as it would be to strive to assimilate the female to the male body by the same kind of physical training and by the adoption of the same pursuits. Without doubt there have been some striking instances of extraordinary women who have shown great mental power and these may fairly be quoted as evidence in support of the right of women to the best mental culture; but it is another matter when they are adduced in support of the assertion that there is no sex in mind, and that a system of female education should be laid down on the same lines, follow the same method, and have the same ends in view, as a system of education for men."[163]

It is hard to guess to what extent the imagination of enthusiastic proponents of "sex in education" might have gone in demonstrating by *a priori* reasoning the very divergent characteristics of male and female minds had not the rise of more exact psychological study offered some questions and facts for their consideration. As one final example of their analysis, which was to determine a divergent education, note the statement of Marbury:

"Finally, we claim that there is sex in mind, or, in other words, strongly marked mental differences between the sexes, and we will content ourselves by mentioning a few characteristics that are peculiarly feminine. . . . First: Woman's love of the helpless affecting her thoughts and sentiments and appealing more to pity than to equity. Second: The aptitude of the female mind to dwell on the concrete and proximate, rather than on the abstract and remote. Third: Woman's prevailing awe of power and authority swaying her ideas and sentiments about all institutions. Fourth: In reasoning, a woman is synthetic rather than analytic.

"To state the truth broadly, we should say that in woman the receptive faculties, in man the originative, are predominant, and though there are conspicuous exceptions to this general rule, it nevertheless is true, and is not refuted by the ordinary erroneous simile made between the average man and the superior woman. Yet a more serious mistake arises in overlooking the normal mental power, for in order to institute a just comparison between the sexes, we must not lose sight of the fact that under strong

[163] *Ibid.*, 7–8.

emotion, undue pressure, or extraordinary discipline, the mind of either sex is at times capable of abnormal expansion; therefore, with such a forcing and unnatural process, it may be quite possible for a woman's intellect to produce work of a higher excellence than that yielded by the brain of an average man. But it must ever be remembered that if the mental energy is thus strained and artificially impelled, the physical system must lose in proportion as the nervine force is misapplied and misdirected.

"We also believe that the loss of sex in intellect would be a loss of power. The law of creation runs with two, not one, and by an identical education the world might lose its variety of thought."[164]

III. Reaction against Coeducation

About the beginning of this century occurred what has generally been referred to as a "reaction against coeducation." So far as the theories pro and con, advanced during the reaction, are concerned, they were as old as the history of coeducational practice in the United States. The "reaction" may therefore be characterized first as a revival of century-old arguments against a practice which had become well-nigh coextensive with the elementary and secondary schools, and pervaded about seventy per cent of all institutions of higher learning, excluding the women's colleges. In the second place, there occurred practical changes, or attempts at such, in certain institutions that had been considered strongholds of coeducation. These practical changes were in the direction of "segregation" of the sexes. Segregation was a variable, both in the minds of its proponents and in its practical application. Those who favored coeducation to some extent, or pretended to, favored what they regarded as a relatively slight amount of segregation (as at Wisconsin and the University of Washington). Some who had little or no faith in coeducation were inclined to the "coördinate college" idea.[165] Some who were real friends of coeducation came to accept the coördinate college as the best they could obtain. Thus one may recognize four favored types of collegiate organization for women, ranging from what was regarded as the most radical,

[164] Marbury: Education of Women [*Education* (1887), VIII, 237].

[165] The development of coördinate colleges is discussed in the following chapter.

coeducation, through "segregated" instruction, and "coördinate colleges" to the entirely independent woman's college.

We have already dealt with the two extremes, the origin of coeducation and the separate woman's college. Let us examine the slight modifications of coeducation proposed under "segregation." While treating the segregation plan and the coördinate college separately, it may be proper to keep in mind that the former, in the minds of some proponents at least, was a John the Baptist movement to prepare for eventual coming of the coördinate college. *The School Journal*, speaking of the changing policy at the University of Chicago (1902), stated: "The work of segregation will be gradual, but when it has been completed men and women will never meet in class, at lectures, or at chapel."[166] Professor Small's statements, too, to name no others, make clear that, in his judgment, the way was open, so far as Chicago's charter and the new policy were concerned, for any degree of segregation that might become desirable.[167]

In general, the beliefs, so-called facts, and arguments against co-instruction, that formed the basic soil from which an active revolt against it might spring, have been sufficiently presented. All of them that could bear the light of day were unearthed, refurbished, and made to do service. But it was manifestly impossible to propose, for example, at the beginning of the twentieth century, that women's minds were not strong enough to compete with men in Latin, Greek or mathematics; or that, physically, they could not stand the pace of a college education. Indeed, every study had seemed to indicate that college girls were at least as strong and athletic as their non-collegiate sisters. Miss Thomas stated: "Now we have tried it [college], and tried it for more than a generation, and we know that college women are not only not invalids, but that they are better physically than other women in their own class of life."[168] As for scholastic ability, numerous professors had testified to its high quality. A senior, opposed to coeducation, was said to have given as his reason that "they drag all the prizes." A great deal was made of the unfair competition into which boys were forced. An

[166] LXXIII, 361.

[167] *N. E. A. Proceedings*, 1903, 289 *ff*.

[168] Present Tendencies in Women's Education [*Ed. Rev.* (1908), XXXV, 69–70].

opponent of coeducation went so far as to write that: "Girls are better students than boys, surpassing them in the power of application and the will to learn. They read more, write more, have a wider range of ideas and are proportionally more intellectual."[169] So, obviously, intellectual shortcomings of women could not be urged again as an argument against coeducation. But, thanks to the agility of man's mind, women's *excellence* of scholarship could be, and often was, used just as effectively.

The specific reasons usually urged for the practical change were (1) the rapid increase of women at the universities concerned (general feminization was feared), (2) election of certain courses of the liberal arts college to such an extent as to effect the flight of men from the same, (3) objection of men students to the attendance of women, and (4) the need for a peculiar education for woman that should have regard for her nature and her vocation. The first two reasons appeared most prominently in the actual changes at Chicago, Wisconsin, Stanford, and elsewhere. The third was not excluded, by any means, but was more theoretical in nature. Practical results, in accord with this theory, are certainly to be noted in the development of special vocational schools and courses attended mostly, if not exclusively, by women. Harris' segregation plan in the high school at Cleveland was chiefly on the basis of manual, or vocational, work. For the most part the institutions, undertaking a change, made no reference to failure of coeducation on the grounds on which its downfall had been earlier prophesied. Like the Boston Girls' High School it seems to have suffered because of its success.

The University of Chicago, at the time of its founding (1890) gave great hopes for the higher education of women inasmuch as its charter offered "opportunities for all departments of higher education to persons of both sexes on equal terms." Its position as leader of women's education was also enhanced by its being the first great university to offer a woman a professorship. Alice Freeman Palmer was tendered the chair of history and declined it, though consenting to serve as dean of women.[170] Also a number of other positions were held by women, such as Julia E. Buckley, Martha Foote Crow, and Marion Talbot. But,

[169] *School and Society* (1919), IX, 262.
[170] Palmer: *Life of Alice Palmer*, 232 f.

after about ten years' operation on this basis, the question of
separate instruction was raised, due to the fact of a tentative
offer of an endowment, provided women should be segregated.
Unwilling to accept a gift, and change a practice of such standing, without an examination as to what was the best policy from
an educational standpoint, the trustees referred the question of
coeducation versus segregation to the university senate; it was
also brought before a committee of the Junior College faculty.
This committee was the first to report, the majority favoring "as
far as possible . . . separate sections for men and women"; the
minority report desired continuation of "coinstruction" "as
heretofore." When the question was put before the "Congregation," which represented both faculty and graduates of the
institution, that body was found to favor the old system rather
than the new proposal. In the matter of the minority and
majority votes in the faculty of the Junior College, many felt
Dr. Harper had been too domineering, and, as a result, the
alumnae prepared a circular pointing out just what action he
had taken. His action, described in the following extract, was
in accord with university ruling as to voting, but it was believed
by some that the rule had been invoked because of his own
preference for the segregation plan. As early as January 18,
1902, *The School Journal*[171] had published a lengthy and rather
perplexing statement by Harper, with the comment: "His view
seems to be something like this: 'Coeducation is a good thing,
yes; and then again it isn't. . . .' Perhaps the next time
President Harper . . . will speak straight out and tell what he
means." Dr. Harper's further remarks are quoted from the
Journal named:

"The problems which are connected with the life of women in
a university located in a great city are numerous and complicated. The experience of our nearly ten years of work has furnished an important contribution toward the testimony in favor
of co-education. Not a few members of our faculties, unfamiliar
with the advantages of co-education, came to the university
prejudiced against it. A large majority of these have become
ardent advocates of the co-educational policy. An extended
statement might be made of the arguments and considerations
drawn from our own experience, which speak unmistakably in

[171] LXIV, 68.

favor of the successful working of the system.   That co-education is a permanent feature of higher education, not only in the West, but also, within a few years, in Eastern sections, no one can doubt, and there are few to-day who, with an actual knowledge of the facts, would have it otherwise.   It is the simple and natural method of conducting educational work, and the benefits are equally great to men and women.

"But it should be remembered that no apparent progress has been made during twenty years in adjusting the application of the general principles of co-education in special situations.   It may also be said that no very definite forward steps have been taken in securing a development of the principles and practice in co-education along higher lines.   As a strong believer in co-education, convinced by an experience, which has included work in connection with typical institutions of three kinds— those open only to men, those open only to women, and those open to both men and women—I am confident that in the future important progress is to be made in this department of educational thought and practice.   It is hardly possible to suppose that the full significance of co-education has yet been appreciated, or that its most complete form has yet been attained.

"The direction in which such forward steps may lead us cannot, of course, be accurately predicted; but they will certainly include (1) a closer definition of the term itself; (2) a larger elective privilege on the part of the women as to the extent to which they shall or shall not mingle with men; (3) a similar larger election on the part of the men; (4) a larger possibility for the cultivation of what has properly been termed the feeling of corporate existence in the institution concerned on the part of both men and women; (5) a larger opportunity for cultivating the life which is peculiarly woman's life, and, on the other hand. the life which is peculiarly man's life.

"Certain limitations have already clearly fixed themselves. It is not deemed proper that men and women should take physical exercise together in the gymnasium.   It has never been proposed that they should occupy the same halls or dormitories. It is possible that experience will call attention to other limitations.   It is enough, perhaps, to say that while co-education is unquestionably to be recognized as a permanent element in American higher education, its exact nature and the limitations which attend it will, for a long time, furnish excellent subjects for consideration and experiment. It is important that our own university, situated in the heart of a great city, drawing its students from almost every state, enrolling almost as many women as men, should be one of the institutions which shall undertake to make contributions to the present knowledge and experience on the subject of co-education.''

The *Journal* continued: ''The committee's majority report was disapproved by a vote of 19 to 14. After the adjournment of the meeting, President Harper spoke to two members of the faculty, and their votes were then changed from negative to affirmative, making the vote 17 to 16 still against separation. President Harper himself then voted, and threw out the opposing votes of six other persons. This was done on the ground that they were disqualified because they were on one-year appointments only—a rule of the University, so far as can be ascertained, never before enforced. The President then, several hours after adjournment, announced the final vote as 17 to 11 in favor of separation of sexes.''

The attitude of the University Senate was at first antagonistic to a change of policy, but the final vote was substantially in favor of it.[172] Action by the Board of Trustees, effecting "segregation," was taken Oct. 22, 1902. This action involved, in Dr. Harper's estimation, the following: (1) developing separate instruction for men and women, in the junior college (first two years) as far as possible, but 'extending equal privileges to both sexes'; (2) where courses (elective or required) are given in several sections, some of them shall be for women and others for men, only; (3) certain courses may be restricted one quarter to men, another quarter to women; (4) continuation of separation in Chapel, which had already been begun; (5) attendance of men and women in the same classes, in case not enough students entered to justify more sections; (6) separate laboratories, just as separate accommodations were provided for physical training; (7) teachers to divide their time approximately equally between the sexes; and (8) freedom of women to enjoy all university privileges and to reside either in the ''present women's halls'' or the ''proposed women's quadrangle,'' ''at

172 *The Nation*, Aug. 21, 1902, 147.

their pleasure.''[173]   Dr. Harper urged also that certain things were *not* involved under the new plan: (1) one policy for women and another for men; (2) extension of separation beyond the junior college; (3) separate faculties and special rules for one sex or the other; or (4) separate administrative heads for women and men.   To those things involved and not involved under the new system, Dr. Harper added three considerations that made the change necessary at Chicago, which would not affect coeducation elsewhere:

"(a) *Urban location.*—No coeducational institution which is likely to have an equal number of junior college students in the near future is in a large city.

"(b) *Number of students.*—Coeducation has been in operation, as a rule, with smaller bodies of students than we must provide for, and the numerical ratio of men to women has differed from that which is certain to prevail in the future.

"(c) *Youth of students.*—Until very recently the young women who went to college, and especially those who went to coeducational colleges, have represented a higher average of maturity and fixity of character than is to be expected when it becomes as much the rule in families above a certain level of competence for the daughters to go to college as for the sons, or even more so.   Our junior college students are sure to average younger than those of institutions to which a great city population is not immediately tributary.''[174]

The new proposal caused numerous questions and complaints both before and after adoption.   Editorials and articles appeared in periodicals and newspapers.   Even when there was no outright complaint it was felt that, at least, more solid reasons for segregation should have been offered.   Professor Vincent asked his classes what they thought of the plan.   Some favored it, but the young women generally opposed it strongly, expressing the belief that it would be the death of educational equality.[175]   *The Nation* was of the opinion that there existed a "fundamental opposition to coeducation *per se*," and that this step might

[173] See *Report* of Dr. Harper, 1904, xcvii–cxiii; an abstract of the same in *R. C. E.* (1903), I, 1073–4.

[174] *Ibid.*

[175] *The School Journal,* LXIV, 312.

"prove to be only an entering wedge."[176] Dr. Draper, of the University of Illinois, spoke somewhat derisively, before the Century Club of Boston, concerning the "intellectual entertainment" over coeducation in which Chicago had but recently indulged. He felt that with "all the explanations and assurances" offered, there could really be no danger, for "the University is co-educational, and has no thought of anything else." But "why make the explanations and assurances necessary? Why have to defend the apparently illogical position that coeducation is the natural method for conducting educational work up to the time of going to college; then it is not so for two years; and then it is again for the last two years? And if the association of the young men and women is to be interrupted only so far as recitations are concerned, why do away with it in the only place where each gets the benefit of the serious work, measures the intellectual capacity, and sees the moral attitude of the other.

"The wiser course is upon lines parallel with the highways of nature. The less of the artificial and the unnatural in educational work the safer we are.

"Let us work for well rounded institutions and for equal rights for all. . . . Why should they not be educated together? There is no reason. We have made practical demonstrations and the results are good, and it is not for us now to turn the hands back on the great dial which registers the progress of democratic institutions."[177]

Great interest was shown in the "reaction." Angell reviewed the "reaction from coeducation" in the *Popular Science Monthly*.[178] Thompson, of Ohio State University, viewed the experiment with good humor, feeling that if Doctor Harper could find some one to pay for it there was no "legal reason" why he should not try it. "The mistake occurs when people argue that because coeducation is good for some people therefore it is good for everybody"—or that separate education is best for everybody. "The Chicago boys that desire to be vaccinated so they cannot take the girls or to be educated in quarantine will not be disturbed by the rest of the world. On the other hand if there

176 Aug. 21, 1902, 147.
177 The *Intelligence*, Feb. 15, 1903, 129–30.
178 LXII, 5–26.

are boys who are not afraid of being 'feminized' and who have
the necessary courage let us by all means retain institutions where
they may face the dangers of ruin at the hands of the weaker sex.
As a member of the sterner sex the writer sounds his alarm and
makes a plea for protection for the boys.   The girls have been
taking too many prizes in the college classes and we are told that
the boys conscious of their 'ultimate superiority' feel discouraged
over the condition in the first few years of the contest.''[179]   Jesse,
of Missouri, apparently convinced by the validity of one of the
reasons offered by Harper, said, ''There is no reason known to
me why any university should segregate its women at all unless
it be situated in a large city.''[180]

In addition to questions and criticisms, efforts were made, besides those of Dr. Harper, to explain the reasonableness of
Chicago's position.   Such was the paper by Dr. Small.[181]   He
urged first that ''the new administrative measure . . .   was
devised and supported and carried by men who believe in coeducation''; second, that ''coeducation is not like the form of a
geometrical figure, yesterday, today, and forever the same'';[182]
third, he defined what he meant by coeducation as ''instruction,
under a single management, of males and females, upon equal
terms, under conditions which promise to prove in the long run
most advantageous to all concerned.''   For many, of course, such
an interpretation removed the essence of coeducation.   Dr. Small,
then, gave this explanation, which is inserted here because not
mentioned in Dr. Harper's statement, of the way segregation
came to be:

''The movement in question was occasioned immediately, not by
any speculative theory about coeducation, but by reaching a point
in the growth of the university at which it became an inexorable
necessity to recognize an axiom of physics, namely, two bodies
cannot occupy the same space at the same time.   Our lecture
halls, laboratories, and departmental libraries were overcrowded.
They were wanted by both graduates and undergraduates.   En-

[179] *Ohio Educational Monthly* (1903), LII, 180.

[180] From *Women of a State University*, by Mrs. H. M. Olin, G. P. Putnam's Sons, New York.   Used by courtesy of the publishers.   P. 117.

[181] *N. E. A. Proc.*, 1903, 289 *ff.*

[182] Friends of coeducation saw in such a statement sufficient basis for developing any degree of segregation desired by their opponents.

larged accommodations were imperative. Unless we were to proceed without system and regardless of the future, the question was forced upon us: Looking ahead as far as we can, what principle of assigning ground space for the needed buildings will best provide for all the interests of the university? Time would not permit rehearsal of the many considerations which had to be weighed and it is not necessary for the present purpose. It soon became clear to every one, however, that the four blocks to which the university had been confined would be needed for the higher work alone, and should be reserved accordingly. This meant, in other words, that removal of all freshman and sophomore work—that is, in our terms, the Junior College—from our present base of operations, and provision for it elsewhere, was judged to be the wisest method of relieving our overcrowded condition. When so much was clear, every one taking it for granted that the higher work was anchored by the laboratories, etc., the questions were forced upon us: How can we best provide for the Junior College? Shall we plan to develop in the future an indefinite number of quadrangles, in imitation of the central university quadrangle, with dormitories for women on one side, for men on another, and with intermediate buildings for common instruction; or shall we adopt some other principle? The moment this was recognized as a practical and urgent administrative question, some of us saw that we could not do our full duty in answering it unless we reconsidered on its merits, and in all its bearing, the whole traditional machinery of coeducation, which we had inherited. In other words, it was not sufficient to inquire: How can we most conveniently continue to do the thing we are already doing? The more important question was: Is this the best thing possible? Would any changes in our system improve it in the interest of both men and women?"[183] In closing, Dr. Small remarked that the university was "irrevocably committed" to coeducation.

Although many regarded such statements as equivocal, and Chicago was popularly considered for a time as an exponent of segregation, it is clear that, practically, coeducation lost ground but slowly. Marion Talbot, after five years under the new plan (1907), said that the students of the Junior College were separated in only about a fifth of all work. A few years thereafter,

[183] *N. E. A. Proc.*, 1903, 289 *ff.*

I am advised by the authorities of the University, there was little separation of the sexes except as the sectioning of large elementary courses made it possible.

The second important storm center was the University of Wisconsin. In support of natural segregation, President Van Hise declared two difficulties had been experienced, both of which had sprung from a large number of women attending the state universities.[184] The first was the social difficulty:

"The presence in the same institution of a certain percentage of men and women, both with no very serious purpose, has undoubtedly led to a co-educational problem, that of social affairs, upon which this association has been seriously at work for some years past and which is yet far from a satisfactory solution. In the State universities a number of steps have been taken during the past few years towards the regulation of social affairs, and it is my expectation that we shall go farther before the conditions are reasonably satisfactory.

"In reference to this problem I shall mention merely one difficulty which seems to me to have been frequently overlooked and which must be fully considered in working out a solution. In women's colleges the women set their own standards. That woman is successful who takes a leading part in scholastic work— in the literary society, in dramatics, in athletics, and other forms of college life. The young woman to be a success in a women's

[184] His argument was designed to deal with facts in other schools besides his own, the following figures being given:

University	No. of women	No. of men
California	987	582
Illinois	420	475
Indiana	654	912
Iowa	497	473
Kansas	393	382
Michigan	699	992
Minnesota	879	465
Missouri	396	404
Nebraska	725	314
Ohio	292	324
Texas	448	369
Washington	487	209
Wisconsin	838	1,008

—*Ed. Rev.*, Dec., 1907, 512.

college must win her success by exactly the same qualities of
leadership and of service in the college to the college community
required by the young man to win a prominent position. In the
co-educational institution there is a tendency for the men to fix
the standards not only for themselves but for the women. With
the increase in numbers of men and women in coeducational institutions with no very serious purpose, there is undoubtedly
a tendency among the women to regard as successful the one who
is attractive to the young men—in other words, social availability
rather than intellectual leadership is regarded by at least a considerable number of the young women as the basis of a successful
college career. While this view may seem absurd, a little reflection will convince one that the tendency is perfectly natural—
indeed, is as deep-seated as many of the most firmly established
traditions in reference to the relations between the sexes. So
far as I can see, this obstacle will always be a real one in coeducational institutions.''[185]

From the figures given in the above table, and the tenor of
Van Hise's argument, it is at once clear that Dr. Harper's belief, that segregation would chiefly be needed in the large city,[186]
was not necessarily true. Dr. Van Hise argued that where the
numbers of students are large and many sections of required
courses necessary, there takes place a natural segregation; that,
as to electives, such as humanistic studies, they are chosen by
women in such numbers that men desert them almost entirely;
and that women do not elect engineering, law, commerce, agriculture, as a general rule, nor, up to the present time, have the
men tended ''to crowd women out of home economics.'' Of these
two forms of segregation one is fortunate and the other unfortunate. Segregation by choice of vocational or technical school
is good, and will ''go farther.'' ''At the present time, provision
has been made for nearly complete segregation on a large scale
by the establishment of courses and colleges which are practically
for the one sex or the other. The colleges of engineering, law,
commerce, agriculture, and medicine are essentially men's colleges. While open to women, their opportunities have been taken
advantage of only to a very limited extent. Similarly courses for

[185] Address to Collegiate Alumnae [*Ed. Rev.* (Dec., 1907), XXXIV,
514–15].

[186] See p. 286.

training the heads of households have been established for the women. Whether such courses be called home economics, household science, or domestic science, they are the first of the professional schools for women. Already in a considerable number of state institutions such courses are provided, including the following: Ohio, Illinois, Minnesota, Nebraska, Tennessee, Kansas, Wisconsin."[187] But the natural segregation in the liberal arts has been harmful. These studies are needed by all. And, since in "language, literature, political economy, history and mathematics" there are, in large institutions, many sections, "there is no reason whatever why a course already given in a number of sections should not provide divisions primarily for the men and others primarily for the women." This was practically what Harper had done. Van Hise calls attention to beginnings elsewhere:

"At the University of Washington, President Kane says that in some of the subjects in which there are a large number of students the sections are so scheduled that women only are in certain sections and men only in others. He goes on to say in effect: 'I am strongly in favour, also, of a division of the sexes into separate classes in the departments in which our freshmen and sophomores work. There are in many departments a half-dozen or more sections doing the same work, so that a division can be made with very little difficulty and without added expenditure for the instructional force. In these departments I shall favour, unless our experience goes contrary to my conjecture, the definite plan of separate sections for the men and women.'"[188] Another case was cited by Dr. Van Hise, that of Kansas, whose charter provided that "separate classes" might be maintained "whenever it shall be found convenient."

It was as an exponent of coeducation that Dr. Van Hise wished to appear. Provision for such "natural" segregation as was desired, he believed, would help coeducation at the state universities. ". . . Natural segregation is . . . an undoubted educational tendency . . . [and] it seems to me that in arranging for natural segregation in those subjects attractive to both men and women, steps will be taken which will be likely to preserve coedu-

187 From the address cited above.
188 *Ibid.*; extracts from the address of Van Hise may also be found in Burstall: *Impressions of American Education*, 263 *ff.*

cation in the college of liberal arts. That this may remain the situation at Stanford and Wesleyan has been assured by the limitation of the number of women that are admitted. By Chicago the problem has been handled by segregating the women and men for the first two years. I believe a better solution of the problem than these somewhat arbitrary regulations, is to provide for natural segregation by the development of professional courses, such as engineering, agriculture, commerce, and law, for men, and other courses, illustrated by home economics, for women; and in the college of liberal arts providing for separate divisions, which to a certain extent may be specialized, in those subjects which are attractive to both sexes as rapidly as experience shows that this plan really enlarges the opportunities for both women and men.

"Blindly ignoring facts, and persisting in an old policy regardless of results, will weaken rather than strengthen coeducation. Believing as I do that the adoption of coeducation in the West, which has led to the higher education of tens of thousands of women who would otherwise have had no opportunity to obtain a college training, has been of immeasurable importance to the nation; believing as I do that coeducation gives satisfactory scholastic results for both sexes, I am in favor of taking such steps as are necessary to maintain coeducation in full vigor in the colleges of liberal arts."[189]

Friends of complete coeducation were not inclined to agree exactly with Dr. Van Hise that "natural" segregation was the best way to preserve it. A petition was circulated by the graduates, and presented to the regents. Dr. Bascom, addressing Wisconsin alumnae, on May 1, 1908, declared emphatically: "Segregation is directly opposed to coeducation . . . the method implies adaptation of instruction to the differences incident to sex, and so far as segregation is favoured, implies that these differences are of more moment than effort directed exclusively to the best instruction. This attitude is sure, sooner or later, in a less or greater degree, to issue in a course fitted, according to some one's notion, for women, and less comprehensive than the courses designed for men. There is no end to the limitations which will spring up under this notion, till we reach courses which exclude women from the freest and most profitable forms of study. In

[189] *Ibid.*

the case of political economy what the young woman needs is knowledge as broad as the problem, and the same for all who are occupied with it."[190]   Apropos of segregation, Angell, of Michigan, wrote April 13, 1908:

"The burden of proof is on those who propose segregation, and I know of no sufficient arguments to sustain their proposition. We have never thought for a moment of resorting to it here. . . . I should suppose the conditions there [Wisconsin] were much the same as here [Michigan], and I know of no reason which can be produced for their project."[191]

In June, 1908, the Board of Regents allayed the fears of those who had been agitated by the discussions following upon the President's address in 1906, by the following resolution:

"Men and women shall be equally entitled to membership in all classes of the University, and there shall be no discrimination on account of sex in granting scholarships and fellowships in any of the colleges or departments of the University."[192]

The *Commissioner's Report* for 1909 stated: "The general movement for the higher education of women has apparently not been affected by the action of particular institutions in regard to coeducation," though, it remarked, the "sensitiveness with respect to this subject obscures sometimes the importance of efforts on the part of University authorities to bring about a fuller and better adjustment of their facilities to the requirements of professional and social life."[193]   A few instances of the "action of particular institutions" may be mentioned. Leland Stanford undertook to limit the number of women students in attendance at any time to five hundred.[194]   Hamilton, of Tufts College, had spoken definitely, in his annual report of 1907, pointing to the growing professionalization of the work at Tufts College, the decline of men taking the A.B. degree, and the need for the segregation of women in a "separate department or college."[195]   Edmund J. James, of Northwestern, in his first communication

[190] From *Women of a State University*, by Mrs. H. M. Olin, G. P. Putnam's Sons, New York. Used by courtesy of the publishers. Pp. 130–1.
[191] *Ibid.*, 117.
[192] *R. C. E.* (1909), I, 182.
[193] *Ibid.*, 183.
[194] *Ibid.* (1902), II, 2388–9.
[195] *New Eng. Jour. of Ed.* (1907), LXVI, 485–6; see also Ch. VI.

to the trustees, told them coeducation had "ceased to make new converts" and was "losing ground in the very territory which it had so completely won."[196] Again, in 1910, the old question of segregation versus coeducation arose in Virginia, where there were three institutions for the higher education of boys, but none for girls. Bills favoring a woman's annex, approved by the educational commission, were sent repeatedly to the Legislature for action; while they deliberated, all parties, from the out and out coeducationists to the segregationists, used their best efforts to influence the outcome. The result was that women were, after ten years, admitted on the coeducational plan in graduate and professional schools.[197]

IV. Results of Coeducation.

Not so much is attempted under this head as might be anticipated. Coeducation has been subjected to practical tests and has continued to exist, presumably, because it has helped fill a peculiar need. It has been maintained that it is in harmony with our democratic ideal. Coeducation has been tried in practice (many claiming its success and many its failure) but little or no effort has been made to study it in a scientific way. Such results as are claimed, therefore, are known chiefly as a product of observation by those who have either had opportunity to work intimately with the system or who have watched the labors of others. Among those whose only means of knowing is personal observation there may be expected many differences of opinion; those who know by direct personal experience, plus observation, vary less. This partly explains the unanimity of judgment of heads of coeducational schools, and the divergent opinions of those who have only looked on. In both cases, the judgments are apt to be colored by some personal preference but the results of experience, especially when vouched for generally by men of sound judgment, weigh much more heavily than theoretical objections or results which are only reported by onlookers. In these pages it is possible only to point out results judged to have been obtained, recognizing the liability to error on the part of the observers. It is of especial interest to note the results

196 *The School Journal*, LXVI, 468–9.
197 *Am. Ed. Rev.*, XXXII, 441; and pp. 319 *f*.

bearing upon the *a priori* arguments that coeducation would be a failure.

Moral decline was feared by many. The testimony is, however, overwhelmingly against such a development. It is also difficult to understand why such great moral disasters were feared, when coeducation had for so long been a practice of secondary schools. Higginson called attention to this fact.[198] Later Doctor Gray, of the Mosely Commission, speaking of secondary education, said: "The spirit of camaraderie between the two sexes . . . is, on the whole, vastly beneficial to the American boy and girl alike. . . ."[199] Mr. Armstrong and Mr. Fletcher were especially unfavorably impressed because of the relation they felt existed between a low standard of work and coeducation. Oberlin's experience, reported by Fairchild, was that "there has been an entire absence of the irregularities and roughness so often complained of in college commons."[200] From Oberlin's beginning to the present day, the judgments of presidents of the largest universities, as well as those in small colleges, have generally been of the same kind. We can mention but a few here. Thwing thought: "Coeducation . . . tends to promote the pure moral type."[201] Canfield, of Kansas, said that in sixteen years there was not "a whisper of scandal," while the President of Butler College, Indiana, found that "on no occasion whatever has discipline been made necessary by the association of the sexes."[202] Cutler, at Western Reserve, felt coeducation had done away with "the greatest difficulties and evils of the old monastic system."[203] At the University of Iowa it was found it was "an invaluable feature" in restraining indecorum and an "incitement to every virtue";[204] and Missouri's President, R. H. Jesse, contrary to his preconceptions, found "that the sexes were regulating themselves in the most admirable manner, and there did not seem to be a gap anywhere for my fine spun theories and

198 See *Common Sense about Women*, 227–8; also an editorial in the *New England Journal of Education* (1880), XI, 168–9.

199 *R. C. E.* (1905), I, 8–9.

200 *Ibid.*, 1867–8, 391; also Orton: *op. cit.*, 233.

201 *The College Woman* (1894), 111–18.

202 Thwing: Women's Education [*Education* (1883), IV, 59–61.]

203 *R. C. E.*, 1883, CXLI–CXLIII.

204 *Ibid.*, 1878, 71.

chivalrous intentions.''[205]   Magill, of Swarthmore, after but a
few years' experience (1872) believed that "morally and socially,
young persons are improved by coeducation. . . .''[206] Draper,
of Illinois, believed "these young people are quite as safe in this
environment and atmosphere as in their own homes.''[207] Hosmer, of Antioch, stated that "as to character and conduct, I am
sure that our young men have been improved, rendered more
orderly, gentle and manly, and our young women stronger and
more earnest, by being members of the same institution and meeting in the recitations.''[208] Angell, of Michigan, declared women
should be admitted "unless some serious practical objections can
be shown. In fact, all who try the experiment report *there are
none*. We have not had the slightest embarrassment from the
reception of women." Van Hise, too, during the discussion
about coeducation versus segregation, declared in his address to
the collegiate alumnae that "none of the evils and few of the
difficulties which were suggested against coeducation in advance
of its trial have been confirmed by experience." Again, "The
moral standards of young women and men have not deteriorated
in coeducational institutions." But Van Hise did feel sure that
at the present day, with the increase of "numbers of men and
women in coeducational institutions with no very serious purpose," a social problem had arisen for the state university.[209]
His view would be amply corroborated today by deans of women
and presidents of many institutions. They also agree with him,
however, that the problems arise not from coeducation *per se* but
from the presence of men and women "of no very serious purpose." Apropos of the moral objection to coeducation it is
significant to note the statement of Sachs who raised many objections to coeducation. He pointed out, "We are not likely
often to get distinct admissions from within coeducational institutions that the promiscuous student body sometimes falls quite
short of ideal conditions," and interpreted Van Hise's move for
segregation as "grave occasion for doubt" whether the moral

[205] *N. E. A. Proc.*, 1904, 543–4.
[206] *Pa. Sch. Jour.* (1872), XXI, 102 *ff.*
[207] *The Intelligence*, Feb. 15, 1903, 129 *f.*
[208] Quoted by Duffey: *No Sex in Education*, 128.
[209] Van Hise: Tendencies in State Universities [*Ed. Rev.* (1907), XXXIV,
514–15].

influences, attributed to the presence of women, were not "superficial rather than intensive."[210] Two years earlier, however, he had admitted that "experience has demonstrated that no moral injury accrues to either of the two sexes from an education in common. . . ."[211] Charles A. Selden expressed the change that has come about: "We have recovered completely from the last-century habit of insulting young men and young women by intimating that they could not go to college together without disgracing themselves."[212]

What effect had coeducation on scholarship? On this point the judgments are fairly unanimous; and, whatever may be said about the low-grade work of college students today, there may be found a better explanation than the presence of the two sexes.[213] Fairchild taught Latin, Greek, Hebrew, mathematics, philosophy, and ethics, at various times, but "never observed any difference in the sexes as to performance in the recitations."[214] Cooley, of the law department, at Michigan, declared: "You are misinformed if you are told that the standard of admission is lowered by admitting women to the university. The tendency has been in the other direction." Magill, of Swarthmore, expressed a similar view. Angell, at Michigan, said, "It was soon demonstrated that there were no studies in which some women did not excel." Again, "women graduates are doing their full part in winning a reputation for Michigan University, and are justifying the wisdom of the regents who opened to them the opportunities for a thorough classical training."[215] Carroll Cutler, at

210 *Ibid.* (1908), XXXV, 469–70.

211 *Ibid.*, XXXIII, 298–9.

212 Sex and Higher Education [*Ladies' Home Journal*, Nov., 1924, 15].

213 British critics have often assigned coeducation as a cause of low-grade work. See Reports of the Mosely Commission in *R. C. E.* (1905), I, 1–39; also H. A. L. Fisher: "Under the system of coeducation, which generally prevails, there is less intense intellectual activity than would probably be the case under a system of segregational culture."—*Sch. & Soc.* (1925), XXI, 102.

214 *R. C. E.*, 1867–8, 392; also Duffey: *No Sex in Education*, 135.

215 *N. E. A. Proc.*, 1904, 548–9; *Education* (1883), IV, 59 *ff.*; also *The Nation* (1870), XI, 384, in which it was said, "better recitations have never been made, and in the severest studies, than have been made by the ladies." In fact, unless something goes wrong, Young's 'ungallant lines' may come true:

"Is't not enough plagues, wars, and famines rise
"To lash our crimes, but must our wives be wise?"

Western Reserve, gave as a reason for not abandoning coeducation, that "their presence elevates scholarship."[216] Similar views were expressed by presidents Beach and Warren of Wesleyan and Boston Universities, respectively,[217] and by Gregory of the "Illinois Industrial University."[218] At the time when Cornell was investigating the question as to whether women should be admitted there, President White wrote:

"If it be said that the presence of women will tend to lower the standard of scholarship, or at all events to keep the Faculty from steadily raising it, it may be answered at once that all the facts observed are in opposition to this view. The letters received by the Committee, and their own recent observations in the class-rooms, show beyond a doubt that the young women are at least equals of the young men in collegiate studies. As already stated, the best Greek scholar among the thirteen hundred students of the University of Michigan, a few years since, the best mathematical scholar in one of the largest classes of that institution today, and several among the highest in natural science and in the general courses of study, are young women.

"It has been argued that the want of accuracy and point, the 'sloppiness' of much of the scholarship in some of the newer colleges, is due to the admission of women. The facts observed by the Committee seem to prove that this argument is based on the mistake of concomitancy for cause. If 'sloppiness' and want of point are inadmissible anywhere, it is in translation from the more vigorous and concise ancient and modern authors. Now, the most concise and vigorous rendering from the most concise and vigorous of all,—Tacitus himself,—was given by a young lady at Oberlin College. Nor did the Committee notice any better work in the most difficult of the great modern languages than that of some young women at Antioch College."[219] Orton of Antioch College stated:

"As to the intellectual result of co-education, I have seen nothing to warrant the belief that the general average of scholarship is lowered by it. Young women, as we find them, have not the same powers of endurance, in severe and protracted study, that

216 *R. C. E.*, 1883, CXLI–CXLIII.
217 Dana: *Woman's Possibilities and Limitations*, 47–8.
218 *R. C. E.*, 1871, 45.
219 Quoted by Thwing in *Education* (1883), IV, 57 *ff*.

young men have; but, on the other hand, they do much of their work with greater facility. In the languages, in rhetoric, and belles-lettres, for instance, they are apter pupils than their brothers. Perhaps we do not find them as strong or original mathematicians as young men, but still it must be said that if the two most successful scholars of the last seven years, with us, were to be named in this department both sexes would be represented. They recite what they know better, on the average, than young men. The sexes seem to take different results from the same course. The philosophic phases of a subject always seem to me to take deeper hold of young men. They have 'Darwinism,' for instance, harder. It seems to me that a more symmetrical view is obtained when a subject has been brought under both points of vision.''[220]   Even Doctor Eliot was finally brought by his own observations to admit that "we have learned by actual trial that young women can learn all the more difficult subjects of education just as well as young men; and there is some evidence to show that on the average they will master these subjects better than the average young men.''[221]   Van Hise, too, to name no more here, while recommending segregation, declared coeducation gave satisfactory scholastic results. He did qualify this somewhat by pointing out certain "exceptions and reservations with reference to graduate work."

"While all of the state university presidents, from whom I have had communications, hold the view exprest as to undergraduate work, there are certain exceptions and reservations with reference to graduate work. The president of one large state university says that the presence of women does tend to lower the standard of graduate work, for the simple reason that women do not incline to research. While I should hesitate to assent to this statement, it does appear to be a fact that the percentage of women who are willing to work at the same subject six hours a day for three hundred days in the year is much smaller than among the men. But this quality is essential for success in research. Thus while the intellectual success of the women in undergraduate work is unquestioned, there is still question on

220 *Ibid.*

221 From *Women of a State University*, by Mrs. H. M. Olin, G. P. Putnam's Sons, New York. Used by courtesy of the publishers. Pp. 106–7.

the part of some as to the rank they are to take in the graduate school and in creative work.''

The bugaboo of women's delicate health and inability to endure the physical strain was exploded by practical tests as readily as the moral and intellectual theories. The experiments of Oberlin, Antioch, Wisconsin, Michigan, and other state universities revealed nothing to negate the statement of Dr. Angell:

''We were at first often told that the health of the girls could not endure the strain of college work. But many of the girls in college obstinately persisted in growing stronger with each year of study, and in general the girls who did not attempt to do other things carried their work with as little injury to health as did the boys.''[222]

A fourth calamity, very widely advertised by those who opposed any dealing with coeducation, was the inevitable decline of feminine charm and the rise of mannish women. On this subject there will always be varied opinions. President White's committee, in all its ''observations, failed to detect any symptoms of any loss of the distinctive womanly qualities so highly prized.''[223] But, in 1887, in a symposium on *Coeducation in Colleges* it was declared: ''There yet remains . . . a doubt in the minds of many whether something may not be lost of that indefinable charm of gentle and graceful womanhood by too close contact with the sterner sex. . . .''[224] Individual cases may be taken that seem to show now one, now the other view to be true; but there is a vast amount of truth in the statement of Alice Freeman Palmer that it is not possible ''to annihilate the womanliness of our American girls by anything that you can do to them in education.''[225]

A fifth fear, that coeducation would be conducive to mating, was better grounded than most, if we may judge from the number of colleges that have admitted this realization openly and gladly. Angell, to mention but one by name, says ''this prediction was fulfilled. Many of the happiest marriages I have known resulted. Are we not justified in maintaining that an acquaintance of four years in the class room furnishes as good

[222] *N. E. A. Proc.*, 1904, 548–9.
[223] *Education* (1883), IV, 59 *ff*.
[224] *New Eng. Jour. of Ed.* (1887), XXV, 89.
[225] *Sch. Rev.*, VII, 593.

ground for a wise choice of husband or wife as a chance acquaintance in a ball room?''[226]

The broader social influence of coeducation has been frequently commented upon. Men and women come to know each other better. ''There is no sentimental halo about the classmate who misses his lessons, who blunders in his examples. There is no disrespect and scorn of 'girls' from a youth who sees them well able to hold their own, and to stand beside, if not above, him in intellectual exercises . . . both learn the true, the honest, the natural way of looking at each other, and are prepared to enter life together as they should and must.''[227] These results, while claimed by many, are denied by some who favor separate education. Generally, however, there is agreement with Mr. Bryce's judgment that ''The practice of educating the two sexes together in the same college tends in those sections of the country where it prevails to place women and men on a level as regards attainments, and gives them a greater number of common intellectual interests. It does not, I think, operate to make women either pedantic or masculine, or to diminish the differences between their mental and moral habits and those of men. Nature is quite strong enough to make the differences of temperament she creates persistent, even under influences which might seem likely to diminish them.''[228] The Commissioner's *Report*[229] also pointed to ''the very great influence of coeducation upon the social and business relation of men and women in after years. It explains in great measure the freedom that women enjoy in this country with respect to the pursuit of careers, and especially the large share which they take in the educational work of the country.'' Whether the social significance of coeducation reaches so far as suggested by John H. Phillips[230] it is impossible to say. He raised the question whether there was not a connection between exclusive segregation of men and women in English schools and universities and the ''violent and spectacular type of the militant 'suffragette.' ''

[226] *N. E. A. Proc.*, 1904, 548–9; also McConn: *College or Kindergarten?* 168–83.

[227] Higginson, quoted by *Educational News*, June 14, 1890, 373, from *Harper's Bazaar*.

[228] *American Commonwealth* (1895), II, 734.

[229] 1901, II, 1228.

[230] *Am. Ed. Review*, XXXIV, 316.

"Coeducation develops a mutual understanding between the sexes, and through this, a mutual respect that renders the militant and spectacular features unnecessary and even ridiculous. We will venture the assertion that few, if any of the radical extremists in the suffrage cause, and especially of those who seek opportunities to emphasize their convictions by window smashing, hiking and similar diversions, were educated with men in coeducational institutions."

Aside from the foregoing, certain results may be named which are not open to any question. It is clear that through coeducation as a means, the right of every woman to the highest educational facilities was established; and that by their admission to universities on equal footing the service of women to the public schools, elementary and secondary, where they were becoming almost supreme in importance, was greatly improved.

CHAPTER VI

COÖRDINATE COLLEGES FOR WOMEN

The separate women's college arose, in part, as a result of the distrust of coeducation, held chiefly by those in the East. Where coeducation was accepted and no tradition stood against it, there was little demand, and less wealth, to create the separate institution. In time, a third type of institution for the education of women—the coördinate college—arose, partly as a protest against the completely separate institution. Tradition hindered the older universities of the East from opening their doors on the coeducational plan; but a compromise, midway between coeducation and the separate college, was effected. This step was taken at the moment when some enthusiastic proponents of coeducation were looking for its extension into the oldest universities.[1]

The coördinate college was one more way, and some thought a better one, of providing higher education for women. Doctor Barnard, in 1879, reviewed the satisfactory results of coeducation in many schools; and raised the question whether women's education could best be promoted by improving the seminaries or by establishing separate women's colleges. The former, he answered, "cannot be improved except by reconstruction," and "the objection to these [women's colleges] is that they cannot, or at least in general will not, give instruction of equal value, though it may be the same in name, with that furnished to young men in the long established and well-endowed colleges of highest repute in the country; and that it is unjust to young women, when admitting their right to liberal education, to deny them access to the best."[2]

It is true that the suggestion of the coördinate college plan came from English practice. Barnard, in his report to the Columbia trustees in 1879, dealing with the "Higher Education of Women," recounted the experience of Queen's College, Lon-

[1] Coeducation at Swarthmore College [*Pa. Sch. Jour.* (1872), XXI, 59–60].

[2] Barnard's *Am. Jour. of Ed.*, XXXI, 385.

FREDERICK A. P. BARNARD

don (1854), and of Cambridge University, where "Girton College has now been for a number of years in existence (1869), and of its success the most glowing accounts have been made public. So encouraging have been the results . . . that . . . the University of Oxford has been enlisted in a similar undertaking. . . ."[3] Lander, writing of the university examinations for women given by Harvard, since 1874, called attention to the English system, "on the success . . . [of which], without any doubt, depends the establishment of a regularly equipped college for women in a similar relation to Harvard as that of Girton to Cambridge University."[4] The connection between the Harvard examinations, the subsequent "Annex," and the "countenance of foreign example" was also recognized by Warner.[5]

In 1873, the *Report* of the Commissioner of Education contained the announcement of the Harvard examinations for women "on the plan of the local examinations carried on by the Universities of Oxford, Cambridge and London. . . ."[6] These examinations had been planned by Harvard at the request of the Boston Woman's Educational Association; they were to be conducted by the University, but were "under the auspices" of the Association.[7] These were to be held first in June, 1874, and were of two grades: preliminary (for girls not less than seventeen years old) and advanced (for girls not less than eighteen). The preliminary examination covered English, French, physical geography, either elementary botany or physics, arithmetic, algebra (through quadratics), plane geometry, history, and either German, Latin, or Greek. The advanced examination was divided into five sections, to one or more of which a candidate might be admitted after passing the preliminary. The sections were 'Languages, Natural Science, Mathematics, History, and Philosophy.' Upon satisfactorily passing the tests, of either or both grades, a certificate of the same, "with distinction" or "with the highest distinction," was to be issued by the Univer-

3 *Ibid.*, XXXI, 386.

4 *Education* (1880), I, 62.

5 *Harvard Grad. Magazine* (March 1894), II, 331; consult also Ellen Dean on the "Harvard Examination for Women"—*Report, Supt. Pub. Instruction*, Mich., 1879, 142 *ff.*

6 *R. C. E.*, 1873, LVIII–LIX.

7 Address by Dr. Eliot [Orton: *Liberal Ed. of Women*, 323].

sity and signed by the President of the institution.[8]   These
examinations set up a standard of academic work.   After they
were passed, Harvard did nothing more for the young women
students.[9]   Meantime, the demands of prominent men and
women that the latter be admitted to Harvard became more in-
sistent.   In 1871, Higginson had suggested that the only fair
thing was to admit women openly,—not permit them to enter by
the side door, which he averred had been the case with some
women students, whose names were not, however, allowed to be
published in the catalog.   He had just received a letter from a
friend who "can not see why my child must be exiled to the
University of Michigan for an education simply for the crime
of being a girl instead of a boy."[10]

In 1873, Higginson read a paper on the "Higher Education of
Women" before the Social Science Convention,[11] which deftly
disposed of the argument that because men and women differ
physically there must be a different mental cultivation.   The
other arguments—women's hopeless mental inferiority, their
physical weakness, and that there is really enough higher education provided for them already—were quickly answered, and
the conclusion drawn that "all the problems of education seem
to present themselves in the same way at Harvard for boys, at
Vassar for girls, at Michigan and at Cornell for the two united.
The logic of events is sweeping with irresistible power to the
union of the sexes for higher education."[12]

Higginson was answered very mildly by Agassiz, while Dr.
Eliot defended the conservatism of Harvard and declared he interpreted the facts (common both to himself and Higginson) to
mean exactly the opposite.   Coeducation was really on the wane;
as communities grew richer, separate schools would be established
even in the West where coeducation now prevailed.[13]   To Dr.
Eliot's defense of the non-admission policy, Wendell Phillips
replied that Harvard College belonged to the public, not to a
small group of men, and that women could claim admittance as

[8] *Ibid.*

[9] *Littell's Living Age* (1876), CXXXI, 248–9.

[10] Orton: *Liberal Ed. of Women*, 183–6.

[11] May 14, 1873, reprinted in appendix of Orton's *Liberal Ed. of Women*.

[12] *Ibid.*, 316.

[13] *Ibid.*, 319 *f.*

The Fay House, Radcliffe College

readily as they could claim the right to travel on a public highway. Dr. Eliot could advise them not to come, tell them "it would injure their health, . . . but he should not bar them out. . . . If President Eliot tells a young woman ardent for education 'your sex bars you' she might justly answer 'Hang my sex, I don't care for that.' "[14] James Freeman Clarke declared: ". . . We do not wish any of our grand Massachusetts institutions to lag behind in the advance of society. . . . We have inherited the present system from monastic times, when priests were the only teachers, when the college was a cloister, and when it was thought the only way to preserve purity was a separation of the sexes." On the other hand, Clarke would not undertake to say "whether the proper time has come for introducing this change at Cambridge."

The mild suggestion of Agassiz, "the best thing we can do is to act and let time work," seems to have suited Harvard officials. After the "examinations" had been in operation four years,[15] a suggestion was made by Arthur Gilman to Professor Greenough, that certain Harvard professors repeat some of their courses systematically for women. This proposal was enthusiastically received by Greenough, Child, Goodwin, Gurney, and several other professors. Having thus secured a teaching body of thirty-seven members, practical arrangements were made by Mrs. Agassiz, including the raising of a fund of $15,000, which, it was expected, would carry the experiment for four years. The first circular, *Private Collegiate Instruction*, set forth the essential fact that no instruction would be given "of a grade lower than that given in Harvard College." A later announcement gave the admission requirements and described the courses, which were limited as to number but exactly the same in character as those given by the same professors to Harvard men.

The success which attended the instruction of the few students who at first appeared (27 the first year, 1879, and 47 the second) led to the formation of a corporate body: The Society for the Collegiate Instruction of Women. This society had no degree-

---

[14] *Ibid.*, 324.

[15] In 1877, they were held simultaneously in Cambridge, New York and Cincinnati, notice of intention to appear at the examinations being sent to the Woman's Education Association of Boston, or its New York local committee.—*R. C. E.* (1876), LXXXII–IV.

conferring powers. At the end of four years, those who had
completed the required studies received certificates stating that
they had ''pursued a course of study equivalent in amount and
quality to that for which the degree of-Bachelor of Arts is conferred in Harvard College, and had passed in a satisfactory
manner examinations on that course, corresponding to the college
examinations.''[16]   This practice of allowing women to do, and
admitting that they did do, the same work as men, gave rise to
the question, first in England and then in the United States,
''O, Why should a Woman not get a degree?''

''How ungrateful of You, whose best efforts depend
''On the aid certain ladies in secret may send:
''CLIO here writes a lecture, URANIA there,
''And more Muses than one prompt the Musical Chair.
''CALLIOPE sheds o'er the Classics delight,
''And the lawyers have meetings with THEMIS by night;
''Yet if VENUS de Medici came even She
''Could among her own Medici get no degree.

''In Logic a woman may seldom excel;
''But in Rhetoric always she bears off the bell.
''Fair PORTIA will show woman's talent for law,
''When in old Shylock's bond she could prove such a flaw.
''She would blunder in Physic no worse than the rest,
''She could leave things to Nature as well as the best;
''She could feel at your wrist, she could finger your fee;
''Then why should a woman not get a degree?

''Yet without a degree see how well the Sex knows
''How to bind up our wounds and to lighten our woes.
''They need no Doctor's gown their fair limbs to enwrap,
''They need ne'er hide their locks in a Graduate's cap.
''Then I wonder a woman, the Mistress of Hearts
''Would descend to aspire to be Master of Arts:
''A Ministering Angel in Woman we see,
''And an Angel should covet no other Degree.[17]

In its report for 1884, the Woman's Education Association
proposed a discontinuance of the system of examinations, the
reasons being (a) the falling off of the number of candidates,
(b) the opening of many new opportunities for higher education

16 Quoted by Warner: Radcliffe College [*Harvard Grad. Mag.* (March
1894), II, 334].

17 Quoted from *Blackwood's Magazine* in *Littell's Living Age* (1869), C,
578.

such as Smith College, Wellesley, Boston University, Vassar, Michigan, Cornell, and the "Annex," and (c) the fact that standards of education in high schools had been elevated and fixed during the preceding twelve years. While the proposal was objected to by the New York and Cincinnati committees, which petitioned for their continuance, it was clear that perpetuation of the examinations was undesirable when so many genuine college opportunities were open to women, beside which the mere certificate of passing an examination was a very pale accomplishment.[18]

About this time the "Annex" began to take on some of the attributes of other American colleges. In 1882, Mrs. Agassiz was elected president; and, in 1885, more commodious accommodations were provided by the purchase of the Fay House. Under this leadership, the college experienced a slow but consistent growth, and it was early realized that its graduates should have a more substantial reward than a mere certificate of having done work equal to that of Harvard men. As the University was still unwilling to give its own degree to women, measures were taken to secure degree-conferring powers for the new institution, while still maintaining the close relation that had previously existed between it and Harvard. The Woman's Education Association began raising an endowment, publishing the following reasons (signed by Mrs. Agassiz, Mrs. Palmer, and Katharine P. Loring) in justification of their action:

"(1) As the funds of Harvard College were given for the instruction of young men, the members of the Corporation and Board of Overseers cannot use them for the teaching of young women. The Annex must, therefore, be self-supporting. (2) In view of the larger number of students likely to follow such a change of standing in the Annex, additions in educational outfit, apparatus, etc., would be necessary and would greatly increase expenses. (3) That the present income of the Annex is not large enough to pay for the post-graduate courses, which are very expensive, and for which Harvard offers large opportunities. These advanced studies are in frequent demand by women who are anxious to fit themselves for the higher positions which such preparation would enable them to obtain."[19]

[18] R. C. E., 1883, CXXXIX–CXL.
[19] The Nation (1893), LVI, 28-9.

In 1893, the Society for the Collegiate Instruction of Women proposed, and it was assented to by the Harvard President and Fellows, that the name of the Society be changed to Radcliffe College—in honor of Anne Radcliffe, later Lady Mowlson, who had been the first woman to make a gift to Harvard, in 1641.[20] It further proposed that power be sought to grant degrees, that the President and Fellows of Harvard be "appointed the visitors of this corporation," that no one be employed to teach "without the approval of the visitors," and that the President of Harvard be authorized to "countersign the diplomas of this corporation."[21]

By the new charter,[22] Radcliffe was authorized to grant degrees. Since 1894, degrees have been issued to those applying for them, who had previously been granted the certificate of completion of work equal to that of Harvard men. From 1885 to 1926, 3,399 degrees were conferred.[23] Besides the holders of degrees, some 2,000 women have received instruction in one or more courses during this period. At the opening of the session of 1926–7, there were 727 students. Scholarship funds, available in 1926–7, amounted to over $50,000.[24]

We have previously noted Barnard's advocacy of the education of women, in 1879. The *Report* of 1880 presented his arguments more fully.[25] President Eliot's attitude was, as someone has said, like that of the mother who, though she did not encourage her daughter's education, she did not prohibit her reading. The Columbia President, on the contrary, took a very advanced position. He favored out and out coeducation and regarded the "Annex" merely as a "necessary concession to a deeply-rooted but probably mistaken notion of the fitness of things."[26]

In 1882, there was formed in New York an Association for Promoting the Higher Education of Women, having as its primary object to "secure the admission of women to Columbia

[20] *Harvard Grad. Mag.*, II, 343.

[21] *Ibid.*, 330–1.

[22] *Laws of Mass.*, 1894, 141–2.

[23] 2,578, A.B.; 710, M.A.; 73, Ph.D.; 2, M.S.; 2, D.S.; 34, A.A.

[24] Information supplied by Radcliffe College authorities, June 29, 1926, and March 29, 1927.

[25] See also the *Report* for 1881; extracts from the reports of the President, 1879–1881, relating to *The Higher Education of Women*, reprinted 1882, 46 pages.

[26] *Columbia Univ. Quarterly* (March 1910), XII, 149–50.

College," and also "to raise the standard of instruction in existing schools for girls."[27] Among the members of the Association were: Mrs. Joseph Choate, Dr. and Mrs. W. H. Draper, E. L. Godkin, Mrs. W. E. Dodge, and Mrs. Herman S. LeRoy. At its first public meeting, April 22, 1882, a resolution, presented by Dr. William H. Draper, was adopted, setting forth: (1) that women have conclusively proved their mental and physical ability to do college work; (2) that for lack of college facilities many women are unable "to develop their natural capacity for literature, science, and art . . ." and, for these, collegiate education is a vital need; and (3) that the opening of colleges to women would greatly benefit general education.[28] The Association affirmed its belief in "the undoubted right of women to have as complete and unfettered an opportunity for developing . . . their mental faculties as men now have" and expressly recognized "its obligations to President Barnard of Columbia College for pointing out, in his recent reports, how an ancient and nobly endowed institution like Columbia College can increase its field of usefulness by adapting itself to these requirements."[29] After full deliberation, the following petition for admission of women to Columbia College was approved:

"We, the undersigned, residents of New York City and its neighborhood, beg leave to present our respectful petition: That, in view of the present state of public opinion both here and in other countries touching the justice and expediency of admitting women to the same educational advantages as men, a state of opinion especially evidenced by the recent action of the English universities of Cambridge and London, and in view of the influential position of Columbia College as among the oldest and most richly endowed educational institutions in the United States and preeminently representing the intellectual interests of the city of New York, you will be pleased to consider how best to extend, with as little delay as possible, to such properly qualified women as may desire it, the many and great benefits of education in Columbia College by admitting them to lectures and examinations."[30]

[27] R. C. E., 1883, CXL–CXLI.
[28] Ibid., 1882–3, CXXVIII–CXXX.
[29] Ibid.
[30] Proceedings of the First Meeting of the Association for Promoting the Higher Education of Women in N. Y., 36–7.

The work of the Association and the efforts of Dr. Barnard soon proved effective. By a resolution of the Columbia Trustees, June 8, 1883, there was established "a course of collegiate study equivalent to the course given to young men in the college," to be open to "such women as desire to avail themselves of it." "A general and very strict preliminary examination" was to give admission to a four-year college course. None were to enter under seventeen years of age, except "in case of extraordinary proficiency." Studies were arranged in groups, one of which was required in each of the first two years; with each required group another had to be elected; in the third and fourth years, all studies were elective. The groups were "English language and literature, modern languages and foreign literature, Latin language and literature, Greek language and literature, mathematics, history and political science; physics, chemistry and hygiene; natural history, geology, paleontology, botany and zoölogy; and moral and intellectual philosophy."[31]

A student admitted by the examination was to be "entirely free as to where and how to pursue her studies, whether in some school, private or public, or at home, or under the auspices or direction of any association interested in her welfare and advancement, and providing her with the means of education." Examinations were to be held "as often as may be necessary" and by the "officers of the college or their duly appointed representatives." Having passed such examinations in a "course of study fully equivalent to that for which the same degree is conferred in the School of Arts," young women would receive the Bachelor of Arts degree, admitting them to graduate courses leading to "higher degrees under the direction of the faculty of the college." Women graduates, holding satisfactory degrees of other institutions, were also admitted to the advanced courses. "Certificates of proficiency," signed by the president, were to be issued to those who did not complete the entire requirements for the A.B.[32]

It scarcely need be said that the arrangement proposed by the Columbia Trustees fell far short of what the Association and its friends wanted. Least of all did the plan measure up to Barnard's idea. But, as Draper said, they would take what was

[31] As given in the *R. C. E.*, 1886, 643–4.
[32] *Ibid.*

offered, recognizing the truth of the adage about "half a loaf." As it turned out, it appeared the trustees had really offered something very substantial—the degree—to women who would complete, somehow, somewhere, certain subjects and pass satisfactory examinations. No other large university had done this, either abroad or in the United States. The women at the "Annex," it was noted, were instructed by Harvard professors but did not get the Harvard degree.

In 1884, Dr. Barnard stated in his *Report* that six women were making use of the opportunities offered by the Board of Trustees. Though some received degrees under the first plan, it proved so difficult for young women to get adequate instruction to prepare themselves for the examination, that efforts were soon made to establish a teaching agency to prepare women for the "suitable academic honors" promised by the trustees. In 1889, Barnard College was organized and a provisional charter granted to twenty-two women and men.[33]

These trustees secured physical accommodation for the young college at 343 Madison Avenue, where it remained till 1897. In 1896, a new site was purchased for $160,000 and new buildings erected: Milbank Hall, given by Mrs. A. A. Anderson, and Brinckerhoff Hall, built by the Brinckerhoff fund. Other early and valuable material assets were a sum of $100,000 given for an endowment fund, and $38,000 given for scholarships.[34] At present (1927) the total value of the scholarship funds is $528,000.[35]

To promote instruction of high grade, and to maintain a standard equivalent to Columbia, the staff of professors was made up either of regular Columbia teachers, or others approved by its president. Ella Weed was made chairman of a committee of the board dealing with academic administration, and this part she filled admirably. Examinations were under the direction

[33] The following were named: "Mrs. Francis B. Arnold, the Rev. Dr. Arthur Brooks, Miss Helen Dawes Brown, Silas B. Brownell, Mrs. William C. Brownell, Mrs. Joseph H. Choate, Frederick R. Coudert, Noah Davis, George Hoadley, Hamilton W. Mabie, Mrs. Alfred Meyer, George A. Plimpton, Mrs. John D. Rockefeller, Jacob A. Schiff, James Talcott, the Rev. Dr. Henry Van Dyke, Miss Ella Weed, Everett P. Wheeler, Miss Alice Williams and Mrs. William Wood. . . ."—*Columbia Univ. Quart.* (June 1900), II, 212.

[34] *Columbia Univ. Quart.*, II, 217.

[35] Official information given by the College, April 7, 1927.

of Columbia College and generally the same as given in the college classes. Barnard students had unrestricted access to the Columbia Library. Instruction for the first three years was given in Barnard College, but in the senior year graduate courses in Columbia College were open as electives to Barnard girls. One by one various faculties were authorized by the Board of Trustees to open their work to young women as auditors: in 1889, the faculties of Philosophy and Political Science; and in 1897, the faculty of pure Science, which opened certain courses the next year. In general this system has continued, Barnard contributing some professorships of her own and also benefitting by the instruction of those regularly a part of the Columbia staff.

Growth in point of numbers was slow; but every effort was made to maintain a high standard of work. At the close of the first four years (1893), there were 27 in the first year, 10 in the second, 7 in the third, and 8 in the outgoing class. There were 33 special students. In 1899, there were 312 matriculates. From the time the Columbia degree was first granted to women to 1926, 3,229 Bachelor's degrees were awarded. Up to and including 1900, sixty-eight Master's and six Doctor's degrees were likewise granted. Since that date, the two advanced degrees have been conferred, by the Columbia graduate faculties, on women just as on men. In 1926, there were 957 students enrolled in the four undergraduate classes.[36]

Shortly after educational facilities in coördinate colleges were made available to women at Cambridge and New York City, a similar step was taken in New Orleans. It was natural that the coördinate college idea should appeal to the South as well as to the East; in both sections there had been, from the earliest days, an opposition to the coeducational plan, whether in secondary school or college.

Sophie Newcomb Memorial College for Women was founded "upon an endowment made by Mrs. Josephine Louise Newcomb, of New York City . . . [who] vested this endowment in the administrators of the Tulane Educational Fund. . . . By the act of the administrators, it . . . [was] established as a department of Tulane University."[37] The new institution was to ". . . supplement, not to interfere with . . ." the schools for girls

---

[36] *Ibid.*

[37] *Announcement* of Sophie Newcomb College, 1887–8.

already existing in the city. The purpose of the benefactress, as stated in the official announcement, was "to offer to the young women of Louisiana and the adjoining States a liberal education, similar to that which is now given to young men by the Tulane University, and to young women also by other institutions of the first rank in distant parts of the United States." The establishment of the new college was recognized by its officers to be but an action taken in accord with "an extraordinary impulse in the cause of female education elsewhere; colleges similar to this have sprung up in various localities and have been filled to overflowing; . . . in our own community the increasing desire that such an enterprise should be undertaken has arisen to an imperative demand."[38]

To this end a faculty was selected and a plan of studies drawn up which was "believed to be liberal, thorough and specially adapted to the prevailing conditions." The courses were described as "Classical, Literary, Scientific and Industrial," being designed to contribute to "solid learning" while offering "opportunities for practical and industrial studies." Special encouragement was offered to graduates of normal schools and those already engaged in teaching. The college was opened to "white young women and girls," who had to be fourteen years of age when entering the "Academic year" and pass a satisfactory examination in English grammar (including analysis), history of the United States, elements of rhetoric and composition, elements of English and American literature, geography, physical geography, and arithmetic.[39] After the Academic, came the Collegiate, Sophomore, Junior, and Senior years, the completion of which entitled the candidate to receive the Baccalaureate degree. Latin was required in the academic year of the Classical course, while Greek and Latin were continued throughout the four succeeding years. Four years of two modern languages (French, German, or Spanish) were required for the Literary course; Latin was required in the Academic year, French and Latin in the Collegiate year, and both French and German in the last three years of the Scientific course. The Industrial course required four years of French and three of either German or Spanish.[40]

38 *Ibid.*
39 *Ibid.*
40 *Ibid.*

Since its opening, Sophie Newcomb College has granted 1,155 Bachelor's degrees in Arts and Science, and 155 Bachelor's of Design and Music. Higher degrees are granted only by the graduate faculties of Tulane University. Fifty-nine students enrolled the first year (1887) in the Classical course, twenty-five in the Literary and Scientific courses, and sixty-six in the Art course. Since opening, a total of over 12,000 students have been in attendance. In 1926, there were 719 students: 307 Freshmen, 178 Sophomores, 107 Juniors, and 88 Seniors. Thirty-nine others were doing special and advanced work.[41]

The tendency to favor the plan of segregation, the coördinate, or "affiliated" college, as it has been called more recently, has continued to increase since the early days of the "Annex" and Barnard College. Sophie Newcomb was opened in 1887. In 1891, Brown University, through the Women's College, was opened to women on the coördinate plan, and in 1894 the first Bachelor's degree was granted to a woman. The early growth and success of the Women's College was due, in considerable measure, to the work of the Rhode Island Society for the Collegiate Education of Women, which received a charter in 1896. This group of women, under the leadership of Sarah E. Doyle, secured subscriptions for Pembroke Hall, the first building erected, which they turned over to Brown University in 1897, with all bills paid.[42] The same organization contributed a loan fund of $1,800 and an endowment of $34,000 (1901).[43]

The new college began at once to exert a powerful influence on collegiate education of women within the state. Before its opening, 336 Rhode Island women had entered colleges of other states, and 192 had graduated. Between 1891 and 1907, 776 registered at Brown and 272 took degrees.[44] Two women graduated in the first class, 1894; and to the present (1926) about 2,300 have been in attendance. Approximately 1,700 have been granted the Bachelor's degree. Brown University has conferred the Master's degree on more than 300 women and the Doctorate

---

[41] Information supplied by the officials of Sophie Newcomb College, April 5, 1927.

[42] Amounting to $37,900.

[43] *The School Journal*, LXXV, 517.

[44] King: Women's College in Brown University [*Education* (1907), XXVII, 478 *ff.*].

(Courtesy of the Rhode Island School of Design)

SARAH E. DOYLE

on thirteen.[45]   Dean Lida S. King, in 1907, pointed out the service rendered by the College to young women.   The alumnae records showed 209, out of a total of 272 graduates, chiefly women of the state, holding positions open only to college graduates.   Supporting her statement by what had already been accomplished in the brief period of its existence, Dean King saw the following as the services to be rendered by the Women's College: To provide "opportunity for college work of the highest grade in the section of the country which offered practically none"; to make a college education and professional training possible for many Rhode Island women who could not secure them otherwise; and, finally, to extend the interest in woman's higher education "till it shall reach every town and village in the state."[46]

Besides appearing at universities long open to men only, the coördinate college idea has, in several instances, appeared at coeducational institutions.   There it has been recommended as a means of getting rid of complete coeducation.   The argument generally presented was the age-old one, that though women needed to be educated they did not have to have an identical education.

The reaction against coeducation at Wisconsin, and the attempt to set up a separate woman's college which never functioned, have been mentioned.[47]   A similar, though not so marked, reaction took place at Stanford, Chicago, and other coeducational institutions.   In 1902, president-elect Edmund J. James is said to have written the trustees of Northwestern University that there were "many signs of a reaction in the public mind on the subject of Coeducation. . . . Not only has the system ceased to make new converts, but there are indications that it is losing ground. . . . One hears oftener of the claim that the increasing number of women tends to feminize the institutions where they are, in some cases to such an extent as to discourage the attendance of men.   It is urged with increasing persistence that the social distractions and dissipations form a serious problem, while

[45] Information furnished by officials of the Women's College, March 24, 1927.

[46] King: *op. cit.*, 483.

[47] Pp. 240 *f.* and 290 *ff.*

others emphasize the fact that the broad differences in the future careers of the two sexes should find a more adequate recognition in the College curriculum." The views of James were quoted as antagonistic to coeducation and were approvingly commented on in several Eastern papers.[48] The press comments probably exaggerated his views. An examination of his communications to the Board of Trustees reveals the following statement, which is clearly an argument used in favor of developing technical education and not as a blow at coeducation. As is known, the School of Engineering at Northwestern was founded a few years after this date. President Scott gives it as his judgment that "there has never been any change in attitude about women in the College."[49] It was doubtless the idea of doing something "to restore the balance" which reporters seized upon as indicating hostility to too many women on the campus. President James said, in 1904:

"In my opinion this tendency [the increase in proportion of women] is a permanent one, and is likely to increase more rapidly in the future than it has in the past. The College of Liberal Arts of Northwestern University is distinctly a literary college; its emphasis is placed upon the study of the classics, ancient and modern history, mathematics and pure science. These are subjects which are likely to appeal with increasing force to the women of the country as they become more educated, and as public opinion demands for them a higher standard of education. As long as the curriculum of the College contains so few elements of practical or applied science we may expect to see the relative number of women increase until they constitute fully three quarters of the total registration. The establishment of a school of technology and in general, courses in applied science in the large sense, would doubtless prove attractive to young men and through the increase in such courses, we might expect to restore the balance."[50]

In 1907, President Hamilton, of Tufts College, noting the growing professional tendency and the decline of the liberal arts college, declared: "The average young man will not go to a co-

<hr>

[48] *The School Journal* (1902), LXIV, 468–9.

[49] Letter, April 14, 1927.

[50] As quoted in the letter mentioned above.

educational institution if other things are anywhere near equal.''
Turning to Tufts' problem, he said:

"I am confident that there is one way in which the problem
may be very successfully solved, and I am equally confident that
there is no other. The future of the academic department of
Tufts College as a man's college depends upon the immediate
segregation of the women into a separate department or college.
I do not believe Tufts ought to go out of the business of educating
women, but I do believe that Tufts should educate its women
separately. They should have their own lecture rooms, and their
department should have some distinguishing name. I should
like to see the number of men in the arts courses rapidly increasing, and I should like to see the building up of a strong and successful woman's department. Such action as I have indicated
requires, of course, a considerable expenditure of money, and
some friend or friends of Tufts must be found to endow and perhaps to name our women's department. I should say that it
would be safe to begin operations on the new plan if $250,000
could be available for buildings and salary funds.

"I regard this as the most pressing educational problem we
have before us. I have no fear that a failure to solve it would
involve disaster to Tufts College considered as a university, but
I have no doubt that failure to solve it involves imminent disaster
to the College of Liberal Arts.''[51]

The outcome of this feeling, shared not only by the President
but by many of the faculty, trustees, and students as well, was
the discontinuance of full coeducation, which had been the practice since the admission of women in 1892, and the opening of
Jackson College, an affiliated institution, in 1910.

An interesting controversy has been carried on for many years
relative to the admission of women to the University of Virginia.
As early as 1889, the chairman of the faculty stated, in reply
to a definite query on the subject: "I would say that opinion
is much divided both in our faculty and in our board of Visitors on the question of opening the university to women.''[52]
In 1911, the attempt of women to gain a foothold at the Univer-

[51] *Annual Report*—quoted in *New Eng. Jour. of Ed.* (1907), LXVI,
485-6.

[52] Reply to a letter, quoted in Meyer: *Woman's Work in America*, 95.

sity attracted public notice. Some favored coeducation, others segregation, others no women at the University under any arrangement. A bill was prepared, and approved by many women of the state, proposing the establishment of a women's department or "annex." This met the approval of the educational commission and was sent to the Legislature for action; but, as noted, every effort met failure until 1920–21.[53]

[53] See p. 295.

CHAPTER VII

HIGHER PROFESSIONAL EDUCATION

I. General Lack of Professional Opportunity

The entrance of women into their first great profession outside the home has been described. The rapid development of the public school movement offered them a notable opportunity which they quickly grasped. The public elementary schools were new institutions and needed a new group of professional teachers to serve them. We may say that teaching in the lower schools, as a profession for women, marks its beginning, in the United States, at the rise of common schools and in the normal schools, established to prepare teachers for them. Being a new and, necessarily, a rapidly expanding profession, women entered it with relatively little opposition, compared with that which met their efforts to enter medicine or law.

Long after women had attained the preliminary education, in seminary or college, that would prepare them adequately to pursue advanced professional study, it was impossible for them to do so. Elizabeth Blackwell, after great exertion, succeeded in gaining entrance into a college of medicine, in 1848. The first women's medical college, was incorporated in Philadelphia in 1850, but was for many years discredited by the statements of numerous doctors, medical societies, and journals. There was a world of truth in the words spoken by Z. C. Graves to his graduates of the Mary Sharp College in 1855:

"Having completed it [this course of study]—how different is your situation . . . from that of the young man in the same condition?

"The schools of Law, Theology and Medicine open their doors to him, inviting his entrance. They offer to him a thousand inducements to use all his natural and acquired abilities in appropriating to him their garnered truths. This having been accomplished, society calls him to take a stand upon her contested fields and by using the results of his intellectual labors to gain wealth for the gratification of his tastes in manhood and for the

321

supplying of his wants in age, together with a name that shall be the honor of his descendants.

"But the doors of these schools are barred to your entrance. No public institution offers to you the means of ascending higher. Society has no inducements to offer in any of the learned professions, if we except that of teaching."

Since the doors to professions were generally barred to them, Graves could offer his graduates no more specific guidance than that they should avoid the "light literature," so plentiful in the country, and continue "in the great school of self education . . . a school that has many degrees but no final ones."[1] The last half of the nineteenth century, however, witnessed the gradual opening of medical, law, and theological schools, as well as the graduate departments of universities, wherein women were to be given the chance to prove that they could master not only the literary and scientific studies to the extent developed by men, but also assist in extending the boundaries of that knowledge. It is intended to set forth here, very briefly, significant facts connected with the opening of these paths to professional advancement.

It is worthy of notice that, in the first few decades of the experiment with women's collegiate education, relatively few college graduates entered professions. This was true for some time after professional schools were open to women. Jane Bancroft, in 1885, called particular attention to law and medicine which, among others, she considered proper avenues for college women to enter.[2] But of the 1,235 women preachers, 208 lawyers, and 4,555 doctors, said Thwing, in 1895, there are "only a few who are college women. A lamentably small proportion of the physicians of the country are college-bred. Out of the more than 4,000 women who are physicians it is probable that not more than 200 have had a college training. Out of the more than 1,800 women who are members of the Collegiate Alumnae Association there are only 34 physicians. The law, the ministry and journalism command a far smaller proportion, for, in the same association of college women, there are only half a dozen lawyers, preachers and journalists."[3]

[1] Z. C. Graves and the Mary Sharp College, 70 and 72.

[2] Education (1885), V, 486-95; see also Claghorn: College Training for Women (1897).

[3] What becomes of College Women [N. A. R., Nov. 1895, 549].

Of 633 women listed in *Appleton's Cyclopedia of American Biography*, only nineteen had had a college education. This is not remarkable, inasmuch as at the time of its publication (1886–1889) women had not long had many opportunities for college education opened to them. Thwing estimated that of about 8,000 college women (1895) probably 5,000 were married or would marry.[4] The remaining 3,000 were to be found in every kind of employment, but about two-thirds were engaged in school teaching.[5] Further suggestions as to the slow assimilation of college women by the medical, legal, and other professions are obtained from the figures of certain women's colleges. Rachel Kent Fitz, writing of the *College Woman Graduate*, in 1907, pointed out that of 3,800 alumnae of two large colleges there were but thirty-three doctors, seven lawyers, and two ministers. Twenty-one were nurses, fifty were writers, one hundred were in philanthropic work, eighty-five in library work, five were actresses, and two were architects. About 16 per cent were in these or similar professions, whereas 84 per cent were "either home-makers or teachers." Fitz concluded that, "as the two colleges chosen are pre-eminent for their standards of scholarships, it would seem to be a fair inference that the college woman graduate of today is in general either a home maker or a teacher. Many teachers, however, are but teachers in passing, since notably through marriage, they subsequently become home makers. The home, even more than teaching, is therefore seen to be the ultimate goal and fruition of the life of the majority of college women."[6] Although this estimate of 84 per cent of college women as home makers is somewhat above that reported by other students of the question, is based on but two women's colleges, and rests, partially, on the assumption that those who are now unemployed will become home makers eventually, the fact is perfectly clear that colleges were not recruiting many women for advanced professional positions. Gambrill, studying the men and women graduates of eleven institutions (1922), found that of the "37 per cent of [women of] the class of 1903, engaged in paid occupations at the end of $12\frac{1}{2}$ years, about 7/10 were teachers." About 50 per cent of the women studied were listed

[4] Compare with pp. 204 *ff*.

[5] *N. A. R.*, Nov. 1895, 546–53.

[6] *Education* (1907), XXVII, 601 and 610.

as "home makers.'"[7]   The smallness of the number entering professions would be partly accounted for by these factors: first, that many college women were drawn from leisure classes; second, that the general disciplinary conception of education in women's colleges did not conduce to the development of professional interests and insights; and, third, there was then considerable, and still is some, antipathy towards women who desire to enter such higher professional positions.

Even in the profession of teaching, the lower ranks of which were early opened to women, there has been a marked tardiness and coldness of welcome to those who would enter the higher and better paid branches of it. This may be accounted for by (1) a lack of collegiate training to prepare adequately for higher teaching posts and (2) antipathy of those in colleges and universities to the admission of women to a field once occupied almost exclusively by men. As colleges and graduate departments of universities have gradually made it possible for women to attain to equal scholarship with men, the first obstacle has been disposed of; the second still stands in many places, and can only be removed by time, which undermines prejudices, and a long and thorough demonstration, on the part of women trained in research, that they can do the work as well or better than men.

Though women have entered the higher ranks of the teaching profession very slowly, the importance of collegiate training, from the professional standpoint, was early recognized. Beecher advocated women's institutions "on the college plan" in order that they might be prepared to enter into their true professions.[8] McCabe prophesied, a little.later, in the *American Girl at College*, that "the scholastic standard of common-school teachers will eventually be elevated to such a point that only the woman with A.B. can hope for a position, while the aspirants for college professorships will find Ph.D. imperative!"[9]

Many of the early colleges, even when the classical departments were open only to men, established "ladies' department" and "normal" or, sometimes, "scientific" courses which were open to women and prepared them for lower school posts. Gradually, from the "normal" or other departments as an intermediate step,

[7] Gambrill: *College Achievement and Vocational Efficiency*, 85.
[8] See pp. 143 *ff*.
[9] Page 10.

they were enabled to obtain access to the college proper. Olin showed that the normal department of the University of Wisconsin was first created with the idea of preparing teachers for the common schools, thus linking the University with a problem of general public interest. But, during the Civil War and after, women stepped into the men's places as teachers, came to constitute most of the normal student body, and were eventually admitted to full recognition in the college department.[10] In 1850, the Regents' *Report* declared: "It is proper, however, to subjoin in this connection, that the normal department of the University will be made to embrace suitable provisions for the professional training of female teachers"; and, the next year, that the 'plan contemplates the admission of female as well as male teachers to all the advantages of the normal department of the university, and offers to the members of the teachers' class access to the instructions of the other departments."[11] The history of woman's advancement in other institutions admitting men is very similar, and goes to show that her access to a college education depended largely upon its necessity as a preparation for her vocational fitness.

Instead of decreasing in importance, the movement to professionalize higher education continued to increase. In colleges and universities there were founded chairs of pedagogy[12] and departments of education (more elaborate than the early "normal" departments), and in these women found more advanced professional preparation offered them as freely as to men.[13] Even in the women's colleges, which, as a general rule, were inclined to cleave to the idea of general discipline, the notion appeared that women should be given specific preparation for teaching, which was preeminently their profession. It has been noted that Wellesley College made a particular appeal to those who were teachers.[14] F. A. Walker, 1892, although taking the position that the women's colleges "should, at least in the present and the

[10] From *Women of a State University*, by Mrs. H. M. Olin, G. P. Putnam's Sons, New York. Used by courtesy of the publishers. Pp. 11–13; 23–24.

[11] *Ibid.*, 14 and 15.

[12] Hall: The Training of Teachers [*The Forum* (1890–1), X, 11–22].

[13] "Chairs of Pedagogics," by W. T. Harris, chairman [*Proc. Nat. Council of Ed.*, 1882, 24–31].

[14] See p. 196.

immediate future, confine themselves to the proper college function of mental discipline," made "one important exception,"—namely, relating "to the training of teachers. Already the leading colleges and universities for men are turning their attention to this urgent need of the times, and are establishing chairs of pedagogy for the instruction of their undergraduates in the theory and history of teaching. I believe that the colleges for women should go still further in this direction, so that each one of them shall become, in a high sense, a normal school."[15] That this was not a popular doctrine in 1892 need scarcely be said, but it did indicate a line of development to be followed more and more in the succeeding years.

It was shown in a previous chapter[16] that though women became teachers in elementary schools at an early date they did not often become administrators. More recently, this field has come to be regarded as one for which they may be well qualified when given the necessary training. Horn, writing but a short time ago, noted that though normal schools prepare women for elementary classroom teaching and the college for high-school teaching, "there is practically no agency for the training of elementary school administrators. The college woman is selected for native ability. She has a broad training. Her natural faculties have been developed. She possesses a measure of initiative. She should come into her own as a leader and administrator of the American elementary school."[17] Such preparation as is needed would presumably be best afforded in the educational departments of colleges and universities.[18]

Women held some teaching positions, though generally of minor importance, in the first institutions that experimented with college education for women. The names of Anna P. Sill and Lucinda Stone are indeed worthy of remembrance. Sophia Jex Blake pointed out, in her *Visit to American Schools and Colleges*, that there were "several lady-professors" at Antioch College, one in mathematics, another in natural science and history,

[15] *Educational Review* (1892), IV, 334–8.

[16] Vol. I, 514 *ff*.

[17] College Women as Elementary Teachers [*Ed. Adm. and Supervision*, X, 145–6].

[18] See p. 338 for figures of women attending this type of higher professional school.

MARIA MITCHELL

and others in modern languages.[19]   But neither Mrs. Dean, Mrs. Fay, nor Miss Hitchcock were as well known as Lucretia Crocker, who served for a time as professor of mathematics and astronomy; and none of them attained, and few approached, the scholarly recognition accorded to Maria Mitchell, of Vassar, or Alice Freeman Palmer, of Wellesley College.   Describing conditions of 1884, Dr. Thomas, of Bryn Mawr, asserted that "women were teaching in Wellesley, Mount Holyoke and Smith without even the elementary training of a college course behind them.   Men in general, including highly intelligent presidents of colleges for women, as well as highly intelligent presidents of colleges for men, held in good faith absurd opinions on women's education. When I protested to the president of the most advanced college for women in regard to this lack of training, he told me that we could never run Bryn Mawr if we insisted on the same scholarly attainments in women professors."[20]   A quarter century later (1908) Miss Thomas declared: "The old type of untrained woman teacher has practically disappeared from women's colleges . . . [being supplanted by] ardent young women scholars who have qualified themselves by long years of graduate study for advanced teaching."

It was the rapid expansion of better college facilities in the last years of the old century, the opening of such new institutions as the University of Chicago, as freely to women as to men, and the expansion of post-graduate work in many older universities, that began to put a new complexion on the woman-professor question.   By 1901, Harper, of Chicago, was willing to assert that "the women now being graduated, with the Doctor's degree, from our strongest institutions, are, in almost every particular, as able and as strong as the men.   If opportunity were offered, these women would show that they possess the qualifications demanded."[21]   It was perfectly evident to him that prejudice, and not women's incompetence, was the reason for failure to offer them appointments:

"In colleges and universities for men only, women may not find a place upon the faculty.   In a certain great State university, in which there are as many women students as men stu-

[19] Butler: *Woman's Work and Culture*, 71–2.
[20] Tendencies in Women's Education [*Ed. Rev.* (1908), XXXV, 67].
[21] *R. C. E.* (1901–2), I, 661–2.

dents, women are represented in the faculty by a single individual, and she has been appointed within the last three years. In some of the women's colleges women find a place. In others, second-rate and third-rate men are preferred to women of first-rate ability. The number of faculties of colleges and universities on which women have appointments in any number is very small, and even in certain institutions in which women have gained secure footing there is often greater or less distress among the men of the various departments if even one or two women are appointed. And yet, is it possible that the heads of our State institutions—institutions which are established by the people and conducted with the people's money; institutions which are professedly democratic beyond all others—deliberately refuse to recommend the appointment of women even when they have attained equal rank with men in scholarship and efficiency? So far as I can ascertain, during the past year the appointment of women, east and west, even in coeducational institutions, have numbered very few—fewer, perhaps, than ever before. Is this progress? Or is it rather a concession to prejudices which, instead of growing weaker, are growing stronger? I venture to ask the regents of our State universities and the trustees of our coeducational institutions to consider this question; and I think it is not inappropriate to suggest for the consideration of the trustees of certain women's colleges the question whether, in this matter, they have given to women the full opportunity which they deserve."[22]

Ten years later (1911) figures for state colleges and universities showed an average of about nine per cent women teachers; west of the Mississippi the average was thirteen per cent per institution, while to the east the average was but six. Extreme variation was to be noted in several institutions. In Florida State College for Women, fifty-six per cent of the teachers were women; in Ohio University, forty-one per cent; and at the University of New Mexico and Kansas Agricultural College, thirty and twenty-eight per cent of the teachers, respectively, were women. The University of California, Massachusetts Institute of Technology, University of Maine, and Cornell had a total teaching staff of 1258, of whom but twenty-five were women.[23]

22 *Ibid.*
23 *Am. Ed. Rev.* (1911–12), XXXIII, 268.

ALICE FREEMAN PALMER

In 1921, the Association of University Professors published a preliminary report of the status of women in college and university faculties, covering most of the 176 institutions represented by its members. Twenty-nine colleges and universities for men had only two women among nearly two thousand professors. One of these was in Harvard Medical School and the other in the Yale School of Education. In fourteen colleges for women, however, men were well represented, there being 251 men in a total faculty group of 989—more than 25 per cent. In 104 institutions for men and women together, there were 12,869 faculty members (of all grades), with a total of 1,646 women or nearly 13 per cent.[24] Only 4 per cent of the full professorships, 7.9 per cent of all professorships, and 23.5 per cent of the instructorships were held by women, although more than 31 per cent of the students at the institutions were women. Twenty-six per cent of these institutions had no woman holding professorial rank in the arts college; 12 had but one each. Forty-seven per cent had "no woman holding a professorship of the first rank in the academic faculty." In 25 of the 104 institutions there was no dean of women. Replies from men's colleges often stated that, being non-coeducational, they had no women professors. Men were, however, well represented in the faculties of the women's colleges. The reason for the unequal employment of men and women seems to have been prejudice against the latter—except, in some instances, when they were appointed to teach such subjects as home economics or nursing.

That prejudice is beginning to weaken is indicated by some replies sent in to the investigating committee. One dean replied: "When we discover a woman who can handle some subject in our course of study better than a man could handle it, we shall not hesitate to urge the appointment of the woman and we shall, in all probability, be successful in getting it confirmed. . . . President —— has admitted that we must in time have women on our Faculty. There is, of course, a general prejudice at —— against the appointment of women, but it is a prejudice that arises out of the traditional masculinity of the institution. It is neither a violent antagonism nor a judgment based on study

[24] See *Biennial Survey*, 1920–22, I, 74–5; see also *Report* of the Association of University Professors, *Bulletin*, Oct. 1921, No. 6, Vol. VII, 21–32.

or experience.''[25]   There may be some significance in the statement that the woman who can do the work *better than a man*
will be urged for appointment.   She ought to stand an *equal*
chance with the man if she has *equal* qualifications, but it will
probably be some time before ''traditional masculinity'' is so far
reduced in potency.   The Trustees of the University of North
Carolina voted, April 12, 1927, that, to facilitate the work of the
School of Education, it may employ women on its faculty.[26]

The further weakening of the masculine tradition, while not
universal, is, however, suggested in numerous expressions found
in replies, as: ''The attitude of our faculty and regents is rapidly
changing''; ''there has been a decided tendency in the last five
years to more and more recognition of women in high places of
responsibility''; and ''until recently we have been unable to
secure women with the Ph.D. degree.''   The investigating committee attributed the changing attitude to (1) the introduction
of women into higher teaching positions in war emergencies, (2)
the scarcity of men due to the keen competition of other better
paid work, (3) development of schools of education (in which
women have found facilities for their professional preparation),
(4) new realization of rights and capacities of women, and (5)
the success of the woman suffrage movement.[27]

Not only have women entered professorships at universities
infrequently, but their promotion has been much ''slower than
that of men.''   Little study has been devoted to this question,
but H. D. Kitson published some facts which were ascertained in
an examination of their situation at Chicago and Columbia Universities.   Though the number of cases was small, but fifteen
women being among the number studied, Dr. Kitson felt the fact
of slower progress in coeducational institutions was ''pretty
firmly established.''   These women ''began their academic careers
later than the men and reached the professorship much later—
at Columbia at the age of forty-seven and at Chicago in their
fifty-third year, nine years later than the corresponding age of
the Chicago men.''[28]

25 *Report*, Association of University Professors, *Bulletin* VII, 22.

26 Extract from Trustees' Minutes, furnished by the Secretary, Mr. R. B.
House, June 27, 1927.

27 *Report*, Association of University Professors, *Bulletin* VII, 25.

28 Relation between Age and Promotion of University Professors [*Sch.
and Soc.*, Sept. 25, 1926, 400–4].

The committee of the Association of Professors found that women received equal pay for equal work in 73 per cent of the eleven women's colleges and in 53 per cent of the coeducational institutions. In the others, it was "frankly admitted that women are given a less salary and lower rank than men for the same work . . . ," the differences ranging from 10 to 50 per cent, and averaging 18. The reasons offered to justify the different salary schedules were fundamentally the same, presented elsewhere, to justify the same practice in lower schools: the law of supply and demand; families depending on men for support; and the need of keeping men in college teaching.[29]

In connection with the questions of equal pay and rank for equal work and the rate of promotion, the question naturally arises as to whether women are able to perform the services of university professors as well as men. This question was also investigated by Committee W of the American Association of University Professors, to ascertain whether lower pay, slower promotion, and lower rank were due to inferiority of women in some respect or simply to the general acceptance of the idea that men were more desirable. Twenty-four questions were sent "to the dean and to one male and one female professor [where there were such] in each institution connected with the American Association." While the results represent only opinions, they are significant since the generally accepted opinions determine the status of women in college faculties. The results published[30] were "based upon 130 answers from 86 coeducational institutions and 22 answers from 13 colleges for women. Of the reports from coeducational institutions, 20 are from male presidents, 32 from male deans, 13 from deans of women, 43 from male professors, 18 from female professors, 3 from male secretaries, one from a male registrar. Of the reports from colleges for women, 3 are from male presidents, one from a female president, 5 from female and 2 from male deans, 6 from female, and 5 from male professors. Nearly all of the reports are from representative faculty men and women of high rank and distinction."

Comparing the teaching of women with that of men, 63 (15 women and 48 men) thought women equal to men, 12 (7 women and 5 men) thought them better, 29 (12 women and 17 men)

[29] *Bulletin* of the Association, VII, 27; compare also Vol. I, 495–6.
[30] *Ibid.*, Nov. 1924, X, No. 7, 65–73.

considered it merely an individual matter, while 16 (0 women and 16 men) held that women were not equal to the men. As to the amount of work men and women are able to handle in colleges, 110 (37 women and 73 men), out of 121, thought women had "shown themselves physically able to handle as much or more" than men, while 11 (1 woman and 10 men) held that the opposite was true. Relative to the preference of students for men or women, 46 (3 women and 43 men) "from coeducational faculties" stated that men preferred men teachers, and 44 (4 women and 40 men) said that girls, too, preferred men as teachers. "No one reported that either boys or girls preferred women as teachers." That it was a matter of indifference was held by 50 (21 women, 29 men). Three (0 women, 3 men) from women's colleges said girls preferred men, and 5 (4 women, 1 man) stated it was merely a question of the individual teacher.[31]

As to women's success in teaching advanced classes, 64 (25 women, 39 men) thought it equal to or greater than that of men, 8 (4 women, 4 men) believed it an individual matter, while 42 (5 women, 37 men) thought it less than that of men. To the question as to the continuance of study and improvement of their scholarship, 79 (29 women, 50 men) held that women were equal to men or better, 7 (3 women, 4 men) thought it an individual matter, while 43 (5 women, 38 men) thought women did not continue to improve themselves as did men.[32]

So far as productive scholarship was concerned, 47 (20 women, 27 men) stated women were equal to men, or that it was "an individual matter"; but 72 (12 women and 60 men) thought women inferior.

That women were more conscientious about their work was thought by 29 (11 women, 18 men); that they were less conscientious was the opinion of five (men); that they were about the same as men was the judgment of 92. Women's work on committees was held by 101 (33 women, 68 men) to be equal to, or better than, that of men, or that it was an individual matter, and by 26 (2 women, 24 men) to be not so good. As to active interest in the larger affairs of the institutions, 78 (30 women, 48 men) thought it as great in women as in men, or a matter of individuals; 7 thought women took a greater interest (3 women, 4 men);

31 *Ibid.*, 66, 68, 69.
32 *Ibid.*, 70.

while 44 (2 women, 42 men) held that they took less interest in such things. As to interest in "social, civic and economic problems of the day," 77 (33 women, 44 men) thought women equal to men, one woman thought they surpassed the men, and 57 (6 women, 51 men) thought them below men. As to efficiency "in developing a social consciousness and a social conscience," 72 (26 women, 46 men) thought women equal to men, 21 (8 women, 13 men) thought them more so, and 24 men thought them less. As to the employment of married women, or the employment of the wife of a man on the staff, one of thirteen women's colleges reporting forbade, by rule, the employment of married women, and four said it was the custom not to employ such. Seven, of the thirteen, had no teachers with living husbands, and five had "an average of 8% of their faculties . . . with husbands living." Seventy-seven, of seventy-eight answering the question, stated there was no rule against employing married women; but in 16 the employment of married women was "contrary to custom," whereas in 51 it was not. In 13 institutions there were regulations against employing a man and wife at the same time; in the other 67 there was no such regulation.[33]

II. Graduate Instruction for Women

One of the most important developments, influencing the entrance of women into college teaching, was the growth of graduate instruction in American universities. In these departments for advanced study and research, there could not be raised the same objections which had stood in the way of their entering the lower schools of many old universities. The maturity of the students and the definiteness of purpose with which they came offered double assurance to the institution that their presence would not cause the troubles, real or imaginary, that many associated with undergraduate coeducation.[34]

Graduate instruction in American universities is itself of recent origin, and for many years it did not cut much of a figure in the education of either men or women. Yale established graduate courses in philosophy and arts, in 1846. The Harvard Graduate School of Arts and Sciences was established in 1872, that of the University of Pennsylvania in 1882, and graduate

33 *Ibid.*, 71–3.
34 Thwing: *The College Woman*, 130–1.

work in philosophy and in pure science was begun by Columbia University in 1890 and 1892, respectively. Johns Hopkins emphasized graduate research from its beginning in 1876. Considering the late date of their opening, that women's collegiate education was a well established practice, and the fact that the new departments were anxious to build themselves up, it would have been unusual indeed if women had long been excluded. As it was due partly to the small prestige of the new departments, the limited number of them, and the fact that in some quarters women were not welcome, many American women followed the example of American men and pursued advanced studies abroad, chiefly in Germany and France. The need for greater attention to research in American universities was stressed by some of these returned scholars. In 1894, G. Stanley Hall pointed out that home institutions were not yet doing what they should, otherwise 411 American students would not have been found in Prussian universities the year before.[35]

Bryn Mawr College, in its first catalog of 1885, acknowledged its indebtedness to the Johns Hopkins University, and proceeded to offer graduate instruction to students who "presented a diploma from some college of acknowledged standing." Candidates were to pursue work for three years beyond the A.B., write a dissertation, be able to read Latin, French, and German, and be not "wholly unacquainted with Greek." The thesis was to be printed. Only women from Bryn Mawr College could obtain the Master's degree after one year of advanced study.[36] Up to and including 1900, Bryn Mawr College had granted forty-four Master's and eighteen Doctor's degrees.[37] Considering the prominence of the institution from the very outset, the fact that the standards set were equal to those of the best, and better than those of some graduate departments in older universities, and that many women holding her highest degree became teachers elsewhere, much credit must be given for influencing the development of this higher branch of education for women.

The Faculty of Philosophy, of the University of Pennsylvania, "organized for the supervision of advanced studies in the several

[35] American Universities and the Training of Teachers [*The Forum*, XVII, 148–59].

[36] *Catalog*, 1885, 6, 11, 12 and 13.

[37] Information furnished by the college authorities, May 14, 1927.

departments of literature and science," and leading to the degree
of Doctor of Philosophy, was announced in the catalog of 1882–3.
Two women and two men entered in 1885. The courses leading
to the degree were "to cover a period of at least two years."[38]
The candidate had to hold a Bachelor's degree from some recognized institution and present a thesis on some original investigation.[39] The catalog of 1888–9 announced that "women are admitted to any course for the Ph.D. degree on the same conditions
as men."

The *Annual Report* of President Low, of Columbia College
(1890), recorded the facts of the newly organized graduate
studies in philosophy and letters;[40] and two years later, two
women students, one holding the degree of Barnard, the other a
certificate from Harvard, had taken advantage of the new opportunities.[41]

In 1891, the report of President Dwight, of Yale University,
set forth the action taken by a committee of the philosophical
faculty and approved by the corporation, relative to the admission of women to graduate studies. Thereby it was "recommended that in the academic year 1891–92, and afterwards, the
courses of graduate study, leading to the degree of doctor of
philosophy, should be open to the graduates of all colleges and
universities without distinction of sex. . . . It is believed that
the opening of these opportunities to young women who have
previously advanced to such a point in their studies in the institutions founded especially for them will prove to be a great advantage to the cause of the higher education. . . . The University becomes by the offering of this privilege, not a rival or opponent of the colleges for women, but an ally and helper to
them. . . ."[42] Such action, Hadley pointed out,[43] served to
sanction officially the presence of women, which had occasionally
and by "special arrangements" been secured before. The work
done by women thus admitted had been "generally good" and

38 *Report of the Provost*, 1883, 54.

39 *Catalog*, 1883–4, 102.

40 P. 8.

41 *Catalog* of Columbia College, 1892–3, 32–5.

42 The President's *Report* of 1891, quoted in the *R. C. E.* (1891–2), II,
814–15; an article on Education for Women at Yale, by Timothy Dwight,
appeared in *The Forum* (1892), XIII, 451–63.

43 *Educational Review* (1892), III, 486–7.

had "helped rather than hindered the efficiency of the classes. It seemed only fair to give such students official recognition as members of the University; to encourage them instead of barely tolerating them; and to award them the degree of Doctor of Philosophy if their work was such as to deserve it." In 1893, Yale reported 125 graduate students, of whom 22 were women.[44]

In the year 1891–2, the faculty of Brown University took action relative to the admission of women to graduate courses, it being provided that "to women holding bachelors' degrees and, by special permission, to other women of liberal education, all the courses of instruction in the University, intended for graduate students, be opened on the same terms as [to] men."[45]

In 1894, the overseers of Harvard University authorized the admission of "properly qualified women" to courses designed "primarily for graduates."[46] These first students of the graduate department did not, however, become candidates for the Harvard degree, but received the Radcliffe degree "with the approval of the President and Fellows of Harvard College." Recently when the new graduate school of education was opened (1921), women were admitted as candidates for the degrees of Master and Doctor of Education on the same conditions as men.[47]

The University of Chicago, opened in 1892, offered the same opportunities to women as to men. Dr. Marion Talbot, in her report to the President, 1898, stated that ten women had received the doctorate and eleven the Master's degree, between 1892 and 1897; and that nine received the doctorate and five the Master's in the year 1897–8. Of the nineteen granted the doctorate, one obtained the "rite" degree, thirteen the "cum laude," and five the "magna cum laude." Five women were represented in the University faculty in 1892–3, and ten in 1897–8.[48] Of these women, Alice Freeman Palmer, Marion Talbot, Myra Reynolds, Katherine Bates, and Martha Foote Crow are among the best known.

Summarizing the experience of the University of Chicago as to the "status of women in graduate work and their future in

44 *Ibid.* (1893), V, 202.

45 *R. C. E.* (1890–1), II, 814–15.

46 By letter, May 4, 1927; also *Ed. Rev.* (1894), VIII, 99.

47 *Sch. and Soc.*, XII, 349; and letter, May 4, 1927.

48 *President's Report*, University of Chicago, 1897–8, 111–12, 115, and 117.

academic positions," as seen in their work at the University of Chicago, between 1910 and 1915, Dr. Talbot stated:

"(1) A larger proportion of women than of men admitted to candidacy for the master's degree complete the course and a smaller proportion for the doctor's degree; (2) the proportion of women taking the doctor's degree with the lowest grade is smaller than of men, with the highest grade larger and approximately the same for the intermediate grades; (3) a smaller proportion of women than of men hold college and university appointments, a larger proportion hold normal and high-school appointments, and the same proportions are in miscellaneous occupations; (4) nine per cent of the men holding the doctor's degree from the university occupy faculty positions and 5 per cent of the women; (5) eighty-seven per cent of men Doctors of Philosophy holding faculty positions in the University of Chicago are of professorial rank of different grades and sixty-six per cent of women."[49]

In 1907, the President of Johns Hopkins University announced the step taken by the last of the great graduate institutions of the country to admit women. This action was first recommended by the Academic Council April 1, 1907, and subsequently approved by the trustees. "Women who have taken the baccalaureate degree at institutions of good standing" are to be "admitted to graduate courses . . . provided there is no objection on the part of the instructor concerned. . . ."[50] It was particularly emphasized that there was "no intention of admitting women to the undergraduate classes of the University."

The rapid growth of graduate instruction for women is indicated by the following figures, which, though not entirely complete, represent the facts in broad outline.

According to the reports sent in to the office of the Commissioner of Education, 189 Ph.D. degrees were granted by American universities in 1892–3.[51] In 1900–1901, the same degree was granted, upon examination, by 42 institutions, to 312 men and 31 women; in the same year the Master of Arts degree was granted to 1,106 men and 295 women.[52] In 1909–10, the doc-

[49] N. E. A. Proc., 1922, 770.
[50] Report of the President of the Johns Hopkins University, 1907, 18–19.
[51] R. C. E., I, 81–2.
[52] Ibid. (1901), II, 1613.

TABLE I

GRADUATE STUDENTS IN PUBLIC AND PRIVATE INSTITUTIONS

Date	Resident students	Non-resident students	Total
1892–3			
Men	2,235	846	3,081[53]
Women	390	94	484
1900–01			
Men	4,090	793	4,883[54]
Women	1,876	106	1,982
1909–10			
Men	6,506	1,002	7,508[55]
Women	2,865	126	2,991
1919–20			
Men	9,837	....	9,837[56]
Women	5,775	....	5,775

torate was conferred on 362 men and 44 women, while the Master's degree was granted to 1,172 men and 465 women. The Master of Science was granted 278 men and 39 women.[57] The doctorates were conferred on women by the following institutions: University of California, Clark, and the University of Wisconsin, one each; Illinois, Michigan, and New York Universities, two each; Radcliffe College, four; Chicago University and Bryn Mawr, five each; Cornell and the University of Pennsylvania, 6 each; and Columbia University, nine. In 1919–20, 439 doctorates were conferred on men and 93 on women; the Master of Arts was conferred on 1,650 men and 1,180 women; and the Master of Science on 585 men and 103 women.[58]

When women first undertook serious college studies there was much speculation as to whether they could master them. Similar queries have been raised as to their ability to carry on research work successfully, even by those who most readily admit their success in undergraduate study. That the wish is father of the

[53] *Ibid.*, (1892–3), I, 74.
[54] *Ibid.* (1900–1), II, 1618–19.
[55] *Ibid.* (1910), II, 850–1.
[56] *Biennial Survey of Education*, Bulletin 1923, No. 29, 291–2.
[57] *Ibid.* (1910), II, 846.
[58] *Biennial Survey of Education*, 1918–20, Statistics, 298–9.

thought is clear, however, in some cases. Hyde declared: "Productive scholarship should remain and will remain in men's hands."[59] Dr. Eliot, too, when graduate instruction for women was still in its infancy, was of the opinion that women had not shown ability to do more than "learn from teachers and practice what they have been taught."[60] Van Hise, of Wisconsin, while apparently skeptical as to the reliability of his information, said: "It does appear to be a fact that the percentage of women who are willing to work at the same subject six hours a day for three hundred days in the year is much smaller than among men. But this quality is essential for success in research. Thus while the intellectual success of the women in undergraduate work is unquestioned, there is still a question on the part of some as to the rank they are to take in the graduate school and in creative work."[61] E. E. Slosson, writing about twenty-five years after the opening to women of graduate facilities in large universities, undoubtedly summarized quite accurately when he observed that the ability of women to do advanced work was generally unquestioned, "but it is the prevailing opinion that they are as a rule inferior to men in work requiring initiative and originality."[62]

That such has been the "prevailing opinion" is no doubt true. But if one were to take the pains to examine a great array of pieces of research, such as have been presented to meet requirements for the doctorate, it would be difficult to determine, on the basis of their originality of conception and execution, whether they had been presented by women or men. Among the women in graduate groups of recent years, there appear many whose work measures up to or, indeed, exceeds the quality of that of men. And as for the ability and willingness to work six hours a day for three hundred days in the year, which Van Hise doubted, there are many undaunted by ten or twelve hours a day, for one, two, or three years, as may be necessary. There is little question today but that, given the same incentive to research as men (economic and professional rewards), women can, will, and do, show a comparable capacity for scientific work.[63]

[59] *College Man and College Woman*, see Chaps. 9 and 10.

[60] Tetlow: Education of Women for the Learned Professions [*Ed. Rev.* (1896), XI, 124–5].

[61] Quoted by Burstall: *Impressions of American Education* (1908), 206.

[62] *Cyclopedia of Education*, V, 673.

[63] Compare Hughes: Can Women Make Good? [*Sch. and Soc.*, II, 336–7]; Thomas: Future of Women as Research Workers [*Jour. Coll. Alumnae*, Feb.

Marion Talbot, speaking recently of the results of advanced graduate work for women, and basing her opinion on work done at the University of Chicago, held that "from certain points of view . . . [the] results are very discouraging, but it must be remembered that graduate schools have been open to women for a comparatively short period of time and considering all the circumstances, women have made satisfactory progress and have ground to believe that in time recognition will come to them in proportion to the thoroughness and scholarly quality of their attainments."[64]

III. Entrance of Women into Medical Schools

The entrance of women into college teaching, and study in graduate schools as a preparation for it, represented an extension of woman's first-found public profession. To this extension there was considerable opposition. The objections to this professional advancement of women were of small moment, however, compared with those raised when women attempted to secure preparation to enter the medical profession.

From an historical point of view, the movement made by women to study and practice medicine in the nineteenth century may be considered an effort to re-enter a field of usefulness in which they were once employed, but from which they had been excluded. In the Colonial period of our history, as well as in ancient times and in modern foreign countries, women held a traditional position as attendants upon the sick, and as midwives. The cases of Mrs. Wiat, who, throughout a lifetime of 94 years, had assisted women in the birth of more than 1100 children; Mrs. Thomas Whitmore, of Marlboro, Vermont; Mrs. Fuller, of Rehoboth; Elizabeth Phillips, of Charleston, and Anne Hutchinson may be mentioned, as representative of a host of women who, throughout the colonies, were allied to the medical profession, albeit in the most humble ranks.[65] In Virginia, in 1748, Mary Johnson presented a petition to the House of Burgesses to the effect that "for several years past" she had been "very success-

---

1903, 13 ff.]; and Neilson: Do Women Learn Faster? [Collier's, Oct. 3, 1925, 25]. See also Mozans: Woman in Science.

[64] N. E. A. Proc., 1922, 770.

[65] Gregory: Letter to Ladies in Favor of Female Physicians, 1–48; Jacobi: Woman in Medicine [in Meyer (Ed.): Woman's Work in America, 141].

ful in curing cancers,'' and that she was willing to ''communicate her method of performing the cure to the public,'' relying on the House ''for such a Reward as they shall think reasonable.''[66] The petition was referred to eight gentlemen ''to examine into the matter thereof.'' Shortly they reported several cases investigated, in which she had effected cures where other doctors had failed, and recommended that she ''ought to be rewarded, if she will communicate . . . her method of curing Cancers.'' It was subsequently voted by the House and the Council that one hundred pounds should be paid to her upon her production of a certificate signed by any two of the three men named to ''make an experiment of the efficacy of the medicine. . . .''[67] In 1766, Constant Woodson announced a willingness, ''for a valuable consideration,'' to make known ''an effectual remedy for curing cancers.'' As in the first case, the petition was agreed to and one hundred pounds set aside as a reward as soon as the cure should be tested and ''published in the *Virginia Gazette.*''[68]

The period of the Revolution brought an important opportunity to the medical profession, with a resultant quickening of interest in the scientific aspect of it. Just before the War, a few doctors, Lloyd, of Boston, and Shippen, of Philadelphia, among them, studied in England and became familiar with the latest development of obstetrical science there. Those who studied abroad could not but be impressed by the contrast with the ignorant old women who acted as midwives at home. Upon taking up his lectures in Philadelphia, Dr. Shippen showed his willingness to improve conditions by offering a course of ''lectures'' with a ''proper apparatus'' prepared for that purpose ''in order to instruct women who have had virtue enough to own their ignorance and apply for instruction. . . .'' The ''female pupils'' were to be taught privately, and ''assisted at any of their private labours when necessary.'' A ''convenient lodging'' was provided for ''a few poor women who might otherwise suffer for the want of the common necessities on those occasions, to be under the care of a sober, honest matron, well acquainted with lying-in women, employed by the doctor for that purpose.''[69]

[66] *Journal, House of Burgesses of Va.*, Nov. 24, 1748, 303 (Ed. by H. R. McIllvaine).

[67] *Ibid.*, 314 and 318.

[68] *Ibid.* (1766), 42, 124, 128 and 131.

[69] *Pa. Gaz.*, Jan. 31, 1765; quoted Vol. I, 227 *ff.*

To what extent the midwives responded to the offer of such advantages is not known. Perhaps the price of "ten guineas" was too much for them. It is known, however, that the offer was also made by Doctor Shippen to "all those young gentlemen now engaged in the study of that useful and necessary branch of surgery who are taking pains to qualify themselves to practice in different parts of the country, with safety and advantage to their fellow creatures." The period from the Revolution to about the middle of the nineteenth century witnessed the increase of men as accoucheurs, and a decrease of women.

As we have already noted, the second quarter of the nineteenth century was marked by woman's entrance into many fields of labor outside the home.[70] The first significant profession opened to them was teaching. But among the advocates of women's education there were those who were not content with demanding a general education, nor with the one profession of teaching. Those who associated themselves with the woman's rights movement asserted that, in justice, woman should be allowed to enter any occupation or profession whatsoever, so long as she was qualified by abilities and prepared equally with men. Such was the view of Caroline H. Dall and later of Olive Schreiner. Catherine Beecher, who was more conservative in certain respects, exerted, through the Women's Education Association (1852), a great influence on the opening of professions other than teaching. In particular, she urged that the care of children and the sick was woman's age-old profession and she should, therefore, be prepared for it.

The position taken by Beecher, Dall, Mott, Preston, Blackwell, Adamson, and many others, was strengthened by a reaction, on the part of a few medical men, against the employment of men in the capacity of midwives. The leader was Samuel Gregory who, in 1848, published, in Boston, *Man-midwifery Exposed and Corrected; or the Employment of Men to attend women in childbirth, shown to be a modern innovation, unnecessary, unnatural, and injurious to the physical welfare of the community, and pernicious in its influence on Professional and Public Morality.* From the appearance of this attack on men as midwives, which was seconded by some doctors[71] and numerous publications, it

[70] Pp. 8 ff.

[71] Thomas Ewell, of Virginia, and W. Beach, of New York, were quoted by Jacobi: *op. cit.*, 143.

was but a short step to the idea that the whole field of medicine should be opened to women. In fact, publications such as *Godey's Lady's Book* approved the views of Gregory, and continued in the same breath to advocate medicine as one of the most natural professions for women. In 1852, "a few ladies of Philadelphia," organized "for the purpose of advancing educational and Christian improvement," stated their belief that "the BIBLE recognizes and approves *only woman* in the sacred office of *midwife*" and united in the following purposes:

"*1st.* To co-operate with the efforts now being made in this city of Philadelphia, to qualify women to become physicians for their own sex and for children.

"*2d.* To give kindly encouragement to those females who are engaged in medical studies.

"*3d.* To give aid and sympathy to any among them who may desire to become missionaries, and go, in the spirit of love, to carry to the poor suffering women of heathendom, not only the blessings of the healing art, which Christian men can rarely, if ever bear to females in those lands, but also the higher and holier knowledge of the true God, and of salvation through his Son, Jesus Christ."[72]

The issue of March, 1852, contained another statement of the "three important vocations" of women which required them to be properly educated: teaching, medical science (that they may "become physicians for their own sex and for children"), and management of charities and banking.[73] Again and again they returned to hammer at the old prejudice against women in the field of medicine. In 1853, writing on "Woman the True physician," they declared: "So far as the practice of midwifery is concerned, we have only to say, in the language of the Report of the Sanitary Committee of the Commonwealth of Massachusetts, for 1850, 'For the first one hundred and fifty years after the settlement of this country, this branch of practice was mostly in the hands of females.' We believe not only mostly, but wholly. . . ." More at length, answers were made to several of the stock objections to women as physicians:

"But, it is said, 'Women cannot go abroad to attend the sick— their domestic employment precludes them from practice. What

[72] *Godey's Lady's Book* (1852), 185.
[73] *Ibid.*, March 1852, 228.

shall they do, when they are called for, and cannot go?' Just what the male doctor does when he is called for, and cannot go— stay at home. Just what everybody else does, when he is asked to do a thing and cannot—let it alone. 'But the people will not employ them if you make them doctors.' Very well, then, let them employ others. We don't expect people to employ those whom they do not choose to employ; and we are willing to say that, if woman never practises medicine, she would be amply repaid for studying it. Another says, 'You will break up the medical profession, you will drive all the men out of it, and even those who are now in it will starve.' They may as well starve as the women. They have as much physical strength, and as many hands and feet, to earn their daily bread, as women have, and, if they cannot cope with women in the medical profession, let them take an humble occupation, in which they can. . .

"We admit that woman has her own sphere in which to act, as much as man. She is better calculated for some duties than for others, and we maintain that there are none, within the whole range of these duties, for which she could have been better de- signed, or more in her sphere of usefulness, than in this of medi- cine. Talk about this being the appropriate sphere of man, and his alone! With tenfold more plausibility and reason might we say, it is the appropriate sphere of woman, and hers alone. The order of nature—the constitution of families—the nature of hu- man society—the earthly origin of the race—the commission of the child first to the care of woman—the delicacy of females—all these proclaim her fitness to be the good physician.' "[74]

Attention was given the fact that too many women were enter- ing, or preparing to enter, the teaching profession. This was criticized, for "female physicians are more needed than school teachers. Everywhere the profession is open to them. Those who have entered this noble duty find full employment. It is more remunerative than teaching. It is equally woman's field of employment.' "[75] "Female physicians will produce an era in the history of women. . . . How will this reform be effected? . . . We would, in all deference, suggest that, first of all, there will be candor in the patient to the female physician, which could not be expected when a sense of native delicacy and modesty existed to

[74] *Ibid.*, Jan. 1853, 82–3.
[75] *Ibid.*, Sept. 1853, 273–4.

the extent of preferring to suffer rather than divulge the symptoms.

"Female physicians we regard as designed alone for the department of women and children. Through their agency we believe that mothers will be enabled to rear their children in the paths of physical, and, consequently, intellectual and moral health. We say moral health, alas! Many delinquencies, and, even more melancholy, many crimes, might be traced to physical causes. Some morbid or irritating action, imperceptible to all but acute and practised eyes, has often consigned its captive to degradation, misery, imprisonment, and death."[76]

But while the advocates of woman's rights, and others interested especially in medicine, were urging women's entrance into medicine as a profession, there was a great deal of opposition on the part of old medical schools, managers of hospitals, and various medical societies, to the admission of women. This opposition made study so disagreeable and difficult that, as Woolson said, in 1873, it was still hard to get a first-rate medical training in this country[77] and friends would not "hear of her exiling herself to Paris to fit herself for its practice."[78] As a result, many took the inferior degree at home, or as much training as they could get, and began to practice—sometimes illegally, as did Harriett K. Hunt.[79] Dall and Livermore praised the accomplishments of Blackwell, Safford, Jacobi, Sewall, Zakrzewska, Ross, and others for what they had accomplished; and the former urged that they should form a Woman's Medical Society "with an examining board whose diploma should attest the character of the member."[80]

The opposition to women's medical education may be classified under two heads: those who opposed it entirely, as contrary to

[76] *Ibid.*, Nov. 1853, 465–6.—A letter from S. H. Waddell.

[77] It should be noted, however, that handbooks on women's vocations, in the seventies and eighties, generally called attention to opportunities in the medical field. Rayne, in *What Can a Woman Do?* discussed at some length the "Requisites for a Physician" and named schools where training could be secured. This appeared in 1884.

[78] Woolson: *Woman in American Society*, 30–3.

[79] Meyer: *Woman's Work in America*, 147.

[80] Dall: *College, Market and the Court*, 26–7, touched on the evils pointed out by Dr. Storer's pamphlet, *Why Not?*; also Livermore: *What Shall We Do with Our Daughters?* 21–2.

the native delicacy of the sex and designed to overturn established social usage; and those who spoke favorably of women's medical education, but emphasized the view that they did not need a complete medical training. The first group was represented by those who voiced their objections vigorously, as well as those who merely stood in the way, refusing to express themselves, but by their position in the profession serving as a barrier to women's entrance.

An editorial of the *Buffalo Medical Journal*[81] stated: "If I were to plan with malicious hate the greatest curse I could conceive for women, if I would estrange them from the protection of women, and make them as far as possible loathsome and disgusting to man, I would favor the so called reform which proposed to make doctors of them." The *Medical and Surgical Reporter* declared: "The opposition of medical men arises because this movement outrages all their enlightened estimate of what a woman should be. It shocks their refined appreciation of woman to see her assume to follow a profession with repulsive details at every step, after the disgusting preliminaries have been passed." Again, it was asserted that "many of our more delicate feelings, much of our refined sensibility must be subdued before we can study medicine; in females they must be destroyed."[82] Nowhere were women who sought entrance to medical schools met by solid objections. Their requests were refused as indelicate and inspired by a desire to attend to affairs outside their sphere. A type of opposition most difficult to meet, that of noncommittal aloofness, has been described by Elizabeth Blackwell in her account of her visit to Dr. Darrach:

". . . Felt gloomy as thunder, trudging round to Dr. Darrach. He is the most non-committal man I ever saw. I harangued him, and he sat full five minutes without a word. I asked at last if he could give me any encouragement. 'The subject is a novel one, madam, I have nothing to say either for or against it; you have awakened trains of thought upon which my mind is taking action, but I cannot express my opinion to you either one way or another.' 'Your opinion, I fear, is unfavourable.' 'I did not say so. I beg you, madam, distinctly to understand that I ex-

---

81 1869, 191—quoted by Jacobi: *Women in Medicine,* 143.

82 Quoted from *Remarks on Employment of Females as Practitioners* (Boston, 1820), by Jacobi.

press no opinion one way or another; the way in which my mind acts in this matter I do not feel at liberty to unfold.' 'Shall I call on the other professors of your college?' 'I cannot take the responsibility of advising you to pursue such a course.' 'Can you not grant me admittance to your lectures, as you do not feel unfavourable to my scheme?' 'I have said no such thing; whether favourable or unfavourable, I have not expressed any opinion; and I beg leave to state clearly that the operation of my mind in regard to this matter I do not feel at liberty to unfold.' I got up in despair, leaving his mind to take action on the subject at his leisure.'[83]

That there was objection to women in the profession based on economic grounds—the crowding of the profession—is quite clear. In England, as in the United States, the entrance to medical faculties was far more difficult to obtain than entrance into those of arts and science.[84] A letter to the *Boston Journal*[85] deplored the action taken by Geneva Medical faculty, and declared "the profession was quite too full before." Probably the economic question lurked in the minds of those who appeared favorable to women physicians but urged that "by adopting, as their sphere of action, the hygiene of female and infantile life, ladies would be in their right social position; and assuredly they could have no higher vocation than that of teaching their own sex the important duties which devolve upon them as mothers. . . . If ladies, properly educated for such duty—*they need not be fully educated physicians*—would devote their time and energies to this noble work, they would confer an inestimable benefit on the rising generation, and merit the lasting gratitude of posterity." As for those who "have gone through a systematic course of medical education, with the view to qualify themselves as medical practitioners," he raises the question whether "the instruction of their own sex in the laws of health would not form an equally useful and a more appropriate profession than that of physician or surgeon.'[86]

[83] Taken by permission from the Everyman's Library edition of Blackwell's *Pioneer Work for Women*, published by J. M. Dent & Sons, Ltd., London, and E. P. Dutton & Co., Inc., New York. Pp. 48–9.

[84] Lange: *Higher Education for Women* (1890), 42.

[85] Feb. 1849—quoted by Jacobi: *op. cit.*, 144.

[86] Sir James Clark, in *Littell's Living Age* (1862), LXXV, 494.

The opening of the medical profession to woman owed much
to the spirit of the times, the general sentiment that was beginning to develop in favor of her emancipation, and the fact that
for the previous half century the way tŏ-a general education had
gradually been opened to her. Upon this first rung of the ladder
woman stood, and demanded the right to ascend higher. Voicing
this demand for admission into a new profession was the contribution made by Elizabeth Blackwell, the first woman granted
a degree of Doctor of Medicine in the United States, 1849.

The Blackwells arrived in New York, in 1832, lived there for a
time and in Jersey City, and removed to Cincinnati in 1838.
While in New York, Elizabeth came to know the Garrison family
and thus came under the influence of the great anti-slavery
reform and its kindred movement, the emancipation of women.
The expansion of general educational opportunities for women,
too, enlisted her interest, for she wrote: ". . . We three sisters
threw ourselves with ardour into the public conferences held in
Cincinnati on this subject. . . ."[87] To support the family, after
their father's death (1838), the three elder sisters opened a
girls' boarding school. Six years later, Elizabeth went to teach
in Henderson, Kentucky, for a year; then in the school of John
Dickson, Asheville, North Carolina; and finally in the girls'
school of Mrs. Du Pré at Charleston, South Carolina.[88]

It was during the interval between her teaching at Henderson
and Asheville that the idea of becoming a physician was suggested
to her by a friend, who said:

"You are fond of study, have health and leisure; why not
study medicine? If I could have been treated by a lady doctor
my worst sufferings would have been spared me." The idea
did not make an appeal—was, in fact, repulsive—and she "reso-
lutely tried for weeks" to put it away; "but it constantly recurred to me." Moreover "other circumstances" caused her to
think of finding "some absorbing occupation." She was "impatient of the disturbing influence exercised by the other sex"
and "suffered more or less from the common malady—falling in
love." But she shrank from "a life association," disappointed

[87] Taken by permission from the Everyman's Library edition of Blackwell's *Pioneer Work for Women*, published by J. M. Dent & Sons, Ltd.,
London, and E. P. Dutton & Co., Inc., New York. Pp. 7–9.

[88] *Ibid.*, 11, 27 and 37; see also Arthur: *Western North Carolina*, 424.

or repelled at what it might mean. She says it was during an "acute attack" that she wrote in her journal: "I felt more determined than ever to become a physician and thus place a strong barrier between me and all ordinary marriage. I must have something to engross my thoughts, some object in life which will fill this vacuum and prevent this sad wearing away of the heart."[89]

Gradually her resolution hardened. Letters were written asking how to get a medical education, and all received the same answer, "that the idea was a good one, but . . . impossible to accomplish; . . . [there was] no way of obtaining such an education for a woman." Thus it developed that the study of the human body and its ailments, the mere thought of which had disgusted her, gave promise of being a real challenge, offering her bold spirit the opportunity of breaking a path into an uncharted territory, opening a profession not only for herself but for all women. It appears from numerous comments that it was this challenge, this opportunity, which determined her choice. As she said, "The idea of winning a doctor's degree gradually assumed the aspect of a great moral struggle, and the moral fight possessed attraction for me."

With the earnings of a few years' teaching, in 1847, she left Charleston for Philadelphia, where she hoped to enter some medical school. But the encouragement and assistance of her Quaker friends, though important to her, were insufficient to enable her to succeed. One by one, the applications for entrance to four medical colleges of the city were refused; and similar answers were the outcome of applications made in New York. Finally she applied to smaller "country schools,"—twelve of the best—and, October 20, 1847, received a favorable reply from Geneva, New York. The dean's letter stated they had "thought it important to submit your proposal to the class" and a transcript of their action was inclosed. Their answer was unique, breathing a spirit of justice not met with generally in the expressions of medical men of that day; it espoused the principle of equal "universal education of both sexes," declared that

[89] Ibid., 21, 23. Taken by permission from the Everyman's Library edition of Blackwell's Pioneer Work for Women, published by J. M. Dent & Sons, Ltd., London, and E. P. Dutton & Co., Inc., New York.

"every branch of scientific education . . . should be open equally to all," and guaranteed that their conduct should not "cause her to regret her attendance."[90]

Two years later Elizabeth Blackwell graduated, having made a high record in every department of her work, and was granted the degree of M.D.[91] During her vacation she had gained entrance to Blockley Almshouse in Philadelphia, for the sake of practical experience and observation. Immediately after graduation, realizing the need of "much wider opportunities for study than were open to women in America," she resolved to return to England. During two years abroad she visited hospitals and made the acquaintance of famous physicians in England. For more advanced study she turned to Paris, in May, 1849, where she was advised by M. Louis to enter *La Maternité*,[92] which she did on June 30. After four months' training, which she recognized later as of the greatest importance to her successful practice, she left *La Maternité*. After some months of idleness, due to the injury of one eye, she returned to London and was admitted to study in St. Bartholomew's Hospital.[93]

She would gladly have settled down to the practice of medicine in London, but circumstances seemed to favor America. Two years had passed since she had taken the first doctor's degree, public sentiment in America was being changed somewhat, new schools for women were already struggling to give women that training which the best older medical colleges still denied them, her family was in America, her sister Emily had taken up medical study at Cleveland Medical College and they hoped to work together. Accordingly, she returned to New York, in July, 1851, and devoted her time to preparing lectures, which were published (1852) as *The Laws of Life*—dealing with the question of physical education of girls. Her first practice was chiefly among the Quaker ladies of New York, many of whom attended these lectures when first given and later (1853) assisted in open-

[90] *Ibid.*, 53. Taken by permission from the Everyman's Library edition of Blackwell's *Pioneer Work for Women*, published by J. M. Dent & Sons, Ltd., London, and E. P. Dutton & Co., Inc., New York.

[91] *Ibid.*, 70-2.

[92] *Ibid.*, 95.

[93] *Ibid.*, 133 *ff.*

ELIZABETH BLACKWELL

ing the dispensary which was incorporated, in 1854, as the New York Dispensary,[94] to which a hospital was added in 1856.[95]

Into the opportunity presented by the Civil War the medical women of the country entered with enthusiasm. The Ladies' Sanitary Commission was established and sought to forward supplies and nurses to the front. While the War enabled trained women to render a valuable service, it hindered the advance of the dispensary for the time being. In 1865, steps were taken by trustees to secure a college charter, though it was contrary to the sentiment of the women doctors, who believed the oldest and best schools should be opened to them rather than new, inferior, separate medical colleges.[96] The expediency of the women's college, however, was not to be doubted. Three important innovations were made, according to Blackwell: the establishment of the chair of hygiene—to encourage the diffusion of sanitary information, which she had always held to be one of the chief functions of the family physician; the creation of a Board of Examiners, apart from the teaching staff; and the extension of the time of study from three to four years.

In 1869, Dr. Blackwell returned to England, attended the Social Service Congress, delivered numerous lectures, and established herself in practice. She died in 1910. No other woman had exerted such an influence over the medical profession, the advancement of the right of her sex to such labor, or injected into the minds of so many people, both in England and the United States, the lessons of the "Religion of Health." The chief visible monuments to her labor are her writings, the Blackwell Medical Society of Rochester, New York, the Elizabeth Blackwell House at Hobart College, and the institutions which she founded, or helped to found, in New York City. In 1925, a movement was started to found the Elizabeth Blackwell Professorship in the London School of Medicine for Women, University of London.[97]

Among other women who played the rôle of pathfinders, should be mentioned Harriett K. Hunt, Sarah Adamson, Ann

[94] *Ibid.*, 158–9; $1000 was granted the N. Y. Dispensary in 1854—*Laws of New York*, 1854, 624.

[95] *Pioneer Work*, 168.

[96] *Ibid.*, 192.

[97] Circular issued by Murray Bartlett, President, Hobart College, March 26, 1925.

Preston, Marie Zakrzewska, Emily Blackwell, Lucy Sewall, Helen Morton, and Mary Putnam Jacobi. The last, along with Emily Blackwell and others, followed the precedent of Elizabeth by going to Paris to study and was graduated with a certificate of *trés satisfait*, the highest rank given, and awarded that year to no one else.[98]

Harriett K. Hunt, who had undertaken to practice medicine without a diploma, first sought admission to Harvard Medical School lectures in 1847, but was refused. Three years later the request was repeated, and acted upon favorably; but, due to the fact that three Negroes had just been admitted, and the addition of a woman to the student body seemed likely to result in great discontent on the part of students, the faculty requested the candidate to withdraw her application. She acquiesced but continued to practice medicine successfully.[99]

In 1845, Dr. Samuel Gregory and his brother George began to promote the idea of admitting women to the medical profession, and to attack the custom of "man-midwifery." In 1847, the plan of starting regular instruction was announced; and was begun November 1, 1848, twelve pupils attending. Dr. Enoch C. Rolfe and, later, Dr. William M. Cornell were lecturers; chief attention was given to midwifery and the diseases of women and children.[100] The first term's work lasted only three months; but, according to a quoted statement of Dr. Jacobi, the pupils successfully attended "above 300 midwifery cases."

The success achieved by the struggling school was no doubt due to the support of the Female Medical Education Society, organized November 23, 1848, for the express purpose of assisting the school, and incorporated "for the purpose of providing for the education of midwives, nurses and female physicians," in 1850.[101] Membership cost one dollar a year; life members paid twenty. With six members to start with, the number increased, in one year, to one thousand. In 1855, there were one hundred and sixty life members. In 1852, the name was changed from the Boston Female Medical School to the New England

---

[98] See an account in *Godey's Lady's Book*, Oct. 1870, 374–5.

[99] Meyer: *Woman's Work in America*, 148.

[100] *Ibid.*, 145; and an account in the *New York Teacher*, July 1855, 245 *ff.*

[101] *Laws of Mass.*, April 30, 1850, 444; the Ladies' Physiological Institute was incorporated the same year.—*Ibid.*, 481.

Female Medical College; and, as such, it was reorganized and re-incorporated, in 1856.[102] In 1852, the course was extended to cover three years, of four months each, and some professors from the college in Philadelphia were called to lecture for a brief time. In 1855, more than a hundred had been in attendance and six had finished the three-year course. This was held to show that very high standards of work were maintained; that the faculty aimed "to raise instead of lowering the standard of professional attainments."[103] In 1854, the legislature granted the College $1,000 annually for five years, to be used to pay professors; and, in 1855, $10,000, in case a like amount was raised by subscription, to erect buildings, library, and apparatus.[104] After a checkered career, the college ceased to exist, being merged with Boston University with the provision that the latter's medical school be opened to women on the same basis as to men.[105]

In Philadelphia, liberal-minded men, following a suggestion which was advanced by Dr. Bartholomew Fussell, a Quaker physician of Chester county, took up the cause of women's medical education in much the same manner as Gregory and the Female Medical Education Society had done in Boston. While Dr. Gregory's school, which was later made the New England Female Medical College, and re-incorporated May 28, 1856, deserves credit as a pioneer effort in organizing regular medical instruction for women (courses having opened Nov. 1, 1848), the Female Medical College of Pennsylvania was the first regularly incorporated institution, its powers being granted and approved March 11, 1850.[106] In 1867, the name was changed by court decree to "Woman's Medical College of Pennsylvania."[107] It is significant that the lead was taken by men who were fair-minded enough to ask, with Dr. Fussell: "Why should not women have

---

[102] *Ibid.*, May 28, 1856, 115–16.

[103] The *New York Teacher*, July 1855, 246.

[104] A description, and an appeal for assistance in raising the funds, *Godey's Lady's Book*, Oct. 1855, 372–3.

[105] *Laws of Mass.*, May 29, 1874, 188–9; and Meyer: *op. cit.*, 146.

[106] *Laws of Pa.*, March 11, 1850, 171; Dr. Emily White discussed the claims of the institutions for priority in an address, published in the *Medical News*, Aug. 3, 1895.

[107] Marshall: *Woman's Medical College*, 9; the desirability of changing the name had been urged in an article in *Godey's Lady's Book*, Oct. 1866, 355 *f*.

the same opportunities in life as men?'' In 1867, a woman was named as one of the corporators; others were added later; and in 1893, Mary E. Mumford was president. The initial success of the institution was due in no small measure to the energetic action of William J. Mullen, the first president, who secured the lease of a building and "at his own expense" made it ready for the admission of students, October 12, 1850. There was a faculty of six "regular practitioners, and graduates of regular schools,"[108] and a student body of forty. The first graduating class consisted of eight ladies. About fifteen hundred witnessed the conferring of "full degrees of Doctor of Medicine," in accord with the rights and privileges vested in the college by the legislature.

In this class was Ann Preston (1813–1872), who became, shortly thereafter, the first woman member of the faculty, as Professor of Physiology and Hygiene,[109] and later (1866) served as dean of the faculty. She was active as an abolitionist, interested in philanthropic work, and possessed a considerable degree of poetic and literary ability; but her greatest service was in the support rendered to the struggle of women for a professional existence. She was by no means as well qualified for teaching or practicing medicine as was Elizabeth Blackwell, having had small opportunity for study; but she was an ardent and indefatigable worker for the success of the institution. Especially did she strive to impress upon her students the need of propriety in their actions: "Ladies, I am very jealous for the honor of my sex in its connection with the study of medicine. I would have it . . . clear even from the taint of suspicion. . . . Every woman who enters this department of life will be the more narrowly watched and severely criticized because she is a woman. If she bear not herself wisely and well, many will suffer for her sake."[110]

Other women, deserving of mention for their excellent service, were Dr. Hannah Longshore and Professors Emeline Cleveland and Rachel Bodley. The former, following in the footsteps of Blackwell, studied at *La Maternité* in Paris (1860), receiving, on the completion of her work, five prizes, and honorable men-

---

108 Quoted from *Godey's Lady's Book*, Oct. 1866, 355.
109 Marshall: *op. cit.*, 10–11.
110 Quoted by *Godey's Lady's Book*, Dec. 1856, 559–66.

Ann Preston

tion for her "clinical observation."[111] She was declared by one authority[112] to have been "the first adequate teacher to appear in the [Philadelphia] school. . . ."

The Female Medical College of Pennsylvania was criticized, and justly, as that of Boston had been, for its inadequate teachers, equipment, lack of thoroughness, and length of preparation offered. For a time, instruction did not go beyond textbooks and lectures. Four months' study constituted the year's work, at first; but this was increased to 17, 19, 21, and 23 weeks in the second, third, fourth, and fifth years, respectively. At this time it was stated, though the authority may be questioned, that the standard for graduation was increased to equal "that of the University of Pennsylvania and other old and respectable colleges."[113]

The graduates numbered eight in the first class, nine in the second, four in the third, six in the fourth, and twenty-seven in the fifth. By 1866, seventy-one had received the degree, while nearly 300 had been registered as students. Of these graduates, three were on the college staff, and others were practicing in various parts of the country (several were said to have made over $1,000 the first year); still others turned to public lecturing on physiology and hygiene, or employment by schools[114] and hospitals. The New York *Tribune*, commenting on the success of the schools in Boston and Philadelphia, asserted: "Requests for their alumnae to settle in different parts of the Union are frequently received by each, and it will be long before the supply can equal the demand."[115]

The above statements must be taken with some salt. They speak eloquently of the enthusiasm that was beginning to be felt by many people. Still more evidence of growing enthusiasm is found in the numerous societies, associations, and schools set up to teach or encourage the teaching of medicine to women. In 1853, *Godey's* chronicled the opening of Penn Medical College— destined to be much weaker than the "regular female medical

---

[111] Marshall: *op. cit.*

[112] Jacobi: *op. cit.*, 157.

[113] Quoted from the *New York Teacher*, July 1855, 248.

[114] "Graduates of the New England College fill the responsible positions as professors of anatomy, physiology and hygiene in Mount Holyoke Seminary and Vassar College. . . ."—*R. C. E.*, 1871, 514.

[115] Quoted by the *New York Teacher*, July 1855, 248.

college'' of Philadelphia—and exultantly declared that ''every graduate from the medical schools finds herself in practice at once. It is a noble pursuit for women, this of the healing art; it belongs to our sex more than to men, because women and children mostly require its exercise and care.''[116]   Other early initial efforts were mentioned, such as the Eclectic Medical Institute, Cincinnati, ''a new medical institution'' organized by Dr. Freese

''WHEW! I HADN'T CALCULATED ON A WOMAN DOCTOR''

at Bloomington, Illinois, and the Ohio Female Medical Education Society, organized on a plan similar to that in Boston. Meantime Harvard had agreed to admit a woman but had subsequently asked the withdrawal of her request; the Cleveland Medical College (Ohio) graduated a lady in 1852;[117] and Elizabeth Blackwell began her work in New York, which led eventually to the founding of the Woman's Medical College.

[116] August 1853, 178; also July 1854, 80.
[117] *New York Teacher, loc. cit.*

The first step was taken in the establishment of a small dispensary in 1853. In 1854 an act of incorporation was passed by the legislature, and in 1857 this became the New York Infirmary for Women and Children, with Dr. Marie Zakrzewska and Dr. Emily Blackwell filling the positions of resident physician and surgeon, respectively.[118] In 1864, two years after the founding of the Woman's Hospital of Philadelphia, the State of New York granted the corporation of the New York Infirmary the power "to grant and confer the title of Doctor of Medicine upon the recommendation of the board of professors of such college."[119] It was specifically provided that degrees should be granted only to persons over twenty-one years of age who had "pursued the study of medicine for at least three years previous to applying for the degree . . ."; the institution was to be subject to "the visitation of the regents" and to make an annual report to them.[120] This was the fourth medical college established for women, with power to grant medical degrees.[121]

Women requested admission to Rush Medical School in 1865, but were not admitted. Three years later, however, the Chicago Medical School, a rival, admitted women for a year, and then discontinued the practice. The next year (1869) the Women's Hospital Medical College was opened, later merging with Northwestern University. The Women's Hospital was founded through the efforts of Dr. Mary Thompson, a graduate of the Philadelphia College, who began practice in Chicago about 1863.[122]

While the Women's Medical College of Chicago was beginning its career, a more significant advance was made for women by the opening of the medical department of the University of Michigan to them, the same as to men. On the Pacific coast, the first woman, Mrs. Lucy Wanzer, was admitted to the Toland Medical School—of the State University—in 1874.

The admission of women to the same medical instruction as men, and in company with them, raised all the objections that had been made to coeducation in academic departments, and in

[118] Blackwell: *Pioneer Work*, 168.

[119] *Laws of New York*, April 13, 1864, 360–1.

[120] *Ibid.*, 1866, 644.

[121] See comments on the opening of the new school, *Godey's Lady's Book*, 1866, 92.

[122] *R. C. E.* (1892–3), I, 1108; Meyer: *Woman's Work in America*, 174.

more vigorous terms.[123] The opening of Michigan Medical School did not attract much attention, since but few students attended and the school was not widely known. But twenty years later, when the Johns Hopkins University[124] made provision for women, arguments pro and con were heard on every hand. The admission of women was provided for by the gift of about $350,-000 (total) by Mary E. Garrett. To this were added funds collected by women all over the United States and the gift of $10,000 by Marian Hovey, originally offered to Harvard, to secure the medical instruction of women, "on equal terms with men." The Medical School opened Oct. 2, 1893, with sixteen students, of whom three were women.[125]

Admission to this great medical school marked the close of the experimental period of women's medical education in the United States. This period had covered over forty years. By some critics it was urged that the victory at Johns Hopkins was very incomplete, inasmuch as the minute which admitted women "upon the same terms as may be prescribed for men" went on to explain that "such preliminary training in all its parts shall be obtained in some other institution of learning devoted in whole or in part to the education of women, or by private tuition."[126] Dr. Martha Carey Thomas pointed out that whatever shortcomings were to be found in the conditions specified were chargeable to the committees of women who had made the request; that the resolution of the university trustees granted exactly what had been asked.[127]

The Commissioner's *Report* for 1871 gave the data (Table II) with reference to the medical institutions opened to women at that date.[128]

Twenty years later, when the Johns Hopkins Medical School was opened to women, the Commissioner's *Report* showed 132 medical schools, with 1,302 women and 18,514 men students of medicine in the United States. These women were enrolled in 64 medical schools, 36 of which were regular, 9 eclectic, 13 homeo-

123 Hershberger: Coeducation in Medicine [*Educational News*, Nov. 12, 1892, 643–4]; *The Nation* (1891), LII, 131.

124 *Fifteenth Annual Report*, Johns Hopkins University, 1890, 7–9, 23–4.

125 *Eighteenth Annual Report*, Johns Hopkins, 1893, 8–9, and 91–105; *R. C. E.*, 1879, CI–CII; see also *Educational Review* (1893), V, 202.

126 *The Nation* (1891), LII, 71.

127 *Ibid.*, 114.

128 Pp. 664–7.

TABLE II

Name	Place	Men and Women	Women	Date Opened	Students	Library	Faculty	Alumnae
Women's Hospital Medical College	Chicago		x	1870	12	......	13[?]	4
New England Female Medical College	Boston		x	1848	26	......	5	83
University of Michigan (Medical Dept.)	Ann Arbor	x		1850	315[129]	......	9	......
Women's Medical College of New York Infirmary	New York		x	1865	36	......	17	......
Woman's Medical College of Pa.	Philadelphia			1850	60	1,300	8	138
Medical Dept. of Howard University	Washington, D. C.	x		1867	......	......	10	......
New York Medical College for Women	New York		x	1863	47	......		......
Homeopathic Hospital College	Cleveland, O.	x		1849	86	2,000	17	780

¹²⁹ Few women.

pathic, 2 physio-medical, and 4 graduate.[130]   There were seven schools for women only. In 1899–1900, there were 151 medical schools, and 23,757 men and 1,456 women students.[131] By 1919–1920 the medical schools reporting had decreased to 77, having 13,354 men and 888 women students.[132] In 1919–20, 2,691 men and 115 women were granted medical degrees in the United States.[133] The United States census for 1870 showed 525 women and 61,858 men physicians and surgeons; that of 1890, 4,555 women and 100,248 men; that of 1910, 9,015 women and 142,117 men; and, in 1920, 8,882 women and 141,125 men.[134]

By the end of the experimental period (1890), the standards of medical education had been greatly improved, but the requirements for admission were still very low. Of 24 schools, replying to an enquiry of the United States Commissioner of Education, only 10 had a regular entrance examination and "14 demanded some slight proof of capacity . . . to study medicine." Most schools demanded nothing more than "knowledge of all branches of a good English education, including composition, mathematics, elements of physics, of chemistry and natural sciences." Some schools specified such subjects as Latin, algebra, grammar, arithmetic, geography, history, reading, writing, and ciphering; that is, an elementary education was usually enough to qualify for entrance.[135]

At this date, the length of the medical course in the best schools was usually three years; but at Johns Hopkins and a few other institutions plans for the four-year course, of six months each, were being put into operation. Preparatory courses for the medical faculty had been established in eight universities.[136] Notwithstanding these progressive steps, the conditions, twenty years later, were considered by Flexner to be not inspiring, but rather "commonplace," "bad," and in some places "scandalous." Over 150 schools were visited and examined. Of these, about 25 required two or more years of college work for entrance; about 50 required four years of high-school study; and

130 *R. C. E.* (1892–3), II, 1627; also I, 99.
131 *Ibid.*, II, 1970.
132 *Biennial Survey*, 1918–1920, Bulletin 1923, No. 29, 294.
133 *Ibid.*, 300.
134 *Abstract of the Fourteenth Census*, 1920, 494.
135 *R. C. E.* (1892–3), I, 601 *ff.*; also (1894–5), II, 1263–4.
136 *Ibid.*

the remainder, chiefly in the Southern states but found also in Chicago, San Francisco, St. Louis, and Baltimore, required less than four years of high-school preparation. The worst features of medical education appeared to the investigators to be commercialization and "over production of uneducated and ill-trained medical practitioners." Germany was getting along with one doctor to every two thousand of her population; while the United States had one to every five hundred and sixty-eight.[137]   Dr. Flexner was of the opinion that 31 medical schools, rightly operated, would be better for the United States than the 150 in existence.[138]

One of the most difficult obstacles in the development of women's medical education was encountered in gaining clinical instruction. At the very outset there was little or none. When women sought entrance they were rebuffed because it was said to be "indecent" for them to observe cases in the presence of men. Being excluded from existing hospitals, there developed a need for women's hospitals, not only for the sake of patients, but for the opportunities for instruction which they afforded to women medical students.

The vigor of the opposition to women's use of existing clinical facilities is illustrated in the case of the Pennsylvania Hospital in 1869. Ladies were welcomed by Dr. Stillé to clinical lectures on Jan. 2, 1869, and the managers of the Pennsylvania Hospital gave permission to about thirty women in the early autumn. The male students expressed their disapproval "with insolent and offensive language."[139]   In spite of the presence and efforts of Dr. William Biddle, "during the last hour missiles of paper, tinfoil, [and] tobacco quids" were thrown at the women. Shortly thereafter the medical faculties of Jefferson Medical College and of the University of Pennsylvania declared "their deliberate conviction . . . adverse to conducting clinical instruction in the presence of students of both sexes."[140]   Dr. Preston and Dr. Cleveland answered ably that at Blockley, when forty women had attended, "the tone and bearing of the students were generally improved"; and that in attending the Pennsylvania Hos-

[137] Ibid. (1910), II, 1027–31.

[138] Medical Education in the United States and Canada, 149.

[139] Evening Bulletin (Phila.), Nov. 8, 1869.

[140] Nov. 15, 1869—quoted by Marshall: Woman's Medical College of Pa., 22–3.

pital women were not seeking to interfere "with the legitimate advantages of other students," but had purchased tickets in accordance with the regulation of the board of managers.[141]   The final result was the establishment of a separate clinic which women attended for a time until, becoming dissatisfied with the partial offering, they resumed their attendance at the Philadelphia Hospital.

The Woman's College in New York (1864) had the good fortune to be preceded by the dispensary and hospital.   In Philadelphia, the founding of the Woman's Hospital was due, in part at least, to the embarrassing experience of young women who had attended the wards of Blockley Almshouse in 1861.   Funds were collected, a house purchased, and the hospital opened on a miniature scale in 1862.[142]   In Boston, the New England Hospital for women and children was incorporated in 1863.[143]   A similar institution was opened in Chicago (1865), largely due to the labors of Dr. Mary Thompson; and another in San Francisco (1875).

Objections, equal to those met in entering clinics, and in some respects even greater, were raised against women's entrance to medical societies.   In 1859, the Philadelphia County Medical Society passed a resolution that any member who consulted with women doctors should lose his membership.   This action was endorsed by the State Society in 1860.   The Medical Society of Montgomery County refused to accept this position and, led by Dr. Hiram Corson, adopted a resolution that women, "if properly educated, should receive the same treatment as males."   This view did not prevail, however, until 1871, when the State Medical Society rescinded its previous action by a vote of 55 over 45.[144]   In 1869, the Blackwell sisters were admitted to the Medical Library and Journal Association; and in 1879, after a long struggle, the Massachusetts Medical Society was opened to women, by action of the councillors.   A year later, Dr. Emma Call, a graduate of the University of Michigan Medical School, was examined and admitted.

[141] The action of the managers was severely criticized in a pamphlet: *Men and Women Medical Students and the Woman Movement*, Phila., April, 1870.

[142] Meyer: *op. cit.*, 165.

[143] *Laws of Mass.*, 1863, 412.

[144] Corson: *History of . . . Recognition of Women Physicians by the Medical Profession* (1888).

IV. Women in the Christian Ministry

Notwithstanding the prominent place in early Christian history filled by such women as Mary, Martha, Susanna, Dorcas, Monica, Eusebia, Paula, and Cecilia, one of the oldest learned professions, the Christian ministry, has long retained a hostility to the service of women. This hostility has continued in spite of the fact that some of the more recent denominations, arising since the Reformation, have owed much to the power of women preachers. Methodism in England was jointly indebted to the Countess of Huntingdon and to Whitefield; Wesleyan Methodism of England has been considered the result of the influence of Susanna Wesley; and Barbara Heck may be considered the foundress of Methodism in the United States.[145] The promise given by this early prominence of women in Methodism has not been fulfilled. Even in Wesley's time it was clear that, while he recognized the power of women, he would have men achieve the public glory. Wesley objected to women holding religious services during his absence and "suggested that, to avoid the scandal of having a sermon read in public by a woman, she should find some man to read it."[146] His interpretation was undoubtedly in accord with the views generally entertained at that time. Ada C. Bowles declared, in her survey of woman in the ministry in America (1890), that "the Methodist Episcopal Church of America is singularly backward in recognition of its women."[147] The Primitive Methodists and the so-called German Methodists, or United Brethren in Christ, were more liberal; but they exerted little influence. It was asserted a generation ago that in many American churches, a woman class leader "would be almost as great a curiosity as John the Baptist, with his raiment of camel's hair."[148] Buckley, in the *History of Methodists in the United States* (1896), recounted that "a woman had been presented for license as a local preacher, but the presiding elder had decided it to be unauthorized by the Discipline and usages of the Church. An appeal was taken to Bowman, presiding at the North Indiana Congress, who sustained and affirmed the decision. An appeal was taken to the General Conference, which body declared the

---

145 Stevens: *Women of Methodism*, 175 ff.
146 Daniels: *History of Methodism*, 67.
147 In Meyer: *Woman's Work in America*, 210.
148 *Ibid.*, 210–11.

"said decision to be correct and agreeable to the letter and spirit of the discipline." At the same conference was adopted the report of the committee on the "state of the church adverse to the licensing and ordaining of women as ministers of the gospel."[149]

As for women's education in early Methodist colleges, that was out of the question. Cokesbury College, founded in 1787, specifically limited admission to sons of traveling ministers, sons of annual subscribers, sons of members of the church, and orphans. Girls might have gotten in under the last head, but apparently they did not.[150]

In seeking to find an explanation of this antagonism to women in the public work of the church, we may find it, partially, in the emphasis laid by Reformation leaders on the home duties of women. Luther, speaking of the women whom he planned to release from the nunnery of Nimptsch, referred to "that sex in itself so weak, and united to ours by nature," which "perishes by this cruel seclusion from ours."[151] To his wife "Katy" he referred as one "gentle, kind, and obedient in all things, far beyond my hopes—thanks be to God. . . ."[152] Calvin, when ready to marry, asked friends to present candidates, hoping to find one that would be "economical, patient, and who is likely to interest herself about my health." This he appears to have found in Idelette de Bures, for whom, at her death, he had these words of praise: "I have never experienced from her any hindrance, even the smallest."[153] The expressions of these men are brief and to the point; they show their general idea of the function of women.

Knox, in his *First Blast of the Trumpet Against the Monstrous Regiment of Women*, 1558, unquestionably had in mind such as "that horrible monster Jesabel of England," Mary; but if she motivated his thinking, he carried his conclusions sufficiently far to include all of womankind. He maintained, for example, "that woman, in her greatest perfection, was made to serve and obey man, not to rule and command him." As Paul said: "Man is not of the woman but the woman of the man." According to the doctrine of Paul it is "plain, that frome all

[149] Buckley: *op. cit.*, 541, 550 and 555.
[150] Bangs: *A History of the Methodist Episcopal Church*, I, 229–40.
[151] Anderson: *Ladies of the Reformation*, 51.
[152] *Ibid.*, 66.
[153] *Ibid.*, 266, 271.

ANNE HUTCHINSON

woman, be she married or unmarried, is all authoritie taken to execute any office, that appertaineth to man. Yea plain it is that all woman is commanded, to serve, to be in humilitie and subjection. . . . I meane the same of the authoritie of all women.''[154]

The idea of the wife as an obedient servant, rather than an equal partner, was stressed in marriage forms: ''Wilt thou obey him, and serve him, love, honor, and keep him in sickness and in health . . . ?''[155] On his part, the husband declared his willingness to ''love,'' ''comfort,'' ''honor,'' and ''keep'' the wife ''in sickness and in health.''

The opposition of one denomination has been similar to that of others. In New England, the tenets held by Anne Hutchinson were declared by a synod of 1637 to be erroneous, and she was shortly thereafter banished from Massachusetts. This action resulted from her insistence on her right to preach, that the ''Holy Spirit dwells in every believer, and that the inward revelations of the spirit, the conscious judgment of the mind, are of paramount authority.'' Her exclusion from the ministry was not less rigid and immediate than it would have been had she offered to become a priestess of the Catholic Church. The attitude of the German Lutheran Church is hardly more yielding. Bowles,[156] in 1890, cited a decision of the Missouri Conference, held at Baltimore, to the effect that ''they must not teach at all in the pulpit nor in the congregation.'' That the situation is still fundamentally the same is indicated by a recent letter[157] from the president of Red Wing Seminary (Minnesota) to a prospective woman student, which stated: ''The Lutheran Church in this country will not employ women as pastors (ordained clergymen).''

The problem of woman's utterance, and the seriousness with which arguments were advanced covering it, is well illustrated by the action of the Philadelphia Baptist Association in 1746. The question and answer need to be read in entirety to be appreciated:

[154] Knox: *The First Blast of the Trumpet* (Ed. by Edward Arber), 15 *ff.*
[155] As in the *Book of Common Prayer,* approved by the convention of 1789, Phila., 1873, 234–5.
[156] *Op. cit.,* 212.
[157] Dated April 15, 1926.

"3. Query: Whether women may or ought to have their votes in the church in such matters as the church shall agree to be decided by votes?

"Solution. As that in I *Corinthians* xiv: 34–35, and other parallel texts, are urged against their votes, as a rule, and ought, therefore, to be maturely considered.

"If, then, the silence enjoined on women be taken so absolute, as that they must keep entire silence in all respects whatever; yet, notwithstanding, it is to be hoped that they may have as members of the body of the church, liberty to give a mute voice, by standing or lifting up of the hands, or the contrary, to signify assent or dissent to the thing proposed, and so augment the number on the one or the both sides of the question. . . .

"Hence the silence with subjection enjoined on all women in the church of God, is such a silence as excludes all women whomsoever from all degrees of teaching, ruling, governing, dictating, and leading in the church of God; yet may their voice be taken as above said. . . .'"[158] In 1890, Reverend Bowles wrote that no steps had been taken "leading to the admission of women to its ministry," with the exception of the Free Will Baptists.[159]

From an examination of the practice of religious denominations it appears that, though there were some exceptions, it was founded, in general principle at least, on the doctrine of St. Paul:

"Let your women keep silence in the churches: for it is not permitted unto them to speak; but they are commanded to be under obedience, as also saith the law. And if they will learn anything let them ask their husbands at home: for it is a shame for women to speak in the church."[160] Only with great reluctance, and due to other changes in woman's sphere, did some of the Protestant churches begin slowly to modify their positions.

The Presbyterian Church, which long occupied a conservative position with reference to the public service of women, gave evidence of recognition of the changing times when, in 1889, it "decided by a vote of 93 to 34 that the ordination of women as deacons is in harmony with the New Testament and the constitution of the Apostolic church."[161] Today, there is an indication that

158 Phila. Baptist Association, *Minutes,* 1746, 53.

159 *Op. cit.,* 211.

160 I *Corinthians* xiv: 34–5.

161 Reported by Bowles: *op. cit.,* 211.

the ancient Pauline prohibition against women may be set aside; for, in March, 1929, the Presbyterian General Council voted, by a large majority, to recommend to the General Assembly that a general referendum be held in presbyteries to permit equality of women in church affairs. In Congregational circles, too, signs of an awakening appeared in the last quarter of the nineteenth century. Reverend Louise S. Baker was ordained by the Orthodox Congregational Church of Nantucket, Massachusetts, in 1884. The Hartford Theological Seminary was opened to women in 1889, being the first in the United States;[162] and a scholarship was given to be awarded only to women. The Reverend Antoinette Brown Blackwell, first woman theological graduate of Oberlin College, was ordained by an orthodox Congregational church of South Butler and Savannah, New York, in 1853; but she stated, in a letter to the editor of *Woman's Work in America*, 1891, that ''doubtless the Congregational body as a whole never would have ordained a woman either then, thirty seven years ago, nor yet today.''

The Free Will Baptist Conference, in 1886, took the position that ''intelligent, godly women, who are so situated as to devote their time to the ministry, and desire to be ordained, should receive such indorsement and authority as ordination involves, provided there are no objections to such indorsement other than the matter of sex.''[163]

Among all the numerous Protestant bodies that were represented in the founding of the American colonies, the Society of Friends was the most liberal in its attitude towards the ministry of women. Women's meetings were organized to provide a channel for their free expression and action in 1660.[164] A clear call to women to be active in the meetings was sounded in these words: ''Encourage all the women that are convinced, and minds virtue, and loves the truth, and walks in it, that they may come up into God's service, that they may be serviceable in their generation and in the Creation.''[165] Schools were established for girls and boys; women served on school committees; and many

---

[162] Steiner: *Hist. Ed. in Conn.*, 294.
[163] Bowles: *op. cit.*, 211.
[164] Brailsford: *Quaker Women*, 14 *f*.
[165] *Ibid.*, 15.

other services of general significance in the Society were performed by them.[166] Fox's first convert, in 1647, was a woman,
Elizabeth Hooton. Quaker women preachers appeared at an
early date, 1656, in the persons of Mary Fisher and Ann Austin,
to test the nature of the freedom of the Colony of Massachusetts and found it no better than that of the land from whence
they came. Their books and baggage were burned; they were
imprisoned, examined for witchcraft, and banished for their
heretical ideas.[167] The Quakers had no paid ministry; they did
not require an educated one; but the ministry among them was,
nevertheless, a field of larger service outside the sphere of domestic duties. This opportunity for a larger service was embraced by many women who became, not so much theologians, as
crusaders for social reforms such as emancipation of slaves,
woman suffrage, and temperance. The freedom with which
Quaker women preached—and, more than that, the freedom with
which they entered the public platform in one reform and another—had, undoubtedly, a liberalizing effect on woman's position in the United States in the nineteenth century, and may
have influenced other religious denominations somewhat to accord woman a more active part in their affairs.[168]

The first woman to graduate from a theological school in the
United States was Antoinette Brown Blackwell, who completed
the three years' course at Oberlin College in 1851.[169] The practice thus inaugurated by the infant college was not repeated,
however, for many years. Reverend Olympia Brown Willis, who
had already studied at Mount Holyoke and Antioch, requested
admission to Meadville Unitarian Theological School in 1859,
and was refused. When her request was presented to St. Lawrence University, in 1860, she was admitted, though there was no
precedent, as a student in its theological department and subsequently ordained. This action marked the attitude of the Uni-
versalists as most liberal. By 1890, a half hundred women had
been ordained and all its schools and colleges, save one, were coeducational.[170]

166 Woody: *Early Quaker Education in Pennsylvania*, 22, 54, 72–3, and
204 *ff.*; *Quaker Education in the Colony and State of New Jersey*, 297.
167 Ellis: *The Puritan Age and Rule*, 434 *ff.*
168 Bowles: *op. cit.*, 207.
169 *R. C. E.*, 1867–8, 387; Bowles: *op. cit.*, 212.
170 Bowles: *op. cit.*, 214.

The following figures show, to some extent, the situation with regard to women in theological schools. In 1871, 94 schools of theology reported 3,204 students—women not being listed separately.[171] Thirty years later, 154 schools reported 8,009 students, of whom only 181 were women.[172] In 1921–22, only 121 schools[173] of theology reporting, there were 8,430 students, of whom 1,177 were women; and of 752 graduates, 12 were women.[174]

The foregoing pages have set forth facts regarding the attitude of schools and churches towards the preparation of women for, and their entering into, the ministry. To what extent have changes been made in recent years? In 1926, a young lady, about to graduate from an Eastern college for women, and desirous of ascertaining what were the best facilities open to her, as a preparation for the ministry, secured answers to certain pertinent questions from sixty, out of eighty-two, theological schools of the United States to which requests were sent. It is probably safe to assume that the 27 per cent not replying did not admit women. The replies were not very encouraging as a general rule; but there were some notable exceptions. The significant contents of the letters[175] are summarized here briefly, so far as they refer to the three topics: whether women would be admitted as students; whether they would advise against, or whether the attitude of the church was opposed to, the ordination of women as ministers; and whether women should seek some other form of Christian service rather than the ministry, assuming they were qualified, for either or both, by ability and preparation. Of the sixty replies, forty-two (70 per cent) stated that women were admitted or would be admitted if they applied. Several stated they had admitted women only recently; some that women were allowed to enter as "special students"; in a few, they could take any courses wanted but could not be

[171] R. C. E., 1881, CLXXXII.

[172] Ibid. (1909–10), II, 1018–19; and (1899–1900), II, 1967.

[173] The decrease in numbers is due to the dropping out of "institutions, such as Bible schools, which should not perhaps have been included in the list in the first place."—[Letter, June 8, 1927, Commissioner of Education].

[174] Biennial Survey (1920–22), II, 310 and 316.

[175] Kindly loaned me by the applicant, Miss Lydia Kern, New Jersey College for Women, New Brunswick, New Jersey, and deposited in the Penniman Memorial Library of Education, University of Pennsylvania.

candidates for degrees; one or two had never had a woman applicant but would admit them; another would be willing to consider a woman as a candidate for admission. Thirty-one of the forty-two institutions (about 74 per cent) admitting, or willing to admit women, stated explicitly that they granted, or would grant, the same degrees to women as to men—*i.e.*, the B.D., B.Th. or the B.S.T., or even the D.D.

Forty-one of the sixty replies contained either (1) advice against going into the ministry or (2) a warning that churches, or "the church with which this seminary is connected," do not want, or will not ordain, women as ministers. This discouraging advice and warning came, in twenty-four, or 58.5 per cent of the cases, from the schools admitting women as students and for degrees. A few quotations are given showing prevailing sentiment, as to the reality of which the seminary heads are in a fair position to judge. The position of the Presbyterian church is made clear in a great number of letters, one from the South stating: "The attitude of the Southern Presbyterian Church is opposed to women being ordained in the ministry. . . . In my opinion it will be thirty years before a woman preacher could have much success in the Southern states."[176] From another, located in the North: "The constitution of our church makes no provision for this [ordaining of women] and for any presbytery to ordain a woman to the ministry of our denomination would be considered irregular and would be disapproved."[177] A note of hope was stressed by a few, one of them writing: "I think the time will come when the Presbyterian church will ordain women as elders and ministers, but the attempt to ordain them as elders has recently failed."[178]

Very vigorous discouragement came from some Lutheran school heads, with whom it was a personal conviction as well as the church practice that women should not enter the ministry. One writes: ". . . It is contrary to the word of God for a woman under ordinary circumstances to become a minister";[179] another, "only a few denominations allow women pastors and preachers; nearly all refuse them on Biblical grounds; the ministry is *not*

176 Letter No. 23, April 16, 1926.
177 Letter No. 33, April 19, 1926; No. 18, April 15, 1926, states the same view.
178 Letter No. 18, April 15, 1926.
179 Letter No. 5, April 12, 1926.

for women'';[180] still another advises that it is a ''fact to be faced'' and assures that there is ''no reflection of inferiority . . . cast upon women in the candid statement that . . . nowhere in the Lutheran church do congregations˜call women as their pastors or intrust to them the preaching of the Word and the administration of the Sacraments.''[181] Another head advised: ''We never have had any application from a woman for admission and . . . with existing sentiment in this part of the church such . . . is not expected. . . . I know not what developments there may be in the church in the future; but for the present the Lutheran church is not ready to entertain the question whether women should be called to the ministry.''[182]

From a Southern Baptist school, the information comes that ''we do not recognize women preachers. We are very glad for the women to serve in any of the great phases of our Kingdom work, except the ministry. Practically all Southern Baptists interpret the word of God as against women entering the ministry. . . .''[183]

The heads of several schools merely advised that ''when it comes to ordination to the ministry and to the filling of pastorates that is a matter for church judicatories to decide,'' or ''it makes no difference to this institution what service the women may render after graduation. This will depend on the will of the local church.''[184] A Moravian says: ''We have no ordained women. . . . I doubt . . . whether the Moravian church as such is ready to admit women to the ministry.''[185]

Others stated that it might be done, but that much prejudice and opposition must be overcome; the labor of overcoming such opposition would not leave much energy for good work. ''The only difficulty . . . is the prejudice which exists in the majority of the churches.''[186] Again, ''you would encounter immense publicity and immense opposition merely for the sake of trying to become a minister.''[187]

[180] Letter No. 26, April 16, 1926.
[181] Letter No. 27, April 17, 1926.
[182] Letter No. 30, April 15, 1926.
[183] Letter No. 53, April 15, 1926.
[184] Letters No. 17, April 16, 1926; and No. 21, April 16, 1926.
[185] Letter No. 44, April 20, 1926.
[186] Letter No. 49, April 20, 1926.
[187] Letter No. 25, April 17, 1926.

A very few letters spoke encouragingly, looking on the ministry as a profession in which women might overcome the monsters of prejudice, even as they have done so largely in medicine and elsewhere. According to one, a personal view, contrary to the usage of the church, "the day is not far distant when all denominations will ordain women."[188]   Another was "fully committed to the idea of ladies entering the ministry. . . . They are entering all other professions and advocations [sic] and making good and why not in the Ministry."[189]   A similar view was expressed by the dean of a prominent theological seminary: "I see no reason why women should not be on the same level as men, not only with reference to the ministry but with reference to any profession or occupation."[190]   Some of the most encouraging letters, as that just quoted, came from schools which, being non-coeducational, had to refuse admittance though the school officer was most favorably inclined to equality of treatment for women.

Another point is worthy of note. Twenty-five (61 per cent) of the forty-one institutions advising specifically against the ministry, or warning that the attitude of churches would not be favorable to women as ministers, suggested the consideration of social service, educational work, religious education, evangelistic work, pastors' assistants, church secretaries, deaconesses, sisterhoods, and the mission field as substitutes for the regular ministry. Some said directly it was the will of God; others implied that women should thus serve, rather than as regular ministers. When the foreign mission field is suggested as a less taxing sphere of endeavor for women than a local home church, at least the penetration of the writer is open to question. In many of the letters there is a dictatorial tone which suggests that the arbitrary authority of men equals, if it does not exceed, that of God. When a young woman minister, although ordained, declares she will not take a pastorate, preferring to do social work, young people's work, or what not, it is quite possible that the choice is dictated—not openly but just as effectively—by the prevailing sentiment of the men ministers, as well as congregations, against the ministry of women.[191]

[188] Letter No. 11, April 13, 1926.

[189] Letter No. 35, April 22, 1926.

[190] Letter No. 39, April 19, 1926.

[191] A case mentioned in the *Evening Public Ledger* (Philadelphia), Jan. 18, 1927.

V. Women in the Profession of Law

Law, as a profession for women in the United States, was not opened until near the close of the seventh decade of the past century, and then only after stubborn opposition had been overcome. While schools for the medical preparation of women opened as early as 1848, and Elizabeth Blackwell took the first medical degree in 1849, the first woman graduate of a law school, Ada Kepley, of Illinois, received the degree of the Union College of Law, Chicago, in 1870.[192] The growth of numbers in law schools, and in law departments of universities, since that date, has been slow, compared with the rapidly expanding field of medical study and practice. Reasons for the slow development of law practice among women are discussed later.[193] So far as objections to women entering law schools are concerned, they have been fewer and less violent than those urged against their entering medical schools. Their subsequent admission to the bar, however, was met by opposition and arguments very similar to those urged against the admission of women to medical societies, consultation, and practice.

Snow states that the Law School of Washington University, at St. Louis, established March 9, 1860, was not opened until 1867, due to the disturbances of the Civil War. This school was opened to both sexes alike;[194] and, in 1869, Lemma Barkaloo, who had previously been refused admission to Columbia College, was admitted. The first woman was granted the law degree from the St. Louis school in 1871.[195]

In 1870 the Commissioner's office received information regarding 28 law schools, with 1,653 students; in the next report, several new schools were included and old ones not before reporting, there being a total of 40 institutions and 1,722 students. No report was made as to the number of women among them.[196] While it is certain a few attended here and there, the number was not considerable enough to be thought worthy of separate

[192] Young: Law as a Profession for Women [*Jour. Assoc. Coll. Alumnae,* Feb. 1902, 15].

[193] See p. 380.

[194] *Higher Educ. in Mo.,* 133–4, 140–1.

[195] *Ibid.;* see also Bittenbender: "Women in Law" [in Meyer: *Woman's Work in America,* 231].

[196] *R. C. E.,* 1870, 521; and 1871, 662–3.

tabulation or notice. Twenty years later (1890), the schools reporting numbered 54, with 5,252 students.[197] No report was made of the number of women attending. The number was still, no doubt, small, though it is certain that some prominent schools had admitted them. Among the older universities, that of Pennsylvania had, upon the "request of the law-school faculty" and the approval of the trustees, admitted women since 1881, granting them the same degrees as to men. Carrie Burnham asked admission in 1871 and was refused; but her second request, 1881, was granted. She graduated in 1883. From 1883 to 1895 no women entered the Law Department. Since then a considerable number have attended lectures and a few have graduated.[198]

The decade 1890–1900 witnessed an unprecedented growth in the number of law schools and students. In the period of 1870–1890, law schools reported to the Commissioner almost doubled; a decade later they had nearly doubled again, 96 being reported.[199] Commenting on the rapid increase of students seeking to prepare themselves, in schools, for the profession of law, rather than in the offices of lawyers as was the old custom, Franklin M. Dannaher, of the New York Board of Examiners, said, in 1900, after careful study of the question: "It is due to the general raising of the standard of education among the students themselves; they know that under existing conditions a thorough education in the law cannot be obtained in a law office . . . [that] it is almost impossible to qualify unless . . . fully prepared and they know that they cannot get adequate preparation outside of a law school. Seventy per cent who apply have been at law schools; 14 per cent fail who have had law school training; and 26 per cent fail, who have been trained in law offices only."[200]

This transition of the seat of law study from the practitioner's office to a school was an immense advantage to woman. It was difficult, if not impossible, to study law in an office, unless hus-

197 *Ibid.* (1890–1), II, 878.

198 Nitzsche: Hist. of the Department of Law [*Proceedings at the Dedication of the New Building of the Law Department* (1901), 230]; see also *Sch. and Soc.*, VII, 286.

199 *R. C. E.* (1899–1900), II, 1968.

200 *Ibid.* (1899–1900), II, 1962.

band, father, or brother invited her to do so. In the school she could have an even chance with men. At the end of this decade of rapid growth, the 94 law schools reporting in 1899–1900 showed 151 women and 12,365 men students.[201] Up to 1901, 108 women had been granted law degrees by the schools connected with the Association of Collegiate Alumnae. This list of course included the best schools granting the law degree to women, but not all. It is fair to assume that not more than twice that number had been granted by all schools since 1870.[202]

In 1891, New York University announced "Lectures on Law for non-matriculants, and in particular for Business Women." These had been founded by the Woman's Legal Education Society, incorporated June 14, 1890, whose president was Mrs. Leonard Weber and the treasurer, Dr. Mary Putnam Jacobi. While forming no part of the University Law School, they were under the direction of the Council and Vice-Chancellor of the University. Four courses were opened, each containing twelve lectures. While giving practical training to women of the business world, the lectures also furnished "preparation for entrance upon the professional study of the law, with a view to active practice at the bar."[203] Ten free, and twenty half-free, scholarships were provided by the Legal Education Society.[204] At the end of its seventh year, fifteen were in the senior, and about twenty-five in the junior law classes for women.[205]

In 1897–98, according to the Commissioner's *Report*, "the major part of the law schools of the United States" were admitting "women to their law classes when application is made. . . ." Those that stood out against the movement most steadfastly were Harvard, Yale, Columbia, Washington and Lee, and the University of Virginia. Yale opened to women in 1918. Women have been admitted to the University of Virginia Law School on the same basis as men since 1920–21.[206] As late as 1925, the National Woman's party was still trying to persuade the Colum-

[201] *Ibid.*, II, 1968.

[202] Young's article in *Jour. Assoc. Coll. Alumnae*, Feb. 1902, 15–23.

[203] *R. C. E.* (1897–8), I, 636–7; also *Catalog*, University of the City of New York, 1895–6, 217.

[204] *Catalog*, University of the City of New York, 1890–91, 174 *f.*

[205] *R. C. E.* (1897–98), I, 636–7.

[206] Letter, May 16, 1927.

bia president to open the law department to women.[207]   Women
are not admitted to the law school of Washington and Lee University.[208]

In 1909, 114 schools of law were reported, with 19,567 students,
of whom 205 were women.[209]   Of the 4,233 graduated in 1910,
forty-four were women.[210]   In 1919–1920, 107 law schools reported 19,821 men and 1,171 women; in the same year, the
schools conferred 3,094 degrees on men and 179 on women.[211]

Admission to the bar was achieved, but not without more pains
than admission to schools of law.   Some of the newly established
law schools welcomed women, because they needed students and
had no tradition to combat.   The bar had many traditions and
more candidates than needed.   An anonymous author, writing of
her early struggle to enter law practice, said: When "I pointed
my pencil toward the court house and became a 'crack' court
reporter, I was flattered by my lawyer friends as the wonder
of the verbatim shorthand world. . . . But when I began to talk
of studying law, they called me impractical and visionary."[212]

The reluctance of the American courts regarding the pleading
of cases by women has been traced back, through the English
custom, to the days of ancient Rome, when Calphurnia, because
of "excess of boldness," and being unable to "endure that her
side should be beaten," was excluded from the forum.   The
common law of England being transplanted to this country, it
was held that women were unable to plead in the courts.   With
one exception, it appears, it was not until the last half of the
nineteenth century that women in America made any test of the
traditional usage.

Margaret Brent came to the Colony of Maryland in 1638.   On
the governor's death, in 1647, she was named sole executrix and,
according to the ruling of the court, accepted as "attorney both
for recovering of rights unto the estate and paying of dew debts
out of the estate and taking care for the estate's preservation:

207 Editorial in *The Nation*, Feb. 18, 1925, 173; see also *Sch. and Soc.*,
XII, 349.

208 Letter, May 14, 1927.

209 *R. C. E.* (1910), II, 1017.

210 *Ibid.;* also 1052–7.

211 *Biennial Survey*, 1918–1920, Bulletin 1923, No. 29, 294 and 300.

212 *The Nation*, Dec. 15, 1926, 634.

But not further . . .'' till another be substituted.[213] She appeared in court frequently thereafter, exercising her office of attorney, and no objection was raised to her sex. Shortly after receiving the power to act as attorney, and forgetful or heedless of the warning, "but not further," she demanded a voice and vote in the House, on the ground that she was acting as his Lordship's attorney. This demand was refused; and she entered her protest "against all proceedings in this present assembly, unlesse shee may be present and have vote as aforesaid.''[214]

About two and a quarter centuries later, in keeping with the general movement for the complete emancipation of women in America, which had already opened up several professions to a greater or less degree, the demand for the right to practice law was revived. A series of significant efforts were made to gain admission to the courts: Arabella Mansfield, of Iowa, 1869; Myra Bradwell, of Chicago, who sought admission to the Illinois bar at the same time; Belva Lockwood, who sought admission to the bar of the United States Court of Claims in 1873; Lavinia Goodell, who sought to enter the Supreme Court of Wisconsin in 1875; and the cases of Lelia Robinson and Mary Hall, who sought the right to practice in Massachusetts (1881) and Connecticut (1882), respectively.[215]

A few of the cases will suffice to set forth the arguments against the admission of women, as also to illustrate the method whereby the admission of women to the courts was finally gained. The admission of Miss Mansfield was accomplished without opposition, the committee asserting that "in her examination she has given the very best rebuke possible to the imputation that ladies cannot qualify for the practice of law."

When Mrs. Bradwell applied for a license, it was refused on the grounds that (1) as a married woman her contracts would not be binding; (2) the admission of a female to be attorney-at-law would not be in accord with the common law; (3) to license a woman would be to admit that women should be governors, judges and sheriffs and this the court was not ready to accept; (4) possibly the "delicacy" of the female sex would be endan-

[213] *Archives of Md.*, IV, 358.

[214] *Ibid.*, I, 215.

[215] The details of each case are given in some completeness by Meyer: *Woman's Work in America*, 221–31.

gered; and (5) what influence women lawyers would have on the "administration of justice" was a question, and it could only be answered by experience.[216] The case was appealed to the Supreme Court of the United States, where the first decision was confirmed.[217] In 1872, belated justice was brought to Mrs. Bradwell by the passage of a bill which provided that no person should be debarred from any employment or profession, save the military, because of sex.[218]

Belva Lockwood graduated in law at the National University Law School, established in 1870, and was admitted to practice in the Supreme Court of the District of Columbia, 1873. She desired, the same year, admission to the United States Court of Claims as well. Her request was refused, and it was concluded that "a woman is without legal capacity to take the office of attorney."[219] In 1876, she asked admission to the Supreme Court of the United States, which was also refused. In the meantime she worked for the passage of a bill which would make it impossible for the courts to disbar qualified women from practice. In 1879 her bill was passed, which provided "that any woman who shall have been a member of the bar of the highest court of any state or territory, or of the supreme court of the District of Columbia, for the space of three years, and shall have maintained a good standing before such court, and who shall be a person of good moral character shall, on motion, and the production of such record, be admitted to practice before the Supreme Court of the United States."[220]

In 1875, the Supreme Court of Wisconsin refused to admit Lavinia Goodell, who had been practicing in a circuit court of the state.[221] To remedy the situation a law was passed by Wisconsin, in 1877, whereby women might be admitted to practice in the courts.[222] In similar fashion, in 1881, Lelia Robinson was held by the Massachusetts Supreme Court to be disqualified by sex;[223] and not until the legislature had passed a law removing

[216] *Supreme Court Reports*, Ill., LV, 535–42.
[217] Wallace's U. S. *Supreme Court Reports*, XVI, 130–42.
[218] *Laws of Illinois*, approved March 22, 1872, 578.
[219] *U. S. Court of Claims Reports*, IX, 346–56.
[220] *Laws of the U. S.*, Feb. 15, 1879; *Supplement, Rev. Stat. U. S.*, I, 217.
[221] *Wisconsin Supreme Court Reports*, XXXIX, 232–46.
[222] *Laws of Wisconsin*, March 8, 1877, 616.
[223] *Mass. Supreme Court Reports*, CXXXI, 376–84.

BELVA LOCKWOOD

the restriction and permitting women to appear for bar examinations (1882) was she admitted.[224] In the same year, Mary Hall was licensed to practice by the Hartford County (Connecticut) Superior Court, by virtue of a liberal interpretation of existing law handed down from the supreme court of the state, in the decision rendered by Chief Justice Park.[225] Pennsylvania furnished most stubborn resistance to the entrance of women, Mrs. Kilgore having labored for twelve years, 1874 to 1886, to secure her right to plead in the Supreme Court.

As noted before,[226] the number of women who had taken the law degree by 1900 was probably in the vicinity of two hundred. It has been said that in 1882 there were 56 women admitted to the practice of law, and of these, 31 had come from the law schools; the others had studied privately and in law offices. After examing these first cases in which the admission of women to the bar was questioned, one may say the arguments advanced against it were found: first, in the legal tradition; second, in the terminology employed in existing laws and constitutions; third, in the law of nature which seemed to have put upon women duties incompatible with public life; and, fourth, in the prevailing notion that womanly delicacy and character had no place in the coarse, brutal, and repulsive affairs with which the law must deal.

The legal obstacles could be, and were, fairly readily removed. The other handicaps persisted much longer. Women showed, by their work as students, that they could do work equal to that of men: at Michigan they were said to have compared favorably with men;[227] and at the Union Law College, where women had attended for a long time and in considerable numbers, it was said that "no difference in the capacity of the sexes to apprehend and apply legal principles" had been found.[228] The many successful women lawyers are a far more conclusive proof. Their success as practitioners has been achieved in face of far greater difficulties than those met by men.[229] Men are assisted in build-

---

[224] Laws of Massachusetts, April 10, 1882, 100; see also Jour. Assoc. Coll. Alumnae, Feb. 1902, 15–23.

[225] Conn. Supreme Court Reports, L, 131–9.

[226] P. 375.

[227] R. C. E. (1897–8), I, 636 f.

[228] Robinson: Women Lawyers in the United States [The Green Bag, Jan. 1890, 10–32].

[229] Young: The Law as a Profession [in Jour. Assoc. Coll. Alumnae, Feb. 1902, 15–23].

ing up a practice by their associations and friendships with men of various business interests and with politicians; women of the legal profession, too, find that in proportion as other business and political circles have been opened to women, the path to success in the law is made easier for them. Their number has increased rapidly in the past thirty years. From fifty-six, in 1882, the number of women lawyers rose to 208 in 1890, 1,010 in 1900,[230] and 1,738 in 1920. Male lawyers numbered 89,422 in 1890, 113,450 in 1900, and 120,781 in 1920.[231]

What do women do after they study law? Young found, in 1902, that few of the women thus prepared were actually practicing attorneys. Questions sent to 108 holders of the LL.B. were answered by 59, of whom 29 were not in practice.[232] A majority of those not answering were probably not practicing law. The 1,738 women lawyers listed in 1920[233] represent but a small part of those granted degrees since 1900.

The women who first entered the profession of law in the United States achieved greater fame as editors than as practicing lawyers. The names of Myra Bradwell, founder and editor of the *Chicago Legal News,* and Catharine Waite, of the *Chicago Law Times,* are well known; but their reputations were made by their editorial work rather than by their practice of law. Preparation in law has been valuable to women going into business and other professions; valuable, also, in enabling them to manage their property intelligently and removing them from the clutch of the unscrupulous who preyed upon their ignorance; it is of greater importance today than ever before, due to the admission of women to equal political privileges with men.

The oldest learned professions—teaching, law, medicine—have admitted women after considerable protest. Numerous other professions, requiring more or less of advanced preparation, have likewise been opened. There is nothing more significant for the position of women today than the fact of their steady increase, in recent years, in the professions which were once held almost exclusively by men. Woman's entrance into the highest professions, demanding the best powers, physical and mental,

[230] *Stat. Abstract,* 1910, 225.
[231] *Ibid.,* 1924, 54.
[232] *Jour. Assoc. Coll. Alumnae,* Feb. 1902, 21.
[233] *Statistical Abstract of the United States,* 1924, 54.

as well as the best educational facilities, is a more certain mark of her emancipation from the dominion of man and her freedom from the drudgery of life than her recent political privileges. These did but come when, having achieved the others to such a great extent, it became patent to the poorest intelligence that it was folly to insist on her incompetence to participate in government.

The following table[234] shows the number of women engaged in several of the professions for which technical training is required, since 1890; and the total number of men in professional service at the same dates:

TABLE III

	1890	1900	1910	1920
Architects, designers, and draftsmen	327	1,041	3,314[237]	7,801
Artists and teachers of art	10,815	11,021	15,429	14,617
Clergymen	1,143	3,373	685	1,787
Dentists	337	807	1,254	1,829
Engineers	124	84[235]	584[236]	1,755[236]
Journalists	888	2,193	4,181	5,730
Lawyers, judges	208	1,010	558	1,738
Physicians and surgeons	4,557	7,387	9,015[238]	8,882[238]
Teachers and professors	246,066	327,614	480,985	640,316
Total	264,465	354,530	516,005	684,455
Others listed under professional service	47,222	76,067	217,880	332,043
Grand total	311,687	430,597	733,885	1,016,498
G. T. for men	632,046	827,941	929,684	1,127,391

The population of the United States, since 1890, increased from 62,947,714 to 105,710,620 in 1920.[239] The ratio of men to women in this period has been about the same.[240] The population increased 68 per cent between 1890 and 1920; men in professional service for the same period increased 78 per cent; while women increased 226 per cent.

[234] *Statistical Abstract of the U. S.*, 1910, 225; 1914, 233; 1924, 54.
[235] Did not include electricians as did the figures of 1890.
[236] 579 are chemists, assayers, and metallurgists.
[237] 44 inventors.
[238] Including osteopaths.
[239] *Stat. Abstract of the U. S.*, 1914, 41; and 1924, 39.
[240] In 1900, 104.4 men to 100 women; 1910, 106 men to 100 women; 1920, 104 men to 100 women.

CHAPTER VIII

EMANCIPATION AND EDUCATION

I. Introduction

"Man for the field and woman for the hearth:
"Man for the sword and for the needle she:
"Man with the head and woman with the heart
"Man to command and woman to obey. . . ."

"Male and female created he them and gave them dominion."

"The woman's cause is man's: they rise or sink
"Together, dwarfed or godlike, bond or free."

The foregoing quotations present the subject at issue. The question, raised in the United States in the nineteenth century, concerned the tenability of the age-old theory of "outside" duties for man, "inside" duties for woman.

"The clock of time has struck the woman's hour": this may be considered an epitome of the sentiment of those who, for the past seventy-five years, have endeavored to realize woman's complete emancipation.[1] From the days of Plato, who caught a vision of the equality of men and women, down to the middle of the nineteenth century, the world witnessed no effective measures to secure for her that equality. Theorists did appear who voiced their belief in her equality; but, if judged by practical results, they were men of faith, rather than of works. Agrippa Von Nettesheim's *De Nobilitate et Praecellentia Foeminei Sexus* (1532), the *True Copy of the Petition of the Gentlewomen and Tradesmen's Wives* (1641), Norris' *Haec et Hic, or the Feminine Gender more worthy than the Masculine* (1683), Astell's *Defense of the Female Sex* (1697), Condorcet's *Lettres d'un*

---

[1] For general account, giving background of suffrage movement, and relating it to others, compare Schlesinger's *Polit. and Soc. Hist. of the U. S.*, Chaps. V and XVIII; excellent brief accounts of the period 1830 to 1850 are given in Fish's *Rise of the Common Man*, chaps. dealing with "Manners and Morals" and "Education for the People"; see, too, Adams: *New England in the Republic*, Chaps. XIV and XV.

382

Bourgeois de New Haven (1787) and his essays, *Sur l'Admission des femmes au droit de cité* (1790), Wollstonecraft's *Vindication of the Rights of Women* (1792), Grimké's *Letters on the Equality of the Sexes* (1838), Mott's *Discourse on Woman* (1849) and Mill's *Subjection of Women* (1869) are but representative of a faith in some cases, a reasoned conclusion in others, that continued to maintain itself in the face of opposition and ridicule. None of these and their kindred (unless an exception be made of the Quakers) knew, in practice, the equality of women and men which they so ardently advocated.[2]   Walt Whitman expressed the spirit of revolt when he wrote: ''The female equally with the male I sing;'' but he had to look into the future to see women enter ''the public assembly and take places the same as the men.'' Of these ideal women, ''children of Adam,'' he proclaimed:

''They are not one jot less than I am,
''They are tanned in the face by shining suns and blowing winds,
''Their flesh has the old divine suppleness and strength,
''They know how to swim, row, ride, wrestle, shoot, run, strike,
    retreat, advance, resist, defend themselves,
''They are ultimate in their own right—they are calm, clear,
    well-possessed of themselves.''

II. Position of Woman

That Whitman spoke of future women is clear from a brief examination of the position filled by women up to his day. Legally, said Blackstone, ''husband and wife are one person . . .'' so that ''the very being or legal existence of the woman is suspended during marriage, or, at least, incorporated and consolidated into that of the husband.''[3] This was no mere verbal claim; it described accurately actual practice. Another authority declared: ''The husband has the right of imposing such corporeal restraints as he may deem necessary for securing to himself the fulfillment of the obligations imposed on the wife. He may, in the plenitude of his power, adopt every act of physical coercion which does not endanger the life or health of the wife.''[4]

[2] *Westminster and Foreign Quarterly Review*, July 1851, quoted in *Woman's Rights Tracts*, No. 3, 7.

[3] *Commentaries*, I, 442.

[4] Higginson: *Woman and her Wishes* [*Woman's Rights Tracts*, No. 4, 17].

Early laws generally made it clear that the husband was to be assured the possession of his wife. The following provision in the *Duke of York's Laws* fairly presents the spirit and intent of the early statutes; with minor variations, of course, one finds women thus bound by law to their husbands in all colonies; and the latter were empowered to deal with them very much as with other servants. Against the protection of such masters, whose hands were strengthened by law, about the only satisfactory redress was in flight. Many women absconded and were advertised for; but the law put as many obstacles in their way as possible. Apparently only in case of "barbarous cruelty" was any one to receive the fleeing wife— and then only some public officer. Thus the laws for New York and Pennsylvania territories, in 1676, stated that:

"No man shall harbour, conceal or detain Contrary to the consent of the Husband any Married woman, upon penalty of five Shillings for every hour that such Married woman remains under his Roof; after demand made by her Husband at the Dwelling house where his wife is so harboured concealed or detained.

"Provided always that any woman flying from the barbarous Cruelty of Her Husband to the House of the Constable or one of the Overseers of the same Parish; may be protected by them in the manner as is Directed for Servants in such Cases, and not otherwise."[5]

The churches generally, in harmony with the common law, had held women in a state of subjection. With the exception of the Quakers they held them bound to be silent and submissive unto their husbands, as Paul had commanded. Catholic opinion was definitely expressed and diametrically opposed to the woman's rights movement.[6] Doctor Dix, whose views attracted much attention in the last quarter of the nineteenth century, no doubt expressed the past and current attitude of his church when he declared: "The place and work of woman in this world are, then, a place and a work in social life. And her place and work are not those of the man. His work lies outside, hers within."[7]

The formal restraints, exhibited in the views held by churches, found ready expression in social usage, which denied freedom to

5 *Duke of York's Laws,* Sept. 22, 1676 (Linn), 36.

6 *Catholic World* (1869), IX, 145–6.

7 Quoted in *Pop. Sci. Mo.* (1883), XXIII, 121.

women but granted it to men. Such partiality was deplored by
many, doubtless, but few expressed it better than the young lady
who complained:

> "How wretched is a Woman's Fate,
> "No happy change her fortune knows,
> "Subject to man in every state,
> "How can she then be free from woes?"

Recognizing, however, the impossibility of escape from the
clutches of Fate, she concluded:

> "Oh, cruel Powers! since you've designed,
> "That man, vain man! should bear the sway,
> "To a slave's fetters add a slavish mind,
> "That I may cheerfully your Will obey."[8]

The character and temper which male society uniformly expected in the wife were doubtless described in the following bit
of advice:

"A wife must learn how to form a husband's happiness; in
what direction the secret of his comfort lies; she must not cher-
ish his weaknesses by working upon them; she must not rashly
run counter to his prejudices. Her motto must be never to
irritate.

"She must study never to draw largely upon the small stock of
patience in man's nature, nor to increase his obstinacy by trying to drive him: never, if possible, to have scenes. I doubt much
if a real quarrel, even if made up, does not loosen the bond between man and wife, and sometimes, unless the affection of both
be very sincere, lastingly. . . .

"If irritation should occur, a woman must expect to hear from
most men a strength and vehemence of language far more than
the occasion requires. Mild as well as stern men are prone to
this exaggeration of language: let not a woman be tempted ever
to say anything sarcastic or violent in retaliation. The bitterest
repentance must needs follow such an indulgence if she does.

"Men frequently forget what they have themselves said, but
seldom what is uttered by their wives. They are grateful, too,
for forbearance in such cases; for, whilst asserting most loudly
that they are right, they are often conscious that they are wrong.

---

[8] *S. C. Gaz.*, Nov. 21, 1743, 2, col. 2; see "The Lady's Complaint," *Va.
Gaz.*, Oct. 15–22, 1736, 3, col. 2.

Give a little time, as the greatest boon you can bestow, to the
irritated feelings of your husband.''[9]

That women should free themselves from this domestic servitude and seek to earn their living elsewhere, was enough to disgrace the individual and her family as well. The difficulty of
entering the legal, medical and ministerial professions has already been referred to; even to become a teacher was scarcely
tolerated by those who prided themselves on the social position
of their family. In *Pratt Portraits* (1892) Anna Fuller described the grandmother, ''Old Lady Pratt,'' who still believed
''a woman toiling early and late for husband and children was
but fulfilling the chief end and aim of her being, but a woman
who set out to wrest a living from the world when she 'need want
for nothing at home' was clearly flying in the face of Providence.''[10]

An interesting and instructive, though not entirely reliable,
view of the position of women in America, to the middle of the
nineteenth century, may be gleaned from the observations and
criticisms of foreign visitors.[11]

Darusmont, in her *Views of Society and Manners in America*
(1819), was impressed with the gaiety of women's life in the
large cities, especially New York;[12] and Brissot de Warville was
shocked at the elegance of dress, even among the Quaker ladies
of Philadelphia,[13] which was not to be reconciled with the teach-
ings of Fox and Penn. The daughters of a family were observed
to be ''beautiful, easy in their manners, and decent in their
deportment . . . [assisting] their mother in the management
of the family.'' But most indicative of the advancement of
society, he thought, was the school for Negroes at Philadelphia
where ''the black girls'' were being educated for ''good servants

[9] From the *Evening Public Ledger* (Philadelphia), Feb. 6, 1926.

[10] Portrait of ''The School Marm'' in *Pratt Portraits*, 175.

[11] Besides those mentioned, or quoted at some length, reference might be
made to such as Kemble: *Journal of a Residence on a Georgian Plantation,*
1838–1839; Stevens: *The Land of the Dollar* (1897); Muirhead: *America
the Land of Contrasts* (1898).

[12] Pp. 31–3.

[13] *New Travels*, 319; compare also Calhoun: *Soc. Hist. of the Am. Family*,
I, 246, quoting Abbé Robin on the subject of ''Female Luxury''; II, 226–9;
also Nevins: *Am. Soc. Hist.*, 21, 36–7.

FRANCES WRIGHT

and virtuous housekeepers,'' who elsewhere would have been formed ''but to debauchery and ignominy'' by the planters.[14]

Darusmont was impressed with the ''peculiarly liberal'' education of women in New England and other Eastern states. Elsewhere she found girls' education too much after the ''European manner,'' too much emphasis being placed on ''French, Italian, dancing, [and] drawing,'' which are taught ''too commonly in a lax and careless way.'' Personal accomplishments, she thought, ought in America to be subordinated to ''solid information,'' inasmuch as in a republic, the mother must form the infant mind which, in the future, will ''judge of the laws and support the liberties'' thereof. She was able to see in the new seminary education, which she felt must ''become, more and more, the concern of the state,'' a means to still further enhancement of woman's character and the increased amelioration of her condition.[15]

Frances Trollope had no such faith in the education of the ''collegiate institutes'' established for young ladies or the academic degrees conferred on them. ''It is after marriage, and when these young attempts upon all the sciences are forgotten, that the lamentable insignificance of the American women appears. . . .''[16] James S. Buckingham, too, was impressed with the apathy and indifference in American women's society. He did not find the ''same passionate admiration'' of the things they engaged in, which was to be found in English ladies. ''Neither painting, sculpture, poetry, nor music; neither the higher topics of intellectual conversation, nor the higher beauties of the belles lettres, seem to move them from the general apathy and indifference, or coldness of temperament, which is their most remarkable defect. . . .''[17]

Reich was impressed with the shallowness of American women, and remarked that many of the earlier travelers in America had been deceived by it. Particularly he mentions the brothers Goncourt (1867) who saw, in American men and women, a people destined to become the conquerors of the world. They were misled, he believed, by the ''dash and verve'' of American

[14] *New Travels*, 263 and 142.
[15] *Op. cit.*, 420–4, 428.
[16] Trollope: *Domestic Manners of the Americans* (1832), 230.
[17] Quoted by Nevins: *op. cit.*, 326.

women. The succeeding years had not made good their prophecy. Reich's criticism of American women is linked up with
their education, which, he believed, had accomplished little:

"In spite of the most extraordinary measures and institutes
for the development of the intellectual or artistic faculties of
women in America; in spite of numberless colleges, universities,
'female academies,' libraries, societies, debating clubs, papers,
magazines, and—isms; woman has in America done none of those
remarkable deeds of a literary, scientific or artistic character
for which the Somervilles, Fawcetts, Brontës, George Eliots,
Madame de Staëls, George Sands, Madame Jules Adams, etc.,
etc., are famous in Europe. There are over twelve million pianos
in American houses, used mostly by women; yet there is not a
single American pianiste of even the third order. There are
thousands of schools for American women; yet there is not a
single American woman of note as a scholar. Amongst singers,
indeed, there have been a few American women whose voices were
striking, sensational and technically remarkable. But of voices
soulful, endowed with that mysterious *timbre* that alone gives
fascination to a voice, there has never been a case. The voices
of American women are like themselves: stunners. They bring
about what the French call *des effets à coups de pistolet*. Music
there is little in them."[18]

Harriett Martineau observed in *Society in America* that, "if
a test of civilization be sought, none can be so sure as the condition of that half of society over which the other half has
power. . . . Tried by this test, the American civilization appears
to be of a lower order than might have been expected from some
other symptoms of its social state. The Americans have, in the
treatment of women, fallen below, not only their democratic
principles, but the practice of some parts of the Old World."
Especially was Miss Martineau shocked to see the "unconscious-
ness of both parties as to the injuries suffered by women"; and
she held this to be sufficient proof of the "low degree of civilization . . . at which they rest." In spite of the confinement of
her intellect, the harm to her morals, the encouragement of her
weakness, and the punishment of her health, "she is told that her
lot is cast in the paradise of women"; and there is more boasting
here as to chivalrous treatment than anywhere else in the world.

[18] Reich: *Woman through the Ages*, II, 253-5.

The advantages of women were, however, according to Martineau's observations, chiefly material, external and superficial:

". . . She has the best place in stage-coaches: when there are not chairs enough for everybody, the gentlemen stand: she hears oratorical flourishes on public occasions about wives and home, and apostrophes to woman: her husband's hair stands on end at the idea of her working, and he toils to indulge her with money: she has liberty to get her brain turned by religious excitements, that her attention may be diverted from morals, politics, and philosophy; and, especially, her morals are guarded by the strictest observance of propriety in her presence. In short, indulgence is given her as a substitute for justice. Her case differs from that of the slave, as to the principle, just as far as this; that the indulgence is large and universal, instead of petty and capricious. In both cases, justice is denied on no better plea than the right of the strongest."[19]

As to her labor, "Wifely and motherly occupations may be called the sole business of women there. If she has not that she has nothing."[20] Many are, of course, unfit to make homes and these "shirk some of their labours and cares, by taking refuge in boarding houses." Though she deplored the boarding-houses, she admitted the servant shortage as a real factor in encouraging it. For leisure occupations she found American ladies chiefly concerned in charities, "doing good or harm" as the case might be; attending "preachings and other religious meetings"; and in "paying visits, for religious purposes, to the poor and sorrowful." "All American ladies," she found, "are more or less literary: and some are so to excellent purpose." But though readers and linguists were plentiful, "thinkers" were rare. Most of the learning she encountered, she held was not "of much use to them, except as a harmless exercise." "More intellectual activity, more general power" was found among those who gave little time to books than those who were "distinguished as being literary." Good artists were entirely lacking. Their attainments in natural, moral, and intellectual

[19] *Op. cit.*, II, 226–7.

[20] Hall, in his *Travels in North America* (1827–1828), Vol. II, 153 *ff.*, noted that men and women mingled little in social functions and that there was a tendency "to give to the men and the women of America such different classes of occupations, that they seldom act together. . . ."

philosophy, though studied almost universally in female seminaries, she thought did not even merit discussion.[21]

Chief among the causes of woman's low position, though a
change was beginning to take place, she believed was the "chivalrous taste" which made it so "difficult" if not "impossible for
women to earn their bread. Where it is a boast that women do
not labour, the encouragement and rewards of labour are not
provided. It is so in America. In some parts, there are now
so many women dependent on their own exertions for a maintenance, that the evil will give way before the force of circumstances. In the meantime, the lot of poor women is sad. Before
the opening of factories, there were but three resources; teaching,
needle-work, and keeping boarding-houses or hotels. Now, there
are the mills; and women are employed in printing-offices; as
compositors, as well as folders and stitchers.

"For women who shrink from the lot of the needle-woman—
almost equally dreadful, from the fashionable milliner down to
the humble stocking-darner—for those who shrink through pride,
or fear of sickness, poverty, or temptation, there is little resource
but pretension to teach."

There was, then, nothing in the United States to indicate that
the principles of the Declaration of Independence had any significance for the females of the race. It was truly a primitive
society she witnessed in the "families of many settlers" where
there was always "plenty to eat and drink" but "no servants"
and so much work as to make an education of little use had it
been attained. Nothing more could be expected till families
were able to provide more than the necessities of life. Even in
the wealthier sections, society, so far as women were concerned,
had not passed beyond the transition stage between primitive
life and that of civilization, if we understand by the latter, a
state in which society takes a critical interest in, and passes
critical judgments on, its conditions. Martineau declared "all
women should inform themselves of the condition of their sex,
and of their own position" and expressed a belief that "the
noblest of them will, sooner or later, put forth a moral power
which shall prostrate cant, and burst asunder the bonds . . . of
feudal prejudices and usages."[22] The chief positive evidences

[21] Martineau: *op. cit.*, II, 245–59.
[22] *Ibid.*, II, 219–22, 259.

of the "emergence" of women in the United States were the "greater freedom of divorce," the tendency to make marriage more and more a reciprocal relation, and to make the husband less and less the owner of his wife.

Bodichon, a leader of the English educational movement, was, however, more hopeful for the future of American women, for "the men are not so dead set against the rights of women as in the old country." She had been assured by "men of position and reliable sources of information" that when a majority of women in any state "shall claim the suffrage, it will be granted them." She noted that the education of women was gradually changing; a real interest was being taken in it. The opening of seminaries, attendance on public lectures, and the numerous publications for ladies, she believed would assist in the change; and the more liberal attitude of men in a country where "evils do not go on forever dragging their slow length as in England," would abet in the process.[23]

No writer of the nineteenth century succeeded more ably in his efforts to interpret social and political life in America than did de Tocqueville. In his work (1840) there is a breadth and thoroughness of view, a lack of bitterness in criticism, a combination of information and judgment, that convinces the reader that he understood American life. The position of women here he saw clearly.

Of the young lady he says, before she "arrives at the age of marriage, her emancipation from maternal control begins: she has scarcely ceased to be a child, when she already thinks for herself, speaks with freedom, and acts on her own impulse. The great scene of the world is constantly open to her view; far from seeking concealment, it is every day disclosed to her more completely, and she is taught to survey it with a firm and calm gaze. Thus the vices and dangers of society are early revealed to her; as she sees them clearly, she views them without illusions, and braves them without fear; for she is full of reliance on her own strength, and her reliance seems to be shared by all who are about her.

"An American girl scarcely ever displays that virginal bloom in the midst of young desires, or that innocent and ingenuous grace which usually attend the European woman in the transi-

[23] *Women and Work*, 20.

tion from girlhood to youth. It is rarely that an American woman at any age displays childish timidity or ignorance. Like the young women of Europe, she seeks to please, but she knows precisely the cost of pleasing. If she does not abandon herself to evil, at least she knows that it exists; and she is remarkable rather for purity of manners than for chastity of mind.

"I have been frequently surprised, and almost frightened, at the singular address and happy boldness with which young women in America contrive to manage their thoughts and their language, amid all the difficulties of stimulating conversation; a philosopher would have stumbled at every step along the narrow path which they trod without accidents and without effort. It is easy indeed to perceive that, even amid the independence of early youth, an American woman is always mistress of herself; she indulges in all permitted pleasures, without yielding herself up to any of them; and her reason never allows the reins of self-guidance to drop, though it often seems to hold them loosely."[24]

As to the moral education of the daughter, he asserted that "believing . . . they had little chance of repressing in woman the most vehement passions of the human heart, they held that the surer way was to teach her the art of combating those passions for herself. As they could not prevent her virtue from being exposed to frequent danger, they determined that she should know how best to defend it; and more reliance was placed on the free vigour of her will, than on safeguards which have been shaken or overthrown. Instead then of inculcating mistrust of herself, they constantly seek to enhance her confidence in her own strength of character. As it is neither possible nor desirable to keep a young woman in perpetual and complete ignorance, they hasten to give her a precocious knowledge on all subjects. Far from hiding the corruptions of the world from her, they prefer that she should see them at once and train herself to shun them; and they hold it of more importance to protect her conduct, than to be over-scrupulous of her innocence."[25]

He depicted faithfully the life of the pioneer woman, whose "whole physiognomy bears marks of a degree of religious resignation, a deep quiet of all the passions, and some sort of natural

24 *Democracy in America*, II, 209.
25 *Ibid.*, II, 210–11.

and tranquil firmness, ready to meet all the ills of life, without fearing and without braving them.'' With her ''true children of the wilderness'' clustered, nay crowded, around her, in the one room house, he could still detect ''a lingering taste for dress'' in her apparel and a certain superiority to her condition.

The position of married women formed quite a contrast with that of their unmarried sisters. ''In America the independence of women is irrevocably lost in the bonds of matrimony: if an unmarried woman is less constrained there than elsewhere, a wife is subjected to stricter obligations. The former makes her father's house an abode of freedom and pleasure; the latter lives in the house of her husband as if it were a cloister.''[26] As to the American interpretation of ''democratic equality . . . between the sexes,'' he said: ''They admit that as nature has appointed such wide differences between the physical and moral constitutions of man and woman, her manifest design was to give a distinct employment to their various faculties; and they hold that improvement does not consist in making beings so dissimilar do pretty nearly the same things, but in getting each of them to fulfil their respective tasks in the best possible manner. Americans have applied to the sexes the great principle of political economy which governs the manufactures of our age, by carefully dividing the duties of man from those of woman, in order that the great work of society may be the better carried on.

''In no country has such constant care been taken as in America to trace two clearly distinct lines of action for the two sexes, and to make them keep pace one with the other, but in two pathways which are always different. American women never manage the outward concerns of the family, or conduct a business, or take a part in political life; nor are they, on the other hand, ever compelled to perform the rough labor of the fields, or to make any of those laborious exertions which demand the exertion of physical strength. No families are so poor as to form an exception to this rule. If on the one hand an American woman cannot escape from the quiet circle of domestic employments, on the other hand she is never forced to go beyond it. . . .

[26] *Ibid.*, II, 212.

"Nor have the Americans ever supposed that one consequence of democratic principles is the subversion of marital power, or the confusion of the natural authorities in families. They hold that every association must have a head in order to accomplish its object, and that the natural head of the conjugal association is man. They do not therefore deny him the right of directing his partner; and they maintain, that in the smaller association of husband and wife, as well as in the great social community, the object of democracy is to regulate and legalize the powers which are necessary, not to subvert all power.

"This opinion is not peculiar to one sex, and contested by the other: I never observed that the women of America consider conjugal authority as a fortunate usurpation of their rights, nor that they thought themselves degraded by submitting to it. It appeared to me, on the contrary, that they attach a sort of pride to the voluntary surrender of their own will, and make it their boast to bend themselves to the yoke, not to shake it off. Such at least is the feeling expressed by the most virtuous of their sex; the others are silent; and in the United States it is not the practice for a guilty wife to clamour for the rights of woman, while she is trampling on her holiest duties."[27]

By the close of the century the situation was changing decidedly. Due to liberal as well as professional education, due to increased opportunity for work, due to freedom from earlier property disabilities, and certain few, though definite, gains as to suffrage, women, both married and single, were better able to be themselves. A previously unknown equality of husband and wife had begun to prevail. Day declared, in his *Life and Society in America*, that married women had equal or greater freedom than the unmarried; and Dugard, too, asserted that the married woman lost none of her independence.[28]

Particularly oppressive were the laws relative to property holding by married women. A contributor to the *Southern Ladies' Book*, in 1840, pointed to the difficulty of making changes, and regretted that though our ancestors, when they came to America, had abolished "the very unnatural law of primogeniture," they had left the "remnants of barbarism" in "that law

[27] *Ibid.*, II, 224–6.
[28] Day's work was published in London, 1880; Dugard's *La Société Américaine* appeared in Paris, 1896.

which deprives married women of all right to their own personal property'' by the simple act of marriage.[29]   A single woman, under English law, was far more fortunate; though she could not hold office in church or state, unless one except the sovereign, she was allowed to vote on parish questions and for parish officers, if duly qualified as a holder of a specified amount of property.   She could secure, hold, and dispose of property the same as any man, was entitled to the protection of the law, and had to pay the same taxes.   In general, the laws in the United States provided that the husband be entitled, at marriage, to the goods and chattels of the wife, the rents and profits from all her holdings; in return he was liable to settle her debts, and perform whatever she contracted.

Dall[30] summarized the details as follows:

''1. If the wife have an inheritance in land, he takes the rents and profits during their joint lives.   He may sue in his own name for an injury to the profits of the land; but, if the husband himself chooses to commit waste, the wife has no redress at common law.

''2. If the wife, at the time of her marriage, hath an estate for her life, the husband becomes seized of such an estate, and is entitled to the profits during marriage.

''3. The husband also becomes possessed of the chattels real of the wife; and the law gives him power, *without her consent*, to sell, assign, mortgage, or otherwise dispose of, the same as he pleases.   Such chattels real are liable to be sold on execution for his debts.   If he survive his wife, the law gives him her chattels real by survivorship.

''4. If debts are due to the wife before marriage, and are recovered by the husband afterward, the money becomes, in most cases, absolutely his own.

''On the other hand, the husband is—

''1st, Obliged to provide for his wife out of his fortune, or her own that he has taken into custody, of what the court calls 'necessaries'—these again, of course, to be dependent on the *'man's notion'*! and,—

29 *Op. cit.*, II, 363–4; also a discussion of the question Ought A Married Woman Hold Property? [*Godey's Lady's Book*, Dec. 1852, 542 *ff.*]; Cook: The Law's Partiality to the Married Woman [*At. Mo.*, LVIII, 311–13].

30 *College, Market and the Court*, 344–6.

"2d, Becomes liable for her frauds and torts during coverture—the law understanding, as well as a merchant, that it is useless to 'sue a broken bench!'

"The *indulgence* of the law toward the wife, we are then told, is founded on the idea of force exercised by the husband; a presumption only, which may be repelled. What this indulgence is, we may well be puzzled to guess, unless the phrase indicates that she is not to be prosecuted for theft, where *both* are guilty; and yet, if the presumption that he compelled her to steal be *repelled*, she may be prosecuted, and found guilty.

"A wife cannot devise her lands by will; nor can she make a testament of chattels, except it be of those which she holds *en autre droit*, without the license of her husband. It is not strictly a will, then, only an appointment, which the husband is bound to allow.

"The laws are essentially the same in Pennsylvania, Virginia, North Carolina, South Carolina, Kentucky, and New York; in the latter State, of course, only as applicable to marriages contracted before the passage of the new bill. It is the same in all the States, with one or two Western exceptions; because the passage of a new law never annuls *pre-existing* contracts. In consequence, practice becomes contradictory and intricate; and most lawyers not only *feel*, but *show*, a great dislike to new laws on that account."

Pierson, in a recent discussion of property rights of married women in Pennsylvania, called attention to the "well defined institutional and historical basis" of the law which fixes the rights of married women. "Marriage, as an institution," he stated, "seems to have passed through three stages: first, the physical; second, the legal; and third, the personal or moral stage." Under the first, "woman was practically a slave, the purchase of her master. Mutual rights were unknown. The rights were with the strong—the man. The duties were with the weak—the woman." In spite of increasing "ceremony in selecting the wife, . . ." recognition of the husband's supremacy continued. "In the second stage, permanence was secured by assigning to the husband a property right in his wife. He continued his control over his wife's person and took dominion of her property. In the third stage," the present, "the relation approximates that of two individuals on a basis of equality.''[31] Judged on the basis of this question alone, it appears that society in the United States, in the past seventy-five years, has been slowly sloughing off the vestigial traits of primitive and barbarian peoples.

The early nineteenth century witnessed several efforts at the amelioration of laws affecting women, both single and married. In 1809, Connecticut gave married women the power to will property;[32] in 1845, an act to protect the rights of married women provided that ''the interest of any married man in the real estate of his wife,'' held by her at marriage or acquired during marriage, ''shall not be liable to be taken by levy of execution against him,'' during her life or the lives of her children by the said marriage;[33] and, in 1846, it was enacted that, ''whenever any married woman shall hereafter earn wages by her own labour, payment may be made to her for the same, and when made shall be good and valid in law as though made to the husband of said married woman. . . .''[34]

In Massachusetts, progress was slow indeed. Up to 1776, said Bowditch, contrary to the English law, ''no woman, married or single, had . . . ever voted even in parish matters.'' A married woman's property became ''absolutely her husband's''; he could will it ''entirely away from her'' but if he left no will, a third of it reverted to her and two-thirds went to the children. If without children, a half came back to the wife and the other half went to his relations. Not until 1787 was a woman, whose husband had left her, able ''to convey her own real estate'' and then only by the authorization of the Supreme Court.[35] In 1833, married women were empowered to receive payments, with the Supreme Court's approval, in case the husband had absented

[31] *University of Pennsylvania, Public Lectures* (1915–1916), 340–1.

[32] *Laws of Conn.*, 1809; *Statutes of Conn.*, 1821, Tit. 31, Ch. 1, 145.

[33] *Laws of Conn.*, June 10, 1845, 36.

[34] *Ibid.*, June 6, 1846, 28–9; other laws relating to her property rights were passed April 14, 1881 [*Ibid.*, 1881, 93], and Mch. 9, 1882 [*Ibid.*, 1882, 122]; by law of 1886, her deeds were to be valid without signature of her husband, though signed in his presence [*Ibid.*, 1886, 599–600]; see also the law concerning women as trustees, guardians and executrices [*Ibid.*, 1882, 152–3].

[35] *Laws of Mass.*, 1787, Ch. 32. Barnes held, contrary to Bowditch, that women voted in Massachusetts for nearly a hundred years prior to the Revolution.—*Women in Modern Society*, 174.

himself or abandoned her without "sufficient provision for her support."[36] Sixty-two years after the adoption of her constitution (1842) Massachusetts authorized women to make wills;[37] in 1845, married women were empowered to hold property separately and "to sue and be sued" on contracts made with reference to such property as if unmarried;[38] in 1846, they were "allowed to give a valid receipt for their own wages";[39] and, by law of 1874, they were put substantially on an equality with men so far as contracting, selling real estate, giving notes, making mortgages, suing and being sued, were concerned.[40] "Why has progress been so halting?" asked Bowditch. "Because men alone have had the ballot; men alone have had the making; expounding and executing of the laws. . . ."[41] We are, he declared, "far too civilized to harness our women" as some peasants still do abroad, "but not at all unwilling to imprison them if they do not quietly submit to our tyranny."[42]

Elsewhere, similar slow reform efforts were being translated into law. Mississippi gave married women control of their property as early as 1839.[43] Maine, Mississippi and Pennsylvania, between 1844 and 1849, made some modifications of the property laws affecting women, and these made excellent ammunition for use in the general agitation which was carried on from 1850 to 1860.[44] The California constitution (1849) recognized the right of married women to continue to hold as their separate property

---

36 *Ibid.*, 1833, 693.

37 *Ibid.*, 1842, Ch. 74.

38 *Ibid.*, 1845, Ch. 208.

39 *Ibid.*, 1846, Ch. 209.

40 *Ibid.*, 1874, Ch. 184; see the summary of Bowditch: *Taxation of Women in Mass.*, 14–16, wherein he shows that, in spite of the progress made, it was still possible for a husband to own his wife's clothes, though bought with money earned in part by her labor.

41 *Op. cit., loc. cit.*

42 *Ibid.*, 18–19.

43 Fish: *The Rise of the Common Man*, 271; also Schlesinger: *Polit. and Soc. Hist. of the U. S.*, 75.

44 Cook: Law's Partiality to Married Women [*At. Mo.*, LVIII, 311–13]; see also the *Revised Statutes of Maine*, 1857, Ch. 61, 397–9; *Laws of Mississippi*, 1846, Ch. 13, 152–5; *Laws of Pennsylvania*, 1848, No. 372, 536–7; also Catt and Shuler: *Suffrage and Politics*, 21; and Calhoun: *Soc. Hist. Am. Fam.*, II, 126–7.

such as they had held before marriage.[45]   Similar guarantees
were made to women by the constitution of Texas.[46]

On April 7, 1848, New York State passed a "Law to protect
Property of Married Women," which became an objective for the
women's rights agitators in other states. The text of the law is
given below.[47]   Its passage marked a turning point and must have
lent courage to the little group that called the convention the
same year, at Seneca Falls, where the declaration of women's
rights was published to the world.

Not alone did church, state and general social usage bind
woman to her limited activities of the home; many of the best
known and influential writers lent their voice to the strengthen-
ing of the chains of custom. Rousseau's traditional education for
Sophie need only be mentioned. Ruskin, in his *Letters and Advice to Young Girls and Young Ladies,* declared the duties of
women were to please people, feed them in dainty ways, clothe
them, keep them orderly and teach them.[48]   McIntosh, in *Woman
in America* (1850), declared: "There is a political inequality,
ordained in Paradise, when God said to the Woman, 'he shall
rule over thee' and which has ever existed, in every tribe, and
nation and people of earth's countless multitudes. Let those
who would destroy this inequality pause ere they attempt to

[45] *Statutes of California,* 1850, 33.

[46] Constitution, 1845, Art. 7, Sec. 19.

[47] "1. The real and personal property of any female who may hereafter
marry, and which she shall own at the time of marriage, and the rents issues
and profits thereof shall not be subject to the disposal of her husband, nor
be liable for his debts, and shall continue her sole and separate property, as
if she were a single female.

"2. The real and personal property, and the rents issues and profits
thereof of any female now married shall not be subject to the disposal of
her husband; but shall be her sole and separate property as if she were a
single female except so far as the same may be liable for the debts of her
husband heretofore contracted.

"3. It shall be lawful for any married female to receive, by gift, grant,
devise or bequest, from any person other than her husband and hold to her
sole and separate use, as if she were a single female, real and personal property, and the rents, issues and profits thereof, and the same shall not be
subject to the disposal of her husband, nor be liable for his debts.

"4. All contracts made between persons in contemplation of marriage
shall remain in full force after such marriage takes place."—*Laws of N. Y.,*
1848, 307–8.

[48] *Op. cit.,* 41–3.

abrogate a law which emanated from the all-perfect Mind. And
let no woman murmur at the lowliness of her lot."[49]

Even the Positivists who regarded it as essential that woman
should be educated equally with man, and that the old education
of adornment was a disgrace to woman's intellect, believed that
the family was so important—more important than the state—
that woman must always devote herself to it. "To keep the
family true, refined, affectionate," said Harrison, "is a grander
task than to govern the state; it is a task which needs the whole
energies, the entire life of woman. To mix up her sacred duty
with the coarser occupations of politics and trade is to unfit her
for it as completely as if a priest were to embark in the business
of money lender."[50]

As for their education, girls had been treated as a parasitic
class from early Colonial days. As the wealth of communities
and families increased, the education of accomplishments was
afforded. In spite of the efforts of the greatest leaders, only the
best of the seminaries arrived at a rational education; and college education, at the middle of the century, was still in its
infancy.

The new higher education could not gain much of a footing as
long as the old idea of woman's inferiority and her domestic
sphere continued to prevail. As one expressed it, in 1812:
"Born to a life of uniformity and dependence, what they have
occasion for is reason, sweetness, and sensibility; . . . were it
in your power to give them genius, it would be . . . useless . . .
and a dangerous present."[51] A contributor to the *American
Annals of Education* declared there was one virtue, "often overlooked, so self denying and humbling . . . too frequently neglected or despised . . . it is the spirit of submission. Real or
apparent subjection is the lot of woman, in the regular course
of Providence, and by the early appointment of her Creator. . . .
Let then our daughters, especially be taught from their childhood, cheerfully to submit their choice . . . in everything lawful
and prudent to that of the presiding power. In this lies the
great strength of female influence. . . ."[52] Coxe, in *Claims of*

49 Pp. 22–3.

50 Article by Harrison: The Emancipation of Women [*Fortnightly Review*, N.S. (1891), L, 437–52].

51 Sketches of the *History, Genius and Disposition of the Fair Sex*, 262–4.

52 *Am. Annals*, V, 415–17.

the Country on American Females (1842), also upheld the conception of women in "the maternal relation" and, at the most, would only extend her sphere to include the office of teacher.[53] It was through this channel that women must exercise public influence and not in other labors, or politics.[54] To this sentiment might be added the support of a great array of witnesses, but it is scarcely necessary.[55] Some comments on the education of ladies of the White House may, however, be added, as they depict the range of the prevailing idea of the education of girls.

Emily Donelson, mistress of the White House in the days of Jackson, "finished" her education at the "Old Academy, in Nashville." She was credited with "rare personal loveliness and superior intellect" and "no expense or care was spared to fit her for the high position she was destined to fill in Society."[56] Mrs. Andrew Jackson was favored by a knowledge of "all the accomplishments."[57] The daughter-in-law of Van Buren was "a lady of rare accomplishments, very modest, yet perfectly easy and graceful in her manners, and free and vivacious in her conversation" and had completed her education "superior to the generality of her sex at that day" at "Madame Grelaud's Seminary in Philadelphia."[58] So successful was it that she was able to bear "the fatigue of a three hours' levee with a patience and pleasantry which . . . [seemed] inexhaustible to last one through so severe a trial." Mrs. Tyler's education was completed at Chegary Institute, in New York City.[59] Mrs. Polk was educated at Salem, North Carolina. She was "highly cultivated, without being a literary woman"; and though she was "interested in all that related to her husband" and informed "herself fully in political affairs" she avoided discussing "a subject [politics] in relation to which her sex were expected to be entirely ignorant."[60] Mrs. Zachary Taylor was trained "with special care in

53 I, 36–7 and 42–3.

54 *Ibid.,* II, 6–8 and 24–5.

55 Compare Webster on the Influence of Woman [*Godey's Lady's Book,* Jan. 1852, 90]; Todd: *The Daughter at School,* 206–8; also Minnigerode: *Fabulous Forties,* 74–8.

56 Holloway: *Ladies of the White House,* 333.

57 *Ibid.,* 339.

58 *Ibid.,* 349–50.

59 *Ibid.,* 436.

60 *Ibid.,* 439, 440–1, and 461–2.

all the accomplishments of domestic duties'' and ''finished'' her schooling at a seminary in Philadelphia.[61] Harriet Lane, niece of Buchanan, was educated at Charlestown, Virginia, and later at a convent in Georgetown.[62] The most notable exception to the general rule was Mrs. Fillmore who, because of the ''reduced circumstances'' of her mother, after her father's death, prepared herself to be a teacher. She was, indeed, more than a reader; she was a student. Her daughter is credited with having left a ''celebrated select family school'' because she felt the ''necessity of an education, not merely of grace and ornament. . . .'' Her chronicles state she was ''uncommonly familiar with English literature,'' spoke French, knew Italian and some German; she was also skilled in drawing and music, and gave some attention to sculpture.[63]

Politically, women had no voice. Most of the colonies passed laws whereby women were barred from suffrage. Margaret Brent tried to gain the right to vote in Maryland, but failed.[64]

Jefferson, though a most thorough believer in democracy, said: ''Were our State a pure democracy, in which all the inhabitants should meet together to transact all their business, there would yet be excluded from their deliberations:

''1. Infants, until arrived at years of discretion;

''2. Women, who, to prevent depravation of morals, and ambiguity of issue, could not mix promiscuously in the public meetings of men;

''3. Slaves, from whom the unfortunate state of things with us takes away the rights of will and of property.''[65]

New Jersey was an exception among the states. Her constitution of July 2, 1776, gave the voting privilege to ''all inhabitants of full age who are worth fifty pounds proclamation money.'' Few women took advantage of this freedom but in some closely contested elections they attempted to vote and no law was found to stop them. Finally, to stop women's voting the legislature took action in 1807.[66]

61 *Ibid.*, 468–9, and 485.

62 *Ibid.*, 537–9.

63 *Ibid.*, 495–517.

64 *Harper's New Mo. Mag.* (1898), XCVII, 229 and 230; *William and Mary Coll. Quarterly*, VI, Ser. 2, 164; and *Archives of Md.*, I, 215.

65 Quoted by Martineau: *Society in America*, I, 148 *ff.*

66 Porter: *Suffrage in the United States*, 136.

It was the too agile minds of legislators, who readily admitted women as equal to men on one occasion and denied them, just as readily, on another, which Alice D. Miller satirized in the following dialogue:

"Father, what is a Legislature?
"A representative body elected by the people of the state.
"Are women people?
"No, my son, criminals, lunatics and women are not people.
"Do legislators legislate for nothing?
"Oh, no; they are paid a salary.
"By whom?
"By the people.
"Are women people?
"Of course, my son, just as much as men are."[67]

Considering the foregoing statements concerning the place of women in society, it is not strange that such a man as Doctor Bushnell admitted, in his discussion of woman suffrage, that, "If I were a woman, in the present lot of women, I think I should certainly wish to be a man, and that any change giving but a semblance of a chance that way I should hail with delight and accept with eagerness. The wages allowed their industry are so unequal; their employments so restricted; their subjection, so often, when married, to an overbearing tyrant will they have no counter-force to resist; the crime it is for them to be heart-broken, and publish their woes by the sad look of their silence; and, what is worst and saddest of all, the worse than broker's corner wherein all unmarried women are penned by restrictions they cannot escape—unable to work, because it will humble their position; unable to venture on great operations in trade, because a woman cannot get the necessary credit; subject to indignities and much laughter when they undertake a profession; wanting marriage as the proper woman's place, with a conscious ability to fill it, and with no ambition save to be the ornament and cherished love of a worthy and true husband, yet chained fast under bonds of delicacy which well-nigh forbid so much as the being approachable by a man. When, I say, these things are duly considered as pertainings of a woman's lot, we might almost justify

[67] *Are Women People?* by Alice D. Miller, copyright, 1915, by George H. Doran Company.

them in a riot against natural sexhood itself, if there were anything to be gained by it.'[68]

This much he admitted, though he denounced the suffrage movement as a "reform against nature."

Livermore, in 1883, quoted what she believed a fitting summary of the conditions woman had endured—the conditions against which she rebelled in a supreme effort to find that justice which knows no sex: " 'In marriage she has been a serf; as a mother she has been robbed of her children; in public instruction she has been ignored; in labor she has been a menial, and then inadequately compensated; civilly she has been a minor, and politically she has had no existence. She has been the equal of man only when punishment, and the payment of taxes, were in question.' ''[69]

In their emancipation from these disabilities, women owe much to the movement for equal education which developed slowly from 1800 to 1850; and, thereafter, found its completest realization in the best coeducational colleges and universities. Though women's colleges contributed much to the independence of woman, it must be admitted that by coeducation, both in secondary and higher institutions, a greater step was taken to place her on a plane of absolute equality with man.[70]

III. The Revolt

The suffrage movement began as a reaction against the narrowness of woman's position. Wollstonecraft bewailed the lot of those who "thus waste life away, the prey of discontent, who might have practiced as physicians, regulated a farm, managed a shop, and stood erect, supported by their own industry, instead of hanging their heads surcharged with the dew of sensibility.'"[71] She struck the keynote of the whole movement. Notwithstanding the numerous forms in which the new demands of woman have been made, in all there is found the thread of discontent with the old limited functions mixed with the positive demand for the privilege of working in all fields of human in-

[68] Review in The Nation, VIII, 497.

[69] What Shall We Do with Our Daughters? 9–10.

[70] Grant and Hodgson: The Case for Coeducation, 164–5; Bryce: Am. Commonwealth, II, 732 ff.; and the R. C. E. (1903), I, 1048.

[71] As quoted by Hutchins, who sets forth well the conflict between the new and the old in Conflicting Ideals, 15–16.

terest.[72] Woman was to come out of the shadow of that legal *coverture,* by virtue of which she had been subjected to husband and home and forced to lose her identity in him. As the ''Lawe's Resolution of Woman's Rights'' (1632) explained:

''. . . In this consolidation which we call wedlock is a locking together. It is true, that man and wife are one person; but understand in what manner. When a small brooke or little river incorporateth with Rhodanus, Humber, or the Thames, the poore rivulet looseth her name; it is carried and recarried with the new associate; it beareth no sway; it possesseth nothing during coverture. A woman, as soon as she is married, is called *covert;* in Latine, *nupta*—that is, 'veiled'; as it were, clouded and over-shadowed: she hath lost her streame. I may more truly, farre away, say to a married woman, her new self is her superior; her companion, her master. . . . Eve, because she had helped to seduce her husband, had inflicted upon her a special bane. See here the reason of that which I touched before—that women have no voice in Parliament. They make no laws, they consent to none, they abrogate none. All of them are understood either married or to be married, and their desires are to their husbands. I know no remedy, that some women can shift it well enough. The common lawe here shaketh hand with divinitye.''[73]

Dissatisfaction with these limitations of sphere is suggested by a story of the early suffrage movement. ''In a London omnibus some men were talking about the nerve and skill of William Tell in shooting an apple off his son's head. To vex a lady who was listening, and who was a well known suffragette, one of them said: 'That was Mr. Tell. But what did his wife amount to? Why doesn't history mention her?' 'I'll undertake to answer that,' said the lady: 'She sat up half the night to patch the boy's pants so he might be decent to go out.' ''

There was a decided revolt against the idea that women should live only to marry. Gail Hamilton wrote, in 1865: ''They inhale, they imbibe, they are steeped in the idea that the great business of their life is marriage, and if they fail to secure that they will become utterly bankrupt and pitiable. Naturally this idea becomes their ruling passion; all their Course is bent to its guid-

[72] See p. 2.

[73] Quoted in Dall: *College, Market and the Court,* 288–9; also 77; compare Channing: *Review of Hist. of Woman Suffrage,* 15.

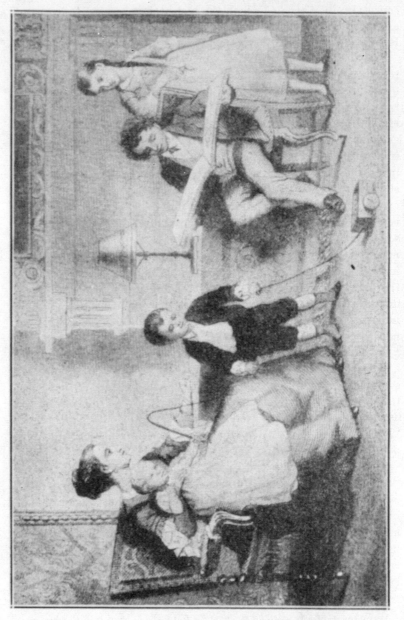

WOMAN AS QUEEN OF THE FAMILY (1869)

ance.''[74] In "Homes," Stetson poked fun at this single objective of woman's life:

> "And are we not the woman's perfect world,
> "Prescribed by nature and ordained of God,
> "Beyond which she can have no right desires,
> "No need for service other than in homes?
> "For doth she not bring up her young therein?
> "And is not rearing young the end of life?"[75]

Women were urged to find and assert themselves, be their own guides, and above all to be women. Margaret Fuller, in *The Great Lawsuit*, advised: "The time is come when Euridice is to call for an Orpheus . . . I would have woman lay aside all thought, such as she habitually cherishes, of being taught and led by men. I would have her, like the Indian girl, dedicate herself to the Sun, the Sun of Truth, and go nowhere if his beams did not make clear the path. I would have her free from compromise, from complaisance, from helplessness, because I would have her good enough and strong enough to love one and all beings, from the fullness, not the poverty of being."[76] Hamilton similarly urged the need of independence and self-respect. In one of her letters, she replied to her sister: "You say, 'if we females' . . . Hannah Augusta Dodge, never let me hear you call yourself a female; never call me a female. Would you rank yourself with the brutes? *Are* you a female? So is a cow—so is a hog. Do not degrade yourself. Stand up in all the glory of your birthright. Call yourself a woman! Be a woman!"[77]

The subservience and inferior position of women as mere housekeepers was held up to ridicule. Stetson, in "Wedded Bliss," contrasted the home talent and quietude of the female with the wide range and freedom of activity of the male:

> " 'O come and be my mate!' said the Lion to the Sheep;
> " 'My love for you is deep!
> " 'I slay, a Lion should,
> " 'But you are mild and good!'
> "Said the Sheep, 'I do no ill—
> " 'Could not, had I the will—
> " 'But I joy to see my mate pursue, devour, and kill.'

[74] *A New Atmosphere*, 5–6.
[75] From *In This Our World*, 7–8.
[76] *The Dial*, July, 1843, No. 13, 7; and 45.
[77] Hamilton: *Life in Letters*, I, 38.

"They wed, and cried, 'Ah, this is Love, my own!'
"And the Sheep browsed, the Lion prowled, alone.'"[78]

Charles Follen Adams suggested, in "Der Oak und der Vine,"
that the supremacy and strength of the male was, if not an actual
error, at least a 'little joke':

"I don't vas preaching voman's righdts,
"Or anyding like dot;
"Und I likes to see all beoples
"Shust gondented mit dheir lot;
"Budt I vants to gondradict der shap
"Dot made dis leedle shoke,
" 'A voman vas der glinging vine,
"Und man der shturdy oak.'

"Berhaps, sometimes, dot may pe true,
"Budt den dimes oudt off nine,
"I find me oudt dot man himself
"Vas peen der clinging vine;
"Und vhen hees frendts dhey all vas gone,
"Und he vas shust 'tead proke,'
"Dot's vhen der voman shteps righdt in
"Und peen der shturdy oak.'"[79]

In *A Woman's Career*, Myrtle Reed recently commented on
the household slavery of women. The "eighty six per cent of
. . . women in this prosperous country" who "do their own
housework" do not do it "you may be sure, of their own
volition."[80]   With somewhat the same sentiment, but more
effectively, Stetson heaped ridicule upon the cookstove, "the
altar of the home," which seemed a last remaining symbol of
woman's former servitude.

"O the soap-vat is a common thing!
"The pickle-tub is low!
"The loom and wheel have lost their grace
"In falling from the dwelling-place
"To the mills where all may go!
"The bread-tray needeth not your love;
"The wash-tub wide doth roam;
"Even the oven free may rove;
"But bow ye down to the Holy Stove,
"The Altar of the Home!

[78] *In This Our World*, 157 *f.*; see also the poem, "Nature's Answer," 4.
[79] Strothers: *Manual of Exercises in Elocution* (Lynchburg, Va., 1888.)
[80] Pp. 17–20.

MARGARET FULLER

"Speak not to us of a fairer faith,
"Of a lifetime free from pain.
"Our fathers always worshipped here,
"Our mothers served this altar drear,
"And still we serve amain.
"Our earliest dreams around it cling,
"Bright hopes that childhood sees,
"And memory leaves a vista wide
"Where Mother's Doughnuts rank beside
"The thought of Mother's Knees."[81]

In the minds of many men—and women too—there have been numerous questions, either real or professed, as to just what it is that modern women want. Is it "latch keys, that they may be free to be out after dark like their brothers; is it freedom from marriage; is it higher education; equal wages; or merely freedom from the necessity of runing households?"[82] Somewhere, in the development of present civilization out of the dim vistas of the past, women, according to such authorities as Bachofen[83] and Morgan,[84] lost the freedom and prominence they once had. Accepting this view, one might regard the recent revolt as an effort to regain what was theirs. From another point of view it may be simply regarded as the natural effort of human beings—with substantially the same capacities as men—to find that freedom wherein they may be unrestricted in their development. Given the torch of learning, women were enabled to look more critically into the nature of that authority which, since the days of Aristotle, had averred that they had no faculty higher than that of the child or the slave; that in them there was only an "obeying" or "submitting" principle, while in man there resided a "directing" and "commanding" one. The factors of economic change, coupled with those of educational nature, in the eighteenth and nineteenth centuries, were instrumental in producing this new insight.

As to the demands of women, there was, in reality, a great deal of plain speaking; there was, in fact, little reason for misunderstanding, except as tradition blinded the eyes and muffled the ears so that new ideas could not be readily apprehended and

[81] "The Holy Stove," from *In This Our World*, 160.
[82] Bisland: The Cry of Women [*N. A. R.* (1894), CLVIII, 757–8].
[83] *Das Mutterrecht*, I–XCII.
[84] *Ancient Society*, 55 and 67.

assimilated. Emancipationists in the United States continued to hammer on the same point made by Mary Wollstonecraft, that woman could do, and ought to do, many things that were then done only by men. Openness of mind and ability to read English were the only prerequisites to an understanding of woman's demands. Angelina Grimké stated them briefly, yet comprehensively:

"Whatever it is morally right for a man to do, it is morally right for a woman to do. I recognize no rights but *human* rights. I know nothing of men's rights and women's rights; for in Christ Jesus there is neither male nor female. Sure I am that woman is not to be, as she has been, a mere *second-hand agent* in the regeneration of a fallen world, but the acknowledged co-equal and co-worker with man in this glorious work."[85]

Lucretia Mott, sometimes called the "Soul of the woman suffrage movement," was the product of that policy of equality, inaugurated by Fox, in order that women "may be useful in their generation and the Creation."[86] She usually spoke extemporaneously and little remains to show exactly what she said. The following, however, an answer to an opponent who denied and ridiculed the movement for political rights and an extended sphere of activities, expressed her fundamental view, that it was a desire for freedom to be a woman, and not to be like man, that was the motivating idea.

"Why should not woman seek to be a Reformer? If she is to fear to exercise her reason and her noblest powers, lest she should be thought to 'attempt to act the man,' and not to 'acknowledge his supremacy;' if she is to be satisfied with the narrow sphere assigned her by man, nor aspire to a higher, lest she should transcend the bounds of 'female delicacy,' then truly the prospect is mournful for woman. We would admit all the difference that our beneficent Creator has made in the relation of man and woman, nor would we seek to disturb this relation. But we deny that the present position of woman is her true *sphere of usefulness;* nor will she attain to this sphere, until the disabilities and disadvantages, religious, civil, and social, which impede her prog-

[85] Channing: *Review of the Hist. of Woman Suffrage* (Edited by Stanton, Anthony and Gage), 3.

[86] Compare also Work of Quakers for Woman's Emancipation [*The Nation* (Dec. 31, 1924), CIX, 729].

LUCRETIA MOTT

ress are removed. These restrictions have enervated her mind and paralysed her powers. . . . So far from her 'ambition leading her to attempt to act the man,' she needs all the encouragement she can receive by the removal of obstacles from her path, in order that she may become the 'True Woman.' As it is desirable that man should act a manly and generous part, not a *'mannish'* one, so let woman be urged to exercise a dignified and womanly, not a *'womanish'* bearing. Let her cultivate all graces and accomplishments proper to her sex, but let her not degenerate through these into an effeminacy in which she is satisfied to be the mere plaything and toy of society. . . . When it is asked, What does woman want more than she enjoys? Of what rights is she deprived? What privileges are withheld from her? I answer, She asks nothing as a *favour*, but as a RIGHT! She wants to be acknowledged as a *moral responsible being!* She is seeking not to be governed by laws in the making of which she had no voice! She is deprived of almost every right in *civil* society, and is a cipher, except in the right of presenting a petition. And in *religious* society . . . her exclusion from the ministry, her duties marked out for her by her equal brother-man, and her subjection to creeds, rules, and disciplines made for her by him are unworthy of her true dignity.'[87]

The demand for freedom of political activity was an extension of an early demand for a field of social usefulness. A generation earlier Willard, Beecher and others had urged that women should become teachers, because as such, their influence would extend through the home and the school, to the great benefit of society. This objective of the teaching profession had been gained. There was no reason, real reason, many thought, for drawing an arbitrary line. As Theodore Parker explained: "The domestic function of woman, as a housekeeper, wife and mother, does not exhaust her powers. Woman's function, like charity, begins at home; then, like charity, goes everywhere. To make one half of the human race consume all their energies in the function of housekeeper, wife and mother, is a monstrous waste of the most precious material that God ever made.'[88]

In her denunciation of the parasitism[89] of woman and her demand for the right to labor, Olive Schreiner described the changes

[87] Channing: *op. cit.*, 3–4.
[88] Parker: *Sermon on the Public Functions of Woman* (1853), 1.
[89] *Woman and Labor*, 69 *ff.*

that had come to pass as men and women advanced from the savage state. These changes explain the reason for woman's unrest. At first, both men and women labored; but, with the advancement of science and invention, men reduced labor, removed much of it from the home, leaving little there for her to do.[90] Even woman's labor in child-bearing has no longer great demand. The modern woman movement, then, is a result of woman's restlessness growing out of increasing unemployment. She demands that she have real work to do. "Give us labor and the training that fits for labor: we demand this, not for ourselves alone but for the race."[91]

It is recognized that it is impossible to return to ancient practice. We must go forward, not backward. "We do not demand that our old grindstones and hoes be returned to us, or that man should again betake himself entirely to his ancient province of war and the chase, leaving to us all domestic and civil labor. We do not even demand that society shall immediately so reconstruct itself that every woman may be again a child-bearer (deep and overmastering as lies the hunger for motherhood in every virile woman's heart!); neither do we demand that the children whom we bear shall again be put exclusively into our hands to train. This, we know, cannot be. The past material conditions of life have gone forever, no will of man can recall them, but *this* is our demand: We demand that, in that strange new world that is arising alike upon the men and the women, where nothing is as it was, and all things are assuming new shapes and relations, that in this new world we also shall have our share of honored and socially useful human toil, our full half of the labor of the Children of Woman. We demand nothing more than this, and we will take nothing less. *This is our* 'WOMAN'S RIGHT!' "[92]

The range of woman's activities is to be wide—as wide as man's—for the newly educated woman knows she has capacity as well as man. She will see how far this capacity may be developed. "For the present, *we take all labor for our province!* From the judge's seat to the legislator's chair; from the statesman's closet to the merchant's office; from the chemist's labora-

90 *Ibid.*, 64.
91 *Ibid.*, 27.
92 *Ibid.*, 64–5.

Abigail Adams

tory to the astronomer's tower, there is no post or form of toil
for which it is not our intention to attempt to fit ourselves; and
there is no closed door we do not intend to force open; and there
is no fruit in the garden of knowledge it-is not our determination
to eat. Acting in us, and through us, nature will mercilessly ex-
pose to us our deficiencies in the field of human toil and reveal
to us our powers."[93]

It was not until the decade of the forties that the suffrage
movement became crystallized. Colonial women had demanded
the right to vote in a few instances. Mrs. Adams had appealed
to her husband, in 1776, to "be more generous to them [the
ladies] than your ancestors;" had suggested the possibility of
ladies fomenting a revolution; and declared we "will not hold
ourselves bound by any laws in which we have no voice or representation."[94] But these views, if expressed seriously, were not
taken so. The Declaration of Independence had emphasized that
government must derive its "just powers from the consent of the
governed"; Franklin had stated that those "who have no voice
nor vote in the electing of representatives do not enjoy liberty,
but are absolutely enslaved to those who have votes and their
representatives"; and Madison had declared it "indispensable
that the mass of the citizens should not be without a voice in making the laws which they are to obey." But American statesmen
did not go so far as Condorcet, who stated explicitly that
"women, having the same qualities, have the same equal rights."
They did not go so far until they were pressed to do so. Thirty-
five years after the declaration of women's rights, Thomas W.
Palmer was ready to stand squarely in favor of their political
independence, maintaining that "the Right of women to personal representation through the ballot seems to me unassailable,
wherever the right of man is conceded and exercised. I can conceive of no possible abstract justification for the exclusion of
the one and the inclusion of the other."[95]

The nineteenth-century agitation which, in 1848, culminated
in a definite declaration and demands had begun as early as 1828.

[93] *Ibid.*, 172–3; see Schreiner: "The Woman Question" [*The Cosmopolitan* (1899), XXVIII, 45–54]; and Howe: *Reminiscences*, 372–8.

[94] *Letters* (Ed. by C. F. Adams), 75; *Familiar Letters* (1876), 149–50;
Wharton: *Colonial Days and Dames*, 129–30; and Brown: *Mercy Warren*,
238–45.

[95] *Speech of Thomas W. Palmer in the U. S. Senate*, Feb. 6, 1885, 9.

Preceding it there had been an unmistakable advancement of the conception of woman's education. Frances Wright, a Scotch girl, was the first to lecture publicly on political questions in the United States. Having come, at the age of twenty, and being filled with the beautiful ideal of freedom which she was told was here secured for all, imagine her surprise to find women still degraded by a bondage similar to that existing abroad. The justice of this inequality she challenged openly, and for that, and her radical ideas on theology and slavery, she was roundly condemned by press and pulpit, but continued "at the risk of her life."[96]

Lydia Maria Child, in 1832, published a *History of Women;* in 1833, Lucretia Mott brought the capacities of women to public attention by speaking with force and cogency at the first convention of the American Anti-Slavery Society, held at Philadelphia; and three years later, Ernestine L. Rose, a Polish Jewess, lectured in the larger cities on the "Science of Government," boldly advocating suffrage for women.[97] Abby Kelly, a gentle Quakeress from Lynn, Massachusetts, had risen to calm a tumultous crowd, declaring it is the " 'still small voice within' which may not be withstood, that bids me open my mouth for the dumb; that bids me plead the cause of God's perishing poor; aye! God's poor." These and many others had proved, or were just ready to prove, woman's power on the public platform. The anti-slavery movement was participated in by numerous women. From an offensive against the slavery of the black man it was easy to turn to rescue their own sex from what was soon to be admitted, by the best minds of the country, to be the most ignominious servitude.

It was at this time (1845) that Judge Hurlbut of New York published his *Essays on Human Rights,* which he had begun as a refutation of the arguments advanced by others in favor of woman suffrage. Finding that he could overthrow all arguments he had presented against woman suffrage, he came forth in this publication as an advocate of equal suffrage. Such a voice com-

---

[96] Stanton, Anthony and Gage: *Hist. of Woman Suffrage,* I, 35 *f.*; Ferrall, in his *Ramble of Six Thousand Miles Through the United States* (Pp. 15 *f.*) referred to the powerful influence of Frances Wright on her American audiences.

[97] *History of Woman Suffrage,* I, 38.

ELIZABETH CADY STANTON

manded attention. In the meantime (1836), a bill had been introduced in the New York Legislature by Judge Hertell to relieve married women from odious property restrictions. The furtherance of this bill gave women a new opportunity to become acquainted with public affairs and, before the final passage in 1848, enabled them to understand better the conservative nature of politicians with whom they must deal to secure their freedom. It is said that while "exerting herself to strengthen their convictions" in favor of this property bill (1844–1846), Elizabeth Cady Stanton "resolved at no distant day to call a convention for a full and free discussion of woman's rights and wrongs."[98] In 1837, eight states were represented at a National Woman's Anti-Slavery Convention in New York City. This was the beginning of a united woman's effort to bring about a critical examination of the wrongs of the Negro. Three years later, Margaret Fuller published *Man Versus Woman or the Great Lawsuit,* wherein she set forth more forcefully and clearly than any one had before, in the United States, the servitude of women and the need for their complete emancipation.

It was in connection with anti-slavery societies that women began to agitate the question of their right to speak, vote, and serve on committees. This question divided the American Anti-Slavery Society, in 1840. In the same year, the question was brought before the World's Anti-Slavery Convention, held in London. The call had been sent out to all societies in many lands to send delegates. Several women—Lucretia Mott, Sarah Pugh, Abby Kimber, Elizabeth Neal, Mary Grew, Ann Phillips, Emily Winslow, and Abby Southwick—went as delegates from the United States but, after long discussion, were refused recognition by the convention, by a large majority. The reasons offered were chiefly traditional custom and that women had not really been included in the invitation. The effect of this exclusion was far reaching. The ladies sat through the convention; with them sat William Lloyd Garrison and Nathaniel P. Rogers who refused to participate in a convention which was so illogical as to harangue against white tyranny over black but did not recognize any wrong in the sex tyranny of male over female. The effect of exclusion was that women leaders were caused to see clearly the necessity of taking a definite stand on their own

[98] *Ibid.,* I, 38, 39.

behalf. It is said that as Elizabeth Cady Stanton and Lucretia Mott went from the convention "they agreed to hold a woman's rights convention on their return to America, as the men to whom they had just listened had manifested their great need of some education on that question."[99] This belief, as far as Elizabeth Cady Stanton was concerned, was confirmed by her experience when urging the passage of the married women's property bill in New York State. In 1848, shortly after the successful issue of the fight for the new bill, and possibly inspired by this success to take a new step, Mrs. Stanton and Mrs. Mott, who met again at Seneca Falls, took up the "propriety of holding a woman's rights convention," to which they had both been committed. The "Call," issued by Lucretia Mott, E. C. Stanton, Martha Wright and Mary Ann McClintock, who were neither "sour old maids," "childless women," nor "divorced wives," and published in the *Seneca County Courier*,[100] has been called by Susan B. Anthony "one of the most courageous acts on record."[101]

The convention, to be held on July nineteenth and twentieth, was to discuss the "social, civil, and religious condition and rights of woman." The "Declaration of Sentiments" which, it was finally agreed, should be presented to the convention, was an imitation of the Declaration of Independence; it asserted the belief that "all men and women are created equal"; continued with the enumeration of wrongs that now caused "them to demand the equal station to which they are entitled"; and expressed, finally, their determination to carry on the fight by agents, tracts, petitions to legislatures, pulpits and the press, and their hope that this first convention would be followed by others "embracing every part of the country." No campaign was ever launched more successfully; no plan more complete than that upon which the crusaders embarked. For nearly three quarters of a century, women's organizations continued to use the means here suggested to secure redress of the grievances named in the first manifesto of the rights of women.

The grievances listed were as follows:

"The history of mankind is a history of repeated injuries and usurpations on the part of man toward woman, having in direct

99 *Ibid.*, I, 61.
100 July 14, 1848.
101 Harper: *Life and Work of Susan B. Anthony*, III, 1265.

object the establishment of an absolute tyranny over her. To prove this, let facts be submitted to a candid world.

"He has never permitted her to exercise her inalienable right to the elective franchise.

"He has compelled her to submit to laws, in the formation of which she had no voice.

"He has withheld from her rights which are given to the most ignorant and degraded men—both natives and foreigners.

"Having deprived her of this first right of a citizen, the elective franchise, thereby leaving her without representation in the halls of legislation, he has oppressed her on all sides.

"He has made her, if married, in the eye of the law, civilly dead.

"He has taken from her all right in property, even to the wages she earns.

"He has made her, morally, an irresponsible being, as she can commit many crimes with impunity, provided they be done in the presence of her husband. In the covenant of marriage, she is compelled to promise obedience to her husband, he becoming, to all intents and purposes, her master—the law giving him power to deprive her of her liberty, and to administer chastisement.

"He has so framed the laws of divorce, as to what shall be the proper causes, and in case of separation, to whom the guardianship of the children shall be given, as to be wholly regardless of the happiness of women—the law, in all cases, going upon a false supposition of the supremacy of man, and giving all power into his hands.

"After depriving her of all rights as a married woman, if single, and the owner of property, he has taxed her to support a government which recognizes her only when her property can be made profitable to it.

"He has monopolized nearly all the profitable employments, and from those she is permitted to follow, she receives but a scanty remuneration. He closes against her all the avenues to wealth and distinction which he considers most honorable to himself. As a teacher of theology, medicine, or law, she is not known.

"He has denied her the facilities for obtaining a thorough education, all colleges being closed against her.

"He allows her in Church, as well as State, but a subordinate position, claiming Apostolic authority for her exclusion from the ministry, and, with some exceptions, from any public participation in the affairs of the Church.

"He has created a false public sentiment by giving to the world a different code of morals for men and women, by which moral delinquencies which exclude women from society, are not only tolerated, but deemed of little account in man.

"He has usurped the prerogative of Jehovah himself, claiming it as his right to assign for her a sphere of action, when that belongs to her conscience and to her God.

"He has endeavored, in every way that he could, to destroy her confidence in her own powers, to lessen her self-respect, and to make her willing to lead a dependent and abject life."[102]

The "Declaration" was adopted, except for slight modifications, as originally written. Thereafter, a series of resolutions were discussed and adopted, the substance of which follows: First, that laws conflicting with the true happiness of women are contrary to nature and "of no validity"; second, all laws preventing women from following the dictates of their own conscience, or which place woman on a plane inferior to man, are contrary to nature, and invalid; third, woman was created as man's equal and "the highest good of the race" demands she be so recognized; fourth, that women should be so enlightened about the laws under which they live as to no longer publish to the world that they are satisfied with their present status and have all the rights they want; fifth, since man, though he claims mental superiority, admits woman's moral equality with him, he should secure for her freedom of speaking and teaching in religious bodies; sixth, that there should no longer be a double standard of "virtue, delicacy and refinement of behavior"; seventh, that it ill becomes those who encourage or tolerate women in public circuses, theatricals and concerts to object to her on the public rostrum; eighth, that woman should enter the larger sphere for which endowed by her Creator, and cease to be satisfied with the narrow sphere, to which a "perverted application of the Scriptures" has condemned her; ninth, "that it is the duty of the women of this country to secure to themselves their sacred right to the elective franchise"; tenth, that equality of human rights

102 Stanton, Anthony and Gage: *History of Woman Suffrage*, I, 70–1.

springs from the identity of the race in capacities and responsibilities; eleventh, being invested with the same capacities and a consciousness of responsibilities "it is demonstrably the right and duty of woman, equally with man, to promote every righteous cause by every righteous means," by teaching, speaking, "both in private and in public," and writing. Any custom or authority to the contrary, new or old, is "self evident falsehood, and at war with mankind."[103] A final resolution discussed by Lucretia Mott, and adopted by the convention, declared "the success of the cause" depended on the efforts of men and women to overthrow the "monopoly of the pulpit" and to secure "to woman an equal participation with men in the various trades, professions and commerce."

The ninth resolution alone failed to secure unanimous endorsement, as some feared such a demand for the vote might defeat other more reasonable demands. Only by the ceaseless activity and advocacy of Mrs. Stanton and Frederick Douglass, who felt this was the key to success in all other demands, was it finally carried.

These resolutions had some of the anticipated results; public discussion was aroused and the adult population, men and women, were thereby educated; conventions were called shortly in Ohio, Indiana, Massachusetts, Pennsylvania and at many points in New York State. The bitter opposition which was called forth by such a clear statement of demands had, in itself, the result of steeling the nerves of women's rights advocates to greater efforts. At Rochester, a second convention was held August 2, 1848, to continue the deliberations begun at Seneca Falls. Here further attention was given to the inequalities of women in the business, religious, and professional world.

A further happy outcome, for the success of the women's cause, was that, after so definite a stand had been taken, men of leadership were compelled to take one side or the other of the question; and the woman's cause enlisted many of the best. Lucy Stone, the silvery-voiced orator of woman suffrage, has recounted a conversation between Wendell Phillips and Theodore Parker. The latter, hearing the former had been to the Woman's Rights Convention, said: "Wendell, don't make a fool of yourself." He replied: "Theodore, this is the greatest question of

[103] *Ibid.*, I, 72–3.

the age. You ought to understand it.'' As a result, Parker studied it, and soon published four sermons in favor of woman's rights, one of the most powerful being *The Public Functions of Woman*. Other powerful statements, by men whose influence was worth much, came from Phillips in his speech at the Worcester Convention; from Higginson, in *Woman and her Wishes;* from Mrs. Nichols, in *The Responsibilities of Woman;* from John Hooker, in *The Bible and Woman Suffrage;* from E. H. Heywood in *The Injustice and Impolicy of Ruling Woman without her Consent;* from T. Walker, in *The Legal Rights of Woman;* from W. I. Bowditch, in *Taxation of Women in Massachusetts;* from Daniel P. Livermore in *Woman Suffrage Defended by Irrefutable Arguments;* and from the Honorable George F. Hoar in his presentation of *Woman Suffrage; Essential to The True Republic*. Especially was it true that after the abolition of Negro slavery, thinking men could no longer find very satisfactory reasons for opposing the enfranchisement of women.

As noted, there was some opposition at Seneca Falls to the resolution demanding the right of suffrage. It is significant that the convention, called at Worcester, October 15 and 16, 1851, placed equal suffrage as its first objective, ''the cornerstone of this enterprise,'' though not undervaluing ''other methods.''[104] From that time onward, the fight was waged continuously, first in state associations, and later in national conventions as well. In 1869, the first state victory was won for equal suffrage, in Wyoming.[105] The next three were Colorado, Utah and Idaho.[106]

The dream of equal suffrage by federal amendment was encouraged by the events following the Civil War; and, after the successful adoption of the fourteenth and fifteenth amendments, which had secured the franchise for Negro men but denied it to all women, federal action appeared to be all the more justified. There must be a woman suffrage amendment to raise woman from her degraded political slavery. From this time on, women and men labored at the problem of emancipation, attacking it from the standpoint of full suffrage in additional states and also by federal amendment. But from the date of the first introduc-

---

104 *Woman's Rights Tracts*, No. 1, 1.

105 Catt and Shuler: *Woman Suffrage and Politics*, 74 *ff.*

106 Anthony: Summary of the Results of Fifty Years' Labor [*The Arena*, XVII, 901 *f.*].

tion of the proposed amendment, Jan. 10, 1878, it took forty years of agitation to secure its passage.[107] During this long drawn out process many, doubtless, came to feel, with the London Bobby, that it was time to "give women the vote and get on with the traffic." But the politicians were of a different mind and quite willing to sacrifice all semblance of principle to party advantage.[108] Senators Wadsworth and Moses were conspicuously unwilling to obey the mandate of their people. "What," said the suffrage leaders of New York State, "is a representative for if not to represent?"[109] While noticing the keen competition of the two parties, angling for such advantage as might be derived from the success of woman suffrage, it is pertinent to recall that the memory of the election of 1916 was still freshly in mind. None could fail to note that the hand that rocked the cradle had also rocked the political barque in that election; that the woman suffrage states, with the exception of Oregon and Illinois, had stood for Wilson; and that California, with her woman suffrage, had finally tipped the balance for the democratic candidate.

At length, after passage by the House (January 10, 1918), and after failure in the senate (October 1, 1918), and again, on reconsideration (February 10, 1919), the federal suffrage amendment was brought before the special session, called for May 19, 1919. On June 4, 1919, the vote was taken by the Senate, the result being favorable, sixty-six to thirty.[110] Ratification of the amendment was secured by the action of the thirty-sixth state, Tennessee. Thirty-five had ratified; eight had taken action, refusing ratification; and five, Vermont, Connecticut, Tennessee, Florida, and North Carolina, had taken none. The battle in Connecticut and Vermont was hopeless, since the governors refused to call special sessions. After a bitter fight, Tennessee ratified, the certificate was signed by the Governor, August 24, 1920, and the proclamation of the amendment's ratification was signed two days later.

IV. Antagonism to Woman Suffrage

Opposition to woman suffrage was at first far more common than agitation for it. After the first convention, the attack of

107 Catt and Shuler: *op. cit.*, 227 *ff.*; and 316 *ff.*
108 *Ibid.*, 322.
109 *Ibid.*, 334 *f.*
110 *Ibid.*, 341.

the opposition was sharpened and redoubled.   Truly, it may be said that the opposition to women in politics was based on the thesis that women should not, because of their tender nature, go into the rude world of affairs.   It was the old argument, regarding the inner and outer spheres, which was refurbished to do new service: just as in the old Greek comedy, wherein one character asked of another, "Where is your wife?" and, receiving the reply, "She has gone out," shouted, "Death and fury! What has she to do out?"

This elopement from their proper sphere seems first to have impressed most men and women.   The proposed woman's property bill in Massachusetts (1848) was reported adversely because it would "destroy their sensibility, weaken their dependence on man and thereby take away one of the loveliest of their charms." Senator John Ingalls, who indulged in a great deal of rhetoric, declared: "The doctrines of female suffrage and the equality of the sexes are undermining the foundation of our social structure."   Coxe criticized those women's rights agitators who had led some women to believe they had been "subjected to a rigorous and oppressive vassalage for near six thousand years"; and to "exhaust all their energies in furthering a cause . . . falsely deemed fraught with blessings to those whose rights are normally espoused."[111]   In Peoria, Illinois, about 1870, the women antisuffragists resolved "that woman's sphere of duty is distinct from man's and is well defined; and that, as going to the polls forms no part of it, we will strenuously oppose this movement as an invasion of our right not to do a man's work."[112]

Woman suffrage failed to enlist the hearty cooperation of many excellent women because it was thought to be too much an anti-man movement.   Thus Elizabeth Blackwell, though she felt some sympathy for, and would help the suffrage movement incidentally, could not work with it "heart and soul," could not "sympathize fully with an anti-man movement.   I have had too much kindness, aid and just recognition from men to make such an attitude of women otherwise than painful; and I think the true end of freedom may be gained better another way."[113]

[111] *Claims of the Country on American Females*, 15–16.

[112] *Godey's Lady's Book*, Sept., 1870, 278.

[113] Taken by permission from the Everyman's Library edition of Blackwell's *Pioneer Work For Women*, published by J. M. Dent & Sons, Ltd., London, and E. P. Dutton & Co., Inc., New York. P. 145.

Though some ministers took the side of woman suffrage, it was, at the beginning of the movement, more common for them to dissent, pointing to the alleged Biblical justification for woman's exclusion from public affairs. A book was published, as late as 1913, inscribed to anti-suffrage folks who had with wisdom and brave hearts opposed the terrible doctrine, striving to preserve the ideal woman, the gift of God. The argument presented was based on Biblical statements such as: "Thy desire shall be to thy husband and he shall rule over thee"; "For thy Maker is thy husband"; "For the woman which has a husband is bound by the law of her husband as long as he liveth"; "and the wife see that she reverence her husband"; and "wives, submit yourselves unto your husbands, as unto the Lord" for "I would have you know that the head of every man is Christ; and the head of the woman is the man. . . . For the man is not of the woman; but the woman of the man."[114] This was but an echo of the voice of the preachers who, in the "Pastoral Letter," spoke for the General Association of Massachusetts to their churches, in 1837. Therein, they invited "attention to the dangers which at present seem to threaten the female character with widespread and permanent injury." The proper "duties and influence of women are clearly stated in the New Testament" and are "unobtrusive and private. . . . When the mild, dependent, softening influence of woman upon the sternness of man's opinions is fully exercised, society feels the effects of it in a thousand forms. The power of woman is her dependence, flowing from the consciousness of that weakness which God has given for her protection, and which keeps her in those departments of life that form the character of individuals, and of the nation. There are social influences which females use in promoting piety and the great objects of Christian benevolence which we can not too highly commend.

"We appreciate the unostentatious prayers and efforts of woman in advancing the cause of religion at home and abroad; in Sabbath-schools; in leading religious inquirers to the pastors for instruction; and in all such associated effort as becomes the modesty of her sex; and earnestly hope that she may abound more and more in these labors of piety and love. But when she assumes the place and tone of man as a public reformer, our care and protection of her seem unnecessary; we put ourselves

[114] Quoted by Sams: *Shall Women Vote?* 15–17.

in self-defense against her; she yields the power which God has
given her for her protection, and her character becomes unnatural. If the vine, whose strength and beauty is to lean upon
the trellis-work, and half conceal its clusters, thinks to assume
the independence and the overshadowing nature of the elm, it
will not only cease to bear fruit, but fall in shame and dishonor
into the dust. We can not, therefore, but regret the mistaken
conduct of those who encourage females to bear an obtrusive
and ostentatious part in measures of reform, and countenance
any of that sex who so far forget themselves as to itinerate in the
character of public lecturers and teachers. We especially de-
plore the intimate acquaintance and promiscuous conversation
of females with regard to things which ought not to be named;
by which that modesty and delicacy which is the charm of
domestic life, and which constitutes the true influence of woman
in society, is consumed, and the way opened, as we apprehend,
for degeneracy and ruin.

"We say these things not to discourage proper influences
against sin, but to secure such reformation as we believe is Scrip-
tural, and will be permanent."[115]

In answer to this "Pastoral Letter," Whittier wrote a spirited
reply under the same title:

"A 'Pastoral Letter,' grave and dull—
"Alas! in hoofs and horns and features,
"How different is your Brookfield bull,
"From him who bellows from St. Peter's!
"Your pastoral rights and powers from harm,
"Think ye, can words alone preserve them?
"Your wiser fathers taught the arm
"And sword of temporal power to serve them."[116]

Mrs. Chapman's poem, "The Times That Try Men's Souls,"
signed by the "Lords of Creation," answered the clergy's attack
with ridicule:

"Confusion has seized us, and all things go wrong,
"The women have leaped from 'their spheres,'
"And, instead of fixed stars, shoot as comets along,
"And are setting the world by the ears!
"In courses erratic they're wheeling through space,
"In brainless confusion and meaningless chase.

115 Stanton, Anthony and Gage: *Hist. of Woman Suffrage*, I, 81–2.
116 *Ibid.*, I, 84.

"In vain do our knowing ones try to compute
"Their return to the orbit designed;
"They're glanced at a moment, then onward they shoot,
"And are neither 'to hold nor to bind';
"So freely they move in their chosen ellipse,
"The 'Lords of Creation' do fear an eclipse."[117]

Though St. Peter did not exactly 'bellow,' Catholic sentiment was certainly as much against woman suffrage as that of the most conservative Protestant churchmen. "The women in question," said the *Catholic World*, "claim for women all the prerogatives of men; we shall, therefore, take the liberty to disregard their privileges as women. They may expect from us civility, not gallantry.

"We say frankly in the outset that we are decidedly opposed to female suffrage and elegibility. The woman's rights women demand them both as a right and complain that men, in refusing to concede them, withhold a natural right, and violate the equal rights on which the American Republic professes to be based. We deny that women have a natural right to suffrage and eligibility; for neither is a natural right at all, for either men or women. Either is a trust from civil society, not a natural and indefeasible right, and civil society confers either on whom it judges trustworthy, and on such candidates it deems expedient to annex. As the trust has never been conferred on women, they are deprived of no right by not being enfranchised."[118]

When the news of the Seneca Falls convention was published, consternation was expressed generally in the editorial comments. Most of them ridiculed the idea, but there were notable exceptions such as *The North Star*, with an article by Frederick Douglass; and the *New York Herald*, owned by James Gordon Bennett. Mrs. Stanton declared there was no danger of the movement dying for want of press notices; and ridiculed the generally adverse character of the comments when she said it was apparently the belief of most editors that the object of the convention was to "seat every lord at the head of a cradle, and to clothe every woman in her lord's attire."[119] The *Mechanics Advocate*, Albany, New York, regarded the movement as "unwomanly," "impracticable," "unnecessary," "uncalled for"; it

[117] *Ibid.*, I, 82.
[118] The Woman Question [*Catholic World* (1869), IX, 145–6].
[119] *History of Woman Suffrage*, I, 806.

would "set the world by the ears," and "demoralize and degrade from their high sphere and noble destiny, women of all respectable and useful classes, and prove a monstrous injury to all mankind." The *Lowell Courier*, of Massachusetts, declared that women "should have resolved at the same time, that it was obligatory also upon the 'lords' aforesaid, to wash dishes, scour up, be put to the tub, handle the broom, darn stockings, patch breeches, scold the servants, dress in the latest fashion, wear trinkets," and "look beautiful. . . ." The *Rochester* [New York] *Democrat*, to mention but another instance, declared: "This has been a remarkable convention. It was composed of those holding to some one of the various *isms* of the day, and some, we should think, who embraced them all. . . . Verily, this is a progressive era!"[120]

A host of books and pamphlets appeared to correct the evils and wrong notions of these "misguided" women; and have continued to appear to the present. Only a few can be mentioned here. In *The Sphere and Activities of Women*, Burnap, in 1848, maintained woman's true position was that of "wife, the mistress of a home, the head of a family"; that God had designed men and women for "spheres of action entirely different"; that "political rights are determined by expediency" and are not inherently natural; and that "woman has a right" only to "that position which is most conducive to the welfare of that community to which she belongs. . . ." Clearly, political rights are not for her.[121] William B. Sprague, in 1851, celebrated the *Excellent Woman*, as described in the Proverbs, which was clearly counter to the suffrage movement. He lauded the active, educated, businesslike woman, but assured her that "her activity must be guided by discretion and animated by benevolence; she must be content to work within her own sphere and to occupy her own quiet throne."[122] Brockett, though loud in his praise of *Woman's Work in the Civil War*, found numerous reasons against her suffrage. First, she is already represented through her family;[123] second, the suffrage of woman "would be an at-

120 *Ibid.*, I, 803-4.

121 *Op. cit.*, 98 *ff*. and 190 *ff*.

122 P. XIII.

123 This argument appeared frequently. Said one woman, "I control seven votes, why should I desire to cast one myself?" [*Godey's Lady's Book*, March 1852, 293].

tempt to make suffrage individual instead of representative, and so against the natural order of things''; third, by suffrage they will gain nothing but lose much—''all that chivalric regard for their interests which now prompts our legislators to grant all their reasonable and some of their unreasonable requests''; fourth, she needs no vote for her protection—the interests of man and woman are one and neither need fear ''aggressions of the other''; fifth, her vote, if she had it, could not remedy the evils against which she complains—low wages, long hours, want of employment, and overcrowding all operate according to inexorable laws, not affected by ballots; finally, the greatest is the social objection. ''They will become partizans; zealous, earnest, indefatigable in their way . . . forgetful of that womanly modesty and grace which is the highest ornament of womanhood . . . what bickerings, . . . acrid debates . . . bitter feelings would be engendered in the family circle! How unseemly would be such contests in the presence of their children, if they had any!''[124]

In *Ecce Femina, or An Attempt to Solve the Woman Question,* the woman's rights agitators were condemned for having ''urged the employment of men and women together, without regard to the extra danger to virtue and morality; when a little reflection ought to convince anyone that an increase of temptation is equivalent to an increase of sin.'' In their present position in the home they ''will continue to exert a great influence for good over men, but . . . the surest method of increasing crime and misery is to mingle the sexes indiscriminately in politics.''[125]

Among those who opposed woman suffrage, it is clear, then, that general adherence was given to the belief that it was ''useless, expensive, detrimental to the best interests of women, inimical to marriage and the best interests of the home''; that many and, perhaps, the best women did not want it and were not fitted for it mentally and physically; that it would be immoral for women to go to the polls; it would debase their delicate nature and defeat the best interests of the Republic. Moreover, they

[124] Brockett: *Woman: Her Rights, Wrongs, Privileges and Responsibilities,* 269 *ff.*

[125] *Ecce Femina,* published at Hanover, New Hampshire, quoted in a pamphlet, *Men and Women Medical Students and the Woman Movement,* Philadelphia, April 1870.

WOMEN AT THE POLLS AS SOMEONE IMAGINED (1869)

were already well represented; they could not back their ballots with bullets; and, finally, woman suffrage was a "reform against nature."[126] The argument of bullets back of ballots was greatly overworked. The Constitution of the United States lays emphasis on the fact that it rests on "wisdom and knowledge, as well as virtue diffused generally among the people." Neither in England nor in America had suffrage been limited to those males who were able to fight.

Recognizing the strength of other arguments, it is, nevertheless, probably true, that the belief that it was a "reform against nature" held more people aloof or made more positive opponents than any other. The fearful consequences were foreseen by Ouida: "Where will this pleasant gaiety and smiling radiance go when, harassed, heated, and blown by the bitter winds of strife, the woman seeks to outshriek the man on political platforms . . .? There is in every woman, even in the best woman, a sleeping potentiality for crime," and, apparently, it was thought this unnatural proposal of going to the polls, and studying anatomy, would release all these potentialities for "fiendish evil."[127]

Horace Bushnell sought to prove the antagonism of woman suffrage to nature, and that women were not "created or called to govern," by reference to history, the Scriptures, and to the fallacies in the doctrine that the right of suffrage is absolute in either man or woman. Rousseau, Voltaire, and the American Fathers, he declared, had fallen into the use of "these catchwords of liberty" with greater ease "than was to be desired." He recognized the demand for woman suffrage as but the logical application or extension of that "cheap imposture of philosophy" which declared that "government is founded in consent" of the governed and "therefore terminable by them." Woman suffrage he regarded as a step just one degree worse than the state's rights rebellion which, also, had proceeded from the false premise that government is founded on consent. Turning to the woman suffrage proposition he found it was based on two fallacious assumptions: first, that women are equal to men, which

126 Abbott: A Comparative View of the Woman Suffrage Movement [*N. A. R.* (1895), CLX, 142–3]; also Buckley: *Wrong and Peril of Woman Suffrage*, 94 ff.

127 *N. A. R.* (1886), CXLIII, 304.

could not be proved; and, the second, which is more important than the first, for it stands, even though women be shown by science to be the equals of men, that there is no such thing as a natural, inherent right of suffrage, even for males. Men have never received the right of suffrage because of any absolute principle, but, on occasion, because they were taxed; again, because they were liable to be taxed; again, because they did military duty; again, to encourage virtue or to relieve the state of their animosity which might be aroused if suffrage were denied them. His final conclusion is that "if women ever have the right of voting accorded to them, it must be for a like variety of reasons, and not on the ground of any absolute principle."[128]

V. Woman Suffrage Closely Connected with Other Movements

The political suffrage agitation was only one phase of the nineteenth century movement towards woman's emancipation; it was closely interwoven with other changes, some of which were fundamental; without them, political enfranchisement of women would never have become an issue. Foremost among these were the change in woman's economic position and the advancement in her education. Besides these, the woman suffrage movement was linked up with our fundamental political doctrine of equality and faith in representative government; the first labor movement;[129] the emancipation of slaves and the Civil War which it involved; and other reforms, such as temperance.

Numerous advocates of woman's better education, such as Rush, Beecher, and Joseph Emerson, had urged its necessity to improve the home and school influence on the morals of the next generation. Many had urged the view that the salvation of the nation depended on the womanhood and motherhood of the country. Any reform, it was felt, could be effected by good, intelligent, educated women, by their indirect influence through their families. This faith in indirect influence was gradually abandoned by some in favor of direct action at the polls. Leading

[128] Bushnell: *Woman's Suffrage; The Reform Against Nature*, 32 ff.

[129] The demands of labor, published in *Young America*, an organ of the first labor movement, were clear-cut in favor of "equal rights for women with men in all respects."—As quoted by Ely: *The Labor Movement in America*, 42.

suffragists were temperance advocates. E. C. Stanton shocked some decidedly when she proposed a resolution that no woman should remain the wife of a drunkard;[130] and a broadside, issued by the Women's Christian Temperance Union at Newark, New Jersey, urged "give women the ballot" and "the Lord himself shall reign from sea to sea." Their votes are necessary to conquer the monster "oligarchy" made up of "ninety-nine out of every hundred Irishmen, nineteen of every twenty German saloon keepers . . . [and] every Jesuit in the Land."[131]

The granting of the vote to women, as a weapon to use in their own defense and as an instrument of social reform, may be considered as a natural, some say, an inevitable, result of our fundamental democratic principles. It has been seen that Bushnell, for example, traced woman suffrage to an extension of the doctrine of equality and to our theory of government by consent of the governed. Travellers in the United States were early, and almost universally, impressed with the freedom and independence of women here, even at a time when American women felt themselves very greatly oppressed.[132] The social freedom, it was felt, was in harmony with our tradition and consonant with our doctrine of equality.

To the effect of the industrial revolution and the development of factory labor, reference has already been made. Briefly we may recall that women were relieved of many of their household occupations and followed them into the factory. As a worker outside the home, woman became directly concerned with questions outside the home, but which affected it. She was interested in property and wages, which she now acquired by her own labor; no longer was she willing to turn over all earnings to her husband, though, as shown before, her wages have gone to the support of the family. As a laborer, she became interested in the labor movement, interested in higher wages and shorter hours. And, as labor came to see the need of organized political action, it was but natural that women needed political strength as well. As the laborer felt he could no longer rely entirely on his employer's ballot to get him his just reward, and that he must get

---

[130] See Coolidge: *Why Women Are So*, 202.

[131] A leaflet by H. W. Adams, in a volume of pamphlets, University of Pennsylvania Library.

[132] Compare Calhoun: *Soc. Hist. Am. Fam.*, II, 70 *ff.*

it for himself, so also women began to see the necessity of the vote to secure their rights, and that they could not always rely on the chivalrous protection afforded by men. Not only her personal welfare, but that of her children, she came to see, was dependent on her power: questions of education, sanitation, child labor, and so on, became vital concerns. Once she controlled or helped control things under her own roof; now she must legislate to control them. What may, or may not, have been the effectiveness of woman's vote in these matters, it remains that they were urged as reasons for her participation in politics. From this angle, woman suffrage looks much less fundamental than other phases of her emancipation. The economic changes, and the educational, emerge as the most fundamental, conditioning her entrance into the world of politics.[133] "The woman movement," said Jessie Taft, "viewed not as an isolated phenomenon but as an integral part of the vaster social evolution, is seen to be only the woman's side of what from the man's angle is called the labor movement."[134] This relationship has frequently been either ignored, misunderstood, or misrepresented.

Another event, intimately connected with the emancipation of women, was the Civil War.[135] Old habits, traditions and prejudices regarding the functions of women were broken down. What men once had declared women could not, should not, do, they were now glad to have them do; and women proved their ability to do them. "Delicate" women of the South began to do their own work; others worked in the field and in the factory.[136] Women in the West labored on farms because men were scarce. In some schools and colleges, women received an opportunity for an education such as they had not had when men were there to occupy the professor's attention and all the seats. In numerous places, and probably very generally, women went forward to teaching positions, which formerly had been filled by men. The Germans of Pennsylvania had thought women could not handle their difficult schools, but the experience of the war period taught them otherwise.[137]

[133] Compare Schlesinger: *Political and Social Hist. of the U. S.*, 73 *ff.*
[134] Taft: *The Woman Movement from the Point of View of Social Consciousness*, 53.
[135] Schlesinger: *op. oit.*, 315 *f.*
[136] Pp. 8 *f.*
[137] Vol. I, 503.

Besides the performance of tasks formerly done by men, women entered into new positions and rendered service which was considered valuable. In 1863, Gail Hamilton, in a stirring "call to my countrywomen," urged them to do many other things besides praying, making coats, scraping lint, making bandages, and sewing sheets and pillow-cases. These "ye ought to do . . . but . . . others . . . not to leave undone. The war cannot be finished by sheets and pillowcases."[138] In 1864, *Littell's Living Age* published an urgent appeal to women to curtail all extravagance and wasted energy and bend all efforts to a successful termination of the war; to establish a "Loyal Ladies League" whose objects should be economy, discouragement of importation of expensive materials, and the establishment of a Sanitary Commission.

The sacrifices, heroism, and constructive work rendered by the women of the war period have been completely catalogued and need not be reviewed here. It is worth while noting, however, that a large number of these workers, such as Clara Barton, Sarah P. Elson, Mary Vance, Mrs. E. J. Russell, Phoebe Allen, Mary Livermore, Mrs. H. L. Colt, Anna L. Clapp, Miss H. A. Adams, Maria Mann, Carrie Sheads, Eliza Porter, Amy Bradley, Nellie Taylor, Mrs. Hoge, Delphine Baker, Mrs. Stearns, and others, were well educated according to the standards of the day. Many were teachers or had taught; some were heads of prominent girls' schools, or teachers in public schools. Not many were college women, for there were few places where they could get such training; but many had had the best seminary or academy education available. These rendered intelligent and useful service, even as judged by those who were opposed to their labors.[139] What was done by Northern women was also done by the women of the South.[140] In recent travels of nine thousand miles through the Southern states, white-haired old ladies told me proudly, yet modestly, of their sacrifices during the war.[141]

[138] *At. Mo.* (1863), XI, 345–6.

[139] For references to training and position of many women see Brockett and Vaughan: *Women's Work in the Civil War,* 112–13, 163–4, 212–13, 235–6, 239, 429, 479, 502, 562, 577, 578–9, 609, 634, 636, 697, 755, 760 and 776; also Moore: *Women of the War,* 19, 238–9, 384, etc.

[140] Underwood: *The Women of the Confederacy* (1906).

[141] Summer, 1926 and 1927, travels in Maryland, Virginia, North and South Carolina, Georgia, Alabama, Mississippi, Louisiana, Kentucky, and Tennessee.

That their service was judged to be of very high and genuine character is evidenced by memorials such as the Resolution of the Virginia legislature, which inscribed on its journals, "a lasting memorial of their exalted worth, that history may present to posterity so shining an example, and that our children's children, to the latest generation, may be incited thereby to deeds of heroism and public virtue."[142]   Many instances of such recognition occur.[143]   Hurn, in her study of *Wisconsin Women in the War*, has set forth their accomplishment and enables one to see their distinguished achievements as a step towards greater public recognition.   In the states, generally, such recognition was earned.   With it, women were in a better position to demand political voice in a society which depended on them for such valuable aid.   Thenceforth it could be said, if that were a valid argument, that women could back their ballots with bullets—in as complete a sense as could any army doctor, nurse, stretcher-bearer or engineer.   Many women came from war service to work heartily for the suffrage movement; some of them had not previously been awake to its importance.

So much for the War as a factor in setting aside old prejudices and opening new activities to many women.   In the larger sense, the movement for the emancipation of the Negro may be said to have furnished the soil and atmosphere in which the seed of the early woman's movement developed.   Such leaders of suffrage as Lucretia Mott, the heroic Grimké sisters, Abby Kelly, Lucy Stone and Susan B. Anthony were first emancipators of the slave.   They asserted their right and accepted their duty to speak in public, in the face of great opposition, that they might "plead for black men in chains."   They made common cause with the Negro, asserting their condition too was one of slavery. Garrison's *Liberator,* for years, carried the likeness of a kneeling female slave, with the legend, "Am I not a Woman and a Sister?"   In speaking of Susan B. Anthony at her death, Garrison referred to "a·half century ago, when the fresh and earnest Quaker schoolmistress entered upon her consecration to the cause of the imbruted slaves and to the uplifting of oppressed womanhood.   Out of the first movement," he declared, "the second grew, and what was more natural than the impulse which led

[142] *Laws of Va.* (1863), Resolution No. 2, adopted March 26, 1863, 121.
[143] See *Laws of New York,* 1886, 365.

‘Am I not a Woman and a Sister?’

An Illustration Carried in *The Liberator*

the new disciple to seek acquaintance with the abolition leaders.''[144]

Thus did the suffrage movement, to a certain extent, "grow out of" its predecessor. More than that, its leaders learned something from the experiment. Before the War, few ever thought of extending suffrage throughout the United States by an amendment. But when the amendment was adopted, arming the one-time slave with the ballot, and women were still disfranchised, there arose an instant and persistent demand for federal action, which continued without abatement of vigor. From 1878 to 1919 the woman suffrage amendment was brought regularly before Congress.

The movement for woman's better education was of prime significance for the success of her politial emancipation. "Educate and agitate" might well have been the motto of women in the nineteenth century. As a matter of fact, it was the accepted doctrine of many of the greatest suffrage leaders, even though not always emblazoned on the banners carried by suffragists in the streets. The suffrage movement could not have carried on without educated leadership; that leadership was provided by the educational reform, in favor of women, which had been going on since about the period of the Revolution, and which, in the nineteenth century, though still incomplete, had changed the entire outlook of woman's life. Those women, such as Margaret

[144] Harper: *Life and Work of Susan B. Anthony*, III, 1435.

Fuller, Susan Anthony, Lydia Child, Abby Kelly, Lucretia Mott, Lucy Stone, E. C. Stanton, Antoinette Brown Blackwell, Julia Ward Howe and the Grimké sisters, who were the organizers, publicists and spokesmen of the movement, approached their work with more than a firm determination and emotional response born of the injustice which confronted them. They had gained insight into affairs, which was impossible when women were utterly uneducated. A great change took place between 1820 and 1870. When Emma Willard presented her plan for female education she appealed to the "enlightened rulers"; by 1870, many women were enlightened enough to pray that their rulers might be so. The gift of equal, or nearly equal, education to woman was the first sign of a recognition of her rights and capacities as a human being. With this gift she forced her way to a recognition of her equality, legally and politically.

The steps toward political equality had to be taken gradually. The earliest advocates of women's education were not even able to see a small part of the future opportunities that were to follow. Neither Emma Willard nor Mary Lyon dreamed of a "college like a man's" but of a "female seminary." Beecher went so far as to demand that her institution should be "on the college plan," have endowments, lead to professions besides teaching, and have permanent and well paid professorships: an institution that would educate women to be truly independent.[145] As to the franchise, said Beecher, later in life, let it be given to women "on condition that they are duly qualified by paying taxes and a certain measure of education, and then every woman will have new stimulus to fit herself for these responsibilities."[146] Dall declared the nature of women's education should be changed; it should prepare definitely for medicine, law, the ministry or any other profession or work, in which humans might engage. She attacked the content of studies, particularly the classics, which, she maintained, perpetuated the old Greek and Roman notions of female inferiority.[147]

Mrs. J. Ellen Foster, speaking of "Woman's Political Evolution," pointed to popular education as a potent evolutionary force. Coeducation in colleges had put women on the same foot-

---

[145] *True Remedy*, 29–30, 32–4, 45 and 55; also pp. 143 *f*.

[146] *Reminiscences*, 200 *ff*.

[147] Dall: *College, Market and the Court*, 61–2; 48–9; and 51.

ing as men; and the time would come, as a result of education, when society would welcome woman to any position she desired and could acceptably fill.[148] Edward Everett, too, in 1867, recognized educational privileges granted as the most important instance of justice to women and believed that "equal participation" therein was the "best guaranty that if in any thing else the sex is unjustly or unfairly dealt with, the remedy will come in due time."[149] Theodore Parker, before his conversion to outright advocacy of suffrage, stressed the necessity of equalization of educational, economic, and professional opportunities.[150] Some who opposed woman's change of sphere were greatly disturbed at the tendency towards equal education, fearing that once gained it would lead women into all sorts of activities outside the home. In 1852, while advocating woman's education, many doubtless felt, with the author of an article in the *Pennsylvania School Journal,* that education ought not to tempt them away from the home:

"We are not among those, however, who would take woman from her natural position, and send her forth to address audiences, to command armies, to fill offices under Government, or to join in the clamor of elections. These things we believe foreign to her nature; nor do we think them coveted by many women who possess a cultivated and well regulated mind. We believe that those who advocate such a change forget that no good would result from it, while the evil consequences would be incalculable."[151]

Thirty years later (1882), Charles W. Eliot expressed himself in a similar vein, seeing clearly that with education as a stepping-stone women would enter any profession, even the Senate and the pulpit: "Girls are being prepared daily, by 'superior education,' to engage, not in child-bearing and house-work, but in clerkships, telegraphy, newspaper-writing, school-teaching. . . . And many are learning to believe that, if they can but have their 'rights,' they will be enabled to compete with men at the bar, in the pulpit, the Senate, the bench."[152]

[148] *N. A. R.,* CLXV, 603–4.
[149] *R. C. E.,* 1867–8, 384 *f.*
[150] Howe: *Reminiscences,* 165–6.
[151] An Essay on Female Education [*Pa. Sch. Jour.* (1852), I, 251].
[152] *N. A. R.,* August 1882, 146–61.

In a day when higher education for women has become so common, it is easy to forget the debt which political suffrage owed to its first handful of educated women; easy to forget the interdependence of each upon the other. Perhaps the obligation of the political movement to the intellectual leadership of such a woman as Margaret Fuller can never be estimated. But the testimony to her influence, given by Mary Livermore, could doubtless be repeated by many others. The truths proclaimed in *Woman in the Nineteenth Century* and the reforms therein advocated, said Livermore, "were far in advance of public acceptance" and "its appearance was the signal for an immediate, widespread newspaper controversy that raged with great violence. I was young then; and as I took the book from the hands of the bookseller, [I wondered] . . . what the contents of the thin little volume could be, to provoke so wordy a strife. . . ."[153]

By force of her example, as well as by her writing, Miss Fuller stirred women to a realization of the untruth of the old doctrine of their incapacity. She was born in 1810, studied Latin at six, and, at thirteen, was a precocious child. At twenty-four, she published "A Defense of Brutus," in the *Daily Advertiser,* which was well received and gained the attention of serious critics. At twenty-six, she taught in the new school of Alcott in Boston, which Emerson said was killed by public criticism because it aimed to teach children to think. For such a school, Margaret Fuller was well fitted. Later she was a teacher at Providence. She was a student of Latin, French, German, Italian, philosophy, metaphysics, logic, and was a brilliant conversationalist. She was a friend of Emerson and Channing and highly regarded by them for her critical judgment. Like them, she exerted an important influence on the thought of the century. But more than that, she stirred the hearts of her sex and communicated to them a new vision.[154]

While it is impossible, and perhaps unnecessary, to review here the personal history of suffrage leaders to show how they combined in themselves an interest in educational and political reforms, one or two cases may be noted. The educational background of at least a few leaders is significant, inasmuch as it

---

[153] Livermore: *What Shall We Do with Our Daughters,* 7–8.

[154] Howe: *Margaret Fuller,* 4–5, 16–17, and 49–50; Higginson: *Margaret Fuller Ossoli,* 83 *ff.*

Susan B. Anthony

accounts for the fact that they wrote into the first suffrage documents their educational belief. A recent article has pointed out that only two contributors to a series of articles on "These Modern Women" were not college products.[155] It should be recalled, among other things, that Lucy Stone was a product of Oberlin College; that Antoinette Brown Blackwell came from the theological school; and that Susan B. Anthony was first a teacher, and interested in that work always, even to her death.

Susan B. Anthony had a "phenomenal memory," learned to read and spell at three years of age, and at the district school insisted on learning long division, much to the consternation and embarrassment of the master who did not himself understand it.[156] She became a teacher at fifteen years of age and extended her education at a "home school" and by private instruction in algebra.[157] About 1840, she taught at New Rochelle, New York, and, later, was head of the female department of the Canajoharie Academy. She was very early interested in many reforms such as temperance and emancipation; indignant that the prevalent notion assigned women only to work in the home; and, while still a teacher, became incensed at the unequal pay for women's services.[158] She believed that, as teachers, women's voices should be heard in their conventions, and at a teachers' meeting (1853) she fought for the right to speak. It was granted, and the next day a resolution was adopted granting women the right to share in the deliberations; and another favoring equal pay for equal work.[159]

Miss Anthony was always a firm advocate of coeducation; and she, Mrs. Stanton and Lucy Stone were actively interested in establishing the People's College, on the coeducational basis.[160] This venture, before consummated, was merged in Cornell University; but, at Rochester University, Miss Anthony was successful, by dint of great personal exertion, sacrifice, and a pledge of $2,000, in having provision made for the admission of young women.[161] As a final expression of her belief in the education

155 *The Nation* (July 6, 1927), CXXV, 8 *ff.*
156 Harper: *op. cit.*, I, 13–14.
157 *Ibid.*, I, 35 and 43.
158 *Ibid.*, I, 40, 45.
159 *Ibid.*, I, 100; and 221.
160 *Ibid.*, I, 64.
161 *Ibid.*, III, 1224–6.

of girls, she declared her hope that no "shaft or any monument of that sort" would be erected in her memory; and added, "The best kind of a memorial would be a school where girls could be taught everything useful that would help them to earn an honorable livelihood; where they could learn to do anything they were capable of, just as boys can. I would like to have lived to see such a school as that in every great city of the United States."[162]

There can be no doubt that the college leaders of to-day have recognized their debt to the suffrage movement. Education opened the way for, promoted and supported suffrage; in turn that movement has increased the opportunities, and made undeniable the demand for equality of education. At a meeting in 1906, Mrs. Moore expressed the tribute of college women to the labors of Susan B. Anthony, and Mrs. Park stated that one object of the College Women's League was to cause them to realize their debt to the women who have labored hard; as well as to cause them to see the necessity of continuing "to fight the battle in the quarter of the field . . . still unwon." Miss Anthony's "courage and strength, the patient devotion of a life consecrated to the education, advancement and elevation of womanhood, her invincible honor, her logic, her power to touch and sway all hearts, are recognized by every student of woman's progress. We perceive in her the advocate of that liberty which knows no limitations, a freedom which means the certain advancement of the race."[163]

Not only in the work and words of individual leaders was the connection between education and suffrage stressed, but in official platforms and resolutions as well. Reference has already been made to those of the Seneca Falls Convention. The *Westminster and Foreign Quarterly Review*, in summarizing the principal demands of the first suffrage convention, pointed out that education in all schools and colleges held an important place.[164] The seventh resolution, offered by Wendell Phillips, in 1851, stated:

"7. *Resolved*, That we deny the right of any portion of the species to decide for another portion, or of any individual to decide for another individual, what is and what is not their 'proper sphere'; that the proper sphere for all human beings

[162] *Ibid.*, III, 1420.
[163] *Ibid.*, III, 1390–5.
[164] *Woman's Rights Tracts* No. 3, 2–3.

Lucy Stone

is the largest and highest to which they are able to attain; what this is, cannot be ascertained without complete liberty of choice; woman, therefore, ought to choose for herself what sphere she will fill, what education she will seek,-and what employment she will follow; and not be held bound to accept, in submission, the rights, the education, and the sphere which man thinks proper to allow her."[165]

The direction that suffragists' thought on education was taking is indicated in the resolution offered by Dall, in 1859:

"*Resolved,* That it is our bounden duty to open, in every possible way, new vocations to women, to raise their wages by every advisable means, and to secure to them an education which shall be less a decoration to their persons than a tool to their hands."[166]

VI. School Suffrage

As noted, struggle for political voice began earnestly in 1848. Before this was achieved in the fullest measure, small but significant concessions were made in several states. Women had gradually taken a prominent place in the teaching profession, in the elementary schools. Everywhere they were demonstrating their capacity as teachers; and, in some places, were becoming superintendents and principals of schools. Because of their prominence in this, their first great public profession, it came to be generally recognized that they should have a voice in the control of school affairs. While each state was a law unto itself, it may be stated that a measure of participation in the control of school affairs was granted in most of them during the last half of the nineteenth century. In some states school suffrage came at the same time as full suffrage; in others, the former was regarded as a wedge to force the extension of complete suffrage. The granting of school suffrage as a gradual step to full suffrage was a test of a legislature's generosity and at the same time a test of the public opinion of women. In a gradual way it accustomed them to the idea of voting. When Massachusetts first conferred the right of voting for members of public school committees, a privilege long sought by the Woman's Suffrage

[165] *Woman's Rights Tracts* No. 1, p. 2; also Phillips on the relation of suffrage and education, at the *Ninth National Woman's Rights Convention,* 1859, 17; and the address of Ernestine L. Rose at the same convention, 7–8.
[166] *Proceedings of the Ninth National Convention,* 3.

Party, women throughout the state showed no great interest in voting. This initial indifference was regarded by some as an indication that "woman suffrage will never be a success."[167]

Partial school suffrage was granted by Kentucky in 1838, when any widow or *femme sole*, owning property subject to taxation for school purposes, was allowed to vote;[168] likewise, in 1888 the privilege was extended to any spinster having a ward between those ages. It was, however, the judgment of the state superintendent of instruction that the "exercise of the power was so little insisted upon" as to make it difficult to see its effect on the schools.[169]

School suffrage was granted women of Kansas in 1859.[170] There, the superintendent believed that, because of the mother's interest in, and contact with, school affairs, "the schools have been made better."[171] In Wyoming, women had full suffrage after 1869.[172] Provision was made by Minnesota (1876) whereby women could vote in school elections;[173] and Michigan (1875) passed a similar law.[174] Colorado provided (1877) that no one should be denied the right to vote at school elections on account of sex.[175] Oregon[176] and New Hampshire[177] provided for school suffrage in 1878.

In 1874, Massachusetts declared women eligible for membership in school committees;[178] five years later they were granted the right to vote for members on such committees.[179]

[167] *The Nation* (1879), XXIX, 272.

[168] *Laws of Kentucky*, 1857–8, 282; Sumner: *Equal Suffrage*, 2–3; see also Anthony and Harper: *Hist. of Woman Suffrage*, IV, 674.

[169] *R. C. E.* (1893–4), II, 1416–19; there are, however, conflicting views on this point: Supt. of Public Instruction, McHenry Rhodes, tells me that "women have always exercised the right under this law. . . ."—Letter, Nov. 14, 1927.

[170] *Laws of Kansas*, 1862, Ch. 181, Sec. 20, 808.

[171] *R. C. E.* (1893–94), II, 1416–19.

[172] *Laws of Territory of Wyoming*, 1869; *Hist. of Woman Suffrage*, IV, 994 *ff*.

[173] *Laws of Minnesota*, 1876, Ch. 14, 29–30.

[174] *Laws of Michigan*, 1875, No. 106, 143.

[175] *Laws of Colorado*, 1877, Ch. 30, Sec. 1.

[176] *Laws of Oregon*, 1878, 67–8.

[177] *Laws of N. H.*, 1878, Ch. 87, sec. 6, 210.

[178] *Laws of Mass.*, 1874, 443.

[179] *Ibid.*, 1879, 559–60; also 1881, 502–3; and 1886, 124, for law extending eligibility to women to act as overseers of the poor. Beginning of ser-

CAROLINE H. DALL

New York, in 1880, declared no one should be deemed ineligible to serve as any school officer or to vote at any school meeting "by reason of sex," provided they had all other qualifications required by law.[180] Vermont granted school suffrage the same year.[181] Three years later Nebraska granted school suffrage.[182] In 1885, Wisconsin took the same step;[183] four more states, Arizona, Montana, New Jersey, and North Dakota provided for school suffrage, in 1887;[184] and South Dakota by her Constitution of 1889.[185] In 1891, Illinois; in 1893, Connecticut; and, in 1894, Ohio, offered the privilege of school suffrage to women.[186] By 1910, there were twenty-four states which gave women suffrage on school questions.[187]

In many states women were made eligible to school offices—beyond that of teacher—before they had the right to vote. In 1879, the Commissioner reported the extent of such privileges as were granted by California, Colorado, Illinois, Iowa, Kansas, Louisiana, Massachusetts, Michigan, Minnesota, New Hampshire, New Jersey, Rhode Island, Vermont, Washington Territory, Wisconsin and Wyoming. At that date only nine of the sixteen had any school suffrage.[188]

When Ohio passed her law permitting women to vote, April 24, 1894, the Commissioner of Education, recognizing the need of information as to the existence, operation and effect of similar laws elsewhere, sent out a circular letter of inquiry. The answers from thirty states showed ten—Alabama, Arkansas, Delaware, Georgia, Missouri, North Carolina, South Carolina, Tennessee, Virginia, and West Virginia—in which women had no right to vote on school questions. An analysis of the replies,

---

vice of women on school boards was described in the *R. C. E.* (1880), LXXXII.

[180] *Laws of N. Y.*, 1880, 10; also the law of 1886, 938.

[181] *Laws of Vermont*, 1880, No. 103, 102.

[182] *Laws of Nebraska*, 1883, Ch. LXXII, Sec. 4, 289–90.

[183] *Laws of Wisconsin*, 1885, Ch. 211, 184.

[184] *Laws of Montana* [*Code* of 1895, I, 148]; *Laws of New Jersey*, 1887, Ch. CXVI, 149; *Revised Code of North Dakota*, 1895, Art. 672, 199.

[185] Letter of C. G. St. John, Supt. of Pub. Instruction, Nov. 8, 1927.

[186] *Laws of Illinois*, 1891, 135; *Laws of Connecticut*, 1893, Ch. CCLXVI, 411–12; *Laws of Ohio*, 1894, 182.

[187] Sumner: *Equal Suffrage*, 3.

[188] *R. C. E.*, 1879, 14, 21, 47, 64, 72, 85, 103, 118, 128, 153, 159, 212, 237, 256, 287, and 290.

where suffrage had been granted, shows that it was not taken very seriously and did not, at least to the chief school officer, appear to be of much influence. Indiana still doubted whether the suffrage statute was constitutional; in Massachusetts, it was reported women did not generally avail themselves of the right to vote, but were a "kind of reserve force that seldom goes into action"; New York was not aware that "any serious effect on the school interests of this state" had been wrought; in Vermont, after six years' trial, the voting of women had had "no particular effect" on the schools "for the women have not availed themselves of the right, except in a few instances. . . ." While the above were either unfavorable or indefinite judgments, there were other very positive and favorable estimates of the influence women exerted on the schools. This was true of Wyoming, Wisconsin, Minnesota, Michigan, Kansas and Louisiana. In the last, women were office-holders, but not voters. Wisconsin reported the school system had certainly gained "by the extension of these privileges to women"; Kansas found "schools have been made better"; while, in Michigan, women were reported to be active "in many localities"; in "many instances their work and influence" had "done much good" and "no intelligent man in Michigan" who had the interests of the schools at heart, it was asserted, would wish "to deprive women of this right."[189]

VII. After Suffrage, What?

Woman was warned, throughout the campaign for suffrage, of the dire consequences of her going to the polls; that her finer sensibilities would be destroyed; she would lose the chivalrous deference of men; going to vote in bad weather and over poor roads would ruin her health; and that the experiences would make her harsh and competitive, whereas she should be soft and yielding. The cartoons of suffragists depicted them as devoid of all charm of person and manner, and addicted to manly vices as well as mannish dress.[190] This prevalent argument as to the certain degradation of women, once they had the vote, led to the laughing ridicule of Alice Duer Miller in "A Consistent Anti to her Son":

[189] *Ibid.* (1893–94), II, 1416–19.
[190] See, for example, Dall: *College, Market and the Court,* 212–14; Crothers: *Meditations on Votes for Women,* 62; Hardy: *The Five Talents of Woman,* 17.

"You're twenty-one to-day, Willie,
"And a danger lurks at the door,
"I've known about it always,
"But I never spoke before;
"When you were only a baby
"It seemed so very remote,
"But you're twenty-one to-day, Willie,
"And old enough to vote.

"You must not go to the polls, Willie,
"Never go to the polls,
"They're dark and dreadful places
"Where many lose their souls;
"They smirch, degrade and coarsen,
"Terrible things they do
"To quiet, elderly women—
"What would they do to you!"[191]

THE EFFECT OF EMANCIPATION AS SEEN BY A CARTOONIST

Besides the disasters to come upon them personally, the un-avoidable decay of the home, the neglect of children, and the increase of domestic quarrels and divorce were prophesied.[192]

[191] From *Are Women People?* by Alice Duer Miller, copyright 1915 by George H. Doran Company. Pp. 11–12.

[192] Sumner: *Equal Suffrage*, 2.

WOMEN CAMPAIGNING FOR OFFICE UNDER THE REGIME OF WOMAN SUFFRAGE

Those who advocated suffrage were just as certain that none of these results would materialize. On the contrary they believed that rather than degrade women the new reform would elevate men. Thomas Palmer, in a speech before the Senate (1885), declared: "I believe the tone of our politics will be higher; that our caucuses will be jealously guarded, and our conventions more orderly and decorous. I believe the polls will be freed from the vulgarity and coarseness which now too often surround them, and that the polling booths, instead of being in the least attractive parts of a ward or town, will be in the most attractive; instead of being in stables, will be in parlors. I believe the character of candidates will be more closely scrutinized and that better officers will be chosen to make and administer the laws. I believe that the casting of the ballot will be invested with a seriousness—I had almost said a sanctity—second only to a religious observance."[193] Henry W. Beecher believed "that politics are still in need of some improvement," though some think them perfect already, and expressed a firm faith that great benefit would flow from the votes of women.[194] Others, as well as he, saw suffrage also as a means to the final attainment of freedom. Put the vote into woman's hand and she need no longer petition for her rights but may "assume and exercise them." Besides the reform of politics and the attainment of her complete personal freedom as a citizen, others saw a great success of reform movements such as temperance, child labor, improvement of schools, marriage laws, divorce laws, property laws and even the outlawing of war.

Schreiner declared: "We pay the first cost on all human life. . . Men's bodies are woman's works of art. Given to us power to control, we will never carelessly throw them in to fill up the gaps in human relationships made by international ambitions and greeds. The thought would never come to us as women, 'Cast in men's bodies; settle the thing so!' Arbitration and compensation would as naturally occur to her as cheaper and simpler methods of bridging the gaps in national relationships, as to the sculptor it would occur to throw in anything rather than statuary, though he might be driven to that at last!"[195]

[193] P. 6.

[194] Beecher: *Women's Influence in Politics*, 8–9.

[195] *Woman and Labor*, 173–5, and 179–80; and Howe: *Reminiscences*, Ch. XV.

The vote has been gained. Some results prognosticated have come about, though it is impossible to say exactly to what degree they are the result of woman's influence as a voter; or to what extent they are the result of other factors affecting them, such as women's increasing prominence in every field of labor and her gradually equalized educational opportunities. All the improvements that have come about can no more be credited to woman's vote than can all the evils which hasty moralists have laid at the door of suffragists.

Women have entered politics and have secured the opportunity of service in public capacities: as governors of states; as representatives in legislatures and Congress; as judges of higher as well as lower courts; as collectors of customs; as attorney-general; as investigators; as magistrates; as policewomen; and so on.[196] In spite of ridicule heaped upon them in their new rôles, women have gone steadily forward, where opportunity offered. Some have taken a decided interest in their political education; others have not. Women's influence is credited with the passage of the Maternity Bill, for the protection of mothers and babies; the Cable Bill, fixing the rights of married women to citizenship independently of the husband; the Woman's Bureau, as a recognized part of the United States Bureau of Labor, has been established and, through its work, that light is being shed on the condition of women as laborers in all fields which is necessary before improvement can be sought intelligently. According as one is inclined to favor the former system of liquor control, or the present bootlegging operations, one may condemn or praise the influence of women with reference to prohibition. At present, much attention is directed toward a uniform divorce law, a national secretary of education, and Americanization agencies.

Women have shown a willingness and ability to organize and play the game of politics like men. Here they have followed the patterns set by men rather consistently, being instructed by them. They found politics muddy water; muddy it still is. They have lined up with old parties that have nothing but rotten platforms; no great reform planks have been provided by the new members. The statement, credited to Mrs. Ross, of Wyo-

196 Many prominent women listed in numerous fields of public service [Philadelphia] *Evening Bulletin,* Oct. 24, 1925.

ming, that "women plan no upheaval" in politics may be taken as indicating the general nature of what is to be anticipated in the immediate future. This is perhaps not to be decried. Slow evolutionary changes are best. But the spirit of such a statement is contrary to the glowing, enthusiastic pictures of whitewashed politics, published when suffragists were first striving for the vote. To make good the advance claims, women must add something besides numbers to politics—a new thought—for the old ones are threadbare and decidedly unproductive. Whether they can make such a contribution through existing party machines, notoriously skittish as these are about innovations, is a grave question. The swinging pendulum in its arc gets nowhere, though it does mark time! Will women remain content to swing in the old arc; mark time with the old parties; or, will they be bearers of the divine fire that is to blaze the path to true freedom and social justice?

Again, what bearing has the equality of women on the riddle of perpetuity which has perplexed nations from ancient times to modern? Man has repeatedly failed to bear up and carry on amid the refinements of civilization. But such civilizations have been half civilizations. The question naturally arises whether the free and equal economic, educational and political participation of the other half will materially affect the stability and endurance of the modern state. The question waits for answer.

Instead of finding a direct answer to this question of remote social consequences, it is necessary first to deal with immediate effects. The political emancipation of women must be regarded as only one phase of the great transformation taking place in American life—the decline of the patriarchal ideal and the rise of the individualistic.[197] Seen in this light, political emancipation of women appears more selfishly than socially inclined and would be expected, first of all, to contribute to the freedom of women as individuals rather than, indiscriminately, to the reform of social evils. From this new individual freedom, according to a democratic view, larger social benefits may be expected to flow. Helen Sumner's findings, in a study of the effects of equal suffrage in Colorado, substantiate the truth of the first part of the proposition—that women as individuals are gainers. In summary, she declared the effect on party politics had been slight;

[197] Compare Hutchins: *Conflicting Ideals*, London, 1913.

but that women had experienced a "broadening in their outlook, a glimpse of wider interests than pots and kettles, trivial scandal and bridge whist." No evil effect on woman's character was noted; and Miss Sumner was forced to conclude that casting votes was no more damaging to woman's character "than purchasing a garden hose." Thus, there was no loss and some gain; for through those broadened interests leads the way, Sumner thinks, to "a better citizenship . . . and a closer understanding and comradeship between men and women."[198]

That woman's voice can be turned effectively against evils is sufficiently shown in the case of Adams County, Ohio, where women were the first to rebel against the wholesale vote selling that had been going on for years.[199]

Granted, says the opponent of woman suffrage, that woman has gained greater freedom for herself, and that through her broader interests she has been, or will be, enabled to exert a wholesome influence in politics; but what has been the effect on the home? What of the visions of divorce, uncared for children, unfed husbands? Did not fathers have to croon their children to sleep, when Wyoming women first did duty on the public jury in '69?

> "Don't cry baby, don't be in a fury;
> "'Cause mama's gone to sit on the jury."

There can be no denial of the fact of the decline of the home home authority and increasing divorce. But that suffrage is responsible, many would hesitate to assert. What made run-a-way wives in Colonial days, when there was no woman suffrage? Economic changes of the past century have provided the most fundamental cause of decline of the patriarchal home; economic independence and education have enabled women to be franker in rejecting undesirable marriage, both before and after the ceremony. Divorce has become easier because of changing social sanction, as well as changing divorce laws. With the growth of a materialistic philosophy, the religion of the fathers has declined. One no longer forbears to break asunder what God has joined together. Some churches have even decided to relax the bonds themselves, to meet the changed notions of man,

198 Sumner: *op. cit.*, 242–4.

199 *McClure's Mag.* (1911), XXXVIII, 35; also, on results of woman's suffrage, see Schirmacher: *Modern Woman's Rights Movement*, 39–40.

by striking out the word "obey." Thus the authority of an oriental concept slowly crumbles before the onslaught of a materialistic civilization which has no part with it; which will not tolerate it, when it stands in the way. Since 1870, when the number of divorces granted was 11,207, they have increased by leaps and bounds. In 1900, there were 55,502, an increase from 29 to 73 per 100,000 of population. At this rate, some looked forward to the time when one out of sixteen or even one out of twelve marriages will be dissolved by the courts. The only country having more than the United States was Japan, where they were three times as numerous.[200] Lichtenberger, after his study of divorce (1909), was hopeful, however, declaring that because of industrial change and expansion it was to be expected that the family experience turmoil as well as any other institution. He concluded: "The higher education and more systematic development of woman will result in better training of youth but the home will continue to be the only school adequate for the development of a strong personality and the attainment of life in all its highest manifestations . . . the ultimate effect will be not to increase divorces but to make them more rare."[201] The increasing rarity is not evident in figures up to date, however, and various schemes, such as "marital vacations" and companionate marriage, are proposed to reduce the mounting divorce list. By 1924, divorces had steadily mounted to 170,952, which was 1.52 per thousand of our population. In 1927, divorces increased 6.2 per cent, making about one to every six marriages.

As suggested, many hesitate to blame the increase of divorce and other infelicities on the absence of mother's pies,[202] jury duty of women, or the marking, folding and dropping of ballots. Others, of whom C. W. Sams is representative, do not hesitate to proclaim our indebtedness, for various social evils, to the emancipation of woman:

". . . During these years the aims and ideals which underlay that movement have been made manifest by what has transpired since the agitation began. We have seen men's places in the business world taken by women; divorces multiplied, and still

---

[200] World's Work, XIX, 12426-7.

[201] Instability of the American Family [Annals of the Am. Acad. Polit. & Soc. Sci. (1909), XXXIV, 97-105].

[202] Compare article by Wells in the Atlantic Mo. (1880), XLVI, 817-23.

increasing—most of them brought by women against their husbands; household duties neglected; the care and the training of the children slighted; the children growing up unruly, ill-mannered, disrespectful; the parents largely subordinated to their children; prolonged absences of wives in the summer; husbands put in jail on preposterous grounds; then put under rules which tend to destroy utterly their influence and their authority in their families; disorder and violence unheard of before in the home, and the family hearth often stained with the blood of the wretched members by whom and for whom death was preferred to the domestice anarchy in which they were living.''[203]

Many, however, are apparently not content with marking time, whether with Mr. Sams or the Republican party. They believe much is still to be sought before "the woman's cause is man's," in the completest sense. The National Woman's Party, founded in 1913 to work for the franchise amendment, has been reorganized (1921) "to secure the removal of all the remaining forms of the subjection of women," claiming, with propriety, that of those things women of 1848 declared they were deprived, the modern woman has won only one in clear-cut fashion—the right to vote. To secure that perfect freedom from subordination to men, whether in religion, law, labor or social life, which is at present denied by existing practices, they concentrate all forces on an equal rights amendment: *"Men and women shall have equal rights throughout the United States and every place subject to its jurisdiction."*

[203] *Shall Women Vote?* 273–4. Quoted by permission of the author.

CHAPTER IX

WOMAN'S CLUB MOVEMENT AND EDUCATION

I. Beginning of "Female Associations"

The woman's club movement, as it is understood to-day, is said to have originated about 1866.[1] That decade did mark the rise of such organizations as Friends in Council, Quincy, Illinois; Sorosis, of New York; and the New England Woman's Club, of Boston. Viewed from the standpoint of her complete emancipation, however, woman's clubs and associations of different sorts may well be considered, if one would understand the evolution of the movement. Earlier associations need to be studied. Women's organizations were founded as a result of new interests; as the range of interests and activities expanded, so the woman's club of to-day, with its numerous departments, gradually came into being. The early associations were educational and philantropic; the clubs of the sixties, under the leadership of such women as Jennie Croly, of the *World*, Kate Field, of the *Tribune*, Alice Cary, and Harriet K. Hunt, had clearly more catholic interests, including various professions besides teaching. Moreover, they aimed at culture of the members. Later, an emphasis was placed on certain reforms which were to be encouraged by the clubs. Changing as they have been, from generation to generation, women's clubs have contributed largely to adult education—both of those whose education was lacking or broken, and those who had completed the seminary or college course. They have helped turn women's minds to present problems. The club movement is, at once, an outgrowth of woman's gradual emancipation from the realm of the household and an indication of her continuance of interest in all of her household, though she has gone to labor outside of it. Thus, it is part and parcel of woman's emancipation: it is linked with her oldest profession, as well as her newest; it aims to make her feel at home in the new, wider world as well as to render her more effective.

[1] Croly: *Hist. of Woman's Club Movement*, 54; and Wood: *Hist. of the General Fed. of Women's Clubs*, 23.

The first women's associations date back to the opening up of educational facilities for her, and these associations seem to have depended on her enlarged views and interests; it extends from the latter part of the eighteenth century to about 1860. The interests were almost wholly philanthropic and educational, though the latter, especially, varied from time to time. A few of these beginnings may be mentioned. Anne Parrish began a school for poor Christian girls, in 1796, and soon formed an association of Quaker ladies who managed, supported and taught the Aimwell School in Philadelphia.[2] In New York, the Female Association was formed, about 1795, which shortly thereafter educated girls on the Lancasterian plan,[3] and was incorporated in 1813.[4] Under the leadership of Joanna Bethune an Infant School Society, of New York ladies, was organized about 1827, for the "instruction of children from two to six or seven years of age."[5] About forty years later, women's associations were very active in promoting the establishment of kindergartens.

In the first half of the nineteenth century a large number of societies were incorporated for philanthropic purposes. In New York, the Society for the Relief of Indigent Women and Children,[6] the New York Female Assistance Society,[7] and the American Female Guardian Society[8] may be named. The Ladies' Depository was opened by prominent ladies of New York, in 1834, for "supplying work to respectable Females of every Religious Denomination."[9] In Massachusetts, the Female Society of Boston for Promoting Christianity among the Jews,[10] The Beverly Female Charitable Society,[11] the New England Female Moral Reform Society,[12] and the Needlewoman's Friend Society[13] for the "purpose of providing employment for indigent females," are fairly typical of those incorporated between 1800 and 1860.

2 See Vol. I, 202.

3 Reigart: *Lancasterian System in N. Y. C.*, 24.

4 *Laws of N. Y.*, Ch. LXXXVII, 91–2.

5 Randall: *Hist. of Com. Sch. System of N. Y.*, 72–3.

6 *Laws of N. Y.*, 1821, 175.

7 *Ibid.*, 1840, 170.

8 *Ibid.*, 1849, 364.

9 Reports of the Society, for the years 1856–1858 are in N. Y. Pub. Lib.

10 *Laws of Mass.*, 1834, 228.

11 *Ibid.*, 1836, 814–15.

12 *Ibid.*, 1846, 100.

13 *Ibid.*, 1851, 572–3.

Connecticut incorporated the Female Beneficent Association of Fairfield, in 1833, and extended its power in 1838 ;[14] a year later, the Ladies Beneficent Society for the Relief of Colored Children in the City of Hartford ;[15] and in 1847; the Widow's Society for the Relief of Destitute Widows, which had been in existence since 1825.[16]

In the South, female societies were no less common. Perhaps they were more so. Petersburg Female Association for providing "support and education of poor females" was incorporated by Virginia, in 1813.[17] In 1816, the Female Orphan Society of Norfolk ;[18] in 1846, the Anne Norvell Orphan Asylum Association ;[19] and in 1849, the Lynchburg Female Orphan Asylum, were incorporated for philanthropic and educational purposes.[20] All the foregoing are but a handful of the vast number incorporated in the states named and elsewhere during this period. After 1860, they increased in number and in the variety of purposes to be served.

Besides the associations established to further the Lancasterian system, infant schools, and other specifically beneficent and educational enterprises, there were those which grew directly as a result of the girls' seminary and the common school movements. At the Female Seminary of New Hampton, New Hampshire, a Literary and Missionary Association, with about two hundred members, and at Miss Grant's seminary at Ipswich, a Society for the Promotion of Knowledge, were formed; and similar literary societies became the rule in most female seminaries. These associations, formed in the seminaries, anticipated the cultural, intellectual interests of the later woman's clubs which developed, outside the schools, in the decade of the sixties. The leaders were educated women. What was more natural than that they should carry over into adult life the interests of the school and, perhaps, too, the idea of a club for the pursuit of those interests? At Troy, Mrs. Willard established a society of ladies whose object was the opening of a school in Athens, Greece, for the

[14] *Laws of Connecticut*, 1838, 17.

[15] *Ibid.*, 1839, 60–1.

[16] *Ibid.*, 1847, 16 *ff*.

[17] *Laws of Va.*, 1813, Ch. LV, 35.

[18] *Ibid.*, 1816, Ch. LXXIX, 198.

[19] *Ibid.*, 1846, Ch. CLIII, 116.

[20] *Ibid.*, 1849, CCXLVII, 178.

"education of female teachers."[21]   Later (about 1840), at Kensington, Mrs. Willard was responsible for the suggestion of
"female associations," which were to be a component part of
"the scheme she had devised for the benefit of common schools."
The result of these female associations was not only to enlist
women's interest but that of "their partners and brothers" who
evinced "a greater willingness . . . to provide the means of improvement."[22]   Four similar associations were founded in other
towns besides Kensington.   Barnard declared that from the outset he sought to enlist the coöperation of women; and that "by
their associated, or even individual, efforts, a revolution in our
common schools can be effected."[23]

Specific efforts were made to improve the common schools
through women teachers; and, to encourage their entrance into
teaching, women's associations were formed.   Such was the
Ladies Association for Educating Females, established at Jacksonville, Illinois, about 1833.[24]   A missionary effort may be seen
in the Boston Ladies' Society for Evangelizing the West, established in 1842.[25]   The forming of an association for the training
of teachers for Western schools was one of the chief interests of
Catherine Beecher.   In 1846, she published an *Address on the
Evils Suffered by American Women and Children,* wherein she
set forth how the "destitute American children" were to be educated "by the agency of American women."   Negotiations were
carried on with Governor Slade, of Vermont, who finally headed
the Central Committee for Promoting National Education.[26]
The results of this movement are recorded in the annual *Reports,*
the first of which appeared in 1847.

In an *Address* to The Ladies Society for the Promotion of
Education at the West (1846), Edward Beecher showed that
one of the motives was to counteract the Catholic influence in
that section.   "Look now and see what the Catholics have been
doing in this same state of Indiana, where there is not one good
Protestant female high school.   Though the Catholic population

21 *Am. Annals,* III, 189.
22 *Conn. Com. Sch. Jour.,* IV, 193–4.
23 *Ibid.,* IV, 187.
24 Beecher: *True Remedy,* 186 *ff.;* see also *Am. Annals,* VII, 185–6; and
V, 81–4.
25 *First Annual Report,* 1843.
26 *Address,* 34 *ff.;* see also *Educational Reminiscences,* 262–5.

JENNIE C. CROLY

of the State is but 25,000, they have five female seminaries established at the most important points in the State:—at Fort Wayne, at Vincennes, and at Jasper, Dubois County, and at Madison, and one near Terre Haute; and this is but a specimen of what they are doing all over the West. Indeed, out of sixty-eight Catholic female seminaries, forty-five are at the West. What does this look like but a deliberate purpose to proselyte the West, by the power of the female mind?''[27]

In 1852, the Women's Education Association was founded, which adopted as its principal objectives those general improvements for which Catherine Beecher had been striving, and contributed much to the success of the Seminary in Milwaukee as well as other schools of the West.[28] The continuation of similar women's efforts to effect certain definite results is to be noted in the establishment of the Woman's Education Association of Boston and the Association for Promoting the Higher Education of Women in New York, in 1882.[29]

II. Progress of the Club Movement

The second period of the association, or club, movement saw the rise of an organization very similar to many that exist today. It was an outgrowth of earlier educational opportunities and labors; it was influenced by the opening of new occupations and professions, the emancipation of slaves and the agitation for woman suffrage. Though, at first, an emphasis was put upon cultural programs, more and more attention was gradually directed to reform. With this new many-sidedness of interest, the old favorite, education, was not forgotten, but reappeared in new forms. From one point of view the woman's club, since the sixties, with its manifold activities, is symbolic of the new freedom of woman. Its "diversity with unity" reflects her new varied life.

The Sorosis of New York was established in 1868, under the influence of Jennie Croly, due to the exclusiveness of the Press Club of New York.[30] In its foundation there was expressed the

27 P. 9.

28 See Vol. I, 325 *f*.

29 *N. E. Jour. Ed.*, I, 90–1; *R. C. E.* (1883), CXL–CXLI; and (1882) CXXVIII–CXXX.

30 Croly: *Hist. of the Woman's Club Movement*, 15 and 21.

spirit of independence of woman, which marked it as different from earlier associations. Moreover, in place of definite reform, philanthropic or educational program, this new club was distinguished by having none save general ends. Alice Cary, in her first and only address, declared: "We have, then, to begin at the beginning," proposed the innoculation of deeper and broader ideas among women, proposed to teach them to think for themselves, and get their opinions at first hand, not so much because it is their right as because it is their duty. "We have also proposed to open out new avenues of employment to women, to make them less dependent and less burdensome, to lift them out of unwomanly self-distrust, disqualifying diffidence, into womanly self-respect and self-knowledge; to teach each one to make all work honorable by doing the share that falls to her, or that she may work out to herself agreeably to her own special aptitude, cheerfully and faithfully. . . . We have proposed to enter our protest against all idle gossip, against misuse and waste of time, saying and doing what we are able to say and to do, without asking leave, and without suffering hindrance. . . ."[31]

The New England Woman's Club originated in the same year as Sorosis, but, unlike the latter, it included men and was not a protest against them. Under the leadership of Mrs. C. M. Severance, Julia W. Howe and Ednah Cheney, a large number of women and men were brought together, interested in "literary, charitable, philanthropic, educational, reformatory, political, religious . . . [and] recreative" objectives but not exclusively attentive to any one. They were "kindred spirits" but "drawn together by no ties of family, neighborhood, or church." The catholic nature of interests is shown in the Club's efforts to establish a horticultural school, the lectures provided by the committee on art and literature, the Woman's Industrial and Educational Union, the work of classes in various subjects, and the array of social questions to which it gave attention.[32]

Friends in Council, the woman's club of Quincy, Illinois, began in the weekly meetings of twelve ladies (1866), who spent their time reading and discussing Lecky's *History of the Rise and Influence of the Spirit of Rationalism in Europe* and Mrs. Child's *Progress of Religious Ideas*. The next two years they

31 *Ibid.*

32 *Ibid.*, 37 *ff.*

read Plato; and, in 1869, realizing the need of organization, a meeting for that purpose was held by twenty-two ladies in the Quincy Young Ladies Seminary.[33]   The continued academic tendency of the club is shown in the list of topics studied, about 1875, which began with the "State of [the] Roman Empire at the appearance of Christ," continued through the "Saracens in Spain," the "Character of the Fifteenth Century," and concluded with the "Present Aspect of Italy" and the "Present Aspect of Russia." A like interest in intellectual culture was taken by the Fortnightly Club of Chicago, founded, in 1873, by the efforts of Kate Nevell Doggett, and carried on by such women as Ellen M. Mitchell, Jane Addams and Mrs. Ellen M. Henrotin. The Chicago Woman's Club, formed in 1876, by twenty-one women called together by Caroline M. Brown, had six departments—reform, home, education, philanthropy, art and literature, and philosophy and science.   The Civic Club of Philadelphia (1893), said to be the "first civic club proper, in name and purpose," aimed, according to its president, Sarah Yorke Stevenson, to promote, "by education and active coöperation, a higher public spirit and a better social order."   The scope of work was to be limited to the departments of "municipal government, education, social science, and art."   The club, though interested in and "sympathetic" with the work of the Anti-Spoils League of New York City and that of the National Civil Service Reform Convention, refused to take an active part, referring to the fact that "as disfranchised citizens, we regard it as incompatible with our dignity to take an active part in politics. . . ."[34]   In the meantime, they hoped to do all possible good by "quiet individual influence."

Between 1868 and 1889, many clubs were founded in various states of the Union.   When Sorosis, wishing to celebrate her twenty-first birthday, sent out a call for a general conference of women's clubs, it went to ninety-seven known organizations and was accepted by delegates from sixty-one.[35]   In these were included some of the associations founded earlier, such as the Ladies' Education Association of Jacksonville, Illinois (1833);

33 *Ibid.*, 54.

34 *Ibid.*, 77.

35 Wood: *op. cit.*, 32; a list of clubs, with their foundation dates, is given, 350 *ff.*

the Ladies' Physiological Institute of Massachusetts (1848) ; the Ladies' Library Association of Kalamazoo, Michigan (1852) ; the Randolph Ladies' Library Association (1855) ; the Fénelon Street Circle of Dubuque, Iowa (1857) ; the Minerva of New Harmony, Indiana (1858) ; and the Brontë of Madison (1864). The variety of interests in these early associations must have been partly responsible for Mrs. Clymer's pointed declaration, which became the motto of the General Federation: "We look for unity, but *unity in diversity.*" A roll call of the prominent women in these clubs reveals the names of those associated with one or another of the great fields opened to women—teaching, medicine, law, the ministry, journalism, and others.

The convention discussed the woman's club: the idea, its growth, its essence, its difference from clubs of men, its methods, influence and future. Out of it came the General Federation of Women's Clubs, for which a constitution was drawn up by a committee of fourteen. Seven of the fourteen were constituted an Advisory Board, and a Ratification Convention, to approve their work, was held in New York City in 1890. Sixty-three delegates, from seventeen states, attended; the constitution was adopted; Charlotte Emerson Brown was elected President; and, with its other officers, Mary B. Temple, Jennie C. Croly, Phoebe A. Hearst, Kate T. Woods, and an advisory board of nine members, the new Federation began its career. On March 3, 1901, the General Federation was granted a charter by Act of Congress.[36] Throughout its brief history there has been a remarkable unanimity, in spite of diverse interests, the only serious division having been threatened at the Milwaukee Biennial on the color question, on which Northern and Southern clubs especially held divergent views. This was settled amicably, in 1902, by an amendment which preserved state sovereignty and made it possible for any club, a member of a state federation, to become eligible to the General Federation.[37]

The organization of a General Federation stimulated a growth of state and territorial organizations, which, beginning in 1892, had, by 1911, extended to include every state in the Union.[38] Thirty-two state organizations had been established before 1900.

[36] *Ibid.*, 342 *ff.*
[37] *Ibid.*, 130 *f.*, 157 *f.*, and 163.
[38] *Ibid.*, 353.

In each state movement there were capable women, but probably none greater than Lucinda Hinsdale Stone, of whom the General Federation said in its resolution, in 1900, that in her death "the woman's club movement and the cause of woman and education, humanity and progress, have lost one of the foremost workers of the age, and one who made an impress on the life and thought of her time not exceeded by any other woman."[39]

III. Purposes of Women's Clubs

As noted, the purpose of early associations was educational, either in the public or the personal sense. With Friends in Council, as with numerous others, the objective was personal culture through extensive reading and discussion. On the other hand, the Ladies Association at Jacksonville aimed to keep the nation from growing up "under the predominating influence of ignorance and fanaticism, anarchy and misrule." They wished that men might see that "unless means and efforts are almost miraculously increased, the coming generation will soon, as a majority, be ignorant and debased, and then our country is lost." Realizing that "the work of saving the nation" must be undertaken, they saw the need for "some organized system of operation . . . to prepare female teachers" and hastened to provide it.[40]

These two objectives, the individual and the social, have been pursued by different clubs, according to the needs and wishes of their members. Helen Starrett noted in her *Letters to Elder Daughters* (1888) that the objects of clubs were various, but chiefly literary. Mrs. Henrotin regarded the club movement as an important new agency for women's education, which recognized "the fact that education is not limited to the school period but continues to the last day of . . . life." The club continues to add to that limited education given by the school. The slogan of one club holds true for most, if not all: "The education of women in all lines affecting their especial work in the home and their influence in the community."[41]

In more recent years, the club for personal improvement,—"a school where they might teach and be taught, a mutual improve-

---

[39] Perry: *Lucinda Stone*, 172–3.
[40] *Am. Annals*, V, 81–4.
[41] *Woman's Club of Swarthmore*, Pennsylvania, organized in 1898.

ment society,''—has given way, in larger centers at least, to the club of many departments, all having a bearing on public affairs. Mrs. Croly, of Sorosis, as early as 1869, was striving to direct the club to public education, reformatory schools, hygienic and sanitary reforms, women's labor, domestic economy, and other matters connected with the public welfare.[42]   Even in the New York Club, her proposal was defeated.   Women were not yet educated to the point, were not yet sure enough of themselves, to enter such undertakings.   And if not in the great city, certainly not in the small towns and villages.   The first efforts had to be small and local; had to be directed to the broader education of the members themselves before they could undertake boldly a work of wider significance.

The organization of the General Federation, in 1890, marks the turning of women's clubs' attention to certain definite objectives of wide significance.   These were, many of them, not new; but it was a novelty for women's clubs everywhere to attend to them.   In many quarters there began to develop a feeling that the whole effort of a club should not be spent on study of the fifteenth century when the problems of the twentieth were staring them full in the face.

The formation of the Civic Club of Philadelphia (1893) signified the turning to municipal affairs in a larger way than before. At the third Biennial (1896), Mary E. Mumford expressed her belief that ''the great movement toward municipal housecleaning and housekeeping'' would ''find a steady propelling force in the woman's club.''   For the benefit of her fellow members, she defined a civic club as follows: ''The woman who plants a tree and cleans the street in front of her door is a civic club of one.   The woman who follows her child to school and demands sanitary conditions in the school room, mental discipline and moral culture, is a civic club of one.   When, from the home and the school, she begins to study the administration of all public charity and the principle of government, she is still a civic club of one.   A number of such women banded together make a civic club.''[43]

The number of specific questions in which the General Federation has taken an interest is legion.   The impelling motive has been a desire to perform some service.   Without presuming to discuss them, it is worth while to call the roll of the more impor-

42 Wood: *op. cit.*, 27.

43 *Ibid.*, 72 and 75.

tant: education, child labor, public health, reforestation, conservation of natural resources, reclamation of arid lands, art education, marriage laws, divorce laws, laws securing the possession of children to the mother, civil service reforms, traveling libraries, industrial conditions, pure food laws, woman suffrage, school hygiene, social hygiene, Americanization, the Bible as literature, the establishment of a secretariat of education, and so forth.[44]

As education was the oldest, so it has continued to be among the most permanent and engrossing activities of the woman's club. The opening of new activities since 1890 has scarcely diminished the attention given to that subject. It has had a prominent place at each Biennial meeting of the General Federation. At the third (1896) the "Uses of University Extension Lectures," and women in various occupations and professions requiring special education, were discussed. The Department of Education, under Mary E. Mumford, presented such topics as "The Philosophy of the Kindergarten," "The Schools a Moral Factor in the Nation" and the "Relation of College to the Lower Schools."[45] A resolution declared: "We recommend to the clubs a study of the science of education and of educational conditions existing in their home cities, to the end that the united influence of women's clubs may be exerted for the betterment of the state system of education from the Kindergarten to the University." Systematic instruction in ethics was also urged as a necessary part of the school curriculum.[46] The convention, in 1898, listened to a program dealing with "Transitions of Modern Education," "Ethical Education in the Schools," and "Manual Education"; and numerous reports on school decoration, education in patriotism, legislation for improvement of schools, women on school boards, education of defectives, instruction in home economics, truant laws, manual training, vocational schools, night schools, kindergartens, visitation of schools and the coördination of educational efforts.[47] The establishment of a national university in Washington was endorsed. The Education Department reported, in 1900, that women had "visited schools systemati-

---

[44] See the programs of the Biennial conventions in Wood: *op. cit.*, 43 *ff.*; and such books as Cass: *Practical Programs for Women's Clubs* and Benton: *Woman's Club Work*, etc.

[45] Wood: *op. cit.*, 84.

[46] *Ibid.*, 87; also *Proc. N. E. A.*, 1897, 74 *ff.*

[47] *Ibid.*, 102 and 108.

cally . . . studied school laws and conditions and aided in preventing truancy; coöperated with local, state and national associations; united . . . home and school by means of mothers' clubs, child study circles . . . ; maintained vocation schools . . . ; served . . . [on] school boards . . . and as county and state superintendents of schools; maintained free kindergartens and secured their adoption into the public school system; . . . [promoted] manual training, . . . domestic science, . . . sewing . . . and equipped model kitchens; provided for reading rooms, play rooms, and public playgrounds; improved . . . sanitary conditions of schoolhouses and grounds; [and] cultivated the aesthetic sense by the artistic decoration of school rooms, . . . gifts of pictures and casts, by instruction in outdoor art and prizes for flower culture."[48]

In 1906, state federations were urged to encourage their congressmen to pass a compulsory school law for the District of Columbia. Realizing that education was a state, rather than a national, affair, a stand was taken for "equalization of educational advantages" so that "any child in any nook or corner of the nation may receive as good an education as any child in the most favorable locality now receives."[49] Since 1906, national influence on education in the states has increased in a number of ways and women's clubs have taken a stand in favor of a national department of education with a secretary in the President's cabinet.

The coöperation of various clubs, for the improvement of education, may be noted in a single state, which will illustrate the tendency to unification of efforts along this line. In 1903, Celeste Bush, of Niantic, Connecticut, brought together sixty women, representatives of the Women's Christian Temperance Union, The Collegiate Alumnae, Daughters of the American Revolution, State Federation of Women's Clubs, Motherhood Club, Wellesley Club, Mount Holyoke Club, and the women teachers of the state, and founded the Connecticut Woman's Council of Education, later the National Council of Education. The objectives of this organization were stated to be: "To become acquainted with the true condition of education in Connecticut; to study the educational work in other states and nations; to improve the schools throughout the commonwealth; to secure

48 *Ibid.*, 124.
49 *Ibid.*, 205.

the coöperation of the educational agencies of the state; [and] to raise the standard for admission to the profession of teaching."[50]

In child labor, school hygiene, and also social hygiene, the work of women's clubs has come to bear on educational problems. At the ninth Biennial (1908), the principles of the education committee, formulated by Miss Abbott, stressed the point that the aim of "equal educational opportunities for all children in the United States," meant nothing until strong and well enforced child labor laws, as well as compulsory school laws, existed in every state.[51] Club efforts have been consistently directed toward securing the enactment of a child labor amendment. The following women's organizations were among the active supporters of the proposed amendment, in 1924: American Association of University Women, General Federation of Women's Clubs, Girls' Friendly Society in America, National Council of Catholic Women, National Council of Jewish Women, National Council of Women, National Federation of Business and Professional Women's Clubs, National League of Women Voters, National Women's Christian Temperance Union, National Women's Trade Union League, and the Young Women's Christian Association.[52] The sub-committee on School Hygiene, in 1912, urged the appointment of a committee "whose interest should be the promotion of the health of school children" and that they should coöperate "with state and local officials" and "club and community workers" for the accomplishment of their ends. The committee on Social Hygiene for the restriction of "the spread of social diseases among the innocent, especially women and children," urged that adults be reached by "lectures and pamphlets" and caused to "instruct their children early enough to save them from the possibility of infection." The Health Committee urged the naming of a School Hygiene Committee, which should, among other things, "endeavor to reach school teachers collectively, and interest the school authorities in the proper education of the children in their classes on these important subjects. . . ."[53]

[50] Jenkins: Origin of the National Council of Education [*Educational Foundations* (1909–10), XXI, 579].

[51] Wood: *op. cit.*, 230.

[52] Watson: *The Proposed Twentieth Amendment* (1924), 8–9.

[53] *Ibid.*, 283–5.

IV. Estimates of Women's Club Work

Women's clubs have attempted many works of improvement. Though, on first examination, they may seem remote, it will appear that these reforms are chiefly connected with functions formerly performed by women in their homes. Their four walls have expanded to include the walls of the city, the boundaries of the state and the nation. As many things which concerned men in the early nineteenth century had no more than local bearing, but have now become of national importance, so also have those things which pertained to the accepted sphere of woman. Many efforts of women to meet these problems on the larger scale cannot appear as more or less than hasty, ill-considered, the result of faulty education, and, so far, futile. The same must be said of many efforts made by men. The woman's club movement is no more to be judged a failure, because it has known failures, than other movements and organizations that have learned success by failure.

While prejudged to failure, by the men of New York in 1868, Sorosis grew rapidly and found herself not alone in the world. Women did not know, but they found out, that their clubs could teach them what to do and how to do it. The clubs became both the instrument for locating the public task and the machine for performing it, or bringing others to do so. With some, of course, the club became merely a pastime, a place where one could 'take up art' or music or literature, or something else, and dispose of each in an evening. But the great programs of reform, on which the state and national organizations have embarked, indicate the presence of a serious-minded group, and an enlightened leadership, which may be expected to continue to accomplish much.

In keeping with the early spirit of antagonism to the woman's club movement, there have been critics with little perception who have not hesitated to blame the prevalence of divorce and remarriage on the development of women's clubs.[54] Some have declared, and probably others have felt, with Mrs. O'Harra, that "many women busy themselves with running meetings while their own children's morals are neglected" or they spend their time "soaking themselves in the cheap magazines of the day."[55]

[54] *N. C. University Magazine* (1886), N. S., V, No. 6, 244.

[55] [Phila.] *Evening Public Ledger*, Jan. 4, 1926.

But others point out that such women would neglect their families even though there were no women's clubs to go to; and that women who are seriously inclined to accept responsibility are much more adequately prepared for it through the educational, political, and civic programs of their clubs. For such as these there cannot be too many women's clubs; they improve her life, her home; whether she be from college or the elementary school, the club extends and perfects the education of the woman as well as that of the man.[56] Benton declared, in 1913, that:

"The time has long since passed when a special plea is needed for the existence of women's clubs, for actual demonstration has proved their worth to the individual and to society. Multitudes of women on farms, on remote ranches, in little villages, in great cities, have felt their impetus to a broader and more useful life. They have instructed those of limited education; they have given a wider horizon to those hemmed in by circumstance; they have trained the timid to speak, and, of late years, they have prepared the way for women of leisure and influence to take up what is called 'the larger housekeeping,' the bettering of social and civic conditions."[57]

Howe, too, saw women's clubs as "the sign and seal of the advance of woman in health, in sound life, and in rational enjoyment and service. . . . I know of many of them, and I do not know of one which does not keep in view serious and worthy objects."[58] There is, doubtless, too great a tendency to confuse change, and increase of numbers, with progress. Even though the General Federation has long passed the mark of a million members, one is scarcely to be condemned for a lack of enthusiastic appreciation who fails to catch the vision of the early "coming of a kingdom not made with hands."[59]

Mrs. Jennie de la M. Lozier summarized, without exaggeration, the contribution of the early club movement, when she said:

"It gives to woman, first, a sense of individuality; second, some conception of true democracy; third, sympathetic understanding; fourth, a development of the judicial faculty; fifth, a power of expression. In other words, the early club life may be said to have laid the foundation necessary for the proper devel-

[56] *Ibid.*, Feb. 6, 1926.
[57] Benton: *Woman's Club Work and Programs*, 11.
[58] *Educational News*, June 28, 1890, 406.
[59] Wood: *op. cit.*, 295.

opment of that civic power with which organized womanhood should in the twentieth century prove its usefulness.''[60]

Club members, though the best judges of its worth to them as individuals, may easily have exaggerated the public worth of the woman's club. But there are many others who have corroborated the judgment that the influence was great. Hammond pointed out recently the significant work of Southern women's clubs for racial adjustment.[61] In ''awakening public sentiment, improving schoolhouses, and even in effecting school legislation'' women's clubs had (1903) rendered ''invaluable assistance.'' The Federation of Women's Clubs in Alabama had aided in the establishment of a girls' normal and industrial school at Montevallo, campaigned against child labor and led a movement for improvement of schoolhouses and grounds. McIver reported to the Virginia Conference that a woman's association had been formed in North Carolina for the improvement of schoolhouses; that twenty counties had such organizations; and that they planned to form an association of women around every school.[62]

For a wider circle of educators, W. T. Harris (1894) spoke of the importance of the ''federated clubs'' for the ''extension of schools and colleges.'' Governor Adams declared enthusiastically, in 1898, that ''the Nation owes a debt of gratitude to women's clubs. They have been an inspiration to its members, they have been centers from which radiate electric currents of moral and political reform. They have broadened their own horizon and that of the race. . . .'' That there is something substantial resulting from women's clubs is also the belief expressed by Carlton, who noted in his *Education and Industrial Evolution* (1908) that they ''are beginning to exert a powerful directive influence upon social, political and educational affairs.'' Today every propagandist movement knows the importance of securing the backing of women's clubs, whether local or national. First, by giving women opportunities for self-exploration and development and, second, by uniting them to face, more effectively, social problems of the modern world, the women's club movement has contributed largely to their emancipation in the broadest sense.

[60] *Ibid.*, 50–1.

[61] Hammond: *Southern Women and Racial Adjustment* [J. F. Slater Fund, Occasional Papers, 1917, No. 19].

[62] *R. C. E.* (1903), I, 371–2.

CHAPTER X

CONCLUSION

In early Colonial days, the conception of women's position, socially, politically, and educationally, was determined primarily by foreign antecedents. Throughout this period the education of girls was a somewhat variable, but generally meager, quantity. In the Northern colonies, due to English tradition, a narrow Puritanism, pioneer conditions which made hard work an absolute necessity, and a firm reliance on Christian theology, the Colonial maid found few opportunities for learning. In the Central colonies, due to a more liberal religious conception, so far as Quakers were concerned, and a somewhat more favorable tradition in Holland and Germany, which affected colonists from thence, it is found that girls generally shared elementary school privileges, though a higher education was not accessible to them. In the South, daughters of the wealthy were usually given opportunities for education by private tutors; but, so far as the lower class was concerned, education was chiefly through apprenticeship and philanthropic agencies and generally did not extend beyond the merest rudiments of reading and, perhaps, writing. Everywhere crude conditions of pioneer life militated against great educational achievements, for boys as well as girls.

With the advancement of the eighteenth century beyond its noon, a change is noted, proceeding from numerous private schools which had appeared somewhat earlier, chiefly in cities. Many "adventure" masters and mistresses began to cater to popular demands. Gradually the seminary or academy took definite form as a well-organized institution. This institution was frequently open to boys and girls together. A vast number of seminaries and academies were established especially for girls. This was true in all parts of the United States east of the Mississippi, and, to a considerable extent, west of it, between 1780 and 1870. In the female seminary, women had their first general opportunity to gain an intellectual insight into the problems of life. No longer were they compelled to rely wholly on the hard

469

experience gained from everyday drudgery. It was on the foundation of a seminary education that women built the super-structure of a higher education and prepared for manifold activi-ties in various professions. With this somewhat superficial preparation they frequently entered the profession of teaching. Having proved their native ability in that field, they found many advocates ready to urge that they be given a much more adequate preparation for this profession. The result was the establish-ment of normal schools, which took place coincidently with the rise of the common school movement, and one of whose primary purposes was the preparation of an economical teacher supply. As women were willing to work for a lower wage, having no other professional openings outside the home, the normal schools soon looked to women for their students,—and the common schools, to women for their teachers.

Following upon the success of the seminary, came the develop-ment of two other important institutions: the first, a new sec-ondary school, the high school, which may be regarded as a pub-lic embodiment of the old private seminary; the second, the female college, which was destined in time to extend the range of women's education beyond the somewhat superficial studies of early seminaries. The public high school, developing rapidly after 1870, came to have an even larger enrollment of girls than boys. In time, its general course became so diversified as to offer vocational preparation, enabling thousands of girls to at once take up some occupation. The establishment of the female college upon a plane comparable with the male college required a period of experimentation extending over about fifty years, the development of the idea having begun at least as early as 1825, and the first college for women, which was able to duplicate the male college curriculum, being opened in 1875. Work, worthy of the name "collegiate," comparable in varying degrees with that done at men's colleges, and rewarded by an A.B. degree, had been available to women for twenty-five years: first, at Mary Sharp College; and then at Elmira and Vassar. The successful out-come of the college movement, culminating in the establishment of a high-grade institution with a curriculum as broad and solid as that of the men's institution, owed much to the increase of academies, seminaries and high schools between 1820 and 1870. Without these preparatory institutions, many of the earlier collegiate experiments found it impossible to establish work of true college grade.

A change, of utmost consequence to the life of women, took place in the establishment and gradual development of the factory system of production in the early part of the nineteenth century, and continued throughout to the present time. Prior to this great economic readjustment, woman had labored in the home as producer. The life of her children, and even their education, was her intimate concern. The new factories, ofttimes in the hands of unscrupulous and avaricious men, demanded cheap labor. Operating on a large scale, they began to produce goods in such quantities that the housewife could no longer compete with them as a producer in the home. Women have always been producers since the days of the most primitive human societies. It was not to be expected that all of them should be content to eat the bread of idleness. Even had they been content, the income of the poor, and even of the moderately circumstanced, family would not have been equal to the support of the women—the mothers—in idleness. It was but natural, then, that women should withdraw in increasingly large numbers to enter into work of various kinds outside the home. Having undertaken the drudgery of the factory, it would have been strange, indeed, had they not seen the possibility and the desirability, of preparing themselves for higher occupations than those of the manual laborer. The mill girls, we find,—at least many of the most intelligent,—were desirous of preparing themselves to enter a profession. Many of them entered teaching.

The economic changes of the past century, the shifting of woman's sphere from the hearth to the outside world, have contributed much to the development of several grave problems: the decline of the family as an effective social factor in stabilizing society; the marriage and divorce question; the care of the children; and the education of children. Likewise, in connection with the manifold complexities of life in an industrial society, which no longer depends upon a system of apprenticeship training, there has come the extremely perplexing problem of vocational preparation and vocational guidance.

Having entered into the work-a-day world outside the home, having secured admission to the lowliest of public professions— that of teaching—women gradually forced their way into the more exclusive professional fields of medicine, law, and even sacred theology. These steps were not taken without a vast and painful struggle on the part of individuals who saw the necessity of women having the opportunity to go into the highest and the best paid professions if they were to be allowed—yes, even compelled by force of circumstances—to go into the lowest. Besides entering these four most ancient professions, women have gradually found a place in practically every profession recognized by the United States Bureau of the Census.

When women went into these new and untried activities, they found themselves facing difficulties over which they had no control. They found themselves interested directly in certain things which formerly had concerned them, for the most part, indirectly. They became workers for wages, involved in the question of hours of labor, condition of manufacturing establishments, and so on *ad infinitum*. Moreover, having turned their children over to an hireling nurse—the public schools—they became vitally interested in the laws governing those institutions, the preparation of teachers for them, the sanitary condition of schoolhouses, and the employment of their children in factories. It was inevitable, then, that women should henceforth be made competent, in the legal and practical sense, to exercise a guiding influence over these affairs by direct political action.

This final revolution had to take place first in the minds of women themselves. Once they grasped the idea firmly and began to propose such an enormous change, the vast majority of male society in the United States was turned against them as against some loathsome thing. For was not here, in their proposed political equality, a complete negation of the principles of God himself? Thus it was felt by the multitude, without a doubt; and thus it was expressed by the leaders who opposed granting the political franchise to women. In 1850, there were comparatively few leaders among men in the United States who would agree that the "honorable rights of woman" were "the reasonable rights of man," and that the perfect rights of both were the "supreme will of God." Rather than agree to such an equality, the vast majority were inclined to the notion that woman suffrage constituted a "reform against nature," was antisocial and anti-Christian. Due, however, to heroic leadership on the part of women themselves and the assistance of the gradually augmented numbers of men who became convinced of the righteousness of woman's demands, woman suffrage finally succeeded. The intimate connection between woman suffrage and the education of children is to be seen in the fact that the earliest provisions for exercise of the franchise were in connection with the settlement of school questions. The full suffrage granted by Wyoming, in 1869, was a pattern which most other states hesitated long about imitating. Having gradually won over a number of individual states, the question was finally settled on a nation-wide basis by the equal suffrage amendment, despite the chicanery of politicians.

This does not represent the sum of all things for which women have striven during the past seventy-five years. It has about it, however, a certain degree of finality which other successes, already achieved, did not possess. With it in her hands, woman has the same opportunity to control the various agencies that affect her life, as has man. Looking back over the past three hundred years, it is clear, however, that though political emancipation is the great symbol of women's victory, their intellectual emancipation, because of its priority and fundamental character, was of vaster significance. Without freedom from thoroughgoing subjection to the drudgeries of life, without the opening of even a few, and, at first, inferior, institutions of higher learning, women would never have been able to conceive of their complete emancipation as citizens; nor been able to profit by it, had it been given them. With native powers sharpened by education and experience, comparable with that available for men, and ofttimes identically the same (but here and there they must still fight for it), the progressives of today demand that the elimination of the last barriers to their emancipation be guaranteed by an equal rights amendment to the constitution.

The modern woman, if she rightly estimates the value of the heritage she has gained in the past hundred and fifty years, might with propriety express her sentiments as did a little school girl of long ago:

"Next unto God, dear Parents, I address
"Myself to you in humble thankfulness
"For all your care and pains on me bestowed
"And means of learning unto me allowed.
"Go on I pray and let me still pursue
"These golden paths the vulgar never knew."

APPENDICES

APPENDIX I

TEXTBOOKS MENTIONED BY WOMEN'S COLLEGE CATALOGS SINCE 1850

Aesthetics
Alison on Taste
Bascomb: Aesthetics

Algebra
Bailey: Algebra
Davis: Algebra
Davies' Bourdon: Algebra
Davies: Elementary Algebra
Davis: Algebra
Day: Algebra
Loomis: Algebra
Olney: University Algebra
Ray: Algebra
Robinson: Algebra
Robinson: University Algebra

Analysis
Bullion: Parsing
Green: Analysis

Anglo-Saxon
Anglo-Saxon Bible
Beowulf and Judith
Sweet: Reader

Arithmetic
Davies: Arithmetic
Emerson: Arithmetic
Ray: Higher Arithmetic

Astronomy
Burritt: Geography of the Heavens
Kiddle: Astronomy
Mattison: Descriptive Astronomy
McIntire: Astronomy

Astronomy (Cont'd)
Olmstead: Astronomy
Olmstead: Astronomy (University edition)
Olmstead and Mattison: Astronomy
Robinson: Astronomy
Smith: Astronomy
Snell's Olmstead: Astronomy
Young: Astronomy

Bookkeeping
Mayhew: Bookkeeping

Botany
Darby: Botany
Eaton: Botany
Gray: Botany
Lincoln: Botany
Wood: Botany

Calculus
Olney: Calculus
Robinson: Calculus

Chemistry
Beck: Chemistry
Draper: Chemistry
Eliot and Storer: Manual
Gray: Chemistry
Johnston: Chemistry
Silliman: Chemistry
Stockhardt: Chemistry
Turner: Chemistry
Wells: Chemistry
Youmans: Chemistry
Youmans: Inorganic Chemistry
Youmans: Organic Chemistry

474

Composition
Boyd: Composition
Parker: Aids to Composition
Quackenbos: Composition and Rhetoric

Conic Sections
Bridge: Conic Sections
Loomis: Conic Sections

Constitutional History
Stubbs, Hallam and May: Constitutional History of England

Criticism
Boyd's Kames: Criticism
Kames: Criticism

Elocution
Russell: Elocution

English Grammar
Bullion: Grammatical Analysis
Fowler: English Grammar
Kerl: English Grammar
Smith: English Grammar

English Literature
Botta: English Literature
Boyd: English Literature
Boyd: Notes on Cowper
Boyd: Notes on Paradise Lost
Boyd: Notes on Thomson's Seasons
Boyd: Notes on Young's Night Thoughts
Burke on the Sublime
Chambers: English Literature
Chaucer
Cleveland: English Literature
Fowler: English Literature
Goldsmith: Analysis of Prose and Poetry
Hallam: English Literature
Harrison: English Language
Mills: English Literature
Milton: Paradise Lost
Montgomery: Lectures on Poetry
Piers the Ploughman
Reed: English Literature

English Literature (cont'd)
Schlegel: General Literature
Schlegel: History of Literature
Shakespeare
Shaw: English Literature
Spalding: English Literature
Spalding: History of English Literature

French
Albert: Littérature Française
Andrews and Batchelor: French Instructor
Andrews and Batchelor: French Pronouncer and Key
Arnold: French Composition
Bocher: Modern French Plays
Bolmar: Colloquial Phrases
Bolmar: Grammar
Boyer: Dictionary
Buffet: Littérature
Chapsal: Littérature Française
Chardenal: Translation from English into French
Charles XII
Callot: Dramatic French Reader
Corneille
De Fiva: French Reader
Fasquelle: Colloquial French Reader
Fasquelle: Corinne
Fasquelle's Dumas: Napoleon
Fasquelle: Grammar
Fasquelle: Racine
Fasquelle: Télémaque
French Testament
George Sand
Henriade
Howard: French Prose Composition
Knapp: French Grammar and Reading Book
La Fontaine: Fables
L'Allemagne
Lamartine
La Sainte Bible
Le Cid
Le Grand-Père

French (cont'd)
  Madame de Sèvigné
  Merimée
  Molière
  Molière: Les Femmes Savantes
  Noel and Chapsal: French Grammar
  Ollendorff: French Grammar
  Otto: French Grammar
  Perrin: Fables
  Picciola
  Picot: French Reader
  Pinney and Arnoult
  Rowan: French Reader
  Victor Hugo
  Vie de Washington
  Williams: English into French

General Science
  Bigelow: Application of Science to Useful Arts

Geography
  Barrington: Physical Geography
  Colton: Physical Geography
  Dew: Ancient and Modern Geography
  Fitch and Colton: Physical Geography
  Guyot: Physical Geography
  Long: Atlas of Ancient Geography
  Mitchell: Ancient Geography
  Mitchell: Geography
  Ritter: Physical Geography
  Somerville: Physical Geography

Geology
  Dana: Geology
  Gray and Adams: Geology
  Hitchcock: Geology
  St. John: Geology
  Tenney: Geology
  Wells: Geology

Geometry
  Chauvenet: Solid and Spherical Geometry
  Davies: Analytical Geometry

Geometry (cont'd)
  Davies: Geometry
  Davies' Legendre: Geometry
  Davies' Legendre: Spherical Geometry
  Loomis: Geometry
  Robinson: Geometry
  Smyth: Analytical Geometry

German
  Adler: Dictionary
  Adler: Handbook of German Literature
  Adler's Ollendorff: Grammar
  Adler: Progressive German Reader
  Boker: Introduction
  Egmont
  Follen: Grammar
  German Testament
  Goethe: Faust
  Goethe: Iphigenie
  Herder
  Lessing: Minna von Barnhelm
  Lessing: Prose
  Otto: German Grammar
  Schiller: Jungfrau
  Schiller: Maria Stuart
  Schiller: Thirty Years' War
  Schiller: William Tell
  Storm: Immensee
  Uhland
  Webber: Dictionary
  Wenckebach: Grammar
  Whitney: Grammar and Reader
  Woodbridge: Eclectic German Reader
  Woodbury: Elementary Reader
  Woodbury: Grammar and Reader
  Woodbury: Method
  Woodbury: Shorter Course

Greek
  Adams' Lemprier: Antiquities
  Aeschines: De Corona
  Aeschylus: Prometheus Bound
  Arian
  Aristophanes: Birds
  Aristophanes: Clouds
  Aristotle: Ethics

Greek (cont'd)
  Aristotle: Politics
  Arnold: Greek Prose Composition
  Boise: Xenophon's Anabasis
  Brooks: Greek Lessons
  Brooks: Collectanea Evangelica
  Bullion: Grammar
  Bullion: Greek Reader
  Crosby: Greek Grammar and Lessons
  Demosthenes: De Corona
  Demosthenes: Oedipus Tyrannus
  Euripedes: Alcestis
  Euripedes: Medea
  Graeca Majora
  Graeca Minora
  Greenfield: Greek Testament
  Harkness and Goodwin: Greek Grammar
  Herodotus
  Jones: Greek Prose
  Kendrick: Grammar
  Liddell and Scott: Greek Lexicon
  Longinus
  Lucian
  Merry's Homer: Odyssey
  Ollendorff: Grammar
  Owen: Homer
  Owen's Xenophon: Anabasis
  Pindar
  Plato: Apology
  Plato: Crito
  Plato: Gorgias
  Plato: Phaedo
  Plato: Protagoras
  Plato: Republic
  Potter: Grecian Antiquities
  Robbins' Xenophon: Memorabilia
  Septuagint
  Sophocles: Antigone
  Sophocles: Electra
  Strong's Harmony: Greek Testament
  Taylor's Kuhner: Elements of Greek Grammar
  Thucydides
  Tyler: Demosthenes on the Crown
  Tyler: Selections from the Greek Lyric Poets

Greek (cont'd)
  Xenophon: Hellenics
  Xenophon: Isocrates

History
  Eadie: Oriental History
  Goldsmith: England
  Goldsmith: France
  Goldsmith: Greece
  Goldsmith: Rome
  Goodrich: Ecclesiastical History
  Grimshaw: France
  Liddell: Rome
  Smith: Greece
  Student's Hume (Hist. of England)
  Weber: General History
  Whelpley: General History and Chronology
  Willard: Universal History
  Wilson: Ancient History
  Wilson: Modern History
  Wilson: Philosophy of History
  Worcester: Elements

International Law
  Woolsey: International Law

Italian
  Foresti: Reader
  Ollendorff: Grammar
  Tasso: Jerusalem Delivered

Latin
  Adam: Roman Antiquities
  Allen and Greenough: Ovid
  Andrews: Latin Reader
  Andrews and Stoddard: Grammar
  Anthon: Aeneid
  Anthon: Cicero
  Anthon: Horace
  Anthon: Nepos
  Anthon: Sallust
  Anthon: Tacitus
  Arnold: First and Second Books
  Arnold: Latin Prose Composition
  Beck: Hercules Fureus
  Brooks: Caesar
  Brooks: Expurgated Ovid
  Brooks: Latin Lessons

Latin (cont'd)
Brooks' Ross: Latin Grammar
Bullion: Caesar
Bullion: Cicero
Bullion: Latin Grammar
Bullion: Latin Reader
Butler: Sallust
Catullus
Chase and Stewart: Cicero
Cooper: Virgil
Crowell: Selections from the Latin
  Poets
Dillaway: de Senectute and de
  Amicitia
Excerpta Latina
Frieze: Virgil
Grotius
Juvenal
Lincoln: Horace
Lincoln: Livy
Lucan
Lucretius
Moore: Virgil
Persius
Pliny
Plutarch
Propertius
Proudfit: Captives of Plautus
Quintilian: Dialogues
Schmitz and Zumpt: Livy
Terence
Thatcher: Cicero's de Officiis
Tibullus
Tyler: Tacitus

Logic
Everett: Science of Thought
Harris: Theory of the Syllogism
Hedge: Logic
Jevon: Logic
Kant: Prolegomena
Mansel: Prolegomena Logica
Tappan: Logic
Whateley: Logic
Wilson: Logic

Mechanics
Gray: Mechanics

Mensuration
Day: Mensuration

Mental Philosophy
Abercrombie: Intellectual Powers
Abercrombie: Mental Philosophy
Bigelow on Reason
Church: Mental Philosophy
Hamilton: Metaphysics
Harris: Introduction to the Study
  of Philosophy
Haven: Intellectual Philosophy
Haven: Mental Philosophy
Hickok: Mental Philosophy
Porter: Intellectual Science
Schmucker: Mental Philosophy
Upham: Mental Philosophy
Watts on the Mind
Wayland: Mental Philosophy

Meteorology
Brocklesby: Meteorology

Mineralogy
Brush: Mineralogy
Comstock: Mineralogy
Dana: Mineralogy
Emmon: Mineralogy

Moral Philosophy
Abercrombie: Moral Feelings
Abercrombie: Moral Philosophy
Boyd: Moral Philosophy
Haven: Moral Philosophy
Hickok: Moral Philosophy
Hopkins: Moral Philosophy
Paley: Moral Philosophy
Valpy's Paley: Moral Philosophy
Wayland: Moral Science

Natural History
Ruschenburg: Natural History
Smellie: Natural History
Smellie: Philosophy of Natural
  History
Ware's Smellie: Natural History

Natural Philosophy and Physics
Atkinson's Ganot: Physics
Ganot: Physics

Natural Philosophy (cont'd)
  Gray: Natural Philosophy
  Johnston: Natural Philosophy
  Lardner: Natural Philosophy
  Olmstead: Natural Philosophy (2 vols.)
  Olmstead: Natural Philosophy (University Edition)
  Parker: Natural Philosophy
  Renwick: Natural Philosophy
  Silliman: Natural Philosophy
  Wells: Natural Philosophy

Natural Theology
  Chadbourne: Natural Theology
  Paley: Natural Theology
  Potter's Paley: Natural Theology

Philology
  Graham: Synonyms
  March: Philological Study
  March: Study of Anglo-Saxon
  Oswald: Etymological Dictionary

Philosophy
  Harris: History of Philosophy
  Parker: Philosophy
  Olmstead: Mathematical Philosophy
  Schwegler: History of Philosophy
  Spencer: First Principles of Philosophy
  Ueberweg: History of Philosophy

Physiology
  Comstock: Physiology
  Cummings: Physiology
  Cutter: Physiology
  Dalton: Physiology
  Draper: Physiology
  Hitchcock: Physiology
  Lambert: Physiology
  Luce: Physiology

Political Economy
  Hart: Constitution of the United States
  Mansfield: Constitution of the United States
  Mansfield: Political Grammar

Political Economy (cont'd)
  Story: Constitution
  Townsend: Analysis of Civil Government
  Wayland: Political Economy
  Young: Civil Government
  Young: Civil Jurisprudence and Political Economy
  Young: Principles of Government

Psychology
  Browne: Psychology
  Dewey: Psychology
  Hickok: Psychology
  Hopkins: Psychology
  Ladd: Psychology
  Porter: Psychology

Religion
  Alexander: Evidences of Christianity
  Bascom: Ethics
  Butler: Analogy
  Emory and Crook's Butler: Analogy
  Flint: Theism
  Gregory: Evidences of Christianity
  Harris: Self-Revelation of God
  Hopkins: Evidences of Christianity
  Horne: Introduction to the Study of the Bible
  McCosh on Divine Government
  Nevius: Biblical Antiquities
  Nichols: Biblical Analysis
  Nicholl: Introduction to the Study of the Bible
  Paley: Evidences of Christianity
  Pearson: Essay on Infidelity
  Pierce: Biblical History
  Porteus: Evidences of Christianity
  Thompson: Theism
  Wardlaw: Christian Ethics
  White: Christian Centuries

Rhetoric
  Bascomb: Rhetoric
  Blair: Rhetoric

Rhetoric (cont'd)
  Day: Rhetoric
  Hill: Principles of Rhetoric
  Jamieson: Rhetoric
  Newman: Rhetoric
  Quackenbos: Rhetoric
  Whateley: Rhetoric

Spanish
  Cubi: Grammar
  Don Quijote
  Newman: Dictionary
  Novelas Españolas
  Ollendorff: Grammar
  Spanish Testament

Spanish (cont'd)
  Traductor Español
  Velasquez: Reader

Trigonometry
  Davies' Legendre: Plane Trigonometry
  Davies: Trigonometry
  Day: Plane Trigonometry
  Loomis: Trigonometry
  Olney: Plane and Spherical Trigonometry

Zoölogy
  Agassiz: Zoölogy
  Chambers: Zoölogy
  Tenney: Manual of Zoölogy

APPENDIX II

BIBLIOGRAPHY[1]

I[2]

Laws, court records, manuscript and printed minutes, records and plans of institutions, reports, student publications, diplomas, catalogs, and other miscellaneous documents

Abbott Female Academy, Andover, Mass. Catalogs, 1832–1870. [Abbott Archives]

Abbott Female Academy. Financial Day Book of David Hidden, containing items relative to its development. [*MS.*, Abbott Archives]

Abbott Female Academy. A Circular to the Friends of Female Education, published at Andover Theological Seminary, Dec. 19, 1834. [Abbott Archives]

Adams, H. W. A leaflet issued by the Women's Christian Temperance Union, Newark, New Jersey, n.d.

Adams Female Academy, Derry, N. H. Catalogs of the officers and members, 1824–26. [Am. Antiq. Soc., Worcester]

Aimwell School, Philadelphia. Mary Wheeler's Account Book for the Society, 1797–1804. [Aimwell School *MSS.*, Vol. I, Mrs. H. E. Yarnall, 4727 Springfield Avenue, Philadelphia]

Aimwell School. Regulations adopted by the Society for the Free Instruction of Female Children. [Aimwell School *MSS.*, Vols. II and III]

Alabama, Laws of, 1818–1900.

Albion [Mich.] Female Collegiate Institute and Wesleyan Seminary. Catalogs, 1843–4; 1850–1, and 1854–5. [Burton Collection, Detroit Public Library]

Amenia Seminary, Dutchess County, N. Y. Address by E. O. Haven, 1848. [Adriance Memorial Library, Poughkeepsie, N. Y.]

American Female Guardian Society. Reports, 1856–58. New York.

American Women's Education Association. Annual Reports, 1853–74.

Amherst College. Catalogs, 1856–78.

[Anderson, S. C.] Male and Female Academy. *MS.* Minute Book of the Trustees, 1835–60. [Anderson Public Library]

Ann Arbor [Mich.] Female Seminary. Catalog, 1844–5. [Burton Collection, Detroit Public Library]

Ann Smith Academy, Lexington, Va. *MS.* account of, drawn from the Minute Book by Harrington Waddell. [Ann Smith *MSS.*, Harrington Waddell, Lexington, Va., High School]

---

[1] A number of special bibliographies are given on page 506.

[2] For II, newspapers, see p. 496; III, books, pamphlets, theses, etc., p. 501; and IV, periodical publications and proceedings, p. 550.

Ann Smith Academy. Minutes of the Trustees, 1807–1871. [Ann Smith *MSS.*]

Ann Smith Academy. Package of *MS.* papers relating to, 1807—. [Ann Smith *MSS.*]

Ann Smith Academy. Subscription list. [Ann Smith *MSS.*]

Antioch College. Catalogs and Announcements, 1853–1880. [College Library]

Antioch College. Articles of Incorporation, Xenia, 1875. [College Library]

Antioch College. Laws and Regulations, containing an address by Horace Mann. n.p., n.d.

Arizona, Laws of, 1864—.

Association for Promoting the Higher Education of Women in New York. *Proceedings of the First Public Meeting,* April 22, 1882. New York, 1882.

Association for the Advancement of the Medical Education of Women. Reports, 1878, 1880–84, 1887, 1896.

Association of Collegiate Alumnae, Committee on Vocational Opportunities (E. K. Adams, Chairman): *Vocational Education.* Gazette Printing Co.: Northampton, Mass., 1913.

Association of Colleges and Secondary Schools of the Southern States. *Proceedings of the 31st Annual Meeting,* 1926.

Augusta [Ky.] College. Catalog, 1828.

Augusta Female Seminary, Staunton, Va. Catalog, 1844.

Bache, Alexander D. *Report on the Organization of the High School for Girls and Seminary for Female Teachers,* Oct. 5, 1840. Philadelphia, 1840.

Baltimore [Md.] Female College. Prospectus issued by the Trustees, 1849; Catalogs, 1850–75, incomplete file. [Md. Hist. Soc.]

Baltimore [Md.] Eastern Female High School. Report of the Principal, 1860. [Md. Hist. Soc.]

Baltimore [Md.] Female High School. Rules for the Government and Discipline, 1859. [Md. Hist. Soc., Educational Pamphlets, Vol. XCVII]

Barleywood Female Seminary, near Frederick, Md. Catalog, 1839–1840. [Md. Hist. Soc.]

Beecher, Catherine E. *Suggestions Respecting Improvements in Education,* presented to the Trustees of the Hartford Female Seminary. Hartford, 1829.

Biddle, Owen. *Plan for a Boarding School.* Philadelphia, 1790.

Bishop Lee Seminary, Iowa. Catalog, 1866. [Dubuque Public Library]

Boston. Reports on High School for Girls. [Documents Nos. 43, 44, 80 and 89]

Boston High School for Girls. Regulations and Catalog, 1827.

Boston University. Yearbooks, 1870–1900.

Boston Young Ladies' High School. Catalog of the Teachers and Scholars, 1829.

Bourbon Academy, Paris, Ky. *MS.* Minute Book of the Trustees, 1799–1853. [Miss Blanche Lilleston, 672 Higgins Avenue, Paris, Ky.]

Bradford Academy. Catalogs, 1815–70, incomplete file. [School Archives]

Bradford Academy. Lucretia Kimball's Copy Book for Practicing Penmanship (1811?) [School Archives]

Bradford Academy. Lucretia Kimball's *MS*. Arithmetic, 1811. [School Archives]

Bradford Academy. *MS*. Record Book of the Trustees, 1803–43. [School Archives]

Bradford Academy. Constitution of the "Sister Society," 1818 (?). [School Archives]

Bradwell, Myra, vs. the state. [Wallace's Reports, Supreme Court U. S., XVI: 130–42]

Bradwell, Myra. Her application to practice law. [Ill. Supreme Ct. Repts., LV: 535–42]

Brockport [N. Y.] Collegiate Institute. Secretary's *MS*. Book of Records, 1841–54. [Dr. Morris Mann, Brockport, N. Y.]

Brookwood Labor College, Katonah, New York. *Leaflets* and *Announcements*, 1921—.

Bryn Mawr College. Bulletin No. 5, May, 1925.

Bryn Mawr College. Circulars, Nos. 1 and 2, 1883 and 1884.

Bryn Mawr College. Programs and Catalogs, 1885—.

Buckland [Mass.] Female School. Centennial, Sept. 10, 1879.

Buckland Female School. Catalog of Teachers and Pupils, Mar. 2, 1830.

Burnham, Carrie S., The Argument of, before . . . Supreme Court of Pennsylvania . . . [with] the Opinion of Hon. George Sharswood . . . also . . . Laws of Pennsylvania Touching the Rights of Women. Philadelphia, 1873.

California High School Teachers' Association: *Report of the Committee of Fifteen.* 1924.

California, Statutes of, 1849—.

Carey, Mathew. Diary [*MS*.], Dec. 15, 1822–June 16, 1826.

Carter, James G. *Essays upon Popular Education and an Outline of an Institution for the Education of Teachers.* Boston, 1826.

Census Reports of the United States, 1790—. Government Printing Office, Washington.

Central Committee for Promoting National Education. Annual Reports, 1847—, incomplete file.

Chandler, Daniel. An address on Female Education. Washington, Ga., 1835.

Charleston [Mass.] Female Seminary. Catalog, 1843–4. [Conn. Hist. Soc.]

Christian and Brotherly Advices . . . by the Yearly Meeting of New Jersey and Pennsylvania, a Collection. [*MS*.] [304 Arch Street, Philadelphia]

Cincinnati [Ohio] Directories, 1819–20; 1825–6; 1829; 1831; 1834; 1836; 1840.

Coburn Classical Institute, Waterville, Me. Historical Sketch. [Coburn Catalog, 1916–17, 13–18]

Collegiate Institute for Young Ladies, Waterbury, Conn. Catalog, 1866.
    [Conn. Hist. Soc.]
Colorado, Laws of, 1856—.
Columbia Athenaeum, Maury County, Tenn. Fourteenth Annual Catalog,
    1867.
Columbia College. Annual Reports of the President, 1886–95.
Columbia College. Catalogs, 1859–93.
Columbia College. *The Higher Education of Women*—Passages from the
    annual reports of the president of Columbia College, June 1879, 1880,
    and 1881. New York, 1882.
Columbia [Mo.] Female Seminary. Catalog, 1853.
Columbia [Tenn.] Female Institute. Annual Catalogs, 1838, 1840, and 1845.
Commissioner of Education of the United States, Reports of the, 1867–1915.
    Government Printing Office: Washington.
Connecticut Historical Society. *Collections,* 1870–1924. 21 vols. Hartford.
Connecticut, Laws of, 1837–93.
Connecticut Supreme Court Reports. Vols. L–LIV.
Connecticut, The Public Records of the Colony of. 18 vols. Hartford,
    1868–1922.
Connecticut, The Public Statute Laws of the State of, in 1821. Hartford,
    1824.
Cottage Hill Female Seminary, Poughkeepsie, N. Y. Descriptive folder,
    about 1856. [Adriance Memorial Library, Poughkeepsie, N. Y.]

Dakota Territory, Laws of, 1867–1882.
De Bow, J. D. B. *Statistical View of the United States: being a com-
    pendium of the 7th Census.* Washington, 1854.
Dickinson College. Catalog, 1855–6.
Due West [S. C.] Woman's College. Treasurer's Report, Bulletin 1924–25.

East Avenue Collegiate Institute, Rochester, N. Y. Catalog, 1857. [Munic-
    ipal Museum Hist. Soc., Rochester]
East Maine Conference Seminary, Bucksport, Me. Third Annual Catalog,
    1853–4. [State Library]
East Tennessee University. Catalog of Officers, Alumni and Students,
    1851–2. [State Library]
Elizabeth Female Academy, Rules of. [*Miss. Hist. Soc. Pub.,* II, 172–4]
Elmira [N. Y.] College. Catalogs, 1855—.
Elmira College. Diploma, 1859. [Supplied by the College]
Emerson's Female Seminary, Byfield and Saugus, Mass. Catalogs, 1818–22.
Emerson's Female Seminary, Wethersfield, Conn. Prospectus; Course of
    Instruction; Maxims on Education; Regulations, with notes on books;
    Branches of Literature and Methods of Instruction, 1826. [Conn. Hist.
    Soc.]
Emma Willard School, Troy, N. Y. Catalog, 1895–6. [School Archives]
Emma Willard School. Circular to the Citizens of Troy, 1871. [School
    Archives]

Farmington [Me.] Academy. Catalog of Officers and Students, 1839. [State Library]

Fayette Street Female Seminary, Syracuse, N. Y. Catalog, 1853. [Public Library]

Female Classical Seminary, Brookfield, Mass. Catalog, 1826. [Conn. Hist. Soc.]

Female Medical College, Philadelphia. Annual Announcements, 1850—, incomplete file.

Female Medical Educational Society. Reports, 1848–56. Boston.

Female Medical Education Society of New England. Reports to the Massachusetts Legislature by a committee favoring appropriations to the Society. [Senate Document No. 70, 1851; and No. 105, 1852]

Female Student and Young Ladies Chronicle, The, 1844–47. Vols. I–III. Wesleyan Female Collegiate Institute: Wilmington, Delaware.

Fisk Female Academy. A manuscript in a folder of Overton County history. [State Library, Tenn.]

Frederick [Md.] Female Seminary. Certificate of Proficiency in Penmanship, 1839. [Florence Trail, Frederick, Md.]

Frederick Female Seminary. Diploma, 1843. [Florence Trail, Frederick, Md.]

Frederick Female Seminary. Catalogs, 1842–90, incomplete file. [Florence Trail, Frederick Md. and at Hood College, Frederick, Md.]

Friends' Academy, New Bedford, Mass. Catalogs, 1859–89, incomplete file. [New Bedford Public Library]

Friends, Rules of Discipline of the Yearly Meeting of, Held in Philadelphia. Philadelphia, 1828.

Gallaudet, T. H. *Plan of a Seminary for the Education of Instructors of Youth.* Boston, 1825.

Georgetown [Ky.] Female Seminary. Catalogs, 1857–89, incomplete file. [Georgetown College Archives]

Georgia, Acts of the General Assembly of the State of, 1823, 1824, 1828, 1832–35, 1837, 1840, 1842–43, 1847, 1851–1858. Atlanta.

Georgia, A Compilation of the Laws of, 1800–10. By A. S. Clayton. Augusta, 1813.

Georgia, The Colonial Records of, 1754–1805. (Compiled by Allen D. Chandler) 3 vols. Published by the State: Atlanta, 1910–11.

Georgia Female College, Macon. Diploma of Catherine Brewer, July 1840 [College Archives]

German Reformed Congregation in Pennsylvania, Minutes and Letters of the Coetus of, 1747–1792. (Ed. by J. I. Good and William J. Hinke.) Reformed Church Publication Board: Philadelphia, 1903.

Granville [O.] Female Academy. Catalogs, 1835–60. [Susan Bawden, Granville, O.]

Granville Female College. Catalogs, 1861–96. [Susan Bawden, Granville, O.]

Greenfield [Mass.] High School for Young Ladies. Outline of the Plan of Education, 1829. [Conn. Hist. Soc.]

[Hallesche] *Nachrichten von den vereinigten Deutschen Evangelisch-Luth-erischen Gemeinen in Nord Amerika.* 2 vols. Halle, 1787.

Hartford [Conn.] Female Seminary. Catalogs, 1851–68, incomplete file. [State Library]

Harvard College. Catalogs, 1850–75.

Hebron [Me.] Academy. Catalogs, 1855 and 1866. [State Library]

Hening, William W. (Compiler). *The Statutes at Large . . . of Virginia,* 1619–1792. 13 vols. Richmond, 1809–23.

Hobart College, Circular, Mar. 26, 1925: Concerning the Elizabeth Blackwell Professorship of Medicine, London University.

Holliston [Mass.] Academy. Rules and Regulations. n.d. [Holliston Hist. Soc.]

Holliston Manual Labor School. Catalog, 1838. [Holliston Hist. Soc.]

Holliston Academy. Catalogs, 1840–56. [Holliston Hist. Soc.]

Home School (Lexington, Mass.). Catalog, 1866.

Howard Female Institute, Gallatin, Tenn. Announcement, 1856. [State Library]

Illinois College. Catalog, 1853–4.

Illinois Conference Female Academy, Jacksonville. Catalogs, 1849–50. [College Archives]

Illinois Conference Female College. Catalogs, 1851–61. [College Archives]

Illinois Female College, Jacksonville. Catalogs, 1863–98. [College Archives]

Illinois Supreme Court Reports. Vol. LV. (N. L. Freeman) Springfield, 1872.

Illinois Territory and State, Laws of, 1788—.

Illinois Woman's College. Catalogs, 1898—. [College Archives]

Indiana, Laws of, 1801—.

Ingham Female University, Leroy, N. Y. Annual Synopsis, 1857. [State Library]

Ingham Female University. Catalog, 1857. [State Library]

Iowa, Laws of, 1838—.

Ipswich [Mass.] Female Seminary. Catalogs, 1828–64, incomplete file. [Ipswich Public Library and American Antiquarian Society, Worcester]

Ipswich Female Seminary. An appeal of Mary Lyon to the friends and patrons, 1834. [Ipswich Public Library]

Ipswich Female Seminary. Record of Internal Concerns, 1827. [Ipswich Public Library]

Ipswich Female Seminary. Maxims for Teachers, n.d.

Ipswich Female Seminary, The Passing of. [Monticello Seminary, Godfrey, Ill., *The Echo,* No. 20]

Jacksonville [Ill.] Female Academy. Catalogs, 1845–1902, incomplete file. [College Archives]

Jefferson, Thomas. Letter to Nathaniel Burwell . . . on girls' education. [*Collections, Missouri Hist. Soc.* (1923) IV, No. 4: 475–8]

Jewett, Milo P. Letter to Augustus W. Cowles (President of Elmira College), May 18, 1861. [Elmira College Archives]

Johns Hopkins University. Circulars and Reports of the President, 1890–1908.

Johnson, Walter R. *Observations on the Improvement of Seminaries of Learning in the United States.* Philadelphia, 1825.

Judson Female Institute, Marion, Ala. Catalog, 1841. [Judson College Archives]

Kansas, General Laws of, 1862. Topeka, 1862.

Kansas, State Department of Public Instruction. Reports, 1873, 1876. Topeka.

Kentucky, Laws of, 1792—.

Kern, Lydia. Unpublished letters relative to her entrance to theological schools in the United States. [Assembled and arranged, with an article by Thomas Woody on "Women in the Christian Ministry," University of Pennsylvania, 1927. In Penniman Library]

Kingsbury, Susan M. *The Records of the Virginia Company of London.* Government Printing Office: Washington, 1906.

Knoxville [Tenn.] Female Academy. Catalogs, 1830–31. [Lawson McGhee Library]

Ladies' Depository. Incomplete file of Reports between 1856 and 1888. New York.

Ladies' Society, of Boston, for Evangelizing the West. Annual Reports, 1843, 1847–53.

Lagrange [Ga.] Female College. Catalogs, 1848–87, incomplete file. [College Archives]

Lagrange Female College. *MS. Records of the Trustees,* 1859—. [College Archives]

Lake Erie Female Seminary, Painesville, O. Catalogs, 1859–90. [Lake Erie Woman's College Archives]

Lancasterian System, Manual of the, . . . as Practised in the Schools of the Free School Society of New York. New York, 1820.

Lasell Female Seminary, Auburndale, Mass. Catalog, 1855–6. [Conn. Hist. Soc.]

Leicester [Mass.] Academy. Catalogs, 1838–69, incomplete file. [Boston Public Library]

Letters, received from various school officials containing information as to school history and the location of sources. In possession of the author.

Lewis' Family School for Young Ladies, Lexington, Mass. Catalog and Circular, 1866. [Mrs. Charles C. Goodwin, Lexington, Mass.]

Lewis' Normal Institute for Physical Education, Boston. Announcements, 1861–62.

Lexington [Mo.] Female Collegiate Institute. Catalog, 1852–3. [E. N. Hopkins, Traders' National Bank, Lexington]

Lindenwood Female College, St. Charles, Mo. Catalog, 1863. [College Archives]

Lindenwood Female College. Diplomas, 1861 and 1869. [Supplied by Lindenwood College]

Linn, John B. *Charter to William Penn and Laws of the Province of Pennsylvania (1682–1700) Preceded by Duke of York's Laws in Force from the Year 1676 to the Year 1682* . . . Harrisburg, 1879.

Litchfield [Conn.] Female Academy. Catalog, 1832. [Conn. Hist. Soc.]

Lockwood, Belva A., Case of. [*U. S. Court of Claims Reports*, IX: 346–56]

Louisiana, Laws of the Territory and State of, 1805—.

Lowell Offering, The. October, 1845. [Reprinted in *Old South Leaflets*, No. 157, VII, 129–52]

Luther's Letter to the Mayors and Aldermen of All the Cities of Germany in Behalf of Christian Schools, 1524. [In Painter's *Luther*, Ch. IX]

Madison Female School, Richmond, Ky. Announcement, 1860.

Maine, The Revised Statutes of. Bangor, 1857.

Maine, Laws of, 1820—.

Maine Wesleyan Seminary and Female Collegiate Institute, Readfield. Catalogs, 1827–70, incomplete file. [School Archives]

Maine Wesleyan Seminary. The *Calliopean*, 1841–73, chiefly *MSS.* 63 vols. [School Archives]

Maine Wesleyan Seminary. *MS.* Records of the Calliopean Society, Dec. 31, 1828. [School Archives]

Maine Wesleyan Seminary. *Kents Hill School Breeze*, 1882–88. [School Archives]

Maine Wesleyan Seminary. *MS.* Report of the Trustees, Dec. 31, 1828. [School Archives]

Marriage agreement, A. [*Va. Mag. Hist. and Biography* (1896–7) IV: 64–6]

Marsh, Ann, a teacher in Philadelphia, Manuscript account book of, 1772 to 1789. [Photostat copy in possession of the author]

Mary Baldwin Seminary (Augusta Female Seminary), Staunton, Va. Catalogs, 1844—. [Mary Baldwin Archives]

Mary Sharp College, Winchester, Tenn. Catalogs, 1853–4, 1858, 1859, 1861, and 1885–6. [Mrs. W. H. Carmack, 1075 Peachtree Street, Atlanta, Ga.]

Mary Sharp College. Diploma, 1855. [Mrs. W. H. Carmack, 1075 Peachtree St., Atlanta, Ga.]

Maryland, Archives of, 1883–1925. 44 vols. Maryland Historical Society, Baltimore.

Maryland, Laws of, 1692—. Annapolis.

Maryville [Tenn.] College. Catalog, 1854. [College Archives]

Masonic Female Institute, Maryville, Tenn. Catalog, 1854.

Massachusetts, Acts and Resolves of the Commonwealth of, 1780—.

Massachusetts, Board of Education. Annual Reports, 1848—. Boston.

Massachusetts, Bureau of Statistics of Labor. Sixth Annual Report, Part IV. Boston, 1875.

Massachusetts, Commonwealth of. *Report of the Commission for an Investigation Relative to Opportunities and Methods for Technical and*

Higher Education in the Commonwealth. [House Document No. 1700, Dec. 26, 1923]

Massachusetts, Health Department. Fifth Annual Report, 1873. Boston, 1874.

Massachusetts Supreme Court Reports. Vol. CXXXI. (John Lathrop) Boston, 1882.

Mercier's Young Ladies' Academy, St. Louis, Mo. Catalog, 1851-2. [St. Louis Public Library]

Miami University. Circulars, 1851—.

Michigan Female Seminary, Kalamazoo. Circular and Annual Catalogs, 1867-1905. [Kalamazoo Public Library]

Michigan, Laws of, 1805—.

Michigan, Superintendent of Public Instruction. Annual Reports, 1837—.

Mills Seminary and College, Oakland, Cal. Catalogs, 1884—. [College Archives]

Minerva College, Nashville, Tenn. Catalog and Announcement, 1856-7. [State Library]

Minnesota, Laws of, 1850—.

Misses Clark's School, Ann Arbor, Mich. Catalogs, 1839-56, incomplete file. [Burton Collection, Detroit Public Library]

Mississippi, Laws of, 1799—.

Missouri, Territory and State, Laws of, 1804—.

Mobile [Ala.] Female Seminary. Catalog, 1850. [State Library]

Monmouth [Me.] Academy. Catalog, 1855. [State Library]

Monroe City [Mich.] Young Ladies' Seminary and Collegiate Institute. Seventh Annual Catalog, 1857. [Library, University of Michigan]

Monroe High School, Rochester, N. Y. Advertisement, 1827. [A Directory of the Village of Rochester, 1827. Municipal Museum, Hist. Soc., Rochester]

Montana, The Codes and Statutes of, 1895. (Compiled by Edwin S. Booth) 2 vols. Butte, 1895.

Montana, Laws of, 1864—.

Montgomery Female Seminary, Perkiomen Bridge, Pa. Catalogs, 1851-80, incomplete file. [Ursinus College Archives]

Monticello Female Seminary, Godfrey, Ill. Catalogs, 1839-48, incomplete file. [Monticello Archives]

Monticello Female Seminary. *The Echo,* 1898-1902. [Monticello Archives]

Monticello Female Seminary. An Historical Address, by Theron Baldwin. [*The Echo,* No. 15]

Mooresville [Ala.] Young Ladies' Seminary. Catalog, 1838. [Furnished by Mr. R. H. Walker, *Limestone Democrat,* Mooresville, Ala.]

Mormon Women of Utah, Memorial of the, to the President of the Congress of the U. S. . . . Washington, 1886.

Mount Holyoke Female Seminary, South Hadley, Mass. Mary Lyon's Plan for the New England Seminary for Teachers, 1832. [College Archives]

Mount Holyoke Female Seminary. Address to the Christian Public, June 15, 1835. Northampton.

Mount Holyoke Female Seminary. Prospectus, 1835. [*Old South Leaflets*, VI, No. 145, 425–40]

Mount Holyoke Female Seminary. Public letter by Mary Lyon, 1836. [College Archives]

Mount Holyoke Female Seminary. Prospectus, 1837. [College Archives]

Mount Holyoke Female Seminary. Catalogs, 1837–87. [College Library]

Mount Holyoke Seminary and College. Catalogs, 1888—. [College Library]

Mount Holyoke Female Seminary. Circular of the Trustees, April 20, 1849.

Mount Holyoke Female Seminary. Circular Letter of Mary Lyon, n.d.

Mount Holyoke Female Seminary. Circular Concerning Admission, Sept. 1840.

Mount Holyoke Female Seminary. Tendencies of the Principles Embraced and the System Adopted, June, 1839.

Mount Holyoke Female Seminary. General view of the Principles and Design, by Mary Lyon. [*Religious Mag. and Family Miscellany* (1837), N.S. I: 184–9]

Mount Holyoke College. Anniversary Addresses, 1839–1849.

Mount Holyoke College. Catalog of the Memorandum Society and the Alumnae, 1877–87.

Mount Holyoke College. General Catalog, 1837–1924.

Nashville [Tenn.] Female Academy. Leaflets. [State Library]

Nashville [Tenn.] Ladies' College. Catalogs, 1852 and 1854. [State Library]

Nebraska, Laws of, 1855—.

Neophagen Male and Female College, Gallatin, Tenn. Catalog, 1877–8. [State Library]

Nevada, Laws of, 1861—.

New Hampshire, Laws of, 1864—.

New Haven [Conn.] Female Seminary. Catalogs, 1824–26, 1828–9. [Yale Library]

New Haven Young Ladies' Institute. Catalog of the Instructors and Pupils, 1830. [Yale Library]

New Haven Young Ladies' Institute. Circular and Catalogs, 1829–33. [Yale Library]

New Jersey, Laws of, 1800—.

New London [Conn.] Female Academy. Catalogs, 1851 and 1852. [Conn. Hist. Soc.]

[New York] *Board of Education, Report of the Select Committee of the, in Relation to the Propriety . . . of . . . a Free Academy for Females.* New York, 1849.

New York, Colonial Laws of, 1664–1776. 5 vols. Albany, 1894–96.

New York High School Society. Reports, 1824–28.

New York, Laws of, 1774—. Albany.

Normal Institute for Physical Education, *Announcement,* 1861. Boston.

North Carolina, The Colonial Records of, 1662–1776. 10 vols. [Collected and edited by William L. Saunders] Raleigh, 1886–90.

North Carolina, Laws of, 1715–90. [Republished as Vols. XXIII to XXV of the *State Records of North Carolina,* collected and edited by Walter Clark] Nasl. Brothers: Goldsboro, N. C., 1904–6.

North Carolina, Laws of, 1790—.

North Dakota, Revised Codes of the State of, 1895. Bismarck, 1895.

North Yarmouth [Me.] Academy. Catalog, 1854. [State Library]

Oberlin [O.] Collegiate Institute and College. Catalogs, 1835—. [Oberlin Library]

Oberlin College. First diploma issued to a woman, 1841. [Supplied by the College]

Ohio, Territory and State, Laws of, 1788–1894.

Ohio Wesleyan Female College, Delaware. Circular and Catalogs, 1853–77, incomplete file. [Furnished by the College]

Ontario Female Seminary, Canandaigua, N. Y. Catalogs, 1826–73, incomplete file. [Hist. Soc. and Public Libraries, Canandaigua; Education Library, Albany, N. Y.]

Oregon, Laws of, 1849—.

Oxford [Ohio] Female College. Catalogs, 1852–65; also those of recent date. [College Archives]

Oxford Female College. Diploma issued to Julia Rogers, June 26, 1856. [Loaned by Miss Rogers, Oxford, O.]

Oxford Female Institute. *The Philalethian,* 1851–53. 3 vols. [Oxford College Library]

Oxford Female Institute. Catalogs, 1849–52. [Oxford College Library]

Oxford Female Seminary. Catalog, 1839. [Oxford College Library]

Oxford Ladies Collegian. Vol. I, No. 10. Oxford, Ohio.

Paris [Ky.] Female Academy. Catalog, 1852. [Paris Public Library]

Paris Hill [Me.] Academy. Catalog, 1866. [State Library]

Park Institute, Syracuse, N. Y. (Cottage Seminary). Catalog, 1852. [Syracuse Public Library]

Patapsco Female Institute, Ellicotts Mills, Md. Catalogs, 1847–53, incomplete file. [Md. Hist. Soc.]

Patapsco Female Institute. Cash Book, 1834–91. [Md. Hist. Soc.]

Patapsco Female Institute. Diploma, 1846. [Florence Trail, Frederick, Md.]

Patapsco Female Institute. Fifteen folders of *MS.* material, 1833–91. [Md. Hist. Soc.]

Patapsco Female Institute. Laws and Resolutions of the General Assembly of Maryland Relating Thereto. Ellicotts Mills, 1855.

Patapsco Female Institute. *MS.* Records of Proceedings, 1833–90. 2 vols. [Md. Hist. Soc.]

P. C. S. M.: Penn Charter School Minutes.

Penn Charter School, Philadelphia. Minutes, for dates as indicated in footnotes. [Provident Life and Trust Company, Philadelphia]

Pennsylvania, Colonial Records of: Minutes of the Provincial Council of Pennsylvania, 1683 to 1790. 16 vols. Philadelphia, 1852–3.

Pennsylvania, Laws of the Commonwealth of, 1700–1890.

Pennsylvania Supreme Court Reports, 1886.

Pennsylvania Female College, Perkiomen Bridge, Pa. Catalogs, 1853-82, incomplete file. [Ursinus College Archives]

Philadelphia [and Burlington] Yearly Meeting of Friends, Minutes, 1681–1777. (*MS.*) [304 Arch Street, Philadelphia]

Philadelphia Baptist Association. Minutes from 1707 to 1807.

[Philadelphia] *Board of Public Education of the First School District of Pennsylvania,* Journal of the, 1818—. Philadelphia.

Philadelphia Female Academy. A pamphlet describing its rise and progress. n.p., n.d. [State Library]

[Philadelphia] *Girls' High School, Scheme for a.* 34 pages. n.p., n.d.

Philadelphia Monthly Meeting Minutes, 1681–1776. [Friends' Book Store, 304 Arch Street, Philadelphia]

[Philadelphia] *Reports on Public Schools,* Vol. II, 1831–41. Philadelphia.

Phipps Union Female Seminary, Albion, N. Y. Catalog, 1865. [Albion Public Library]

Physical Education, Requirements of State Departments for Directors and Supervisors of—. [Mimeographed circular No. 8247. Issued by the Bureau of Education.]

[Pittsfield, Mass.] Young Ladies' Institute. Catalogs, 1844–51, incomplete file. [Conn. Hist. Soc.]

Protestant Episcopal Book of Common Prayer. As adopted by the Convention of 1789. Philadelphia, 1873.

Providence, The Early Records of the Town of. 20 vols. City Council: Providence, 1892–1909.

Public School Society [New York] *Reports,* 1826–1853.

Quaboag Seminary, Warren, Mass. Catalog, 1842. [Am. Antiquarian Soc., Worcester]

R. C. E.: See *Commissioner of Education of the United States, Reports.*

Radcliffe College. Programs of Study, 1879—.

Radcliffe College. Report of Radcliffe Historian for 1903.

Radcliffe College. Report of Private Collegiate Instruction for Women, 1879.

Radcliffe College. Reports of President, 1883—.

Radcliffe College. Reports of the Executive Committee, 1883—.

Randolph-Macon Woman's College, Lynchburg, Va. Catalogs, 1892—.

Reformed Dutch Church of North America, Constitution of the. Philadelphia, 1840.

Rhode Island, Records of the Colony of, and Providence Plantations in New England. Vols. I–X. Providence, 1856–65.

Rhode Island State School Reports, 1870, 1872, 1873, 1883–1921. Providence.

Robinson, Lelia, Case of. [*Mass. Supreme Court Reports,* CXXXI: 376–84]

Rochester [N. Y.], Charter and Directory of the City of, 1834.

Rochester [N. Y.] Female Seminary. Catalog, 1859. [Education Library, Albany]

Rochester High School. Catalog, 1857. [Municipal Museum, Hist. Soc.]

Rochester Seminary. Catalog of Officers and Students, 1833. [Municipal Museum, Hist. Soc.]

Rockford Female Seminary [and later College]. Catalogs, 1854–1925. [College Library]

Rogersville [Tenn.] Female Institute. Seventh Annual Catalog, 1857. [State Library]

St. Louis [Mo.] Female Institute. Third Annual Catalog, 1854. [St. Louis Public Library]

St. Louis High School for the Education of Young Ladies. Catalog and Prospectus, 1850. [St. Louis Public Library]

St. Mary's Hall, Burlington, N. J. Appeal to Parents for Female Education on Christian Principles, with a Prospectus, 1837. [Seminary Archives]

St. Mary's Hall. Catalogs, 1837—. [Seminary Archives]

St. Mary's Hall. *Ivy Leaves*, 1892–1922. [Seminary Archives]

St. Mary's Hall. Programs and Registers. [Seminary Archives]

St. Jerome to Laeta, a letter on the education of her daughter, Paula. [*R. C. E.*, 1867–8: 372–6; and *Barnard's Jour.*, V: 593–8]

Savage School for Physical Education. Catalog, 1927–8.

Schools Enquiry Commission, Report. (Appointed Dec. 28, 1864.) December, 1867. London.

Science Hill School, Shelbyville, Ky. Catalogs, 1852–86, incomplete file. [School Archives]

Science Hill School. *MS.* Notebook, List of Pupils, 1825–26. [School Archives]

Seward Female Seminary, Rochester, N. Y. Catalog of Teachers and Pupils, 1846–7. [Municipal Museum, Hist. Soc.]

Sharon Female Seminary. Circular . . . and . . . description of apparatus . . . with a Catalogue of Pupils, 1852. [H. S. P., Philadelphia]

Shelbyville [Ky.] Female College. Catalog, 1871. [College Archives]

Sherwood, Grace. Trial for witchcraft, 1705. [*Va. Hist. and Phil. Soc. Collections* (1833) I: 73–8]

Smith College. Addresses at the Inauguration of President Seelye, July, 1875.

Smith College. Annual Reports of the President, 1879—.

Smith College. Catalogs, 1879—. [College Library]

Smith College. Inauguration of William A. Neilson, 1918.

Smith College. Official Circulars, 1883, 1885, 1887, and 1895.

Smith College. Prospectus, 1872, 1873, and 1874. [College Library]

Sophie Newcomb Memorial College, New Orleans. Announcements, 1887—. [College Library]

South Carolina, Acts of the Assembly of, 1770—.

South Carolina, Statutes at Large, 1682–1871. 14 vols. Columbia, 1836–1871.

South Carolina Female Collegiate Institute, Barhamsville. Circulars, 1849–50. [University of South Carolina Library]

South Dakota, Laws of, 1890—.
Southern Colleges for Women, The Various Types of. By Elizabeth A.
  Colton. [Bul. No. 2, 1916. Southern Association of College Women]
State Female College, Greenwood, Tenn. Announcement, 1858. [State
  Library].

Teachers College, N. Y. Bulletin, 15th series No. 12, May 24, 1924—
  Courses for Advisers of Women and Girls.
Tennessee, Laws of, 1792—.
Texas, Laws of, 1822–97. H. P. N. Gammel (Ed.). Austin, 1898.
Tracy Female Institute, Rochester, N. Y. Circular, 1857.
Trinity College, Washington. Synopsis of the First Annual Report, 1901.
  [College Library]
Trinity College. Catalogs and Annual Reports, 1901—. [College Library]
Troy [N. Y.] Female Seminary. Catalogs of Officers and Pupils, 1843–64.
  [School Archives]

United States Court of Claims Reports. Vol. IX. (C. C. Nott and A.
  Hopkins) Washington, 1874.
United States, Supplement to the Revised Statutes of the. By William A.
  Richardson. Vol. I. Washington, 1891.
United States Supreme Court Reports. Vol. XVI. (J. W. Wallace) Wash-
  ington, 1873.
United States, Laws of, 1879.
University of Chicago. President's Reports, 1892—.
University of Iowa, *Catalogs,* 1856–70. [Library of University of Iowa]
University of the City of New York. Catalogs, 1890—.
University of Georgia. Catalog, 1834.
University of Michigan. *The Chronicle,* Sept. 25, 1869–June 28, 1873.
  [Univ. of Mich. Library]
University of Michigan. *Daily,* 1890–92. [University of Michigan Library]
University of Michigan. *The Inlander,* Oct., 1891–June, 1892. [University
  of Michigan Library]
University of Pennsylvania. Catalogs, 1828–50, 1880–95.
University of Pennsylvania. Provost's Reports, 1883–90.
University of Pennsylvania. *Daily Pennsylvanian,* 1885—.
University of the State of New York. Regents' Annual Reports, 1787–
  1904. 117 vols. Albany, N. Y.
University of Tennessee. Catalog, 1851–2.
University of Wisconsin. Catalogs, 1860—.
University of Wisconsin. Regents' and Visitors' Reports, 1850—.

Vassar College. Catalogs, 1865—.
Vassar College. Reports of the President, 1865—.
Vassar College. Associate Alumnae, Annual Report and Register, 1895.
Vassar College. Fourth General Catalog of the Officers and Graduates,
  1861–1910. Haight: Poughkeepsie, N. Y., 1910.
Vassar College. Prospectus, 1865.

Vassar Female College. Report on Organization. n.p., n.d.

Vassar, Matthew. *Communications to the Board of Trustees of Vassar College.* New York, 1869.

Vermont, Laws of, 1820—.

Virginia, Journal of the House of Burgesses of, 1619–1776. Virginia State Library: Richmond, 1905–15.

Virginia, Laws of, 1807—.

Wadawanuck Young Ladies' Institute, Stonington, Conn. First Catalog, 1858. [Conn. Hist. Soc.]

Waldo, Fullerton. *The Glen Mills Schools.* Glen Mills, 1926.

Washington [Pa.] Female Seminary. Catalog, 1841–2, 1872–3. [School Archives]

Washington Female Seminary. *The Fair Ephemeral,* 1844. [School Archives]

Washington Female Seminary. Semi-centennial Celebration, 1836–86. [School Archives]

Waterville [Me.] Academy [Later Coburn Classical Institute] Catalogs, 1831–70. [School Archives]

Weller's Seminary for Young Ladies, Nashville, Tenn. Prospectus and Rules, 1835. [State Library]

Wellesley College. Prospectus, Dec., 1874. [College Archives]

Wellesley College. Calendars, 1876—.

Wellesley College. Circulars for 1875 and 1876.

Wellesley College. Circular to Parents, June 1, 1877.

Wellesley College. Circular to Parents and Students, Aug. 1, 1879.

Wellesley College. Occupations towards which Wellesley Courses May Lead. Maugus Printing Co.: Wellesley, 1918.

Wells College, Aurora, N. Y. General Catalog, 1868–94.

Wesleyan Alumnae, The. Macon, Ga., 1925–26.

Wesleyan College, Macon, Ga. The Greater Wesleyan Issue, Bul. No. 6, 1933.

Wesleyan College. Charters, 1836, 1843, 1871. Published by the College, 1924.

Wesleyan College. *MS.* Composition Book of Alice Culler Cobb. [College Library]

Wesleyan College. Catalogs, 1842—. [College Library]

Wesleyan Female Collegiate Institute, Wilmington, Del. *The Female Student and Young Ladies' Chronicle,* 1844. [Delaware Women's College Archives]

Wesleyan Female Collegiate Institute. *MS.* Account of Its Origin, by A. C. M., Nov. 2, 1916. [Delaware College Archives]

Wesleyan Female Collegiate Institute. Steel box of manuscripts and catalogs. [Delaware College Archives]

Wesleyan Seminary, Albion, Mich. Catalog, 1843.

West Bradford [Mass.] Academy. Constitution and Proceedings of the Female Association for the Education of Heathen Youth. [*MS.* in the School Archives, 1832–33]

Westbrook Seminary and Female Collegiate Institute, Stevens Plains, Me. Catalog, 1862. [State Library]

Western College and Seminary, Oxford, O. Catalogs, 1894—. [College Archives]

Western Female Seminary. Catalogs, 1853–90. [College Archives]

Wheaton Female Seminary, Norton, Mass. Catalogs, 1837–79, incomplete file. [Am. Antiquarian Soc., Worcester; and Conn. Hist. Soc.]

White, Andrew D. Report submitted to the Trustees of Cornell University on Mr. Sage's proposal to endow a college for women, Feb. 13, 1872. [Cornell Univ. Library]

Willard, Emma. *An Address to the Public; particularly to the members of the Legislature of New York, proposing a plan for improving female education.* Middlebury, 1819.

Willard, Emma, Principal of Troy Female Seminary, Memorial of, to the Honorable Legislature of the State of New York, Jan. 25, 1823.

William and Mary College. Catalogs, 1841—. [College Archives]

Williams, Hannah. A letter, Feb. 6, 1704–5. [*S. C. Hist. and Genealogical Mag.*, XXI]

Winchester Industrial School for Girls. Rules and Regulations, 1854. [Conn. Hist. Soc.]

Wisconsin, Laws of, 1836—.

Wisconsin Supreme Court Reports. Vol. XXXIX.

Woman's College of Baltimore (Goucher). Annual Programs, 1888—. [College Library]

Women disqualified to be Justices of the Peace. [*Mass. Supreme Court Report*, CVII: 604–5]

Women's Bureau, Director of the. Seventh Annual Report, June 30, 1925. Government Printing Office, 1925.

Women's College, Old Bennington, Vt. Official Circular, 1929.

Wyman's English and Classical High School, St. Louis, Mo. Annual Catalog of the Visiting Committee, Teachers and Students, 1846. [St. Louis Public Library]

Wyoming, Laws and Constitution of, 1869—.

Yarmouth [Me.] Male and Female Institute. Catalog, 1853. [State Library]

Young Ladies' Athenaeum, Jacksonville, Ill. Catalogs, 1865–83, incomplete file.

Zook, George F., and others. *Reports of the Commission for an Investigation Relative to Opportunities and Methods for Technical and Higher Education in the Commonwealth* (Mass.). [House Document No. 1700, 1923]

II

Newspapers

Alabama Sentinel, Greensborough, 1836–38. [State Library]

American Weekly Mercury, Philadelphia, 1719–23, 1727–42. [Hist. Soc. Pa., Philadelphia]

Baltimore Gazette and Daily Advertizer, 1837. [Md. Hist. Soc.]

Baltimore Whig, 1810–13, a few numbers only. [Md. Hist. Soc.; Handley Library, Winchester, Va.]

Berks and Schuylkill Journal, Reading, Pa., 1838. [Berks Co. Hist. Soc., Reading]

Boston Evening Post, 1735–76. [Am. Antiquarian Soc.]

Boston News-Letter, 1704–36. [Boston Public Library]

Boston Transcript, a few issues as indicated in footnotes. [Boston Public Library]

Calhoun County [Mich.] *Patriot*, 1838. [Burton Collection, Detroit Public Library]

Cape Fear Mercury, Wilmington, N. C., 1769–75, a few issues. [University of N. C. Library]

Cincinnati Chronicle and Literary Gazette, 1830. [Cincinnati Public Library]

Cincinnati Daily Gazette, 1831. [Cincinnati Public Library]

City Gazette and Daily Advertizer, Charleston, S. C., 1787–1800. [Charleston College Library]

Clarke County Post, Suggsville, Ala., 1836–37. [State Library]

Cleveland [O.] *Daily Herald*, 1841–43. [State Library]

Columbia [Mo.] *Patriot*, 1838–41, incomplete file. [State Hist. Soc.]

Columbian Centinel, Boston, 1825. [Boston Public Library]

Columbian Herald and General Advertizer (later *Southern Star;* and again, *New Daily Advertizer*), Charleston, S. C., 1793–96. [Charleston College Library]

Columbus [Miss.] *Democrat*, 1836–41, and 1848–53. [State Library]

Columbus [O.] *Sentinel*, 1831–33. [State Library]

Confederate Veteran, 1907. [Virginia State Library, Richmond.]

Courrier de La Louisiane, New Orleans, 1807–08. [Cabildo, New Orleans]

Daily Express and Herald, Dubuque, Ia., 1854–59, incomplete file. [State Hist. Library]

Daily Picayune, New Orleans, 1831–54, and 1859–61. [Cabildo and City Hall, New Orleans]

Democratic Free Press, Detroit, Mich., 1842. [Burton Collection, Detroit Public Library]

Detroit [Mich.] *Courier*, 1832–33. [Burton Collection, Detroit Public Library]

Detroit Gazette, 1819–27. [Clements Library, Univ. of Mich.]

Detroit Journal and Michigan Advertizer, 1831–35, incomplete file. [Burton Collection, Detroit Public Library]

Eastern Argus, Portland, Me., 1812–14. [State Library]

Eclectic, Portland, Me., 1851–52. [State Library]

Edenton [N. C.] *Intelligencer*, 1788, a few issues. [Univ. of N. C. Library]

Evening Bulletin (Philadelphia). A few recent issues quoted in footnotes.

Evening Public Ledger (Philadelphia). Issues indicated in footnotes.

Fayetteville, [N. C.] *Gazette*, 1792–93, incomplete. [Univ. of N. C. Library]
Flag of the Union, Tuscaloosa, Ala., 1835–36. [State Library]
Florida Sentinel, Talahassee, Florida, Aug. 4 and Sept. 10, 1841. [Copy of advertisements loaned by W. H. Kilpatrick]
Free Press, Halifax and Tarborough, N. C., 1824–30, incomplete. [Univ. of N. C. Library]

Greensboro [N. C.] *Patriot*, 1839–40, and 1846–47. [Greensboro Public Library]

Hall's Wilmington [N. C.] *Gazette*, 1797–99. [Univ. of N. C. Library]
Hannibal [Mo.] *Commercial Advertizer*, 1839–40. [State Hist. Soc.]
Hawkeye and Iowa Patriot, Burlington, 1840–41. [State Hist. Library]
Hillsborough [N. C.] *Recorder*, 1820–29, incomplete. [Univ. of N. C. Library]
Hinds County [Miss.] *Gazette*, 1852–62. [State Library]

Iowa Sun, Davenport, 1838–42, incomplete. [State Hist. Library]
Iowa Territorial Gazette and Advertizer, Burlington, 1840–41, a few issues. [State Hist. Library]
Independent Chronicle (*and Universal Advertizer*), Boston, 1784–85, 1802. [Am. Antiquarian Soc. and Boston Public Library]

Kennebec Journal, Augusta, Me., 1825–27. [State Library]
Kentucky Gazette, Lexington, 1810–26, incomplete. [Lexington Public Library]
Knoxville [Tenn.] *Register*, 1816–18 and 1822–30, incomplete. [Lawson McGhee Library]

Labor Letter, The Federated Press. Vols. I–XVI. Chicago, 1920—.
Lexington [Mo.] *Weekly Express*, 1859–60. [Vault, Traders National Bank, Lexington]
Liberator, The, Boston, 1831–60, incomplete file. [Am. Antiquarian Soc. and Boston Public Library]
Liberty Hall and Cincinnati Gazette, 1823–24. [Cincinnati Public Library]
Liberty Hall Chronicle and Cincinnati Gazette, 1827, 1835–37. [Cincinnati Public Library]
London Times Educational Supplement, occasional articles.
Louisiana Courier, New Orleans, 1807–08. [Cabildo, New Orleans]
Louisiana Gazette, New Orleans, 1825–26. [Cabildo and City Hall, New Orleans]

Macon [Ga.] *Telegraph*, 1826–42. [Washington Memorial Library]
Maine Enquirer, Bath, 1832–33. [State Library]
Maine Palladium, Saco, 1826–29. [State Library]
Man, The, Feb. 18–May 16, 1834 and Jan. 1–Mar. 30, 1835. [New York Public Library]
Maryland Gazette, Annapolis, 1728–35 and 1745–95. [Md. Hist. Soc.]

Maryland Journal and Baltimore Advertizer, 1774, 1783, and 1793. [Md. Hist. Soc.]

Massachusetts Spy or Worcester Gazette, 1819, a few issues. [Am. Antiquarian Soc.]

Maury Intelligencer, Columbia, Tenn., 1848–49. [State Library]

Maysville [Ky.] *Eagle,* 1850–60. [Maysville Public Library]

Messenger, The, Fort Hawkins, Ga., 1823–25. [Washington Memorial Library, Macon]

Minerva, The, Raleigh, N. C., 1807–08. [University of N. C. Library]

Mississippi State Gazette, Natchez, 1818–28. [State Library]

Missouri Advocate, St. Louis, 1817–18. [Mo. Hist. Soc.]

Missouri Gazette and Illinois Advertizer, St. Louis, 1818. [Mo. Hist. Soc.]

Missouri Gazette and Public Advertizer, St. Louis, 1818–22. [Mo. Hist. Soc.]

Missouri Intelligencer, Franklin, 1819–29, incomplete file. [Mo. Hist. Soc.]

Missouri Republican, St. Louis, 1822–27, and 1838, incomplete file. [Mo. Hist. Soc.]

Moniteur de la Louisiane, New Orleans, 1802–09, incomplete file. [Cabildo, New Orleans]

[Montgomery, Ala.] *Daily Post,* 1860–61. [State Library.]

Nashville [Tenn.] *Gazette,* 1819–21. [State Library]

National Intelligencer, 1810–13, a few issues. [Handley Library, Winchester, Va.]

Newbern [N. C.] *Gazette,* 1793–1800, incomplete. [Univ. of N. C. Library]

Newburgh [N. Y.] *Gazette,* 1827–29, 1845, 1847–52. [Newburgh Free Library]

Newburgh [N. Y.] *Telegraph,* 1847. [Newburgh Free Library]

Newport [R. I.] *Mercury or the Weekly Advertiser,* 1758–76. [R. I. Hist. Soc.]

New York Weekly Journal, 1733–1749. Incomplete file. [New York Public Library]

New York Post-Boy, Weekly. (With frequently changing title) 1743–1773. Incomplete file. [New York Public Library]

New York Mercury (Later *New York Gazette and Weekly Mercury*) 1752–1783. Incomplete file. [New York Public Library]

New York Gazette, 1725–1751. Incomplete file. [New York Public Library]

New York Times. A few issues as referred to in footnotes.

North Carolina Chronicle or Fayetteville Gazette, 1790, a few issues. [Univ. of N. C. Library]

North Carolina Centinel and Fayetteville Gazette, 1790–91 and 1795, a few issues. [Univ. of N. C. Library]

North Carolina Gazette, Wilmington and Newbern, 1751–97, incomplete file. [Univ. of N. C. Library and State Library]

North Carolina Journal, Halifax, 1792–99, and 1805–07. [Univ. of N. C. Library]

North Carolina Minerva and Fayetteville Advertizer, 1796–99. [Univ. of N. C. Library]

Northern Budget, Troy, N. Y., 1821–24. [Troy Public Library]

Ohio Statesman, Columbus, 1838. [State Library]

Pennsylvania Gazette, Philadelphia, 1728–90, incomplete. [Hist. Soc. Pa., Philadelphia]
Peoples Friend, The, 1810–13, a few numbers. [Handley Library, Winchester, Va.]
Philadelphia Inquirer, a few issues mentioned in footnotes.
Philadelphia Press, a few issues referred to in text and footnotes.
Port Gibson [Miss.] *Correspondent,* 1842–46. [State Library]
Portsmouth [O.] *Courier,* 1831–32. [State Library]
Post, The, Bloomington, Ind., 1835–41, incomplete file. [State Library]
Poughkeepsie [N. Y.] *Eagle,* 1856. [Adriance Memorial Library]
Poughkeepsie Intelligencer and Republican, 1833–36. [Adriance Memorial Library]
Poughkeepsie Telegraph, 1834–38. [Adriance Memorial Library]
Providence [R. I.] *Gazette (and Country Journal),* 1762–76. [R. I. Hist. Soc.]

Raleigh [N. C.] *Star,* 1809–12, incomplete file. [N. C. Hist. Library]
Raleigh Star and North Carolina State Gazette, 1820. [N. C. Hist. Library]
Reporter, The, Lexington, Ky., 1812–14 and 1825. [Lexington Public Library]
Republican Constellation, Winchester, Va., 1811 and 1813. [Handley Library, Winchester]
Republican Vindicator, Staunton, Va., 1849–50. [Court House, Staunton]
Rhode Island Gazette, 1732. [R. I. Hist. Soc.]
Richmond [Va.] *Inquirer,* a few issues as mentioned in footnotes. [State Library]

St. Croix [Me.] *Courier,* 1834. [State Library]
Salt River Journal, Bowling Green, Mo., 1837–39, incomplete file. [State Hist. Soc.]
Seneca County [N. Y.] *Courier,* 1848. [Rochester Public Library]
South Carolina Gazette, Charleston, 1732–92, incomplete. [Library Soc., Charleston]
South Carolina State Gazette and Columbia Advertizer, 1827–28. [Library, Univ. of S. C.]
Southern Advocate and Huntsville [Ala.] *Advertizer,* 1825–31, incomplete file. [State Library]
Spirit of the Age, Tuscaloosa, Ala., 1831–32. [State Library]
Springfield [Mass.] *Republican,* May 11, 1924.
State Gazette of North Carolina, Newbern and Edenton, 1787–99, incomplete file. [Univ. of N. C. Library]
State Gazette of South Carolina, Charleston, 1790–1800. [Charleston College Library]
Staunton [Va.] *Spectator,* 1836–48. [Courthouse, Staunton]
Telescope, The, Columbia, S. C., 1815–16. [Library, Univ. of S. C.]
Thomas' Massachusetts Spy or Worcester Gazette, 1790 and 1797. [Boston Public Library]

Times, Richmond, Va., June 11, 1895, Woman's Edition.

Tobacco Plant, The, Virginia, a few issues as given in footnotes.

Tri-Weekly Eagle, The, Maysville, Ky., 1850–51, 1859–60, and 1869. [Maysville Public Library]

True American, The, New Orleans, 1839. [Cabildo, New Orleans]

Virginia Centinel, The, or the Winchester Mercury, 1789–91. [Handley Library, Winchester]

Virginia Gazette, Williamsburg, 1736–62, 1767–91, incomplete files. [Va. State Library and Univ. of N. C. Library]

Virginia Gazette and General Advertiser, 1809. [State Library, Richmond]

Virginia Gazette and Winchester Advertizer, 1787–91. [Handley Library, Winchester]

Wayne Sentinel, The, Palmyra, N. Y., 1831–45. [Masonic Parlors, Palmyra]

Weekly Chronicle, Athens, Ala., a few issues mentioned in footnotes.

Western Citizen, Paris, Ky., 1826–59, incomplete file. [Paris Public Library]

Western Carolinian, Salisbury, N. C., 1820–23. [Univ. of N. C. Library]

Western Christian Advocate, Cincinnati, O., 1838, a few issues. [State Library]

Western Herald and Steubenville [O.] *Gazette*, 1819–20. [State Library]

Western State Journal, Syracuse, N. Y., 1839–43, incomplete file. [Syracuse Public Library]

Western Union, Hannibal, Mo., 1850, a few issues. [State Hist. Soc.]

Wilmington [N. C.] *Centinel and General Advertiser*, 1788, a few issues. [Univ. of N. C. Library]

Wilmington [N. C.] *Chronicle and Weekly Advertiser*, 1795–96, a few issues. [Univ. of N. C. Library]

Wilson's Knoxville [Tenn.] *Gazette*, 1808–11. [Lawson McGhee Library]

Winchester [Va.] *Gazette*, 1810–13, a few issues. [Handley Library, Winchester]

Winchester Virginian, 1841–42. [Handley Library, Winchester]

Workingman's Advocate, The, 1830–1847. Irregular file. [New York Public Library]

Yankee Farmer, Boston, 1841. [Boston Public Library and Maine State Library]

III

Books, collections, pamphlets, theses, and a few special reports.

Abbott, John S. C. *The School Girl; or the principles of Christian duty familiarly enforced.* Boston, 1840.

Abdy, Edward S. *Journal of a Residence and Tour in the United States.* 3 vols. London, 1835.

Acrelius, Israel. *A History of New Sweden or the Settlements on the River Delaware.* (Trans. of William M. Reynolds), Philadelphia, 1874.

Adams, Charles F. (Ed.). *Familiar Letters of John Adams and his Wife Abigail Adams, during the Revolution.* New York, 1876.

Adams, Charles F. *Letters of Mrs. Adams*. Boston, 1840.

Adams, Elizabeth K. Higher education of women. [Monroe, P.: *Cyclopedia of Education*, V: 795–810. Macmillan: New York, 1913]

Adams, Elizabeth K. *Women Professional Workers*. Macmillan: New York, 1921.

Adams, Herbert B. *Thomas Jefferson and the University of Virginia*. Washington, 1888.

Adams, James T. *Provincial Society*. Macmillan: New York, 1927.

Adams, James T. *New England in the Republic*. Little, Brown: Boston, 1926.

Adams, James T. *Revolutionary New England*. Atlantic Monthly Press: Boston, 1926.

Adams, James T. *The Founding of New England*. Atlantic Monthly Press: Boston, 1921.

Adams, Sherman W., and Stiles, Henry R. *The History of Ancient Wethersfield, Connecticut*. Vol. I. Grafton Press: New York, 1903.

Adams, W. H. Davenport. *Woman's Work and Worth*. London, 1880.

Addison, Daniel Dulany. *Lucy Larcom: Life, Letters and Diary*. Houghton, Mifflin: Boston, 1895.

Aimé-Martin, L. *Education of Mothers*. (Trans. of Edwin Lee) Philadelphia, 1843.

Aitken, George A. *Later Stuart Tracts*. Vol. IV. Westminster, 1903.

Alabama Industries, Women in. [Bul. Women's Bur., No. 34, 1924] Government Printing Office: Washington, 1924.

Alden, Cynthia W. *The Ways of Earning Money*. Barnes: New York, 1904.

Alexander, William. *The History of Women from the Earliest Antiquity to the Present Times*. 2 vols. Philadelphia, 1795–96.

Allen, Frederick F. *Guide to the Study of Occupations*. Harvard Press: Cambridge, 1921.

Allen, Nathan. *Education of Girls, as connected with their growth and physical development*. n.p., n.d.

Allen, William F., and Spencer, David E. *Higher Education in Wisconsin*. [Circular of Information, Bur. Ed., No. 1, 1889] Washington, 1889.

Allen, William H. *Woman's Part in Government, Whether She Votes or Not*. Dodd, Mead: New York, 1911.

Allestree, Richard. *The Ladies' Calling*. Edinburgh, 1675.

Allinson, May. *The Public Schools and Women in Office Service*. Women's Educational and Industrial Union: Boston, 1914.

American Industry, New Position of Women in. [Bul. Women's Bur., No. 12, 1920] Government Printing Office: Washington, 1920.

American Lady's Preceptor, The. Baltimore, 1821.

American Repository of Useful Information, The. Philadelphia, 1797.

Americanization Work Among Foreign Born Women, Suggestions For. [U. S. Dept. of Labor, Bur. Naturalization, Form H–13, 1921] Government Printing Office: Washington, 1921.

Anderson, James. *Ladies of the Reformation*. London, 1857.

Andrews, Benjamin R. *Education for the Home*. [Buls. Bur. Ed., Nos. 36–39, 1914] Government Printing Office: Washington, 1914–15.

Andrews, Benjamin R. *The Girl of Tomorrow, what will the school do for her?* Teachers College: New York, 1911.

Antrobus, Augustine M. *History of Des Moines County, Iowa.* Clarke: Chicago, 1915.

Appleton, Elizabeth. *Private Education, or a practical plan for the studies of young ladies.* London, 1816.

Aristotle. *Politics.* [Everyman's Library] Dutton: New York, n.d.

Arkansas Industries, Women in. [Bul. Women's Bur., No. 26, 1923] Government Printing Office: Washington, 1923.

Arthur, J. P. *Western North Carolina; a history from 1730–1913.* Daughters of the American Revolution: Raleigh, 1914.

Arthur, T. S. *Advice to Young Ladies on their Duties and Conduct in Life.* Philadelphia, 1866.

Ascham, Roger. *The Scholemaster.* Heath: Boston, 1910.

Ashe, S. A. *History of North Carolina.* 2 vols. Edwards and Broughton: Raleigh, 1925.

Ashton, John. *Social Life in the Reign of Queen Anne.* New York, 1883.

Association for the Advancement of Women, Historical Account of the, 1873–1893. Dedham, Mass., 1893.

Astell, Mary. *An Essay in Defence of the Female Sex.* London, 1696.

Astell, Mary. *A Serious Proposal to the Ladies.* London, 1697.

Athletics for Women. Physical Education Series No. 4, April, 1924. Bureau of Education: Washington, 1924.

Atwater, Edward E. *History of the City of New Haven* (Conn.). New York, 1887.

Aurner, Clarence R. *History of Education in Iowa.* 5 vols. State Hist. Soc. Iowa: Iowa City, 1914.

Aveling, Edward and Eleanor. *The Working Class Movement in America.* London, 1891.

Babbitt, Mary K. *Maria Mitchell as Her Students Know Her.* Underhill: Poughkeepsie, 1912.

Bachmann, Friedrich. *Die Königliche Elisabethschule zu Berlin.* Berlin, 1893.

Bachofen, Johann J. *Das Mutterrecht.* Basel, 1897.

Bailey, Ebenezer. *The Young Ladies' Class Book.* Boston, 1831.

Bailey, N. B. *Familiar Coloquies of Erasmus.* London, 1733.

Baldwin, B. T., Messner, H. L., and Greene, G. W. *Present Status of the Honor System in Colleges and Universities.* [Bul. Bur. Ed., No. 8, 1915] Government Printing Office: Washington, 1915.

Baldwin, Simeon E. A Young Man's Journal of a Hundred Years Ago. [*New Haven Hist. Soc. Papers,* IV: 193–208]

Ballagh, James C. *White Servitude in the Colony of Virginia.* [Johns Hopkins University Studies, Thirteenth Series, VI–VII] Baltimore, 1895.

Bamford-Slack, Lady. *Liberal Reasons for a Liberal Reform.* Women's Liberal Federation: London, n.d.

Bangs, Nathan. *A History of the Methodist Episcopal Church.* New York, 1839.

Barnard, F. A. P.   Should American colleges be open to women as well as to men?   [*Twentieth Annual Convocation of the University of the State of New York*, Albany, 1882]

Barnard, Henry.   *Educational Biography: Memoirs of Teachers, Educators, and Promoters and Benefactors of Education, Literature and Science.*   New York, 1861.

Barnard, Henry.   *Memoirs of Teachers and Educators in Germany.*   Hartford, 1873.

Barnard, Henry.   *Normal Schools and Other Institutions . . . for the Professional Education of Teachers.*   Hartford, 1851.

Barnes, Earl.   *Women in Modern Society.*   Huebsch: New York, 1913.

Barney, H. H.   *Report on the American System of Graded Free Schools*   Cincinnati, 1851.

Bartholomew, G. W.   *Record of the Bartholomew Family.*   Austin, Texas, 1885.

Bassett, John S.   *The Writings of Colonel William Byrd.*   Doubleday: New York, 1901.

Bay Psalm Book, The Old.   [Facsimile reprint of the First Edition, 1640] Dodd, Mead: New York, 1903.

Beale, Dorothea, Soulsby, L. H. M., and Dove, J. F.   *Work and Play in the Girls' Schools by Three Headmistresses.*   London, 1898.

Beard, Mary Ritter.   *Woman's Work in Municipalities.*   Appleton: New York, 1916.

Beauty's Triumph, or the superiority of the fair sex invincibly proved, . . showing their minds to be as much more beautiful than the men's as their bodies; and that, if they had the same advantages of education, they would excel their tyrants as much in sense as they do in virtue.   London, 1751.

Bebel, August.   *Woman in the Past, Present and Future.*   (Trans. by H. B. A. Walther)   London, n.d.

Beck, Herbert.   *Linden Hall, 1746–1921.*   n.p., n.d.

[Beecher, Catherine E.]   *American Women, Will You Save Your Country?*   New York, [1845?]

Beecher, Caherine E.   *An Appeal to the People in Behalf of Their Rights as Authorized Interpreters of the Bible.*   New York, 1860.

Beecher, Catherine E.   *Calisthenic Exercises for Schools, Families and Health Establishments.*   New York, 1856.

Beecher, Catherine E.   *Common Sense Applied to Religion.*   New York, 1857.

Beecher, Catherine E.   *The Duty of American Women to Their Country.*   New York, 1845.

Beecher, Catherine E.   *Educational Reminiscences and Suggestions.*   New York, 1874.

Beecher, Catherine E.   *Elements of Mental and Moral Philosophy.*   Hartford, 1831.

Beecher, Catherine E.   *An Essay on Slavery and Abolition, with Reference to the Duty of American Females.*   Philadelphia, 1837.

Beecher, Catherine E.   *An Essay on the Education of Female Teachers.*   New York, 1835.

Beecher, Catherine E. *The Evils Suffered by American Women and American Children: the causes and the remedy.* New York, 1846.

Beecher, Catherine E. *Letters to Persons Engaged in Domestic Service.* New York, 1842.

Beecher, Catherine E. *Letters on the Difficulties of Religion.* Hartford, 1836.

Beecher, Catherine E. *Letters to the People on Health and Happiness.* New York, 1855.

Beecher, Catherine E. *Miss Beecher's Domestic Receipt Book.* New York, 1846.

Beecher, Catherine E. *The Moral Instructor . . . a reading book for schools.* Cincinnati, 1838.

Beecher, Catherine E. *Religious Training of Children in the School, the Family, and the Church.* New York, 1864.

Beecher, Catherine E. *A Treatise on Domestic Economy.* Boston, 1841.

Beecher, Catherine E. *True Remedy for the Wrongs of Women.* Boston, 1851.

Beecher, Catherine E. *Truth Stranger than Fiction; a narrative of recent transactions . . . in a distinguished American university.* Boston, 1850.

Beecher, Catherine E. *Woman Suffrage and Woman's Profession.* Hartford, 1871.

Beecher, Catherine E. *Woman's Profession as Mother and Educator.* Philadelphia, 1872.

Beecher, Catherine E., and Stowe, Harriet B. *The American Woman's Home or Principles of Domestic Science.* New York, 1869.

Beecher, Edward and Kirk, E. N. Two addresses delivered at the formation of The Ladies' Society for the Promotion of Education at the West. Boston, 1846.

Beecher, Henry W. *Woman's Influence in Politics.* Boston, 1860.

Beecher, Henry W., and Brady, James T. Addresses on mental culture for women. New York, 1859.

Beedy, Mary E. *The Joint Education of Young Men and Women in the American Schools and Colleges.* London, 1873.

Belting, P. E. *The Community and its High School.* Heath: Boston, 1923.

Benedict, Mary. *The Higher Education of Women in the Southern States.* [*The South in the Building of the Nation*, Vol. 10] Southern Hist. Publication Society: Richmond, 1909.

Bennett, John. *Letters to a Young Lady.* Philadelphia, 1793.

Bennett, John. *Strictures on Female Education.* Philadelphia, 1793.

Benton, Caroline F. *The Complete Club Book for Women.* Page: Boston, 1915.

Benton, Caroline F. *Woman's Club Work and Programs.* Estes: Boston, 1913.

Bernheim, G. D. *History of the German Settlements and of the Lutheran Church in North Carolina.* Philadelphia, 1872.

Betts, Edward. *History of Huntsville, Madison County, Alabama.* Brown Printing Co.: Montgomery, 1916.

Bevier, Isabel, and Usher, Susannah. *Home Economics Movement.* Whitcomb and Barrows: Boston, 1906.

Bible, The Holy. Cambridge, 1885.

Bibliographies:

Coeducation, A bibliography on. [*R. C. E.* (1903) I: 1075 *ff.*]

Dunlap, Fanny, and Johnson, A. S. *Vocations for College Women* (A reading list). American Library Assoc.: Chicago, 1925.

Education of Women in the United States, List of References on. [Library leaflet, Bur. Ed., No. 19, April, 1923] Government Printing Office: Washington, 1923.

Pierce, A. E. *Catalog of Literature for Advisers of Young Women and Girls.* Wilson: New York, 1921.

Stone, Edna L. *Minimum Wage for Women in United States and Canada, a Bibliography.* [Bul. Women's Bur., No. 42, 1925] Government Printing Office: Washington, 1925.

Vocations for College Women, A Bibliography on. [Reprint from *News Bulletin,* Bureau of Vocational Information] American Library Assoc.: Chicago, 1925.

Biennial Survey of Education, 1916–18. 4 vols. [Bul. Bur. Ed., Nos. 88–91, 1919] Government Printing Office: Washington, 1921.

Biennial Survey of Education, 1918–20. [Bul. Bur. Ed., No. 29, 1923] Government Printing Office: Washington, 1923.

Biennial Survey of Education, 1920–22. 2 vols. [Bul. Bur. Ed., Nos. 13 and 14, 1924 and 1925] Government Printing Office: Washington, 1924 and 1925.

Bingham, Caleb. *American Preceptor.* Boston, 1815.

Bingham, Caleb. *Columbian Orator.* Boston, 1814.

Bingham, Caleb. *The Young Lady's Accidence.* Boston, 1793.

Birney, Catherine H. *The Grimké Sisters.* Boston, 1885.

Bissell, Emily P. *A talk to Women on the Suffrage Question.* State Association Opposed to Woman Suffrage: New York, 1909.

Björkman, F. M. and Porritt, A. G. *Woman Suffrage; history, arguments and results.* National Woman Suffrage Publishing Co.: New York, 1917.

Black, Alexander. *Miss America.* New York, 1898.

Black, W. C. *Christian Womanhood.* Methodist Episcopal Church Publishing House: Nashville, 1888.

Blackmar, Frank W. *Higher Education in Kansas.* [Circular of Information, Bur. Ed., No. 2, 1900] Government Printing Office: Washington, 1900.

Blackstone, William. *Commentaries on the Laws of England.* 4 vols. Oxford, 1778.

Blackwell, Elizabeth. *Lectures on the Laws of Life with Special Reference to the Physical Education of Girls.* London, 1871.

Blackwell, Elizabeth. *Pioneer Work for Women* [Everyman's Library] Dutton: New York, n.d.

Blackwell, Elizabeth and Emily. *Medicine as a Profession for Women.* New York, 1860.

Blake, Mabelle B. *Guidance for College Women.* Appleton: New York, 1926.

Blake, Sophia Jex. *A Visit to Some American Schools and Colleges*. London, 1867.

Blandin, (Mrs.) I. M. E. *History of Higher Education of Women in the South, Prior to 1860*. Neale: New York, 1909.

Boardman, George N. *Importance of Public Institutions for the Education of Young Women*. New York, 1867.

Bodichon, Barbara L. Smith. *Objections to the Enfranchisement of Women Considered*. London, 1866.

Bodichon, Barbara L. Smith. *Reasons for the Enfranchisement of Women*. London, 1866.

Bodichon, Barbara L. Smith. *Women and Work*. New York, 1859.

Bolen, George L. *Getting a Living*. Ch. XVII. Macmillan: New York, 1903.

Book of Common Prayer, Approved 1789. Philadelphia, 1873.

Boone, Richard G. *Education in the United States*. New York, 1894.

Bosworth, Louise M. *The Living Wage of Women Workers* [Supplement to the Annals of American Academy of Political and Social Science, May 1911] Philadelphia, 1911.

Bourne, W. O. *History of the Public School Society of New York City*. New York, 1873.

Bowditch, William I. *Taxation of Women in Massachusetts*. Cambridge, 1875.

Bowditch, William I. *Woman Suffrage a Right not a Privilege*. Cambridge, 1882.

Boyd, W. K. *Some Phases of Educational History in the South Since 1865*. [Studies in Southern History and Politics, 1914, 257–87]

Boyd, W. K. *Story of Durham, City of the New South*. Duke University Press: Durham, 1925.

Boyden, Albert G. *History . . . of the State Normal School, Bridgewater, Massachusetts*. Boston, 1876.

Brace, John P. *Lectures to Young Converts—delivered to pupils of the Hartford Female Seminary during the Revival, 1841*. Hartford, 1846.

Brackett, Anna C. (Ed.). *The Education of American Girls*. New York, 1874.

Brackett, Anna C. *Woman and the Higher Education*. New York, 1893.

Bradford Academy. A Memorial. Congregational S. S. and Publishing Soc.: Boston, 1870.

Bradford, J. E. *Education in the Ohio Valley Prior to 1840*. [Reprint from *Ohio Archeological and Historical Quart.*, Jan., 1916] Herr: Columbus, 1916.

Brailsford, Mabel R. *Quaker Women*. London, 1915.

Brainerd, Ezra. *Life and Work in Middlebury, Vermont, of Emma Willard*. Middlebury, n.d.

Branagan, Thomas. *Excellency of the Female Character Vindicated; being an investigation relative to the cause and effect of the encroachment of men upon women's rights and the too frequent degradation and consequent misfortunes of the fair sex*. Philadelphia, 1808.

Breadwinning Women in Four Selected Cities, Family Status of. [Bul. Women's Bur., No. 41, 1925] Government Printing Office: Washington, 1925.

Breadwinning Women, The Family Status of. [Bul. Women's Bur., No. 23, 1922] Government Printing Office: Washington, 1922.

Bremner, C. S. *Education of Girls and Women in Great Britain.* London, 1897.

Brewer, John M. *The Vocational Guidance Movement.* Macmillan: New York, 1922.

Brickell, John. *Natural History of North Carolina.* Raleigh, n.d.

Briggs, LeBaron R. *Girls and Education.* Houghton: Boston, 1911.

Brissot de Warville, Jean P. *New Travels in the United States of America, in 1788.* Dublin, 1792.

Brockett, L. P. *Woman, Her Rights, Wrongs, Privileges, and Responsibilities; containing a sketch of her condition in all ages and countries . . . her true position in education . . .* Hartford, 1869.

Brockett, L. P., and Vaughan, Mary C. *Woman's Work in the Civil War.* Philadelphia, 1867.

Brooks, Charles, and Usher, James M. *History of the Town of Medford, Massachusetts.* Boston, 1886.

Brooks, Geraldine. *Dames and Daughters of Colonial Days.* Crowell: New York, 1901.

Broome, Edwin C. *A History and Critical Discussion of College Entrance Requirements.* Columbia University: New York, 1902.

Brown, Alexander. *First Republic in America; an account of the origin of this nation.* Boston, 1898.

Brown, Alexander (Ed.). *Genesis of the United States.* Boston, 1890.

Brown, Alice. *Mercy Warren.* New York, 1896.

Brown, E. E. *The Making of Our Middle Schools.* Longmans: New York, 1903.

Brown, William S. *The Capability of Women to Practise the Healing Art.* Boston, 1859.

Browne, William H. *Famous Women of History.* Philadelphia, 1895.

Browne, William H. *Maryland: The History of a Palatinate.* Boston, 1884.

Bruce, Philip A. *Economic History of Virginia in the Seventeenth Century.* 2 vols. New York, 1896.

Bruce, Philip A. *History of the University of Virginia, 1819–1919.* 5 vols. Macmillan: New York, 1921–22.

Bruce, Philip A. *Institutional History of Virginia in the Seventeenth Century.* 2 vols. Putnam: New York, 1910.

Bruce, Philip A. *Social Life of Virginia in the Seventeenth Century.* Whittet: Richmond, 1907.

Brumbaugh, Martin G. *The Life and Works of Christopher Dock, with a translation of his works into English.* Lippincott: Philadelphia, 1908.

Brunet, René. *The New German Constitution.* Knopf: New York, 1922.

Bryce, James. *The American Commonwealth.* 2 vols. New York, 1895.

Buchanan, Joseph R. *The New Education: Moral, Industrial, Hygienic, Intellectual.* Boston, 1882.

Buckingham, J. S. *Slave States of America.* 2 vols. London, 1842.

Buckley, James M. *A History of Methodists in the United States.* New York, 1896.

Buckley, James M. *The Wrong and Peril of Woman Suffrage.* Revell: New York, 1909.

Buckstaff, Florence G. *Married Women's Property in Anglo-Saxon and Anglo-Norman Law.* American Academy Political and Social Science: Philadelphia, 1893.

Budd, Thomas. *Good Order Established in Pennsylvania and New Jersey.* Philadelphia, 1685.

Bühler, G. *The Laws of Manu.* [Vol. XXV of *Sacred Books of the East,* ed. by M. Müller] Oxford, 1886.

Burke, Emily P. *Reminiscences of Georgia.* J. M. Fitch: n.p., 1850.

Burkhead, L. S. *Centennial of Methodism in North Carolina.* Raleigh, 1876.

Burnaby, Andrews. *Travels through the Middle Settlements in North America.* London, 1775.

Burnap, George W. *Sphere and Duties of Woman, a course of lectures.* Baltimore, 1848.

Burns, James J. *Educational History of Ohio.* Historical Publishing Co.: Columbus, 1905.

Burroughs, Charles. An address on female education delivered in Portsmouth (N. H.). Portsmouth, 1827.

Burstall, Sara A. *The Education of Girls in the United States.* London, 1894.

Burstall, Sara A. *Impressions of American Education in 1908.* Longmans: New York, 1909.

Burstall, Sara A. and Douglas, M. A. *Public Schools for Girls.* Longmans: New York, 1911.

Burton, John. *Lectures on Female Education and Manners.* Philadelphia, 1794.

Burton, L. R. *Womanhood and its Development.* Riverside Press: Boston.

Burton, Margaret E. *The Education of Women in China.* Revell: New York, 1911.

Burton, Warren. *The District School as it Was.* Boston, 1833.

Burwell, Letitia. *Girl's Life in Virginia Before the War.* New York, 1895.

Bush, George G. *History of Education in Florida.* [Circular of Information, Bur. Ed., No. 7, 1888] Washington, 1889.

Bush, George G. *History of Higher Education in Massachusetts.* [Circular of Information, Bur. Ed., No. 6, 1891] Washington, 1891.

Bushnell, Henry. *The History of Granville, Licking County, Ohio.* Columbus, 1889.

Bushnell, Horace. *Women's Suffrage: The reform against nature.* New York, 1870.

Butler, Charles. *The American Lady.* Philadelphia, 1851.

Butler, Elizabeth B. *Saleswomen in Mercantile Stores, Baltimore, 1909.* Charities Publication Committee: New York, 1912.

Butler, Elizabeth B. *Women and the Trades, Pittsburg, 1907–8.* Charities Publication Committee: New York, 1909.

Butler, John C. *Historical Record of Macon and Central Georgia.* Macon, 1879.

Butler, Josephine. *Woman's Work and Woman's Culture.* London, 1869.

Butler, Nicholas M. (Ed.). *Education in the United States.* American Book Co.: New York, 1910.

Cable, George W. *The Creoles of Louisiana.* New York, 1884.

Calcutta, History of Native Female Education in. Calcutta, 1858.

Calhoun, Arthur W. *A Social History of the American Family.* 3 vols. Clark: Cleveland, 1917–19.

Campan, J. L. *De L'Éducation.* 3 vols. Paris, 1824.

Campbell, Helen. *Anne Bradstreet and Her Time.* Boston, 1891.

Campbell, Helen. *Household Economics.* New York, 1897.

Cannon, Mary A. *The Education of Women during the Renaissance.* National Capitol Press: Washington, 1916.

Carlton, Frank T. *Education and Industrial Evolution.* Macmillan, New York, 1908.

Cary, Virginia. *Letters on Female Character Addressed to a Young Lady on the Death of her Mother.* Richmond, Va., 1830.

Cass, Alice H. *Practical Programs for Women's Clubs.* McClurg: Chicago, 1915.

Castle, Cora S. *A Statistical Study of Eminent Women.* Science Press: New York, 1913.

Catlin, George B. *The Story of Detroit.* The Detroit News: Detroit, 1923.

Catt, Carrie C. and Shuler, Nettie R. *Woman Suffrage and Politics, the inner story of the suffrage movement.* Scribner's: New York, 1923.

Caullery, Maurice. *Universities and Scientific Life in the United States.* (Trans. by J. H. Woods and Emmet Russell) Harvard Press: Cambridge, Mass., 1922.

Cederborg, Hazel P. *The Early History of Rockford College.* 2 vols. [M.A. Thesis, Wellesley College, June, 1926]

Celnart, Madame E. F. *The Gentleman and Lady's Book of Politeness.* Boston, 1837.

Chadwick, James R. *The Study and Practice of Medicine by Women.* Boston, 1879.

Chancellor, William E. *Our Schools—Their Administration.* Heath: Boston, 1906.

Chandler, Julian A. C., and others (Eds.). *The South in the Building of the Nation.* 12 vols. Southern Historical Publication Soc.: Richmond, 1909.

Channing, Edward. *A History of the United States.* 6 vols. Macmillan: New York, 1905–26.

Channing, W. Henry. *The History of Woman Suffrage.* [From *The Inquirer*, London, Nov. 5, 1881]

Chapman, Maria W. *Harriett Martineau's Autobiography.* 2 vols. Boston, 1877.

Chapone, Hester. *Letters on the Improvement of the Mind Addressed to a Young Lady.* 2 vols. New York, 1819.

Character, Education, Prerogatives, and Moral Influence of Women. Boston, 1837.

Chemistry, Women in. [In New York City Bur. of Vocational Ed., *Studies in Occupations,* Vol. 4]

Chemistry, Industrial, as a Vocation for Women. Women's Educational and Industrial Union: Boston, 1911.

Cheney, Ednah D. (Ed.). *Louisa May Alcott: Her Life, Letters, and Journals.* Boston, 1889.

Chester, Eliza. *Chats with Girls on Self-Culture.* New York, 1891.

Chester, Eliza. *Girls and Women.* Boston, 1890.

Chesterfield, Philip D. S. *Letters . . .* 4 vols. London, 1847.

Chevalier, Michel. *Society, Manners, and Politics in the United States.* Boston, 1839.

Child, Lydia Maria. *Brief History of the Condition of Women.* 2 vols. New York, 1854.

Child, Lydia Maria. *The Mother's Book.* Boston, 1831.

Chirol, J. L. *Enquiry into the Best System of Female Education; or, boarding school and home education.* London, 1809.

Church, Charles A. *History of Rockford and Winnebago County.* Rockford, Ill., 1900.

Church, Ella R. *Money-Making for Ladies.* New York, 1882.

Citizens Suffrage Association. *Tract No. 7.* n.p., n.d.

Claghorn, Kate H. *College Training for Women.* New York, 1897.

Clark, Sue A. and Wyatt, Edith. *Making Both Ends Meet.* Macmillan: New York, 1911.

Clark, Willis G. *History of Education in Alabama.* [Circular of Information, Bur. Ed., No. 8, 1889] Washington, 1889.

Clarke, Edward H. *The Building of a Brain.* Boston, 1880.

Clarke, Edward H. *Sex in Education; or, a fair chance for girls.* Boston, 1874.

Clarke, Ida C. *American Women and the World War.* Appleton: New York, 1918.

Clarke, Mary C. *World-Noted Women; or, types of womanly attributes of all lands and ages.* New York, 1858.

Clay, Jehu C. *Annals of the Swedes on the Delaware.* Philadelphia, 1858.

Clement, J. (Ed.). *Noble Deeds of American Women.* Auburn, N. Y., 1854.

Coal-Mine Workers' Families, Home Environment and Employment Opportunities of Women in. [Bul. Women's Bur., No. 45, 1925] Government Printing Office: Washington, 1925.

Cobb, (Mrs.) John B. *Wesleyan Female College.* [In the *Seventy-Fifth Anniversary of Macon Methodism,* compiled by O. A. Park, Macon, 1904]

Cobbe, Frances P. *The Duties of Women.* Boston, 1881.

Coburn Classical Institute. Seventy-fifth Anniversary, with an historical sketch by E. C. Whittemore. Portland, 1904.

Coeducation. [Circular of Information, Bur. Ed., No. 2, 1883] Washington, 1883.

Coeducation. [*R. C. E.* (1903) I: 1047–78]

Coeducation of the Sexes in the Public Schools of the United States. [Circular of Information, Bur. Ed., No. 2, 1883] Washington, 1883.

Coeducation of the sexes in the United States. [*R. C. E.* (1891–2) II: 783–859]

Cole, Marion S. *The Women's College in Brown University, its Progress and Expansion.* Providence, 1917.

College Graduates, Women, Health Statistics of. [Report of a special committee of the A. C. A., Annie G. Howes, chairman] Boston, 1855.

Collins, Richard H. *History of Kentucky.* 2 vols. Covington, 1874.

Colton, Elizabeth Avery. Materials relating to her work; and an article by W. J. Grinstead in the *Dictionary of American Biography.*

Colton, Elizabeth Avery. *Various Types of Southern Colleges for Women.* [Bul. Tennessee College (October, 1916) X, No. 1] Murfreesboro, 1916.

Combe, George. Female education. [In *Lectures on Popular Education.* Edinburgh and London, 1848]

Comenius, J. A. *Great Didactic* (Trans. by M. W. Keatinge). London, 1917.

Comenius, J. A. *School of Infancy* (Ed. by W. S. Monroe). Boston, 1893.

Comfort, George F., and Comfort, Anna M. *Woman's Education and Woman's Health; chiefly in reply to "Sex in Education."* Syracuse, N. Y., 1874.

Commercial Register for the Country, Mobile, Ala., 1830–31.

Commons, J. R. *History of Labor in the United States.* 2 vols. Macmillan: New York, 1921.

Commons, J. R., Phillips, U. B., *et al* (Eds.). *A Documentary History of American Industrial Society.* 10 vols. The Arthur H. Clark Company: Cleveland, 1910–11.

Conrad, Henry C. *History of the State of Delaware.* 3 vols. Author: Wilmington, 1908.

Converse, Florence. *The Story of Wellesley.* Little, Brown: Boston, 1915.

Cook, Clarence. *A Girl's Life Eighty Years Ago; selections from the letters of Eliza Southgate Bowne.* New York, 1888.

Cook, Ebenezer. *The Sotweed Factor.* London, 1708; reprinted New York, 1865.

Cooke, John E. *Virginia.* Houghton: Boston, 1903.

Coolidge, Mary E. *Why Women Are So.* Holt: New York, 1912.

Coon, Charles L. *Beginnings of Public Education in North Carolina, 1790–1840.* 2 vols. Edwards: Raleigh, 1908.

Coon, Charles L. *North Carolina Schools and Academies, 1790–1840.* North Carolina Historical Commission: Raleigh, 1915.

Corbin, Caroline F. *Socialism and Christianity with Reference to the Woman Question.* Chicago, 1905.

Corson, Hiram. *Brief History of Proceedings in the Medical Society of Pennsylvania to Procure Recognition of Women Physicians.* Norristown, 1894.

Corson, Juliet. *Fifteen Cent Dinners for Working Men's Families of Six.* New York, 1877.

Cosgrave, Jessica G. *Mothers and Daughters.* Doran: New York, 1925.

Costello, Louisa S. *Memoirs of Eminent Englishwomen.* 4 vols. London, 1844.

Courtenay, William A. *Education in Charleston.* Charleston, S. C., 1881.

Cowles, Eunice Caldwell. *Memories.* [Read by Lydia A. Caldwell before Ipswich First Parish Missionary Society, Oct. 7, 1903]

Cox, Walter S. *Lessons in Law for Women.* Brentano: New York, 1900.

Coxe, Margaret. *Claims of the Country on American Females.* 2 vols. Columbus, 1842.

Coxe, Margaret. *The Young Lady's Companion and Token of Affection.* Columbus, Ohio, 1846.

Crawford, Mary C. *The College Girl of America.* Page: Boston, 1904.

Crawford, Mary C. *Old Boston Days and Ways.* Little, Brown: Boston, 1909.

Crawford, Mary C. *Social Life in Old New England.* Little, Brown: Boston, 1914.

Creevey, (Mrs.) C. A. S. *A Daughter of the Puritans.* (An autobiography) Putnam: New York, 1916.

Cressman, Elmer W. *Education of Women in England, France and Germany.* [M.A. Thesis, University of Pennsylvania, 1921]

Croly, Jennie C. *The History of the Woman's Club Movement in America.* New York, 1898.

Cronwright-Schreiner, S. C. *Life of Olive Schreiner.* Little, Brown: New York, 1924.

Crothers, Samuel M. *Meditations on Votes for Women.* Houghton: Boston, 1914.

Cubberley, E. P. *Readings in the History of Education.* Houghton: Boston, 1909.

Cubberley, E. P. *Public Education in the United States.* Houghton: Boston, 1919.

Cubberley, E. P. *Readings in the History of Education.* Houghton: Boston, 1920.

Curtis, George W. *An Address Indicating the Right of Women to the Elective Franchise.* New York, 1858.

Daggett, M. P. *Women Wanted.* Doran: New York, 1918.

Dalcho, Frederick. *An Historical Account of the Protestant Episcopal Church in South Carolina.* Charleston, 1820.

Dall, Caroline H. *The College, the Market and the Court.* Rumford: Boston, 1914.

Dall, Caroline H. *The Legal Rights of Married Women: Woman's rights under the law.* Three lectures. Boston, 1861.

Dall, Caroline H. (Ed.). *A Practical Illustration of Woman's Right to Labor; or a letter from Marie E. Zakrzewksa.* Boston, 1860.

Dana, Daniel. *Hints on Reading.* [Address delivered in the Ipswich Female Seminary, Jan. 15, 1834]

Dana, Stephen W. *Woman's Possibilities and Limitations: A message to the young women of today.* New York, 1899.

Daniels, W. H. *History of Methodism.* Chicago, 1880.

Danville (Va.), Its Origin and Early History Copied from the Manuscript of George W. Dame.

Darusmont, F. W. *Views of Society and Manners in America, 1818–1820.* London, 1821.

Darwin, Erasmus. *A Plan for the Conduct of Female Education in Boarding Schools, Private Families and Public Seminaries.* Philadelphia, 1798.

Davies, Emily. *The Higher Education of Women.* New York, 1866.

Davies, Emily. *Thoughts on Some Questions Relating to Women, 1860–1908.* Cambridge, 1910.

Davies, (Mrs.) Huns. Women and adult education. [*Cambridge Essays on Adult Education,* 1920, No. 7]

Davis, Paulina W. *A History of the National Woman's Rights Movement, 1850–1870.* New York, 1871.

Davis, R. Means. Sketch of education in South Carolina. [*South Carolina: Resources and Population, Institutions and Industries* (Charleston, 1883) 445–549]

Day, Samuel P. *Life and Society in America.* 2 vols. London, 1880.

Dean, A. D. *The Worker and the State.* Century: New York, 1910.

Dean, Ellen. The Harvard examination for women. [*43d Annual Report of the Superintendent of Public Instruction of the State of Michigan,* 1879: 142–7]

Dearborn, Ned H. *The Oswego Movement in American Education.* Teachers College: New York, 1925.

De Beaujour, Felix. *Sketch of the United States.* (Trans. of W. Walton) London, 1814.

De Crèvecoeur, J. Hector St. John. *Letters from an American Farmer.* [Everyman's Library] Dutton: New York, n.d.

De Foe, Daniel. *A Projected Academy for Women—Essays on Projects.* London, 1797.

De Kay, John. *Women and the New Social State.* Basel, 1918.

De la Guard, Theodore. *The Simple Cobbler of Agawam in America.* [Vol. III, No. 8, of Force's *Collection of Historical Tracts.* London, 1713.

Delaware Industries, Women in. [Bul. Women's Bur., No. 58, 1927] Government Printing Office: Washington, 1927.

Dell, Floyd. *Women as World Builders: studies in modern feminism.* Forbes: Chicago, 1913.

Densmore, Emmet. *Sex Equality: a solution of the woman problem.* Funk and Wagnalls: New York, n.d.

Derry, J. T. *Georgia: A Guide to its Cities, Towns, Scenery and Resources.* Philadelphia, 1878.

DeTocqueville, Alexis. *Democracy in America.* 2 vols. New York, 1845.

DeVarigny, C. *The Women of the United States.* (Trans. of Arabella Ward) New York, 1895.

DeWahl, Anne. *Practical Hints on the Moral, Mental, and Physical Training of Girls at School.* London, 1847.

Dewees, W. W. *History of Westtown Boarding School.* Philadelphia, 1884.

Dexter, E. G. *History of Education in the United States.* Macmillan: New York, 1919.

Dexter, Elizabeth A. *Colonial Women of Affairs.* Houghton: Boston, 1924.

Dexter, F. B. *Diary of David McClure.* New York, 1899.

Dickinson, Emily. *Letters.* (Ed. by Mabel L. Todd) Vol. I. Boston, 1894.

Dickinson, Mary L. *From Girlhood to Womanhood.* New York, 1899.

Disraeli, Benjamin. *Sybil; or the two nations.* London, 1920.

Dix, Morgan. *Lectures on the Calling of a Christian Woman and her Training to Fulfill It.* New York, 1883.

Doane, William C. *A Memoir of the Life of George Washington Doane.* New York, 1860.

Documentary History of the American Industrial Society: See Commons, J. R. (Editor).

Doddridge, Philip. *Sermons to Young Persons.* Hartford, 1803.

Dodge, H. Augusta (Ed.). *Gail Hamilton's Life in Letters.* 2 vols. Lee and Shepard: Boston, 1901.

Domestic Workers and their Employment Relations. [Bul. Women's Bur., No. 39, 1924] Government Printing Office: Washington, 1924.

Donaldson, James. *Woman: Her Position and Influence in Ancient Greece and Rome and Among the Early Christians.* Longmans: New York, 1907.

Dorchester, Massachusetts, History of the Town of. By a committee of the Dorchester Antiquarian and Historical Society, Boston, 1859.

Douglas, James. *Status of Women in New England and New France.* Jackson Press: Kingston, Canada, 1912.

Dow, G. F. (Ed.). *The Holyoke Diaries, 1709–1856.* Essex Institute: Salem, 1911.

Doyle, J. A. *English Colonies in America.* New York, 1889.

Draper, Andrew S. *American Education.* Houghton: Boston, 1909.

Draper, Andrew S. *Our Children, Our Schools and Our Industries.* Bardeen: Syracuse, 1908.

Dressler, Von S. *Moderne Mädchenerziehung und die Frauenfrage.* Gotha, 1888.

Dubbs, Joseph H. *History of the Reformed Church in Pennsylvania.* Pennsylvania German Society: Lancaster, 1902.

Dubois, Jean A. *Hindu Manners, Customs and Ceremonies.* (Trans. of H. K. Beauchamp) Oxford, 1906.

Dubuque County, Iowa, The History of. Chicago, 1880.

Dudley, Gertrude, and Kellor, F. A. *Athletic Games in the Education of Women.* Holt: New York, 1909.

Due West [S. C.] Woman's College. Fiftieth Anniversary, 1860–1911.

Duffey, (Mrs.) E. B. *No Sex in Education; or an equal chance for both girls and boys.* Philadelphia, 1874.

Dugard, M. *La Société Américaine.* Paris, 1896.

Dunn, Jacob P. *Greater Indianapolis: the history, the industries, the institutions.* Lewis Publishing Co.: Chicago, 1910.

Dunshee, Henry W. *History of the School of the Reformed Protestant Dutch Church* [of New York]. New York, 1853.

Duppa, B. T. (Ed.) *Scottish Institutions for the Education of Young Ladies.* London, 1837.

Dutton, Samuel T., and Snedden, David. *Administration of Public Education in the United States.* Macmillan: New York, 1916.

Dwight, Timothy. *Travels in New England and New York.* 4 vols. London, 1823.

Dyer, G. W. *Democracy in the South Before the Civil War.* M. E. Church South: Nashville, 1905.

Earle, Alice M. *Child Life in Colonial Days.* New York, 1899.

Earle, Alice M. *Colonial Days in Old New York.* New York, 1896.

Earle, Alice M. *Customs and Fashions in Old New England.* Scribner's: New York, 1902.

Earle, Alice M. *Margaret Winthrop.* New York, 1896.

Early, Ruth H. *By-Ways of Virginia History.* Everett Waddey: Richmond, 1907.

Eastman, Mary F. *The Biography of Dio Lewis.* New York, 1891.

Eby, Frederick. *Education in Texas.* University of Texas: Austin, 1919.

Eckenstein, Lina. *Woman Under Monasticism.* Cambridge, 1896.

Education, Woman in. [International Congress of Women of 1899: Report of transactions of the educational section. London, 1900]

Educational Yearbook of the International Institute of Teachers College, 1924, 1925, 1926. (Ed. by I. L. Kandel) Macmillan: New York.

Eggleston, Edward. *The Transit of Civilization.* Appleton; New York, 1901.

Eggleston, (Mrs.) M. W. *Womanhood in the Making.* Doran: New York, 1923.

Eliot, Charles W. *A Late Harvest.* Atlantic Monthly Press: Boston, 1924.

Eliot, George. *Mill on the Floss.* New York, 1860.

Ellet, Elizabeth F. *The Women of the American Revolution.* 3 vols. New York, 1850.

Ellis, George E. *Life of Anne Hutchinson.* Boston, 1847.

Ellis, George E. *The Puritan Age and Rule in . . . Massachusetts, 1629–85.* Boston, 1891.

Ellis, Mildred. *Education of Young Ladies of Small Pecuniary Resources for Other Occupations Than That of Teaching.* 2 vols. London, 1838.

Ely, Richard T. *The Labor Movement in America.* Macmillan: New York, 1905.

Elyot, Thomas. *The Boke Named the Governour.* (Edited by H. H. S. Croft from the edition of 1531.) London, 1883.

Emerson, George B. *Reminiscences of an Old Teacher.* Boston, 1878.

Emerson, Joseph. *Female Education—a discourse delivered at the dedication of the seminary hall in Saugus, Jan. 15, 1822, to which is added*

The Little Reckoner, consisting principally of arithmetical questions for infant minds. Boston, 1822.

Emerson, Joseph. *Letter to a Class of Young Ladies Upon the Study of History of the United States.* n.p., 1828.

Emerson, Joseph. *Recitation Lectures Upon the Acquisition and Communication of Thought.* n.p., 1826.

Emerson, Ralph W. *Lectures and Biographical Sketches.* [Vol. X of complete works.] Boston, 1889–91.

Emerson, Ralph W. *The Life of Joseph Emerson.* Boston, 1834.

Emerson, Ralph W., Clarke, James Freeman, and Channing, William H. *Memoirs of Margaret Fuller Ossoli.* 2 vols. New York, 1869.

Enfranchisement of Women. Reprinted from the *Westminister and Foreign Quarterly Review* for July 1851. [*Woman's Rights Tracts* No. 3, n.p., n.d.]

English Gentlewoman, The. A practical manual for young ladies and their entrance into society. London, 1861.

Enslow, Charles A. *Law Concerning Women, being a resumé of federal and state laws affecting woman's property and civil rights.* Davidson: Seattle, n.d.

Evans, M. A. *How Should Secondary Mathematics for Girls Differ from that for Boys?* Assoc. of Teachers of Mathematics for the Middle States and Maryland: Lancaster, 1914.

Fairbanks, (Mrs.) A. W. (Ed.) *Emma Willard and Her Pupils.* New York, 1898.

Fairchild, James H. *Oberlin, The Colony and the College.* Oberlin, 1883.

Fairchild, James H. *Oberlin: Its Origin, Progress and Results.* Oberlin, 1871.

Fallet, Celino. *Éducation Des Jeunes Filles.* Paris, 1851.

Family Support, The Share of Wage-Earning Women in. [Bul. Women's Bur., No. 30, 1923] Government Printing Office: Washington, 1923.

Family Support, Women Workers and. [Bul. Women's Bur., No. 49, 1925] Government Printing Office: Washington, 1925.

Farmer, Lydia H. (Ed.). *National Exposition Souvenir; what America owes to women . . .* Buffalo, 1893.

Farmer, Silas. *The History of Detroit and Michigan.* Detroit, 1884.

Farrington, F. E. *French Secondary Schools.* Longmans: New York, 1910.

Fay, Edwin W. *History of Education in Louisiana.* [Circular of Information, Bur. Ed., No. 1, 1898] Washington, 1898.

Fearnley, (Mrs.) John. *Eighty Years of St. Mary's Hall, Burlington, New Jersey.* Philadelphia, 1917.

Fearon, Henry B. *Sketches of America (1817).* London, 1818.

Felt, Joseph B. *Annals of Salem.* Salem, 1845.

Felt, Joseph B. *The Ecclesiastical History of New England.* 2 vols. Boston, 1855–62.

Female Slave, Autobiography of a. New York, 1857.

Fénelon, Francois. *De L'Éducation des Filles.* Paris, 1895.

Fénelon, Francois. *Education of Girls.* [Trans. of Thomas Dibdin] Albany, 1806.

Fénelon, Francois. *Education of Girls.* [Trans. of Kate Lupton] Boston, 1891.

Ferrall, Simon A. *Ramble of Six Thousand Miles through the United States of America.* London, 1832.

Ferris, Helen J. *Girls' Clubs.* Dutton: New York, 1918.

Fields, Annie. *Life and Letters of Harriet Beecher Stowe.* Boston, 1898.

Finding Employment for Girls Who Have to Work. By the Chicago School of Civics and Philanthropy. n.d.

Fish, C. R. *The Rise of the Common Man.* Macmillan: New York, 1927.

Fisher, Sydney G. *Men, Women and Manners in Colonial Times.* 2 vols. Lippincott: Philadelphia, 1913.

Fisk, Fidelia. *Recollections of Mary Lyon, with selections from her instructions to her pupils.* Boston, 1866.

Fiske, John. *The Dutch and Quaker Colonies in America.* 2 vols. Boston, 1899.

Fiske, John. *Old Virginia and Her Neighbors.* 2 vols. Houghton: Boston, 1900.

Fithian, Philip. *Journal and Letters (1767–74).* University Library: Princeton, 1900.

Fitzpatrick, E. A. *The Educational Views and Influence of DeWitt Clinton.* New York, Teachers College, 1911.

Flexner, Abraham. *American College; a criticism.* Century: New York, 1908.

Flexner, Abraham. *Medical Education in the United States and Canada.* Carnegie Foundation: New York, n.d.

Flexner, Abraham. *A modern College and a Modern School.* Doubleday: New York, 1923.

Foote, William H. *Sketches of North Carolina.* New York, 1846.

Forbes, H. M. (Ed.) *The Diary of Rev. Ebenezer Parkman.* Worcester, 1899.

Fordyce, David. *Dialogues Concerning Education.* London, 1745.

Fordyce, James. *Sermons to Young Women.* Philadelphia, 1787.

Forrest, Mary. *Women of the South Distinguished in Literature.* New York, 1865.

Forrest, W. S. *Historical and Descriptive Sketches of Norfolk and Vicinity.* Philadelphia, 1853.

Fortier, Alcée. *Louisiana Studies: Literature, Customs and Dialects, History and Education.* New Orleans, 1894.

Foster, Hannah W. *The Boarding School; or lessons of a preceptress to her pupils.* Boston, 1798.

Franklin, James. *The Philosophical and Political History of the Thirteen United States.* London, 1784.

Franklin, Margaret L. *The Case for Woman Suffrage. . . .* National College Equal Suffrage League: New York, 1913.

Frazier, Cora B. *Social Service as a Vocation for Women.* Women's Educational and Industrial Union: Boston.

Frazier, Cora B. *Talks to Women on Essentials to Success in the Business World.* Palmer-Goodman Company: Philadelphia, 1913.

French, E. R. *History of Maine Wesleyan Seminary.* Smith and Sale: Portland, 1919.

Friends' Academy, New Bedford, Mass. Historical Sketch, 1876. [New Bedford Public Library]

Friends' Library. 9 vols. Philadelphia, 1837–47.

Fries, Adelaide L. *Historical Sketch of Salem Female Academy.* Salem, N. C., 1902.

Fries, Adelaide L. *Records of the Moravians in North Carolina.* 2 vols. North Carolina Hist. Commission: Raleigh, 1922–6.

Frothingham, O. B., *et al. Woman Suffrage Unnatural and Inexpedient.* Boston, 1894.

Fuller, Anna. *Pratt Portraits.* New York, 1892.

Fuller, Margaret. *The Great Lawsuit.* [Reprint from *The Dial*, No. 13, July 1843] Rowfant Club: Cleveland, 1901–02.

Fuller, Margaret. *Women in the Nineteenth Century and Kindred Papers.* . . . Boston, 1860.

Fuller, (Mrs.) Marcus B. *The Wrongs of Indian Womanhood.* Revell: New York, 1900.

Gadesden, F. The education of girls and the development of girls' high schools. [Chapter V in Roberts, R. D. (Ed.): *Education in the Nineteenth Century.* Cambridge, 1901]

Gage, Matilda J. *Woman, Church and State; a historical account of the status of woman through Christian ages.* . . . New York, 1893.

Gaines, B. O. *History of Scott County,* Kentucky. 2 vols. Georgetown, 1905.

Gallaher, Ruth A. *Legal and Political Status of Women in Iowa.* . . . State Hist. Soc. of Iowa: Iowa City, 1918.

Gallaudet, T. H. An address on female education delivered Nov. 21, 1827, at the opening of the edifice erected for the accommodation of the Hartford Female Seminary. Hartford, 1828.

Gallichan, (Mrs.) W. M. *The Truth About Women.* London, 1913.

Galton, Francis, Westermarck, Edward, *et al. Sociological Papers.* London, 1905.

Gamble, Eliza B. *The Evolution of Woman; an inquiry into the dogma of her inferiority.* New York, 1894.

Gambrill, Bessie L. *College Achievement and Vocational Efficiency.* Teachers College: New York, 1922.

Gardiner, Dorothy. *English Girlhood at School; a study of Woman's Education through twelve centuries.* Oxford University Press, 1929.

Garnett, James M. *Lectures on Female Education, comprising the first and second series of a course delivered to Mrs. Garnett's pupils, at Elmwood, Essex County, Va.* Richmond, 1825.

Garnett, James M. *Token of Regard, presented to the pupils of the Elmwood School.* Richmond, 1830.

George, W. L. *Intelligence of Woman.* Little, Brown: Boston, 1916.

Georgia Industries, Women in. [Bul. Women's Bur., No. 22, 1922] Government Printing Office: Washington, 1922.

Gifford, Walter J. *Historical Development of the New York State High School System.* Lyon: Albany, 1922.

Gilchrist, Beth B. *The Life of Mary Lyon.* Houghton: Boston, 1910.

Gilman, Charlotte P. *The Man-Made World; or, our androcentric culture.* Charlton: New York, 1911.

Gilman, Charlotte P. *Women and Economics.* Small, Maynard: Boston, 1898.

Girls' Manual; comprising a summary view of female studies, accomplishments and principles of conduct. New York, 1865.

Gisbourne, Thomas. *An Enquiry into the Duties of the Female Sex.* New York, 1820.

Gladden, Washington. *Woman's Part in Social Questions.* n.p., 1889.

Goerth, Albrecht. *Erziehung und Ausbildung der Mädchen.* Leipsig, 1894.

Good, Harry G. *Benjamin Rush and His Services to American Education.* Berne, Ind., 1918.

Goodloe, Abbe Carter. *College Girls.* New York, 1895.

Goodpasture, Albert V. *Overton County* (Tennessee). Nashville, 1877.

Goodpasture, Albert V. and W. H. *Life of Jefferson Dillard Goodpasture.* Nashville, 1897.

Goodsell, Willystine. *Education of Women, its social background and problems.* Macmillan: New York, 1923.

Goodsell, Willystine. *The Family as a Social and Educational Institution.* Macmillan: New York, 1915.

Goodsell, Willystine. Education of Women. [In *Twenty-Five Years of American Education* (Ed. by I. L. Kandel), Ch. XIII. Macmillan: New York, 1924]

Goodspeed Publishing Company. *Biographical and Historical Memoirs of Mississippi.* 2 vols. 1891.

Goodspeed Publishing Company. *History of Tennessee.* Nashville, 1887.

Goodspeed, Thomas W. *History of the University of Chicago . . . the First Quarter Century.* University of Chicago Press: Chicago, 1916.

Goodspeed, Weston A., and Goodspeed, Kenneth C. *History of Dubuque County, Iowa.* Goodspeed Hist. Assoc.: Chicago, n.d.

Goodwin, Maud W. *The Colonial Cavalier; or Southern life before the Revolution.* Boston, 1897.

Goodwin, Maud W. *Dolly Madison.* New York, 1898.

Gordy, John P. *Rise and Growth of the Normal School Idea in the United States.* [Circular of Information, Bur. Ed., No. 8, 1891] Washington, 1891.

Goretsky, Eva. *Die Theorie der höheren Mädchenbildung bei G. Stanley Hall.* [Ph.D. Thesis, Munich, 1922]

Goucher, John F. *The Woman's College of Baltimore. . . .* Goucher College: Baltimore, 1906.

Grant, Anne. *Memoirs of an American Lady.* 2 vols. London, 1809.

Grant, Cecil, and Hodgson, Norman. *The Case for Coeducation.* London, 1913.

Graves, (Mrs.) A. J. *Girlhood and Womanhood.* Boston, 1844.

Graves, (Mrs.) A. J. *Woman in America.* New York, 1841.

Graves, Frank P. The college education of today; and curriculum of our women's colleges. [In *Addresses and Papers, 1921–26.* University of the State of New York Press: Albany, 1926]

Greene, John M. Origin of Smith College. [Smith College: *Quarter Centennial Anniversary, 1875–1900, 79–93*]

Gregory, John. *A Father's Legacy to His Daughters.* London, 1784.

Gregory, Samuel. *Letter to Ladies in Favor of Female Physicians.* Boston, 1850.

Gregory, Samuel. *Man-Midwifery Exposed and Corrected.* Boston, 1848.

Griffin, Orwin B. *Evolution of the Connecticut State School System.* Teachers College: New York, 1928.

Grimes, J. Bryan. *Abstract of North Carolina Wills.* . . . Uzzell: Raleigh, 1910.

Grimes, J. Bryan. *North Carolina Wills and Inventories.* Edwards and Broughton: Raleigh, 1912.

Grimké, A. E. *Letters to Catherine E. Beecher in Reply to "An Essay on Slavery and Abolition."* Boston, 1838.

Grimké, Sarah. *Letters on the Condition of Women and the Equality of the Sexes.* Boston, 1838.

Grimké, Thomas Smith. *Addresses on Science, Education and Literature.* New Haven, 1831.

Griscom, John. *Monitorial Instruction.* An address at the opening of the N. Y. High School. New York, 1825.

Griscom, John. *A Year in Europe.* 2 vols. New York, 1824.

Griscom, John H. *Memoir of John Griscom.* New York, 1859.

Griswold, Rufus W. *The Female Poets of America.* Philadelphia, 1852.

Grizzell, E. D. *Origin and Development of the High School in New England before 1865.* Macmillan: New York, 1923.

Grote, George. *A History of Greece.* 4 vols. New York, 1881.

Grubb, Sarah, and Woolman, John. *Extracts on Education.* Bristol, 1820.

Guild, (Mrs.) Charles E. *Municipal Suffrage for Women.* Massachusetts Assoc. Opposed to Further Extension of Suffrage to Women: Boston, 1904.

Guilford County Literary and Historical Association, Publications of the. Vol. I. Greensboro, 1908.

Guilford, L. T. *The Use of a Life: Memorials of Mrs. Z. P. Grant Bannister.* New York, 1885.

Habits of Good Society, The: A handbook for ladies and gentlemen. New York, 1865.

Hager, Frank N. *The American Family.* University Publishing Soc.: New York, 1905.

Haight, Elizabeth H. *The Autobiography and Letters of Matthew Vassar.* Oxford Press: New York, 1916.

Hale, Beatrice F. *What Women Want; an interpretation of the feminist movement.* Stokes: New York, 1914.

Halifax, George Savile, First Marquis of. *Ladies' New Year's Gift; or advice to a daughter.* Wessels: New York, 1902.

Hall, Basil. *Travels in North America (1827–1828)*. 3 vols. Edinburgh, 1829.

Hall, C. C. (Ed.) *Narratives of Early Maryland*, 1633–1684. Scribner's: New York, 1910.

Hall, G. Stanley. *Adolescence*. Appleton: New York, 1904.

Hall, S. R. *Lectures to Female Teachers on Schoolkeeping*. Boston, 1832.

Hall, W. S., and Hall, Jeanette. *Girlhood and Its Problems*. Winston: Philadelphia, 1919.

Hallowell, J. Burnette. *Teaching of Mathematics in Philadelphia*. [Master's Thesis, University of Pennsylvania, 1925]

Hallowell, Richard P. *The Quaker Invasion of Massachusetts*. Boston, 1887.

Hamilton, Alexander, The Works of. 3 vols. New York, 1810.

Hamilton, Alice. *Women Workers and Industrial Poisons*. [Bul. Women's Bur., No. 57, 1926] Government Printing Office: Washington, 1926.

Hamilton, Gail. *A New Atmosphere*. Boston, 1865.

Hamilton, Gail. *Woman's Worth and Worthlessness*. New York, 1872.

Hamilton, Gail. *Women's Wrongs: a counter-irritant*. Boston, 1868.

Hamilton, Mary E. *The Policewoman, Her Service and Ideals*. Stokes: New York, 1924.

Hamilton, Peter J. *Colonial Mobile*. Houghton: Boston, 1910.

Hamilton, Thomas. *Men and Manners in America*. Philadelphia, 1833.

Hammond, John. *Leah and Rachel; or the two fruitful sisters, Virginia and Maryland*. London, 1656. [Force's *Collection of Historical Tracts*, Vol. III, No. 14]

Hammond, Lily H. *Southern Women and Racial Adjustment*. [J. F. Slater Fund. Occasional papers, 1917, No. 19.] Bell: Lynchburg, Va., 1917.

Hanaford, Phebe A. *Daughters of America; or women of the century*. Boston, 1883.

Hansen, A. O. *Early Educational Leadership in the Ohio Valley*. Public School Publishing Co.; Bloomington, Ill., 1923.

Hard, William. *The Women of Tomorrow*. Baker and Taylor: New York, 1911.

Hardy, Edward J. *The Five Talents of Woman, a book for girls and women*. New York, 1892.

Hark, J. Max (Translator). *Chronicon Ephratense: a history of the community of the Seventh Day Baptists*. Lancaster, 1889.

Harper, Ida H. (Ed.) *The History of Woman Suffrage*. 6 vols. New York, 1881–1922.

Harper, Ida H. *The Life and Work of Susan B. Anthony*. 3 vols. Hollenbeck Press: Indianapolis, 1898–1908.

Harper, Ida H. *Suffrage A Right*. North American Review Publishing Co.: New York, 1906.

Harper, Ida H. *Woman Suffrage Throughout the World*. North American Review Publishing Co.: New York, 1907.

Harper, William R. *The Trend in Higher Education*. University of Chicago Press: Chicago, 1905.

Hartford Female Seminary. Reunion, 1892. [State Library]

Hartley, C. Gasquoine. *The Age of Mother-Power; the position of woman in primitive society.* Dodd, Mead: New York, 1914.

Harwood, W. S. *Life and Letters of Austin Craig.* Revell: N. Y., 1908.

Hatcher, O. L. (Ed.). *Occupations for Women.* Southern Woman's Educational Alliance: Richmond, 1927.

Hawks, F. L. *History of North Carolina, 1584–1729.* 2 vols. Fayetteville, 1859.

Hayes, Ellen. *Letters to a College Girl.* Ellis: Boston, 1909.

Hazard, Caroline. *From College Gates, 1899–1910.* Houghton: Boston, 1925.

Hazard, Caroline. *Some Ideals in the Education of Women.* Crowell: New York, 1900.

Hazardous Industries, The Employment of Women in, in the United States. [Bul. Women's Bur., No. 6, 1921] Government Printing Office: Washington, 1921.

Healey, Caroline W. *Margaret Fuller and Her Friends.* Boston, 1895.

Heatwole, Cornelius J. *History of Education in Virginia.* Macmillan: New York, 1916.

Hecker, Eugene A. *A Short History of Women's Rights from the Days of Augustus to the Present Time, with Special Reference to England and the United States.* Putnam: New York, 1914.

Henderson, Charles H. *Pay-Day.* Houghton: Boston, 1911.

Hendren, Gilbert H. *Special Report Concerning Common School Funds.* State Printer: Indianapolis, 1918.

Henry, Alice. *Women and the Labor Movement.* Doran: New York, 1923.

Henschke, Frau Ulrike. *Denkschrift über das weibliche Fortbildungschulwesen in Deutschland.* Berlin, 1893.

Herodotus, The History of. (Trans. of George Rawlinson.) 2 vols. [Everyman's Library] Dutton: New York, 1910.

Hertwig, John G. *Woman Suffrage.* Washington, 1883.

Hewes, Amy. *Changing Jobs—study of students in Bryn Mawr Summer School.* [Bul. Women's Bur., No. 54, 1926] Government Printing Office: Washington, 1926.

Heydrick, B. A. *Academies in the United States.* [Master's Thesis, Teachers College, Columbia University, 1907]

Heywood, Ezra H. *Uncivil Liberty; an essay to show the injustice and impolicy of ruling woman without her consent.* Princeton, Mass., 1873.

Higginson, Thomas W. *Common Sense About Women.* Boston, 1882.

Higginson, Thomas W. *Margaret Fuller Ossoli.* Boston, 1887.

Higginson, Thomas W. *Woman and Her Wishes.* London, 1854.

Higginson, Thomas W. *Women and Men.* New York, 1888.

Hill, Lucille E. *Athletics and Out Door Sports for Women.* Macmillan: New York, 1903.

Hillsdale College, History of. [*Collections of the Pioneer Society of Michigan,* VI: 137–66]

Hinsdale, B. A. *History of the University of Michigan.* Michigan University: Ann Arbor, 1906.

Hitchcock, Edward. *A Chapter in the Book of Providence.* Anniversary address at Mount Holyoke Female Seminary. South Hadley, 1849.

Hitchcock, Edward. *The Character of Mary Lyon.* [*Old South Leaflets,* Vol. VI, No. 145]

Hitchcock, Edward. *Power of Christian Benevolence Illustrated in the Life and Labors of Mary Lyon.* Northampton, 1852.

Hoar, George F. *Woman Suffrage Essential to the True Republic.* Boston, 1873.

Hobson, Elsie G. *Educational Legislation and Administration in the State of New York, 1777–1850.* University of Chicago: Chicago, 1918.

Hodgman, Edwin R. *History of the Town of Westford* [Mass.], *1659–1883.* Lowell, 1883.

Hollister, Horace A. *The Woman Citizen.* Appleton: New York, 1918.

Holloway, Laura C. *The Ladies of the White House.* New York, 1870.

Home-Work in Bridgeport, Connecticut. [Bul. Women's Bur., No. 9, 1920] Government Printing Office: Washington, 1920.

Hooker, I. Beecher. *The Constitutional Rights of Women in the United States.* Washington, 1888.

Hooker, John. *The Bible and Woman Suffrage.* [*Tracts of Connecticut Woman Suffrage Assoc.,* No. 1] Hartford, 1870.

Hopkins, Alice L. *A Reminiscence of the Rochester Female Seminary.* [Historical Society Library, Municipal Museum]

Horlacher, Vaneta T. *The Academy in Kentucky.* [Master's Thesis, University of Kentucky, 1925]

Houghton, L. S. Women's work in the church. [In *Schaff-Herzog Encyclopedia of Religious Knowledge.* Funk and Wagnalls: New York, 1912]

Howard, George E. *A History of Matrimonial Institutions.* 3 vols. University of Chicago Press: Chicago, 1904.

Howard, John R. Anniversary address on female education, Henry Academy, 1837. [Tennessee State Library]

Howe, Julia W. *Margaret Fuller.* London, 1883.

Howe, Julia W. *Reminiscences, 1819–1899.* Houghton: Boston, 1900.

Howe, Julia W. (Ed.). *Sex and Education; a reply to Dr. E. H. Clarke's "Sex in Education."* Boston, 1874.

Hoyt, John W. *Address of . . . on Woman Suffrage in Wyoming,* April 3, 1882. n.p.

Hubbell, George A. *Horace Mann, Educator, Patriot and Reformer.* Fell: Philadelphia, 1910.

Hubbs, Rebecca, A Memoir of. Philadelphia, n.d.

Hudson, Charles. *History of the Town of Lexington* [Mass.] Vol. I. Houghton: Boston, 1913.

Humphrey, Heman. *The Shining Path; a sermon preached in South Hadley at the funeral of Mary Lyon, March 8, 1849.*

Humphreys, Mary G. *Catherine Schuyler.* New York, 1897.

Hundley, D. R. *Social Relations in Our Southern States.* New York, 1860.

Hunt, Caroline L. *The Life of Ellen H. Richards.* Whitcomb and Barrows: Boston, 1912.

Hurd, H. B. *The Revised Statutes of Illinois.* Springfield, 1874.

Hurlbut, E. P. *Essays on Human Rights and their Political Guaranties.* New York, 1845.

Hurn, Ethel A. *Wisconsin Women in the War Between the States.* State Printer: Wisconsin, 1911.

Hutchins, B. Leigh. *Conflicting Ideals; two sides of the Woman's question.* London, 1913.

Hutchins, B. Leigh. *Women in Modern Industry.* London, 1915.

Hyde, William D. *The College Man and the College Woman.* Houghton: Boston, 1906.

Illinois Conservatory of Music, Jacksonville. *MS.* Historical Sketch. n.d. [College Archives]

Industrial Accidents to Women in New Jersey, Ohio, and Wisconsin. [Bul. Women's Bur., No. 60, 1927] Government Printing Office: Washington, 1927.

Industrial Opportunities and Training for Women and Girls. [Bul. Women's Bur., No. 13, 1921] Government Printing Office: Washington, 1921.

Industry, Health Problems of Women in. [Bul. Women's Bur., No. 18, 1921] Government Printing Office: Washington, 1921.

Industry, Hours and Conditions of Work for Women in, in Virginia. [Bul. Women's Bur., No. 10, 1920] Government Printing Office: Washington, 1920.

Industry, Women in, Standard and Scheduled Hours of Work for. [Bul. Women's Bur., No. 43, 1925] Government Printing Office: Washington, 1925.

Inglis, Alexander J. *The Rise of the High School in Massachusetts.* Teachers College: New York, 1911.

International Council of Women, assembled by the National Woman Suffrage Association, Dec. 1888. *Report.* Washington, 1888.

International Federation of University Women. *Report of the First Conference, 1920.* [Bulletin International Federation of University Women, No. 1]

Invention, Women's Contribution in the Field of. [Bul. Women's Bur., No. 28, 1923] Government Printing Office: Washington, 1923.

Iowa Industries, Women in. [Bul. Women's Bur., No. 10, 1922] Government Printing Office: Washington, 1922.

Irwin, Inez H. *Story of the Woman's Party.* Harcourt: New York, 1921.

Jackson, Francis. *Coeducation in the Department of Arts of the University of Pennsylvania.* An eight-page pamphlet. Nov. 25, 1882.

Jacksonville Female Academy. *MS.* Historical Sketch, by Sue F. Ellis, June 5, 1906. [College Archives]

Jacksonville Female Academy. Semi-centennial and Anniversary Exercises, 1880. [College Archives]

Jacobi, Mary P. Woman in medicine. [In Meyer, A. N. (Ed.): *Woman's Work in America.* New York, 1891]

Jacobi, Mary P. *"Common Sense" Applied to Woman Suffrage.* New York, 1894.

Jacobi, Mary P. *Life and Letters, 1842–1906.* Putnam: New York, 1925.

Jameson, John F. *American Revolution Considered as a Social Movement.* Princeton University Press: Princeton, 1926.

Jameson, Kate, and Lockwood, Frank C. *The Freshman Girl.* Heath: New York, 1925.

Janes, Thomas P. *Handbook of the State of Georgia.* Atlanta, 1876.

Jastrow, Joseph. *Psychology of Conviction.* Houghton: Boston, 1918.

Jocelin, Elizabeth. *The Mother's Legacie to Her Unborn Child.* London, 1624.

Johnson, Amandus. *The Swedish Settlements on the Delaware, 1638–1664.* 2 vols. Appleton: New York, 1911.

Johnson, Georgia B. *Organization of Required Physical Education for Women in State Universities.* Teachers College: New York, 1927.

Johnson, Edith. *To Women of the Business World.* Lippincott: Philadelphia, 1923.

Johnson, F. W. History of Coburn Classical Institute [In Whittemore, E. C.: *Centennial History of Waterville* (Me.), Ch. X. Waterville, 1902]

Jones, Charles C. *The History of Georgia.* 2 vols. Boston, 1883.

Jones, Charles E. *Education in Georgia.* [Circular of Information, Bur. Ed., No. 4, 1888. Washington, 1889.

Jones, Jane L. A Personnel Study of Women Deans in Colleges and Universities. [Teachers College Ph.D. Thesis, 1927. (*MS.*)]

Jordan, David S. *The Care and Culture of Men: a series of addresses on the higher education.* San Francisco, 1896.

Kalm, Peter. *Travels into North America.* 3 vols. London, 1770–71.

Kandel, I. L. (Ed.). *Twenty-five Years of American Education.* Macmillan: New York, 1924.

Keller, G. R., and McCann, J. M. *Sketches of Paris, Kentucky.* Paris, 1876.

Kelly, Amy. *A Curriculum to Build a Mental World: a proposal for a college of liberal arts for women.* Baltimore, 1927.

Kelsey, Rayner W. *Centennial History of Moses Brown School.* Moses Brown School: Providence, 1919.

Kemble, Frances A. *Journal of a Residence on a Georgian Plantation.* New York, 1863.

Kendall, P. M. *Maria Mitchell: Life, Letters and Journals.* Boston, 1896.

Kentucky Industries, Women in. [Bul. Women's Bur., No. 28, 1923] Government Printing Office: Washington, 1923.

Ketling, Elizabeth. *Helpful Talks with Girls.* (Ed. by Theodore Waters) Christian Herald Bible House: New York, 1910.

Key, Ellen. *War, Peace and the Future.* Putnam: New York, 1916.

Kilbourne, Payne K. *Sketches and Chronicles of the Town of Litchfield, Connecticut.* Hartford, 1859.

Kilpatrick, William H. *The Dutch Schools of New Netherlands and Colonial New York.* Government Printing Office: Washington, 1912.

Kilpatrick, William H. *Source Book in the Philosophy of Education.* Macmillan: New York, 1924.

King, Grace. *New Orleans, the Place and the People.* New York, 1896.

Kingsley, Charles. *Women and Politics.* London, 1869.

Kingsley, Florence M. *Life of H. F. Durant.* Century: New York, 1924.

Kirkland, James H. *Higher Education in the United States of America.* [Reprinted from the *Vanderbilt University Quart.*] n.p., 1913.

Kitchiner, William. *The Cook's Oracle (Adapted to the American Public).* New York, 1838.

Kittredge, George L. *The Old Farmer and His Almanack.* Harvard University Press: Cambridge, 1920.

Klain, Zora. *Quaker Contributions to Education in North Carolina.* Westbrook Printing Co.: Philadelphia, 1925.

Klain, Zora. *Educational Activities of New England Quakers.* Westbrook Printing Co.: Philadelphia, 1928.

Knauss, James O. *Social Conditions Among the Pennsylvania Germans.* New Era Printing Company: Lancaster, 1922.

Knight, Edgar W. *The Influence of Reconstruction on Education in the South.* Teachers College: New York, 1913.

Knight, Edgar W. *Public Education in the South.* Ginn: New York, 1922.

Knight, George W., and Commons, John R. *History of Higher Education in Ohio.* [Circular of Information, Bur. Ed., No. 5, 1891] Washington, 1891.

Knight, Kate Brannon. *History of the Work of Connecticut Women.* Hartford, 1898.

Knight, Lucian L. *Georgia's Landmarks, Memorials and Legends.* 2 vols. Byrd: Atlanta, 1914.

Knight, Lucian L. *A Standard History of Georgia and the Georgians.* 6 vols. Lewis Publishing Co.: New York, 1917.

Knox, John. *The First Blast of the Trumpet.* (Ed. by Edward Arber) London, 1878.

Koos, L. V. *The Junior College.* [Research Publications of the University of Minnesota, 1924]

Kuo, P. W. *The Chinese System of Public Education.* Teachers College: New York, 1915.

Labor Laws for Women in Industry in Indiana. [Bul. Dept. Labor, No. 2, 1918] Government Printing Office: Washington, 1919.

Ladies' Society for the Promotion of Education at the West, History of the Foundation of the. Boston, 1846.

Lady of Charleston. *House and Home; or the Carolina Housewife.* Charleston, 1847.

LaFollette, Suzanne. *Concerning Women.* Boni: New York, 1926.

Lange, Helene. *Die Ethische Bedeutung der Frauenbewegung.* Berlin, 1889.

Lange, Helene. *Entwickelung und Stand des höheren Mädchenschulwesens in Deutschland.* Berlin, 1893.

Lange, Helene. *Higher Education of Women in Europe.* (Trans. of R. Klemm) Appleton: New York, 1890.

Larcom, Lucy. *A New England Girlhood.* Houghton: Boston, 1889.

Larcom, Lucy. *Wheaton Seminary: A semi-centennial sketch.* Cambridge, 1885.

Latham, E. B. *Something New: . . . the honorable rights of woman, the reasonable rights of man: the perfect rights of both the supreme will of God.* New York, 1853.

Latimer, Caroline W. *The Girl and the Woman.* Macmillan: New York, 1918.

Lauderbach, Marian, and Thompson, Katharine. Augusta of Long Ago. [Scrap book of newspaper clippings, *The Augusta Chronicle*, 1921, relative to Augusta College, admission of girls, etc.]

Laurie, S. S. *Historical Survey of Pre-Christian Education.* Longmans: New York, 1895.

Leach, Arthur F. *English Schools at the Reformation, 1546–48.* Westminster, 1896.

Leake, Albert H. *Vocational Education of Girls and Women.* Macmillan: New York, 1918.

Legge, James (Translator). *The Sacred Books of China.* [In the *Sacred Books of the East,* ed. by Max Müller, vols. XXVII and XXVIII] Oxford, 1885 and 1886.

Legislation Limiting Hours of Work for Women, Some Effects of. [Bul. Women's Bur., No. 15, 1921] Government Printing Office: Washington, 1921.

Leicester Academy. Centenary, 1884; with an historical address by W. C. Rice. Hamilton: Worcester, 1884.

Leicester Academy. Festival on the Seventy-first Anniversary, 1855; address by Alonzo Hill. Worcester, 1855.

Leonard, F. E. *History of Physical Education.* Lea and Febiger: Philadelphia, 1923.

Levine, Louis. *The Women's Garment Workers.* Huebsch: New York, 1924.

Lewis, Dio. *The New Gymnastics for Men, Women and Children.* Boston, 1862.

Lewis, Dio. *Our Girls.* New York, 1871.

Lewis, Ida B. *Education of Girls in China.* Teachers College: New York, 1919.

Lincoln, William. *History of Worcester* (Massachusetts). Worcester, 1862.

Lindsey, B. B. *The Companionate Marriage.* Boni and Liveright: New York, 1927.

Livermore, D. P. *Woman Suffrage Defended by Irrefutable Arguments.* Boston, 1885.

Livermore, Mary A. *My Story of the War.* Hartford, 1888.

Livermore, Mary A. *What Shall We Do With Our Daughters?* Boston, 1883.

Livingston Park Seminary: the Story of sixty years, 1858–1918. Rochester, N. Y., n.d.

Lockwood, Belva A., *Argument of, Before the Committee of the House of Delegates on Laws and Judiciary . . . in Support of Bills . . . Looking to the Granting of Suffrage to Women and Equal Pay in Office.* Universal Franchise Assoc.: n.p., n.d.

Logan, (Mrs.) John A. *The Part Taken by Women in American History.* Perry-Nalle: Wilmington, Del., 1912.

Lombroso, Gina. *The Soul of Woman.* Dutton: New York, 1923.

Long, D. A. *Legal History of Antioch College.* Dayton, 1890.

Loomis, Silas L. *Record of Holliston Academy, 1836–44.* Washington, 1876.

Lord, John. *The Life of Emma Willard.* New York, 1873.

Lossing, Benson J. *Vassar College and Its Founder.* New York, 1867.

Lozier, Clemence S., *et al. Arguments of the Delegates of the National Woman Suffrage Association before the Committee on Privileges and Elections of the United States Senate, Jan. 11 and 12, 1878.* Washington, 1878.

Lucian. *Philosophies for Sale.* [Vol. II, *Works of Lucian,* translated by A. M. Harmon. Macmillan: New York, 1915]

Ludlow, J. M. *Woman's Work in the Church.* London, 1885.

Ludovici, Anthony M. *Lysistrata, or Woman's Future and Future Woman.* Dutton: New York, 1925.

Lutz, Alma. *Emma Willard: Daughter of Democracy.* Houghton: Boston, 1929.

Lyon, Mary. *A Missionary Offering.* Boston, 1843.

MacLean, Annie M. *Our Neighbors.* Macmillan: New York, 1922.

MacLean, Annie M. *Wage Earning Women.* Macmillan: New York, 1910.

Maddison, Isabel. *Handbook of British Continental and Canadian Universities, with special mention of the courses open to women. . . .* New York, 1899.

Maddox, William A. *The Free School Idea in Virginia before the Civil War.* Teachers College: New York, 1918.

Magaw, Samuel. An address at the Young Ladies Academy, Philadelphia, February 8, 1787. Philadelphia, 1787.

Magill, Edward H. *An Address Upon the Coeducation of the Sexes.* Philadelphia, 1873.

Maine, State Superintendent of Public Schools. *A Study of the History of Education in Maine and the Evolution of the Present School System.* Published by the State: n.d.

Malcolm, James P. *Anecdotes of the Manners and Customs of London from the Roman Invasion to the Year 1700.* London, 1811.

Manly, Louise. *History of Judson College.* Foote and Davies: Atlanta, Ga., n.d.

Mann, Herman. *The Female Review; or memoirs of an American young lady.* Dedham, Mass., 1797.

Mann, Kristine. The hygiene of women's colleges. [Rapeer, L. W.: *Educational Hygiene,* Ch. XXXII. Scribner's: New York, 1915]

Mansfield, Edward D.   *Legal Rights, Liabilities, and Duties of Women.* . . . Salem, 1845.

Manson, George J.   *Work of Women.*   New York, 1883.

Marks, Jeannette.   *Girl's Student Days and After.*   Revell: New York, 1911.

Marryat, C. B.   *A Diary in America, with Remarks on Its Institutions.*   New York, 1839.

Marshall, Clara.   *The Woman's Medical College of Pennsylvania.*   Philadelphia, 1897.

Martin, Edward S.   *The Unrest of Women.*   Appleton: New York, 1913.

Martin, Eleanor, and Post, M. A.   *Vocations for the Trained Woman.*   Longmans: New York, 1914.

Martineau, Harriett.   *Household Education.*   Boston, n.d.

Martineau, Harriett.   *Retrospect of Western Travel.*   3 vols.   London, 1838.

Martineau, Harriett.   *Society in America.*   2 vols.   New York, 1837.

Mary Sharp College, Z. C. Graves and the, 1850–1896.   Mary Sharp College Club: Nashville, Tenn., 1925.

Maryland Industries, Women in.   [Bul. Women's Bur., No. 24, 1922] Government Printing Office: Washington, 1922.

Mason, Amelia G.   *Woman in the Golden Ages.*   Century: New York, 1901.

Mason, E. V. (Ed.).   *Journal of a Young Lady of Virginia, 1782.*

Maspero, G. C.   *Dawn of Civilization in Egypt and Chaldea.*   (Trans. of M. L. McClure)   New York, 1894.

Mather, Cotton.   *Diary, 1681–1708.*   [Collections, Massachusetts Hist. Soc., Seventh Series, Vols. VII and VIII]

Mathews, Lois K.   *The Dean of Women.*   Houghton: Boston, 1915.

Maudsley, Henry.   *Sex in Mind and in Education.*   Syracuse, N. Y., 1884.

Maulde la Clavière, Marie Alphonse Renè de.   *The Women of the Renaissance.*   (Trans. of George H. Ely.)   Putnam: New York, 1900.

Maury County [Tennessee], A Historical Sketch of, read at the Centennial Celebration in Columbia, Tennessee, July 4, 1876.   Columbia, 1876.

Maury County, Tennessee, History and Directory of; a century review, 1805–1905.   n.p., n.d.

May, Caroline (Ed.).   *The American Female Poets.* . . . Philadelphia, 1848.

May, Samuel J.   *The Rights and Condition of Married Women.*   Syracuse, N. Y., 1846.

Mayes, Edward.   *History of Education in Mississippi.*   [Circular of Information, Bur. Ed., No. 2, 1899.]   Washington, 1899.

Mayo, A. D.   The American common school system in the Southern states during the first half century of the Republic, 1790–1840.   [*R. C. E.* (1895–6) I: 267–388]

Mayo, A. D.   Common schools of New York, New Jersey and Pennsylvania.   [*R. C. E.* (1895–6) I: 219–66]

Mayo, A. D.   *The New Education in the New South.*   Sixteen pages.   n.p., n.d.

Mayo, A. D.   The organization and development of the American common schools in the Atlantic and central states of the South, 1830–1860.   [*R. C. E.* (1899–1900) I: 427–561]

Mayo, A. D.   Public schools during the Colonial and Revolutionary periods in the United States.   [*R. C. E.* (1893–4) I: 639–738]

Mayo, A. D. *Southern Women in the Recent Educational Movement in the South.* [Circular of Information, Bur. Ed., No. 1, 1892] Washington, 1892.

McCabe, Lida R. *The American Girl at College.* New York, 1893.

McConn, Max. *College or Kindergarten?* New Republic: New York, 1928.

McCormac, E. I. *White Servitude in Maryland,* 1634–1820. [Johns Hopkins University Studies, Series XXII, Nos. 3–4] Baltimore, 1904.

McCracken, Elizabeth. *The Women of America.* Macmillan: New York, 1904.

McCrady, Edward. Colonial education in South Carolina. [Meriwether, Colyer: *History of Higher Education in South Carolina,* Appendix II—Circular of Information, Bur. Ed., No. 3, 1888. Washington, 1889]

McCrady, Edward. *The History of South Carolina, 1670–1783.* 4 vols. Macmillan: New York. 1897–1902.

McIntosh, Maria J. *Woman in America: her work and her reward.* New York, 1850.

McIntosh, W. H. *History of Ontario County, New York.* Philadelphia, 1876.

McKeen, Philena. *Sequel to the Annals of Fifty Years; a history of Abbot Academy, 1879–1892.* Andover, 1897.

McKeen, Philena and Phebe F. *A History of Abbot Academy, 1829–1879.* Andover, 1880.

McKeever, William A. *The Industrial Training of the Girl.* Macmillan: New York, 1914.

McKenna, Ethel M. (Ed.). *Education and the Professions.* [*The Woman's Library,* I. London, 1903]

McLaughlin, Andrew C. *History of Higher Education in Michigan.* [Circular of Information, Bur. Ed., No. 4, 1891] Washington, 1891.

McMaster, J. Bach. *History of the People of the United States.* 8 vols. Appleton: New York, 1883–1913.

McMillan, Genevieve. *History of Higher Education of Women in the South.* [Master's Thesis, University of North Carolina, 1923]

Medical Students, Men and Women: the hospital clinics and the woman movement. [Pamphlet No. 2, April, 1870] Philadelphia, 1870.

Melish, John. *Travels in the United States of America.* 2 vols. Philadelphia, 1812.

Meriwether, Colyer. *History of Higher Education in South Carolina.* [Circular of Information, Bur. Ed., No. 3, 1888] Washington, 1889.

Meriwether, Colyer. *Our Colonial Curriculum, 1607–1776.* Capitol Publishing Co.: Washington, 1907.

Merriam, Lucius S. *Higher Education in Tennessee.* [Circular of Information, Bur. Ed., No. 5, 1893] Washington, 1893.

Meyer, Annie Nathan (Ed.). *Woman's Work in America.* New York, 1891.

Michael, Helen A. *Woman and Freedom in Whitman.* Boston, 1897.

Mill, John Stuart. *The Subjection of Women.* New York, 1898.

Mill, (Mrs.) John Stuart. *Enfranchisement of Women.* London, 1868.

Miller, Alice D. *Are Women People? Or a book of rhymes for suffrage times.* Doran: New York, 1915.

Miller, Edward A. *The History of Educational Legislation in Ohio, 1803–1850.* Heer: Columbus, 1918.

Mills, Robert. *Statistics of South Carolina.* Charleston, 1826.

Mind Among the Spindles: a miscellany . . . selected from the Lowell Offering, with an introduction by the English editor and a letter from Hariett Martineau. Boston, 1845.

Minnigerode, Meade. *The Fabulous Forties.* Putnam: New York, 1924.

Miremont, Anne. *Traité De L'Éducation Des Femmes.* Paris, 1779.

Mississippi Industries, Women in. [Bul. Women's Bur., No. 55, 1926] Government Printing Office: Washington, 1926.

Missouri Industries, Women in. [Bul. Women's Bur., No. 35, 1924] Government Printing Office: Washington, 1924.

Mommsen, Theodor. *The History of Rome.* 5 vols. Scribner's: New York, 1923.

Monroe, Paul (Ed.). *Cyclopedia of Education.* 5 vols. Macmillan: New York, 1915.

Monroe, Paul. *Sourcebook in the History of Education.* Macmillan: New York, 1919.

Moore, Frank. *Women of the War.* . . Hartford, 1867.

Moore, John T., and Foster, A. P. *Tennessee, the Volunteer State, 1769–1923.* S. J. Clarke: Chicago, 1923.

Moore, Mary N. *History of Athens College.* Athens College: Athens, Ala., 1916.

More, Hannah. *Coelebs in Search of a Wife.* 2 vols. London, 1809.

More, Hannah. *Strictures on the Modern System of Female Education.* 2 vols. Philadelphia, 1800.

Morgan, Anne. *American Girl; her education, her responsibility, her recreation, her future.* Harper: New York, 1915.

Morgan, Lewis H. *Ancient Society.* New York, 1877.

Mosher, Clelia D. *Woman's Physical Freedom.* Woman's Press: New York, 1923.

Mother, A. *Thoughts on Domestic Education.* Boston, 1829.

Mott, Abigail. *Observations on the Importance of Female Education.* New York, 1825.

Mount Holyoke College. Semi-centennial Celebration, 1837–87.

Mount Holyoke Female Seminary. Memorial Twenty-fifth Anniversary, 1862, with an address by E. N. Kirk, and reminiscences by Rufus Anderson, *et al.*

Mozans, H. J. *Woman in Science.* Appleton: New York, 1913.

Muirhead, James F. *Land of Contrasts.* Leipzig, 1900.

Mulcaster, Richard. *Positions.* London, 1888.

Müller, Max (Ed.). *Sacred Books of the East.* Vols. XXV, XXVII, and XXVIII. Oxford, 1885 and 1886.

Münsterberg, Hugo. *The Americans.* 2 vols. Berlin, 1904.

Münsterberg, Hugo. *Psychology and Industrial Efficiency.* Houghton: Boston, 1913.

Murray, Charles A. *Travels in North America (1834–1836)*. 2 vols. London, 1839.

Musonius on the education of women. [Monroe, P.: *Sourcebook, History of Education*, 401–6. Macmillan: New York, 1914]

Myers, Albert Cook. *Hannah Logan's Courtship*. Ferris and Leach: Philadelphia, 1904.

Myers, Albert Cook. *Sally Wister's Journal*. Philadelphia, 1902.

Nason, Emma H. *Old Hallowell on the Kennebec*. Burleigh and Flint: Augusta, 1909.

National Woman Suffrage Association, An Address of the, to the Friends of Equal Suffrage for Woman, 1878.

National Woman Suffrage Association, Arguments of the Delegates of the, before the Committee on Privileges and Elections of the United States Senate, Jan. 11 and 12, 1878.

National Woman's Rights Convention, Ninth, Proceedings of the (including address of Wendell Phillips). Rochester, 1859.

Nazareth: A Famous Convent School of the Southwest. (Nazareth, Ky.) n.d.

Neal, J. Armstrong. *An Essay on the Education and Genius of the Female Sex* [with account of the Young Ladies' Academy of Philadelphia]. Philadelphia, 1795.

Necker, Madame de Saussure. *Progressive Education Commencing with the Infant*. (Trans. of Mrs. Willard and Mrs. Phelps) Boston, 1835.

Necker, Madame de Saussure. *Study of the Life of Woman*. Philadelphia, 1844.

Negro Women in Industry. [Bul. Women's Bur., No. 20, 1922] Government Printing Office: Washington, 1922.

Neill, Edward D. *History of the Virginia Company of London*. Albany, 1869.

Neill, Edward D. *Virginia Carolorum*. Albany, 1886.

Nettement, M. Alfred. *De la Seconde Éducation des Filles*. Paris, 1867.

Nevins, Allan. *American Social History as Recorded by British Travellers*. Holt: New York, 1923.

Nevins, Allan. *The Emergence of Modern America*. Macmillan: New York, 1927.

New Jersey Industries, Women in. [Bul. Women's Bur., No. 37, 1924] Government Printing Office: Washington, 1924.

Newton, R. H. *Womanhood: lectures on woman's work in the world*. New York, 1881.

Nichols, (Mrs.) C. I. H. *The Responsibilities of Woman; address to Woman's Rights Convention, Worcester, Oct. 15, 1851*. [*Woman's Rights Tracts*, No. 5]

Nichols, Jane H. *A Historical Sketch: Rochester Female Academy, 1837–1912*. n.p., n.d.

Night Work of Women, Laws in the United States Regulating the. [Bul. Women's Bur., No. 7, 1920] Government Printing Office: Washington, 1920.

Nitzsche, George. History of the Department of Law. [*Proceedings at the dedication of the new building of the Law Department* (1901), University of Pennsylvania]

Noble, Stuart G., and Roy, V. L. *Personnel and Progress of High School Teaching Staff of Louisiana* [Educational pamphlets, State Department, Vol. II, No. 2] Baton Rouge, 1926.

Noell, Thomas E. *Woman Suffrage* and *Reconstruction in Massachusetts.* Addresses Feb. 11 and 18, 1867. Washington, 1867.

Nohle, Carl. *A History of the German School System.* Washington, 1899.

North Carolina, University of. *Extension Leaflets,* division for women series. June and April, 1918. Vols. I and II. Chapel Hill.

Norton, A. O. *The First State Normal School in America: Journals of Cyrus Peirce and Mary Swift.* Harvard Press: Cambridge, 1926.

Nursing Education, Twenty Five Years of, . . . in Teachers College, 1899–1925. Teachers College: New York, 1926.

Nutt, J. J. *Newburgh; her institutions, industries, and leading citizens, historical, descriptive and biographical.* Newburgh, 1891.

Nutting, Mary O. *Historical Sketch of Mount Holyoke Seminary.* Springfield, 1878.

Occupational Progress of Women. [Bul. Women's Bur., No. 27, 1922] Government Printing Office: Washington, 1922.

Ohio Industries, Women in. [Bul. Women's Bur., No. 44, 1925] Government Printing Office: Washington, 1925.

Oldmixon, Captain. *Transatlantic Wanderings, or a last look at the United States.* London, 1855.

O'Leary, Iris P. *Cooking in the Vocational School.* [Bul. Bur. Ed., No. 1, 1915] Government Printing Office: Washington, 1915.

Olin, Helen M. *Women of a State University.* Putnam: New York, 1909.

O'Reilly, Bernard. *The Mirror of True Womanhood.* New York, 1878.

O'Reilly, Henry. *Sketches of Rochester* (New York). Rochester, 1838.

Orton, James. *The Liberal Education of Women.* New York, 1873.

Owen, Thomas. *History of Alabama and Dictionary of Alabama Biography.* 4 vols. Clarke: Chicago, 1921.

Owings, Chloe. *Women Police.* Hitchcock: New York, 1925.

Page, Curtis H. *The Chief American Poets.* Houghton: Boston, 1905.

Page, Thomas N. *Social Life in Old Virginia Before the War.* New York, 1898.

Paine, Harriet E. *The Life of Eliza Baylies Wheaton.* Riverside Press: Cambridge, 1907.

Painter, F. N. *Luther on Education.* Philadelphia, 1889.

Palfrey, John G. *A History of New England.* 2 vols. New York, 1866.

Palmer, Alice F. *In Memoriam.* Association of Collegiate Alumnae: Boston, 1903.

Palmer, Alice F. *Why Go to College?* New York, 1897.

Palmer, B. [Address on] *Education of Women.* Albany, 1852.

Palmer, George H. *The Life of Alice Freeman Palmer.* Houghton: Boston, 1910.

Palmer, Thomas W., Speech of, . . . *on Universal Suffrage, in the Senate of the United States.* Washington, 1885.

Pankhurst, E. Sylvia. *The Suffragette; the history of the women's militant suffrage movement, 1905–1910.* Sturgis and Walton: New York, 1911.

Parker, Jenny M. *Rochester* [N. Y.]: *A Story Historical.* Rochester, 1884.

Parker, Leonard F. *Higher Education in Iowa.* [Circular of Information, Bur. Ed., No. 6, 1893] Washington, 1893.

Parker, Theodore. *A Sermon on the Public Function of Woman,* Boston, March 27, 1853. [*Woman's Rights Tracts* No. 2]

Parkman, Francis. *Some of the Reasons Against Woman Suffrage.* Massachusetts Man Suffrage Assoc: Boston, n.d.

Parrish, Edward. *An Essay on Education in the Society of Friends.* Philadelphia, 1866.

Pascoe, C. E. *Schools for Girls and Colleges for Women.* London, 1879.

Paul, Alice. *Abstract of Thesis on the Legal Position of Women in Pennsylvania.* n.p., 1912.

Paulsen, Frederick. *German Education, Past and Present.* Scribner's: New York, 1908.

Peaslee, E. R. *et al. Reply to Dr. J. Marion Sims' Pamphlet Entitled the "Woman's Hospital in 1874."* New York, 1877.

Peck, William F. *History of Rochester and Monroe County, New York.* Vol. I. Pioneer Publishing Co.: New York, 1908.

Peck, William F. *Landmarks of Monroe County, New York.* Boston, 1895.

Peck, William F. *Semicentennial History of the City of Rochester.* Syracuse, 1884.

Pedder, Henry C. *Man and Woman Considered in their Relations to Each Other and to the World.* New York, 1871.

Pellew, W. George. *Woman and the Commonwealth.* Boston, 1888.

Pendered, Anne E. *Remarks on Female Education.* London, 1827.

Pendleton, J. M. *Address on Female Education,* at Mary Sharp College, Winchester, Tenn., June 22, 1856.

Penny, Virginia. *Think and Act: Men and Women, Work and Wages.* Philadelphia, 1869.

Perkins, Agnes F. *Vocations for the Trained Woman.* Women's Educational and Industrial Union: Boston, 1910.

Perrin, William H. *History of Bourbon, Scott, Harrison, and Nicholas Counties, Ky.* Chicago, 1882.

Perry, Belle M. *Lucinda Stone.* Blinn Publishing Co.: Detroit, 1902.

Phelan, James. *History of Tennessee.* Boston, 1889.

Phelps, A. *Louisiana, A Record of Expansion.* Boston, 1905.

Phelps, Almira L. *Caroline Westerly or the Young Traveller from Ohio.* New York, 1833.

Phelps, Almira L. *Female Student; or lectures to young ladies . . . on female education.* Boston, 1833.

Phelps, Almira L. *Hours with My Pupils.* New York, 1859.

Phelps, Edith M. (Compiler). *Selected Articles on Woman Suffrage.* Wilson: New York, 1916.

Philadelphia Normal School for Girls. A Sketch. Government Printing Office: Washington, 1882.

Phillips, Ulrich B., and others. *Plantation and Frontier Documents, 1649–1863.* 2 vols. Clark: Cleveland, Ohio, 1910.

Phillips, Wendell, Address of, on Freedom for Women—Convention at Worcester, Oct. 15–16, 1851. [*Woman's Rights Tracts* No. 1] n.p., n.d.

Physical Education in American Colleges and Universities. [Bul. Bur. Ed., No. 14, 1927] Government Printing Office: Washington, 1927.

Physical Education, Recent State Legislation for. [Bul. Bur. Ed., No. 1, 1922] Government Printing Office: Washington, 1922.

Physician, A. [John Ware]. *Remarks on the Employment of Females as Practitioners in Midwifery.* Boston, 1820.

Pierson, Ward W. Property rights of married women in Pennsylvania. [*University of Pennsylvania Lectures, 1915–16*] Philadelphia.

Plato. *Dialogues.* (Benjamin Jowett, Translator and Editor) 5 vols. New York, 1892.

Plato. *Republic.* (Trans. of J. L. Davies and D. J. Vaughn) London, 1874.

Pope, E. F. *The Practice of Medicine by Women in the United States.* [Read before the American Social Science Assoc., Sept. 7, 1881] Boston, 1881.

Porter, K. H. *History of Suffrage in the United States.* University of Chicago Press: Chicago, 1918.

Porter, Noah. *The Christian College.* Boston, 1880.

Porter, Sarah H. *The Life and Times of Anne Royall.* Torch Press Bookshop: Cedar Rapids, Iowa, 1909.

Potter, Alonzo, and Emerson, George B. *The School and the Schoolmaster.* New York, 1842.

Poughkeepsie [N. Y.] Female Collegiate Institute. Historical Sketch. Lyndon Hall Alumnae: Poughkeepsie, 1848.

Powell, Lyman P. *History of Education in Delaware.* Washington, 1893.

Power, Tyrone. *Impressions of America (1833–35).* 2 vols. Philadelphia, 1836.

Pringle, Ralph W. *Adolescence and High School Problems.* Heath: New York, 1922.

Proctor, W. M. *Psychological Tests and Guidance of High School Pupils.* [Jour. Ed. Research Monographs No. 1. Public School Publishing Co.: Bloomington, 1921]

Professions, Education and. A symposium. [*Woman's Library*, Vol. I] London, 1903.

Professions, Women in. 2 vols. [International Congress of Women, London, 1899] London, 1900.

Proffatt, John. *Woman Before the Law.* New York, 1874.

Pruette, Lorine. *Women and Leisure.* Dutton: New York, 1924.

Public life, Women in. [*Annals Am. Acad. Political and Social Science* (Nov., 1914) LVI]

Public Schools and Women in Office Service. [*Studies in Economic Relations of Women,* VIII] Women's Educational and Industrial Union: Boston, 1914.

Pusey, Pennock. *History of Lewes, Delaware.* [Papers of the Historical Society of Delaware, XXXVIII] Delaware Historical Soc.: Wilmington, 1903.

Quincy, Josiah. *Municipal History of the Town and City of Boston, 1630–1830.* Boston, 1852.

Ramage, B. J. *Local Government and Free Schools in South Carolina.* [Johns Hopkins Studies in Historical and Political Science, I, No. 12] Baltimore, 1883.

Ramsay, David. *History of South Carolina.* 2 vols. Charleston, 1809.

Rammelkamp, C. H. *Illinois College: A Centennial History.* Yale Press: New Haven, 1928.

Randall, Samuel S. *History of the Common School System of the State of New York.* New York, 1871.

Raper, Charles L. *The Church and Private Schools in North Carolina.* Greensboro, 1898.

Rauschenbusch-Clough, Emma. *Study of Mary Wollstonecraft and the Rights of Woman.* New York, 1898.

Ravenel, Harriott H. *Eliza Pinckney.* New York, 1896.

Raymond, John H. Biographical sketch of Matthew Vassar. [Addresses at the celebration of the completion of the twenty-fifth academic year of Vassar College, June 1890]

Raymond, John H. *Life and Letters.* (Edited by his daughter) New York, 1881.

Raymond, John H. *Vassar College: A College for Women; a sketch of its foundation, aims, and resources. . . .* New York, 1873.

Rayne, (Mrs.) M. L. *What Can a Woman Do?* Chicago, 1884.

Roody, Marie M. *Physical Education in American Universities.* [Bul. Bur. Ed., No. 14, 1927] Government Printing Office: Washington, 1927.

Re-Bartlett, Lucy. *The Coming Order.* Longmans: New York, 1911.

Reed, Myrtle. *A Woman's Career.* Putnam: New York, 1914.

Reich, Emil. *Woman through the Ages.* 2 vols. London, 1908.

Reichel, Levin T. *The Moravians in North Carolina.* Salem, N. C., 1857.

Reichel, W. C. *History of Bethlehem Female Seminary.* Philadelphia, 1858.

Reid, (Mrs.) Hugo. *Woman, her Education and Influence.* New York, 1847.

Reigart, John F. *The Lancasterian System of Instruction in the Schools of New York City.* Teachers College: New York, 1916.

Rembaugh, Bertha. *Political Status of Women in the United States; a digest of the laws concerning women in the various states and territories. . . .* Putnam: New York, 1911.

Remo, Felix. *L'Égalité des Sexes en Angleterre.* Paris, 1886.

Remusat, C. E. J. de. *Essai Sur l'Éducation des Femmes.* Paris, 1842.

Reynolds, Myra. *The Learned Lady in England, 1650-1760.* Houghton: Boston, 1920.

Rhees, H. S. *Laurenus Clark Seelye.* Houghton: Boston, 1929.

Rhode Island Industries, Women in. [Bul. Women's Bur., No. 21, 1922] Government Printing Office: Washington, 1922.

Richards, Caroline C., Diary of, 1852-1872. Canandaigua, N. Y., 1908.

Richards, Lysander S. *Vocophy. . . . The New Profession.* Marlboro, Mass., 1881.

Richardson, Hester D. *Sidelights on Maryland History.* 2 vols. Williams and Wilkins: Baltimore, 1913.

Richter, Jean P. *Levana; or the doctrine of education.* London, 1897.

Rightor, Henry. *Standard History of New Orleans, Louisiana.* Lewis Publishing Co.: Chicago, 1900.

Roberts, Robert D. (Ed.). *Education in the Nineteenth Century.* Cambridge, 1901.

Robins, (Mrs.) Raymond. Industrial education for women. [*Bul. Nat. Soc. for the Promotion of Industrial Ed.*, No. 9, 1910: 77-81]

Robinson, Harriet H. *Loom and Spindle; or life among the early mill girls.* New York, 1898.

Robinson, Harriet H. *Massachusetts in the Woman Suffrage Movement.* Boston, 1881.

Robinson, Mabel L. *The Curriculum of the Woman's College.* [Bul. Bur. Ed., No. 6, 1918] Government Printing Office: Washington, 1918.

Rochefoucault-Liancourt, Francois. *Travels through the United States of North America.* 2 vols. London, 1799.

Rockford [Ill.] College. Jubilee Book, the Alumnae Association, 1854-1904. [College Library]

Rogers, Anna. *Why American Marriages Fail.* Houghton: Boston, 1909.

Rohrbach, Q. A. W. *Lutheran Education in the Ministerium of Pennsylvania (MS.).*

Roosevelt, Theodore. *Conservation of Womanhood and Childhood.* Funk and Wagnalls: New York, 1912.

Rose, Ernestine L. Address at the Ninth National Woman's Rights Convention. [*Woman's Rights Tracts* No. 1]

Rousseau, Jean Jacques. *Émile.* (Trans. of W. H. Payne) Appleton: New York, 1914.

Rousseau, Jean Jacques. *Eloisa: or, a series of original letters collected and published by J. J. Rousseau.* 4 vols. London, 1769.

Rousselot, Paul. *Histoire de l'Éducation des Femmes en France.* 2 vols. Paris, 1883.

Royall, Anne. *Black Book; or a continuation of travels in the United States.* 3 vols. Washington, 1828-29.

Rule, William (Ed.). *Standard History of Knoxville, Tennessee.* Lewis Publishing Co.: Chicago, 1900.

Rush, Benjamin. *An Account of the German Inhabitants of Pennsylvania . . . with the notes* of I. D. Rupp revised. (Ed. by Theodore E. Schmauk) Pennsylvania German Soc.: Lancaster, Pa., 1910.

Rush, Benjamin. Thoughts upon female education, 1787. [*Essays, Moral, Literary and Philosophical*] Philadelphia, 1798.

Rusk, Ralph L. *The Literature of the Middle Western Frontier.* 2 vols. Columbia University Press: New York, 1925.

Ruskin, John. *Letters and Advice to Young Girls and Young Ladies.* . . . New York, 1879.

Russell, Bertrand. *Why Men Fight.* Century: New York, 1917.

Russell, Dora. *Hypatia; or woman and knowledge.* Dutton: New York, 1925.

Russell, James E. *Trend in American Education.* American Book Co.: New York, 1922.

Russell, James E. *German Higher Schools.* Longmans: New York, 1907.

Ruttenber, E. M. *History of the County of Orange* (New York). Newburgh, 1875.

Sachse, Julius F. *German Pietists of Provincial Pennsylvania.* 3 vols. Philadelphia, 1895–1900.

Safford, A. E. *A Memoir of Daniel Safford.* Boston, 1861.

Saleeby, C. W. *Woman and Womanhood.* Mitchell Kennerley: New York, 1911.

Salley, A. S. A century of the *Courier.* [*News and Courier* (Charleston, S. C.) Centennial Edition, 1803–1903]

Salley, A. S. *The First Presses of South Carolina.* [*Proceedings and Papers, Bibliographical Soc. of America,* Vol. II] New York, 1908.

Salley, A. S. *Narratives of Early Carolina, 1650–1708.* Scribner's: New York, 1911.

Salmon, Lucy M. *Domestic Service.* New York, 1897.

Salmon, Lucy M. *Progress in the Household.* Houghton: Boston, 1906.

Sams, Conway W. *Shall Women Vote?* Neale: New York, 1913.

Sanderson Academy, Mass. An Historical Address, 1889.

Sanford, Edward T. *Blount College and the University of Tennessee.* Knoxville, 1894.

Sangster, Margaret E. *Winsome Womanhood.* . . . Revell: New York, 1900.

Scharf, J. Thomas. *History of Delaware, 1609–1888.* 2 vols. Philadelphia, 1888.

Schirmacher, Käthe. *The Modern Woman's Rights Movement.* (Trans. of Carl C. Eckhardt) Macmillan: New York, 1912.

Schlesinger, Arthur M. *Political and Social History of the United States, 1829–1925.* Macmillan: New York, 1925.

Schlesinger, Arthur M., and Fox, D. R. (Editors). *A History of American Life.* 8 vols. Macmillan: New York, 1927.

Schreiner, Olive. *Woman and Labor.* Stokes: New York, 1911.

Schuyten, M. C. *L'Éducation de la Femme.* Paris, 1908.

Scoresby, William. *American Factories and Their Female Operatives.* Boston, 1845.

Scott, (Mrs.) C. P. *Women's Suffrage from a Liberal Point of View.* Westminster, 1902.

Scudder, Horace E. (Ed.). *Men and Manners in America One Hundred Years Ago.* New York, 1876.

Secondary Education in California, Report on, 1923. California High School Teachers Assoc.: San Francisco, 1924.

Seelye, L. Clark. *The Early History of Smith College.* Houghton: Boston, 1923.

Seguin, E. *Report on Education.* Milwaukee, 1880.

Severence, C. M., and Dall, C. H. *Report of the Woman's Rights Meeting at Mercantile Hall.* Boston, 1859.

Sewall, May W. *The Domestic and Social Effects of the Higher Education of Women.* [Read before the Western Assoc. of Collegiate Alumnae, Ann Arbor, Dec. 10, 1887]

Sewall, May W. *The World's Congress of Representative Women.* 2 vols. Chicago, 1894.

Sewall Papers, 1673–1729. [*Massachusetts Historical Soc. Collections,* Fifth Series, Vols. V–VII] Boston, 1878.

Sewall, Samuel E. *The History of Woburn, Massachusetts.* Boston, 1868.

Sewall, Samuel E. *The Legal Condition of Woman in Massachusetts.* [*Woman's Suffrage Tracts,* No. 5] Boston, 1869.

Sewell, E. M. *Principles of Education Drawn from Nature and Revelation and Applied to Female Education in the Upper Classes.* New York, 1871.

Seybolt, Robert F. *Apprenticeship and Apprenticeship Education in Colonial New York and New England.* Teachers College: New York, 1917.

Seybolt, Robert F. *The Private School.* Bul. 28, Vol. XXIII, No. 4 (1925) University of Illinois.

Shaw, Anna H., and Jordan, Elizabeth. *The Story of a Pioneer.* Harper: New York, 1915.

Sherwood, Adiel. *A Gazetteer of Georgia.* . . . Phila., 1829; and Macon, 1860.

Sherwood, (Mrs.) John. *Manners and Social Usages.* Harper: New York, 1903.

Sherwood, Sidney. *The University of the State of New York.* [*Circular of Information,* Bur. Ed., No. 3, 1900] Government Printing Office: Washington, 1900.

Shields, Thomas E. *The Education of Our Girls.* Benziger Brothers: New York, 1907.

Shillito, Elizabeth H. *Dorothea Beale.* Macmillan: New York, 1920.

Shirreff, Emily. *Intellectual Education and Its Influence on the Character and Happiness of Women.* London, 1862.

Sibleys, The. Lindenwood College: St. Charles, Mo., n.d.

Sidgwick, (Mrs.) Henry. Higher education of women. [In Roberts, R. D. (Ed.): *Education in the Nineteenth Century.* Cambridge, 1901]

Sigourney, (Mrs.) L. H. *Letters to My Pupils, with narrative and bibliographical sketches.* New York, 1860.

Siljeström, Pehr A. *Educational Institutions of the United States: their character and organization.* (Trans. of Frederica Rowan) London, 1853.

Simon, Joseph. *L'Éducation et l'Instruction des Enfants chez les anciens Juifs d'apres la Bible et le Talmud.* Leipsic, 1879.

Sims, J. Marion. *Story of My Life.* New York, 1885.

Sisters of the I. H. M. By a member of the Scranton community. Kennedy: New York, 1921.

Sketches of the History, Genius, Disposition . . . of the Fair Sex. By "A Friend of the Sex." Gettysburg, 1812.

Slafter, Carlos. Schools and teachers of Dedham (Mass.) 1644–1904. [In *Dedham Historical Register,* Vol. I. Dedham, 1905]

Slosson, Edwin E. *American Spirit in Education.* Yale University Press: New Haven, 1921.

Slosson, Edwin E. *Great American Universities.* Macmillan: New York, 1910.

Small, Walter H. *Early New England Schools.* Ginn: Boston, 1914.

Smith, Charles L. *History of Education in North Carolina.* [Circular of Information, Bur. Ed., No. 2, 1888] Washington, 1888.

Smith College: *Celebration of the Quarter-Centenary.* Riverside Press: Cambridge, 1900.

Smith, Edgar F. *Chemistry in America.* Appleton: New York, 1914.

Smith, Fanny R. (Compiler). *Manners and Conduct in School and Out.* By the deans of girls in Chicago high schools. Allyn and Bacon: Boston, 1921.

Smith, Florence M. *Mary Astell.* Columbia University Press: New York, 1916.

Smith, George G. *Life and Times of George Foster Pierce.* Sparta, Ga., 1888.

Smith, George G. *The History of Georgia Methodism from 1786–1866.* Caldwell: Atlanta, 1913.

Smith, George G. *The Story of Georgia and the Georgia People, 1732–1860.* Macon, 1900.

Smith, Golwin. *Woman Suffrage.* New York, 1894.

Smith, Mary R. *College Women and Marriage.* [Publications, American Statistical Assoc. (1900–01) VII]

Smith, Sydney. Female education. [*Selections from the Writings of . . . ,* I: 45–73. London, 1854]

Smith, T. R. (Ed.). *The Woman Question.* A symposium by Ellen Key, G. Lowes Dickinson and others. Boni and Liveright: New York, 1918.

Smith, W. L. *Historical Sketches of Education in Michigan.* Lansing, 1881.

Smith, William. *A Brief Statement of the Province of Pennsylvania.* London, 1755.

Snedden, David. *Vocational Education.* Macmillan: New York, 1920.

Snow, Louis F. *The College Curriculum in the United States.* Teachers College: New York, 1907.

Snow, Marshall S. *Higher Education in Missouri.* [Circular of Information, Bur. Ed., No. 2, 1898] Washington, 1898.

Somerville, Martha. *Personal Recollections of Mary Somerville.* London, 1873.

South Carolina Industries, Women in. [Bul. Women's Bur., No. 32, 1923] Government Printing Office: Washington, 1923.

South, The educational movement in the. [*R. C. E.* (1903) I: 359–90]

Spalding, Helen F. *Higher Education of Women.* Portland, Ore., 1883.

Sparks, Jared. *Works of Benjamin Franklin.* 10 vols. Boston, 1836–1856.

Sparks, W. H. *The Memories of Fifty Years.* Philadelphia, 1882.

Spencer, Anna G. *History of Rhode Island Public Schools*—an address dealing with women in our public schools.

Spencer, Anna G. *Woman's Share in Social Culture.* Lippincott: Philadelphia, 1913.

Spencer, W. B., and Gillen, F. J. *The Native Tribes of Central Australia.* London, 1899.

Spiers, B. *School System of the Talmud.* London, 1898.

Sprague, William B. *The Excellent Woman as Described in the Book of Proverbs.* Boston, 1851.

Squire, V. Belle. *The Woman Movement in America.* . . McClurg: Chicago, 1911.

Stanard, Mary N. *Colonial Virginia; its people and customs.* Lippincott: Philadelphia, 1917.

Stansfeld, James. *Medical Women; an historical sketch.* Edinburgh, 1878.

Stanton, Elizabeth C. *Address in Favor of Universal Suffrage for the Election of Delegates to the Constitutional Convention,* Before the New York Legislature. Albany, 1867.

Stanton, Elizabeth C. *Address to the Legislature of New York, 1854.* Albany, 1854.

Stanton, Elizabeth C. *Eighty Years and More.* New York, 1898.

Stanton, Elizabeth, Anthony, S. B., Gage, M. J., and Harper, Ida H. *History of Woman Suffrage.* 6 vols. Rochester, 1881–1920.

Starcke, C. N. *The Primitive Family.* New York, 1889.

Starrett, Helen E. *After College What—for Girls?* New York, 1896.

Starrett, Helen E. *Letters to a Daughter and a Little Sermon to School Girls.* Chicago, 1892.

Starrett, Helen E. *Letters to Elder Daughters, Married and Unmarried.* Chicago, 1888.

Statistical Abstract of the United States Census, 1910. Government Printing Office, Washington.

Statistical Survey of Education, 1921–22. [Bul. Bur. Ed., No. 38, 1924] Government Printing Office: Washington, 1925.

Stearns, Charles. *The Ladies' Philosophy of Love.* . . Leominster, Mass., 1797.

Steevens, G. W. *The Land of the Dollar.* London, 1897.

Steiner, Bernard C. *The History of Education in Connecticut.* [Circular of Information, Bur. Ed., No. 2, 1893.] Washington, 1893.

Stephens, Kate. Forerunners of Women's collegiate education; and Mary Astell. [In Stephens, Kate: *Workfellows in Social Progression.* Sturgis and Walton: New York, 1916]

Stetson, Charlotte P. *In This Our World.* Small, Maynard: Boston, 1899.

Stevens, Abel. *The Women of Methodism.* New York, 1866.

Stevens College at Columbia, Missouri, from 1833 to 1900: a history based on newspapers. [*MS.* at Stevens College, Columbia, Mo.]

Stevens, Doris. *Jailed for Freedom.* Boni and Liveright: New York, 1920.

Stevens, Romiett (Compiler). *The Equipment for the Adviser or Dean of Women and Girls.* Teachers College: New York.

Stevens, W. Le Conte. *The Admission of Women to Universities.* New York, 1883.

Stevens, Warden W. *Centennial History of Washington County, Indiana.* Bowen: Indianapolis, 1916.

Stewart, George, Jr. *History of Religious Education in Connecticut to the Middle of the Nineteenth Century.* Yale University Press: New Haven, 1924.

Stiles, Henry S. *History of Ancient Wethersfield, Connecticut.* 2 vols. Grafton Press: New York, 1904.

Stinson, Alvah L. *Woman Under the Law.* Hudson Printing Co.: Boston, 1914.

Stodart, M. A. *Principles of Education, . . . with an especial reference . . . to female education in England.* London, 1844.

Stone, H. E. *Friendly Words to Young Women. . .* New York, n.d.

Storke, Elliot G., and Smith, James H. *History of Cayuga County, New York.* Syracuse, 1879.

Storrs, Henry M. *Address at First Anniversary of the Lake Erie Female Seminary,* July 19, 1860. Boston, 1860.

Stow, Sarah D. *History of Mount Holyoke Seminary, 1834–87.* South Hadley, 1887.

Strabo. *Geography.* (Trans. of H. C. Hamilton and W. Falconer) 3 vols. London, 1903.

Strassburger, B. *Geschichte der Erziehung und des Unterrichts bei den Israeliten. . .* Breslau, 1885.

Strong, Gurney S. *Early Landmarks of Syracuse* (New York). Syracuse, 1894.

Strothers, W. M. *Manual of Exercises in Elocution.* Lynchburg, Va., 1888.

Studley, Mary J. *What Our Girls Ought to Know.* New York, 1878.

Sturtevant, Sarah, and Strang, Ruth. *Personnel Study of Deans of Women in Teachers Colleges and Normal Schools.* Teachers College: New York, 1928.

Sulgrove, B. R. *History of Indianapolis.* Philadelphia, 1884.

Sumner, Helen L. *Equal Suffrage.* Harper: New York, 1909.

Sutcliff, Robert. *Travels in Some Parts of North America.* Philadelphia, 1812.

Swanwick, H. M. *Future of the Women's Movement.* London, 1913.

Swift, Fletcher H. *Education in Ancient Israel.* Open Court: Chicago, 1919.

Swinton, John. *Striking for Life.* Philadelphia, 1894.

Sykes, Frederick H. *The Social Basis of the New Education for Women.* [Address to the Household Arts Section of the Alumni Assoc. of Teachers College, Feb. 24, 1917]

Taft, Jessie. *The Woman Movement from the Point of View of Social Consciousness.* Banta: Menasha, 1915.

Talbot, Emily. *The Boston Girls' Latin School.* [Typewritten copy in Boston Public Library] June, 1901.

Talbot, Marion. *The Education of Women.* University of Chicago Press: Chicago, 1910.

Tappan, Henry P. *A Discourse on Education*—delivered at the anniversary of the Young Ladies Institute, Pittsfield, Mass., Oct. 2, 1846. New York, 1846.

Tarbell, Ida M. *The Business of Being a Woman.* Macmillan: New York, 1912.

Taylor, George R. S. *Mary Wollstonecraft.* London, 1911.

Taylor, James M. *Before Vassar Opened.* Houghton: Boston, 1914.

Taylor, James M., and Haight, Elizabeth H. *Vassar.* Oxford University Press: New York, 1915.

Templin, Lucinda. *Some Defects and Merits in Education of Women in Missouri.* University of Missouri; Columbia, n.d.

Templin, Lucinda. *George C. Sibley and Mary E. Sibley. Two Illustrious Pioneers in the Education of Women in Missouri.* Lindenwood College: St. Charles, Mo., 1926.

Templin, Lucinda. *Reminiscences of Lindenwood College.* Lindenwood College: St. Charles, Mo., 1920.

Ten-Brook, A. *American State Universities and . . . the University of Michigan.* Cincinnati, 1875.

Tennessee, History of. Goodspeed Publishing Co.: Nashville, 1887.

Tennessee College, Murfreesboro. *Mary Sharp College Souvenir Edition,* Vol. III, No. 2, 1910.

Tennessee Industries, Women in. [Bul. Women's Bur., No. 56, 1927] Government Printing Office: Washington, 1927.

Tennyson, Alfred. *The Princess.* [Vol. III of Tennyson's *Works.* Macmillan: New York, 1903]

Teresa, Sister Miriam. *Legislation for Women in Oregon.* Catholic University: Washington, 1924.

Terhune, (Mrs.) M. V. *Our Daughters, What Shall We Do With Them?* New York, 1880.

Tevis, Julia A. *Sixty Years in a Schoolroom; an autobiography.* Cincinnati, 1878.

Thayer, William M. *The True Woman.* Crowell: New York, n.d.

Thiselton-Dyer, T. F. *Folklore of Women.* London, 1905.

Thomas, Arad. *Pioneer History of Orleans County, New York.* Albion, 1871.

Thomas, M. Carey. *Coeducation.* [Reprint from new edition of the *Encyclopedia Americana*]

Thomas, M. Carey. Education of women. [In *Education in the United States,* Monograph No. 7, edited by N. M. Butler. Albany, 1899]

Thomas, William I. *Sex and Society.* University of Chicago Press: Chicago, 1907.

Thomason, W. R. *An Address on Female Education.* Nashville, Tenn., 1836.

Thompson, Helen B. *The Mental Traits of Sex.* University of Chicago Press: Chicago, 1903.

Thompson, Helen B. *Psychological Norms in Men and Women.* University of Chicago Press: Chicago, 1903.

Thorndike, E. L. *Educational Psychology.* 3 vols. Teachers College: New York, 1913–14.

Thwaites, Reuben G. (Ed.). *The University of Wisconsin.* Purcell: Madison, 1900.

Thwing, Charles F. *American Colleges, Their Students and Work.* New York, 1878.

Thwing, Charles F. *The College Woman.* New York, 1894.

Thwing, Charles F. *History of Education in the United States Since the Civil War.* Houghton: Boston, 1910.

Thwing, Charles F. *A History of Higher Education in the United States.* Appleton: New York, 1906.

Thwing, Charles F. *Letters from a Father to His Daughter Entering College.* Platt and Peck: New York, 1913.

Tilton, Theodore. *The Constitution a Title Deed to Woman's Franchise: a letter to Charles Sumner.* New York, 1871.

Todd, Arthur J. *The Primitive Family as an Educational Agency.* Putnam: New York, 1913.

Todd, John. *The Daughter at School.* Northampton, Mass., 1854.

Token of Friendship. Boston, 1845.

Tolman, William H. *History of Higher Education in Rhode Island.* [Circular of Information, Bur., Ed., No. 1, 1894] Washington, 1894.

Trades, General Description of All, by Which Parents, Guardians and Trustees May Make Choice of Trades Agreeable to the Capacity, Education, Inclination . . . of Youth. London, 1747.

Training for the Professions and Allied Occupations—Facilities Available to Women in the United States. Bureau of Vocational Information: New York, 1924.

Trollope, Frances M. *Domestic Manners of the Americans.* London, 1832.

Trotsky, Leon. *Problems of Life.* (Trans. of Z. Vengerova) London, n.d.

Trowbridge, Ada W. *The Home School.* Houghton: Boston, 1913.

Troy Female Seminary. [Described in *Letters about the Hudson Valley,* Letter V: 37–42] New York, 1837.

Tucker, Henry St. George. *Women's Suffrage by Constitutional Amendment.* Yale Press: New Haven, 1916.

Tusser, Thomas. *Five Hundred Points of Good Husbandry . . . with a book of housewifery.* London, 1812.

Tuttle, Florence G. *Awakening of Woman: suggestions from the psychic side of feminism.* Abingdon Press: New York, 1915.

Tyler, Moses C. *A History of American Literature.* New York, 1878.

Tyler, W. S. Smith College. [Address before the citizens of Northampton, Dec. 9, 1872]

Tylor, Edward B. *Primitive Culture.* 2 vols. London, 1903.

Tyson, Hobart W. *Lutheran Education in Pennsylvania.* [Master's Thesis, University of Pennsylvania, 1923]

Underwood, J. L. *The Women of the Confederacy.* Neale: New York, 1906.

Ursulines in New Orleans, The, 1725–1925. Kennedy: New York, 1925.

Vanderpoel, E. N. *Litchfield School; chronicles of a pioneer school from 1792–1833.* Harvard University Press: Cambridge, 1903.

Van de Warker, Ely. *Woman's Unfitness for Higher Coeducation.* Grafton Press: New York, 1903.

Van Doren, Mark (Ed.). *Samuel Sewall's Diary.* Macy-Masius: New York, 1927.

Van Horne, David. *History of the Reformed Church in Philadelphia.* Philadelphia, 1876.

Van Kleeck, Mary. *What Industry Means to Women Workers.* [Bul. Women's Bur., No. 31, 1923] Government Printing Office: Washington, 1923.

Van Rensselaer, (Mrs.) John K. *The Goede Vrouw of Mana-Ha-Ta.* New York, 1898.

Van Vorst, (Mrs.) John and Marie. *The Woman Who Toils.* Doubleday: New York, 1903.

Vassar College. *Historical Sketch.* New York, 1873.

Vassar College. Addresses at the Celebration of the Twenty-fifth Academic Year, 1890.

Virginia Historical Society Collections, 1833–1897. 10 vols. Richmond.

Virginia, Journal of a Young Lady of 1782. (Ed. by E. V. Mason) Baltimore, 1871.

Vocational Training, Handbook of Opportunities for, in Boston. Woman's Municipal League: Boston, 1913.

Vocations Open to College Woman. University of Minnesota: Minneapolis, n.d.

Von Raumer, Karl. *Education of Girls.* [Republished from *Barnard's Jour.,* March and June, 1861] Bardeen: Syracuse, n.d.

Vote, Why the Home Makers Do not Want to. Vindicator Press: Youngstown, O., n.d.

Voters of the Middle West, To the. Illinois Assoc. Opposed to the Extension of Suffrage to Women: Chicago, 1909.

Waddell, Joseph A. *History of Mary Baldwin Seminary.* Staunton, Va., 1908.

Wade, John D. *Augustus Baldwin Longstreet.* Macmillan: New York, 1924.

Walker, Thomas. *Legal Rights of Women.* [Reprint from the *Western Law Jour.,* Jan. 1849] Cincinnati, 1849.

Warwick, Countess of. *Progress in Women's Education in the British Empire.* London, 1898.

Washburn, Emory. *History of Leicester Academy.* Boston, 1855.

Washburn, Henry S. *Woman Suffrage; an argument delivered May 14, 1874, before the Massachusetts Senate.* Boston, 1874.

Waters, Thomas F. *Ipswich in the Massachusetts Bay Colony: 1700–1917.* Ch. XXIV. Ipswich Historical Soc.: Ipswich, 1917.

Waterston, Robert C. *Memoir of George B. Emerson.* Cambridge, 1884.

Watson, Bruce M. *The Proposed Twentieth Amendment to the Federal Constitution.* Philadelphia Public Education and Child Labor Assoc. of Pennsylvania: Philadelphia, 1924.

Watson, John F. *Annals of Philadelphia and Pennsylvania.* 2 vols. Philadelphia, 1856.

Wayland, Francis. *Thoughts on the Present Collegiate System in the United States.* Boston, 1842.

Weathersby, William H. *A History of Educational Legislation in Mississippi from 1798 to 1860.* [University of Chicago, Educational Monographs, III, No. 4, 1921]

Weaver, Eli W. (Ed.). *Vocations for Girls.* Prepared by a committee of teachers. Barnes: New York, 1913.

Weber, Samuel. *The Charity School Movement in Colonial Pennsylvania, 1754–1763.* Campbell: Philadelphia, 1905.

Webster, George W. *Physiological Basis for the Shorter Working Day for Women.* [Bul. Women's Bur., No. 14, 1921] Government Printing Office: Washington, 1921.

[Webster, Noah] *To the Friends of American Literature.* [An answer to Lyman Cobb's Review of Webster's books] 1829 (?).

Weeden, Anne T. *The Women's College in Brown University, its Origin and Development.* Providence, 1912.

Weeden, William B. *Early Rhode Island; a social history of the people.* Grafton Press: New York, 1910.

Weeden, William B. *Economic and Social History of New England, 1620–1789.* 2 vols. Boston, 1890.

Weeks, Ruth M. *The People's School.* Houghton: Boston, 1912.

Weeks, Stephen B. *History of Public School Education in Alabama.* Government Printing Office: Washington, 1915.

Weir, Dorothy. *Training Opportunities for Connecticut Women.* Woman's Division, Connecticut State Council of Defense: Hartford, n.d.

Wellman, J. W. *A Sermon in Memory of Mrs. Maria Brigham Furber.* Boston, 1833.

Wertenbaker, Thomas J. *Patrician and Plebian in Virginia.* Michie: Charlottesville, 1910.

Wertenbaker, Thomas J. *The First Americans.* Macmillan: New York, 1927.

West, Anson. *History of Methodism in Alabama.* Publishing House, Methodist Episcopal Church, South: Nashville, 1893.

Westermarck, Edward. *The History of Human Marriage.* Macmillan: New York, 1903.

Westermarck, Edward. *Position of Woman in Early Civilization.* [London Sociological Soc.: *Sociological Papers,* Vol. I] London, 1905.

Wharton, Anne H. *Colonial Days and Dames.* Lippincott: Philadelphia, 1900.

Wharton, Anne H. *Martha Washington.* New York, 1897.

Wheatley, Phillis, Letters and Poems of. (First collected edition, edited by Charles F. Heartman) New York, 1916.

White, Alain C. *The History of the Town of Litchfield, Connecticut, 1720–1920.* Enquirer Print: Litchfield, 1920.

White, Carlos. *Ecce Femina: an attempt to solve the woman question.* Hanover, N. H., 1870.

White, George. *Historical Collections of Georgia.* New York, 1855.

White, George. *Statistics of the State of Georgia.* Savannah, 1849.

White, Mary C. *The Life-Story of Alice Culler Cobb.* Revell: New York, 1925.

Whitford, Helena. *Thoughts on . . . an Institution for the Support and Education of Unportioned Respectable Females.* London, 1809.

Whitney, M. W. *Eulogy on Matthew Vassar,* April 29, 1869.

Whittier, John Greenleaf. *Margaret Smith's Journal in the Province of Massachusetts Bay, 1678–79.* [Works of Whittier, V] Houghton: Boston, 1910.

Wickersham, James P. *A History of Education in Pennsylvania.* Lancaster, 1886.

Wigglesworth, Michael. *Day of Doom.* New York, 1867.

Wight, William W. *Annals of Milwaukee College.* Milwaukee, 1891.

Wightman, J. M. *Annals of the Boston Primary School Committee.* Boston, 1860.

Wilcox, Hamilton. *Women's Common Law—Right to Vote from the Earliest to the Present Time.* New York, 1885.

Wilderspin, Samuel. *A System for the Education of the Young.* London, 1840.

Wile, Ira S. *Sex hygiene and sex education.* [Rapeer, L. W.: *Educational Hygiene,* Ch. XXIX. Scribner's: New York, 1915]

Will and Doom; or the miseries of Connecticut. [*Collections, Connecticut Historical Soc.,* III, 79–269]

Willard, Emma. *Journal and Letters from France and Great Britain in 1833.* Troy, 1833.

Willard, Emma. *Letter to the Members of the Willard Association for the Improvement of Female Teachers.* Troy, 1838.

Willard, Frances E. *Address . . . at the First Triennial Meeting of the Woman's National Council of the United States.* Washington, 1891.

Willard, Frances E. *How to Win: a book for girls.* New York, 1886.

Willard, Frances E., and Livermore, M. A. (Eds.). *A Woman of the Century.* Buffalo, 1893.

Willard, Frances E., Winslow, H. M., and White, S. J. *Occupations for Women.* . . . New York, 1897.

Williams, E. M. *History of Worcester County, Massachusetts.* 2 vols. Boston, 1879.

Wilson, Calvin D. *Working One's Way Through College and University.* McClurg: Chicago, 1912.

Wilson, Epiphanius (Ed.). *Literature of the Orient.* Colonial Press: New York, 1902.

Wilson, Samuel T. *A Century of Maryville College.* Maryville College: Maryville, 1919.

Wingfield, Marshall. *A History of Caroline County, Virginia.* Trevvet Christian: Richmond, 1924.

Winslow, Helen (Ed.). *Official Register and Directory of Woman's Clubs.* Winslow: Shirley, Mass., 1921.

Winslow, Mary N. *Married Women in Industry.* [Bul. Women's Bur., No. 38, 1924] Government Printing Office: Washington, 1924.

Winthrop, John. *Conclusions for the Plantation in New England.* [*Old South Leaflets*, General Series, II, No. 50] Boston, 1894.

Winthrop, John. *The History of New England, 1630–1649.* 2 vols. Boston, 1853.

Wollstonecraft, Mary. *A Vindication of the Rights of Woman, with strictures on political and moral subjects.* New York, 1856.

Woman Suffrage, Common Sense as to. Boston, 1885.

Woman Suffrage, Debates Upon the Report of the Suffrage Committee on. State Constitutional Convention: New York, 1894.

Woman Suffrage, Hearing Before the Select Committee on, of the United States Senate. Government Printing Office: Washington, 1908.

Woman Suffrage, The Woman's Protest Against, 1912–18. New York.

Woman's Book, The. A symposium. 2 vols. New York, 1894.

Women's clubs and education. [Monroe, P.: *Cyclopedia of Education,* V: 811–13]

Woman's Rights Tracts, No. 1, 1851. n.p., n.d.

Women's Industrial Conference, Proceedings of. [Bul. Women's Bur., No. 33, 1923] Government Printing Office: Washington, 1923.

Women in the Modern World. [*The Annals of the American Academy of Polit. and Soc. Science,* CXLIII, May, 1929. Edited by V. B. Boothe]

Women's Wages in Kansas. [Bul. Women's Bur., No. 17, 1921] Government Printing Office: Washington, 1921.

Wood, Frances A. *Earliest Years at Vassar.* Vassar College Press: Poughkeepsie, 1909.

Wood, Mary I. *The History of the General Federation of Women's Clubs.* General Federation of Women's Clubs: New York, 1912.

Woodburn, James A. *Higher Education in Indiana.* [Circular of Information, Bur. Ed., No. 1, 1891] Washington, 1891.

Woods, Alice. *Coeducation.* London, 1903.

Woods, Alice (Ed.). *Advance in Coeducation.* London, 1919.

Woods, Lucy R. *A History of the Girls' High School of Boston, 1852–1902.* Riverside Press: Cambridge, 1904.

Woods, Robert A., and Kennedy, Albert J. (Eds.). *Young Working Girls.* Houghton: Boston, 1913.

Woodward, W. H. *Vittorino da Feltre and other Humanist Educators.* Cambridge University Press: Cambridge, 1921.

Woody, Thomas. *Early Quaker Education in Pennsylvania.* Teachers College: New York, 1920.

Woody, Thomas. *Quaker Education in the Colony and State of New Jersey.* Philadelphia, 1923.

Woody, Thomas. Vocational education. [*Twenty-five Years of American Education* (Ed. by I. L. Kandel), Ch. XI. Macmillan: New York, 1924]

Woolson, A. G. *Woman in American Society.* Boston, 1873.

Worcester, Alfred. *A New Way of Training Nurses.* Boston, 1888.

Worcester, Alfred. *Nurses and Nursing.* Harvard University Press: Cambridge, 1927.

Working Women, Facts About. [Bul. Women's Bur., No. 46, 1925] Government Printing Office: Washington, 1925.

Working Women, Short Talks About. [Bul. Women's Bur., No. 59, 1927] Government Printing Office: Washington, 1927.

Working Women, State Laws Affecting. [Bul. Women's Bur., No. 40, 1924] Government Printing Office: Washington, 1924.

Wright, A. Edward. *Unexpurgated Case Against Woman Suffrage.* London, 1913.

Wright, G. Frederick. *Oberlin College.* [Reprint from the *New England Mag.*, Sept. 1900]

Wright, Martha (Ed.). *History of the Oread Collegiate Institute, Worcester, Massachusetts, 1849-1881.* Tuttle, Morehouse and Taylor: New Haven, 1905.

Wright, Paul W. *Educational Work in New York Yearly Meeting of Friends, Prior to 1860.* [Master's Thesis, Teachers College, Columbia University, 1913]

Wroth, Lawrence C. *History of Printing in Colonial Maryland.* Typothetae: Baltimore, 1922.

Xenophon. *The Oeconomicus.* (Trans. of E. C. Marchant) Putnam: New York, 1923.

Young Lady's Conduct: Or Rules for Education. London, 1722.

Young Lady's Own Book, The. By the author of the *Young Man's Own Book.* Philadelphia, 1836.

Young Lady's Parental Monitor, The. Reprinted at Hartford, 1792.

Young, William. *History of Lafayette County, Missouri.* Vols. I and II. Bowen: Indianapolis, 1910.

IV

Periodical Publications and Proceedings

Abbott, Edith. A study of the early history of child labor in America. [*Am. Jour. Soc.* (1908-9) XIV: 15-37]

Abbott, Edward. Wellesley College. [*Harper's N. M. Mag.* (1876) LIII: 321-32]

Abbott, Frances M. A comparative view of the woman suffrage movement. [*N. A. R.* (1895) CLX: 142-51]

Abbott, Frances M. A generation of college women. [*Forum* (Nov. 1895) XX: 377-84]

Abbott, Frances M. Three decades of college women. [*Pop. Sci. Mo.* (Aug. 1904) LXV: 350-9]

Abernethy, Julian W. The anomaly of coeducation. [*Sch. and Soc.* (1919) IX: 259-62]

Academies, The old. [*New Englander & Yale Rev.*, Jan., 1885: 104-12]

Adams, Elizabeth K. Psychological gains and losses of the college woman. [*Ed. Rev.* (1910) XXXIX: 238-56]

Adams, Elizabeth K. Some new professional standards for college women. [*Ed. Record*, I: 54-60]

Addams, Jane. The world's food supply and woman's obligation. [*N. E. A. Proc.*, 1918: 108–13]

Agerter, Rose E. The duties of the student adviser. [*Sch. Rev.* (1922) XXX: 37–44]

Aggasiz, Louis, on coeducation of the sexes. [*Ed. Jour. of Va.*, VI: 308 *f.*]

Aggasiz, (Mrs.) Louis. The higher education of women. [*Jour. Ed.* (1897) XLV: 304–5]

Agnew, J. H. Woman's offices and influence. [*Harper's N. M. Mag.* (1851) III: 654 *ff.*]

Agriculture, Women at a college of. [*Pub. Opin.* (Nov. 24, 1898) XXV: 662]

Allan, Evelyn W. The unsociable student. [*Jour. A. C. A.* (Dec. 1908) Series III, No. 18: 74–8]

Allen, Annie T. The economic relation of the college woman to society. [*Education* (1902) XXII: 351–62]

Allen, Grant. A letter on the woman question. [*Pop. Sci. Mo.* (1889–90) XXXVI: 552–3]

Allen, Grant. Plain words on the woman question. [*Pop. Sci. Mo.* (1889–90) XXXVI: 170–81]

Allyn, Robert. The education of girls. [*N. E. A. Proc.*, 1891: 375–8]

Almy, Emma A. A year's progress for college women. [*Education* (1890) X: 476–85]

Alumna. Vols. I–X. Alumnae, Wesleyan Female College of Cincinnati: Cincinnati, 1890–1901.

Alumna: Alumna's children. [*Pop. Sci. Mo.* (1904) LXV: 45–51, 279–81]

Alvord, K. S. Relation of the faculty, and especially of the dean of women, to the student government association. [*N. E. A. Proc.*, 1919: 412]

American Annals of Education and Instruction, 1831–39. 9 vols. Boston.

American Association for the Study and Prevention of Infant Mortality. *Transactions of the Annual Meetings*, 1914–22. Baltimore.

American Association of University Professors. *Bulletins*, 1915–27. Vols. I–XIII. n.p.

American Association of University Women [Association of Collegiate Alumnae]. *Journal* 1884–1927. Ithaca.

American Educational Review, 1909–12. Vols. XXXI–XXXIV. New York and Chicago.

American Institute of Instruction. *Proceedings*, 1830–1908. Vols. I–LXXVIII. Boston.

American Journal of Education, 1826–31. 5 vols. Boston.

American Journal of Sociology, 1895–1928. Vols. I–XXXIII. Chicago.

American School Board Journal, The, 1909–27. Vols. XXXVIII–LXXIV. New York, Milwaukee, Chicago.

American Teacher, The. N. S. Vols. I–II, IV–VII. Boston.

American women, Education of. [*Harper's N. M. Mag.* (1857) XV: 776–83]

American woman and her home, The. [*The Outlook* (1910) XCVI: 111–18]

American women, Two. [*L. L. A.* (1897) CCXV: 90–102]

Ancient, Aunt. Women teachers. [*Ed. Jour. Va.* (Oct. 1888) XXIX: 445–8]

Anderson, Mary. Women in industry. [*N. E. A. Proc.*, 1922: 707–12]

Andrews, Benjamin R. Catherine E. Beecher, the pioneer in home economics. [*Jour. Home Econ.*, IV: 211–22]

Andrews, Benjamin R. The cost of going to college. [*T. C. Record* (Oct. 1925) XXVII: 129–41]

Angell, James B. Coeducation at Michigan University. [*Pa. Sch. Jour.* (1881) XXIX: 281]

Angell, James B. Coeducation in relation to other types of college education for women. [*N. E. A. Proc.*, 1904: 548–9]

Angell, James R. Some reflections upon the reaction from coeducation. [*Pop. Sci. Mo.* (Nov., 1902) LXII: 5–26]

Anthony, Susan B. Status of woman, past, present, and future. [*Arena* (1897) XVII: 901–8]

Antioch College History. [*R. C. E.* (1896–7) I: 758–67]

Armstrong, J. E. The advantages of limited sex segregation in the high school. [*Sch. Rev.*, XVIII: 339–50]

Armstrong, M. F. The mission of educated women. [*Pop. Sci. Mo.* (1889–90) XXXVI: 601–8]

Arnold, Sarah L. The education of girls. [*N. E. Mag.* (Mar. 1907) N. S. XXXVI: 81–4]

Arnold, Sarah L. Some phases of the education of women. [*Jour. Ed.*, LVI: 71–2]

Arps, George F. Social implications of educational selection. [*Nat. Voc. Guid. Assoc. Bul.* No. 4, 1922: 11–17]

Artists, Women, of the South. [*L. L. A.* (1859) LXIII: 616]

Ashe, S. A. Social conditions in North Carolina in 1783. [*N. C. Booklet* (1910–11) X: 200–22]

Atlantic Monthly, 1857–1927. Vols. I–CXL. Boston.

Baer, Clara G. The health of college women. [*N. E. A. Proc.*, 1916: 690–3]

Baer, Clara G. Women and the war. [*N. E. A. Proc.*, 1918: 355–7]

Bailey, Ebenezer, and his relation to the Boston Girls' High School. [*Barnard's Jour.*, XII: 429–52]

Baker, H. Barton. Two women of letters of the last century. [*L. L. A.* (1885) CLXVII: 741–8]

Ball, B. W. Woman's rights in ancient Athens. [*At. Mo.* (1871) XXVII: 273–86]

Ballard, Walter J. Women and coeducation. [*Jour. Ed.* (1903) LVIII: 115]

Bancroft, Jane M. Occupations and professions for college bred women. [*Education* (1885) V: 486–95]

Banker, Howard J. Women's marriage decrease. [*Jour. Heredity* (May 1917) VIII: 208–14]

Bansemer, Caroline S. A Colonial dame. [*Harper's N. M. Mag.* (1898) XCVII: 229–32]

Barnard, F. A. P. Higher education of women. [*Barnard's Jour.* (1879) XXXI: 385–96]

Barnard, Henry. *American Journal of Education*, 1855–1881. 32 vols. Hartford.

Barnes, Earl. New professions for women. [*At. Mo.*, CXVI: 225–34]

Barr, Amelia E. Discontented women. [*N. A. R.* (1896) CLXII: 201–9]

Bascom, John. Coeducation. [*Ed. Rev.* (1908) XXXVI: 442–51]

Beard, Charles A. The woman's party. [*New Republic* (1916) VII: 329–31]

Beecher, Catherine E. How to redeem woman's profession from dishonor. [*Harper's N. M. Mag.* (1865) XXXI: 710–16]

Beecher, Catherine E. Woman's profession dishonored. [*Harper's N. M. Mag.* (1864) XXIX: 766–8]

Bentzon, Theodore. Family life in America. [*Forum* (March, 1896) XXI: 1–20]

Beyer, Thomas P. Creative evolution and the woman question. [*Ed. Rev.* (1914) XLVII: 22–7]

Birge, E. A. What a president may expect from a dean of women. [*N. E. A. Proc.*, 1919: 399]

Birth-rate in New England. [*Independent* (1902) LIV: 1503–4]

Bisland, Elizabeth. The cry of the women. [*N. A. R.* (1894) CLVIII: 757–9]

Bisland, Elizabeth. Educating a daughter. [*N. A. R.* (1894) CLIX: 627–30]

Bisland, Elizabeth. The modern woman and marriage. [*N. A. R.* (1895) CLX: 753–5]

Black, Ruby A. Jobs for women. [*Nation* (Dec. 9, 1925) CXXI: 648–9]

Blackburn, Helen. The relation of women to the state in past time. [From *The National Review—L. L. A.* (1886) CLXXI: 684–8]

Blackwell, Emily. Story of the experience of the first woman students in medicine. [*Boston Herald*, Feb. 1, 1891]

Blair, A. Z. Seventeen hundred rural vote-sellers. [*McClure's Mag.* (Nov. 1911) XXXVIII: 28–40]

Blaisdell, A. F. Physical education of high school girls. [*N. E. Jour. Ed.* (1875) 11: 109–10]

Blumer, J. C. Marriage of Iowa college women. [*Jour. Heredity* (May 1917) VIII: 217]

Bok, Edward. What women's colleges lack. [*Jour. Ed.* (1900) LII: 85]

Bolce, Harold. Does the college rob the cradle? [*Delineator* (1911) LXXVII: 169–70]

Bolles, John A. Mary Wollstonecraft. [*Harper's N. M. Mag.* (1867) XXXV: 737–40]

Bolton, Henry C. *The Early Practice of Medicine by Women*. [Reprint from *Jour. of Sci.*, Feb. 1881] London, 1881.

Bolton, Sarah K. Higher education of women at Oxford University. [*Education* (Nov. 1883) IV: 126–32]

Bolton, Sarah K. Higher education of women in Cambridge, England. [*Education* (1882) II: 553–63]

Bolton, Sarah K. Letter on women in the same college with men. [*N. E. Jour. Ed.* (1884) XX: 379]

Bolton, Sarah K. Women in London University and in University College. [*Education* (May 1884) IV: 476–81]

Boone, Richard G. The high-school dean of girls. [*Sierra Educational News* (April 1922) XVIII: 193]

Borg, (Mrs.) Sidney C. The big sister movement. [*Jour. N. E. A.*, Apr. 1917: 845–6]

Boston public schools, Girls in. [*Barnard's Jour.*, XIII: 243–66]

Boston Woman's Educational Association. [*N. E. Jour. Ed.*, I: 90–1]

Boykin, James C. Women in the public schools. [*Ed. Rev.* (1899) XVIII: 138–43]

Brackett, Anna C. Liberal education for women. [*Harper's N. M. Mag.* (1876–7) LIV: 695–6]

Brackett, Anna C. The private school for girls. [*Harper's N. M. Mag.* (1891–2) LXXXIV: 943–58]

Brackett, Anna C. Vassar College. [*Harper's N. M. Mag.* (1875–6) LII: 346–61]

Bradford, G. Mary Lyon. [*At. Mo.* (Dec. 1918) CXXII: 785–95]

Bradford, M. C. C. The status of the woman teacher in rural districts. [*N. E. A. Proc.*, 1923: 490–1]

Bradwell, Myra. A report on her efforts to be admitted to the Illinois Bar. [*Chicago Legal News*, April 5, 1890]

Breed, Mary B. The control of college social life. [*Jour. A. C. A.* (Dec. 1908) Series III, No. 18: 60–74]

Bremer, Edith T. Education for immigrant women. [*Ed. Foundations*, XXVII: 289 *ff.*]

Brent, J. H. Report on mixed schools. [*N. C. Jour. Ed.*, 1859: 267]

Brewster, William T. Barnard College. [*Columbia Univ. Quart.* (March 1910) XII: 151–71]

Britan, Nellie H. What physical education is doing for women. [*Education* (1908) XXIX: 35–45]

Brown, E. E. The work of women's organizations in education. [*N. E. A. Proc.*, 1908, 1218–22]

Brown, J. H., Gengembre, P. W., and Davis W. V. Coeducation of the sexes. [*Pa. Sch. Jour.* (1854) III: 211–15]

Brown, Mary L. Talks to freshmen—their content and value. [*N. E. A. Proc.*, 1923, 634–5]

Brown University Woman's College. [*Sch. Jour.*, LXXV, 517]

Browne, A. K. Influence of female teachers. [*Pa. Sch. Jour.* (1854) III: 85–7]

Brumbaugh, Martin G. Why women teach. [*N. E. Jour. Ed.* (1907) LXVI: 63–4]

Bryant, Emily J. The Woman's Medical College of Pennsylvania. [*Education* (1890) XI: 12–15]

Bryant, Ethel W. Some reflections on the duties of a dean of girls. [*Sierra Ed. News* (April 1922) XVIII: 198]

Buckle, Henry T. Influence of women on the progress of knowledge. [*L. L. A.* (1858) LVII: 883–93]

Bunce, O. B. Literature for women. [*Critic* (1889) N. S. XII: 67–8]

Burgerstein, Leo. Coeducation and hygiene, with special reference to European experience and views. [*Ped. Sem.* (1910) XVII: 1–15]

Burnap, George W. The health of American women. [*Ladies' Wreath* (1848–49) III: 185–8]

Burrowes, Thomas H. Coeducation of the sexes. [*Pa. Sch. Jour.* (1856) V: 27–32]

Bushee, Frederick A. Declining birth-rate and its causes. [*Pop. Sci. Mo.* (1903) LXIII: 355–61]

Bushnell, Dr., on women's rights. [*Nation* (1869) VIII: 496–7]

Butler, Nicholas M. Barnard College. [*Columbia Univ. Quart.*, June 1915: 201–11]

Butler, Nicholas M. Coeducation a dead issue. [*Jour. Ed.* (1902) LVI: 314]

Butler, Nicholas M. Frederick A. P. Barnard. [*Columbia Univ. Quart.* (March 1910) XII: 137–50]

Butler, Nicholas M., Robinson, J. H., and Earle, M. L. On the education of women. [*Columbia Univ. Quart.*, June 1900: 226–34]

Byerly, William E. Radcliffe College thirty years after. [*Harvard Grad. Mag.*, Dec. 1909: 233–6]

Cady, Helen M. The American college girl's ignorance of literature. [*Jour. Ped.* (June 1907) XIX: 231 *ff.*]

Call, Annie P. The greatest need of college girls. [*At. Mo.* (1892) LXIX: 102–9]

Cambridge, Education of women at. [*Ed. Rev.* (1922) LXIII: 172–4]

Cambridge, Women at. [*Sch. & Soc.* (1920) XII: 498–9]

Cambridge University. [*Nation* (July 21, 1887) XLV: 51–2]

Cambridge University, The conferring of degrees on women at. [*Sch. and Soc.*, XVII: 18–19]

Candler, W. A. Educational progress in the South since 1865. [*Proc. N. E. A.*, 1889: 339–44]

Cardwill, Mary E. Should the education of girls differ from that of boys? [*Education* (1889) X: 33–6]

Careers, new, The effect of, on women's happiness. [*L. L. A.* (1890) CLXXXVI: 190–2]

Carmault, A. M. Manners and morals. [*N. E. A. Proc.*, 1916: 1008]

Carpenter, Elizabeth. More truth about women in industry. [*N. A. R.* (1904) CLXXIX: 215–25]

Carpenter, Mary A. Problems confronting the deans of women in Western colleges and universities. [*Iowa State Teachers Assoc. Proc.*, 1906: 87–94]

Carr, Ezra S. The industrial education of women. [*N. E. A. Proc.*, 1876: 240–9]

Carroll, Mother Austin. Education in Louisiana in French Colonial days. [*Am. Catholic Rev.* (1886) XI: 396–418]

Carroll, Mother Austin. Education in New Orleans in Spanish Colonial days. [*Am. Catholic Rev.* (1887) XII: 253–77]

Carter, Susan N. Women in the field of art-work. [*N. A. R.* (1892) CLV: 381–4]

Case, Thomas. Against Oxford degrees for women. [*Fortnightly Rev.* (July 1895) LVIII: 89–100]

Catholic Educational Review, The, 1911–27. Vols. I–XXV. Washington.

Catholic World, 1865–1928. Vols. I–CXXVII. New York.

Catt, Carrie C. The home and the higher education. [*N. E. A. Proc.,* 1902: 100–10]

Catt, Carrie C. A plea for women. [*Jour. Ed.* (1902) LVI: 136]

Chadwick, F. E. The woman peril in American education. [*Ed. Rev.* (1914) XLVII: 109–19]

Chancellor, W. E. Coeducation in higher institutions, pro and con. [*Jour. Ed.* (Sept. 1920) XCII: 227–31]

[Charleston, S. C.] Girls High and Normal School. [*Barnard's Jour.,* XIII: 620–2]

Charters, Jessie A. ˏ Methods of study used by college women. [*Jour. Ed. Research,* X, 344–55]

Charters, W. W. The reorganization of women's education. [*Ed. Rev.* (Oct. 1921) LXII: 224–31]

Cheney, Ednah D. The place of woman in our public schools. [*N. E. Jour. Ed.* (1875) II: 220, 231, and 243]

Cheyney, May S. Will nature eliminate the college woman? [*Jour. A. C. A.,* January 1905: 1–9]

Clapp, T. Memoirs of a college president—womanhood in early America. [*Connecticut Mag.* (1908) XII: 233–9]

Clark, Charles W. Woman suffrage, pro and con. [*At. Mo.* (1890) LXV: 310–20]

Clark, S. Allen. A dean for high school girls. [*Sierra Ed. News* (March 1920) XVI: 153–4]

Clugston, W. G. The collapse of Kentucky. [*American Mercury* (1925) VI: 265–71]

Coeducation. [*Ed. News,* July 1892: 438–9]

Coeducation. (An editorial by N. C. Schaeffer) [*Pa. Sch. Jour.* (1902) L: 558–60]

Coeducation abolished at Chicago. [*Sch. Jour.,* LXXIII: 361]

Coeducation abolished at Wesleyan Academy, Wilbraham, Massachusetts. [*Am. Ed. Rev.* (1910–11) XXXII: 448]

Coeducation again. [*Sch. Jour.,* LXIV: 468–9]

Coeducation again. [*Sch. Jour.,* LXV: 604–5]

Coeducation, an Americanism. [*Nation* (1894) LVIII: 48–9]

Coeducation and secular education in the United States. [*Ed. Rev.* (1908) XXXVI: 295–305]

Coeducation at Antioch. [*Nation* (1870) XI: 24–5]

Coeducation at Chicago. [*Sch. Jour.,* LXIV: 312]

Coeducation at the University of Chicago. [*Nation* (1902) LXXV: 147–8]

Coeducation, Criticism of. [*Am. Ed. Rev.,* XXXIII: 428–9]

Coeducation, Fighting [at Cornell]. [*Sch. Jour.,* LXXIV: 550]

Coeducation, Horace Mann School to abandon. [*Am. Ed. Rev.* XXXIV: 452]

Coeducation in Chicago. [*Independent* (April 1903) LV: 874]

Coeducation in colleges. [*N. E. Jour. Ed.* (1887) XXV: 89]

Coeducation in Germany. [*Ed. News*, Sept. 1892: 487]

Coeducation in Massachusetts. [*N. E. Jour. Ed.* (1891) XXXIV: 186]

Coeducation in New Orleans. [*Sch. Board Jour.* (Jan. 1914) XLVIII: 31]

Coeducation in relation to other types of college education for women. [*Proc. of the National Teachers Assoc.*, 1904: 549]

Coeducation in Swarthmore. [*Pa. Sch. Jour.* (1872) XXI: 59–60]

Coeducation in the public schools. [*Sch. Jour.*, LXVI: 420–2 and 443–4]

Coeducation in the West. [*Ed. News*, Dec. 9, 1893: 693—Quoted from *N. A. R.* for October]

Coeducation in Virginia. [*Am. Ed. Rev.*, XXXII: 441]

Coeducation in Wisconsin. [*Nation* (1883) XXXVI: 80]

Coeducation of the sexes. [*Ed. Jour. Va.*, Aug. 1873: 414–15]

Coeducation of the sexes. [In a report of the committee on the education of girls—*N. E. A. Proc.*, 1890: 338–47]

Coeducation of the sexes. [*N. E. Jour. Ed.* (1890) XXXII: 216]

Coeducation of the sexes. [*Pa. Sch. Jour.* (1852) I: 9–10]

Coeducation of the sexes, Remarks on. [*Pa. Sch. Jour.* (1854) III: 119–22]

Coeducation of the sexes—The other side. [*Rhode Island Schoolmaster*, Dec. 1872: 397–402]

Coeducation [Reaction against]. [*Sch. Jour.*, LXV: 489]

Coeducation, The coördinate plan of. [*Intelligence*, Sept. 1903: 511–12]

Coeducation, The future of. [*Ed. News*, Sept. 1890: 501–2]

Coeducation, collegiate, The present and future of. [*Nation* (1909) LXXXVIII: 404–6]

Coeducation, The University of Pennsylvania and. [*Sch. and Soc.*, VII: 286]

Coeducation, Theory and practice in. [*N. E. Jour. Ed.* (1880) XI: 168–9]

Coffin, Annie Morrison. John Irwin Morrison and the Washington County Seminary. [*Indiana Mag. of Hist.* (June 1926) XXII: 183]

Coleman, Herbert T. The status of education in the South prior to the war between the states. [*Confederate Veteran*, Oct. 1907: 441–7]

College and university faculties, Preliminary report of Committee W. on status of women in. [*Bul. Am. Assoc. Univ. Profs.* (Oct. 1921) VII: 21–32]

College course for women to be employment managers. [*Sch. and Soc.*, VII: 765]

College for women in New Jersey, A. [*Sch. and Soc.*, I, 126–7]

College life for women. [*Nation* (1889) XLIX: 326–7]

College women. [*Pa. Sch. Jour.* (1904) LIII: 192]

College women (editorial). [*Jour. Ed.* (1900) LI: 360]

Colleges and schools in Richmond, Virginia, newspapers. [*Va. Mag. Hist. and Biography* (1914) XXII: 288–96]

Colleges for women. [*Pa. Sch. Jour.* (1866) XV: 17]

Colleges, Women in the. [*Sch. Jour.* LXVIII: 656]

Columbia University Quarterly, 1899–1919. 21 vols. New York.

Colvin, Stephen S. Present status of mental testing. [*Ed. Rev.*, LX: 320–37]

Coman, Katharine. Preparation for citizenship at Wellesley College. [*Education* (1890) X: 341–7]

Common School Assistant, The, 1836–1840. Albany and New York.

Common School Journal, The, 1838–1849. Boston.

Common School Journal of the State of Pennsylvania, The, 1844. Philadelphia.

Comstock, Ada L. Address on the college curriculum as a matter of teaching. [*Jour. A. C. A.* (May 1917) X: 595–99]

Condon, R. J. The girl in the home. [*Intelligence*, Jan. 15, 1904: 69–70]

Connecticut Common School Journal, 1838–66. Hartford.

Conover, Charlotte R. First work for girl graduates. [*Education* (1897): XVIII: 214–17]

Conway, Clara. The needs of Southern women. [*N. E. A. Proc.*, 1884: 169–76]

Cook, Frank G. The law's partiality to married women. [*At. Mo.* (1886) LVIII: 311–17]

Cooke, Rose, T. The real rights of women. [*N. A. R.* (1889) CXLIX: 347–54]

Cooking in the schools. [*Ed. News*, Oct. 15, 1898: 278–9]

Cooper, Elizabeth. The country girl. [*Ed. Foundations*, XXVII: 181 *ff.*]

Cooper, Elizabeth. The education of women in South America. [*Ed. Foundations* (1916–17) XXVIII: 602–5]

Cooper, Elizabeth. The rural mother. [*Ed. Foundations* (1915–16) XXVII: 34 *ff.*]

Cooper, Elizabeth. Woman and education: the country school teacher. [*Ed. Foundations*, XXVI: 347 *ff.*]

Cooper, Elizabeth: Women in British universities. [*Ed. Foundations*, XXVII: 104 *ff.*]

Cooper, Sarah B. The kindergarten in its relation to motherhood. [*N. E. A. Proc.*, 1889: 467–73]

Corbin, Alberta. Method of obtaining legislative appropriation for women's dormitories at Kansas institutions. [*N. E. A. Proc.*, 1922: 728–31]

Cornell University, Education of women at. [*Sch. and Soc.*, VI: 136]

Cornell University, Legislation at, in regard to women. [*Sch. and Soc.*, I: 237–8]

Cornell's fellowship for women. [*Nation* (1886) XLIII: 9]

Cowley, Elizabeth B. A humanized course in mathematics for the first year in a woman's college. [*Education* (1923) XLIV: 92–9]

Crabtree, J. W. Women and the N. E. A. [*Sch. Board Jour.* (Nov. 1911) XLIII: 32]

Cranfell, Helen L. Women's organizations and public education. [*Sch. Jour.*, LXXV: 40]

Crathorne, A. R. Change of mind between high school and college as to life work. [*Sch. and Soc.*, XI: 28–30]

Crosby, A. University education for woman. [*Mass. Teacher* (1861) XIV: 332–8]

Crow, Martha F. Women in German universities. [*Nation* (March 31, 1892) LIV: 247]

Crozier, L. Graham. Woman's clubs and education. [*Ed. Rev.* (1899) XVII: 184–6]

Cruzat, Helen Hulse. The Ursulines of Louisiana. [*Louisiana Hist. Quart.* (Jan. 1919) II: 5–23]

Cunningham, N. J. The advantages of female teachers. [*Pa. Sch. Jour.* (1856) V: 363–4]

Cutler, H. G. Why do women want the ballot? [*Forum* (1915) LIII: 711–25]

Cutten, George B. Reconstruction of democracy. [*Sch. and Soc.*, XVI: 477–89 and 518–9]

Dabney, Charles B. The new education of women. [*N. E. Jour. Ed.*, LXXXV: 8]

D'Alfonso, Nicolo. The problem of women's education. (Trans. by Victoria Champlin) [*Education* (1886) VI: 360–7, 420–8]

Darling, Evelyn. The necessity of education for the working woman. [*Education* (1883) III: 248–54]

Davey, Richard. Woman's life in old Italy. [*L. L. A.* (1891) CXCI: 451–63]

Davis, Caroline. Female education. [*Pa. Sch. Jour.* (1852) I: 431–2]

Davis, Rebecca H., Owen, Catherine, and others. Are women to blame? [*N. A. R.* (1889) CXLVIII: 622–42]

Dealey, H. L. Problems of the college sorority. [*Sch. and Soc.* (Nov. 1916) IV: 735–40]

Dealey, Hermione L. College women and emotional attitudes. [*Education* (1920) XL: 511–19]

Dealey, Hermione L. A comparative study of the curricula of Wellesley, Smith and Vassar Colleges. [*Ped. Sem.*, XXII: 347–76]

Dean of girls in high school. [*Sch. Rev.* (1923) XXXI: 84]

Dean of women, The office of. [*Ed. Rev.* (Jan. 1924) LXVII: 42]

Deans of women's colleges. [*Sch. Jour.*, LXIII: 188–9]

Deans, Resolution of a conference of. [*Sch. and Soc.*, Aug. 23, 1924: 241–2]

Deans, Women school. [*Pittsburgh Sch. Bul.* (May 1913) VI.

Deaton, E. W. The work of a dean of girls and its relation to that of a dean of women. [*N. E. A. Proc.*, 1919: 420]

DeGarmo, Charles. Differentiation in the higher education. [*Ed. Rev.* (1903) XXV: 341–7]

Degree, O why should a woman not get a? [*L. L. A.*, 1869: 578]

Degrees for women at Cambridge. [*Nation* (March 25, 1897) LXIV: 219–20]

Democracy, Western woman's drive on. [*Literary Digest* (1916) LIII: 444–5, and 1315–16]

Devine, E. T. The economic place of woman. [*Jour. A. C. A.*, Jan. 1905: 13–23; also *Teachers College* (N. Y.) *Bul.*, 2d Ser., No. 3, Oct. 8, 1910]

Dial, The, July, 1843.

Dial, Francis N. The possibilities of the dean of women. [*Proc. North Dakota Educational Assoc.* Oct. 30–Nov. 2, 1917: 70–6]

Dick, George S. What a president may rightly expect from a dean of women. [*N. E. A. Proc.*, 1918: 395–7]

Dickson, Virgil. Use of group mental tests in guidance of eighth grade and high school pupils. [*Jour. Ed. Research*, II: 601–10]

Dike, Samuel W. Sociology in the higher education of women. [*At. Mo.* (1892) LXX: 668–76]

District School Journal of the State of New York, 1840–49. 10 vols.

Educational Administration and Supervision, 1915–27. Vols. I–XIII. Baltimore.

Educational Foundations, 1896–1920. Vols. VIII–XXXI. New York.

Educational Journal of Virginia, The. 1870–91. 22 vols. Richmond.

Educational News, 1890–99. Vols. VI–XV. Philadelphia, Pa. and Newark, Del.

Educational Record, 1920–27. Vols. I–IX. Washington.

Educational Review, 1891–1928. 76 vols.

Educator, Woman as an. [*Ed. Jour. Va.* (July 1884) XV: 277–80]

Educators, Women as. [*N. E. Jour. Ed.* (1887) XXVI: 296–7]

Eggleston, George C. The education of women. [*Harper's N. M. Mag.* (1883) LXVII: 292–6]

Eliot, Charles W. Summary of his report for 1902–3, containing references to Radcliffe College. [*Harvard Grad. Mag.* (1903–4) XII: 417–28]

Eliot, Charles W. Wise and unwise economy in schools. [*N. E. Jour. Ed.,* I: 253–5]

Eliot, Charles W. Woman's education—a forecast. [*Jour. A. C. A.,* Feb. 1908: 101–5]

Eliot, Charles W. Educational reform and the social order. [*Sch. Rev.* (April 1909) XVII: 217–22]

Eliot, Charles W. Woman's work and woman's wages. [*N. A. R.,* CXXXV: 146–61]

Eliot, President, at Smith College. [*N. E. Jour. Ed.* (1879) X: 149]

Ellis, (Mrs.) Don Carlos. The Southern Association of College Women. [*N. E. A. Proc.,* 1915: 1109–11]

Emerick, Charles F. College women and race suicide. [*Polit. Sci. Quart.* (June 1909) XXIV: 269–83]

Emerick, Charles F. Is the diminishing birth-rate volitional? [*Pop. Sci. Mo.* (1911) LXXVIII: 71–80]

Emerson, George B., on the education of females. [*Am. Inst. of Instruction* (1832) II: 15–43]

Emmons, Elizabeth S. Sowing in the public schools. [*N. E. Jour. Ed.,* I: 158]

Engelmann, George J. Education not the cause of race decline. [*Pop. Sci. Mo.* (1903) LXIII: 172–84]

England, Female education in. [*Barnard's Jour.,* XXXI: 375–84]

English woman at school, The. [*L. L. A.* (1878) CXXXVIII: 451–67]

Evans, Margaret J. Women's clubs as an educational factor. [*N. E. A. Proc.,* 1898: 237–43]

Everal, Amy S. The girl delinquent. [*Jour. N. E. A.,* April 1917: 841–5]

Everett, Edward: Female education. [*Barnard's Jour.,* IX: 635–6]

Examinations, external, The influence upon girls' schools of (at the University of Cambridge). [*London Student* (1876) CXXI: 245–8]

Exercise for girls. [*N. Y. Teacher,* June 1858: 394]

Fairchild, J. H. Coeducation of the sexes. [*R. C. E.,* 1867–8; 385–400]

Fairman, M. C. A word for the girls. [*N. E. Jour. Ed.,* I: 159]

Family affections, Decay of the. [*Nation* (1869) VIII: 291–2]

Fawcett, Millicent G. University education for women in England. [*N. E. A. Proc.,* 1893: 853–62]

Fawcett, Millicent G. The use of higher education to women. [*L. L. A.* (1886) CLXXI: 729–34]

Fawcett, Millicent G. Woman in English politics. [*Forum* (Dec. 1892) XIV: 453–64)

Fawcett, Millicent G. Woman's work in war time. [*Contemporary Review* (1914) CVI: 775–82]

Felter, William L. The education of women. [*Ed. Rev.* (1906) XXXI: 351–63]

Female character, Excellence and influence of. A sermon preached at the request of the New York Female Missionary Society, 1825. [*Atlantic Mag.*, II: 348–59]

Female education. By Humanitas. [*Pa. Sch. Jour.* (1866) XV: 111–13]

Female education, An essay on (the report of a committee of the Pittsburg Teachers Assoc.). [*Pa. Sch. Jour.* (1852) I: 250–2]

Female education, Dialogue on. [*Southern Lady's Companion*, Oct. 1847: 160 *ff.*]

Female education in the state of Ohio (1862). [*Barnard's Jour.*, XIII: 267–8]

Female education, Policy of elevating the standard of. [*Am. Annals Ed.*, 1834: 361–4]

Female education, Suggestions on, by German authors. [*Barnard's Jour.*, XIII: 495–502]

Female education and employments, Thoughts on. [*Barnard's Jour.*, XVII: 623–40]

Female school visitors. By Humanitas. [*Pa. Sch. Jour.* (1868) XVII: 17–18, 105–6]

Female sex, Education of the. [*Barnard's Jour.*, XIII: 232–42]

Female suffrage: a letter to the Christian women of America. [*Harper's N. M. Mag.* (1870) XLI: 438–46, and 594–600]

Female teachers. [*N. E. Jour. Ed.*, I: 302, 303–4; also II: 40]

Female teachers. [*Pa. Sch. Jour.*, I: 274–5]

Female teachers in common schools. [*N. Y. Teacher*, Apr. 1859: 298–300]

Fennimore, B. A. Resolution regarding deans. [*Nat. Assoc. Sec. Sch. Princs.* (1921) V: 69]

Fernald, Woodbury M. The working girls. [*L. L. A.* (1863) LXXIX: 482]

Fernow, Olivia R. Does higher education unfit women for motherhood? [*Pop. Sci. Mo.* (1904–05) LXVI: 573–5]

Ferris, Helen J. (Ed.). The new world and the college woman. [*Bookman* (Feb. 1916) XLII: 678–91; (March, April, May 1916) XLIII: 63–74, 183–93, 286–97]

Finck, Henry T. Why coeducation is losing ground. [*Independent* (Feb. 5, 1903) LV: 301 *ff.*; (Feb. 12, 1903) LV: 361 *ff.*]

Findley, W. T. Woman as an educator. [*N. Y. Teacher* (1860) N. S. I: 490–3]

Fisher, H. A. L. Comments on American education. [*Sch. and Soc.* (1925) XXI: 101–2]

Fitz, Rachel K. The college woman graduate. [*Education* (1907) XXVII: 601–11]

Fliedner's Institution at Kaiserswerth, on the Rhine. [*Barnard's Jour.*, III: 487–95]

Force, Anna L. The status of the American woman teacher. [*N. E. A. Proc.*, 1923: 543–4]

Ford, H. A. A quarter century of education in Michigan. [*Michigan Pioneer and Hist. Soc. Collections*, IX: 92–9]

Foreign universities, Women in. [*L. L. A.* (1897) CCXIV: 83–5]

Forum, The, 1886–1927. Vols. I–LXXVIII: New York.

Foster, J. Ellen. Woman's political evolution. [*N. A. R.* (1897) CLXV: 600–9]

Foster, W. T. Agencies, methods, materials and ideals of sex education. [*Sch. Rev.*, XXII: 256–61]

Fowler, Henry. Educational services of Mrs. Emma Willard. [*Barnard's Jour.*, VI: 125–68]

Frank, Glenn. An experiment in education. [*Wisconsin Alumni Mag.*, Dec. 1926; Jan. 1927]

Frank, Louis. University opportunities for women. [*Ed. Rev.* (1894) VIII: 471 *ff.*]

Franklin, Fabian. The intellectual powers of women. [*N. A. R.* (1895) CLX: 40–53]

Franklin, Lucy Jenkins. The dean of women. [*Jour. Ed.* (Jan. 8, 1925) CI: 43–4]

Fraternity women. [*Century Mag.* (Dec. 1913) LXV: 289–90]

Freeman, Mary L. Vassar College. [*Education* (1887) VIII: 73–84]

French, F. G. School suffrage for women in states and territories; compilation from latest school laws. [*Woman's Jour.*, Feb. 15, 1890: 50–1]

Fretwell, E. K. The adviser of girls. [*Ed. Adm. and Sup.*, X: 71–8]

Freyer, Douglas. Occupational intelligence standards. [*Sch. and Soc.* (Sept. 1922) XVI: 273–6]

Fryatt, F. E. The New York Cooking School. [*Harper's N. M. Mag.* (1879–80) LX: 22–9]

Fuller, Margaret, in a new aspect. [*At. Mo.* (1896) LXXVIII: 550–2]

Furst, Clyde. Progress at the women's colleges. [*Ed. Rev.* (1908) XXXVI: 85–91]

Gage, Kitty M. Bryn Mawr College for Women. [*Education* (1886) VII: 25–33]

Gage, Matilda J. Woman as an inventor. [*N. A. R.*, CXXXVI: 478–89]

Galloway, C. B. Elizabeth Female Academy—the mother of female colleges. [*Publications of the Mississippi Hist. Soc.*, II: 169–78]

Garber, John P. Coeducation. [*Education* (1902) XXIII: 235–41]

Gardner, George E. College women and matrimony. [*Education* (1900) XX: 285–91]

Gates, Florence A. Some health conditions of our high school girls. [*Ped. Sem.* (1919) XXVI: 153–61]

Gayler, G. W. Dean of girls in high schools. [*Ed. Adm. and Sup.* (October 1917) III: 496–8]

Geary, Blanche. Considerations governing the preparation of floor plans for women's dormitories. [*N. E. A. Proc.*, 1922: 717–21]

Gennings, Martha G. A unique position in the high school. [*Utah Ed. Rev. Manual*, 1914]

German universities, Women at. [*Notes and News—Ed. Rev.* (1917) XLI: 318–21]

German universities, Women at the. [*Ed. Rev.* (1905) XXIX: 102–6]

Germany, Women students and women teachers in. [*Nation* (Sept. 27, 1894) LIX: 232–3]

Gethmann, C. W. Significance of the work of a real dean of women to the high school principal. [*Nat. Assoc. Sec. Sch. Princs. 7th Yearbook,* 1923: 110]

Gildersleeve, Virginia. Student life at Barnard. [*Columbia Univ. Quart.,* March, 1910: 181–94]

Gildersleeve, Virginia. Present dangers in the education of women. [*T. C. Record,* Nov. 1928: 122–5]

Gildersleeve, Virginia, Park, Marion E., *et al.* The question of the women's colleges. [*At. Mo.,* Nov. 1927: 577–84]

Gill, Laura D. Scope of the department of women's organizations. [*N. E. A. Proc.,* 1909: 70–5]

Gilliam, Bertha B. The education of women. [*Education* (1919) XL: 74–7]

Gilman, Arthur. In the beginning. [*Radcliffe Mag.,* June, 1905]

Girl-adviser plan for high schools, Studying. [*Sch. Life* (Oct. 15, 1919) III: 3–4]

Girl operatives' strike at Lowell. [*N. E. Mag.* (Feb. 1890) N.S. I: 111–12]

Girls again, The. [*N. E. Jour. Ed.,* I: 207]

Girls, The proper education of. [*Nation* (1897) LXIV: 47–8]

Girls' rights. By J. W. B. [*N. Y. Teacher* (1860) N. S. I: 266–8]

Girls' school wanted, A. [*Nation* (1878) XXVII: 55, 83, 97, 145, and 194]

Godey's Lady's Book, 1842–70. Philadelphia.

Goodale, (Mrs.) D. H. R. Mothers as educators. [*Education* (1883) III: 483–7, 630–5]

Goodrich, A. L. Women in education. [*N. E. Jour. Ed.* (1890) XXXII: 100–1]

Goodsell, Willystine. Some effects of the war on the higher education of women. [*N. E. A. Proc.,* 1919: 407–12]

Gordon, (Mrs.) J. E. H. The after careers of university-educated women. [*Nineteenth Century* (June, 1895) XXXVII: 955–60]

Gordon, Kate. Wherein should the education of a woman differ from that of a man? [*Sch. Rev.,* XIII: 789–94]

Goucher, John F. The advisable differences between the education of young women and that of young men. [*Sch. Rev.,* VII: 577–99]

Gould, Elizabeth P. The woman problem. [*Education* (1891) XII: 73–6]

Gove, Aaron. Coeducation in high schools. [*N. E. A. Proc.,* 1893: 297–300]

Grand, Sarah. The new aspect of the woman question. [*N. A. R.* (1894) CLVIII: 270–6]

Greene, Rebecca D. Organization of a high school deanship. [*Sierra Ed. News* (April, 1922) XVIII: 197]

Greenwood, Grace. How to obtain money for dormitories by private gifts. [*N. E. A. Proc.,* 1922: 731–2]

Grenfell, Helen L. The influence of women's organizations on public education. [*N. E. A. Proc.*, 1907: 125–34]

Griffin, C. S. Woman in Mohammedanism. [*Ed. Foundations* (1905–6) XVII: 136 *ff.*]

Griffin, C. S. The women of Homer. [*Ed. Foundations* (1904–5) XVI: 93–9; see also 218, 287, 593, and 733]

Grote, Caroline. Regulation of extra curricular activities. [*N. E. A. Proc.*, 1922: 752–8]

Guides for women. [*Nation* (1886) XLIII: 247–8]

Hadley, Arthur T. Admission of women as graduate students at Yale. [*Ed. Rev.* (May 1892) III: 486–9]

Hailmann, Eudora L. The principles and methods of educating our girls for parenthood. [*N. E. A. Proc.*, 1889: 455–67]

Hall, G. Stanley. American universities and the training of teachers. [*Forum* (1894) XVII: 148–59]

Hall, G. Stanley. Coeducation. [*N. E. A. Proc.*, 1904: 538–42]

Hall, G. Stanley. Coeducation. [*Sch. Jour.*, LXIX: 71]

Hall, G. Stanley. Coeducation in the high school. [*N. E. A. Proc.*, 1893: 446–60]

Hall, G. Stanley. The training of teachers. [*Forum* (1890–1) X: 11–22]

Hall, G. Stanley, and Smith, Theodate L. Marriage and fecundity of college men and women. [*Ped. Sem.*, X: 275–314]

Halladay, Alexander Q. Social conditions in Colonial North Carolina. [*N. C. Booklet* (Feb. 1904) III: No. 10]

Hamann, Albert. The higher education of women in Prussia. [*Ed. Rev.* (1908) XXXVI: 433–41]

Hamilton, Anna J. What kind of education is best suited for girls? [*N. E. A. Proc.*, 1900, 65–72]

Hamilton, F. W. Coeducation. [*N. E. Jour. Ed.* (1907) LXVI: 485–6]

Hamilton, Gail. A call to my countrywomen. [*At. Mo.* (1863) XI: 345–9]

Hamilton, W. T. The importance of the education of woman. [*Pa. Sch. Jour.* (1862) XI: 46–9, 117–23]

Hamman, Anne B. Professor Beyer and the woman question. [*Ed. Rev.* (1914) XLVII: 295–8]

Hammond, William A. Woman in politics. [*N. A. R.* (1883) CXXXVII: 137–46]

Hammond's estimate of woman, a criticism by Mrs. Blake and others. [*N. A. R.*, CXXXVII, 495–519]

Hancock, John. Coeducation of the sexes. [*N. E. A. Proc.*, 1890: 338–43]

Hancock, John A. Mental depression in young women and children. [*Ped. Sem.* (1907) XIV: 460–8]

Hanscom, Elizabeth D. The ethical purpose of a woman's college. [*Ed. Rev.* (1901) XXII: 307–12]

Hardaker, M. A. The ethics of sex. [*N. A. R.* (1880) CXXXI: 62–74]

Harkness, Mary L. The education of the girl. [*At. Mo.*, March 1914: 324–30]

Harland, Marion. The incapacity of business women. [*N. A. R.* (1889) CXLIX: 707–12]

Harland, Marion. Women as human beings. [*N. A. R.* (1892) CLIV: 758–60]

Harper, Ida H. Changing conditions of marriage. [*Independent* (Dec. 6, 1906) LXI: 1329–32]

Harper, William R., on coeducation. [*Sch. Jour.*, LXIV: 68]

Harper's New Monthly Magazine, 1850–1900. 100 vols. New York.

Harris, W. T. Chairs of pedagogics in colleges. [*Proc. Nat. Council of Ed.*, 1882]

Harris, W. T. Coeducation. [*Ed. Foundations* (1908–9) XX: 111 *ff.*]

Harris, W. T. Ought young girls to read the daily newspapers? [*N. E. A. Proc.*, 1888: 86–9]

Harrison, Frederic. The emancipation of woman. [*Fortnightly Rev.*, N. S. (1891) L: 437–52]

Hart, Sophie C. Relation of college experience to present social demand. [*Jour. A. C. A.* (Dec. 1908) Series III, No. 18]

Harvard Annex and the University, The. [*Nation* (1893) LVI: 28–9]

Harvard Annex, The appeal of the. [*Century Mag.* (Sept. 1884) XXVIII: 791–2]

Harvard examinations for women. [*L. L. A.* (1876) CXXXI: 248–9]

Harvard Graduate Magazine, 1892–1927. Vols. I–XXXV. Boston.

Harvard Graduate School of Education, Women in the. [*Sch. and Soc.*, XII: 348–9]

Harvey, G. The war and the woman. [*N. A. R.* (1915) CCI: 344–7]

Harvey, L. D. The education of girls. [*N. E. A. Proc.*, 1912: 425–30]

Harwood, W. S. Constitutional suffrage for women. [*N. A. R.* (1896) CLXII: 632–4]

Haworth, Mary V. A dean of high school girls. [*Sierra Ed. News* (April 1922) XVIII: 195]

Hayes, Alice. Can a poor girl go to college? [*N. A. R.* (1891) CLII: 624–31]

Hayes, H. The social life of the high school and some of its problems. [*N. E. A. Proc.*, 1923: 873]

Health of American women, The. [*Nation* (1885) XLI: 295–6]

Hedges, Anna C. Woman's work in industrial education. [*Bul. Nat. Soc. for the Promotion of Industrial Education*, No. 9, 1909: 116–22]

Henrotin, Ellen M. The cooperation of woman's clubs in the public schools. [*N. E. A. Proc.*, 1897: 73–83]

Herrick, J. R. A fair chance for girls; or a word for American women. [*N. E. Jour. Ed.*, I: 133–5]

Hershberger, G. B. Coeducation in medicine. [*Ed. News*, Nov. 12, 1892: 643–4]

Hettenbaugh, J. Female education. [*Pa. Sch. Jour.* (1859) VIII: 25–28]

Hewitt, Florence H. The woman peril in American education. [*Ed. Rev.* (1914) XLVII: 411–15]

Higginson, Thomas W. The American girl graduate. [*Critic* (Dec. 4, 1886) N. S. VI: 273–5]

Higginson, Thomas W. Coeducation. [*Ed. News,* June 14, 1890: 373]

Higginson, Thomas W. Justice to women teachers. [*N. E. Jour. Ed.* (1876) IV: 229]

Higginson, Thomas W. Ought women to learn the alphabet? [*At. Mo.* (1859) III, 137–50]

Higher education of women. [*Pa. Sch. Jour.* (1874) XXII: 265–6]

Higher education of women, The. [*Sch. and Soc.,* XVI: 303]

Higher education of women and the Harvard examinations. [*Penn Monthly,* Feb. 1878]

Higher education of women in Germany. [*Ed. News,* Nov. 28, 1896: 647]

Higher education of women in Germany. [*Nation* (Nov. 28, 1889) LXIX: 426–7; and (Dec. 5, 1889) LXIX: 446–7]

Hilham [Tenn.] and Fisk Female Academies. [*Am. Hist. Mag.,* II: 17 *f.*; III: 94] Peabody Normal College: Nashville, 1898.

Hilliard, Caroline E. Smith College. [*Education* (Sept. 1887) VIII: 12–18]

Hodgkins, Louise M. The higher education of women in 1912. [*Education* (1913) XXXIII: 610–15]

Hodgson, Elizabeth. Equal salaries for men and women teachers. [*Education* (1915) XXXV: 571–7]

Hollingworth, Leta S. Variability as related to sex difference in achievement. [*Am. Jour. Soc.* (Jan. 1914) XIX: 510–30]

Home Monthly, The. Vol. III, No. 2. Nashville, Tenn., 1867.

Hopkins, Henry. The power of personality as illustrated in Mary Lyon, the teacher saint. [*Ed. Foundations* (1905–6) XVII: 3 *ff.*]

Hopkins, Louisa P. Coeducation of the sexes in Boston public schools. [*Ed. Rev.* (1891) I: 46–8]

Hopkins, Louisa P. Woman's work in education. [*N. E. A. Proc.,* 1884: 157–60]

Horn, John L. College women as elementary school teachers. [*Ed. Adm. and Sup.,* X: 142–6]

Hosmer, J. K. Coeducation of the sexes in universities. [*N. E. A. Proc.,* 1874: 118–33]

Howard, Clare M. Opportunities for women in journalism. [*Columbia Univ. Quart.,* June 1915: 233–5]

Howe, Elizabeth M. The Southern girl: a neglected asset. [*Ed. Rev.* (March 1907) XXXIII: 287 *f.*]

Howe, Julia W. The education of women. [*Ed. News,* June 28, 1890: 405–6]

Howe, Julia W. The industrial nature of woman. [*N. A. R.,* CXXXVI: 433–46]

Howe, Julia W., Higginson, T. W., Stone, Lucy, Stanton, E. C., and Phillips, W. The other side of the woman question. [*N. A. R.* (1879) CXXIX: 413–46]

Hughes, Helen S. Can women make good? [*Sch. and Soc.,* II: 336–44]

Huling, Ray Green. College women and physical education. [*Ed. Rev.* (1894) VII: 78–80]

Hutchinson, Emilie J.   The vocational interests of college women.   [*Columbia Univ. Quart.*, June 1915: 227–32]

Hyatt, Alpheus.   The influence of woman in the evolution of the human race.   [*Natural Sci.*, August 1897]

Hyde, William D.   A letter to women who teach.   [*Intelligence*, Feb. 1, 1905: 86]

Hyre, Sarah E.   Woman's part in public school education.   [*N. E. A. Proc.*, 1906: 51–8]

Independent, The, 1848–1927.   Vol. I–CXIX.   New York and Boston.

Industrial schools for women.   [*Harper's N. M. Mag.* (1870) XL: 885–91]

Intellect of women, The.   [*L. L. A.* (1860) LXIV: 184]

Intellect, The approaching extinction of.   [*Independent* (Feb. 1903) LV: 458–9]

Intellectual men and women.   [*Nation* (1886) XLIII: 135]

Intellectual woman, Why not make her an?   [*Nation* (1886) XLIII: 75]

Intellectual women, The.   [*Nation* (1886) XLIII: 96]

Intellectuality among women.   [*N. Y. Teacher*, Aug. 1859: 489–91]

Intelligence, The: A Journal of Education, 1897–1900.   Vols. XVII–XXV.   Chicago.

Inventors, Women as.   [*Ed. News*, 1899: 246]

Iveson, A. M.   Woman.   [*Pa. Sch. Jour.* (1862) XI: 126 *ff*.]

Jacobi, Mary P.   The higher education of women.   [*Medical News*, LVI: 75]

Jacobi, Mary P.   Shall women practice medicine?   [*N. A. R.*, CXXXIV: 52–75]

Jacobs, Ella.   Woman on the platform.   [*Ed. News*, Feb. 27, 1897: 132–3]

Jacobus, Charles.   Women and men vs. men and women.   [*N. E. Jour. Ed.* (1890) XXXI: 84]

James, H. M.   Report of the committee on [technical] education of girls.   [*N. E. A. Proc.*, 1886: 296–304]

James, H. M.   Men and women as teachers.   [*Ed. News*, August 1, 1891: 452–3]

James, Henry, on marriage.   [*Nation* (1870) X: 366–8]

Jenkins, Mabel I.   Origin of the Woman's National Council of Education.   [*Ed. Foundations* (1909–10) XXI: 579 *ff*.]

Jennings, Elma F.   The work of deans of girls.   [*Ohio Ed. Mo.* (Oct. 1921) LXX: 238–43]

Jennings, Martha B.   A unique position in the high school.   [*Utah Ed. Rev.* (March 1913) VI: 16–17]

Jernegan, M. W.   Beginnings of education in New England.   [*Sch. Rev.* (1915) XXIII: 319–30, and 361–80]

Jernegan, M. W.   Compulsory education in the American colonies.   [*Sch. Rev.*, XXVI: 731–49; XXVII: 24–43]

Jesse, R. H.   Coeducation as it has been tested in state universities.   [*N. E. A. Proc.*, 1904: 542–7]

Jesse, R. H.   The position of household economics in the academic curriculum.   [*Jour. A. C. A.*, Jan. 1905: 24–9]

Johns Hopkins, Women at.   [*Nation* (1891) LII: 71 and 114]

Johnson, Alice.   Some problems for a preceptress to solve.   [*Idaho Teacher* Jan. 1921) II: 234–7]

Johnson, Lilian W.   The higher education of women in the Southern states.   [*Proc. 11th Conference for Education in the South,* 1907: 130–9]

Johnson, Roswell H., and Stutzmann, Bertha.   Wellesley's birth-rate.   [*Jour. Hered.,* June 1915: 250–3]

Jones, Katherine I.   The dean's office a friendly center.   [*Sierra Ed. News* (April 1922) XVIII: 194]

Jordan, David S.   Educating girls.   [*R. C. E.* (1894–5) II: 1280 *ff.*]

Jordan, David S.   The higher education of women.   [*Pop. Sci. Mo.,* Dec. 1902: 97–107]

Jordan, David S.   Question of coeducation.   [*Munsey's Mag.* (1905–06) XXXIV: 683–8]

Jordan, Mary A.   Home and student government.   [*Phila. Inquirer,* Dec. 8, 1926]

Jordan, Mary A.   The college for women.   [*At. Mo.* 1892) LXX: 540–6]

Jordan, Mary A.   The heads of some women's colleges.   [*Outlook* (Aug. 2, 1902) LXXI: 829–33]

Jour. A. C. A.: Journal of the Assoc. of Collegiate Alumnae.

Journal of Education (Formerly *New England Journal of Education*), 1875–1926.   104 vols.   Boston.

Journal of Educational Research, 1920–26.   14 vols.   Bloomington, Ill.

Journal of Heredity (To 1914, the *American Breeders' Magazine*), 1910–1927.   Vols. I–XVIII.   Washington.

Journal of the National Education Association, The, 1916–27.   16 vols.   Washington.

Journal of Pedagogy, The, 1898–1907.   Vols. XI–XIX.   Syracuse, N. Y.

Journalism as a profession for women.   [*Contemporary Rev.* (Sept. 1893) LXIV: 362]

Kahn, Ruth W.   Female education.   [*Education* (1891) XII: 20–6]

Kasson, Frank H.   Mary Lyon.   [*Ed. Foundations* (1910–11) XXII: 591 *ff.*]

Keech, Mabel L.   Housekeeping as a public school study.   [*Education* (1914) XXXV: 164–6]

Kelley, M. D. J.   Women and the labor movement.   [*N. A. R.* (1895) CLX: 408–17]

Kelly, Agnes, on women's colleges in England.   [*Ed. Rev.* (1904) XXVII: 395–405]

Kelly, Florence.   The eight hour day and rest at night.   [*Ed. Foundations* (1916–17) XXVIII: 414 *ff.*]

Kennedy, James S.   Identical education and coeducation.   [*N. E. Jour. Ed.,* II: 63]

Kerr, Mina.   The college community life as an opportunity for socialization.   [*N. E. A. Proc.,* 1918: 402–4]

Kiely, M.   The significance of the dean to the high school girl.   [*Nat. Assoc. High Sch. Princs., 7th Yearbook*, 1923: 115]

Kimball, Ruth L.   Report of the dean of girls, San Jose High School.   [*Western Jour. Ed.* (May 1914) XX: 9]

Kincaid, Jean.   Wellesley College.   [*Education* (Jan. 1887) VII: 305–16]

King, Lida S.   The Women's College in Brown University.   [*Education* (1907) XXVII: 478–83]

King, (Mrs.) S. Noble.   Domestic science—a report.   [*Intelligence,* Jan. 1904: 830 *ff.*]

Kingsbury, John, and the Young Ladies' High School of Providence, R. I.   [*Barnard's Jour.,* V: 9–34]

Kingsbury, Susan.   The economic efficiency of college women.   [*Jour. A. C. A.,* 1909: 19–30]

Kingsland, Gertrude S.   Extra-curricular activities . . . importance . . . position?   [*N. E. A. Proc.,* 1922: 778–83]

Kinnear, M. Elizabeth.   Qualifications of the dean of girls.   [*Sierra Ed. News* (April 1922) XVIII: 197]

Kirchwey, Freda.   Too many college girls?   [*Nation*, May 27, 1925, 597–8]

Kitson, Harry D.   Progress and coördination in vocational guidance.   [*Bul., Nat. Voc. Guid. Assoc.* (1923), I, No. 8: 123–4]

Kitson, Harry D.   Relation between age and promotion of university professors.   [*Sch. and Soc.,* Sept. 25, 1926]

Klemm, L. R.   Women students in German universities.   [*Ed. Foundations* (1905–6) XVII: 232]

Knight, Edgar W.   Some fallacies concerning the history of public education in the South.   [*South Atlantic Quart.* (Oct. 1914) XIII: 371–81]

Knight, M. M.   One reason why our college students do not have world vision.   [*Sch. and Soc.,* VI: 285–8]

L. L. A: *Littell's Living Age.*

Ladd, Jessie S.   Recreation and the university mixer.   [*N. E. A. Proc.,* 1922: 732–7]

Ladies and lady teachers.   [*Pa. Sch. Jour.,* I: 26–7]

Ladies' Companion, 1835 and 1836.   New York.

Ladies' Magazine, 1819.   Savannah, 1819.

Ladies' Repository, The, 1841, 1845, 1847, 1848, and 1849.   Cincinnati.

Ladies' Wreath, The, 1847–50.   Vols. I–III.   New York.

Lambert, Lillian V.   Oxford as an educational center for women.   [*Education* (1908) XXVIII: 632–8]

Lander, E. T.   University examinations for women.   [*Education* (1880) I: 48–62]

Lange, A. F.   The problem of professional training for women.   [*Sch. and Soc.* (April 1916) III: 480–5]

Lansing, M. F.   Seventy-five years of higher education for women.   [*Outlook* (Oct. 19, 1912) CII: 363; (Jan. 11, 1913) CIII: 96]

Larcom, Lucy.   Among Lowell mill-girls: a reminiscence.   [*At. Mo.* (1881) XLVIII: 593–612]

Laurvik, John N.   American girl out-of-doors.   [*Woman's Home Companion* (1912) XXXIX: 17–18]

Lawton, William C. Womanhood in the *Iliad*. [*At. Mo.* (1893) LXXI: 784–801]

Lazarus, Josephine. Higher education: a word to women. [*Century Mag.* (Dec. 1890) XLI: 315–16]

Leach, Abby. Hindrances to the intellectual life in college. [*Jour. A. C. A.*, Feb. 1908: 76–83]

Leach, Abby. The ideal curriculum for a woman's college. [*Jour. A. C. A.*, Dec. 1898: 16–21]

Leahy, E. M. Some aims in the education of girls. [*Ed. Foundations* (1911–12) XXIII: 270 *ff.*]

LeBon, Gustave. The education of women and its effects. [*Ed. Rev.* (1891) I: 101–3]

Leigh, Mildred B. Vocational guidance for college women. [*Ed. Rev.* (1921) LXII: 34–45]

Leipzig, Women at. [*Nation* (Oct. 4, 1894) LIX: 247–8]

Leland, Abby P. Scouting education for girls. [*Jour. N. E. A.*, June 1918: 756–60]

Lester, Lucy. New title and old task. [*Jour. N. E. A.* (Dec. 1924) XIII: 326]

Letters, Woman's place in the world of. [*L. L. A.* (1897) CCXIV: 300–7]

Lewis, C. T. An "every girl" supper. [*Sch. Rev.*, Feb. 1924: 134]

Lewis, Charles H. Physical defects of school girls. [*Sch. Jour.*, LV: 390–2]

Lewis, Dio, Stanton, E. C., and Chadwick, James R. The health of American women. [*N. A. R.* (1862) CXXXV: 503–24]

Lichtenberger, James P. The instability of the family. [*Annals of the American Academy of Political and Social Science* (1909) XXXIV: 97–105]

Lighter, Thomas. The pretty woman in the school room. [*Ed. Foundations* (1910–11) XXII: 600 *ff.*]

Linton, (Mrs.) E. Lynn. The higher education of women. [*Pop. Sci. Mo.* (Dec. 1886) XXX: 168–80; also *Fortnightly Rev.*, Oct. 1886: 498–510]

Literary work, No sex distinction in. [*Ed. News*, March 18, 1899: 83–4]

Littell's Living Age, 1844–1924. 323 vols. Boston.

Livermore, Mary A. Cooperative womanhood in the state. [*N. A. R.* (1891) CLIII: 283–95]

Livermore, Mary A. Woman Suffrage. [*N. A. R.* (1886) CXLIII: 371–81]

Livermore, Mary A., and others. Women's view of divorce. [*N. A. R.* (1890) CL: 110–35]

Lloyd, Alice. Education for Southern women. [*Proc. 10th Conference for Education in the South*, 1907: 220–8]

Lockwood, Laura E. College women as wives and mothers. [*Sch. and Soc.* (March 4, 1916) III: 332–8]

Louisiana State University, Plan for. [*DeBow's Review*, III: 311 *ff.*; also IV: 414]

Loyal ladies of the land, To the. [*L. L. A.* (1864) LXXXI: 140–1]

Lumry, O. F. Identical education and coeducation. [*N. E. Jour. Ed.* (1875) II: 81]

Lumsden, Louisa I. On the higher education of women, in Great Britain and Ireland. [*Jour. Soc. Sci.* (1885) XX: 49–60]

Lyon, Mary, and Mount Holyoke Female Seminary. [*Barnard's Jour.*, X: 649 *ff.*; and 670 *ff.*]

Mackintosh, May. An ideal education for girls. [*Education* (1886) VI: 647–51]

Mackintosh, May. Women as professional teachers. [*Education* (1887) VII: 556–8]

MacLean, George E. Women's colleges in Great Britain. [*Sch. and Soc.*, VII: 37–43]

Macvay, Anna P. Cooperation between school and college in character formation. [*N. E. A. Proc.*, 1918: 414–17]

Magill, Edward H. Coeducation of the sexes. *Pa. Sch. Jour.* (1872) XXI: 101–4]

Magill, Edward H. Coeducation of the sexes. [*Pa. Sch. Jour.* (1874) XXIII: 80–4]

Mann, Horace. The female teacher. [*N. Y. Teacher* (1859) N. S. I: 157–8]

Mann, Kristine. Hygiene in the woman's college. [*Ed. Rev.* (1921) LXII: 45–54]

Marbury, Elizabeth. Education of woman. [*Education* (1887) VIII: 235–9]

Marks, Jeannette. The American college girl's ignorance of literature. [*Critic*, Oct. 1905]

Marriages of women college graduates. [*Nation* (1890) L: 330–1]

Marshall, Florence M. How to conduct a trade school for girls. [*Bul. Nat. Soc. for the Promotion of Industrial Education*, No. 9, 1909: 90–100]

Martin, George H. The early education of girls in Massachusetts. [*Education* (1900) XX: 323–7]

Martin, Gertrude S. The education of women and sex quality. [*Proc. American Academy of Political Sci.* (1914) LVI, 38–46]

Martin, Gertrude S. Position of the dean of women. [*Jour. A. C. A.* (March 1911) Series IV: 65–78]

Marshall College. [*Collections and Researches, Michigan Pioneer and Hist. Soc.*, XXX: 528–9]

Marvel, L. H. How does college life affect the health of women? [*Education* (1883) III: 501–11]

Maryland Historical Magazine, 1906–26. 21 vols. Baltimore.

Massachusetts, Female education in, after the Revolution. [*Barnard's Jour.*, XXX: 581–604]

Mathews, Lois K. Training women for social responsibility. [*N. E. A. Proc.*, 1914: 40–5]

May, Julia H. Mount Holyoke College. [*Education* (1888) VIII: 477–88]

Mayo, A. D. Woman as teacher. [*N. Y. Teacher*, Apr. 1857: 308 *ff.*]

McAndrew, William. Aids to girl study. [*Ed. Foundations* (1903–04) XV: 589–93]

McAndrew, William. Women school teachers. [*N. E. Jour. Ed.*, LXV: 340–1; and 372–3]

McCarron, Anna T. Trial of Prudence Crandall for crime of educating Negroes in Connecticut. [*Connecticut Mag.* (1908) XII: 225–32]

McClure's Magazine (1911). Vol. XXXVIII.

McCurdy, Persis H. The history of physical training at Mt. Holyoke College. [*Am. Phys. Ed. Rev.*, March, 1909: 138–50]

McDonald, Jeannette. The needs of high school girls and how these needs are met by a dean of girls. [*N. E. A. Proc.*, 1924: 520 *ff.*]

McDougall, H. R. Vocational guidance in high school. [*Industrial Arts Mag.* (April 1922) XI: 133–5]

McFarland, H. H. What are they doing at Vassar? [*Scribner's Mag.* (Aug. 1871) II: 337–53]

McGlauflin, Isabelle. Vocational training for girls. [*Education* (1911) XXXI: 523–6]

McIlquham, Harriett. Of women in assemblies. [*L. L. A.* (1896) CCXI: 577–88]

McKeag, Anna J. The department of education in colleges for women. [*Ped. Sem.* (1910) XVII: 70–3]

McKeen, Catharine. Mental education of woman. [*Barnard's Jour.*, I: 567–78]

McLean, Kathryn S. Effect of war on the education of women. [*N. E. A. Proc.*, 1919: 214–17]

McLean, Kathryn S. The place of the educational institution for women. [*Jour. N. E. A.*, May, 1918: 687–90]

McMurray, Frank M. Crticism of women's colleges. [*Am. Ed. Rev.*, XXXIV: 447–8]

McNaught, Margaret S. The enfranchised woman teacher: her opportunity. [*N. E. A. Proc.*, 1917: 244–9]

McVea, Emilie W. The effect of recent educational developments upon the higher education of women. [*Education* (1915) XXXVI: 11–19]

McVea, Emilie W. The present curricula of colleges for women. [*Sch. and Soc.* (Sept. 25, 1920) XII: 241–5]

Mearkle, A. L., and White, M. A. Higher education of women—education and marriage and women in journalism. [*Arena* (June 1900) XXIII: 661–72]

Medical and Surgical Journal, Dec. 1837. Boston.

Medical education of women, Public demands and the. By C. B. [*Nation*, March 20, 1890: 237–8]

Medicine, Women in. [*Nation* (1891) LII: 131]

Meiklejohn, Alexander. A new college. . . . [*Century Mag.*, January, 1925, 312–20; and *New Republic*, Apr. 14, 1926, 215–18.]

Messinger, C. S., Spafford, Harriet P., and others. Shall our daughters have dowries? [*N. A. R.* (1890) CLI: 746–9]

Michell, Elene M. The life career motive and the dean of girls. [*Sch. and Soc.* (July 19, 1924) XX: 70–4]

Middle Ages, Woman's work in the. [*At. Mo.* (1886) XVIII: 274–88]

Mission of woman to the common schools. [*Pa. Sch. Jour.* (1862) XI: 49]

Mitchell, Maria. The collegiate education of girls. [*Education* (1881) I: 433–8]

Modern women. [*Nation* (1868) VII: 332–4]

Monroe, (Mrs.) H. E. The North London Collegiate and Camden School for Girls. [*Education* (1890) X: 347–55]

Monroe, (Mrs.) H. E. Woman's educational movement in England. [*Education* (1890) X: 489–93]

Moody, Lucy B. The American college girl's ignorance of literature. [*Jour. Ped.* (1905–6) XVIII: 257–64]

Morais, Nina. The limitations of sex. [*N. A. R.* (1881) CXXXII: 79–95]

Morford, Henry. Womanhood and chivalry in America. [*Lippincott's Mag.* (1868) I: 417–21]

Morgan, L. O. Ladies and learning. [*At. Mo.* (1889) LXIV: 518–27]

Morrison, Martin A. The employment of women in technical and scientific positions. [*Sch. and Soc.*, XIII: 174–5]

Mosso, Professor A. The physical education of woman. (Trans. of A. F. Chamberlain) [*Ped. Sem.* (1892) II: 226–35]

Movements, The two, among women. [*Nation* (1871) XII: 39–40]

Mudge, E. Leigh. Girls' collections. [*Ped. Sem.* XXV: 319 *ff.*]

Muir, Edwin. Women—free for what? [*Nation*, Aug. 6, 1924: 140 *ff.*]

Murphy, A. A. The coeducation of the sexes. [*Ed. Jour. Va.*, VI: 64–71]

Murray, Gilbert. The weaker sex. [*Ed. Rev.* (1910) XL: 512–16]

N. A. R.: See *North American Review*.

N. E. A. Proc.: See *National Education Association Proceedings*.

Nashville Female Academy. [*Southwestern Monthly* (1852) II: 63–4]

Nation, The, 1865–1927. Vols. I–CXXV. New York.

National Education Association, Proceedings of the, 1857–1927.

Nearing, Scott. Race suicide vs. overpopulation. [*Pop. Sci. Mo.* (1911) LXXVIII: 81–3]

Neilson, W. A.: Do Women Learn Faster? [*Collier's*, Oct. 3, 1925]

Nelson, Harriet O. Bradford Academy. [*Education* (1902) XXII: 555–60]

New England women, Two. [*At. Mo.* (1890) LXV: 418–20]

New Student, The, 1925–1928. New York.

New York Grammar School for Girls. [*Barnard's Jour.*, I: 408–12]

New York, Messages from the Governors of. (Ed. by C. Z. Lincoln) Vols. I–XI. Lyon: Albany, 1909.

New York Teacher, The, 1852–1860. 9 vols. Albany.

Newnham College and the higher education of women in England. [*Sch. and Soc.*, XIV: 107–8]

Niles' *Register*, 1811–1849. 75 vols. Baltimore, Washington, and Philadelphia.

Nordfelt, Margaret D. The woman's foundation for health. [*N. E. A. Proc.*, 1923: 627–31]

North American Review, 1820–1927. Vols. XI–CCXXIII. Boston and New York.

North Carolina University Magazine, 1859–60 and 1866–86. Chapel Hill, N. C.

Oakley, Charles S. Of women in assemblies. [*L. L. A.* (1896) CCXI: 572–7]

O'Connor, Mildred. The growing girl. [*Education* (1924) XLIV: 377–84]

Ohio Educational Monthly, The, 1897–1922. Vols. XLVI–LXXI. Columbus.

Ohio Female College. [*Barnard's Jour.*, XIII: 503–6]

O'Keefe, Emily A. The organization of athletics for girls in the elementary school. [*N. E. A. Proc.*, 1916: 693–5]

Old Northwest Genealogical Quarterly, Vol. VIII, No. 4, Oct. 1905. Columbus.

Olin, Helen R. Coeducation again. [*Ed. Rev.* (1909) XXXVII: 199–200]

Olin, Helen R. The undergraduate women of the Wisconsin University. [*Ed. Rev.* (1908) XXXVI: 503–12]

Olivet College, Early history of. [*Collections, Pioneer Society of the State of Michigan* (1881) III: 408–14]

Orton, James. Four years in Vassar College. [*Proc. N. E. A.*, 1874: 109–17]

Ossoli Margaret Fuller. [*Harper's N. M. Mag.* (1861) XXIII: 220 *ff.*]

Ouida. Female suffrage. [*N. A. R.* (1886) CXLIII: 290–306]

Ouida. The new woman. [*N. A. R.* (1894) CLVIII: 610–19]

Our daughters. [*Harper's N. M. Mag.* (1858) XVI: 72–7]

Oxford and Cambridge, Women at. [*L. L. A.* (1898) CCXVI: 219–33]

Oxford University, Women at. [*Andover Rev.* (June 1884) I: 658–9]

Packer Collegiate Institute for Girls, Brooklyn, New York. [*Barnard's Jour.*, I: 579–86]

Palmer, Alice F. A review of the higher education of women. [*Forum* (Sept. 1891) XII: 28–40]

Paris, School for girls at. [*Barnard's Jour.*, I: 394–6]

Park, Maud W. The women of America and the democratic awakening. [*N. E. A. Proc.*, 1922: 216–17]

Parker, Mary E. Report of the educational department, General Federation of Women's Clubs. [*N. E. A. Proc.*, 1917: 633–6]

Parkman, Francis. The woman question again. [*N. A. R.* (1880) I: 16–30]

Parlor Visitor, The—A Monthly Devoted to Religion and General Literature, 1857. Vols. VI VII. Nashville, Tenn.

Parrish, Celestia S. Shall the higher education of women be the same as that of men? [*Ed. Rev.* (1901) XXII: 383–96]

Parsons, Alice B. Sex and Genius. [*Yale Rev.*, July 1925: 739–52]

Parsons, Edward S. The social life of the coeducational college. [*Sch. Rev.*, XIII: 382–9]

Passano, Leonard M. The woman peril: a reply. [*Ed. Rev.* (1915) XLIX: 407–9]

Passano, Leonard M. The woman peril in American education. [*Ed. Rev.* (1914) XLVIII: 184–6]

Patrick, Mary M. Higher education for women in the Orient. [*Education* (1900) XX: 291–4]

Patterson, Herbert P. The logical problem of coeducation. [*Education* (1916) XXXVII: 112–15]

Payne, W. H. Coeducation of the sexes. [*Ed. Jour. Va.* (Nov. 1891) XXII: 484–5]

Peace, Women for. [*Independent* (1915) LXXXI: 120]

Pedagogical Seminary, The, 1891–1923. 30 vols. Worcester.

Pennsylvania Magazine of History and Biography, 1877–1927. Vols. I–LI. Philadelphia.

Pennsylvania School Journal, 1852–1927. Vols. I–LXXVI. Lancaster.

Perry, Arthur C. Woman and equal pay. [*Ed. Rev.* (1912) XLIII: 344–53]

Phelps, Almira L. [*Barnard's Jour.*, XVII: 611–22]

Phillips, John H. Coeducation and equal suffrage. [*Am. Ed. Rev.* XXXIV: 315–16]

Physical culture at women's colleges. [*Ed. News*, Dec. 7, 1895: 695]

Physical education of girls. [*Ed. News*, Nov. 1890: 660–1]

[Physical] education of girls. [*N. Y. Teacher*, 1858: 148]

Physical training for girls and women. [*Ed. News*, Sept. 12, 1891: 500]

Physical training for women. [*Ed. News*, June 11, 1892: 375]

Physicians, women. [*N. Y. Teacher* (July 1855) IV: 245 *ff.*]

Pickard, J. L. Coeducation in colleges. [*Education* (1893) XIII: 259–66]

Pierce, B. K. Mary Lyon and her seminary. [*Nat. Repository*, Feb. 1877: 119–28]

Pierce, George F. Georgia Female College—origin, plan and prospects. [*So. Ladies' Book*, 1840]

Pitman, Robert C. Woman as a political factor. [*N. A. R.* (1884) CXXXIX: 405–16]

Plummer, (Mrs.) George W. The relation of the college woman to the General Federation of Women's Clubs. [*N. E. A. Proc.*, 1922: 758–61]

Political morality of women, The. [*Nation* (1876) XXII: 205–6]

Political Science Quarterly, 1886–1927. Vols.I–XLII.

Politics, A woman's influence on. [*Nation* (1876) XXII: 317–18]

Pomeroy, S. J. The service of the women's fraternities. [*Independent* (Sept. 21, 1914) LXXIX: 413–14]

Popular Science Monthly, The, 1872–1927. 111 vols. New York.

Porter, Charlotte W. The opportunity of the girls' private school. [*N. A. R.* (1897) CLXV: 252–6]

Porter, Maria S. Recollections of May Alcott. [*New England Mag.* (March 1892) N. S. VI: 3–19]

Post, (Mrs.) Louis F. The rôle of women in the new internationalism. [*N. E. A. Proc.* 1918: 74–7]

Pound, Louise. Considerations to be taken into account in the stimulation of graduate work for women. [*N. E. A. Proc.*, 1922: 769–70]

Pound, O. The social life of high school girls: its problems and its opportunities. [*Sch. Rev.* (1920) XXVIII: 50]

Pound, O. The social problems of high school girls and how to meet them. [*Sch. and Soc.*, May, 1924: 584]

Powell, J. R. Social problems in the high school. [*Nat. Assoc. Sec. Sch. Princs., Fifth Yearbook*, 1921: 15]

Power, C. The social program of the unsocial high school girl. [*Sch. Rev.*, Dec., 1924: 773]

Powers, S. R. Intelligence as a factor in election of high school subjects. [*Sch. Rev.*, XXX: 452–5]

Preston, Josephine C. Women and Preparedness, their part in national life, especially in time of war. [*N. E. A. Proc.*, 1917: 63–7]

Price, Ellen E. More women on school boards. [*Pa. Sch. Jour.* (1898) XLVI: 299–300]

Priddy, Bessie L. Relation of the dean of women to the professional life of the student. [*N. E. A. Proc.*, 1922: 788–93]

Prince, Lucinda W. College women in business. [*N. E. A. Proc.*, 1918: 409–11]

Professional courses at Michigan, Large co-ed enrollment in. [*Am. Ed. Rev.*, XXXIV: 79–80]

Professional service, Report of the committee on training women for. [*Ed. Record*, II: 143–4; III: 216–17]

Public School Journal, The. [After 1897, *School and Home Education*], 1889–1898. Vols. IX–XLI. Bloomington, Ill.

Public schools, Women and the. [*Ed. News*, Feb. 2, 1895: 69–70]

Public Schools, Women in our. [*Am. Ed. Rev.* XXXIV: 289–90]

Purdue, Janet M. Deaning in the public high school. [*N. E. A. Proc.*, 1918: 404–6]

Putnam, Emily J. The rise of Barnard College. [*Columbia Univ. Quart.* (June 1900) II, 209–17]

Rand, E. A. A visit to Harvard Annex. [*Education* (1882) II: 415–19]

Raper, Charles L. Social life in Colonial North Carolina. [*N. C. Booklet* (1903) III, No. 5] Raleigh, 1903.

Raymer, J. W. Advisory systems in high school. [*Ed. Rev.*, 1912: 466]

Raymond, John H. Matthew Vassar. [*Galaxy* (Aug., 1869) VIII: 240–8]

Reed, Amy L. Female delicacy in the sixties. [*Century Mag.* (Oct. 1915) LXVIII: 855–64]

Reinhardt, Aurelia H. National aspects of the American Association of University Women. [*N. E. A. Proc.*, 1922: 761–5]

Reitzel, Charles E. Trend of colleges for women. [*Harper's Weekly* (1914) LIX: 310–11]

Religion, Women and. [*Nation* (1869) IX: 170–1]

Repplier, Agnes. Women and war. [*Atlantic* (May 1915 CXV: 577–85]

Richards, Ellen H. Desirable tendencies in education for women. [*Jour. A. C. A.*, Feb. 1908: 25–30]

Richards, Florence L. The dean of women. [*American Schoolmaster* (June 1916) IX: 241–51]

Richards, Florence L. The teaching load of a dean of women in a state teachers college: what shall it be? [*N. E. A. Proc.*, 1923: 635–6]

Richards, Florence L. What a dean may rightly expect from a president. [*N. E. A. Proc.*, 1918: 399–402]

Richards, H. M. The curriculum and equipment of Barnard College. [*Columbia Univ. Quart.* (March 1910) XII, No. 2: 172–80]

Richmond, Winifred. Present practices and tendencies in the secondary education of girls. [*Ped. Sem.*, XXIII: 184–98]

Rickert, Edith. The fraternity idea among college women. [*Century Mag.*, LXIII: 97–106]

Rideing William H. Working women in New York. [*Harper's N. M. Mag.* (1880) LXI: 25–37]

Rider, Linda. The emancipation of the woman teachers. [*Education* (1918) XXXIX: 46–54]

Rights of women, The. [*L. L. A.* (1845) II: 480–94]

Robinson, Lelia J.   Women lawyers in the United States. [*Green Bag,* Jan. 1890: 10–32]

Rogers, Agnes L.   What women in colleges of liberal arts specialize in. [*Sch. and Soc.,* XX: 700–2]

Rogers, Anna.   Why American mothers fail. [*At. Mo.* (March 1908) CI: 289–97]

Ross, E. A.   Western civilization and the birth-rate. [*Am. Jour. Soc.* (1906–07) XII: 607–32]

Rowell, Elizabeth.   The girl problem in the high school. [*N. E. A. Proc.,* 1917: 258]

Runyon, Laura L.   The woman peril in education. [*Ed. Rev.* (1914) XLVII: 507–12]

Sachs, Julius.   Coeducation again. [*Ed. Rev.* (1909) XXXVII: 89–93]

Sachs, Julius.   Coeducation in the United States. [*Ed. Rev.* (March 1907) XXXIII: 298–305]

Sachs, Julius.   Intellectual reactions of coeducation. [*Ed. Rev.* (1908) XXXV: 466–75]

Safford, Irene A.   The decision of Columbia College. [*Overland Monthly* (May 1883) 2d Series, I: 544–5]

St. John, Jane A.   Woman's influence. [*N. Y. Teacher* (1860) N. S. I: 306–7]

Salmon, Lucy M.   Does the college curriculum promote scholarship? [*N. E. A. Proc.,* 1922: 737–45]

Salmon, Lucy M.   The woman's exchange: charity or business. [*Forum* (1892) XIII: 394–406]

Sanford, Bernice E.   Organization of social life when there are no dormitories, and housing students under such conditions. [*N. E. A. Proc.,* 1918: 393–5]

Sangster, Margaret E.   Editorship as a career for women. [*Forum* (Dec. 1895) XX: 445]

Sangster, Margaret E.   Marriage: a question of cash. [*Cosmopolitan* (Sept. 1911) LI: 458–64]

Santa Borghese, Princess.   Women in education. [*N. E. A. Proc.,* 1923: 228–31]

Saunders, Louise S. B.   Government of women students in colleges and universities. [*Ed. Rev.* (1900) XX: 475–98]

Schaeffer, N. C.   Women as teachers. [*Pa. Sch. Jour.* (1903) LI: 360–1]

School and Society, 1915–1927. Vols. I–XXVI: Garrison, N. Y.

School board, Women on the. [*N. E. Jour. Ed.* (1905) LXI: 206]

School boards, Women on. [*Sch. Jour.,* LXXII: 211]

School curricula, changing, Woman's influence in. [*Am. Ed. Rev.,* XXXI: 670]

School directors, Women. [*Pa. Sch. Jour.* (1874) XXII: 365–6; XXXV: 407; (1893) XLI: 517–18]

School Gazette, 1897–1902. Vols. IX–XIV. Harrisburg, Pa.

School Journal, The, 1897–1914. Vols. LIV–LXXXI. New York and Chicago.

School officers, Women as. [*N. E. Jour. Ed.* (1875) II: 222–3]

School Review, The, 1893–1925. Vols. I–XXXIII. Chicago.

School suffrage for women. [*N. E. Jour. Ed.* (1880) XI: 296 *f.*]

School, Women at. [*L. L. A.* (1873) CXIX: 765–7]

Schreiner, Olive. The woman question. [*Cosmopolitan* (1899–1900) XXVIII: 45–54, 182–92]

Scruggs, William L. Restriction of the suffrage. [*N. A. R.* (1884) CXXXIX: 492–502]

Scudder, Vida D. Woman and socialism. [*Yale Rev.* (1914) N. S. III: 454–70]

Sedgwick, Ora G. A girl of sixteen at Brook Farm. [*At. Mo.* (1900) LXXXV: 394–404]

Seelye, L. Clark. Collegiate education for women. [*Am. Inst. of Instruction,* July 28, 1874; *92d Report of the Regents of New York,* 1879: 563–9]

Seelye, L. Clark. The higher education of women: its perils and its benefits. [*59th Annual Meeting, Am. Inst. of Instruction,* 1888: 69–97]

Seelye, L. Clark. The college woman and home life. [*Sch. Jour.,* LXXII: 145]

Selden, Charles A. Sex and higher education. [*Ladies Home Jour.,* Oct. 1924]

Semple, Patty B. An old Kentucky home. [*At. Mo.* (July 1887) LX: 32–43]

Senex (William Woodbridge). Reminiscences of female education. [*Barnard's Jour.,* XVI: 137–40; first appeared in *Am. Jour. Ed.,* Sept. 1830, and *Am. Annals,* Nov. 1831]

Sergeant, Elizabeth S. Education for what? [*New Republic* (Jan. 1916) V: 219–20]

Sewall, May W. Woman's work in education. [*N. E. A. Proc.,* 1884: 153–7]

Sewing in the public schools. [*N. E. Jour. Ed.,* I: 170]

Seybolt, Robert F. Notes on the curriculum in Colonial America. [*Jour. Ed. Research,* Dec. 1925]

Shanks, W. F. G. Woman's work and wages. [*Harper's N. M. Mag.* (1868) XXXVII: 546–52]

Sherwood, (Mrs.) John. Why women marry. [*N. A. R.* (1891) CLII: 292–8]

Sherwood, M. P. Undergraduate life at Vassar. [*Scribner's Mag.* (June 1898) XXIII: 643–60]

Shinn, Millicent W. The marriage rate of college women. [*Century Mag.* (Oct. 1895) L: 946–8]

Sill, E. R. Shall women go to college? [*Century Mag.* (June 1886) X: 323–6]

Sioussat, Anna. Colonial women of Maryland. [*Maryland Hist. Mag.* (1907) II: 214–26]

Skelding, Eugenia. The first principal of Newnham College. [*At. Mo.* (Aug. 1893) LXXII: 224–30]

Slavery, A reply to women in Great Britain on the subject of. [*At. Mo.* (1863) XI: 120–33]

Sleman, Emily F.   A progressive step in the higher education of women. [*Sch. and Soc.*, IV: 772-5]

Slosson, Edwin E.   Coeducation from another standpoint. [*Independent* (1903) LV, Pt. I: 366-70]

Small, Albion W.   Coeducation at the University of Chicago. [*N. E. A. Proc.*, 1903: 288-97]

Small, W. H.   Girls in Colonial schools. [*Education* (1902) XXII: 532-7]

Smith, A. Lapthorn.   Higher education of women and race suicide. [*Pop. Sci. Mo.* (1904-05) LXVI: 466-73]

Smith, Charles F.   The higher education of women in the South. [*Ed. Rev.* (Oct. 1894) VIII: 287 *f.;* also (Feb. 1895) IX: 187-8]

Smith, (Mrs.) E. Oakes.   Woman and her needs. [*DeBow's Rev.*, XIII: 267 *ff.*]

Smith, Elsie M.   Chicago correspondence . . . deans of girls. [*Jour. Ed.* (April 1913) LXXVII: 433]

Smith, Eliza C.   History of the Michigan Female College and a sketch of the life and work of Miss A. C. Rogers. [*Collections, Pioneer Soc. of Michigan* (1883) VI: 284-90]

Smith, H. M.   What the dean may rightly expect from the president. [*N. E. A. Proc.*, 1918: 397]

Smith, Hilda W.   Bryn Mawr Summer School for women workers in industry. [*N. E. A. Proc.*, 1922: 713-14]

Smith, Mary R.   Shall the college curriculum be modified for women? [*Jour. A. C. A.*, Dec. 1898: 1-15]

Smith, Minna C.   The Harvard Annex. [*Education*, VI: 568-74]

Smithies, W. M.   The qualities essential to a dean of girls. [*Sch. Rev.* (March 1924) XXXII: 203-8]

Snowden, (Mrs.) Philip.   Woman and war. [*N. E. A. Proc.*, 1915: 54-6]

Social condition of woman, The. [*N. A. R.* (1836) XLII: 489-513]

Socialistic state, Woman in the. [*Nation* (1894) LVIII: 359 *f.*]

Sollers, Basil.   Transported convict laborers in Maryland during the Colonial period. [*Maryland Hist. Mag.* (1907) II: 17-47]

Somers, Florence A.   The right kind of athletics for girls. [*Am. Phys. Ed. Rev.* (June 1916) XXI: 369-75]

Somerset, Lady Henry.   Coeducation. [*Jour. Ed.* (1895) XLII: 59]

Somerset, Lady Henry.   Frances E. Willard. [*N. A. R.* (1895) CLX: 429-36]

Somerset, Lady Henry.   The Renaissance of women. [*N. A. R.* (1894) CLIX: 490-7]

South, Education in the, Proceedings of Tenth Conference for, 1907.

Southern Ladies' Book, 1840-41.   Vols. I and II.

Southern Lady's Companion, The—A Monthly Periodical Devoted to Literature and Religion, 1847-49.   Vols. I and II.   Nashville, Tenn.

South-Western Monthly, July 1852.   Nashville, Tenn.

Spaulding, J. L.   Woman and the higher education. [*Jour. Ed.*, L: 12-13]

Spencer, A. G.   Woman and war. [*Independent* (1915) LXXXI: 121-4]

Spencer, Sara A.   The world's need of business women. [*N. E. A. Proc.*, 1893· 800-3]

Sprague, Robert J. Education and race suicide. [*Jour. Heredity*, VI: 158–62]

Stahr, J. S. Women vs. men as teachers. [*Pa. Sch. Jour.* (1880) XXIX: 114–18]

Stanton, Elizabeth C. Has Christianity benefited woman? [*N. A. R.* (1885) CXL: 389–99]

Stanton, Elizabeth C. Progress of the American woman. [*N. A. R.* (1900) CLXXI: 904–7]

Starrett, Helen E. The future of our daughters. [*Forum* (1890–91) X: 185–96]

Stayt, Grace A. Retirement systems for women members of college faculties. [*N. E. A. Proc.*, 1922: 771–5]

Steinem, Pauline. Women's work on the board of education. [*Ohio Ed. Mo.*, LV: 226 *ff.*]

Stephens, Kate. Advanced education for women. [*Forum* (March 1889) VII: 41–51]

Stevens, Romiett. The adviser of girls in high school. [*T. C. Record* (Sept. 1919) XX: 301–23]

Stevens, Romiett. What constitutes social ethics? [*N. E. A. Proc.*, 1918: 407–9]

Stevens, W. LeConte. University education for women. [*N. A. R.* (1883) CXXXVI: 25–39]

Stevenson, Louisa. Women students in the Scottish universities. [*N. E. A. Proc.*, 1893: 877–9]

Stewart, Anne B. The "woman peril" again. [*Ed. Rev.* (1914) XLVIII: 380–3]

Stewart, Jane A. The educational work of the woman's clubs. [*N. E. Nat. Jour. Ed.* (1908) LXVII: 536–8]

Stewart, Jane A. Some firsts in woman's progress. [*N. E. Nat. Jour. Ed.*, XC: 34]

S[tillé], C. J. The higher education of women, and the Harvard examinations. [*Penn Monthly* (Feb. 1878) IX: 93–104]

Stoddard, T. H. Women in English universities. [*New England and Yale Rev.* (July 1886) N. S. IX: 573–93]

Stone, Lucinda H. History of coeducation in the University of Michigan. [*Collections, Michigan Pioneer and Hist. Soc.* (1891) XVIII: 411–18]

Stone, Lucinda H. Influence of a foreign education on American girls. [*Education* (1882) III: 14–23]

Sturgis, (Mrs.) E. O. P. Schools for girls in Worcester in former days. [*Proc. Worcester Soc. of Antiquity*, XIX: 760–4]

Sturtevant, Sarah M. Educational implications of the social program of the high school. [*N. E. A. Proc.*, 1923: 878]

Sturtevant, Sarah M. The qualifications and preparation of deans of women. [*T. C. Record* (May 1924) XXV: 179–87]

Sturtevant, Sarah M. The relation of the work of a real dean of girls to the high school girls. [*Nat. Assoc. Sec. Sch. Princs., 7th Yearbook*, 1923: 121]

Subjection of Women, A criticism of Mill's. [*Nation* (1874) XVIII: 311–12]

Swayze, Minnie C. Education for women. [*Pa. Sch. Jour.* (1877) XXV: 351–3]

Tagore muses on woman's soul. [*N. Y. Times Mag.*, Aug. 14, 1927: 1–2]

Talbot, Marion. Present day problems in the education of women. [*Ed. Rev.* (1897) XIV: 248–58]

Talbot, Marion. Some results of graduate work by women. [*N. E. A. Proc.*, 1922: 770]

Tannahill, Anna L. How may the dean best apportion her time among the academic, advisory and social sides of college? [*N. E. A. Proc.*, 1922: 775–7]

Tanner, Amy E. The college woman's code of honor. [*Ped. Sem.* (1906) XIII: 104–17]

Tarbell, H. S. Coeducation. [*Education* (1884) IV: 427–34]

Taylor, Graham. A new force in Chicago politics. [*Survey*, XXXVI: 34]

Taylor, James M. College education for girls in America. [*Ed. Rev.* (1912) XLIV: 216–33; and 325–47]

Taylor, James M. The education of women. [*World's Work* (August 1903) VI: 3751–3]

Taylor, John O. Women as teachers, More of. [*Jour. Ed.* (1892), XXXV: 42]

Teachers College Record, 1900–27. Vols. I–XXVII. New York.

Teachers, Married women as. [*Ed. Rev.* (1903) XXV: 213–4]

Teachers, Men or women—which? By an ex-school officer. [*Education* (1917) XXXVIII: 28–9]

Teachers, Preponderance of women as. [*Ed. Jour. Va.* (1887) XVIII: 21–2]

Teachers, Women. [*Pa. Sch. Jour.* (1878) XXVII: 210–11]

Teachers, women, A work for. [*Intelligence*, June 1, 1903: 415]

Teachers, Women, and mollycoddles. [An answer to G. S. Hall] [*Sch. Jour.*, LXXV: 672]

Teachers, women, Are there too many? [*Ed. Rev.* (1904) XXVIII: 98–105]

Teachers, Women as. [*Ed. Rev.* (1891) II: 358–62]

Teachers, Women as. [*N. E. Jour. Ed.*, II: 105]

Teachers, women, Do [they] feminize boys? [*Am. Ed. Rev.*, XXXI: 690]

Teachers, Women high school. [*Jour. Ed.* (1900) LI: 328]

Teachers, Women, in California. [*N. E. Jour. Ed.* (1918) LXXXVIII: 239]

Teachers, Women, in higher education. [*Am. Ed. Rev.*, XXXIII: 268]

Temperance question, The women and the. [*Nation* (1874) XVIII: 135–6]

Tetlow, John. The eastern colleges for women: their aims, means, and methods. [*Education* (1881) I: 465–84, and 544–55]

Tetlow, John. The education of women for the learned professions. [*Ed. Rev.* (1896) XI: 105–25]

Tetlow, John. Some aspects of the higher education of women. [*Am. Inst. of Instruction*, 1882: 95–124]

Thacher, Mary P. The school mistress. [*Harper's N. M. Mag.* (1878) LVII: 607–11]

Thomas, Calvin. Social life at Barnard. [*Columbia Univ. Quart.*, June 1900: 218–25]

Thomas, M. Carey. The Association of Collegiate Alumnae in its relation to woman's education. [*Jour. A. C. A.*, Dec. 1898: 40–6]

Thomas, M. Carey. The curriculum of the woman's college. [*Jour. A. C. A.* (May 1917) X: 585–91]

Thomas, M. Carey. The future of women in independent study and research. [*Jour. A. C. A.*, Feb. 1903: 13–19]

Thomas, M. Carey. Present tendencies in women's college and university education. [*Jour. A. C. A.*, Feb. 1908: 45–62]

Thomas, M. Carey. Present tendencies in women's education. [*Ed. Rev.* (1908) XXXV: 64–85]

Thomas, M. Carey. Should the higher education of women differ from that of men? [*Ed. Rev.* (1901) XXI: 1–10]

Thomas, M. Carey. Higher education of women. [*Sch. Jour.*, LXVIII: 699–700]

Thomas, M. Carey. Place of Bryn Mawr in the education of women. [*N. E. Jour. Ed.*, XCIII: 488]

Thompson, Flora M. Retrogression of the American woman. [*N. A. R.* (1900) CLXXI: 748–53]

Thompson, R. H. Suffrage in Mississippi. [*Publications of Mississippi Hist. Soc.* (1898) I: 25–49]

Thompson, W. O. Coeducation. [*Ohio Ed. Mo.*, LII: 180–1]

Thorndike, E. L. The decrease in size of American families. [*Pop. Sci. Mo.* (1903) LXIII: 64–70]

Thorntown, Natalie. The women's forum. [*T. C. Record*, XXIII: 305–26]

Thwing, Charles F. The advantages of coördinate (annex) method in education. [*N. E. A. Proc.*, 1904: 547–8]

Thwing, Charles F. The college education of young women. [*Public Opinion* (Oct. 1893) XVI: 9–10]

Thwing, Charles F. Recent movements in woman's education. [*Harper's N. M. Mag.* (1880–81) LXII: 101–7]

Thwing, Charles F. Training the girl to think. [*Sch. Jour.*, LXVIII: 699]

Thwing, Charles F. What becomes of college women? [*N. A. R.* (1895) CLXI: 546–53]

Thwing, Charles F. Woman's education. [*Education* (1883) IV: 53–61]

Tillett, Wilbur F. Southern womanhood as affected by the war. [*Century* (1891) N. S. XXI: 9–16]

Tufts, Edith S. Organization of the work of the heads of halls. [*N. E. A. Proc.*, 1922: 725–8]

Turner, Charles Q. Women who founded ancient seats of learning. [*Ed. Foundations* (1905–6) XVII: 97 *ff.*]

Tuttle, Edith M. Vocational education for girls. [*Education* (1914) XXXIV: 445–58]

Tuttle, Kate A. A plea for scholarships for the young women of the South. [*Jour. A. C. A.*, Feb. 1906: 24–5]

Tutweiler, Julia S.   The technical education of women.   [*Education* (1882) III: 201–7]

Tyler, Eleanor.   Some problems of the dean of women.   [*Ed. Outlook* (April 1916) II: 206–11]

Tyler, John M.   The boy and girl in the high school.   [*Education* (1906) XXVI: 462–9]

Tyler, John M.   The girl in the grammar grades.   [*Education* (1906) XXVI: 404–12]

Tyler, Lyon G.   Education in Colonial Virginia.   [*William and Mary College Quart.*, V: 219–23]

Tyler, M.   Vassar Female College.   [*New Englander* (Oct. 1862) XXI: 725–46]

Tyler, Moses C.   Women at Michigan University.   [*Independent*, Dec. 1870]

Universities, The women and the (in England).   [*L. L. A.* (1874) CXXI: 693–6; *Ed. News*, Sept. 1890: 517–18; *Sch. and Soc.*, XIII: 475; and XVI: 93]

University degrees for women. By an Oxford B.A.   [*Fortnightly Rev.* (June 1, 1895) O. S. LXIII: 895–903]

University of the State of New York: *Proceedings of the Seventh Convocation.* University of the State of New York. Albany.

University of Virginia and a college for women, The.   [*Sch. and Soc.*, III: 274]

University studies, Admission of women to.   [*Ed. Rev.* (1892) IV: 207]

Valbert, G.   German professors on university women.   [*L. L. A.* (1897) CCXIV: 83–91]

Valentine, A. F.   The American [college] woman and her home.   [*Outlook* (Sept. 17, 1910) XCVI: 111–12]

Valentine, J. T.   The coeducation of the sexes.   [*Pa. Sch. Jour.* (1875) XXIV: 183–8]

Van Buren, A. D.   The old academy and seminary; the classic schools of our pioneer days.   [*Collections, Michigan Pioneer and Hist. Soc.* (1892) XVIII: 405–11]

Van Etten, Ida M.   Working women.   [*N. A. R.* (1887) CXLIV: 312–15]

Van Hise, Charles R.   Educational tendencies in state universities.   (Address to the Association of Collegiate Alumnae)   [*Ed. Rev.* (Dec. 1907) XXXIV: 504–20]

Van Kleeck, Mary.   A census of college women.   [*Jour. A. C. A.* (May 1918) XI: 557–91]

Van Rensselaer, M. G.   The waste of women's intellectual labor.   [*Forum* (1892) XIII: 616–28]

Vassar College.   [*Nation*, X: 315–17]

Vassar College, Change in entrance requirements to.   [*Sch. Rev.*, V: 242–3]

Vassar, Matthew, and the Vassar Female College.   [*Am. Jour. Ed.* (1862) XI: 53–6]

Vincent, G. E. University of Chicago. [*Outlook* (Aug. 2, 1902) LXXI: 839–51]

Virginia, Colonial, Books in. [*Va. Mag. of Hist. and Biography* (1902–03) X: 389–405]

Virginia Magazine of History and Biography, 1893–1927. Vols. I–XXXV. Richmond.

Vocation, A new, for women. [*L. L. A.* (1879) CXLII: 728–32]

Vocational guidance and placement of professional women, Agencies other than academic appointment bureaus concerned with the. [*Ed. Record*, III: 66–109]

Vote, Reasons why women should. [*Nation* (1867) V: 416–17]

Voters, women, The. [*Outlook* (1916) CXIII: 641–2]

Voting, A woman's thoughts about. [*Nation* (1867) IV: 136–7]

Wage earners, Women. [*Nation* (1906) LXXXII: 152–3]

Wagenseller, George W. Education of women. [*Ed. News*, Feb. 14, 1891: 99–100]

Wages, Demand for equal, for equal work. [*Nation* (1907) LXXXIV: 72–3]

Waite, Davis H. and Crounse, Lorenzo. Woman suffrage in practice. [*N. A. R.* 1894) CLVIII: 737–44]

Walker, Francis A. Normal training in women's colleges. [*Ed. Rev.* (1892) IV: 328–38]

Warfield, E. Dudley. The moral influence of women in American society. [*Annals of Am. Acad. of Political and Social Sci.* (1909) XXXIV: 106–14]

Warner, Joseph B. Radcliffe College. [*Harvard Grad. Mag.* (March 1894) II: 329–45]

Warren, L. Y. The program of a dean of high school girls. [*Sch. and Soc.* 1923) XVII: 693]

Wasson, Pearl R. Methods of promoting ideals of scholarship among average students. [*N. E. A. Proc.*, 1922: 745–9]

Weisman, Sara. Use of Stanford revision of the Binet-Simon test as a guide in selection of high school courses. [*Jour. Ed. Research*, VII: 137–44]

Webster, Nesta H. On woman and civilization. [*Nineteenth Century Mag.* (1920) LXXXVIII: 741–59]

Welch, Margaret H. Club women and club work. [*Harper's Bazaar* (1897) XXX: 272, 360, 548, 652, and 889]

Wellesley College. [*N. E. Jour. Ed.*, II: 52]

Wellesley College and its relationship to lady teachers. [*N. E. Jour. Ed.* (1879) X: 44]

Wells, D. Collin. Some questions concerning the higher education of women. [*Am. Jour. Soc.* (May 1909) XIV: 731–9]

Wells, Kate G. The transitional American woman. [*At. Mo.* (1880) XLVI: 817–23]

Wells, Kate G. Women in organizations. [*At. Mo.* (1880) XLVI: 360–7]

Werntz, A. J. Should females have the same salary as males? [*Pa. Sch. Jour.* (1858) VII: 24 *ff*.]

Wesson, Cynthia M.   Purposes of the committee on women's athletics of the American Physical Education Association and its progress up to the present.   [*Proc. N. E. A.*, 1922: 1095–8]

West, Mary A.   Lucretia Mott: a reminiscence.   [*N. E. Jour. Ed.* (1881) XIII: 3 *f*.]

Westerman, Frieda.   Social activities for high school girls.   [*Am. Schoolmaster* (Dec. 15, 1918) XI: 433–9]

Wetherell, Leander.   The liberal education of woman.   [*Am. Inst. of Instruction*, 1861: 79–125]

Wheelock, Lucy.   Education of women.   [*Child-Welfare Mag.*, VIII: 4–8]

White, E. E.   Segregation of sexes in high schools.   [*Nat. Teacher*, 1872]

White, Emily.   Women's medical colleges.   [*Medical News*, Aug. 3, 1895]

White, Greenough.   The South, past and present.   [*Sch. Rev.* (1899) VII: 148–53]

White, President, of Cornell University.   Coeducation in colleges.   [*Pa. Sch. Jour.* (1872) XX: 313–15]

Whiting, Harriet L.   Granville Female College.   [*Old Northwest Genealogical Quart.* (Oct. 1905) VIII, No. 4: 317]

Whitley, (Mrs.) W. H.   A glimpse of Paris (Kentucky) in 1809.   [*Register of the Kentucky State Hist. Soc.* (January 1922) XX, No. 58: 49–57]

Whitney, (Mrs.) M. M.   Scientific study and work for women.   [*Ed. Rev.* (1882) III: 58–69]

Whittelsey, Sarah S.   Women and the study of the social sciences.   [*Education* (1902) XXIII: 98–108]

Wickersham, James P. and Thompson, James.   Committee report on coeducation of the sexes.   [*Pa. Sch. Jour.* (1854) III: 87–92]

Wilcox, S.   Conduct of college girls.   [*Independent* (Aug. 7, 1913) LXXV: 320–2]

Wilkins, William D.   Traditions and reminiscences of the public schools of Detroit.   [*Collections, Michigan Pioneer and Hist. Soc.*, I: 448–66]

Wilkinson, Marguerite O. B.   Education as a preventive of divorce.   [*Craftsman* (1912) XXI: 473–81]

Willard, Emma, Educational services of.   [*Barnard's Jour.*, VI: 125–68]

Willard, Frances E.   [*Intelligence*, March 1, 1898: 170–1]

Willard, Frances E.   Woman's work in education.   [*N. E. A. Proc.*, 1884: 161–8]

Willard, (Mrs.) J. H.   A memorial of the late Emma Willard.   [*Proc. Seventh Anniversary of the University Convocation, State of New York*, 1870: 73–81]

Willard, (Mrs.) J. H.   A sketch of the history of Troy Seminary.   [*Proc. Thirteenth Anniversary of the University Convocation, State of New York*, 1876: 169–82]

William and Mary College Quarterly, 1892–1919, Vols. I–XXVII; 1921–26, Vols. I–VI.   Williamsburg.

Williams, Jesse.   The education of emotions through physical education.   [*T. C. Record*, May 1920: 205–8]

Willis, Annie I.   A noted woman educator—Alice Freeman Palmer.   [*Education* (1890) X: 469–72]

Willson, Anna. The need of standardizing the qualifications of deans for high schools. [*N. E. A. Proc.*, 1920: 215]

Winship, A. E. The future of women teachers. [*Jour. Ed.* (1902) LV: 99–100, 105]

Winship, A. E. Woman. [*Jour. Ed.*, XLII: 395]

Winship, A. E. Woman educators. [*Pa. Sch. Jour.* (1916–17) LXV: 169–71]

Winship, A. E. Woman's personality in teaching. [*N. E. A. Proc.*, 1923: 544–5]

Wirt, Lulu E. Student leadership. [*N. E. A. Proc.*, 1922: 783–7]

Witham, R. Adelaide. The American college girl's ignorance of literature. [*Jour. Ped.* (1906) XIX: 13 *ff.*]

Witte, A., on the education of girls. [*Education* (1893) XIV: 229–36]

Witte, A. The woman's educational movement in Germany. [*Education* (1892) XIII: 37–43]

Woman. [*L. L. A.* (1858) LIX: 483–99]

Woman and education: the woman of the East. [*Ed. Foundations*, XXVI: 551 *ff.*; and 612 *ff.*]

Woman question, The. [*Catholic World* (1869) IX: 145–57]

[Woman] suffrage and the higher education of women. [*Nation* (1879) XXIX: 364–5]

Woman suffrage in Massachusetts. [*Nation* (1887) XLIV: 269]

Woman suffrage in Michigan. [*Nation* (1874) XVIII: 311–12]

Woman suffrage in operation. [*Nation* (1887) XLIV: 310]

Woman suffrage on school questions in Massachusetts [*Nation* (1879 XXIX: 272]

Woman, The new. A symposium by C. C. Catt, L. S. Hollingworth, *et al.* [*Current History* (Oct. 1927) XXVII: 1–48]

Woman suffragists, Progress of the. [*Nation* (1879) XXIX: 327]

Woman superintendent in the school of average size. [*School Board Jour.* (June 1915) L: 10 and 79]

Womanhood, The outlook for. [*N. E. Jour. Ed.* (1877) V: 30]

Woman's cause, The advocates of the. [*Nation* (1869) IX: 434]

Woman's clubs, Cooperation of. [*Pub. Sch. Jour.* (1898) XIII: 473–4]

Woman's college and culture, The. [*Am. Ed. Rev.*, XXXIII: 504]

Woman's education in various parts of the world. [*N. E. A. Proc.*, 1893: 853–914]

Woman's emancipation. [*Harper's N. M. Mag.* (1851) III: 424]

Woman's Journal and Suffrage News, The, 1870–1915. Boston.

Woman's question, A tilt at the. [*Harper's N. M. Mag.* (1863) XXVI: 350 *ff.*]

Woman's reason, A (for having a family). [*Independent* (April 1907) LXII: 780–4]

Woman's rights agitation, Notes on the. By a looker-on. [*Nation* (1870) X: 38–9, 88–9, 101–4]

Woman's rights camp, The feud in the. [*Nation* (1870) XI: 346–7]

Woman's rights convention. [*L. L. A.* (1848) XVIII: 423–4]

Woman's rights convention, A. [*L. L. A.* (1853) XXXVI: 289–94]

Woman's sphere. [*N. Y. Teacher*, June 1857: 387 *ff*.]

Woman's sphere. [*Pa. Sch. Jour.* (1858) VII: 72]

Woman's university club of New York, The. [*Am. Ed. Rev.*, XXXII: 279–82]

Woman's work. [*Nation* (1869) IX: 561]

Woman's work and wages. [*Harper's N. M. Mag.* (1868) XXXVII: 546 *ff*.]

Woman's work and wages. By a working woman. [*Harper's N. M. Mag.* (1869) XXXVIII: 665–70]

Women actually in office. [*Nation* (1916) CIII: 581]

Women and women's colleges. [*Am. Ed. Rev.*, XXXIII: 435 *f*.]

Women college graduates, Marriages of. [*Nation*, April 24, 1890: 330–1]

Women in Europe, Education of. [*Ed. Foundations*, XXVI: 430 *ff*.]

Women, The influence of. [*L. L. A.* (1886) CLXXI: 191–2]

Women to the front. (Admission of women to the University of Pennsylvania) [*Pa. Sch. Jour.* (1877) XXVI: 177–8]

Women vs. women. [*Nation* (1867) V: 276–7]

Women's college for Connecticut, A. [*Am. Ed. Rev.*, XXXI: 737 *f*.]

Women's colleges, The aim of. [*Nation* (1907) LXXXIV: 150–1]

Women's colleges, Entrance requirements in. [*Nation* (April 1888) XLVI: 320–1]

Women's colleges, Funds for. [*Sch. and Soc.*, XIV: 72]

Women's colleges, The. [*Sch. and Soc.*, XI: 353–4]

Wood, William. Physical education. [*Ladies' Repository*, Jan. 1845: 18–19; 44–6; 73–5]

Woodberry, George E. Mary Wollstonecraft. [*At. Mo.* (1880) XLVI: 838–46]

Woodruff, Anna C. One woman on a school board. [*N. E. Jour. Ed.*, LXI: 568]

Woods, Alice. Coeducation up to the age of twelve. [*Ed. Foundations* (1904–5) XVI: 588 *ff*.]

Woodward, Mary V. Higher education of women in the South. [*Ed. Rev.* (1895) IX: 187 *ff*.]

Woodward, Mary V. Woman's education in the South. [*Ed. Rev.* (1894) VII: 466–78]

Woody, Thomas. Entrance of women into the teaching profession. [*Ed. Outlook* (1928) II: 72–88, and 138–63]

Woody, Thomas. Women and the Christian minstry. [*Voc. Guid. Mag.*, Dec. 1927, 115–21]

Wooley, Mary E. The civic responsibility of the college woman. [*Jour. A. C. A.* (Jan. 1914) VII: 11–16]

Wooley, Mary E. The college curriculum as a preparation for life. [*Jour. A. C. A.* (May 1917) X: 591–5]

Wooley, Mary E. Educational problems in the colleges for women. [*Education* (1918) XXXVIII: 650–4]

Wooley, Mary E. The effect of college training on character. [*Jour. A. C. A.* (Jan. 1905) Series III, No. 10: 10–12]

Wooley, Mary E. Preparation of women for twentieth century life. [*N. E. A. Proc.*, 1914: 56–60]

Wooley, Mary E. Some ideals for deans. [*N. E. A. Proc.*, 1918: 411–14]

Woolman, Mary S. The making of a girls' trade school. [*T. C. Record* (1909) X, No. 4: 1–67]

Woolman, Mary S. Training of girls and women for trade and industry. [*Jour. N. E. A.*, Feb. 1918: 427–9]

Woolsey, T. D. Divorce and divorce laws in the United States. [*New Englander* (July 1868) XXVII: 517–50]

Working woman's statement, A. [*Nation* (1867) IV: 155–6]

Worthington, Daisy L. Higher education for women. [*Ed. Rev.* (1906) XXXII: 405–14]

Wright, Carroll D. Why women are paid less than men. [*Forum* (1892) XIII: 629–39]

Wright, Helen. The special honors plan at Smith College. [*N. E. A. Proc.*, 1922: 750–2]

Yost, Mary. The extra-mural activities of a dean of women—what shall they be? (Abstract.) [*N. E. A. Proc.*, 1923: 631–2]

Young, Ella Flagg. Dean of girls. [*Jour. Ed.* (Nov. 13, 1913) LXXVIII: 486]

Young, Ella Flagg, editorial reference to. [*Jour. Ed.* (April 17, 1913) LXXVIII: 436]

Young, Elva H. The law as a profession for women. [*Jour. A. C. A.*, Feb. 1902: 15–23]

Young Ladies' Institute, Granville, Ohio, 1860–1900. [Article by N. S. Burton, in *Old Northwest Genealogical Quart.* (Oct. 1905) VIII, No. 4: 368–70]

Zimmern, Alice. Women at the German universities. [*Athenaeum*, May 18, 1895: 642–3]

Zueblin, Charles. The effect on woman of economic dependence. [*Am. Jour. Soc.* (1908–9) XIV: 606–21]

INDEX TO VOLUMES I AND II*

Abbé D'Ancourt's book for ladies, 234

Abbot Female Academy, 343, 356 *f.*

Abbot, Frances M., ii, 204, 207, 429

Abbot, John, 44 *f.*

Abbot, Sarah, 356

Abbot's Teacher, 475

Abbott, Lyman, ii, 152, 193

Abbott, Miss, woman's club leader, ii, 465

A B C Büchlein, 211

Abercrombie's Mental Philosophy, 475

Ability, for college work, ii, 150, 154 *ff.*; of girls in Dutch schools, 197; of men and women professors, compared, ii, 331 *ff.*

Abington, George, schoolmaster, 288

Abituriénten, girls prepared for, 85 *f.*

Academy, beginning of, 108, 137, 153, 217, 225, 227, 234 *f.*, 236; ii, 227, 469 *f.*; criticism of, 441 *ff.*; duration, 108 *f.*, 234; failure of, in teacher training, 471; forerunners of, 281 *ff.*, 292 *ff.*, 301, 329–459; influence of, 457 *ff.*; methods used in, 422–34; purpose of, 397–409; rise and decline of, 395 *f.*; studies pursued in, 409–22; superficial education at the, 148 *f.*

Accomplishments, ii, 151, 178, 181, 192 *f.*, 194, 387, 400 *ff.*; among Chinese, 4 *f.*; beginning of, in New England, 129 *ff.*, 134, 149 *ff.*; condemned, 32, 51, 79, 108, 110 *f.*; criticized, 308 *ff.*, 340, 357, 390, 397, 399, 405, 411 *f.*, 415, 422, 431, 441, 443 *f.*, 450 *ff.*; desired among early peoples, 2; education of, 96; in Colonial days, 185, 234; in Willard's ''Plan,'' 309 *ff.*; made unnecessary by machine production, 112 *f.*; not prized by German settlers, 183; opposed by Quakers, 271; stressed in England, 47; stressed in the South, 244, 271 *f.*, 281 *ff.*

Account book, of Aimwell School, 206 *f.*; of Ann Marsh, 200

Accounts, 148, 224 *f.*, 290, 293 *f.*

Acrelius, Israel, 209

Activity, man's tendency towards, 44

Actresses, ii, 12

Adams, Abigail, 93, 122, 129, 133 *f.*, 175; ii, 260, 413

Adams Academy, 342, 347 *f.*, 350, 358, 455

Adams, Charles Follen, ii, 408

Adams, Charles Francis, ii, 413

Adams, Charles Kendall, ii, 247

Adams, E. K., ii, 95

Adams, Governor, ii, 468

Adams, Miss H. A., ii, 433

Adams, H. W., ii, 431

Adams, Jacob, 347 *f.*

Adams, James Truslow, 136; ii, 6, 382

Adams, John, 344; ii, 260

Adams, Mrs. John Q., 131

Adams, Madame Jules, ii, 388

Adams, W. H. D., 56

Adamson, on need for women in medical service, ii, 342

Adamson, Sarah, ii, 351

Addams, Jane, 123; ii, 459

Addison, Joseph, 31, 136

Address on the Evils Suffered by Women and Children, ii, 456

Administration, women in school, 514–18; ii, 326

Admission of girls to New England schools, 92

Admission requirements, of medical schools, ii, 360 *f.*; of men's colleges, ii, 137; of normal schools of physical education, ii, 135; of seminary, 359, 411; of the high school, 538 *f.*; of women's higher institutions, ii, 146, 163 *f.*, 167 *f.*, 170 *f.*, 173 *ff.*, 188, 190

Adolescence, ii, 154

Adult education, in women's clubs, ii, 453 *ff.*, 467 *f.*

''Advanced women,'' condemned, 45

Adventure schools, 149 *ff.*, 217–30, 271, 281–300; ii, 469; classified, 217, 281 *ff.*; importance of, 153, 217; taught by women, 460

Advice of W. P. to Mr. Samuel Hartlib for the Advancement of Learning, 52

Advice to Young Ladies, 44

Adviser of Women and Girls, special diploma for, 549